SLAVERY RACE AND THE AMERICAN LEGAL SYSTEM 1700-1872

A SIXTEEN VOLUME FACSIMILE SERIES
REPRODUCING OVER ONE HUNDRED
AND SEVENTY RARE AND
IMPORTANT PAMPHLETS

Edited by
Paul Finkelman
*State University of New York
Binghamton*

A GARLAND SERIES

CONTENTS OF THE SET

S O U T H E R N
S L A V E S   I N
F R E E   S T A T E
C O U R T S
THE PAMPHLET LITERATURE

SERIES I
VOLUME 2

Edited with an Introduction by

Paul Finkelman

GARLAND PUBLISHING, INC.
NEW YORK & LONDON 1988

Design by Renata Gomes

Library of Congress Cataloging-in-Publication Data

Southern slaves in free state courts: the pamphlet literature/edited with
an introduction by Paul Finkelman.

p. cm. — (Slavery, race, and the American legal system, 1700-1872)
1. Slavery—United States—Legal status of slaves in free states-Cases.
 2. Slavery—Law and legislation—United States—Cases.
I. Finkelman, Paul, 1949-
KF4545. S5A5 1988d   342.73 0872—dc19
[347.302872]   87-35970
ISBN 0-8240-6718-5

All volumes in this series are printed on acid-free,
250-year-life paper.

Printed in the United States of America

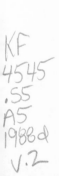

C O N T E N T S

Volume 1

Introduction

Volume 2

Volume 3

SPEECH

OF

SALMON P. CHASE,

IN THE CASE OF

THE COLORED WOMAN, MATILDA,

WHO WAS BROUGHT BEFORE THE COURT OF
COMMON PLEAS OF HAMILTON
COUNTY, OHIO,

BY WRIT OF HABEAS CORPUS;

March 11, 1837.

CINCINNATI:

PUGH & DODD, PRINTERS,—MAIN & FIFTH STS.

1837.

1

THE CASE.

On the 10th day of March, A. D. 1837, application was made to the Court of Common Pleas of Hamilton County, for a writ of habeas corpus, in behalf of Matilda, a colored woman, confined and detained, as was represented to the Court, in the county jail, without lawful authority. The Court granted the writ, returnable on the next day at half past nine o'clock, A. M.; whereupon the writ issued as follows:

STATE OF OHIO, ⎱ ss.
Hamilton County, ⎰

To SAMUEL FOSDICK, *Sheriff of our said County*, GREETING:

We command you, that you have the body of Matilda, a colored girl, by whatever name she may be called, (detained in your custody as is said,) together with the cause of the caption and detention of the said Matilda, before the Honorable, the Judges of the Court of Common Pleas, at the Court House in Cincinnati, at half past nine o'clock, A. M. on the 11th inst., then and there to do, receive, and be subject to whatsoever shall then and there be considered concerning her in that behalf, and have then there this writ.

Witness the Hon. D. K. ESTE, President Judge of our said Court, at Cincinnati, this 10th day of March, A. D. 1837.
W. H. HARRISON, Clerk.

NOTE. The reporter does not pretend to recite the commitment, affidavit, or state's warrant, in the precise terms of the originals. Having made diligent inquiry for the paper which contained them, at the offices of the Clerk and the Sheriff without success; and having been unable to obtain a copy from the magistrate, he is obliged to trust to his memory, aided by the printed forms. But as he carefully and repeatedly perused the originals, he thinks he may assert, with some confidence, that the variance is but slight, and, in no instance, alters or modifies the legal effect.

At the time specified in the writ, it was returned by the Sheriff, with the following indorsement:

" I have the body of the within named Matilda, here before the Court, as directed. The cause of her caption and detention is a commitment from Wm. Doty, a Justice of the peace, that is herewith produced."

The commitment produced by the Sheriff was in the following words:

STATE OF OHIO, } ss.
Hamilton County, }

To the Keeper of the Jail of said County, GREETING :

I hereby command you, in the name of the state of Ohio, to receive into your custody, in the jail of the said county, Matilda, a colored girl, who has been arrested and brought before me for trial, which trial has been postponed on the application of said defendant; and the said Matilda is committed until further trial, at the request of defendant's counsel. March 10, 1837.

WILLIAM DOTY, J. P.

On the same paper on which this warrant of commitment was written, but on the other side, appeared an affidavit and a state's warrant, partly printed and partly written, (being the ordinary blanks for affidavits and warrants used in criminal cases, filled up to suit this case,) as follows :

STATE OF OHIO, } ss.
Hamilton County, }

Before me, William Doty, a Justice of the Peace within and for said county, personally came John W. Riley, agent and attorney for Larkin Lawrence. who, being duly sworn, deposeth and saith, that the said Larkin Lawrence is a citizen and resident of the state of Missouri, and that Matilda, a mulatto woman, and the slave of said Lawrence, did, on the 20th day of May, 1836, escape from the service of said Lawrence, and is now concealed or lurking within said county, as this deponent verily believes : and further this deponent saith not.

JOHN W. RILEY.

Sworn to and subscribed before me, this 8th day of March, 1837.

WILLIAM DOTY, J. P.

STATE OF OHIO, } ss.
Hamilton County, }

To any Constable of said County, GREETING :

WHEREAS complaint has been made before me, William Doty, a Justice of the Peace within and for said county, upon the oath of John W. Riley, of said county, that Matilda, a mulatto woman and the slave of one Larkin Lawrence, of the state of Missouri, did, on the 20th day of May, 1836, escape from the service of said Lawrence, and is now concealed or lurking within said county :

These are therefore to command you, to take the said Matilda, a slave, if she be found in your county, or, if she shall have fled, that you pursue after the said Matilda, a slave, into any county within the state, and her take and safely keep, so that you have her body forthwith before me, William Doty, or some other Justice of the Peace, to answer said complaint and be further dealt with according to law. And you are also required to summon the complainant, and also —— ——, and —— ——, to appear and give evidence relative to the subject matter of said complaint, when and where you have the said Matilda, a slave.

[L. S.] Given under my hand and seal, this 8th day of March, 1837,

WILLIAM DOTY, J. P.

1*

THE ARGUMENT.

———

The case, as presented by the Sheriff's return, was argued to the Court by Mr. S. P. CHASE, and Mr. S. EELLS, in behalf of the petitioner, and by Mr. M. N. McLEAN, Gen. R. T. LYTLE, and Mr. N. C. READ, in behalf of the claimant. Mr. CHASE addressed the Court as follows:

It is very manifest that the questions, involved in this case, are regarded with deep interest by the community. Many seem to feel something of a personal interest in its event: some, as if their own liberty were at stake: others, as if their own rights of property were in peril. There is a topic, also, with which the discussion of this case is thought by many to be closely connected, though in fact no such connection exists: a topic on which an intense and still increasing interest and excitement prevails—interest and excitement not unfelt within these walls. I feel the responsibility which is upon me as an advocate: I perceive the responsibility which rests upon the Court; —responsibility, not to the community alone—not alone to the humble individual who sues for protection here;—but to conscience and to God. It is an awful and affecting responsibility. But how vast the disparity between the opposite consequences of erroneous decision! If there be error on the one hand, it may consign to hopeless bondage, a human being, rightfully free: on the other, it would but deprive a master of the services of a single individual, legally a slave.

In discussing the questions which present themselves in this case, I seek no aid from feeling. I invoke no sympathy for condition or for sex. True, a fellow being sues to this honorable Court for that protection against slavery, which she can look for, no where else upon earth. True, it is a helpless and almost friendless woman who sues for this protection: but

7

I know, that, however much individuals of the Court may feel for her, she can expect no aid from such feelings. This Court will administer the law ; not that law, sublimely described as receiving the homage of all creatures, both in heaven and in earth,—of the very least as feeling her care, and of the very greatest as not exempt from her power: but that other and far less perfect law, which is written in the books and statutes of fallible men. A poetical imagination may indulge the contemplation of the golden scales of immortal, passionless justice, held forth, evenly poised, on high : but the poet will be sadly disappointed if he expects that his cause will be weighed, in those balances, by a human tribunal. I shall confine myself, therefore, to the legal and constitutional aspects of the case before the Court. I shall enter in to no discussion of the merits or demerits of slavery. I shall not touch the exciting topic of abolition. I shall enquire, only, whether the petitioner, Matilda, is, or is not now unlawfully restrained of her liberty. If she is, it is the duty of this Court to discharge her from that restraint : if not, she must be recommitted to the custody of the Sheriff.

One preliminary observation, however, or two, I will make. Slavery is admitted, on all hands, to be contrary to natural right. Wherever it exists at all, it exists only in virtue of positive law.* The right to hold a man as a slave is a naked legal right. It is a right which, in its own nature, can have no existence beyond the territorial limits of the state which sanctions it, except in other states whose positive law recognises and protects it. It vanishes when the master and the slave meet together in a state where positive law interdicts slavery. The moment the slave comes within such a state, he acquires a legal right to freedom. The petitioner, Matilda, is now within the limits of Ohio, by whose fundamental law slavery is positively and forever interdicted. Admitting then, that she was once a slave, and is now claimed as such: admitting that if she is a slave, the present detention is lawful, still, it by no means follows that she is now a slave, or now legally restrained. On the contrary, she is now legally free:

---

* Lunsford vs. Coquillon, 14 Martin's (Louisiana) Reports: Rankin vs. Lydia, 3 Marshall's (Ky.) Reports, 470: Sommersett's case, 20 Howell's State Trials, 1.

legally restored to her natural right; unless some exception to the great interdict can be clearly shown. And is there a man of all who hear me, who would rejoice that this poor woman, if legally free, should nevertheless be given up because once a slave! Is there a citizen of Ohio within these walls, who regards this woman as a mere article of property, the title to which is founded in natural right, and is recognised by the law of nations, and is protected by the positive laws of all states, and as bound to her owner by the same permanent ties which connect him with his horse or his ox!—If there be, let me tell that individual, that the constitution of Ohio frowns upon him, and that the soil of Ohio is dishonored by his tread.

But what is the case before the court! On application, made yesterday, in behalf of the petitioner, a writ of habeas corpus was issued to the Sheriff, commanding him to bring her before the court, together with the day and cause of her caption and detention. The Sheriff has obeyed this writ—he has brought the body of the petitioner into Court—and for the cause of her commitment he refers to a paper, which he also produces, on one side of which is a warrant of commitment, directed to the jailer of this county, commanding him, in the name of the state of Ohio, to receive Matilda, a colored woman, into custody, and keep her safely until further trial; and on the other, an affidavit, purporting to have been made by John W. Riley, the agent and attorney of one Larkin Lawrence, that his principal was a citizen of Missouri, and that Matilda, a colored woman and the slave of Lawrence, having escaped from her master, was concealed or lurking in this county ; and also a state's warrant, founded upon this affidavit, directed to any constable of the county, and commanding him, in the name of the state of Ohio, to arrrest Matilda and bring her before some Justice, to answer the complaint and be further dealt with according to law. The affidavit and the state's warrant pursue the forms which the state law prescribes to be used in criminal cases, so far as circumstances permitted. The warrant of commitment departs slightly from the common form ; and no cause of caption or detention is expressed upon its face.

Two general questions arise upon these facts : Is the warrant of commitment sufficient to warrant the caption and de-

tention of the petitioner, admitting that the magistrate had
power to commit? Had the magistrate such power?

It is a well settled and universal principle, that the matter
for which any person is committed to prison, shall be plainly
and specially expressed in the warrant of commitment. Hawkins says,* "the commitment ought to set forth the crime with
convenient certainty ; otherwise the officer is not punishable
for suffering the party to escape, and the court, before whom
he is removed by habeas corpus, ought to discharge or bail
him ; and this doth not only hold where no cause at all is expressed in the commitment, but also where it is so loosely set
forth that the court cannot judge whether it was a reasonable
ground."

The same doctrine is distinctly recognized in our own habeas corpus act, and is regarded as one of the surest safeguards
of personal liberty.† The statute also which prescribes the
form of commitment to be used by justices of the peace, requires the magistrate to "describe the crime or offence in the
warrant."‡ If then a man charged with murder, were committed upon a warrant shewing no cause of commitment—
shewing nothing but an arrest, a partial trial and the color of
the party—must he not be discharged from custody upon habeas corpus? Might not the officer having him in custody,
suffer him to escape without liability for the escape? Would
not the very act of detention under such a warrant render the
officer liable in trespass? If the passage cited from Hawkins
be sound law, and the statute be any thing but a dead letter,
then, without doubt, all these questions must be affirmatively
answered. But if a man arrested upon a charge of murder,
and committed upon such a warrant must be discharged, can
the petitioner be detained? What offence known to the laws
of this State, or of any State, has she committed? For what
cause is she imprisoned? This Court cannot regard the allegations of counsel or the rumors of the day. It must look to
the commitment and the commitment alone. And what cause
of detention is there plainly and sufficiently expressed, or expressed at all? None. Absolutely none, unless color be a sufficient cause of detention: and if so—if color be sufficient

* Hawkins' Pleas of the Crown, 179.
† 29 O. L. 164. ‡ 29 O. L. 202.

cause of imprisonment, let us know the exact shade. Who in this court house is guilty? Who is innocent? How shall the question be tried? Who shall try it? I remember, that in a case, tried in the supreme court in this county, two gentlemen of this bar, eminent alike for their private virtues and professional attainments, but of complexions rather darker than usual, insisted that the court should determine by inspection, whether certain children were white, within the meaning of the school-law; but the court told them that " the color of the party did not sufficiently mark the distinction between the two races of people," and intimated, that the general application of their favourite test might occasion serious inconvenience to the learned gentlemen themselves. Color, then, affords no presumption against any body. It is no cause of detention or imprisonment. The time has not yet arrived in Ohio, when color implies either crime or bondage. And far distant be the day! For that day will not come, till the solid foundations of our state institutions shall be upheaved and scattered by the volcanic energies of revolution.

The counsel for the claimant will, however, probably concede, that the commitment itself shews no cause of detention: but they will perhaps refer me, and refer the Court to the affidavit and warrant of arrest. I question the propriety of such a reference. I deny that the court can look any where for the cause of commitment out of the commitment itself. " Expressed in the warrant with convenient certainty," is the language of Hawkins;—" plainly and specially set forth in the warrant," is the language of our own statute. More perspicuous language than this could hardly be employed. The terms are precise and definite, and completely exclude the idea of looking out of the commitment for the cause of detention.

But were this otherwise, still the court could not notice the warrant of arrest or the affidavit of Riley, for the warrant was illegal and the affidavit extra-judicial.

The warrant of arrest was illegal:—Because the act of congress concerning fugitives from labor, authorizes no arrest by any officer, and of course no warrant of arrest.

Because no act of congress could authorize the issuing of a state process, in the name of the state, in any case whatever.

Because no case is made by the affidavit, or disclosed by any paper now before the Court, which would warrant any proceeding on the part of the magistrate, under the act of congress.

The act of congress authorizes no arrest by an officer. It authorizes the party claiming the services of a fugitive from labor, to seize or arrest him. This is the first step. The claimant is, then, to take the fugitive before a magistrate and make proof of his claim. The act provides no process to be issued by the magistrate, and no ministerial officer to execute it, if issued. Until the fugitive is brought before the magistrate, he is supposed to know nothing of the matter. Until then he has no duty to perform—no authority to exercise. It is plain therefore, that the issuing of a warrant for the arrest of a fugitive from labor has no sanction in the act of congress. And if none there, none any where; for it will not be pretended, that there is any other act, which confers any authority whatever in relation to fugitives from service.

But it is not enough to say that the act of congress does not sanction the issuing of process: I go further, and assert, that no act of congress could authorize the issuing of such process as has been employed in this case. The main object of the framers of our national constitution was, to establish a government which should act on the persons of the citizens through federal courts, issuing federal process, to be executed by federal officers;—a government complete in itself, independent of the state governments, and capable of effecting its end, without their intervention. In their respective spheres of action, the government of the United States, and the several State governments are entirely distinct and independent. Neither can control or regulate the action of the other. Neither can enlarge, diminish or vary the powers or duties of the officers of the other. If then the process, in the present case, was state process, it is plain that no act of congress could authorize the employment of it: And that it was state process is evident, not only from the consideration that no federal process is provided by the act, and of course no other process than state process could be used, but also from the style of the warrant, which is that prescribed in the constitution for state process, and the command of the writ which is in the name of the State of Ohio.

But if I admit, for argument's sake, that process might issue in a proper case, and that the process issued, was legal, if the case warranted it, a serious difficulty remains to be conquered by the counsel for the claimant. If we admit that process may be issued in all cases, in which the act authorizes the claimant himself to seize or arrest his fugitive servant, how will they show a case for the issuing of process here? The act authorizes such arrest or seizure in those cases only, where a person held to service in one state escapes thence into another. Does the affidavit, or warrant, or any paper, now before the court, disclose such a case? Not at all. The utmost that can be ascertained is, that the claimant is a citizen and resident of Missouri, and that the petitioner escaped from his service; but when, where, or how the escape was effected, nothing informs us. For aught that appears, the petitioner may have escaped from the service of the claimant during a journey through this state; or after being brought into the state as an attendant, during a visit; or after being sent into the state to labor. The affidavit of Riley and every paper before the court is perfectly consistent with either of these suppositions. There is nothing which shows, that the petitioner was held to labor in one state and escaped into another; and the court cannot supply, by intendment or conjecture, this most important circumstance. It is clear, therefore, that the papers before the court, if taken together, do not show a case for any action of the magistrate, under the act of congress. But if the magistrate had no authority to act at all, he had no authority to issue process. The process then, actually issued, was illegal and void.

I need not labor to prove that the affidavit was extra-judicial. If the magistrate had no authority to issue process—which seems clear—he had no authority to take an affidavit as a foundation for the process. It follows, therefore, that the affidavit was extra-judicial.

If I have been fortunate enough to satisfy the Court that the warrant of arrest and the affidavit of Riley were nugatory and void, no argument will be needed, I trust, to demonstrate the impropriety of referring to them for any purpose connected with this cause. It may well be questioned, indeed, whether, even if both were legal and valid, the Court could properly notice them; partly, because they are matters foreign to the commitment; and partly, because neither the commitment nor sheriff's return at all refer to them. The sheriff refers to the

2

commitment for the cause of the detention of the petitioner, and to nothing else: and nothing in the commitment would suggest the existence of the warrant or affidavit. It would be going very far, therefore, to supply total omissions in the commitment, by a sort of volunteer reference to the warrant and affidavit, even if they were valid parts of a valid legal proceeding, of which the commitment, also, was a proper and valid part. But it is not necessary, in order to the present purpose, to contend for a principle so broad as this. It is enough to say, that the Court cannot aid a defective commitment, by any reference to a void warrant, or to an extra-judicial affidavit. The Court cannot, judicially, notice either. They have no more proper connection with the cause than any other warrant or affidavit which might accidentally be found among the papers. The paper, on which they are written, is blank to the eye of the Court.

And here I must be allowed to say, that it is the duty of this court, to scrutinize, very closely, the proceedings of justices under the act of Congress. Taking it now for granted that the act is valid and constitutional, it confers upon the magistrate a jurisdiction, special and very limited indeed, but liable to great abuse. It authorizes him to hear and decide upon claims adverse to the sacred right of personal liberty. It makes his certificates valid warrants, for confining and carrying out of the state, men and women, who may nevertheless be entitled to all the rights of citizenship. It recognizes no distinction of color. It exposes the magistrate to fearful temptations, and at the same time shields him from all responsibility. The jurisdiction which it confers is exclusive of the jurisdiction of the state courts. No state court can control its exercise within the limits prescribed by the act. No state court can review or reverse any decision made in pursuance of it. And yet the state courts were created for the very purpose of protecting personal liberty, and all the provisions of the habeas corpus act were intended as its muniments and safeguards. Vain purpose and intention, if the courts of the state are to presume in favor of the jurisdiction of the magistrate! If a person brought before the court by habeas corpus may be remanded to custody, as a fugitive from labor, although the return does not disclose a state of facts within the jurisdiction conferred by the act of congress, the provisions of our statute are miserable mockery. Let the state courts then scrutinize narrowly every such return. Let the well known and well established rules of law, in regard to courts of special jurisdiction, be applied to the magistrate. Let nothing be presumed in favor of his proceedings; and let nothing be supplied by conjecture or intendment. Thus much at least is due to liberty.

I have thus far argued against this commitment, upon the hypothesis that the act of congress confers on the magistrate power to commit. But does the act confer any such power? Admit that this commitment was made in a case of which the magistrate had jurisdiction—admit that the cause of caption and detention is sufficiently expressed, still there is the fatal defect of power to commit. The arguments already urged against the power to issue a warrant of arrest, apply in full force to the power to commit. The act confers no power to issue the warrant of commitment. It provides no ministerial officers to execute it. Nor could the act authorize the commitment here relied on ; for it was issued in the name of the state—it is directed to an officer of the state—it commands in behalf of the state. It is, in short, state process, and no act of congress can authorize its employment, in any case, without a palpable violation of state rights. So far as the jurisdiction in cases of fugitive servants extends, the magistrate is a federal officer, and cannot, while acting in that capacity, issue state process. He cannot commit. No constable has authority to convey any person to jail, by virtue of a commitment issued by him. No jailer is warranted in receiving any person into jail, or detaining him in custody, under such a commitment. Authorities and duties of this sort must be conferred or imposed by state laws. Acts of congress can neither authorize nor require state officers, as such, to do any act either judicial or ministerial.— The contrary proposition involves the absurdity that the legislative branch of one government may control and regulate the action, of the judicial and executive branches of another.

All this seems very clear, and yet it is contended that the power to commit must exist, because its exercise must be generally beneficial to the person claimed as a fugitive. The commitment, it is said, usually takes place at the instance of his counsel, and in order to allow time for the collection of testimony in his behalf. This argument might possess much force if addressed to congress, but it is little better than futile when addressed to a court. The judicial power cannot amend a law. It cannot interpolate any provisions, however necessary or beneficial. It is the province of courts to construe statutes; not to make them. If then the act contains no provision authorizing a commitment, and none can be inserted by construction, it follows that the commitment, in virtue of which the petitioner is detained, is void.

It may be urged that this would defeat the intention of congress; but, in my judgment, nothing can be clearer, than that congress never intended, that the magistrate should have power to commit. The silence of the act as to any such power, and the entire absence of any provision for the execution of any such power, furnish, to my mind, conclusive evidence that the whole intention of congress is expressed in the act itself. What then was that intention, as gathered from the plain import of the law? Obviously this, and no more: that the master of an escaping servant might arrest him, wherever found, and bring him before a judge or magistrate; that the judge or magistrate should examine the proof of the claim, and, if satisfied of its validity, grant the master a certificate to that effect: and that this certificate should protect the master against legal responsibility for the arrest and removal of his servant. The act anticipates no regular suit—no formal trial—no continuance—no delay. It presumes the claimant to be ready with his proofs, and does not contemplate the introduction of rebutting testimony. It permits the master to establish his claim by affidavits, and of course allows neither opportunity nor time for cross examination. It does not indeed require the magistrate to decide on the claim at once. If not satisfied one day, he may hear further evidence the next. In the mean time, the custody of the person claimed remains with the claimant. The same reasons which induced him to submit his claim to the magistrate in the first instance, will induce him to bring the party again before him for further trial. If he was afraid of the penalties against kidnapping at first, he will continue afraid of them, until he gets the magistrate's certificate. If a sense of propriety and justice, and a proper regard for law, were motives for seeking a legal sanction to his claim, the same motives will

induce him to use no unnecessary control over the party claimed, until that sanction is obtained. But nothing in the act affords the slightest countenance to the idea, that the magistrate
is to exercise any power over the person of the individual
claimed as a servant. That power is expresly confined to the
master or his agent. He alone can bring him before the magistrate: he alone can have custody of him pending the trial:
he alone can remove him after the certificate is granted. The
whole power of the magistrate embraces but these particulars:
the hearing of the proofs, the deciding upon the claim, and the
grant or refusal of the certificate. If he exercises any other
power, he usurps authority.

I now approach another and more important aspect of this
case. I have hitherto discussed the effect of the act of congress: I now propose to examine the constitutionality of that
act.

Here Mr. C. gave way to Gen. R. T. LYTLE, who inquired
of the court ,whether they would, at this late day, permit any
discussion as to the constitutionality of the act of congress,
and urged that such discussion was irrelevant to the case before the court. The court remarked that they were disposed
to hear counsel with patience, and had, perhaps, indulged unnecessary latitude of discussion, but they would not prescribe
to counsel what course of argument should be pursued.

Mr. C. resumed: The constitutionality of the act of congress
is not relevant to this case! What are we then discussing? Is
it not the validity of the magistrate's commitment! But the
commitment cannot be valid if the magistrate had no power
to commit. The magistrate can have no power to commit unless derived from the act of congress, and the act of congress
can confer no power at all, if unconstitutional. Not relevant!
It is the controlling point of the case. If the act of congress
be unconstitutional, then this commitment is no better than
waste paper; the whole proceedings of the magistrate have
been illegal, and the petitioner must be discharged.—I thank
the court for its indulgence; but I mean not to trespass upon
its patience. I have hitherto aimed, and in what yet remains
to be urged, I shall aim, to express myself as concisely as possible. I may be permitted to observe, however, that the questions involved in this case are of sufficient magnitude, inte-

2*

rest and importance, to demand the exercise of higher qualities than patience. They call for deep consideration, severe investigation, and comprehensive judgment. They must be approached in a spirit of enlarged patriotism and right judging philanthropy: for they touch at once the most delicate state relations and the most sacred personal rights.

In attempting a discussion of the constitutional aspect of this case, I have the satisfaction of knowing that other and abler men have been before me. The constitutionality of the act of congress is not, as the counsel on the other side seem to think, now, for the first time, drawn in question. I hold in my hand a newspaper report of a case decided by the supreme court of New Jersey last summer. It arose under the law of New Jersey which authorized the justices of the inferior courts to issue warrants for the arrest of escaping servants, on the application of the master, and to try in a summary way, the validity of the claim. It came before the supreme court upon certiorari: and the question as to the constitutionality of the act of congress was very fully debated. In giving judgment, according to the reporter, who was of counsel in the case, the Chief Justice and Justice Ryerson, (a majority of the court) "expressed a strong inclination, and it was evidently their opinion, (although they said it was not necessary so to decide in that particular case;) that the law of congress regulating the apprehension of fugitives from labor, was unconstitutional, no power being given to congress by the constitution of the United States to legislate on this subject: and their reasoning," says the reporter, "carried conviction to every mind." The precise point, however, on which that case turned was, that the act of New Jersey authorizing the arrest and summary trial of escaping servants, was itself unconstitutional; because it violated the right of trial by jury. The case was argued in behalf of the colored man who had been arrested under the state law, by Mr. Frelinghuysen. a gentleman, not less eminently distinguished by the vigor of his intellect than by the purity of his life. I have no means of knowing by what argument he convinced the court which he addressed; but it is gratifying to know, at least, that I have to maintain here, successfully or unsuccessfully, the same propositions, which he, there, triumphantly asserted and established.

I maintain, then, that the act of congress which authorizes justices of the peace, without a jury, to try and decide the most important questions of personal liberty, which makes the certificate of a justice a sufficient warrant for the transportation out of the state, of any person, whom he may adjudge to be an escaping servant,—is not warranted by the constitution of the United States, is repugnant to the ordinance of 1787 for the government of the Northwestern territory, and is therefore, null and void.

It is not warranted by the constitution of the United States. The leading object of the framers of our federal constitution was to create a national government, and confer upon it adequate powers. A secondary object was to adjust and settle certain matters of right and duty, between the states and between the citizens of different states, by permanent stipulations having the force and effect of a treaty. Both objects were happily accomplished. The constitution establishes a form of government, declares its principles, defines its sphere, and confers its powers. It creates the artificial being, denominated " the government," and breathes into it the breath of life, and imparts to each branch and member, the necessary energies and faculties. It also establishes certain articles of compact or agreement between the states. It prescribes certain duties to be performed by each state and its citizens, towards every other state and its citizens: and it confers certain rights upon each state and its citizens, and binds all the states to the recognition and enforcement of these rights. These different ends of the constitution—the creation of a government and the establishment of a compact, are entirely distinct in their nature. Either might be attained independently of the other. If all the clauses of compact in the constitution were stricken out, the government created by it would still exist. If the articles and sections, establishing a form of government, were blotted from the constitution, the clauses of compact might still remain in full force, as articles of agreement among the states. The clauses of compact confer no powers on the government: and the powers of government cannot be exerted, except in virtue of express provisions, to enforce the matters of compact. In this view of the national constitution, I am fully sustained by the high authority of chief justice Shaw of Massachusetts. In his recent opinion in the case of the slave child, Med, that eminent justice says, " The constitution of the United States partakes both of the nature of a treaty and of a form of government. It regards the states, to a certain extent, as sovereign and independent communities, with full power to make their own laws and regulate their domestic policy, *and fixes the terms upon which their intercourse shall be conducted.* In respect to foreign relations, it regards the people of the United States as one community, *and constitutes a form of government for them.*" Now what is the clause in the constitution in regard to fugitives from labor, but an article of agreement between the states? It is expressed in these words, "No person held to service or labor in one state, under the laws thereof, escaping into another, shall, in consequence of any law or regulation thereof, be discharged from such service or labor; but shall be delivered up on claim of the party to whom such service or labor may be due." Does this clause confer any power on government, or on any officer or department of government?— Clearly not. It says nothing about the government, or its officers, or its departments. It declares that the citizens of no state in the Union, legally entitled to the service of any person, shall be deprived of that right to service, by the operation of the laws of any state into which the servant may escape; and it requires such state to deliver him up, on the claim of the lawful master. The clause, then, restrains the operation of state constitutions and state laws in a particular class of cases; and it obliges, so far as a compact can oblige, each state to the performance of certain duties towards the citizens of other states. The clause has nothing to do with the creation of a form of government. It is, in the strictest sense, a clause of compact.* The parties to the agreement are the states. The general government is not a party to it, nor affected by it. If the clause stood alone in the constitution, it would mean precisely what it does now, and would be just as obligatory as it is now. Nothing can be plainer, then, than that this clause cannot be construed as vesting any power in the government, or in any of its departments, or in any of its officers; and this is the only

---

* This view of the clause in question is also sustained by Chief Justice Shaw in the opinion already cited.

provision in the constitution which at all relates to fugitives from labor.

Now the whole legislative power of congress is derived, either from the general grant of power, "to make all laws, necessary and proper for carrying into execution all the powers vested by the constitution in the government of the United States, or in any department or officer thereof;" or from special provisions in relation to particular subjects. If congress has any power to legislate upon the subject of fugitives from labor, it must be derived from one of these sources,—from the general grant, or from some special provision. It cannot be derived from the general grant, because the clause in regard to fugitives from labor, vests no power in the national government, or in any of its departments or officers; and the general grant of legislative power is expressly confined to the enactment of laws, necessary and proper to carry into execution the powers so vested. Nor can it be derived from any special provision: for none is attached to the clause relating to fugitives from service. The conclusion seems inevitable, that the constitution confers on congress no power to legislate in regard to escaping servants. Where then is this power? Undoubtedly it is reserved to the states; for "all powers not delegated to the United States, nor prohibited to the states, are reserved to the states or to the people." The constitution restrains the operation of the state constitutions and the state laws, which would enfranchise the fugitive. It also binds the states to deliver him up on the claim of the master, and by necessary inference, it obliges them to provide a tribunal before which such claim may be asserted and tried, and by which such claims may be decided upon, and, if valid, enforced: but it confers no jot of legislative power on congress.

This construction of this clause in the constitution, is strengthened by reference to another provision. The first clause of the first section of the same article, in which the provision in regard to escaping servants is found, is in these words: "full faith and credit shall be given, in each state, to the public acts, records, and judicial proceedings of every other state." This clause, so far, is of the same nature with the clause in regard to fugitives from labor. It is a clause of compact, and it pledges the faith of each state to the faithful observance of it. But it confers no power on government, or any of its departments or officers. Congress, therefore, could not legislate in reference to the subject of it in virtue of the general grant of legislative power. Aware of this, the framers of the constitution annexed to this first clause, a second, specially providing that congress might "prescribe, by general laws, the manner in which such acts, records, and proceedings shall be proved, and the effect thereof." Am I not right in saying that the framers of the constitution were aware, that without this special provision, congress would have no power to legislate upon the subject of the section? If the first clause, *proprio vigore*, confers on Congress legislative power, why add the second? Why add it, if legislative power is conferred by the general grant, or by any other provision in the constitution? I think the counsel for the claimant will find some difficulty in answering these questions. The framers of the constitution were men of large experience, comprehensive knowledge, sound judgment, and great ability. Among them were Hamilton, and Madison, and Washington. Such men, in framing such an instrument would avoid all needless repetition. They would not incorporate into the constitution a special provision upon any subject unnecessarily. To them, therefore, the second clause of the section under consideration, must have appeared not only fit, but necessary. But if a special provision was necessary to enable congress to legislate in regard to the authentication and effect of records, why is not a special provision necessary to enable congress to legislate in regard to fugitive servants? Can the counsel explain? Both clauses of the constitution are of the same nature. Neither has any thing to do with creating, organizing, or energizing a form of the government. Both are articles of compact. If then, the framers of the constitution had intended that congress might legislate in reference to the subjects of both, would not special provisions, conferring such legislative power, have been annexed to both? Is not the annexation of such a special provision to one clause, and not to the other, decisive evidence that the convention intended to confer legislative power in regard to the subject of one clause, and to withhold legislative power in reference to the subject of the other? This conclusion seems to me inevitable. I see not how the counsel for the claimant, with all their ability and ingenuity, can frame an argument which will conduct to any other.

Nor is it difficult to assign valid and substantial reasons why the convention should not entrust to congress any legislative power upon this subject. Let us suppose that, when this clause about escaping servants was under discussion, a member had proposed to annex another clause in these words, "And congress shall have power to appoint officers in each state to try and determine the validity of such claims; and to provide by law for the apprehension and re-delivery of persons so escaping." Would not the answer have been, "What! give congress power to appoint officers to try questions of personal liberty, and to provide for the arrest and redelivery of all persons who may be claimed as escaping servants! Who would be safe under such a constitution! What personal right, conferred by God and guarantied by the state constitutions, might not be prostrated under it! Who might not be claimed as a fugitive from labor! Who would be secure against condemnation to servitude! To little purpose has liberty been achieved, if only to be placed in jeopardy like this." And if this answer had failed to satisfy the convention, and the clause had been incorporated into the constitution, can any one believe that it would have received the assent of the states! Let it be remembered that the states existed before the federal constitution, and that the fundamental law of each asserted and guarantied the absolute, inherent, and unalienable rights of every citizen. Among these were reckoned "life, liberty, and the pursuit of happiness:" and can it be supposed that any state, especially any nonslaveholding state, would have assented to a constitution which would withdraw from either of these rights, the ample shield of the fundamental law, and leave it exposed to the almost unlimited discretion of congress, and of officers appointed by congress! I think not.

But a power vested in congress by a special provision as just stated, would not be half so objectionable as the power actually exercised. Under such a provision, congress would have appointed officers by name: and the officers so appointed would have been known and responsible. Process would have been provided for bringing the persons claimed as fugitives before the proper authority, and the benefit of a regular trial would have been secured to those whose personal liberty might thus be called in question. But how is it in point of fact? Has congress selected individuals fitted by nature and by education for this important trust? Persons of sufficient knowledge, sound judgment and undoubted integrity? Not at all. By one sweeping enactment, it has appointed all the magistrates of all the counties, cities and towns corporate throughout the Union, judges of these grave questions; judges, too, in the last resort; judges from whose decision lies no appeal; judges with whose proceedings, so long as they strictly pursue the act, no state court and no court of the United States can interfere. And as if this were not enough, the magistrates, in the exercise of this special jurisdiction, are effectually shielded from all responsibility from malconduct. As state magistrates they are not liable to federal impeachment, and as federal officers they are not liable to state impeachment. And if criminally prosecuted, they may protect themselves under their judicial character. Congress cannot remove them from office, for they exercise their powers under the act of congress in virtue of their offices as magistrates, and they derive their appointment as magistrates, not from congress, but from the states. Some of them are elected by the people,— some are appointed by the executive authority—some are appointed by town or city councils:—some hold their offices for a term of years—some are elected annually—some hold during good behavior:—some are compensated by salaries— others by fees—but none by the United States. For their services under the act of congress, they must make the best bargain they can with the claimants who seek their aid.— To complete the picture, the act omits to require them to hear the proofs of claim in public, or to pronounce a public judgment, or to keep any record of their proceedings. And before these magistrates, thus generally unqualified, thus always and completely irresponsible, and thus exposed to temptation, this act of congress provides that any person may be dragged, by any other person who chooses to set up a claim to him as a fugitive servant, to undergo trial for his personal liberty. And can it be that the framers of the constitution intended to confer on congress power to enact such a law as this! To suppose it, would be to rob their names of that reverence with which they have ever been pronounced. Can it be that the states adopted this constitution, knowing and understanding that it authorized the enactment of this or any similar law! If they did, the great principles which had hallowed their recent struggle, were strangely forgotten. We have little cause to boast of the security with which our institutions surround personal rights, so long as this act is held to be sanctioned by the constitution of the United States.

But this act is not only unauthorized by the federal constitution, but is directly repugnant to some of its plainest provisions. By the second section of the second article, it is made the duty of the President of the United States, with the advice and consent of the Senate, to appoint all judicial officers.— Congress, it is true, may vest the appointment of inferior officers in the President alone, in the courts of law, or in the heads of departments; but there is no clause in the constitution which authorizes congress to retain the appointment of a single officer in its own hands: and yet, here we have congress appointing thousands of federal officers at once. The act on which I am commenting, appointed all who then were, and all who might afterwards become magistrates of counties, cities, and towns corporate throughout the Union, judges of the United States, with a special jurisdiction. What law can be repugnant to the constitution if this be not! What law may not congress enact, if they can enact this law! Can the learned counsel for the claimant inform us!

But perhaps we shall be told that this act does not appoint the state magistrates to be federal officers, but merely transfers to them a certain portion of federal judicial power, to be exercised concurrently with the judges of the circuit and district courts. It is obvious that this a mere formal distinction, founded on no substantial difference. To confer on state magis trates federal powers, is to make them, so far, federal officers. But if we adopt the suggested phrase, will that remove the difficulty! Can the learned counsel tell us, in what clause of the constitution they have discovered the power to transfer the judicial power of the United States, or any part of it, to state magistrates! The discoverer of that power, would merit the title of the Columbus of the constitution.

The act relating to fugitives from service, is also repugnant

3

to the fourth and fifth amendments of the constitution, proposed by congress, at the instance of Virginia,* to the states, and by the states adopted and ratified as parts of that instrument. The first clause of the fourth amendment, is in these words: "The right of the people to be secure in their persons, houses, papers, and effects, against unreasonable searches and seizures, shall not be violated." Now how could the people be more completely exposed to "unreasonable seizures," than by this act of congress! Under its sanction, any man who claims another as his servant, may seize and confine him. It is idle to say that none but escaping servants can be seized. The first step is to seize: the next is to take the person seized before a magistrate: and then the validity of the claim is to be tried. It may turn out to be invalid: and in that case, personal rights have been grossly violated. Very frequently instances occur, in which personal rights are thus violated. And when we reflect, that the questions on which the validity of the claim depends, are often nice and intricate; that it may be the interest of the magistrate to resolve every question as the claimant may desire; that the claimant is permitted to make out his case by affidavits; that these affidavits, there being no cross-examination, will always be strongly in his favor, and may often be false; can we wonder that these outrages against personal rights do not always terminate at the threshhold of the magistrate! Can we wonder that, "upon pretence of seizing fugitives from labor, under the provisions of this act, unprincipled persons have kidnapped free persons, transported them out of the state, and sold them into slavery!"† Is not "this inhuman and infamous practice,"‡ the natural and inevitable consequence of this act! And can such an act consist with that security from unreasonable seizure, which the constitution solemnly guaranties to the people? I think not.

The third clause in the fourth amendment, of the constitution, is in these words: "No man shall be deprived of life, liberty, or property, without due process of law." But

---

* 4 Elliott's Debates, 216, 217. † Chases Statutes of Ohio, 1052
‡ Ib.

the act of congress provides, that persons may be deprived of their liberty without any process of law. It provides no process for the apprehension; none for the detention; none for the final delivery of the escaping servant. Every thing is to be done by the claimant. He is to arrest the fugitive, or the person whom he may take to be the fugitive; he is to bring him before the magistrate: he is to keep him in custody while the magistrate examines the evidences of the claim; he is to remove him when the certificate is granted. From beginning to end of the proceeding, there is nothing like legal process. And yet, the whole proceeding is recognized by the act of congress. The act then, is palpably and utterly repugnant to the very letter, as well as the whole spirit of the constitution. And not only so, but it is subversive of the fundamental principles on which all civil society rests. Let such acts be passed in reference to other civil rights. Let each man be authorized to reclaim property, and enforce rights, in this summary way. If one claims a horse found in the possession of another, instead of resorting to his old fashioned action of replevin, and to "due process of law," let him "seize or arrest" him and take him before the nearest magistrate, and there prove his claim. If a man claims services of another, which he will not perform, instead of going to law about the matter, let him drag his recusant neighbor before a justice, prove his claim to service, and then remove him to his task. How long would society hold together, if this principle were carried into general application!

I might here rest this case, but I feel bound to present it under another aspect. As citizens of Ohio, we are accustomed to hear eulogies upon the ordinance of 1787, for the government of the territory northwest of the Ohio, and certainly, that ordinance merits all the encomiums which have been passed upon it. It lies at the foundation of all our institutions. It was passed by the congress of the confederation, when all that vast region, now occupied by the states of Ohio, Indiana, Illinois, and Michigan, and the territory of Wisconsin, was yet a wilderness. The country had then just emerged from the war of independence. The soil which had been drenched with patriot blood, was hardly dry: and the echoes of that devout thanksgiving, which burst from every lip and from every heart, at the glorious termination of our great struggle, still lingered throughout the land. The great principles of personal right, and of free government, were then familiar to all minds, and dear to all hearts. The struggle which had just terminated, had been a struggle for these great principles. They had been consecrated by the blood of patriots, and attested by the death of martyrs: and the congress resolved to establish them, in the territory then recently acquired from Virginia, as the unalterable basis of all future government and legislation. In pursuance of this resolution, the ordinance of 1787 was framed. It provided for the formation of not less than three, nor more than four states within the territory, and for the admission of these states into the Union. It declared also, certain great fundamental principles of governmental duty, and private right to be maintained, in these states, inviolate forever. It established the freedom of conscience, the sacredness of personal liberty, and the inviolability of private contracts: it recognized and enforced the duty of government to foster schools, and diffuse knowledge: it enjoined the observance of good faith towards the Indians, and the performance towards them, of those offices of kindness and peace which should ever adorn and grace the intercourse of the mighty with the weak: and finally, that nothing should be omitted which might be thought justly to belong to an instrument providing for the creation of free states, it declared that there should be "neither slavery nor involuntary servitude within the territory, otherwise than in the punishment of crimes." And in order to ensure the permanent inviolability of these great first principles, it declared that the articles of the ordinance by which they were established, should "be considered as *articles of compact* between the original states and the people and states in the territory, AND FOREVER REMAIN UNALTERABLE, unless by common consent."

This remarkable instrument was almost the last act of the congress of the confederation; a body of men, which, as the illustrious Chatham declared, "for genuine sagacity, for singular moderation, for solid wisdom, manly spirit, sublime sentiments, and simplicity of language, for every thing respectable and every thing honorable, shone unrivalled." And as much as any other of their great acts, this ordinance justifies this splendid eulogy. In the name of the nation, it declared the terms upon which the then vacant territory should be settled: and those terms were—not the payment of tribute, nor the render of military service—but the perpetual maintenance of the genuine principles of American liberty. It pronounced, for the first time in the history of the world, a solemn national censure upon slavery, by interdicting forever, its existence in the only district, subject, in this respect, to the control of congress. So long as the ordinance endures, the people of the states, formed within this district, cannot introduce slavery, nor can it be introduced by the people of the other states. "The ordinance," as one of our own great statesmen has most truly said, "impressed on the the soil itself, an incapacity to bear up any other than freemen. It laid the interdict against personal servitude in original compact, not only deeper than all local law, but deeper also than all local constitutions." Every settler within the territory, by the very act of settlement, became a party to this compact, and bound by its perpetual covenants, and forever entitled to the benefit of its provisions, for himself and his posterity. No subsequent act of the original states could affect it, without his consent. It could not be affected, therefore, by the adoption of the federal constitution, for that was the act of the people of the original states, to which the people of the territory were not parties. The constitution of the United States neither did, nor could repeal, impair, abridge, or alter the terms of this compact. It left them as it found them, in the full force of their original obligation.

Faithful to the letter and spirit of the compact, the framers of our state constitution, incorporated its leading provisions into that instrument, thereby claiming for the people of Ohio the benefit of those provisions, recognizing their perpetual obligation, and imparting to them an additional sanction. The interdict against slavery is transferred to the constitution in the very words of the ordinance: and, as if to manifest as plainly as possible, the sense of the people on this subject, an additional provision is inserted, declaring that no alteration of the constitution shall ever take place, so as to introduce slavery or involuntary servitude.

3*

The provisions of the ordinance therefore, are the birthright of the people of Ohio. It is their glorious distinction, that the genuine principles of American liberty are imbedded, as it were, in their very soil, and mingled with their very atmosphere. And who of us is insensible to this distinction! Who would willingly forfeit or tarnish it!

Keeping, then, the fundamental interdict against slavery in view, and remembering that no act of congress, in conflict with the ordinance, can be valid, let us inquire how far and under what circumstances we are bound, by that instrument, to recognize the right of masters under the slave systems of other states; and whether the act of congress, relating to fugitives from labor, be consistent with its provisions. The sixth article of compact in the ordinance provides that any person, escaping into the territory, from whom labor or service is lawfully claimed, in any one of the original states, may be lawfully reclaimed. This provision may be said to limit the interdict against slavery; but it would be more proper to say that it introduced a new rule of law in regard to persons held to service, whether as slaves or apprentices, or hired servants, and escaping into the territory from the state in which they might be lawfully so held. At common law, if a servant escape from his master, the remedy is by action for breach of contract; but under this provision, in certain cases, the master may compel the servant to return to his service. The provision was introduced undoubtedly, for the purpose, mainly, of enabling masters in the slaveholding states to reclaim their escaping slaves; but it avoids all recognition of the condition of slavery, and, indeed, impliedly, denies the existence of such a condition, by placing all "persons held to service," upon the same footing. Now, if this provision be regarded as a new rule of law, applicable to the relation of master and servant, then it introduces a course of proceedings *unknown* to the common law, and is an exception to the general provision in the ordinance, that the inhabitants of the territory shall always be entitled to the benefit of judicial proceedings, *according* to the course of the common law. If, on the other hand, this provision be regarded as a qualification of the fundamental interdict against slavery, then it introduces an exception to the general prohibition of involuntary servitude. But the compact reaches all cases, other than those excepted. It secures the benefit of common law proceedings, and of the interdict against slavery, to all persons within the territory, except persons who may be lawfully held to service within one of the original states, and may have escaped thence into the territory. Now the act of congress takes up this provision, and carries it much farther, and applies it to a new class of cases. It provides for the re-caption, not only of servants escaping from the original states, but from all the new states and from all the territories. It is plain, therefore, that the act violates, in this respect, the compact contained in the ordinance, and is so far null and void. In this very case, even if the Court refer to the affidavit of Riley for evidence that the petitioner was a slave, and take for granted that she escaped from Missouri, where her master resides, still the compact guaranties to her the full benefit of common law proceedings, and of the interdict against slavery, for she did not escape from one of the original states. It is no answer to say that the case comes within the constitutional clause in regard to escaping servants: for the constitution could not abrogate or impair the compact.

Again, the ordinance stipulates that the inhabitants of the territory shall always be entitled to the benefit of the writ of habeas corpus and of the trial by jury. But the act of congress provides a mode, in which every inhabitant may be tried for his personal liberty, without a jury. Under the act any man who claims another as a fugitive servant, may subject him, and that, as I have already said, without process, to trial before a single magistrate, without a jury. Is not this so? Who is exempt from being thus tried? What constitutes the exemption? Color! The act says nothing about color: it reaches white apprentices, as well as negro slaves. Condition or character? The act is wholly irrespective of both. There is then no exemption. If any man is safe from such a trial, the act does not make him safe. If any man is secure, he is not indebted for his security to the law. The rich, the intelligent, and the well known may be safe and secure, for their personal rights could hardly be violated with impunity: but there is no safety,—there is

no security for the poor, the ignorant and the unfriended.*
I feel alarmed when I contemplate what has occurred. I see
the solemn pledge in the ordinance, that every settler in the
territory shall be protected in his rights by the jury trial. I
see, notwithstanding this pledge, that this protection is withdrawn, in a most important class of cases, by an act of congress. I know not when the encroachment will stop, if not
now arrested. But I look with confidence to the judiciary of
the country. I feel assured, that, though my reasoning may
fail to convince this Court, other courts, and perhaps this
Court at another time, if not now, will pronounce this act
UNCONSTITUTIONAL, REPUGNANT TO THE ORDINANCE OF 1787,
SUBVERSIVE OF THE FIRST PRINCIPLES OF CIVIL LIBERTY, AND,
THEREFORE, NULL AND VOID.

But it may be said, as I know it has been sometimes said,
that the act of congress is incorporated into the legislation of
the state, and is valid, in consequence of such incorporation,
as an act of our own legislature. I deny the matter of fact,
and I deny the matter of inference. I deny that the act of
congress is incorporated into our state legislation, or is so
recognized as to impart to it the form of an act of our state
legislature ; and I deny that, if so incorporated and recognized, it would acquire any additional validity.

Only four acts have been enacted by the legislature of
Ohio which have the remotest connexion, direct or indirect,
with the subject of the act of congress. These are "an act to
regulate black and mulatto persons," passed, Jan. 5, 1804 ; †
"an act to amend the act regulating black and mulatto persons," passed, January 25, 1807 ; ‡ "an act to punish kidnapping," passed, January 25, 1819; § and "an act to prevent
kidnapping,"‖ passed, February 15, 1831. The first of these

---

* Last summer, a person, from Maryland, caused a young woman,
(Mary Gilmore) to be arrested in Philadelphia, as his fugitive slave. A
legal investigation ensued, when it was established by the most unquestionable testimony, that the alleged slave had been brought up in Philadelphia, and was the child of POOR IRISH PARENTS.
It is well known, and indeed it has been decided by the supreme court
of Ohio, (a) as already stated, that color does not sufficiently mark the
distinction between the negro and the white races.
† Chase's Statutes, 393.   ‡ Ib. 555.   § Chase's Statutes, 1052.
‖ Chase's Statutes, 1878.
(a) 1 Wright's Rep. 578

acts contains no allusion whatever to the act of congress. The most diligent exa:.ination of its provisions would never suggest the idea of the existence of such an act, to a person otherwise ignorant of it. It is true that the act of 1804 proposed to give a remedy to the master, whose slave might be found within the state, but it was a remedy very different from that provided in the act of congress, and entirely independent of it. It went far beyond even that act. It provided that, on the application of any individual in person, or byhis agent, claiming any black or mulatto person, within the state, and making satisfactory proof of *property*,, any judge or justice of the peace should, by his precept, direct the proper officer to arrest and deliver the person claimed to the claimant, or his agent. It did not even require, that the individual, thus claimed, should have any notice of the proceeding. The first intimation that a man would receive, under this section, that his liberty was questioned, would be from the arrest by the sheriff, to be delivered up as a slave! The act, which contained this section, was passed within fourteen months after the constitution had been adopted. And one important lesson may be derived from this startling fact. We may learn from it how little weight is due to contemporaneous, or nearly contemporaneous cconstrutions of constitutional powers, by legislative acts. Nothing could be more dangerous or unconstitutional than this provision; and yet the ink, with which the constitution had been written, was hardly dry, before it found a place in the statute-book. It did not, however, long disgrace our legislation. It was repealed, about two years after its enactment, by the amendatory act of 1807. This act, like that of 1804, is entirely silent in regard to the act of congress. The whole scope and object of both was to enforce a rigid policy of exclusion, in regard to people of color, early adopted in this state, and still persisted in,—whether wisely and justly, or otherwise, need not now be argued. Neither of them adopted the act of congress, or recognized it, or even alluded to it. Whoever, therefore, wishes for evidence of the incorporation of the act of congress into our system of legislation, must seek it elsewhere, than in these acts.

In 1819, the first act against kidnapping was passed. This act recited the act of congress at length, and provided, that

any person who should unlawfully seize, confine, or attempt
to carry out of the state, any black or mulatto person, without
first "proving his right" to such person, agreeably to the act
of congress, should be imprisoned in the penitentiary, not less
than one, nor more than ten years. It is evident, that the
legislature which passed this statute, regarded the act of
congress as a valid and subsisting law. They found it in the
statute book, and without scrutinizing very closely the constitutional power of congress to enact it, legislated in reference to it, as valid. But they did not make it part or parcel
of the law of Ohio. No trace of any intention to incorporate it
into our system of legislation, is discernable in the statute.
They provided, that persons, proceeding under it, should not
be held liable to be punished as kidnappers; and that was all.
It is unnecessary, however, to enquire particularly into the
effect of the act of 1819, for it was repealed in 1831 by the
existing statute against kidnapping. I may say, however, in
passing, that the act of 1819 seems to have been framed in the
spirit of the ordinance, and of our state constitution. Its
phraseology indicates the clear sense of the legislature as to
the true import of the constitutional provision in regard to
fugitives from labor, and that it was understood as providing
for the reclamation of escaping negroes and mulattoes—not as
slaves, not as property—but as persons obliged to service.
The statute of 1831, provides for the punishment of persons
who should attempt to carry any black or mulatto out of the
state, without first taking him before some judge or justice,
and establishing by proof "agreeably to the laws of the United
States," a right of "property" in him. Is the act of
congress incorporated into the legislation of Ohio by this
statute? It exempts from punishment for kidnapping those
persons, who, before removing a black or mulatto out of the
state, take him before a judge or justice, and prove "property"
in him, "agreeably to the laws of the United States." It
admits, that blacks and mulattoes may be lawfully carried
out of the state on proof of property, under federal laws; and
this is all. But, it is hardly less than absurd, to say, that it
adopts these federal laws, and authorizes the magistrates, and
obliges the ministerial officers of the state, to execute them. It
might as well be maintained, that a statute exempting the

marshal of the district of Ohio, from criminal punishment for the arrest of persons violating the revenue laws of tne United States, would have the effect of incorporating into our state legislation, the whole federal revenue code.

But, were this otherwise, is it quite certain, that the act of congress is regard to fugitives, is even referred to in the act of 1831! Is the act of congress "a law of the United States," agreeably to which, " property " may be proved in negroes and mulattoes! The act provides a mode for the reclamation of fugitive servants. It is an attempt, (unauthorized, in my judgment,) on the part of congress, to carry into effect the provision in the federal constitution, in respect to persons held to service in one state, and escaping thence into another. But neither the constitution, nor the act, say any thing about escaping property in negroes and mulattoes. The constitution, (and in this respect the act follows it,) contains no recognition whatever, of any right of property in man. It neither affirms, nor disaffirms the existence, possible or actual, of such property. It leaves this whole matter of property in human beings, precisely where the articles of confederation left it, with the states. It establishes no rule with regard to escaping negroes or mulattoes, which does not equally apply to escaping white apprentices. It takes up and deals with the broad and general relation of master and servant: but it has nothing whatever, to do with the relation of owner and property. It obliges the states to recognize the former relation, and to deliver up the escaping servant: but it does not oblige them to recognize the latter relation, as subsisting at all between man and man. It is plain, therefore, that if we think that the statute of 1831, even refers to the act concerning fugitives from labor, our opinion must be based upon historical facts, rather than upon the plain import of the statute. But, if the act of 1831 can hardly be said to refer to the act of congress, and much less to adopt it, then there is no foundation for the idea, sometimes advanced, that justices of the peace have jurisdiction in cases of escaping servants, not in virtue of the act of congress indeed, but in virtue of the incorporation of that act into our own system of legislation; for there is no act in the statute book, besides the act of 1831, which contains the remotest allusion to it.

And if the act of congress were a part of our own system of legislation; if our legislature had passed a law expressed in the same identical words, what force could it have, so long as the great command of the people remained, legibly written in the constitution, " the right of trial by jury shall be inviolate ?" I need not repeat the arguments already urged to prove that the act of congress is a violation of the right of trial by jury.— It is enough to say, that the act of congress, if incorporated into our state legislation, would violate the provision in the state constitution and in the ordinance, securing, to all persons within the territorial limits of Ohio, this inestimable right, in the same degree and to the same extent, that it violates, if considered as depending on the authority of congress, the provision in the ordinance alone.

I arrive then at the conclusion, that the return of the Sheriff shows no sufficient cause for the caption and detention of the petitioner, and that she must be discharged from custody:

Because the jurisdiction of the magistrate, in cases of escaping servants, if he has any, is very special and limited, and all the facts set forth, in all the papers, connected with the Sheriff's return, do not show a case within that jurisdiction:

Because the commitment of the magistrate to the custody of the Sheriff *is not* warranted by any act, and being a state warrant in the present case, *could not be* warranted by any act of congress:

Because the commitment, even if made by competent authority is utterly insufficient, no cause, whatever, of caption or detention being expressed upon its face, or indicated by reference to any other writing: and substantial defects in the commitment cannot be supplied by volunteer references to any papers or writings not referred to by it, especially when such papers and writings possess, themselves no legal validity:

Because the act of congress, which alone purports to confer on the magistrate jurisdiction in cases of escaping servants, not being necessary or proper to carry into execution any power vested in the government of the United States, or in any department, or officer thereof, is not warranted by the constitution of the United States:

Because this act of congress, being an exercise by congress of the power of appointment, or a transfer of federal judical power to state tribunals, is in one or both these respects, repugnant to the constitution of the United States:

Because this act of congress, authorizing, as it does, the arrest confinement, trial and removal of escaping servants, " without due process of law," is, in this respect, also repugnant to the constitution of the United States:

Because this act of congress, authorizing, as it does, a course of proceedings, unknown to the common law, and the recaption of fugitives from labor, in a class of cases not within the exceptive provision of the ordinance of 1787, violates the fundamental compact contained in that ordinance:

Because this act of congress, exposing as it does, every citizen to trial for his dearest rights, without a jury, violates, in this respect, also, that fundamental compact:

Because this act of congress derives no validity from any act of the state legislature; nor is in any sense incorporated into our state legislation: nor could, even if it were so incorporated, acquire, thereby, any obligatory quality, inasmuch as it would then be repuguant, not only to the provision in the ordinance, but also to the provision in the state constitution, securing, inviolably, the right of trial by jury:

Because this act of congress, exposing as it does, every member of the community to arrest, confinement and forcible transportation, without process of law, by every other man who may claim him as a fugitive from service, is repugnant to the first principles of civil liberty and subversive of the very ends of civil society.

I have now done with this case. I have presented, feebly perhaps and unsuccessfully, but honestly and fearlessly, the great principles, legal and constitutional, which, in my judgment, ought to govern it. I have not asked—I do not now ask, in behalf of my humble client, deliverance from imprisonment, because that imprisonment is against natural right, but because it is against the constitution and against the law. I claim, however in her behalf, that it be borne in mind that there is such a thing as natural right, derived, not from any civil constitution or civil code, but from the constitution of human nature and the code of heaven. This court, I am sure, need not to be reminded of the original, paramount truth, written upon the hearts of all men by the finger of God, the same in all ages

4

and in all climes, and destined to no change, proclaimed by our fathers, in the declaration of independence, to be selfevident, and reiterated in our state constitution as its fundamental axiom, that all men are born "equally free." And if the petitioner at the bar cannot expect, here, the full benefit of this fundamental truth; if her right to freedom must, here, be vindicated upon narrower grounds, let her have, at least this advantage from it. Let her be regarded as free, until it be shown by the fullest and clearest evidence, that her case falls within some exception to the universal law of human liberty. Let the proceedings by which she is now, without the accusation of crime, and without the suspicion of guilt, deprived of freedom and driven a suppliant to this bar, be narrowly scrutinized. Let every provision, unfavorable to liberty, whether legal or constitutional, receive a strict and rigorous interpretation. And if, when thus scrutinized, these proceedings shall be found insufficient, and especially if they shall be found to be warranted by no law and repugnant to the most vital principles of our social system; if, when thus interpreted, those provisions, which exclude a certain class of persons from the benefit of these vital principles, shall be found not broad enough to reach the case of this petitioner; I demand her discharge in the name of justice, of liberty, and of our common humanity.

I am aware that some excitement has connected itself with this case;—excitement, perhaps, not wholly unmingled with prejudice. I trust, however, that this tribunal is beyond the reach of these feelings. The wave of perverted impulse, which so frequently bears down the sense of natural right and the love of constitutional liberty, will break, I trust, harmlessly and noiselessly, at the foot of this seat of justice. Yet the existence of excitement and prejudice may well admonish us to caution. If a hasty judgment be pronounced, in this case, it will afford little consolation, hereafter, to reflect that "feeling had some share in it. Passion and feeling are transitory: we shall survive their influence: but the judgment, which this Court shall this day pronounce, in its lasting consequences, will survive both them and us. The eclipse, which for a few moments hides the sun, passes away; but he, who during the temporary obscuration, makes a false step from the precipice, is lost forever.

Vitally important as the issue of this cause is to the petitioner—for liberty is sweet even to the humblest, and slavery, disguise it as you will, is still a bitter draught,—the community has in it even a deeper stake. If she may be held in custody, though charged with no crime, upon a commitment, which shows, upon its face no cause of caption or detention, and which, even when aided by reference to every paper within reach of the court, still fails to show any legal or sufficient cause, then is it manifest that the habeas corpus act—that grand bulwark of psrsonal liberty,—is virtually repealed. If such a commitment is a sufficient warrant for imprisonment, the whole legal security of personal freedom is gone. If under the act of congress, this petitioner must be remanded to custody, in order that she may be delivered over to the magistrate, then it is clear that every person who may be arrested as a fugitive from labor, must be committed to the same irresponsible authority. If the act must be respected as valid and constitutional in this case, it must be in every other. And I see not how, in this case, or in any other case, the provisions of that act can consist with the proper security of individual rights. I call upon the counsel for the claimant to exert all their ingenuity, and put forth all their ability, and tell me, if they can, upon what principle the provisions of that act, and the provisions of the constitution and the ordinance can be reconciled. I call upon them to tell me and to tell the community who is safe under that act? If the most honored citizen shall be seized and dragged before a magistrate, upon the pretence that he is a fugitive from labor, what redress can this Court afford him, which this petitioner may not equally demand? And what security has he, any more than this petitioner, against a hasty or an unjust decision by the magistrate? Shall I be told that such a man is in no danger of such seizure. He may be in no danger; but what right has he to greater security, than the very humblest man in the community? Shall it be said here, that a man is to be indebted for his personal liberty—not to the constitution, but to his wealth, his intelligence and his many friends! Is there then, indeed, one rule for the intelligent and influential and another for the unlettered and the humble—one measure of liberty for the rich and another for the poor!

I trust that the decision of this day will establish no such odious distinction, and will tend, in no degree, to alienate from the constitution the affections of the people. I trust that the judgment, this day to be pronounced, will assure to all, even to the humblest, the most ample legal security for personal rights, and the full benefit of every provision in the constitution and in the ordinance.

REPORT

OF THE

HOLDEN SLAVE CASE,

TRIED AT THE

JANUARY TERM OF THE COURT OF COMMON PLEAS,
FOR THE COUNTY OF WORCESTER, A. D. 1839.

Published by the
Board of Directors of the Holden Anti-Slavery Society.

WORCESTER:
PRINTED BY COLTON & HOWLAND.
1839.

41

INTRODUCTION.

In the present state of our country, every fact, which has a direct or even indirect and remote bearing on the momentous subject of American Slavery, is of some importance. Few, if any of our Northern citizens profess to hold slavery in any other estimation than the profoundest abhorrence ; and yet, it is undeniable that very many either tolerate its existence in silence, or exert but a very inadequate influence for its removal.

Abstract Slavery every one abhors ; but of slavery, as it exists, so little is even yet known that most seem to regard it as mainly a nominal evil, and, therefore, experience very little sympathy with those who are called slaves. To dissipate this darkness and overcome this apathy, the enlightened and active friends of the slave ought to stand ready to seize upon, and skilfully use, such facts as are evolved by the providence of God, adapted to illustrate the necessary operation of the inhuman system.

The following Report exhibits several facts of this class, and we simply allude to them in this brief introduction, in order to turn the reader's attention to them as he examines the testimony in the case. The facts to which particular allusion is made are the following.

The claimant of " the girl Anne " is a native of Worcester County, and so was her husband, who, on going to reside at the South, lost so much of his New England abhorrence of slavery as himself to become a slave-holder. The same is true of Mrs. Eames. We are not to ascribe this lamentable and forbidding fact to any peculiar cruelty of disposition in these persons, or to any stronger love of money than is common among us. It must be ascribed to the natural operation of the *system* of slavery, as it exists interwoven with all the domestic and social relations of the community among whom these persons went to reside.

43

'There are, also, subordinate facts, which are to be accounted for in the same way ; as, for example, the apparent unconcern of Mrs. Eames touching the health of the girl, and her being overtasked ; the severity with which punishment for trivial faults, called "crimes," was inflicted ; and the entire neglect of the literary and religious education of Anne, during her stay in Holden.

These facts serve to show how important it is that the youth of New England receive early and full instruction in the true nature of the system of slavery ; and how intimately connected are such citizens of the North as have relatives at the South, with the evils of the system ; and how liable are the Northern citizens to regard Slavery with moderated abhorrence and even with favor. It is well known that numerous persons in New England, among whom are ministers and other professors of the benign religion of Jesus Christ, are, at this moment, so connected with the South ; and that these persons almost uniformly stand aloof from all interference with this foulest of moral evils with which the land is polluted, or even strenuously oppose, as " fanatical and incendiary and mad," every effort made to awaken the people to a consideration of the subject. It was under the conviction that the facts of the present case may contribute to undeceive our citizens on some important topics belonging to the great subject of slavery, that the publishers were prompted to publish the following Report.

And here it may be important to remark, that the Report may be relied on as correct, since it has been compiled from minutes taken at the time by a reporter and those of the Hon. Charles Allen, Counsel for the defendants. Mr. Allen has, by request, furnished the publishers with a succinct statement of the points in evidence which would have been more fully established, if the trial had not been arrested by the District Attorney, when only *two* of twelve or fourteen witnesses on the defence had given their testimony.

The law of personal replevin, being new, and this, as is believed, being the first trial under it, the present Report is deemed of the more importance to the community. Neither should it be supposed by any that this law is limited to the removal of slaves or colored persons from duress. Its powers and applicability extend to every class of the people.

COMPILER.

REPORT.

The case of Commonwealth *vs.* SAMUEL STRATTON, SAMUEL FOSTER, JAMES E. CHENEY, and FARNUM WHITE, Jun., who were charged in the indictment with a *conspiracy* to defraud OLIVIA EAMES of Holden, of the *voluntary* services of her servant girl, named ANNE, without her consent,—came on in the Court of Common Pleas, in this town, (Worcester) on Tuesday, January 29th, 1839, Judge STRONG presiding. PLINY MERRICK, Esq., District Attorney, conducted the prosecution ; and CHARLES ALLEN, Esq., appeared for the defendants.

Mr. Merrick, in opening the case, stated that Mrs. Eames, the party aggrieved, was a native of Worcester County—that she was married to Mr. Eames, also a native of this County, who a few years since removed with her to New Orleans. There he acquired some property, and, among other articles, came in possession of a number of slaves. In 1837, he died ; after which, Mrs. Eames sold her property, excepting the girl Anne, then 12 or 13 years of age. She was retained as a house servant and nurse ; and accompanied Mrs. Eames in that capacity, on a visit to Mrs. Eames's friends in Grafton and Holden, in Massachusetts.

Of course, as soon as she came into this State, she was as free as any native born citizen of this State, and had the right to remain with or leave her mistress, as she saw fit. The highest tribunal has decided, that, if a person come here on business or pleasure, and bring a slave, the slave becomes free.

In the session of 1837, an important Act was passed by the Legislature of this State.* By that act any person is entitled to the Writ, unless indicted for some offence. He may go to the Clerk and demand it. No power of

---

* See said Act at the end of this Report.

45

Attorney is to be required and no express form is necessary. Any person for and in behalf of the plaintiff may
sue out this writ.

If Mrs. Eames did imprison her, she might be brought
into Court, and she might apply to the Court for security.
But the allegation, in the indictment, is, *first*, that Anne
was *not* restrained of her liberty *at all.* Anne was there
voluntarily. She did not suppose that her liberty was infringed. Yet the defendants sued out the writ, while
there was no duress. It is alleged that Anne had no
knowledge of the writ. This is an offence, and it is the
offence charged in the indictment. No persons, claiming
to be the friends of Anne, had a right to sue out this writ,
without her consent. Still, we must be careful not to in-
fringe on the rights of minors. Few, if any, children of
those who are educated, know any thing of the writ of
personal replevin, much less, one brought up in bondage.
If Anne, in any way intimated a desire, directly or indirectly, that aid in some form should be granted, the defendants are not only excused but justified. If it was
done without her knowledge or consent, the defendants
are liable, Anne not being in bondage. Undoubtedly, the
defendants understood and believed that it was the purpose of Mrs. Eames to carry Anne back to Louisiana,
where she would be in bondage. The defendants thought
this was wicked, and the dictates of humanity required
that they should interfere. But the motive may be good,
and yet the laws must not be violated from such motives.
Some think the business of distillation is pernicious.
Now, suppose a philanthropist should think that a laborer in the distiller's employ was endangering his health
and his soul, and should sue out this writ, for the purpose of removing the laborer from the service of the distiller. The motive would be good, but the act would be
a violation of the law. So, if a slave should be brought
here, and prefer to go back into slavery, we have no
right to prevent it. It was so with Anne. She had a
right to return and be a slave. *The offence charged is the
conspiracy.* No subsequent ratification by Anne could justify the act of the defendants. If the defendants did design to take Anne and educate and christianize her, if she
did not desire it, though she afterwards ratified it and
blessed God for their efforts, still the defendants would
not be justified. *Instances have occurred in this Commonwealth, where individuals having had their freedom here, and*

having been treated kindly, have voluntarily gone back into slavery.

We should proceed in this trial as we do in other trials, whatever are our sentiments on the subject of slavery. I hope no prosecutor will be found who will abridge the right of personal liberty. If these individuals were actuated by philanthropic motives, these things will be considered by the Court. I enter on my duties with feelings neither elevated nor depressed.

Mr. Merrick exhibited the Writ above-named, dated Sept. 7, 1838, and a bond signed by S. Stratton, S. Foster, and James E. Cheney, and witnessed by Farnum White, Jun.

He then called upon Charles Allen, Esq., who testified, that Samuel Stratton and Elnathan Davis applied for a writ of personal replevin two or three days before date of the writ. They said that Mrs. Eames had in her custody a SLAVE, brought from the South, whom she intended to carry back and sell—they did not like to take the girl by force from Mrs. Eames, but wished to do it in a legal way. He understood from them that the girl desired her liberty. He told them of the legal remedy—had several interviews with them—the writ was made out under his direction, and the bond was written by him, but not executed at his office. Mr. Foster called to see about signing the bond as surety.

Mrs. OLIVIA EAMES being sworn, testified, that she spent the summer of 1838 in Holden and Grafton. Her mother is Mrs. Betsy Sherman of Holden. She, (Mrs. E.) came to New York in 1837, and to Holden in May, 1838. Her husband was Lowell Eames, formerly of Upton. He went to New Orleans in 1835, and died there in 1837. Anne was in her employment as her slave, and all the time, since she left New Orleans, she never knew her to express a wish to leave her, in any instance. Anne *often expressed a wish to return to New Orleans.* I proposed to leave my babe at the North. Anne *wanted* to go back—was 14 years old then. I was in Holden at my father's house. Anne's employment was to take care of my child, and to go of errands; went to the neighbors freely, sometimes went with the babe. I was absent from home occasionally; don't keep house; none of the family were at home but my mother, and a brother 10 years old, and a brother 7 years old. Mr. Flagg lived in the house at that time. Mrs. Flagg was at home. I saw Stratton,

Foster, Cheney, White, and Hinds at Judah Wright's first. When F. White passed the house, the girl was in the garden picking apples. Jim Cheney came to the house and went to go where the girl had been, but she had come to the house. I went out to see what they were looking after—did not think it was the black girl. Cheney came to the door and asked for mother—I asked them to sit down—Hinds said that he understood that I had a colored girl in my possession—I said I had—he said that he had come to take her away. I told him I could'nt help it, he couldn't have her. He said he had authority to take her, and read a paper. I told him I didn't know any thing about it—didn't care who authorized him—he had no right to take her. He asked to see her. I told him she was in the back room—went to call her. He followed. I went for her, but she wasn't there. I went up chamber—Anne was out back with my child. Hinds and Jim Cheney were attending to their business the best way they could. I called her in, told her, Mr. Hinds wanted to speak to her—Hinds asked her age, she did'nt know—he asked me, but didn't find out—he said to Anne, will you go with me ? She said, no. Mr. Hinds patted her on her head—told her he would not hurt her—he would take her to Worcester—Worcester is a beautiful place. I told him if he took Anne he must take me and the child too. He didn't seem inclined to take us. Cheney went out and came back with Stratton and Foster. You have been out for more help, I said ; if you get more help you will not frighten me. Anne went into the bed-room ; Hinds went in after her, and Jim Cheney next. Anne began to cry—Hinds told her not to be frightened, and like of that—coaxing her. Hinds told me to take the child. I wouldn't take it, and mother wouldn't. Then Mrs. Flagg took it, so he got rid of it. He asked for pen and ink—refused. F. White brought in pen and ink. I took hold of Anne, and Anne took hold of me. Sam Stratton was in the room. Cheney was called back—said they had help enough, but Hinds commanded him to assist. Jim Cheney took hold of me; Hinds took me round the waist. Hinds threw me on the bed. I told them they ought to be in better business—they were insulting—they separated us. Foster and Stratton were trying to hold a pen in Anne's hand to make her make her mark—I don't know nothing what the paper was, and nothing about it. I scrabbled round and got away from Hinds—Anne was in the road and Stratton had hold of her—I was so flustered that I did'nt see Cheney, guess he was about somewhere, Foster was writing on the wall—went to see what he was up to—took hold of the paper and pulled it away from him. He said it was well I didn't tear that paper, I should have had to go to State Prison during my life, if I had—I went back into the house to see my child, and they carried Anne off. Stratton said in the bedroom, well, well, enough has been said, take her along. I didn't see her after they carried her off. Saw her in Grand Jury room, have not seen her since. When at the table, told my brother to run for father and Mr. Putnam. I always lived in Upton till I went to New York six years ago, remained there till 1835.

Examined by Mr. Allen.—Said, Anne went out with other children. There was a school in the neighborhood—she didn't go to school, or to meeting since she came from Louisiana. Her principal work was to nurse the child, and to do other chores, such as I chose to have her do. She sometimes went to Judah Wright's and got a pail of water. We lived at the top of the hill, and Wright down the hill—it was'nt so steep a hill as I have seen—the hill is there and you can see it. She did not bring 10 pails of water in a day—some days, not any, she carried it on her head—I told her to, as she could bring it easier, she was most used to that way—didn't see her spill the water.

Question was then put to Mrs. Eames by Mr Allen, whether she intended to carry Anne back as a slave. This question was objected to by Mr. Merrick, who remarked—Mrs. Eames has not ventured to say that she was in her voluntary service. Objection was overruled by the Court.

Question by Mr. Allen.—What did you intend to do with her? *Ans. I did not intend to compel her against her will.* I suppose she would tell me what she wished. *I never considered her property, after I came to the North—never called her property after I came into this free country.* I never made no application to any one in New Orleans to buy her afterwards. I gave no commission about the sale of Anne—I had no negociations to sell her there; when she returned. If I went back to live in New Orleans, I should keep her—set very much by her—I don't think I said I should carry Anne back. It was my intention to go back

2

—I don't know that I should have asked her consent to carry her back—can't tell what I should do—should carry her, if she was willing to go—I had no more interest in her than in any other—I always set by her—I never told her she was a slave or free, told her she was to live with sister June, if I did. Her health has not been injured by carrying water and other loads. *I don't recollect saying she would answer my purpose as long as I wanted her.* Mrs. Caldwell said, I had better call a physician and do something for her. I didn't say she would answer long enough for my use, *never.* I did not say that no body ever heard of sending for a doctor for a negro. Hinds took me in full possession. *Scratch ? Should'nt think strange if I did. Bite ? They know best if they got bit.*

Col. Hinds *called.*—I made service of the writ of personal replevin. I think, I took it from my table, Mr. Allen did not furnish me with the form of a return, when I took the writ.

The writ and bond I took together. I went to Mr. Judah Wright's, I think Mr. Cheney went with me to Wright's ; neither of the Def'ts was there while I was there. I stopped at the door. I saw the deft's first at Col. Stratton's. Found Stratton, Foster and Cheney there. ' My partner told me to call there, as there would be sureties there to sign the bond. Bond was not signed there. I told them it was necessary for the girl to sign the bond first. The next I saw Stratton and Foster, they came into the house at Mr. Sherman's. I did not see Anne make her mark to the paper. I saw Foster and Stratton sign their names, one did it out of doors, I am not sure but both. Anne stood in the road close by, when Foster and Cheney signed their names. Anne was pretty much alone. I took the paper. They walked down to Cheney's. Stratton, Foster, and Cheney came there, *no one led her.* She walked independently by herself. I was behind her. There was a carriage at Cheney's. Foster, Stratton and Anne were in the carriage. *I took the paper. Asked Anne if she made her mark. She said, she did. I got Mr. White to witness it.* She sat on the back seat. Would not be seen from the houses as she passed. I did not know where she was going. I told her she was going to Worcester. I told Stratton and Foster, they must take charge of her. I don't recollect making arrangements with Foster and Stratton to take her, before I took her from Mrs. Eames. Mr. Stratton lived 2 1-2 or 3 miles from there, Mr. Foster 1-2 a mile, or more, farther. They would come past the meeting-house to get to Stratton's. I told Anne at Mrs. Eames's I think, that she was going to Worcester.

Cross Examined.—I directed Mr. Foster and Stratton to take Anne and put her in some safe place, where she would not be taken away or stolen. We went to the house of Mrs. Eames—were invited in—I inquired for Mrs. Eames. Mrs. Eames came. I asked her if she had a colored girl with her. She said she had. I told her I came to take her. She said she did not know what business I had to take her girl. I told her I would show the authority, I read the writ. She said, I might take my writ and go home—I should not have the girl. I told her I was bound to take her and must take her. I must take her at all events. She said she would call her. She did not find her. We walked out and walked round. Cheney went to the back-house door—it was shut. He called; Anne answered. I told Anne, I had come after her to carry her away. I asked her if she wanted to go. She dropped her head, and said, "I don't know." Her mistress spoke and said, " *don't know, Anne? you know you don't want to go.*" Anne made *no reply.* Mistress spoke very quick. I then talked with Mrs. Eames some time, told her to be quiet. If I did what I ought not, she would have a bond to cover all expense. After trying a great while to persuade her to give her up peaceably, the girl went into a small room. I went there—Mrs. Eames followed, and took the girl round with both hands and held her tight. I asked Mrs. Sherman to take the child. She would not, I took the child myself, and Anne let go of it. I stepped into the kitchen. I saw several young ladies, I asked one to take it. She said she did not know as it would answer. I told her I would stand between her and harm. She took it. I stepped back into the little room. Mrs. Eames still stood clinched round the girl. I called upon her to give her up. She refused. I took hold of one of Mrs. Eames's hands, and Cheney the other. Mrs. Eames resisted violently. She tried to bite and scratch. Our throwing her on to a bed must be a mistake. It must be some other time and person. There might have been a bed in the room, but I think there was not. We were there an hour and a half trying to persuade her. I said every thing I could. *She was very violent the whole time.* I used as little violence as possible to effect the object,

She clinched at the paper once, but did not get hold of it. I was close by, Foster was there with the paper. She was out at the wall, I think, when they signed the paper. I heard no such declaration of Foster at the wall. I heard no such declaration of Mr. Foster at any time as, you would have had to go to State Prison, &c. If such a declaration was made, I must have heard it. I was very close to Foster, when he put his name to the bond. After Anne had left her mistress, she went very willingly—was, perfectly composed and calm. She walked down cheerfully, and after she was in the carriage, *she appeared very cheerful.*

I told Mrs. Eames she had better keep the bond as her security. Mr. White took no part whatever in this, except going after ink. I sent Mr. Cheney to get ink somewhere. Mr. Cheney came without the ink-stand, and Mr. White followed with it. That was the first of Mr. White's being at the house. I don't recollect Mr. Foster's meddling at all. He had the paper at the table, that was the first of Mr. Foster's having any thing to do. Besides this, I don't know any thing that Mr. Foster did.

I told Mr. Foster and Cheney and Stratton, it was necessary for them all to sign the bond. Mr. White witnessed the bond, at my request. Anne looked at the paper, and made her mark. I took the paper and asked her if she held the pen and made the cross. I asked her if she did it voluntarily and freely, she replied, she did. I told them I presumed an effort would be made to arrest her, and told them to take care of her. Cheney did not interfere, except by my command. After I told him he must, at first he rather hesitated.

It is my impression that Mrs. Eames repeatedly said, *Anne was her property,* but I cannot certainly testify. It is my impression she did.

ANNE *called.*—I live with Mr. Edward Earle, in Worcester. I remember Col. Hinds ; I went first to Mr. Morey's, in Worcester. I did not know where I was going. I came with Mr. Foster and Mr. Stratton. I had seen Mr. Stratton at Mr. Cheney's house. I had never spoken to either of them. I had not seen Mr. Foster before that day. I had been at Mr. Cheney's house alone. It was about a week before I left, I went for butter. I was not there but a little while. They told me the way to Mr. Cheney's house. I came from New Orleans with Mrs. Eames, I had not always lived at New Orleans. I washed dishes, and took care of the child. Went to the village, went for whortleberries, sometimes alone, and sometimes with the children. I was in Grafton at Mr. Reuben Eames's with Mrs. Eames. I used to take care of George. I did not go to the neighbors there, I went with the children to one house in Grafton. I never sent any message or errand to Mr. Foster or Col. Stratton. I never asked any one to ask either of them to do any thing for me. I never told Mrs. Eames I wanted to go away and leave her. I was in the house when Col. Hinds and the other men came. I knew who Mr. Cheney was—not who the other men were. I went out of the room.

I had never put my name or made my mark to paper before that day. There was a paper on the table. The paper was not read to me. Nobody there told me what was in the paper. Foster put a pen into my hand. Told me to mark my name on it. I believe I made a mark on it. I believe, he did help me make the mark. After I left the table, I went into the road. I don't know who told me to go, Mr. Cheney or Mr. Foster. I went to Cheney's house. I believe, Mr. Foster went with me. I believe, Mr. Foster took hold of my hand. I went right to the carriage. Got into it. Mr. Stratton and Mr. Foster went with me. They went to Worcester. When I got there, it was dark.

Cross Examined.—I believe, it was Mr. Foster who had my hand, I am not sure. I went from Virginia to New Orleans. I was employed to carry water from Mr. Wright's—I carried a great many pails of water in a day. My mistress told me to carry them on my head. My mistress told me that I was thirteen while I was at Holden. She said she meant to carry me back to New Orleans again. She said she was going to sell me when she carried me there.

Did you express a wish to have your personal liberty ? Objected to by Counsel for Government. Though it was reported to the defendants that she wished her liberty, her mind might have changed.

No person has a right to sue out the writ, unless authorized by the person restrained of his liberty. When a party is restrained of his liberty he is entitled to the writ. No agency can be created but by the act of the principal. *The 15th Section of the law provides that the friends may sue out this writ.* A child cannot have the process because a bond is to be executed. To sue out a writ, unless a person is imprisoned, is an injury to him. Suppose Anne's condition is not improved. When the bond was given by Anne, it was of no validity.

Judge Strong *decided*,—It is not necessary to meet and settle all the difficulties which may arise under this Statute. I am inclined to the opinion that the Legislature does not mean that any person must have an implied authority—but *the act* is an authority.

Anne *resumed*.—I expressed a desire to have my liberty before I was taken from Holden. I told Miss White that I wanted to be free. It was Henrietta White. I told Mrs. Warren I wanted to be free. She sits back by the door.

My mistress knocked me across the head with the toasting iron—my mistress lived in Holden, when she struck me with the toasting iron.

John Morey *called*.—The colored girl came to my house. Mr. Stratton and Mr. Foster brought her there—I did not know which day she was coming—Mr. Stratton and another gentleman told me she was coming. It was two or three days before. After she arrived at my house, Anne was kept up chamber some time. Mr. Stratton thought she would be more contented at my house, than with people who were not of the same color. They wished me to let her go to school—She was kept in my chamber, we were afraid she would be stolen.

[Note.—The witness is inquired of whether there were threats in the community of a rescue. The question is objected to—and the objection is sustained.]

Mr. Morey *resumed*.—Anne was very well contented at my house. She said she desired her liberty. I was not directed to restrain or seclude her any farther than was necessary for her protection. Col. Stratton and Mr. Elnathan Davis offered to pay the expense of her schooling. Col. Stratton was at my house once or twice—cannot tell whether the same person was with him second time or not.

Mrs. Betsey Sherman *called*.—I am the mother of Mrs. Eames. Mrs. Eames lived with me at the village and on the hill.

I recollect the time when Anne was put down cellar. She did something worthy of punishment, Mrs. Eames told her to go down cellar. She refused. Mrs. Eames put her down. One or the other hit the toasting iron, and it fell. She made much ado about it.

Before Hinds came to the house, I did not see any other

person. Cheney and Hinds came together. Anne was in
the house. She had been after apples. Hinds inquired for
Mrs. Eames—I introduced him to Mrs. Eames. They went
back into the room. He asked Mrs. Eames if she had a
colored girl in her possession. She said she had. He asked, if he could see her. She said he could. He told her,
he had come after her. She asked by what authority he
came after her girl? *She told Col. Hinds that Anne was
as free as any person. If he could get her away by flattering, she was willing he should.* She went out to look for
Anne. Anne came in through the kitchen. Hinds asked
her if she wanted to go with him. She said NO, sir. He
told her, Worcester was a pretty place. She faced the plas-
tering and began to cry. Hinds took the babe. I refused
to take it. He carried it to Mrs. Flagg in the other room.
He came back and went into the bed-room. Mrs. Eames
was there. Perhaps, Cheney was there. She took hold of
Anne and Hinds took hold of her. They were all hold of
each other, justling. They got Anne up to the table by
pushing and pulling along. They were all huddled up together. Mrs. Eames was thrown on a bed in the kitchen.
Farnum White brought the inkstand in. I saw Stratton
and Foster put the pen into her hand, and take her hand
into his, as though they meant her to write. Nobody told
what was in the paper in my hearing. They pushed Anne
out. Col. Stratton gave me a push back, as I went to the
door—left a blue mark on my arm. I went down to the
carriage. I saw them as they were going down to the carriage. First, one had her arm, and then the other. I saw
a man at the wall, Mr. Foster. He had a paper and pen.
Mrs. Eames was not amongst them. I don't know that I
saw her at the wall.

Cross Examined.—I don't recollect what Anne had done.
Anne made a fuss about it, (the toasting iron.) I think she
might be heard at Mrs. White's—I did not go towards the
cellar at all. I did not leave my seat. I dont know where
I was sitting—I heard the toasting iron fall—All I know
about its falling, was, I heard it fall. Mrs. Eames was
there when the toasting iron fell. All I know is, the toasting iron fell down cellar and made something of a racket.
I cannot swear that Mrs. Eames did not throw the toasting
iron down cellar. Anne made some fuss a minute or two,
the cellar door was shut. I should not think she was down

cellar over fifteen minutes. I cannot tell the time. I don't recollect about its being said that Mrs. Eames would send for Mr. Sherman, and he would take the horse-whip to her. This affair was when Mrs. Eames first came to Holden.

I did not like it very much to have people come in as they (the defendants) did. *It excited some hard feelings.* I think Hinds was there an hour and a half. Mrs. Eames and Hinds were standing alone, and Hinds threw her on a bed. At that time, I was not doing any thing. I don't know as Hinds let go of Mrs. Eames after they came out of the bed-room—I cannot say.

GEORGE PUTNAM, *a lad, called.*—I am son of Le Barron Putnam. When Anne was taken, I was between Wright's and Stratton's. I saw two men hold of her—one hold of each wrist. I was in the road. They did not go by me. They were a little past Mr. Wright's, when I first saw them. I came from home.

Cross Examined.—Charles Drury was with me. Charles got there a little first. I don't know how far I was from Stratton's house. They were *not* dragging her along. I did not see them dragging her. I don't know that I said they were dragging her. I think, she was hanging back a little. I did not notice whether they were walking fast or not. I don't know whether she was hanging back, or whether they were walking fast, and holding her, and she keeping up as well as she could.

THOMAS RANDALL *called.*—I was near Mr. Stratton's when Anne went away. I was between Stratton's and Wright's; not more than 2 rods from Stratton's. I saw a person hold of each hand of Anne. I did not know them. I cannot tell who they were. They were this side of Mr. Wright's, between Wright's and Stratton's. I followed down a little way. I did not see them until they got to Cheney's. They had hold of her hands as long as I was there. She was hanging back. I heard nothing said.

Cross Examined.—I do not recollect that I have denied all this statement. I do not recollect that I ever said, she was not hanging back. I don't recollect that I ever said that I had told one story before the grand jury, and I must stick to it. I did not notice particularly, whether they were travelling fast or not. I was from 10 to 15 rods from them. I cannot tell whether I was within 30 rods of them or not. I cannot say whether I was within 40 rods or not of them.

I have mentioned it to Le Barron Putnam. I cannot say whether Putnam was here or not, when Grand Jury met. Two of James Stratton's boys were near me—about a rod off—a rod or two. I was going to Mr. Stratton's—boarded there then, and board there now.

GEORGE PUTNAM *called again.*—I was at home when I heard something was going on at Sherman's. I was at the top of the hill with the rest of the boys. When I got to the top of the hill, they were beyond Mr. Wright's. I don't know whether I went half way to Mr. Wright's from the top of the hill or not. I don't know whether I walked or run—I told my father what I saw.

MRS. OLIVIA EAMES *again called.*—I never struck Anne with a toasting iron. Anne had committed some little crime. I was going to shut her down cellar. I took her forward of me and in getting her down, the toasting iron fell down. She cried considerably. *Always did* when I punished her.

HENRY BUTTERFIELD *called.*—It is between 22 and 24 rods from Wright's to Sherman's house. I did not tell Mr. Clifford if I had been present, I should have butchered the officer or run a sword through him. I said if I had been there, and the girl had taken on as I heard she did, I would have died between the gate posts, before she would have gone.

COL. HINDS *called again.*—It is not true that Mrs. Eames told me that if I could persuade Anne to go away, I might. She repeatedly told Anne *she should not go,* and me, that I should not have her. She told Anne a number of times not to give up the child. She said Anne was as free as any girl. She said she had papers to show to that effect. Refused to show any papers. Said she had them.

MRS. PATTY CALDWELL *called by Deft's.*—I live with Judah Wright, my brother. I saw Anne frequently, every day almost, she came for water. She came many times. One day she carried 10 pails full, I counted. Washing days she carried *more.* Carried a great many. It is a very steep hill from my house to Mr. Sherman's. She carried it awhile in her hands as other women do. Then she used frequently to put it on her head. Her back was so weak she did not know how to carry it in her arms. I know nothing but that the pails were full. I told Mrs. Eames, I thought it would ruin the child. I told her, she must doctor her.

3

She was diseased. It was plain enough to be discovered. I told Mrs. Eames, I thought it was occasioned by her lifting and working more than her age would bear. Mrs. Eames replied, doctor a negro! She said, it was almost impossible to doctor a negro. She said, she had boiled a sheep's bladder in some milk and given her. She said, *she was going to sell her, and she would not be of any use to her much longer. She would answer her purpose what little time she wanted her. She was going off with her. Time and again, Anne expressed a great desire that she might be free.* Anne said nothing against the family. After Mr. Richardson talked with her, one day she came to me and said, O, Mrs. Caldwell, do you think they will do any thing for me? I heard her say more to my brother Wright. She would often say, *she was a poor slave and must be sold again.* Anne was there with Mrs. Sherman, she brought a little web of linen diaper. I said, is Mrs. Eames going to cut it up for her babe? Mrs. Sherman said, oh no, she is going to make Anne some aprons. She must clothe her until she *sold* her. I said, then the poor girl is going to be sold. *She said, yes.* This was about a week before she went away. After her mother had washed, Mrs. Eames came down and washed a frock, and the conversation I have before stated, took place. She said, *Anne would be no benefit to her now she got so weak.* She said *there would be a fuss, if she kept her here, and therefore she must sell her.* I told Anne I mistrusted there would be a stir made to take her away. I said, she might have her choice. If she told them she wished to stay, she might, and if she told them she wanted to go, I thought she might. She said, *I want to be free, I want to be free.*

I never saw the day when I could carry the water she did. My health always rather poor. I was in Mrs. Sherman's one day. Anne was told to take a bushel basket and get the refuse of the hoop-poles. The girl looked unwilling. Mrs. E. said, I an't afraid of their hurting you. I did not stay.

I was *summoned* before the Grand Jury. I was not asked *to go before the jury and tell my story.* I was here two days. I said to Mrs. Eames, it is a hard case to be summoned without any fees, and you had no reason to think I should say any thing in your favor. She replied, *hard as it is, it is not so hard as mine, to have all my* PROPERTY *taken away. When they took the girl, they took* THE CHIEF OF MY PROPERTY.

: I told Mr. Cheney, I pitied the poor girl, for she said they were going to carry her off and sell her, and she wanted to be free. I told him I thought christians could not pass over such things. I told him, she said she wanted relief from some body. Mrs. Warren heard me talk about it with Anne.

Cross Examined.—These conversations were all at my brother's house. I did not tell Mrs. Eames that Anne wanted her freedom. I was afraid she would abuse her. The first time I heard Anne speak of the subject, she was at my brother's house, and he asked her where she lived? and she told him. He asked her if she always lived with Mrs Eames? She said no, she was sold to her. He asked her if she was a slave then? She said yes. He asked her if she expected to be? She said she expected to be sold again. He asked if she did not feel bad about being sold? she said she did, but as she must be sold, she had rather go back and be sold at New Orleans, than be a *field slave,* for she understood they fared hard. I cannot say that my brother told her she was free, but *think* he did, at that time. She said, she had been told so before.

Mrs. JULIA ANN FLAGG *called by Defendants.*—I live in the house of Mrs. Sherman. I heard Col. Hinds come in and enquire for Anne, Mrs. Eames called her, came back without her. Told Mr. Hinds if he would be seated, she would call her. She brought her in—Hinds asked Anne, if she wanted to go with him? She seemed frightened and said she " *did not know.*" Mrs. Eames said, yes you do know too. Mr. Hinds asked Anne, if she had a shawl and bonnet? She said, she did not know. He asked how old she was. She said she did nor know. He asked Mrs. Eames her age. She told him, it was none of his business, she was not so very old. Mrs. Eames told Anne to keep the babe. After Mr. Hinds took it, she told Anne she should not go—not to go. She told Anne to go into the bed room. I was present when they were at the table with Anne. Col. Hinds *did not* throw Mrs. Eames on the bed. Mrs. Eames took hold of Anne, not gently, she hurt her very much, I think. She laid hold of her violently. Mrs. Eames was very angry all the time; Mrs. Sherman was also very angry. Mrs. Eames told Mr. Hinds Anne should not go, and he should not take her. She did not say any thing to Mr. Hinds about Anne's being at liberty to go if she wanted to, or if he could persuade her to go. Mrs. Eames scratched and bit. Col. Hinds called Mr. Cheney to help. Mrs. Eames told Anne not to sign the paper. She told her mother not to let her sign the paper. Anne went willingly with the men. I saw them down as far as Mr. Wright's. She did not lean back. That day, before Col. Hinds came, Mrs. Eames wanted to know what ailed the nigger, she was so lively ; said, she had always had to drive her to work, but *that* day, *she had'nt had to speak to her.* Anne did not make a noise or scream, when she went away. She made no disturbance or fuss. Anne was very cheerful that morning, uncommonly so. After Anne had left, more than once Mrs. Eames called Anne to come back, not to go. She did not turn her head round; Before they came, Mrs. Eames told her, she must change her dress and mend the one she wore, as she must wear it back to the South. Mrs. Eames said, *she was going to carry her back to the South, and was going to sell her.* *Have heard her say it more than once.* She said Mr. Eames paid $800 for her two years ago, and she would fetch $1000, now, as she was about two years older. Anne packed up her clothes. Mrs. Eames found them packed up the day before, in two bundles. She came down and told her mother that she had found Anne's clothes tied up, and that, *if it was'nt a nigger, it looked like running away.* I believe she had tied them up the day before. It was that day Mrs. Eames spoke thus.

I heard Mrs. Eames tell Anne that if she ever told any thing out of the house, that happened in it, *she would kill her dead.* Mrs. Eames read in my hearing a letter, I took it to be from New Orleans, informing her that business was dull, that she had better not come back herself, that *she could send Anne, that they had found a place for her, where they could sell her.*

After Anne was taken, Mrs. Eames said, she had fought hard, but not any harder than any one would, *losing their* PROPERTY.

I thought Col. Hinds and those who were with him appeared like gentlemen. Col. Hinds talked long, tried to persuade Mrs. Eames to let her go, He read the bond to Mrs. Eames, she would not hear it.

Cross Examined.—I reside in the house with Mrs. Sherman. I think it likely, I have made communications like these. I told Miss White and Mrs. Caldwell.

At this point in the examination, two witnesses only having been called on the part of the defendants,

Mr. MERRICK said,—*I have come to the conclusion that the evidence abundantly justified the issuing of the process, and that the defendants are fully entitled to a verdict of acquittal.* I shall prosecute the case no farther.

The jury immediately gave a verdict of acquittal.

By this sudden termination of the trial, the defendants are deprived of the opportunity of submitting the rest of their evidence. They had a large number of reputable witnesses in attendance, by whom they would have met most fully every fact and circumstance which could be relied upon to show an impropriety of conduct on the part of any, who were concerned in giving freedom to Anne. By several witnesses they would have confirmed the evidence already in the case that the conduct of Col. Hinds and those who were with him, in executing the process of law, was kind and courteous and as mild as the resistance they met with *permitted* it to be, and in all respects as it should have been —that the witnesses who testified of rudeness to Mrs. Eames, were in a remarkable error—that Anne was not compelled to sign the bond—was not dragged away as was stated by some of the witnesses—that there was no haste in removing her; that the carriage in which she was conveyed was the one, which was ordinarily used by Col. Stratton—that there was no more concealment of her than was rendered necessary for her protection until a trial should be had, in consequence of threats of violence.

They are prepared to prove further, by various witnesses, the often expressed desire of Anne, that somebody would interfere and prevent her removal, and sale as a slave—the hardships she endured—the knowledge she had joyfully received, that men were coming to release her—her preparation for the event, voluntarily and privately made, without the knowledge of any one—and the pleasure she expressed as soon as she was beyond the view of the *eye* she had learned to fear, and dared give utterance to her thoughts and feelings. As the trial was arrested, the defendants can give in the form of evidence nothing more than the testimony of Mr. Judah Wright, a man long known by many, and greatly respected for his virtues and intelligence, and for the acquisitions of knowledge which he has made, having never been blessed with sight. Being prevented from attending as a witness, his deposition was taken on the first day of the trial.

DEPOSITION OF JUDAH WRIGHT.

INTERROGATORIES PUT TO JUDAH WRIGHT.

1. Were you acquainted with Anne, a colored girl in the service of Olivia Eames, in Holden, in the summer of 1838? If yes, state what opportunities, if any, you had of conversing with her, how frequently, and where?

2. Did said Anne ever converse with you before she left Holden, respecting any desire she had for personal liberty, or respecting her condition, or her relation to Mrs. Eames? If yes, state what she said at any such conversation, or conversations relative to the above subjects?

3. How near the time of the departure from Holden of Anne, did any of the conversations aforesaid occur, and which?

4. To whom, if any, did you communicate the above conversations, and did you communicate them before the day when said Anne left Holden? [This was objected to by the Counsel for the Government.]

CROSS INTERROGATIONS, BY THE COUNSEL FOR THE GOVERNMENT.

1. If you state any conversations with said Anne, state where and when each of said conversations took place—who was present at each—how each conversation was introduced, and *all* that was said on each particular occasion, both by herself and yourself, and any other person engaged in such conversation.

2. How near did you live to Mr. Sherman in Holden, while Mrs. Eames was there during the season of 1838? and how often, and how many times did you see said Anne during that time, and where?

3. If you state that said Anne had any conversations with you respecting personal liberty, did you take any

measures whatever to ascertain if she was, in fact, under duress, or held in restraint? if so, please state what you did to ascertain the same.

4. If you state that you communicated any conversation had by you with said Anne to any person, please state the name of any and every person to whom you communicated the same; and at what times you did so.

5. Have you now stated the whole of every conversation of which you have given any testimony? if not please state whatever has been omitted.

6. Has any person other than the Magistrate taking your deposition been present during the taking of the same? if so, state the names of all such persons.

MR. WRIGHT'S ANSWERS.

And now the said Judah Wright, being first duly cautioned, examined, and sworn, makes the following answers to the foregoing interrogatories, to wit:

1. To the first interrogatory, this deponent saith, That he was well acquainted with the colored girl, Anne, mentioned in said interrogatory, in the summer of 1838. Mr. Sherman's family, with whom Mrs. Eames and the colored girl lived, resided within about forty rods of me. The well at Mr. Sherman's house became dry, as I understood, and they applied to me for leave to draw water at my well. I gave them leave, and Anne was the principal person employed in drawing water. As the well was situated in the rear of the house, and as they could not get at it without climbing over the fence, I gave them leave to pass through my house. This circumstance led to a particular acquaintance with Anne, as she used to pass through the kitchen into a back room in which I worked making baskets. She passed through there many times every day; on washing days I should think twenty times.

2. To the second interrogatory, this deponent saith, That he did converse with the said Anne, before she left Holden, as to her wishes for her personal liberty. She said she was a slave, from one of the northern slave-holding States, and was carried to the south, and was there sold as a slave to Mr. Eames; and that after Mr. Eames's death she became the property of Mrs. Eames. She often told me that she expected to be sold again; that Mrs. Eames

told her she was going to New Orleans in the fall, and should dispose of her. She said she wished to learn to read, and to attend meeting, but unless she got her liberty she never expected to. She frequently expressed a strong desire to have her liberty, but I never encouraged her to expect it, lest she should take some steps to work her deliverance, and should fail. She used to say that she did not know as there was any way for her to get her liberty; but if she must be a slave, she hoped she should be sold in New Orleans, or some city, for she had always understood that such slaves fared better than those who were employed in the field. There were a number of these conversations; frequently through the season. I recollect one conversation in particular, which was on Sunday morning, I think early in September, and at the time when Mr. John Richardson came over to read to me.

3. To the third interrogatory, this deponent answers and saith, That he should think the said conversation, in presence of Mr. Richardson, was not more than a week before said Anne left Holden. She was in at my house after this conversation, but there was nothing in particular said. We had an idea that she was watched. The day before she went away, she was in and bid me good bye, and said she did not know as she should see me again; she did not know but she should be called for.

4. To the fourth interrogatory, this deponent answers and saith, That he did communicate these conversations to several before Anne left Holden. That he communicated them to Mr. Richardson, Mr. Cheney, Mr. Farnum White, Jr., Henrietta White, and some others. I do not mean to say that I communicated all the conversations to all these persons. I was cautious about it. I only meant to make it understood that the girl wanted her liberty.

1. To the first cross interrogatory, this deponent answers and says, That the said conversations with Anne, all took place at his house. They commenced when she began drawing water there, and he thinks this was in June. The conversations were had frequently, and mostly in his shop, when no one was present. Sometimes his sister was present, and Mr. Richardson was once present, and the deponent does not recollect that any other one was present at any of the conversations. Deponent cannot state how all these con-

versations were introduced; he sometimes introduced them, and sometimes she did. It is impossible to state all these conversations. The tenor of them was that she wanted her liberty, and I sympathised with her. But I did not give her any hope of her deliverance.

2. To the second cross interrogatory, this deponent saith, That he should think he lived in the season of 1838, about forty rods from Mr. Sherman's. He saw the said Anne several times a day generally, and washing days he should think probably as much as twenty times. He never saw her anywhere, that he recollects, but at his house. I use the words *see* and *saw* just as other folks do. What I mean is, I never *met* with her, &c.

3. To the third cross interrogatory, this deponent saith, That it was understood in Holden, that the said Anne was a slave. She said she was a slave. At first I did not know how much she could be relied on, but on acquaintance, I found her intelligence was such, that I thought she could be relied on. The deponent took no further measures to ascertain whether she was under any restraint.

4. To the fourth cross interrogatory, this deponent saith, That he cannot state more particularly than he has already done, to whom he communicated any of his conversations with the said Anne. Nor can he state definitely, at what times such communications were made. There was a good deal said upon the subject, especially within a few weeks of the time when the girl went away; and he thinks it probable that he communicated most of the conversations within that time, but he cannot state positively.

5. To the fifth cross interrogatory, this deponent saith, That he does not suppose that he has stated the whole of each conversation, for it would be impossible for him to do it. He has meant to give a fair general representation.

6. To the sixth cross interrogatory, this deponent saith, That he is blind; he has heard of no one being present, and he presumes no one was present at the time of his giving this deposition, but the magistrate and Mrs. Betsey Stratton.

HIS
JUDAH ✕ WRIGHT.
MARK.

WORCESTER, ss. On the 29th day of January, in the year of our Lord one thousand eight hundred and thirty-nine, the aforesaid deponent was examined, and cautioned, and

4

sworn, agreeable to law, to the deposition aforesaid, by him subscribed, taken at the request of Samuel Stratton and others, and to be used in an indictment now pending between them and the Commonwealth, before the Court of Common Pleas, and taken upon the interrogatories hereto annexed. The said Judah Wright being unable to attend Court, on account of bodily infirmity, is the cause of taking this deposition. IRA BARTON, *Justice of the Peace.*

CONSTRUCTION OF THE STATUTE.

In the course of the cross-examination of Anne, (see p. 13,) the following discussion arose upon the consrruction of the Statute of 1837, ch. 221.

Enquiry was made of the witness by the counsel of the defendants whether she had communicated to any person her desire to be free.

By the counsel for the Government—Unless the communication was made *to* the defendants, the inquiry is irrelevant.

The counsel for the defendants replied, that it was intended to bring the knowledge of the wishes of the witness home to the defendants. The question was still objected to by the counsel for the Government, and an extended argument was entered into respecting the principles of law, which should govern the case. We have not room for all the reasoning and illustrations of counsel, but will briefly state the questions of law which arose.

It was contended by the counsel for the Government, that the defendants could justify the institution of the process of personal replevin only by showing that the girl, Anne, had in some manner requested *them* to aid her in obtaining her liberty. That they could act only as her agents, and under authority previously conferred by her ; that although no " express " power of attorney was necessary, in some way it must be proved, that Anne desired and authorized them to interfere ; that no subsequent ratification by her of their doings, would be sufficient for the protection of the defendants ; and that no justification could be found for their conduct, in the condition of the girl, while under restraint, nor in the benefits, however great, which they may have conferred upon her; that although the defendants, without doubt, believed that the girl was in bondage, and that they were called upon as philanthropists to assert her rights, yet in law their conduct could not be upheld. The consequences of allowing any other person than the agent of the party principally interested, to institute the process of personal replevin, were urged by way of objection ; particularly, that the individual, in whose favor the suit was commenced, might be subjected to cost, and that the statute of 1837 afforded inadequate protection in this respect. An exception was made, in favor of parents and others, who stood in near relation to the party in duress.

It was replied, by the counsel for the defendants, that they must be acquitted of the crime, alleged in the indictment, if the jury should be satisfied, that the defendants believed, at the time of sueing out the aforesaid process, that Anne was held in duress, and that the purpose of the defendants was, to relieve her from unlawful restraint. They were indicted for a conspiracy to deprive Mrs. Eames " *of the voluntary service of Anne ;*" and the indictment further charged, that *to effect such object*, that is, the removal of Anne from *voluntary* service, the defendants unlawfully availed themselves of a process of law, adapted to obtain the liberty of one, who was in duress. Should it then appear, that the defendants *believed*, that the girl was unlawfully restrained of her liberty ; and that they instituted the process of personal replevin, *for the purpose* of removing the supposed unlawful restraint upon her person, they must be acquitted of the crime alleged against them. Such must be the result, *although the government should prove, that the girl was a voluntary servant of Mrs. Eames.*

But the defendants were prepared to go further than simply to refute the charge in the indictment, and obtain an acquittal of the crime specifically alleged against them. They vindicated their right to institute the process of replevin ; and they vindicated the statute of 1837, in favor of personal liberty, from the construction given to it by the Counsel for the Government, which would narrow the sphere of its operation, and deprive it of much of its usefulness. The Legislature which passed it, intended that it should be an efficient remedy, for every case of unlawful encroachment upon the right of personal liberty. The individual imprisoned might be an infant, incapable of understanding his rights, and unable to delegate authority. Or it might be, a married woman, who is legally disqualified from instituting a suit at law, is suffering some great wrong, through deprivation of her liberty, at a distance from 'her husband and friends. Or, a maniac might be the sufferer. Or, as in the present case, a child brought up in ignorance, and imperfectly discerning her rights, and altogether ignorant of the remedy, might be enduring oppression and bondage. In all such cases the provisions of the Statute would be nugatory, if authority must be given by the person in duress, before the writ can be instituted. Scarcely more effectual would they be for the protection of one who was under no such disqualification. *The injury itself would take away the remedy provided for it. The confinement would deprive the prisoner of the means and opportunity of furnishing the necessary authority.*

So far from admitting the construction contended for, in support of this prosecution, which would render futile a most important and beneficial law, the counsel for the Defendants contend, that it should have such broad operation, that the remedy it held out should meet any possible case of unlawful infringement of personal liberty. If the cry for succor should now be heard from yonder house, and the belief be reasonably had that some human being is there unlawfully deprived of freedom, although that voice of distress should proceed from some unknown person, from the stranger from the "furthest pole," it would be the right of any man who should hear it to institute the writ of personal replevin, and to bring the prisoner and him by, whom he was restrained into a Court of Justice, where the cause of the imprisonment could be investigated, and the wrong, if any had been committed, be redressed. Upon any other construction, the Statute, instead of being a protection to men's rights, would be a trap and a snare. In support of his views, the Counsel for the Defendants read and commented upon several sections of the Statute referred to.

The first section provides that if *any person* is unlawfully imprisoned, restrained of liberty or held in duress, such person shall be entitled, of right, to the writ of personal replevin.

That no abuse be made of the law, the 4th and 5th Sections require a bond to be given, with sufficient sureties, for the payment of any damages which the defendant may sustain by reason of the institution of the suit.

The 15th section authorises any person in behalf of another to sue out the writ and prosecute the suit to final judgment, *without any express power* from the person restrained of his liberty.

The 16th section makes provision for the commencement of the suit WHERE THE NAME OF THE PERSON RESTRAINED IS UNKNOWN OR UNCERTAIN.

The objection that no adequate provision was made by the Statute for costs to which, under certain circumstances, the plaintiff whose name is used might be subjected, was met by a reference to the provision therein made, for security to the plaintiff as well as the defendant, for costs which might be sustained. It is further urged by the defendant's counsel that objections arising from an omission tó provide fully for any injury which might possibly result from the use of the process, in any case which could be suffered to arise, could not avail to defeat the plain enactments of a law. The Legislature of 1837, which passed the law, established a great principle, to wit, the right of a trial by jury in cases affecting personal liberty, and it gave ample means for enforcing the right. It may be, as is often the case, that experience may show the necessity for subsequent Legislation to make perfect the details of the law.

The Court decided that no authority to commence the suit need be given by the person in duress, that the Statute itself was sufficient authority. The objection was therefore overruled, and the evidence was admitted.

———

Note. The writ of personal replevin referred to in this trial was duly entered in Court at the December term of the Common Pleas, and stood on the Docket, Anne vs. Olivia Eames. The defendant appeared by her attorney, but afterwards was defaulted by consent, and judgment for nominal damages (being all that was claimed,) and the costs of Court, was rendered against her. This was proved on trial, but, by mistake, was not inserted in its proper place in this report.

The reader will also observe, that in the testimony of Geo. Putnam and Thomas Randall, on pages 16 and 17, the name of Mr. Stratton was incorrectly introduced instead of that of Mr. Sherman.

APPENDIX.

—

AN ACT TO RESTORE THE TRIAL BY JURY, ON QUESTIONS OF PERSONAL FREEDOM.

SECT. 1. If any person is imprisoned, restrained of his liberty, or held in duress, unless it be in the custody of some public officer of the law, by force of a lawful warrant or other process, civil or criminal, issued by a court of competent jurisdiction, he shall be entitled, as of right, to the writ of personal replevin, and to be thereby delivered in the manner hereinafter provided.

SECT. 2. The writ shall be issued from and returnable to the court of common pleas, for the county in which the plaintiff is confined, and shall be issued fourteen days at least before the return day thereof.

SECT. 3. It shall be directed to the sheriff of the county, or his deputy, or to any of the coroners thereof, and shall be served by either to whom it shall be delivered, without delay. ·

SECT. 4. The said writ shall be in the form following, viz.

CRITICAL COMMONWEALTH OF MASSACHUSETTS.

——ss. *To the sheriff of our county of* ——— *or his deputy, or either of* (L. s.) *the coroners thereof,* Greeting.

We command you, that justly and without delay, you cause to be replevied C. D. who (as it is said) is taken and detained at ———, within our said county, by the duress of G. H., that he the said C. D. may appear at our court of common pleas, next to be holden at ———, within our county aforesaid; then and there in our said court to demand right and justice against the said G. H. for the duress and imprisonment aforesaid, and to prosecute his replevin as the law directs: ·

Provided, the said C. D., shall before his deliverance, give bond to the said G. H., in such sum as you shall judge reasonable, and with two sureties at the least, having sufficient within your county, with condition, to appear at our said court to prosecute his replevin against the said G. H., and to have his body there ready to be redelivered, if thereto ordered by the court; and to pay all such damages and costs as shall be then and there awarded against him. Then, and not otherwise, are you to deliver him. And if the said C. D. be by you delivered at any day before the sitting of our said court, you are to summon the said G. H. by serving him with an attested copy of this writ, that he may appear at our said court to answer to the said C. D.

Witness, L. S. Esq. at B—, the — day of — in the year —. A .B. clerk.

SECT. 5. No person shall be delivered from his imprisonment or restraint, by force of such writ, until he shall give bond in the manner expressed in the preceding section; and the bond shall be returned with the writ, in like manner as a bail bond is returned, and shall be left in the clerk's office, to be delivered to the defendant when he shall demand it.

SECT. 6. The officer, who serves the writ, shall be answerable for the insufficiency of the sureties in such bond, in like manner as he is answerable for taking insufficient bail in a civil action.

SECT. 7. If the plaintiff shall maintain his action, and shall make it appear that he was unlawfully imprisoned or restrained, he shall be discharged, and shall recover his costs of suit against the defendant, as well as damages for the said imprisonment and detention.

SECT. 8. If the plaintiff shall not maintain his action, the defendant shall have judgment for his costs of suit, and also for such damages, if any, as he shall have sustained by reason of the replevin.

SECT. 9. If it shall appear that the defendant is bail for the plaintiff, or is entitled to the custody of the plaintiff, as his child, ward, servant, apprentice or otherwise, he shall have judgment for a redelivery of the body of the plaintiff, to be held and disposed of according to law.

SECT. 10. If it shall appear, from the return of the writ of personal replevin, that the defendant has secreted or conveyed away the plaintiff's body, so that the officer cannot deliver him, the court shall, on motion, issue a capias to take the defendant's body, and him safely keep, so that he may be had at the then next term of the court, to traverse the return of the said writ of personal replevin; but the defendant may give, and the officer serving the same shall receive bail, as in civil case, for his appearance as aforesaid, in such sum as the officer may judge reasonable.

SECT. 11. At the term at which the capias is returned, the defendant may deny, by plea, the return on the writ of replevin, and if it shall appear, on the trial thereof, that he is not guilty of secreting or conveying away the plaintiff, as set forth in the return, he shall be discharged and recover his costs.

SECT. 12. If the defendant shall not traverse the said return as aforesaid, or if, upon the said traverse, the issue, on trial, shall be found against him, then an alias writ of capias shall be issued against him, and he shall thereupon be committed to the common jail, there to remain in close custody until he shall produce the body of the plaintiff, or prove him to be dead; and if the defendant shall suggest such death at any time after committal as aforesaid, then the court shall impannel a jury to try the fact, at the expense of the defendant; and if the death be proved, the defendant shall be discharged.

SECT. 13. If, at any time after such return of secretion and conveying away as aforesaid, the defendant shall produce the body of the plaintiff in the court to which the writ of personal replevin was returned, or in which the suit is pending, the court shall deliver the plaintiff from restraint, upon his giving bond agreeably to the condition of the writ of personal replevin; and for want of such bond the plaintiff shall be committed, to abide the judgment on the replevin; and in either case the suit shall be proceeded in, as if the plaintiff had been delivered on the writ of personal replevin.

SECT. 14. Either party may appeal from any judgment upon either of the matters aforesaid to the supreme judicial court, as in common civil actions; and in case of an appeal from the judgments which may be rendered under the writs of capias aforesaid, the whole case shall be carried up to the supreme judicial court and be there disposed of, as it ought to have been in the court of common pleas, if there had been no appeal.

SECT. 15. The writ of personal replevin may be sued out by any person for and in behalf of the plaintiff, and may be prosecuted to final judgment, without any express power for that purpose: *provided*, that the person so appearing for the plaintiff shall, at any time during the pendency of the suit, when required by the court, give security in such manner as the court shall direct, for the payment of all damages and costs that shall be awarded against the plaintiff.

SECT. 16. If the name of the defendant, or the person to be delivered, be unknown or uncertain, then in any writ, proceeding, or process under this act, they may respectively be described and proceeded with, as is prescribed in the sixth and seventh sections of the one hundred and eleventh chapter of the Revised Statutes, in the writ of habeas corpus.

SECT. 17. The thirty eighth section of the one hundred and eleventh chapter of the Revised Statutes, is hereby repealed. [April 19, 1837.]

THE INDICTMENT.

COMMONWEALTH OF MASSACHUSETTS.

WORCESTER, ss. At a Court of Common Pleas, begun and holden at Worcester, within and for the County of Worcester, on the fourth Monday of September, in the year of our Lord one thousand eight hundred and thirty-eight :

The Jurors for the Commonwealth aforesaid, on their oath present, That Samuel Stratton, Samuel Foster, James E. Cheney, and Farnum White, junior, all of Holden, in the County of Worcester, unlawfully and wrongfully devising and intending to deprive one Olivia Eames of the voluntary service and aid of a certain colored female, named Anne, and to remove the said Anne from the service, care and employment of the said Olivia, into places wholly unknown to said Anne, and without her consent, at Holden aforesaid, in the County aforesaid, on the thirteenth day of September now last past, did, unlawfully and wrongfully, combine, conspire, confederate, and agree together, wrongfully and unlawfully to deprive the said Olivia of the said voluntary aid and service of said Anne, and to remove the said Anne from the service and employment of said Olivia, into places wholly unknown to said Anne, without her consent : and then and there, in pursuance of said conspiracy, combination, and agreement, did unlawfully and without the knowledge or consent of said Anne, cause to be sued out in due form of law, a certain Writ of Personal Replevin in behalf of said Anne, wherein it was alleged that said Anne was restrained and imprisoned by the duress of the said Olivia, which Writ was made returnable to the Court of Common Pleas next to be holden at Worcester, within and for the County of Worcester, on the first Monday of December next : and then and there the same Writ did unlawfully and wrongfully put into the hands of Warner Hinds, without the knowledge or consent of said Anne, to be duly served and executed : and the said Stratton, Cheney, Foster, and White, then and there unlawfully and wrongfully did cause and procure the said Hinds, under color and pretence of making service of said Writ of Personal Replevin in behalf of said Anne, to take the body of the said Anne, by force and violence, without her consent therefor first had and obtained, from the said voluntary service, employment, and care of the said Olivia, and did then and there unlawfully and wrongfully aid and assist the said Hinds in taking the body of said Anne in manner aforesaid : and then and there unlawfully and wrongfully, in manner aforesaid, did deprive said Olivia of said voluntary aid and service of said Anne, and did carry and remove the said Anne into places theretofore to the said Anne wholly unknown : and other wrongs the said Foster, Stratton, Cheney, and White, then and there did, in abuse of the process of law provided for the security of personal freedom, and against the peace of the Commonwealth aforesaid. A true Bill.

SAMUEL DAMAN, *Foreman.*

PLINY MERRICK, *Dist. Attorney.*

ARGUMENT

OF

ROBERT J. WALKER, ESQ.

BEFORE

THE SUPREME COURT OF THE UNITED STATES,

ON THE

MISSISSIPPI SLAVE QUESTION,

AT

JANUARY TERM, 1841.

INVOLVING THE POWER OF CONGRESS AND OF THE STATES
TO PROHIBIT THE INTER-STATE SLAVE TRADE.

PHILADELPHIA:

PRINTED BY JOHN C. CLARK, 60 DOCK STREET.

1841.

73

ARGUMENT.

Mr. Walker said, he appeared only for Moses Groves, of Louisiana, whose defence was meritorious as well as legal. He was a mere accommodation endorser, who had been made a party to this illegal contract, without his knowledge or consent, through an endorsement in blank for the accommodation of the drawer of the note. This is evident from the record; but as the question resolved itself into a decision upon the validity of the contract, the following agreement was filed in the case below. "The case is to be defended solely on the question of the validity and legality of the consideration for which the notes sued on were given. It is admitted that the slaves, for which said notes were given, were imported into Mississippi as merchandise, and for sale, in the year 1835, 1836, by plaintiff, but without any previous agreement or understanding, express or implied, between plaintiff and any of the parties to the note; but for sale, generally, to any person who might wish to purchase. The slaves have never been returned to plaintiff, nor tendered to him by any of the parties to the notes sued on." It must be observed, that it is not alleged or pretended that my client, Moses Groves, ever had the possession or control of any of these slaves, or that it ever was in his power to tender or return them. The notes sued on were dated December 20, 1836, and were given and made payable in Mississippi; and the validity of the contract depends upon the following clause in the amended constitution of Mississippi, adopted October 26, 1832. That clause is in these words—" The introduction of slaves into this state as merchandise, or for sale, shall be prohibited from and after the first day of May, 1833: *Provided*, That the actual settler or settlers shall not be prohibited from purchasing slaves in any State of this Union, and bringing them into this State for their own individual use, till the year 1845."

The question arises only on the first branch of this clause; which, it is said, is but a mandate to the legislature to prohibit the introduction of slaves for sale from and after the 1st of May, 1833. But the clause is not directed to the legislature, and is not a mandate in substance or in form, but an absolute prohibition, operating proprio vigore. It requires no legislation to give it efficacy to avoid this contract; and none such could prevent or postpone its operation. To declare it a mandate, is to interpolate into this provision words of solemn import. No court can introduce into a law, or exclude from it, words not used by the legislature; unless it be clearly necessary to give effect to the law, ut res magis valeat quam pereat. Now the clause—" The introduction of slaves into this state as merchandise, or for sale, shall be prohibited from and after the first day of May, eighteen hundred and thirty-three," is complete of itself, as a prohibition, operating by force of the constitution itself, from and after the day designated by that instrument; and to change it into a mandate, the words "by the legislature" must be interpolated. It was an operative fundamental law, ordained by the sovereign power of the state, which called the legislature itself into being; and though that body might prevent the violation of this prohibition by more effectual guards and penalties, as they

A

have done in 1837; yet as the prohibition could not be repealed by the legislature by positive enactments, neither would their omission to act, expunge this prohibition from the fundamental law. This Court, through Chief Justice Marshall, have said, that the nature of a constitution "requires that only its great outlines should be marked, its important objects designated, and the minor ingredients which compose those objects be deduced from the objects themselves." "The constitution unavoidably deals in general language;" it does not "*enumerate the means*" by which its provisions shall be carried into operation. 4 Wheat. 407, 8. 1 Wheat. 326. Baldwin's Const. Views, 99, 100, 192. So also the constitution of Mississippi contained only the important objects and great outlines of the government, written and ordained by the people acting in their highest sovereign capacity, by their delegates in convention assembled; and all the details of legislation were left to that branch and department of the government to whom that duty appropriately belonged. The legislature, in regarding the objects designated, might well surround a constitutional interdict with appropriate penalties; but they could not render it inoperative, either by positive or negative action; and whatever course they might pursue, all laws and contracts repugnant to the prohibition would be void.

When was this prohibition of the constitution to go into effect? That instrument assigns the day; it is "from and after the first day of May, 1833;" not *after* the 1st of May, 1833, but *from* and after that day and no other. From and after a day specified, fixes absolutely the very day when this prohibition would commence to operate; and to postpone its operation to any future, unknown, indefinite period, at the discretion of the legislature, would be to disregard the plain language and manifest intent of the constitution. Nor were these words, "from and," after the day fixed, introduced by accident. On the contrary, the clause, as originally proposed, was, "the introduction of slaves into this state as merchandise shall be prohibited after the —— day," &c., page 57 of Journal; and the provision was amended subsequently by introducing the words "*from* and" after, &c. Why thus cautiously designate the very day for the commencement of the operation of this prohibition, unless it was certainly to go into effect on that very day, by force of the constitutional interdict? To postpone, then, the operation of this prohibition to any day subsequent to that named in the constitution, is to expunge the time altogether, and leave it dependent upon the fluctuating will of the legislature, obeying or disregarding, at pleasure, this constitutional provision, and giving or refusing operation to it, from time to time, by enacting or repealing laws upon the subject, and thus changing a fixed, permanent, established, fundamental law, into a mere directory provision, operative or inoperative, as the legislature might act or refuse to act, or repeal its action upon the subject. But this provision was not only designed to operate of itself from a day fixed and certain, but unchangeably through all time to come, or to be changed only by the same sovereign power which framed the constitution. The convention have said, "the introduction of slaves for sale shall be prohibited," &c. This language is general; it is addressed to every one, and to all the departments of government; and why should it, by implication or interpolation, be limited to a direction to the legislature? It was competent for the convention itself to prohibit this trade; and if they have used language which, in a statute, all admit would be a prohibition, why shall it receive a different construction in the organic law? Is a state constitution merely a mandate to the legislature? Is it so in its prohibitions, and especially in those which are contained in general provisions, as in this case, and not in the article creating the legislative department, and assigning its appropriate powers and duties? If this construction be adopted by implication, in regard to other clauses equally imperative in the constitution of Mississippi, it will be rendered, in many of its most important provisions, absurd and incongruous, nugatory and repugnant.

These words "from and after the 1st of May, 1833," have received a settled construction by this court, in 9 Cranch, 101, 119, where they say "The act 1st July, 1812, provided that an additional duty of 100 per cent. upon the permanent duties now imposed by law, &c., shall be levied and collected upon all goods, wares and merchandise which shall, *from and after* the passing of this act, be imported into the United States from any foreign port or place. It is contended that this statute did not take effect until the 2d day of July; nor indeed, until it was formally promulgated and published. We cannot yield assent to this construction,"—and the court exacted the double duties upon an importation *on the 1st July.* Here it is decided, that these words, *from and after,* included the day named, and such was the settled legal construction when the words were used in our constitution; and in such cases it is conceded, that the construction is adopted with the words. Why then introduce the word *from* by an amendment in this case, unless the prohibition was to commence on that *very day named,* and in all time thereafter? Thus to designate by an amendment the *very day* when this prohibition *"shall"* commence to operate, clearly proves that this should be an absolute prohibition; and never to put it into operation unless the legislature acted upon the subject, or at such indefinite and distant period as they might designate, is to defeat the meaning of the constitution. Here then the precise date is fixed, and the words are *shall be prohibited* from and after that date. In 2 Wheat., 148, 152, 153, it was decided by this court, that "under the Embargo Act of the 22d Dec. 1807, the words *'an embargo shall be laid'* not only imposed upon the public officers the duty of preventing the departure of registered or sea-letter vessels on a foreign voyage, but, consequently rendered them liable to forfeiture under the supplementary act of the 9th Jan. 1808." In this case the court said, this vessel was "libelled for a violation of the Embargo Act of the 22d Dec. 1807, and the Supplementary Act of the 9th Jan. 1808, the former of which enacts 'that an embargo shall be laid on all ships and vessels in the ports of the United States, bound on a foreign voyage,' and the latter forfeits the vessel that shall proceed to any foreign port or place 'contrary to the provisions of this act, or of the act to which this is a supplement.'" "Was then the sailing to a foreign port, a prohibited act under the embargo law, to a registered or sea-letter vessel? If so, the commission of such an act was a cause of forfeiture under the act of Jan. 9, 1808. And here the only doubt is, whether the words 'an embargo *shall be laid,'* operate any further than to *impose a duty on the public officers* to prevent the departure of a registered or sea-letter vessel on a foreign voyage. The language of the act is certainly not very happily chosen; but when we look into the definition of the word *embargo,* we find it to mean 'a prohibition to sail;' substituting this periphrasis for the word embargo, it reads 'a prohibition to sail shall be imposed, &c.,' or in other words, 'such vessels *shall be prohibited* to sail,' which words, had they been used in the act, would have left no scope for doubt."

Here too, the question raised is whether the words "shall be prohibited," operate any further than "to impose a duty" on the legislature to "prevent" the introduction, or amount to a prohibition. Now the words "an embargo shall be laid" operated in presenti, as an embargo, and not merely as directory to the public officers; the words "a prohibition to sail *shall be imposed,*" operated in the like manner, as also did, beyond all doubt, the words "such vessels *shall be prohibited to sail.*" The words then *shall be prohibited* operated as a prohibition, and in presenti, and if the words *shall be prohibited to introduce* would so operate, what difference is there in the words *the introduction shall be prohibited?* The case then is clear in point, and that too, on the construction of a penal statute inflicting a forfeiture; and the construction of these words *shall be prohibited* had thus been settled when our convention adopted them in 1832. And here it was a traffic that was prohibited. Now what is the meaning of the terms *prohibited traffic?* It is an *unlawful traffic,* for the past participle is thus repeatedly used as an adjective.

The clause would then read, the introduction of slaves for sale, shall be *unlawful* from and after the 1st of May, 1833, and the proviso would then read, Provided, that it shall not be unlawful for the actual settler or settlers to purchase slaves, in any state in this Union, and bring them into this state for their own individual use, until the year 1845. But if the proviso, from the different terms used, and failure to designate the day upon which the prohibition should commence to operate, was susceptible of a different construction, it would only render still more imperative the main provision, by which the *traffic* was prohibited *from* and after the day named in the constitution.

Grants of legislative power mandatory and permissive, frequently occur in the constitution, and the convention well knew how to make such grants, and to distinguish between those which were mandatory or permissive. The first section contains three distinct grants of power, permissive to the legislature, in relation to slaves; and one of these was a power to prohibit the introduction of a certain description of slaves. This power to prohibit the introduction of slaves of one class by all persons, and the positive prohibition in this case of the introduction of slaves as merchandise, demonstrates, that the convention well understood the difference between a power to prohibit, and an absolute prohibition. Throughout the same instrument numerous grants of power occur mandatory to the legislature. Thus in the 26th section of the 4th article, it is declared, that "the legislature shall provide by law for determining contested elections of judges and other officers." The 10th section of the 7th article, declares "the legislature shall direct by law in what manner, and in what courts suits may be brought against the state." These and many other grants in the constitution are mandatory injunctions to the legislature to pass certain laws. Whenever, then, the convention designed to address the legislature in the language either of permission or command, they used invariably appropriate words for that purpose, and differing entirely from those provisions or prohibitions designed to operate by their own authority; and in this as in many other similar cases, operating by virtue of the constitution itself. If the terms in the constitution "*shall be*" are mere directions to the legislature, mandatory or permissive, and inoperative until the legislature shall have obeyed the constitutional injunction, then much the most important part of the constitution, which went into operation immediately, would have remained suspended until the legislature acted upon the subject. Thus the 1st section of the 2d article declared, that "the powers of the government of the state of Mississippi *shall be* divided into three distinct departments;" thus seeming to contemplate a future distribution of these powers; yet we know that this division was made and operated by virtue of the constitution itself. Section 9, article 1, declares: "The people shall be secure in their persons, houses," &c. Section 17, "All persons shall, before conviction, be bailable," &c. Section 2, article 3, "Electors shall in all cases, except, &c., be privileged from arrest during their attendance on elections." Section 4, "The legislative power of this state shall be vested in two distinct branches," &c. Section 19, "Senators and representatives shall in cases except, &c., be privileged from arrest," &c.; not by future legislation, but by this provision of the constitution. Section 1, article 5, "The chief executive power of this state shall be vested in a governor," &c. Section 2, article 6, "All impeachments shall be tried by the senate." "The governor, &c., shall be liable to impeachment." In all these cases, and throughout this constitution, the terms *shall be*, operate proprio vigore. The terms "shall be secure," "shall be bailable," "shall be privileged," "shall be vested," mean *are secure, are bailable, are privileged, are vested*. This is the settled meaning of these terms *shall be*, in the constitution; they operate proprio vigore, and should receive the same construction in the clause now under consideration.

The terms "shall be" operated immediately in all these clauses, and present a much stronger case than the one now under consideration. Here the terms "shall be" are the appropriate and proper terms, requiring no construction by which they shall be made to operate in presenti; but operating from and after a future day fixed unchangeably by the constitution. The day too thus fixed, was but six months distant, a time barely sufficient to give full and fair notice throughout the state and Union, of the existence of this prohibition, conforming in this particular to many similar laws on the same subject in other states, quoted in the concluding branch of this argument. Why name a day at all, and especially a day fixed and certain, and so near at hand, if this clause were merely directory to the legislature? If any doubt could still remain, it must vanish upon an investigation of the legislation of the state on this subject. By the act of the territorial legislature of Mississippi, of the 1st of March, 1808, certain restrictions are imposed upon the introduction of slaves as merchandise, but chiefly designed to prevent the introduction of dangerous or convict slaves. (Tur. Dig. 386.) Thus stood the law, when in 1817, we formed our first constitution, which contained the following clause: "They (the legislature) shall have full power to prevent slaves from being brought into this state as merchandise;" but there was no prohibition of the traffic. By the act of June 18, 1822, the territorial law before quoted was substantially re-enacted. Revised Code, 369.

Thus stood the statutes and the organic law when the convention assembled which adopted the new constitution of 1832. The first contained the fullest grant of power on this subject to the legislature. Why then this important change in this provision from a mere grant of power to the legislature, into the prohibitory terms of the constitution of 1832, unless an absolute prohibition was designed by the framers of that instrument? The one was a grant of power to the legislature, the other was a prohibition. The reason of the change is obvious. The legislature, during the intervening period of fifteen years between the adoption of the old and of the new constitution, had never fulfilled the trust confided.to them by prohibiting the introduction of slaves as merchandise; and therefore the framers of the new constitution determined to confide this trust no longer to the legislature, but to prohibit this traffic themselves, by an absolute constitutional interdict, operating of itself, upon a day very near at hand, fixed and certain, and placed, as were many other subjects by the constitution, above the control of the legislature. The history of that period will also furnish other reasons why the constitution of 1817 was changed by that of 1832 from a direction to the legislature, into a prohibition. Events had occurred in Southampton, Virginia, but a few months preceding the period when the convention of 1832 assembled, which had aroused the attention of the Southern States to the numbers and character of the slave population. The influence of that insurrection is no where more clearly demonstrated than in the extraordinary votes and speeches in the legislature of Virginia, assembled shortly after that catastrophe. If insurrection had not appeared in Mississippi, there had been many apprehensions upon the subject; and looking at the tragedy just enacted in our sister state, the convention introduced this provision, to produce among other good effects, additional security to the people of Mississippi. Whilst, in this constitution, they gave to the governor power to call forth the militia of the state "to suppress insurrection," they guarded against the supposed danger of that event, by this important constitutional interdict. If Virginia had been driven to the very verge of the abandonment of her ancient institutions, by the events which had occurred within her limits, was there not some reason that the convention to which was entrusted the security of the people of Mississippi, should interpose some guards for their protection? In looking at the general census of 1830, then recently published, they saw, that whilst in Virginia the whites outnumbered the slaves 224,541, in Mississippi the preponderance of the whites was but 4784, and that the slave population was increasing in an accelerated ratio over the whites, the former now greatly outnumbering the latter. In looking beyond the aggregates of the two races in the state to particular counties, they found that in an entire range of adjacent counties, the preponderance of the slave over the white population was three to one; in many of the contiguous patrol districts, more than ten to one, and in many plantations more than one hundred to one. In looking at the policy adopted by our coterminous and sister state of Louisiana, they found that, in that state, the legislature, by laws passed the 19th November, 1831, and 2d April, 1832, had under severe penalties prohibited the introduction of slaves as merchandise, and declared the slaves so introduced to be free. Such was the legislation of Louisiana immediately preceding the assembling of our convention, and such the circumstances and example under which we acted. We acted as Louisiana had just done, by introducing a provision designed to operate after the short notice of six months, as an absolute prohibition. The subject had attracted great attention when the delegates were elected to the convention; and the people fully expected and required final and definitive action by the convention itself on this question, and they were not disappointed.

Such was the opinion which prevailed when the first legislature assembled under the new constitution, in Jan. 1833. This legislature was assembled at the time specified by the convention, by virtue of writs issued by that body, to orga-

A 2

nize the government under the new constitution. If this clause be in itself a prohibition, then it did not operate as a command to the legislature. But if it be not a prohibition, then it is conceded to be a mandate, directed specifically to the legislature, commanding them to prohibit the introduction of slaves as merchandise *from* and after the 1st of May, 1833. If that legislature adjourned without fulfilling this injunction, it must have remained forever unfulfilled in one most important particular, namely, the time fixed by the convention from which the prohibition should commence to operate; for, under the provision of the constitution, no other legislature could convene until November, 1833, a period long subsequent to the time designated for the commencement of the operation of this prohibition.

The legislature was a department of the government, created by the convention, and assembled in pursuance of its authority. Under the 7th article of the new constitution, every member of this legislature has taken a solemn oath to support that instrument, and had they conceived the provision in controversy to be a mandate directed to the legislature, they would have disregarded those oaths, if they had failed to make any prohibitory enactment in pursuance of this injunction of the constitution. Had even this mandate been in opposition to their views of public policy, it would still have been obligatory upon them. But this legislature passed no laws in pursuance of this provision, because they did not conceive this clause to be a mandate directed to them, but an operative prohibition of the constitution; and that the omission was not casual, is proved by the fact, that they proposed for the consideration of the people at the next November election, an amendment to the constitution, striking out this 2d section in regard to slaves, and introducing in lieu thereof, the following provision: "The legislature of this state shall have, and are hereby vested with power to pass, from time to time, such laws regulating or prohibiting the introduction of slaves into this state as may be deemed proper and expedient." (Laws of Mississippi, 478; March 2d, 1833.) The legislature thus endeavoured to change a prohibition, by their proposed amendment, into a mere discretionary authority, which they might or might not exercise at their pleasure. This attempt on the part of the legislature to obtain for themselves this discretionary power failed, as they conceded at the succeeding session of 1833. The amendment, in order to be incorporated into the constitution, must have been voted for by "a majority of the qualified electors voting for the members of the legislature;" and it is obvious that 4500 votes given for this amendment, must have constituted a small fraction of the voters of the state at that period. The vote of the state for governor in November, 1839, was 34,532. I have not the vote of Nov. 1833, but 4500 could not have been one-third of the vote then actually given for members of the legislature. A very small vote was given against the amendment, and it is surprising that so many votes were given, as no vote on the question was a vote against the amendment. The legislature, in December, 1833, acknowledged, that their proposed amendment had failed. The subject was then again before them. They had renewed their oaths to obey the mandate of the constitution, and why was obedience again refused? Because this legislature, like its predecessor, did not view this provision as a mandate directed to them, but as a prohibition. It is said, that at the date of this note, the validity of such a contract was not disputed in Mississippi; but this is entirely erroneous, and the mistake is proved by the very quotation made by our opponents, from the message of Governor Lynch, of the 1st Monday in January, 1837. That message declares at that date, that "it has now become a mooted question, under this clause of the constitution, whether contracts for that description of property can be enforced." Now the date of this contract is the 20th of December, 1836, but two weeks preceding the admission thus made in the executive message, that the validity of these contracts was then "a mooted question." There is no fact more notorious in the state, than that the legality of these transactions was disputed at the date of this contract; and the suggestion that this illegality is an ex post facto discovery, when bankruptcy became universal, is entirely erroneous. This message shows no embarrassments at that date. The legislature were then engaged in making banks and paper money. We were then careering onward upon the tide of a delusive prosperity; and the explosion of the succeeding spring, came upon us like some of those tropical hurricanes, whose only warning consists in one sudden overwhelming sweep of ruin and desolation. It is true Governor Lynch did, afterwards, in his message of May, 1837, recommend the enforcement of this prohibition. It is true also that the legislature did then guard against the violation of this prohibition, by punishing the transgressors of it with fine and imprisonment: but all this implies no admission of the previous validity of these contracts, for this court have said that a constitution is not the place in which the minor details of legislation, these pains and penalties are to be found. But if this question was mooted as we have seen at the date of this contract, it was not on the ground that this was a mandate; but that, as a prohibition, it interdicted only the importation and not the sale. The proof on this point is ample; but we need only refer to the opinion of Chancellor Buckner, so much relied on by our opponents, in which he recites all the grounds assumed in behalf of the negro traders, namely :—

"1st. That though the introduction of the negroes may have been illegal, yet that the consequences of that act could not be communicated to the contract of sale and purchase, which was a separate and distinct transaction between themselves and the complainants.

"2d. If the reverse of the first proposition were true, it is contended that the illegality of the contract was a matter of pure defence in the court of law."

Here, even at that late day in this controversy, neither these wealthy and powerful traders, nor their learned counsel, deemed it even a point in the controversy, that this provision was not a constitutional interdict, but that the only question was, whether that interdict affected the sale or the introduction only. Chancellor Buckner also takes up fully the constitutional question, and declares his determination "to put it in train for ultimate decision." In that opinion, which is very elaborate, he does not pretend that this clause in the constitution was not of itself prohibitory; but on the contrary, he says: "Thus we intend to prohibit the multiplication of slaves in this state, but as we do not intend to extend it so far as to prohibit our own citizens from bringing them in for their own use, in order to render the *introduction* illegal, it must appear as a part of the act, that the *intention* existed to use the slave so introduced, as an article of merchandise or for sale. If the framers of the constitution intended any thing beyond this construction, instead of the language employed, we should expect to find them declaring that the sale of negroes in this state, which were introduced as merchandise or for sale, shall be prohibited from and after the first day of May, 1833. Such a construction *would fully sustain the construction contended for by the complainants counsel;* there the 'sale' not the 'introduction' would be the thing prohibited. To show my understanding of it more clearly, I mean to declare, that the *moment* the negroes were 'introduced as merchandise or for sale,' *the offence was at once complete. No further step was necessary to bring it within the meaning of the prohibitory clause of the constitution."* Here it is most distinctly conceded, that the act of importation with intent to sell, is rendered illegal by "the *prohibitory clause* of the constitution;" and that the contract by virtue of the true construction of that clause would have been illegal, if the sale had been embraced in the provision. And not only is this point thus clearly conceded in this case, but no decision, so far as my knowledge extends, has ever been made by any judge against us on this point.

Upon this point then we have the decision of the district judge of the United States for the state of Mississippi (Mr. Gholson); the decision of Chancellor Buckner so much relied on by our opponents; and finally, the decision of the highest court of the state of Mississippi, after the most elaborate argument, the question being sent up for the express purpose of obtaining a final adjudication. That opinion, too, was delivered by a gentleman distinguished at the bar and on the bench, as a statesman and jurist; who had repeatedly served with distinction in the legislature of the state, upon the bench of the circuit court, in the convention which framed this very constitution, in the Senate of the United States, and finally as a member of the highest court of the state. He was not only a member of the convention which framed the constitution, but chairman of the very committee to which this clause was referred. He was a witness of all that transpired in that committee and in that convention; he participated in all the debates upon the question, observed all the modifications of this provision from the imperfect form in which it was originally presented, until it was perfected as it now stands; and his opinion as to the intention of the convention, is the testimony of a witness, as well as the decision of a judge. Concurring with him, was the able and learned Chief Justice of the state, and there was no dissenting opinion.

As authority merely, such a decision under such circumstances, pronounced by the highest court of the state upon a question regarding the construction of a clause in their own constitution, upon a local question with which, and all the proceedings relating to it in the convention and in the legislature, they must be more familiar than this court can be, ought to be conclusive.

In delivering, after solemn argument, the deliberate opinion of the high court of errors and appeals of Mississippi, Judge Trotter says—

"Two questions present themselves for the consideration of this court: 1st. Whether the consideration of the note for which the judgment was given is illegal, and renders it void. 2d. Whether a court of chancery can give relief.

"The constitution of 1832 provides that 'the introduction of slaves into this state as merchandise, or for sale, shall be prohibited from and after the first day of May, 1833.' That it is competent for the people in convention to establish a rule of conduct for themselves, and to prohibit certain acts deemed inimical to their welfare, is a proposition which cannot be controverted. And such rule, and such prohibition will be as obligatory as if the same had been adopted by legislative enactment. In the former case it is endowed with greater claims upon the approbation and respect of the country, by being solemnly and deliberately incorporated with the fundamental rules of the paramount law, and thus placed beyond the contingency of legislation. It has been argued that this provision in the constitution is merely directory to the legislature. This interpretation is opposed, as I conceive, to the plain language of the provision itself, as well as to the obvious meaning of the convention. It cannot surely be maintained that this provision is less a prohibition against the introduction of slaves as merchandise, because it is not clothed with the sanction of pains and penalties expressed in the body of it. That belonged appropriately to the legislature. Their neglect or refusal to do so, might lessen the motives to obedience, but could not impair the force of the prohibition."

Here, then, is the question made for the final adjudication of the court, and clearly determined by them, and with an ability worthy of their high reputation. It was, too, a decision in favour of the trader in slaves, upon the doubtful question of chancery jurisdiction, and he was permitted, for want of a defence at law, to reap the fruits of his unlawful contract; thus vindicating the court in this very decision, from the charge of any bias as judges in favour of our own citizens, so unjustly urged by our opponents, as a reason why that decision should have no weight with this court. The judges of that court, for integrity and impartiality, are universally esteemed by the bar and by the people, and by all men and all parties in the state; any insinuation that these judges or any one of them ever had been or ever could be governed by any unworthy bias, could only subject to just suspicion those by whom such a suggestion could be made, and those upon whom it could have the slightest operation. I am restrained by my respect for this court, from expressing here my indignation at the assault made upon the functionaries and people of Mississippi. It is true, as stated, that great embarrassments pervade the state, and that it is strewed with the wrecks of broken hopes and bankrupt fortunes. But has the honour of the state been tarnished, have the laws been disregarded, the courts overthrown or corrupted, or the constitution subverted? Has rebellion arrested for a time the progress of justice, as it once did from similar causes, in the great state of Massachusetts? Have we followed the evil example of another great state of the west, by enacting laws permitting a tender of worthless paper upon executions for debts payable in gold and silver? Have we, to enforce these enactments, trampled upon the fundamental law of the state and of the Union? Have we entered the sacred halls of justice, and by the strong arm of legislative and popular power, expelled from the bench the highest judicial functionaries, and placed usurpers there upon the broken fragments of the constitution? Have we—but even in retaliation I will darken no more, with the pencil of truth, those scenes of misfortune, delusion and folly, which a thousand glorious deeds and ennobling sacrifices, in war and in peace, should expunge from the history of that patriotic commonwealth. But from that state at least, if not from all the Union, though we have never asked their sympathy for our sufferings, might we not justly challenge their respect for the fortitude with which they are borne. Again and again has the stern mandate of the law entered the dwelling of the husband and wife, and driven forth from it, them and their children, without a roof to shelter or a home to receive them. Again and again have endorsers and sureties for others suffered the fate of the principals, and stood by in silence whilst the sheriff or marshal proclaimed the sale, for the debts of others, of the last remnant of that property, which years of honest industry had accumulated. And was the law resisted? No! These gloomy scenes have been marked, almost universally, by a quiet endurance of suffering, and virtuous submission to the laws of the land. I regret the occasion that has extorted these remarks upon a subject which should never have been introduced into this argument; but, when Mississippi is thus arraigned before this high tribunal, this vindication is just and proper.

But, if this clause be not a prohibition, it is conceded to be a mandate to the legislature, requiring from them implicit obedience. It is admitted, that if the legislature had passed an act repugnant to this provision, that act would have been as clear a violation of their oaths and of the constitution, and as utterly void as if this clause had been an absolute prohibition. The mandate then established a policy which the legislature could not overthrow; and being binding upon the legislature, was obligatory on the judiciary. The government itself, in all its branches, was created by the convention; they were all creatures of the constitution, and no one department of that government could violate any mandate or provision of that constitution. The time was not indefinite, but fixed on the 1st of May, 1833, from which very day, in all time to come, this mandate should be made to operate; and if the legislature neglected to enforce this mandate by penal sanctions, did it therefore follow, that the judiciary should decree a performance of a contract, thus required to be prohibited from and after a certain day fixed by the constitution? A contract contrary to the public policy of a state will not be enforced by the judiciary. This policy may arise from the common unwritten law of a state, from its peculiar situation and institutions, or expressly or by implication, from a statute or constitutional provision. Now the convention had promulgated it as the policy of the state, that from and after the 1st of May, 1833, slaves should not be introduced as merchandise; and was the will of the convention or of the legislature to be obeyed by the courts in regard to this policy? It was the will of the convention that this traffic should cease on a day certain and fixed by the constitution; and if the legislature, which could not change this policy, failed to discharge their duty, that was no reason why the courts should follow their evil example. The courts might well say, and it was their duty to say, that although we cannot act affirmatively against the violators of this policy, they shall not make the judiciary the instruments, by a decree in their favour, to overthrow a great constitutional mandate, designed to accomplish important purposes. The courts of a country will often ascertain without a statute, and often from the mere implication of a statute, or merely from the situation of the country, what is contrary to the policy of a state, and they will enforce no contract repugnant to that policy. To no higher source then, could the courts of a state go, in order to ascertain what was the true policy of a state, than to a mandatory clause in the constitution. Had the clause in question been a mere grant of power to the legislature, the courts might have waited the action of that body; but, when the clause was mandatory, it promulgated the policy of the state, from an authority paramount to that of the legislature, and which policy, the legislature, neither by acting nor declining to act, could expunge from the constitution.

If the will of the legislature were ascertained to be one way in regard to this policy, and that of the convention the other, which should be obeyed by the judiciary, when required to act by decrees affirmatively upon the question? Can there be a doubt that the true answer to such a question should be in the language of this court, in 4 Wheat. 408, "If indeed such be the *mandate* of the constitution,

we have only to obey." This view of the subject is sustained by a late unanimous decision of the Supreme Court of Tennessee, in which they say : " In
the precise state above supposed stood the matter, when the convention in 1834
adopted the 5th section of the 11th article of the reformed constitution, in which
they provide, that the legislature ' shall pass laws to prohibit the sale of lottery
tickets in this state.' This was itself a prohibition, and was announced to the complainants before the formation of their contract with the defendants." Bass vs.
Mayor, &c. Meigs, 421. Upon this ground alone, the court pronounced the contract
invalid, which was dated March 3d, 1835, and no law was passed till the 13th
February, 1836, when a law was enacted prohibiting lotteries; as a law was passed
in 1837 by the legislature of Mississippi prohibiting the introduction of slaves as
merchandise. But independent of the subsequent law in Tennessee, their courts
pronounced the contract invalid, in a case where many thousand dollars had been
advanced to the city of Nashville, upon the sale of this lottery for the useful purpose of improving the streets of that city, and which money would be entirely lost
if the contract were declared invalid. But it was so pronounced upon the sole
ground that the constitutional mandate to pass laws prohibiting lotteries " was itself a prohibition;" because by this mandate the policy of the state " was announced
to the complainants before the formation of their contract with the defendants,'' and
they had no right to ask the court to disregard that policy, upon the ground that
the legislature had failed to provide the proper penalties. The court could not
supply those penalties, but they might well declare that they would not become
instrumental in defeating this great public policy by decreeing the performance of
contracts repugnant to it. If such a construction of the constitution of Tennessee,
upon a mere mandate to prohibit lotteries was proper, how much stronger is the
case before us ? Here the subversion by the courts of the policy promulgated in
the constitution, might involve not merely the property, but the lives of the people
of Mississippi. Had not the people then in such a case a right to require that their
courts should not become auxiliary in encouraging the subversion of this policy, by
the enforcement of contracts repugnant to it ? The legislature might never agree
upon the details of a bill for the punishment of the transgressors of this policy; and
must this mandate therefore be expunged by the courts from the constitution, or
changed into a grant of discretionary power to the legislature ? If so, this clause
might as well never have been inserted in the constitution. It is sufficient for
courts to know in any case, that the enforcement of a contract will be dangerous to
the peace and prosperity of a state; and they have invariably refused, from a regard
to the public good, to enforce such contracts. What better evidence could the
courts of Mississippi desire, that the enforcement of this contract would be subversive of the true policy of the state, and dangerous to its peace and prosperity, than
the prohibitory mandate of the constitution ? If, as a consequence of a refusal of
the courts to maintain this cardinal policy, the state had been filled with insurgent
slaves, or with slaves in an excess too far beyond the white population, and the
scenes of Southampton had been re-enacted within our limits, would the judicial
ermine be unstained with the blood of the innocent victims, who had appealed to
them in vain to discharge their duty, by denying their aid to all these contracts
thus clearly repugnant to the prohibitory policy of the constitution ? Why should
the judicial sanction be given to the violation of a constitutional mandate; and the
legislature, thus encouraged by a co-equal and co-ordinate department of the
government, to persist in refusing to discharge the duty imposed by the constitution ? It is clear then to my mind, that, whether the clause in question be of itself
an absolute prohibition, or a prohibitory mandate, the contract is alike invalid, in
accordance with reason and argument, as well as upon the authority of the unanimous decisions of the Supreme Courts of Mississippi and Tennessee.

Such was the view which those courts took of their duty to the people under these
clauses in their respective state constitutions; and it would be strange indeed if this
court should now inform those tribunals, that they had erred in this respect, and direct them to retrace their steps on this question. The people of Mississippi in convention, when creating a government had said, this traffic " shall be prohibited from
and after the 1st of May, 1833." Was it then competent or proper for the judiciary,

who are but agents for the people under this government, deriving their existence and authority from the constitution, and bound by all its injunctions, to say this trade *shall not be prohibited* on the day fixed by the convention, but shall continue upheld by our decrees, until certain other agents of the people superadd legislative penalties? A "law" against the mandate would be "void," and so must be declared by the courts; and yet negative action, or a failure to act in pursuance of the mandate, it is contended, is obligatory upon the judicial tribunals. These tribunals are not created by nor do they derive their appointment or authority from the legislature, nay more, they are expressly authorized to restrain that department within the constitution, by invalidating all their acts repugnant to that instrument; and it would be strange indeed, if when that paramount law which all were bound to obey, declared this traffic shall be prohibited on a day certain, that the courts who are the guardians and interpreters of the constitution, should say, it shall not be prohibited on that day named by the convention, but only on such other future day, as may be designated by the legislature. Even if legislation, additional and penal, was contemplated by the convention, does it therefore follow that the trade was lawful and proper for judicial sanction? On this second point also our highest court, in the case above quoted, declare it immaterial whether it be a mandate or a prohibition. They say, "in either case it fixes/the policy of the state on this subject, and renders illegal the practice designed to be suppressed."

These views, thus declared unanimously by the supreme courts of two of the states of this Union, are in accordance with just views of constitutional liberty. The formation of the constitution of a state is an act of sovereign power emanating directly from the people. Legislation is not an act of sovereign power. The legislature is not sovereign. It is but a co-ordinate department of the government, created by the constitution from which it derives all its powers; and when the people have inserted therein a mandate, declaring that from and after a day named by them, such a thing *shall be prohibited*, would it not be strange, because one department of the government, to whom this mandate was addressed, had disobeyed it, that it should therefore be considered a dead letter by another co-equal and co-ordinate department of the government, sworn to support the constitution, to maintain inviolate all its provisions, to repudiate all contracts repugnant to its spirit or policy, and to declare void, and render inoperative, all acts of any department or persons opposed to its provisions? The legislature could pass no act of grace or indulgence, dispensing with this mandate, and legalizing contracts repugnant to it; nor would their disobedience and failure to act constitute a just cause of disobedience by that very department which was not only sworn to support the constitution, but whose peculiar duty it was to expound that instrument, and to keep all persons and departments within its limits, whenever a case arose for the exercise of their judicial functions. What is the meaning of the oath taken by the judges of our high court to "*support* the constitution?" It is to maintain the supremacy of the constitution, and to enforce no laws or contracts repugnant to any of its mandates. And if an act giving bounties for the violation of this mandate would have been void, why is a contract repugnant to it, unsanctioned by any law, valid, the first being a legislative enactment, the second a confederacy of individuals to disregard the mandate? Suppose this mandate had been addressed to the Executive, could the legislature, with his concurrence, or without it, by the constitutional majority of two-thirds, have passed a valid law in opposition to such a mandate; and would the judiciary, by affirmative decrees, have enforced such an enactment? Or if the mandate had been addressed to the judiciary, would an opposing law have been valid? Surely not. And the reason in all these cases is the same, because no one of the departments of the government, *when required to act affirmatively*, can disregard any mandate of the constitution. The policy of a state may be announced in the constitution as the will of the people, either in a mandate, or in any other form; and however announced, no court can disregard that will, or subvert that policy. The supremacy of the constitution is the great cardinal principle of American liberty, from which there is no appeal but to force; and to subvert its principles, or disregard its mandates, is anarchical and revolutionary. If the clause in question be converted into a mandate to the legislature by interpolation and implication, why is it not *declaratory* by construction, as well as *mandatory;* declaratory of the policy of the state on a day fixed and certain, and mandatory to the legislature to enforce that policy by appropriate legislation? This clause, marking the will of the convention as to this policy upon the day named by them, was declaratory of that policy; not a policy to be established hereafter by grants of discretionary power to the legislature, but declared in a mandate, imperative upon that body, and announcing to all the will of the convention. The words *shall be prohibited,* on a day named by the convention, did announce the policy designed by them to be established on that very day; and *if,* by interpolation and implication, we change these words into a mandate addressed to the legislature, shall we also so interpret these words, thus interpolated by conjectural construction, as to subvert the policy thus announced in terms clear and explicit, and render the whole clause dependent, from time to time, upon the fluctuating will of the legislature, inoperative without their action, changeable at their pleasure, and amounting to nothing more than the mere grant of discretionary power to the legislature, commencing when they legislate, and ceasing when they repeal the present or any future enactment on the subject.

In 2 Dal. 304, Judge Patterson, of this court, said:—"Every state in the Union has its constitution reduced to written exactitude and precision. What is a constitution? It is the form of government delineated by the mighty hand of the people, in which certain *first principles* of fundamental laws are established. The constitution is *certain and fixed;* it contains the permanent will of the people, and is the supreme law of the land; it is paramount to the power of the legislature, and can be revoked or altered only by the authority that made it. What are the legislatures? Creatures of the constitution." "The constitution is the work or will of the people themselves, in their original, sovereign, and unlimited capacity. The one is the work of the creator, and the other of the creature. The constitution fixes limits to the exercise of legislative authority, and prescribes the orbit within which it must move." "It is a *rule* and *commission* by which both *legislators* and *judges* are to proceed;" and "the judiciary in this country is not a subordinate, but co-ordinate branch of the government."

Was not the prohibition of the introduction of slaves as merchandise from and after a day "certain and fixed" by the constitution, one of those "first principles" announced in that instrument as "the permanent will of the people," "paramount to the power of the legislature," "and furnishing the "rule and commission" by which both *legislators* and *judges* are to proceed?" Now, by disregarding this mandate, the courts would make an act, or the absence of an act, of legislation, paramount to the fundamental law; they would exalt the legislature above the people, the creature above the creator, and elevate the policy of the legislature above that of the constitution.

It is admitted that if this clause were in a law it would be a prohibition, but as it is in a constitution it is said to be a mere direction to the legislature. Now the constitution is *a law,* the sovereign law, the paramount law, the fundamental, the supreme law, the permanent law, the law of highest obligation, the *lex legum,* the law of laws. The constitution of Mississippi of 1817, of which that of 1832 is an amendment, declares that therein and thereby the people "do ordain and establish;" which is quite as strong as *do enact;* and all laws contrary to any of its provisions are declared "void." It is then an act of *sovereign legislation, ordaining and establishing* certain permanent rules and fundamental principles of public policy, of universal obligation throughout the state, and not mere directions to any one department of government. In England, their early and fundamental laws, and especially their Magna Charta, were called constitutions; and before the revolution these were called by our ancestors, "the constitution," the "English constitution," "the constitution venerable to Britons and Americans"—1 Journal American Congress, 60, 65, 138, 148, 149, 163. Many of the fundamental principles of public liberty contained in Magna Charta are copied into the constitution of Mississippi and of the other states. How then is this great constitutional law regarded and construed in England? In the first place, then, it was a law, and is thus described in Dwaris on Statutes, 801—"Magna Charta, 9. H. 3, is the earliest *statute* we have on record"—"It contains 37 chapters." Among the rules of construing this fundamental law here laid down was this, that "*no sanction* was wanting to *enforce its* obligations," that *no judgment could be given by any court* "contrary to any of its points," but that it should be observed with "the most scrupulous care"— Lord Coke says in regard to it, " As the gold finer will not out of the dust, threads, or shreds of gold, *let pass the least crumb*, in respect of the excellency of the metal, so ought not the learned reader to let pass any syllable of this law in respect of the excellency of the matter." But here in our Magna Charta, the fundamental law of the state, consecrated as the act of the people in their highest sovereign capacity, we are to give *less effect* to its provisions than to subordinate legislative enactments. In a statute, it is admitted these words would be a prohibition, but in this fundamental law, these same words are not so to operate, but are to be changed by implication and interpolation, or rather by what Coke calls "divination," guessing, or judicial astrology, into a mere direction to the legislature. Was Magna Charta ever regarded as a mere direction to parliament? No, it was universally interpreted as addressed to the courts, and to be enforced by them with the most "scrupulous observance" of all its provisions. And if by implication or interpolation we shall construe one portion as addressed to the legislature for their direction, where is the rule to stop? Parts of this constitution are addressed in words to the legislature, and other portions are not so addressed; and when the framers of the constitution intended merely to give directions to the legislature, they so declared, and not otherwise. No British court would so construe any clause of Magna Charta as to defeat any of its fundamental principles, or to change them into mere directions to the legislature; and shall an American court regard as less sacred the prohibitory enactments of the constitution? Among the canons for construing Magna Charta is the maxim "Verba ita sunt intelligenda, ut res magis valeat quam pereat;" but here we are asked so to construe this provision that it may perish and be treated as a dead letter. Indeed this clause is asked to be expounded as the young interpret dreams, by contraries; and when our fundamental law says, this traffic "shall be prohibited from and after the first May, 1833,—this is to be construed "shall not be prohibited" on that or any other day but such as the legislature may or may not think proper to designate.

The act of December, 1833, it is said, taxes the sale of these slaves, and therefore this clause is not prohibitory. But this act is merely an amendatory and declaratory statute, passed in pursuance of the auditor's report of November, 1833, to remove "any ambiguity" in the act of 1825. Under the last proviso of the 5th section of the act of 1825, citizens of the state who sold slaves as merchandise, contended that they were not liable to pay the tax. The auditor thought otherwise, and justly so, but to remove all "ambiguity" he recommends the legislature to " *declare the liability* of every person bound to pay the said tax." The three first sections of the amendatory act of December, 1833, merely enforced the collection of the tax authorized by the act of 1825, and both acts would embrace a tax on sales of slaves, provided they had been introduced prior to the first of May, 1833. Now many slaves introduced for sale remained, like all other merchandise, for years unsold; and to enforce the collection of the tax already authorized by the act of 1825, on these *lawful sales*, was the intention of the first three sections of the act of 1833. The fourth section of the act of 1833, if it be a substantive provision, going beyond the act of 1825, applies exclusively to any " citizen of this state." From the construction of our opponents, it would follow, that by this act, the legislature intended to discriminate between residents of the state and non-residents, by imposing upon the former only, and not upon the latter, a tax on the sale of all slaves introduced as merchandise after the date of the act of 1833. Such was not the intention of the legislature. The *fourth section* was declaratory only, and was a legislative construction, not of the constitution of 1832, but of the fifth section of the act of 1825. That section commences as follows : " And whereas it is provided, in the fifth section of the act to which this is an amendment, that nothing in that act shall authorize a tax to be collected on the sale of any slave or slaves, sold by one citizen of this state to another citizen thereof; therefore, and for the *better understanding whereof,*

B

" Be it enacted, That when any citizen of this state, residing permanently therein, shall bring into this state any slave or slaves," &c. That section, then, upon its face, was enacted solely for the "better understanding" of the 5th section of the act of which it was an amendment, and with the view only to obviate all " ambiguity" as regards that section by a legislative construction, applying the act of 1825 to residents as well as non-residents. There is not one word in the act of 1833, demonstrating that the legislature were placing any construction on the prohibition or prohibitory mandate of the constitution; much less that they were engaged in the unholy purpose of enacting laws repugnant thereto. The declaratory and amendatory act of 1833, can well expend the whole force of all its provisions, in aiding the collection of the tax authorized by the act of 1825, and applicable only to such cases, as those to which that act could well apply, consistently with the provisions of the constitution. No new tax was authorized by the act of 1833, but only more adequate provisions to insure the collection of the tax authorized by the act of 1825, and declaratory enactments for the "better understanding thereof."

This court is asked to repose upon a legislative construction of our constitution; and to do so, they must give a construction to the very enactment in question, never intended by its framers. Construction is to be based upon construction. And not only was this act of 1833 never intended as a construction of the constitution, but only of the act of 1825; but such has been its practical interpretation. The journals of the convention and legislature of Mississippi not being here, I am driven to the printed book of our opponents, consisting of such extracts from journals and messages, as they deem favourable to their cause, but which show that this act of 1833 has never been applied to slaves introduced after the 1st of May, 1833, although it may properly have applied to the cases, comparatively few in number, of slaves introduced for sale prior to the 1st of May, 1833, but sold, as they lawfully might be, in such cases, subsequent to that period. Thus, at page 29 of this pamphlet, is quoted the statement of the auditor.

" Amount received on account of slaves sold as merchandise from
    the 1st of Jan. 1833, to 3d March, 1833, inclusive, . $1065 17
" Do. do. from 4th March, 1833, to 19th Nov. 1833, . . $2625 13½"

Does this show, that any of these slaves, thus sold, were introduced subsequent to the 1st of May, 1833? The slaves introduced prior to that date, though *sold* afterwards, were clearly liable to the tax ; and if the tax continued to be collected on all slaves imported afterwards, why this *decrease* in the revenue from that source, when the sales were *increasing?* Why was $2000 collected in *two* months from these sales prior to the 4th of March, 1833, and but $2625 in nearly *nine* months afterwards? As the importations and sales were increasing so rapidly, why this decreasing revenue? Can any other reason be assigned than this, that no tax was collected on the sales of slaves introduced after the 1st of May, 1833, but only on such sales, after that period, as were made of slaves before introduced ? But again, our opponents allege that the principal importations and sales were made in the years 1835 and 1836, and consequently the revenue in those years should have greatly increased from that source. Now, at page 45, of their pamphlet, the auditor's report shows that the amount of tax was as follows :

" Amount received on account of slaves sold as merchandise from
    20th Jan. 1835, to 28th Feb. 1835, inclusive, . . . $ 20 00
" Do. do. from 18th March, 1835, to 4th Jan. 1836, . . . 166 40
                                                         $186 40"

Here is a prodigious decrease in the revenue this year, showing, that the tax must have been confined to the few slaves sold within the period abovementioned, introduced prior to the 1st of May, 1833.

On looking at the next year, at page 45 of the pamphlet, we find, by the auditor's report :

" Amount received on account of slaves sold as merchandise from 5th
    Jan. 1836, to 29th Feb. 1836, inclusive, ... $68 50
" Do. from 1st March, 1836, to 4th Jan. 1837, ...   82 00
    ────────
                                                                    $150 50"

Thus, we find the tax reduced the last twelve months to $150.50, and the last
ten months to $82; thus continually decreasing, when it should have been so
vastly augmenting. No reason can be assigned for this, except that the unsold
slaves introduced as merchandise, prior to 1st May, 1833, became fewer every
year, until, in the last ten months, the sale of four slaves, at less than $1000 each,
would have yielded, at the legal rate of tax of 2½ per cent on the sales, more than
the whole amount of the whole tax received of $82. Now this was the period
within which the plaintiffs *made their sales of these slaves*, the amount of which
sales on 20th Dec. 1836, according to the notes sued on, being $14,875, the tax on
which sales alone, would at the lawful rate have amounted to $371, being not
only more than the whole tax on all the sales in 1836, but more than on all the
sales, by our opponents' own showing, from 20th Jan. 1835 to 4th Jan. 1837; the
totality of which was, as we have seen, but $347.50, which would show taxes re-
ceived on but *sixteen slaves* in these two years, rated at less than $1000 each.
Here, by their own book, it is shown that no tax was paid by the plaintiff on
the sales in this case, and that their counsel in this court have been greatly de-
ceived in their conjecture to the contrary. From 1st May, 1833, till May 31st,
1837, at least forty thousand slaves were introduced and sold. The average price
for working slaves, was then $1000 each, on a credit, and such generally were in-
troduced by the traders; and the total price would thus be forty millions of dollars,
the tax on which, under the act of 1833, had it applied, would have been *one million of dollars*, whereas the amount really received, we have seen, as shown by our
opponents, was less than four thousand dollars. If then this tax was payable under
the act of 1833, the negro traders (for by law *they* were to pay the tax,) have de-
frauded the state of Mississippi, in four years, of one million of dollars.
From 1830 till 1840, the slaves, by our census, increased 130,000, and as the importation commenced chiefly in 1833, and was prohibited in May, 1837, the tax
should have much exceeded one million of dollars. Now is it credible, that if this
tax were due under the act of 1833, that it would never have been assessed, and
that less than $4000, out of one million, would have been collected? And why
was not the prohibition enforced by proper pains and penalties? In 1833 we find
the legislature endeavouring to amend the constitution, so as to get clear of this
prohibition to a certain extent. The sessions of our legislature are biennial. The
next session was in 1834–5, but it failed on account of a disagreement between the
two houses, as to the alleged illegal organization of one house, and was prorogued
by the governor. The next legislature *did prohibit*, in May, 1837; the meeting in
May, 1837, being of the same legislature which first assembled in 1836. On the
14th Jan. 1836, the following entry appears on the journal of the house: " The
committee of revisal and *unfinished* business, have requested me to report as part
of the *unfinished business* of *last* session, the following bills and resolutions
namely: ' a bill to be entitled an act to prohibit the introduction of slaves into this
state as merchandise.'" Page of Pamphlet, 42. At page 43, (436 of Journal,)
Mr. *Gholson* called up this bill, but no final and direct action was then had on it.
In January, 1837, the bill was again brought up, and at page 53 of the Pamphlets,
(102 of the Journal,) a motion to postpone it indefinitely failed, by ayes 13,
noes 56, thus showing a very large majority to be in favour of the bill, although
they could not agree on the details until May, 1837, when the present prohibitory
statute was passed by the same legislature which convened in 1836. And here, it
is worthy of remark, that Mr. *Gholson*, our Federal Judge, who has represented the
state with so much ability, both at the capitol of the state, and of the Union,
served throughout all these successive sessions of the legislature, from 1833 till
1837, and took a leading part in all these bills connected with this subject, at all
these periods; namely, the tax bills, the bill to amend the constitution, and the

prohibition bill, repeatedly serving as chairman in all these sessions. Who then more competent to understand all these bills, and to decide with full knowledge of all these questions? Yet this learned judge of our federal court was the first to decide this entire question in our favour, as quoted in the Free Trader Gazette, produced by our opponents. Here then is a practical construction of this question, by a refusal of *all* the authorities of Mississippi to demand or receive any portion of that immense revenue, which might have been derived from these sales, had they been regarded as legal, and it is a construction which embraces both points of the controversy, namely, the absolute character of the prohibition, and the illegality of the sale, as well as of the introduction for sale. Must not all then have known, that by declining to receive these taxes, the state proclaimed the illegality of the sales; and was not the plaintiff when he made the sales in this case, without the payment of any tax, a wilful transgressor of this great constitutional interdict?

But independent of this practical construction in our favour, it is settled that an act passed for "the better understanding" of a previous law, and declaratory of its meaning, must be connected with the previous act of 20th February, 1825, whose true meaning it expounds, and be considered as though inserted in that law, and *at that date.* In this view of the case, the terms "shall bring" need not be construed *shall have brought*, although such construction has been repeatedly given, to prevent a repugnance between a statute and a constitution, or between two statutes, or to obviate injustice or a violation of fundamental principles; but these words "shall bring," in the declaratory 4th section of the act of 1833, must be referred to the 20th February, 1825, the date of the act expounded so as to impose a tax *under that law* on all sales by citizens (as well as non-residents,) of slaves lawfully introduced after that date for sale before the 1st May, 1833, and *not yet sold*, or on which sales *the taxes had not been paid.* This was the obvious intention of the legislature, for they were expounding the meaning of the act of 1825, and not interpreting the constitution. Thus in the case of Pouget, 2 Price, 381, where the act of 53 Geo. 3, c. 33, imposed a duty on hides, of 9s. 4d., meaning that much per 100 weight, but neglecting to say so, when a subsequent act amendatory of the former law, declared that the duty of 9s. 4d. SHALL BE CHARGEABLE on every 100 weight of such hides, it was decided that the new declaratory provision must be taken as a part of the former law, and as then passed, and operating from that date.

The court said, "The duty in this instance was, in fact, imposed by the first act; but the gross mistake of the omission of the weight, for which the sum expressed was to have been payable, occasioned the amendment made by the subsequent act; but that had reference to the former statute as soon as it passed, and they must be taken together as if they were one and the same act, and the *first* must be read as *containing in itself, in words, the amendment supplied by the last.*" Now let the act of 1825, which really did impose this tax on citizens as well as non-residents, be read as "containing in itself, in words, the amendment supplied for the better understanding thereof," by the 4th section of the act of 1833, and the whole difficulty disappears. Perceiving the difficulty in which they would involve the legislature, by asserting that they had violated their oaths, by passing a law opposed to the prohibition or prohibitory mandate of the constitution, our opponents have suggested that when this tax law passed through the two houses, they believed that their amendment proposed at the preceding session to change this mandate or prohibition into a grant of discretionary power to themselves, had been adopted by the people. If this be so, and the legislature acted under this erroneous impression, how could a law thus passed be regarded as a legislative construction of this clause of the constitution? But if this law did authorize the introduction of slaves for sale after the 1st May, 1833, why had the legislature sought to change the mandate or interdict of the constitution into a mere grant of discretionary power, if as is urged they already possessed that power; and if having failed to effect this change in the constitution, they had nevertheless by this law authorized the introduction of slaves as merchandise, could such an act be called a legislative exposition of the constitution?

The framers of our state constitution have withheld all judicial power from the legislature. They have declared, " the judicial power of this state shall be vested" in the courts of the state; and that "the powers of the government of the state of Mississippi shall be divided into three *distinct* departments, and *each of them* confided to a *separate* body of magistracy ; to wit, those which are *legislative* to one, those which are *judicial* to another, and those which are *executive* to another. No person or collection of persons, being *one of these departments*, shall exercise *any power* belonging to *either* of the others, except in the instances hereinafter expressly directed or permitted." If then, as all admit, to expound a constitution be a judicial power, the legislature was forbidden to exercise it, and so was the executive. It was confided to the judiciary, we have their construction ; and an imaginary and conjectural legislative or executive construction is set up in opposition to an exposition of the constitution, by the very tribunal to whom its interpretation was confided by its framers. If then, a construction by the legislature could be quoted, I deny their jurisdiction ; and pointing to the constitution of our state, declare that it is there expressly withheld. But an executive construction is relied on by our opponents. *None such exists ;* but what think our three distinguished opponents of executive construction ? Shall I quote their eloquent denunciations of such abuse of power ? No, I will spare them the contrast with their present argument; but I will say, that the government which deliberately supersedes judicial by legislative or executive construction, has already sunk into despotism. It has combined in one department two out of the three great powers of government; the third will assuredly follow ; and the centralization of all these powers in the legislature or executive, in the opinion of Mr. Jefferson, in his Notes on Virginia, page 195, " is precisely the definition of a despotic government." We shall see in the progress of this discussion, that, by the highest courts of England, no regard is paid to a construction of the laws by the king, or the king in council. But at one time a British judge declared from the bench, " all power centres in the king," and the laws were overthrown by "twelve men in scarlet," taking "royal auricular opinions" for their guide: but for more than a century, executive construction has had no weight with British judges. I need scarcely appeal to this court to disregard executive construction; nor say to them, that if they do not, the day will have arrived when congressional or presidential construction will trample down the high powers of this tribunal in exercising its great constitutional function of expounding in the last resort the laws and constitution of the Union. The volumes of your decision will be thrown aside, and the exposition of the law and the constitution will be looked for in executive messages and congressional enactments. If then there were a legislative and executive construction on the one side, and that of the highest court of the state on the other, which shall prevail ? To whom is the power assigned by the constitution of the state ? And this court will not disregard the distribution of powers as therein delegated to the several departments of government.

The next question is, can the contract for the sale of these slaves be maintained, if the clause in question be a prohibition of the introduction for sale ? Assuming this as established, the clause in question would prohibit the introduction of slaves as merchandise or for sale. The introduction being thus prohibited, if the sale be sanctioned, the clause would read thus: You shall not introduce slaves into this state as merchandise or for sale, but you, the importer, may make merchandise of them, or sell them to any one as soon as they are landed. Would not such language be strangely repugnant and contradictory ? Would it not seem as though the convention had designed to render their own provision inoperative and nugatory ? Could the importer sell the thing he was forbidden to introduce for sale ? Could he make merchandise of the very thing he was prohibited from introducing as merchandise ? The object prohibited was not merely the introduction of slaves, but their introduction *as merchandise or for sale*. Now, was the object prohibited, and yet the sale permitted ? To introduce the slaves with intent to sell is criminal, but to carry that criminal intention into effect, is declared to be authorized and invited by the constitution. Can the intent be criminal, and yet the fulfilment of the evil intention perfectly lawful ? To maintain this position, is to reverse the rule of law and morals, which always regards the execution of the evil intention, as more

B 2

criminal than the intention itself. If the sale crowns and completes the unlawful purpose, if it executes the illegal intention, if it consummates the violation of the law, if it enables the transgressor to obtain the end and object prohibited, and reap the fruits of his transgression, it must be unlawful. To effectuate the object and intention of the law is the great rule in expounding laws and constitutions.

Now the inter-state slave trade, as carried on by traders in slaves as merchandise, was the thing designed to be prohibited. And yet this very prohibited traffic, by a verbal criticism on the words, overlooking the object of the constitution, is in fact encouraged, if the trader may sell the slaves introduced as merchandise. This court have said, that a fraud upon a statute, is a violation of the statute; that an evasion of the constitution, is a violation of the constitution; and is not this construction an evasion by the slave traders of the constitution of Mississippi? Lord Coke, in Heyden's case, 3 Coke, 7, declares, that the true rule in construing statutes is so to interpret as "to suppress inventions and evasions for *continuance of the mischief*, and *pro privato commodo*, and to add force and life to the cure and remedy, according to the true intent of the makers of the act, *pro bono publico*." The clauses of a statute are to be construed in their popular signification, and this is more pre-eminently the great rule in regard to a state constitution. Who then but an astute critic, on reading this clause, would doubt as to the object designed to be prohibited? To whom of the people at large would the subtle distinction occur, that slaves could not be introduced as merchandise or for sale, but that the importer was authorized to sell at once these slaves that could not thus be introduced for sale? The terms of the constitution are peculiar and comprehensive. These slaves are not only forbidden to be introduced "for sale," but also "as merchandise." Merchandise means *vendible articles*. These slaves then cannot be imported as *vendible articles*. How then can they be rendered vendible articles within the state, when they cannot be landed as such within its limits? In Brown v. State of Maryland, 12 Wheat. 439, the question was whether a state could impose a tax upon the sale by the importer of articles imported into a state for sale. The court decided that the right of the importer to introduce the goods free of a state tax, did embrace the subsequent right of sale free of such tax by the importer. In delivering the opinion of the court, Chief Justice Marshall says: "There is no difference in effect between a power to prohibit the sale of an article, and the power to prohibit its introduction into the country. The one would be a necessary consequence of the other. No goods would be imported, if none could be sold." The mere prohibition then of the introduction of slaves into a country, would render the subsequent sale invalid, and if so, how much stronger is the inhibition of the sale, when the prohibition is of the introduction for sale. Why prohibit the introduction for sale, if the subsequent sale is authorized? The sale is the avowed object of the introduction in this case, and without the authority to sell, there would be no introduction for sale, and thus the law prohibiting the introduction would be enforced; but by the construction of our opponents, the sale is authorized, and the importation for sale so far encouraged and invited. But no such interpretation must be given as will defeat the object of the law, or tend to prevent its practical operation. 1st Story's Com. 411, and Chief Justice Marshall declares, 6 Cranch, 314, that "The spirit as well as the letter of the statute must be respected, and where the whole context of the law shows a particular intent in the legislature *to effect a certain object*, some degree of implication may be called in to aid that intent." The rule is that "The words of a statute are to be taken in their ordinary signification and import, and regard is to be had to their general and popular sense." Dwaris on Statutes, 702. "The sense and spirit of an act, however its scope and intention, are primarily to be regarded in the construction of statutes, and it matters not that the terms used by the legislature in delivering its commands are not the most apt to express its meaning, provided the *object* is plain and intelligible, and expressed with sufficient distinctness to enable the judges *to collect it from any part of the act*. The *object* once understood, judges are so to construe an act as to suppress the mischief and advance the remedy." Ib. 703, 4, 7, 18. And the author adds: "A statute may be extended by construction to other cases within the same mischief and occasion of the act, though not expressly within the words." If the legalizing of the sale would encourage the introduction for sale, it is within "the mischief and occasion of the act;" it is within its "spirit," "scope" and "object;" and therefore as much prohibited as though "expressly within the words of the act." "No construction of a given power is to be allowed which plainly defeats or *impairs* its *avowed objects.*" Story's Com. 411. "A statute made *pro bono publico* shall be construed in such a manner that it may as far as possible *attain the end proposed.*" Dwar. 722. As to a question what was within the prohibition of a certain law, the court say, "It is by no means unusual in construing a remedial statute, to extend the enacting words beyond their natural import and effect, in order to include cases within the same mischief." Dwar. 734, Y. and J.'s 196, 215, and the principle is extended to enlarge the policy of a penal statute, not so as to inflict the penalty, but to avoid the contract. Dwar. 752. "Wherever a statute gives or provides any thing, the common law provides all necessary remedies and requisites." Dwar. 662. "Every thing necessary to the making it effectual is given by implication." Dwar. 652. 2 Inst. 306. 12 Rep. 130, 131. "Quando aliquid prohibetur, prohibetur et omne, per quod devenitur ad illud." Dwar. 663. "Whenever the provision of a statute is general, every thing which is necessary to make such provision effectual is supplied by the common law." Dwar. 663. 1 In. 235. 2 Ib. 222. Bacon, T. Stat. "Whatever enters into the reason of the law, enters into the law itself." Dwar. 665. Ratio est anima legis. "Laws and acts which tend to public utility should receive the most liberal and benign interpretation to effect the object intended or declared, ut res magis valeat quam periat." Bald. Con. Views, 8. Bl. Com. 89. "Courts will look to the provisions of a law to discern its *objects* to meet its intentions at the time it was made; it will be sought in the cause and necessity of making the law; the meaning thus extracted, will be taken to be the law intended, as fully as if expressed in its letter." Ib. 9. 1 Wh. 121. 4 Peters, 432. If then, as is obvious, "the object of the law," namely to prevent the introduction of slaves for sale, will be frustrated by legalizing the sale, the court "will not suffer the law to be defeated" by adopting such a construction, but will so expound the law as to "suppress the mischief and advance the remedy." Ib. 9, 11. Co. 72. 1 Bl. Com. 87.

The clause which prohibited the introduction of slaves for sale, never could have intended to defeat itself, by legalizing the sale of slaves thus unlawfully introduced for sale, and thus encouraging and inviting the violation of the law, by making it profitable to disregard its provisions. But it has been said this prohibition must be strictly construed. Why so? It is not a penal statute, and if it were, it should only be construed strictly when operating on the *offender* in exacting the penalty; but when it acts upon the contract, it must be liberally construed, so as to vacate the contract, if within the mischief designed to be remedied, though not within the letter of the law. Thus, it is declared by Blackstone: "But this difference is here to be taken when the statute acts upon the *offender* and inflicts a penalty, as the pillory or a fine, it is there to be taken strictly, but when the statute acts upon the *offence* by *setting aside* the fraudulent transaction, here it is to be construed liberally." 1 Chitty's Black. 60. In a note it is stated as follows, with a reference to the highest authority: "As the statute against gaming, which enables a loser at play to the amount of ten pounds at one sitting to recover it back within three months; the act also provides a penalty against gaming to the same amount at one sitting. And the court has said in a case where the play was only interrupted by the dinner hour, for the purpose of recovering the money lost, they would hold this to be one sitting, but as against a common informer, suing for the penalty, they would hold it to be two sittings." 1 Chit. Black. 60, note, and 2 Black. Rep. 1226. Here, even in a penal law, the same words are construed strictly when they act on the offender, and liberally when they act on the contract. So in this case, were a penalty even annexed to the prohibition, the law would be construed strictly when the penalty was demanded, but liberally when a contract is sought to be enforced against the spirit or object of the prohibition. But how much stronger is the present case? If the first point be with us, the constitution prohibited the introduction of these slaves for sale or as merchandise, and as no penalty was attached to the prohibition, would not the provision be *entirely inoperative,* if the contract of sale could and must be enforced by the judicial tribunals? The object of the constitutional prohibition was to render the traffic unlawful, so that no contract could be enforced in violation of the prohibition, but the penal sanctions by fine and imprisonment might well be left to subsequent legislation. In the case of the U. S. Bank v. Owens, 2 Peters, 537, it is expressly decided by this court, that laws must be strictly construed when the penalty is exacted, but liberally in vacating the contract.

The doctrine which repudiates contracts against public policy or good morals, long preceded the common law of England, and was incorporated into that system from the civil law. In the note S. to 1 Fonblanque's Equity, Book I. sec. 4, page 186, it is stated, "Pacta quæ contra leges constitutionosque vel contra bonos mores nullam vim habere, indubitati juris est." Code, lib. 2, tit. 3, 1, 6. This rule of the civil law is drawn from the principles of universal justice; which, aiming at the prevention of wrong, prohibits agreements which would *lead to* or *encourage* it. To introduce, then, slaves into Mississippi for sale, was prohibited by the constitution, and was therefore wrong, unlawful and immoral; and none will deny, that to legalize the contract of sale for slaves thus unlawfully introduced, would encourage the introduction for sale; and if so, upon the authority above quoted, such contract would be void. " Considerations against the policy of the common law, or against the provisions of a statute, or against the policy of justice, or the rules and claims of decency, or the dictates of morality, are void in law and equity." Ib. note Y. 189. And here I maintain, that where a contract is against the policy of a state, or against good morals, or detrimental to the public interest, or against the peace, security or welfare of a state, or tending to encourage a violation of the laws or policy of a state, or the prohibition of a statute, it is void; and if it is within the spirit, scope or intention of the act, (though not within its words,) or within the object designed to be promoted or mischief suppressed, it is also void; and the most liberal construction will be given to the law, and every fair implication will be allowed, to prevent a defeat of the full operation of the statute. Thus it is declared by the court, in the leading case of Mitchell v. Smith, 1st Bin. 110, 4th Yates, 84, that contracts are void which " *tend to defeat* the *legislative provisions* for the security and peace of the community, though *not made void by statutes;*" or which tend "*to encourage* unlawful acts or omissions," or which are against principles of sound policy; "so a contract *about* a matter prohibited by statute is unlawful and a void contract, although the act does not expressly say so."—Courts ("will not assist an illegal transaction *in any respect.*" It is "immoral to violate the laws of a country," and the contract will not be enforced if illegal, though to refuse to enforce it is " contrary to real justice as between the parties;" or if the contract " militate " against the "rights" or "peace" of a state, or if against the policy of "self-preservation," or if " against the maxims of sound policy" though "not against the rules of morality," or if "repugnant to the welfare of the state;"—so if against "political arguments" or " public benefit and convenience." So the court declared that " none of the acts against smuggling transactions declare any of the contracts for goods purchased for the purpose of smuggling, to be void ; the decisions are grounded on principles of public policy alone," and, although it be "the case of a just debt as between the parties." 4 Yates, 34. The court decided, that a note given for the sale of land, under the Connecticut title, was void, although the act of 1795 only inflicted a penalty on a *combination* or *conspiracy* to convey or settle lands under such a title, but did not declare the contract void or prohibit the sale, as did the subsequent act of 1802, although the defendant was in the occupancy of the land under the sale, and every argument was urged which has been used in this case. And if the purchase money is paid by the vendor can be recovered, could not the vendee, on tender of the purchase money on a contract for sale, enforce the delivery to him of the slaves introduced for sale? Surely he could, " for the remedies must be mutual or not at all." 1 Bin. 118. In Seidenbender v. Charles, 4 Serg. and Rawle, 151, a land sale by tickets without blanks was held to be within the policy of the law against lotteries, and a note given for the sale of a lot of ground under such a lottery was held void, although the title to the lot was conceded to be valid, and the justice of the case with the plaintiff, and the sales had not been declared void by the law. In 8d T. R. 17, it was decided, that a promise of a friend of a bankrupt on his examination to pay all sums he, the bankrupt, had not accounted for, if not examined as to those sums, is void, as against the policy of the bankrupt laws, though not so declared by those laws, nor embraced within their provisions, on the ground that to enforce such contracts would be " contrary to *the spirit* of the bankrupt laws," and that by such enforcement "one of the great *objects* of the bankrupt laws *would be defeated*" by preventing *full* examination of all bankrupts on oath. In Craig v. State of Missouri, 4 Peters, 410, it was decided by this court, that a note given for bills of credit of a state, loaned to the defendant, was void, although the defendant may have realized full value for the bills, the contract being within the prohibitory policy of that clause of the constitution of the United States, which declares that *no state shall emit bills of credit*. There was nothing in this constitutional prohibition declaring such contracts void, nor any thing in words forbidding the loan of such bills ; but, as upholding a contract for their loan would encourage their emission by the state, the contract was declared invalid. In delivering the opinion of the court in this case, Chief Justice Marshall asked the following question: " Had the issuing or circulation of certificates of this or any other description been prohibited by a statute of Missouri, could a suit have been maintained in the courts of that state, on a note given in consideration of the prohibited certificate? If it could not, are the prohibitions of the *constitution* to be held *less sacred* than those of a state law?" And if such a clause in the constitution of the Union rendered void a contract for the loan of those certificates, how much stronger the implication against the sale in this case? And here, upon the first branch of the question, let me ask, if the language in a statute of Mississippi "shall be prohibited from and after the 1st of May, 1833," would be a prohibition, are the same terms and words " of the constitution to be held less sacred than those of a state law?"

In the case of Hunt v. Knickerbocker, 5 John. 327, it was decided, that a contract for the sale in New York, of tickets in a public lottery of Connecticut, authorized by the laws of that state, was illegal, and the money not recoverable, though a valuable consideration may have passed to the defendant, because it was against the policy of the law of New York, forbidding *private* lotteries. Here was a case clearly not within the words of the act, but it was regarded against the policy and spirit of the act, " and to legalize the sale would be productive of many of the mischiefs contemplated by the legislature;" and the court also say that "a contract which in *its execution*, contravenes the policy and spirit of a statute, is equally void as if made as against its positive provisions."

In Sharp v. Teese, 4 Halsted, 352, the court held, that " a note given by an insolvent debtor to two of his creditors, in consideration of their withdrawing their opposition to his discharge under the insolvent act, is void, it being against the policy of the insolvent law." In this case the debt for which the note was given, was justly due, and there was not one word in the law declaring such a contract void, as will appear in the reasons given by the court, at page 354. They say the policy of the law favours a full and fair disclosure, and equal division of the property among all the creditors, and add, " any transaction or arrangement which tends to defeat either of these purposes, is inconsistent with the policy of the law. The attempt to contravene *the policy of a public statute*, is illegal. Nor is it necessary to render it so that the statute should contain an *express prohibition of such attempt. It always contains an implied prohibition.*"

The same court decided that no action can be maintained on a contract which "contravenes the policy of an act of congress." 5 Hal. 89. The court say " many contracts which are *not against morality*, are still void as being against the maxims of sound policy;" that " if the consideration be against the public policy, it is insufficient to support the contract;" " it is a general principle, that all obligations for any matter, operating against the public policy and interests of the nation are void." See also 2 Southard, 756, 763.

In Nichols v. Ruggles, 3 Day, 145, it was decided, that " a contract to reprint any literary work in violation of a copy-right secured to a third person is void: and *the printer who executes such contract*, with a knowledge of the rights of such third person, *can recover nothing for his labour*." The contract between the two persons in this case, was regarded as repugnant to the policy of the copy-right law of congress, though nothing in that act avoided such a contract. And in Marchant v. Evans, 8 Taunt. 142, it was held, that no recovery can be had for printing a newspaper whose publisher does not first make the affidavit directed by the act, though the act does not avoid the contract. And in Stephens v. Robinson, 2 Crom. and Jer. 209, the court decided under the same statute, that there could be no recovery by the printer, where the affidavit as to the proprietorship was false, either for work and labour done, for money paid, or even "for printing and circulating cards advertising the paper." The court said, if we permitted a recovery, it would *defeat the policy of the law*, by enabling "irresponsible persons to stand forward as publishers," instead of the real proprietors. See Roby v. West, 4 N. Hamp. 285.

In the late case of Spurgeon v. M'Elwain, 6 Ohio Rep. 442, it was decided that "*keeping nine-pin alleys* in a town, by a keeper of a public house, being unlawful, the (carpenter,) builder of such alley cannot recover therefor on general assumpsit." There it was urged, as was the fact, that the carpenter had no interest in the alley, or in its profits, keeping, or use, and there was not a word in the law avoiding the contract, or declaring the *building* such a house unlawful, but only the keeping of it. The court said, "The statute forbids under a penalty, any tavern keeper, or retailer, from keeping or permitting to be kept, a nine-pin alley, in the building occupied for that purpose; can a carpenter, knowing the object, recover the price of erecting it?"

"The principle is of general application, that contracts contrary to sound morals, public policy, or forbidden by law, will not be executed by courts of justice." And upon these principles, and the policy of this statute, the court decided that there could be no recovery, because the plaintiff had *violated the policy of the law* in *building* a nine-pin alley for a third person, *in a state* where no such alley could be *kept*, and therefore could not recover:—as here in our case, the plaintiff had violated the policy of the law, in selling these slaves *in a state* where they could not be introduced for sale, and therefore cannot recover. The keeping the slaves for sale in the state is an adherence to the unlawful intention with which they were introduced, and when kept till sold, the very act of sale is a continuation and consummation of the unlawful purpose, and aggravation of the guilt of the offender; yet it is asked to be received as perfectly lawful, and worthy the sanction and encouragement of judicial tribunals. Nor would the pretended misapprehension of the law avail the plaintiff, for in the case of Craig v. U. S Insurance Company, 1 Peters' C. C. R. 410, Justice Washington of this court, said, in deciding against a contract of insurance on the ground that it was against the policy of the law, "I mean not to impute crime, or even intentional impropriety, to either of these parties. I have no doubt that they acted with the *most perfect innocence, mistaking the law*, as *many legal characters* did, at a later period than that when this contract was entered into."

In Billing v. Pitkin, 2 Caines, 146, it was decided that "an action will not lie upon a contract to pay over half the proceeds of an illegal contract, though the money arising from it has been received by the defendant." This was a case of a sale by an agent of land in Pennsylvania under a Connecticut title, which sale we have seen was void, as contrary to the policy of the law. The principal received the money on the sale, and refused to pay the agent the portion he was to receive for effecting the transaction, but a recovery was refused and the defendant permitted to retain the money. The court said: "It is too salutary and well settled a principle to be in any measure infringed, that courts of justice ought not assist an illegal transaction *in any respect*. To sustain the present action would be in some degree *ratifying, countenancing*, and *sanctioning* an illegal contract." "If the consideration money for this pretended claim had been paid to *the plaintiff*, neither a court of law, or equity, *would have aided the defendant* in recovering it from him." By this doctrine, even an agent who receives money for a principal on an unlawful sale, can retain the money, the contract to pay the money to the principal being void, as growing out of the unlawful sale, yet such a contract is distinct and independent of the original transaction, and in every respect collateral. In Parsons v.

Thompson, the sale of an office not within the words of the statute, was declared void, though in the language of Lord Loughborough, "*it was the practice*" to sell such offices. 1 Hen. Black. 322, 324. In Bryan v. Lewis, 1 Ryan & Moody, 386, it was stated as a general rule, that where, to sanction the sale of goods, "would be attended with the most mischievous consequences;" such sales will not be upheld by the courts, though no statute declares the sale void. See 7 Mas. 112. In Fennell v. Ridler, 5 Barn. & Cres. 406, it was decided, that a horse dealer could not recover the price of a horse sold by him on Sunday, such sale being contrary to the policy and spirit of the act, declaring that no persons "shall do or exercise any worldly labour, business, or work of their ordinary calling, on the Lord's day." And see 4 Bing. 84. 2 C. & P. 544. 12 Moore, 266. A mercer who sells ribands to a candidate for parliament, if he knew that the candidate intended them as presents for voters, which is forbidden by law, the mercer could not recover the price. Richardson v. Webster, 3 Car. & Payne, 128. There is no statute forbidding such sales to candidates, but as to sanction the sales would encourage candidates to violate the law which prohibits them from making presents to voters, such sales are held void. See 3 Taunt. 6. 1 Ashmead, 68. 9 Vermont, 23, 310. 7 Greenleaf, 113.

In Fales v. Mayberry, 2 Gall. 560, it was decided, "that no action can be maintained against master and part owner of a ship engaged in the slave trade by his partners in the concern; nor against an *agent with the proceeds in his hands;*" nor even by an assignee of the note growing out of such transactions; and "if a ship be sold in a *foreign port*, to evade a forfeiture *incurred in the United States*, no action can be maintained for the proceeds." Here the offence had been committed long before the sale, by the voyage for slaves, from Boston to Georgia, thence to Africa, and thence with the slaves to the West Indies—*after all which*, the ship was sold at St. Bartholomews. The sale was subsequent to the illegal voyage, but as it was a consummation by the plaintiff, as in this case, of the original unlawful purpose, the sale was held to be unlawful, though there was no law declaring it so, and *there could be no forfeiture at St. Bartholomews;* and besides the case did not proceed on a failure of consideration, for the vessel was *delivered and held under the sale*, but upon the *illegality of the voyage preceding the sale.* In Morel v. Legrand, 1 Howard, 150, it was decided, by the high court of Mississippi, that a sale by a settler, of his improvement, made on the public lands, in expectation of a pre-emption, was void, as contrary to the policy of the intrusion act of congress, though nothing in that act declared such sale to be void. The opinion of the court was delivered by Chief Justice Sharkey, the same judge who decided in our favour in this case; and the case is chiefly cited as evidence of the impartiality and independence of the court, for, in giving judgment against the sale of this inchoate prospective pre-emption, the court was pronouncing an opinion against their wishes as citizens, and against a system of sales by settlers, universally and deservedly popular in the state of Mississippi. In Blachford v. Preston, 8 T. R. 89, it was held, that "a sale (by the owner) of the command of a ship employed in the East India Company's service, without the knowledge of the company, is illegal; and the contract of sale cannot be the foundation of an action." Lord Kenyon, Chief Justice, said—"a plaintiff who comes into a court of justice to enforce a contract, must come on legal grounds; and if he have not a legal title, he cannot succeed, whatever the private wishes of the court may be. In this case the plaintiffs have relied on the practice that (as it is said) has so long prevailed of selling the commands of ships; but that practice is in violation of the laws and regulations of the East India Company." Lawrence, Justice, after stating *the sale*, said—"*subsequent* to this, the East India Company came to a resolution, for the purpose of abolishing *the practice* of selling the commands of ships, and of making compensation to some of the officers in their service, who had paid for their commands—but this resolution was not made in approbation of the *practice that had prevailed before;* but feeling that *they were blameable* for not having put a *stop to it sooner*, they came to the resolution of abolishing the *practice that had obtained* in defiance of the by-laws of the company." This case shows how unavailing any practice, however long established and universal, is, to give validity to any contract repugnant to the policy of the law.

Whenever the introduction of any article into a country, generally, or for sale, is prohibited, or its use or manufacture forbidden, or its offer for sale—in all these cases the sale is illegal, although the law does not, in terms, prohibit the sale. We have seen that the maxims applicable to this question were borrowed from the civil law, as principles of universal justice. One of the most distinguished writers on this subject says—" In certo loco merces quædam prohibitæ sunt. Si vendantur *ibi*, contractus est *nullus* verum si merx eadem *alibi* sit vendita ubi non erat *interdicta*, emptor condemnabitur,' quia contractus inde ab *initio validus* fuit." Huberus Tit. de Conflictu Legum, Vol. II. page 589 : which, as translated, reads —" In a certain place the introduction of some articles is prohibited. If these are sold *there*, the contract is *void*. But if the same articles are sold elsewhere, where their introduction is not interdicted, there the purchaser shall be condemned to pay the price, because the contract was valid from the beginning :" and Lord Mansfield, in 1 Cowper, approves this doctrine, and applies it to render void the sale, *in England*, of goods on which the duties have not been paid.

The same doctrine is laid down in Erskine's Inst. 478, as follows :—" Things, the importation *or* use of which is absolutely prohibited, cannot be the subject of commerce, nor, consequently, of sale. But where the importation of particular goods is only burdened with a duty, a contract may be effectually entered into concerning them ; for though the law enacts penalties, if they should not be regularly entered, it allows the use of them to all the community, and so leaves them as a subject of commerce. (Kames, 40.) ' Yet even in the sale of *run goods*, no action for damages lies against the seller for non-delivery, if the buyer knew that they were run " Home, 34. Ersk. 478. Here the law is distinctly laid down by those two great jurists, Home and Erskine, that where the *importation* or *use* of any article is prohibited, the sale is void.

In 1st Kames' Equity, 357, referring to the Scotch decisions on sales of smuggled goods, he says, " they are not sustained at present, nor, I hope, will be ;" in which he has been fully supported by the subsequent decisions in Scotland. In speaking of this subject, this able writer says—" The transgression of a prohibitory statute is a direct contempt of legal authority, and, consequently, a *moral wrong*, which ought to be redressed ; and where *no sanction is added*, it must necessarily be the purpose of the legislature to leave the remedy to a court of law :" and the author adds, that in such cases the true mode " of redressing the wrong, is *to void the act*." Here we find this great jurist avowing the true principle, that there is no distinction in the rule for enforcing contracts, between malum prohibitum and malum in se. And if, in a despotic or monarchical government, it be a " *moral wrong*" to violate a prohibitory law, how much more strongly should this principle apply to laws proceeding, not from a monarch's will, but from the free consent of the governed, from the people of a state themselves. To violate such laws is not only a " moral wrong," but an assault upon the sovereignty of the people. We find here, also, a full answer to the difficulty suggested as to the want of any sanction to this clause. The true sanction in all such cases, we here see, " is to void the act."

This subject is discussed with great ability by Mr. Bell, Professor of Law in the University of Edinburgh. Having treated of contraband of war, he then proceeds to consider " contraband of *trade*, or smuggling contracts." 1 Bell's Com. 306. He says—" The contempt and breach of those laws is called *smuggling ;* the goods as to which the evasion is attempted, *contraband ;* and the great rule is, that no action is maintainable on the contract, or for the *price of the goods purchased* in contempt of those laws. In the one case, ' Potior est conditio possidentis ;' in the other, if an action is brought for money, ' Potior est conditio defendentis.' " " When the goods *have come into this country*, the criterion of decision to sustain or dismiss the action, is knowledge of the contraband nature of the goods. The decisions have varied ; but it would seem that where the goods are prohibited, no bona fides can justify the contract : that when the goods are not prohibited, but may lawfully be sold, provided the duties have been paid, action is denied where the party knows the duties to be unpaid : that after the goods are in the circulation of this country, the *bona fide purchaser* has action for the delivery, although smuggled. And he gives it as the settled law, that there can be no action " on bills for the price of contraband goods," the bills " being in the hands of the original parties, or of their trustees." 307. In 3d Brown's Synopsis Scotch Cases, page 1437, it is laid down as the settled law, that although there can be no recovery of the price on a sale " of smuggled goods," " in a question between the *importer* and *purchaser*," yet *other* bona fide vendors can recover " where the goods said to have been smuggled have passed from hand to hand on shore."

Having shown that the law in Scotland and upon the continent of Europe is in our favour, let us now examine the English cases. Law v. Hodgson, 2 Camp. 147, which has been repeatedly recognised in England and America, was an action by a brickmaker for the price of certain brick made and sold by him, and used and retained by defendant, in a house erected by him. The defence was founded solely on the allegation that the bricks were not of the size required by the statute. 17 G. 3, c. 42, sec. 1, vol. 14. The first section of this act declares, that " all bricks which shall be made for sale in any part of England, shall, *when burnt*, be not less than 2½ inches thick and not less than 4 inches wide." The 2d section enacts, " That if any person shall make bricks for sale of less dimensions, he shall forfeit the sum of 20 shillings for every 1000 bricks so made." The defendant contended that the act only prohibited " *the making* of smaller bricks, under a penalty, but did not declare contracts void." That even if liable to the penalty for the offence of making bricks, the subsequent sale was valid. He argued the impossibility of compliance with the statute, "as bricks made in the same mould, shrunk very differently in the burning," and that the "honest intention of the brickmaker was not to be doubted in the present case;" and that the defendant having " himself selected" and *used* the bricks, could not make the objection.   Lord Ellenborough said : " The first section of this statute absolutely forbids such bricks to be made for sale. Therefore, the plaintiff *in making the bricks in question*, was guilty of an absolute breach of the law ; and he shall not be permitted to maintain an action *for their value*."

On re-argument, the court adhered to its decision, declaring " that the best way to enforce an observance of the statute, was to prevent the violation of it *from being profitable*." There, the offence was the making the bricks for sale, not the sale ; and the offence was complete when the bricks were thus made, and the subsequent sale, just as distinct a transaction as in this case. There too, the bricks had been selected and used by the defendant, and constituted part of a house, which was his property, and could be sold by him.   It was also a very hard case, which this is not ; but, as the making the bricks for sale was illegal, *therefore*, the subsequent sale was avoided, as here the introduction for sale was illegal, therefore the subsequent sale was void, both sales having been made by the offender himself. The additional reason for the decision, was that, " the best way to enforce an observance of the statute, was to prevent the violation of it from being *profitable*."

Brown v. Duncan, 10 B. & Cres. 93, Lord Tenterden says: " These cases (breaches of revenue regulations) are very different from those where the provisions of acts of parliament have had for their object *the protection of the public*. Such are the acts against stock jobbing, and the acts against usury. It is different also, from the case where a sale of bricks required by act of parliament to be of a certain size, was held to be void, because they were under the size.   There the act of parliament operated as a *protection to the public*, as well as the revenue, securing to them bricks of the particular dimensions.   Here the clauses of the act of parliament had not for their object to protect the public, *but the revenue only*. Neither is this one of that class of cases where an attempt is made to recover the *price of prohibited goods*." Here the case of Law and Hodgson is recognised and distinguished from the class of breaches of revenue regulations, and is classed with those cases, " where an attempt is made to recover the price of prohibited goods."   Even then, if the sale of goods imported and on which the duty is not paid, were lawful, because the object in that case only was to guard the revenue, we see it is entirely different from the case of the sale " of prohibited goods," where revenue is not the

c

object, but the intention is " to protect the public," by forbidding the introduction of such goods, and especially if the introduction for sale is prohibited.

In Little v. Poole, 9 Barn. & Cres. 192, where the law directed in the sale of coals, that " the vendor of coals, by wharf measure, deliver a ticket to the carman employed to cart the coal, and the carter is to deliver it to the purchaser," under a penalty for non-delivery, the sale of the coal was held void; because, such ticket did not accompany the delivery of the coals, although the sale was fair, the coals of the proper quality and measure, and although there was nothing in the act declaring the sale void, and the defendant had received and still retained the coals. Here the coal was property, and retained as such, and yet the sale was avoided; and the case of Law and Hodgson again expressly recognised, and in both cases the sale was avoided by implication only; there was no forfeiture of the property, and nothing in the statute declaring the sale void.

In Forster v. Taylor, 5 Barn. & Adol. 887, the question arose under the act which declared that, " every dairyman and farmer, who shall *pack any butter for sale*, shall pack the same in vessels (marked as prescribed by law,) and shall brand his name on the vessel and butter, upon penalty for every default of five pounds." The court admitted the sale was fair and the weight proper, and the butter sold by the farmer received and retained, yet the sale was declared void; because, the vessel was not marked according to the direction of the statute; and although there was not one word in that statute prohibiting the sale, it was decided, that the act " *indirectly* prohibited" any sale of butter in vessels not properly marked; and the court, after approving Law and Hodgson, and reviewing the cases, and referring to those "arising out of transactions connected with smuggling," declared the " general principle" to be "that where the provisions of an act of parliament have been infringed, no contract can be supported *arising out of it.*" The court affirm the doctrine previously laid down, 3 Barn. & Adol. 221, that where the contract " is expressly *or by implication* forbidden by the statute or common law, no court will lend its assistance to give it effect."

In Tyson v. Thomas, 1 M·Lellan & Young, 119, sale of corn by the hobbet, an unlawful measure, was declared void, although the court admitted, "that the statute had not been acted on for nearly a century," and that there was " great inconvenience from enforcing it;" but the court said, " no act of parliament is lost by desuetude;" and the court annulled the contract of sale, although they declared, "There is no doubt these parties dealt *bona fide* with each other in making the contract." And this case, sustained by many others, is also a complete answer to the argument urged on this as well as the first branch of the case, that this prohibition as to slaves, was "inoperative," or had not been enforced, or was a " mooted question" in Mississippi, and that the plaintiff acted in good faith. No one of these statements as to the plaintiff in this case is correct, but were it otherwise, we perceive how unavailing it would be to uphold this contract.

In Billiard v. Hayden, 2 Car. & Payne, 472, it was decided, that " If the importation of certain goods be prohibited, and the plaintiff sell such goods in this country to A., who endorses a bill of exchange to him in payment, the plaintiff cannot recover on that bill against the acceptor, although there was no evidence that the plaintiff was the importer of the prohibited goods." That is a much stronger case than this. It would be the same as if Slaughter, the importer, had left these slaves with some commission or auction house in Mississippi, and they had sold the slaves in their name, and taken the acceptance of some other house for the price, and endorsed it to Slaughter, and the suit had been against the acceptors, as in the above case " by the plaintiff, as endorsee." That case was the sale in England, of silks imported from France, against the prohibition of such importation by the statute 50 Geo. 3, c. 55. The plaintiff contended, " the statute only prohibits the importation of foreign silk, and it does not at all appear, that the silks were imported by the plaintiffs. The statute does not make *the sale of them void;* and as there is no evidence that the plaintiff imported them, they are entitled to recover on the bill." Abbott, Chief Justice: " This transaction arose before the late act, the statute of the 50 Geo. 3, c. 55, prohibits the importation of all foreign silks, and I have no hesitation in saying, that if these were foreign silks, and the bill was given in payment of them, the plaintiff cannot recover." The reporters, in their note, refer to this "late act," by which the former act, prohibiting the importation of foreign silks, was repealed, and say : " Although this case is thus rendered less important, as to foreign silks, it appears equally to apply *to any other species of goods,* THE IMPORTATION OF WHICH IS PROHIBITED." The court as well as the reporters, place this case upon the sole ground, that if a statute " prohibits the importation" of any article into England, its sale there when imported is void. Here also it was urged, that the importation only was prohibited, and not the sale ; but the sale was regarded as impliedly forbidden by the prohibition of the importation.

In Langton v. Hughes, 1 Maule & Selwin, 393 ; " Where the plaintiff, a druggist, after the 42 Geo. 3, c. 38, but before the 51 Geo. 3, c. 87, sold and delivered ginger and other articles, knowing that they were to be used in brewing beer ; held, that he could not recover the price." By the act of 42 Geo. 3, under which the question arose, the brewer is prohibited from "using any thing but malt and hops, in the brewing of beer ;" and the act of 51 Geo. 3, c. 87, prohibits the sale of such drugs to brewers. It was contended, that although the sale under the last act would be void, it was not so under the first, as it did not prohibit the sale of the ginger to the brewer, but only *its use by him* in *making beer.* They contended that ginger was an innocent article, and might be *lawfully bought and sold,* and that the improper use subsequently made of it by the defendant, did not avoid the previous sale. But the court held, that as the law was for the protection of the public health, and as to uphold such a sale would be " against the policy of the law," that the sale, though not prohibited expressly, was unlawful, as tending to encourage a violation of the law.

In 3d Vesey, ex parte Mather, it was decided, that in the case of a bill endorsed to a broker, in consideration of money advanced by him, in effecting an illegal insurance, no recovery by the broker can be had against any of the parties to the bill. The cases of Faickney v. Reynous, and Petrie v. Hannay, so much relied on by the other side, but now so entirely exploded, were cited in this case ; but the Lord Chancellor said : " I am perfectly aware of both the cases cited, but I cannot perfectly accede to them. What is called a consent in these cases, is a confederacy to break a positive law. I have often had occasion to think of these cases upon lottery insurances, &c., and it never occurred to me to be possible to state a distinction between them, and a case repeatedly adjudged ; if a man is employed to buy smuggled goods, if he paid for the goods, and the goods come to the hands of *the person* who employed him, *that person* shall not pay for the goods." Here, in this case, the broker was not the insurer, he made no illegal contract, but he advanced the money to the man who did make the illegal insurance ; and yet he could not recover that money so advanced. That case was two removes from the direct illegality, and yet, as it grew out of it, there could be no recovery. First " the voyage from Ostend to the East Indies," was declared to be illegal ; and therefore as a consequence, the insurance of that unlawful voyage was illegal, not as declared so by statute, but as contrary to the policy of the law forbidding such voyages. Then came the contract to pay the broker the money advanced by him, to effect the insurance, the broker having no interest in the voyage or insurance, but being merely a lender of money ; but this loan and second contract, being connected with the insurance, was void, and there could be no recovery. Is there not a more direct connection between the act of sale in this case by the original offender, and the unlawful introduction of the slaves for sale, than in the advancing of the money in this case by the broker ? and yet it could not be recovered as against the policy of the law.

Here, too, the Chancellor put a case, which he declares has been " repeatedly adjudged" as to smuggled goods, which is directly in point. A. employs B. to buy smuggled goods ; B. with his own money, purchases the goods for A., and A. retains them ; yet B. cannot compel A. to pay for the goods thus purchased at his instance, and for his benefit, and received, and retained by him. Why is this? The purchase of the smuggled goods is illegal, and therefore the person advancing the purchase money for another, cannot recover the money so advanced, because in that case, as in this, to sustain such contracts, would be to encourage the smuggling of goods into the country, and would therefore be against the policy of the law.

The ground on which insurance on cargoes illegally exported is void, is stated in 11 East. 502. That was an insurance on naval stores, and the objection was, that under the act of 33 Geo. 3, c. 2, naval stores were forbidden to be exported, but the act did "not avoid the contract of insurance." The court said, "the statute having made the exportation of and trade in naval stores contrary to the king's proclamation illegal, *impliedly* avoids all contracts made for protecting the stores so exported."

In Bensly v. Bignold, 5 Barn & Ald. 335, where the act directed every printer of every book or paper to affix his name to it, under a penalty of £20 for every default, it was decided that the printer who had not complied with the law, could not recover for the labour furnished or for the paper used in printing the book. It was urged, as was the fact, that the law contained "no prohibitory clause whatever, but merely a particular regulating clause protected by a penalty;" and upon the ground of a distinction, also, "between a prohibition and a penal enactment," as well as upon the ground that the act was not *malum in se*, and "that there was no clause whatever making the contract illegal;" it was contended, that they were entitled to recover. It was especially urged, that they could recover for "the paper provided by them for printing." But the claim was overruled both as to the labour and materials. The court said, as to statutes, "if there be an omission to do the thing required, it is not any excuse that the party did not intend to commit a fraud." "The public have an interest *that the thing shall not be done*, and the objection in this case must prevail, not for the sake of the defendant, but for that of the public." Now the prohibitory clause in the constitution of Mississippi, is inserted "for public purposes;" the framers of that instrument considered "that the public have an interest that the thing shall not be done;" that is, that slaves should not be introduced as merchandise or for sale; and if so introduced and sold by the importer, must not the objection to the sale prevail, not for the sake of the defendant, but for that "of the public?" And it is the strongest possible case when the contract is against the prohibitory policy of the *constitution of a state*. The court also declared that "the distinction between *mala prohibita* and *malum in se*, has been long since exploded. It was not founded upon any sound principle, for it is equally unfit, that a man should be allowed to take advantage of what the law says he ought not to do, whether the thing be prohibited because it is against good morals, or whether it be prohibited because it is *against the interest of the state*."

If, then, the introduction of slaves into Mississippi from another state, as merchandise and for sale, would be *malum in se*, none will maintain that the sale of the slaves by the guilty transgressor would be valid, and yet it is just as valid where the importation is *malum prohibitum*, as where it is *malum in se*. It has been decided in England, that no action can be maintained for the copy-right, or for the loss or destruction of the book by another, or for the sale or for the profits of the sale, in whole or in part, or for the printing or labour furnished in printing any book of an indecent or immoral or libellous character, or "injurious to the government of the state," or "slanderous," or for caricature prints or pictures of a similar character, 2 Car & Payne, 136 to 171 and notes; also, 198 to 201; 2 Mer. 437; 7 Ves. 1; 4 Esp. 97; 2 Camp. 29; 7 D. & R. 625; 5 B. & C. 173. There was no prohibitory statute in these cases, but all such contracts were held void as against the policy of the law.

In Wheeler v. Russell, 17 Mass. 258, it was decided, that "no action lies on a promissory note, the consideration whereof was the sale of shingles, not of the size prescribed by the statute." "The statute provided, that no shingles under certain dimensions shall be *offered for sale*, in any town in this commonwealth." The act was passed in 1783, and had remained "inoperative" until 1821, the date of this decision. It was contended for the plaintiff, that there might be "an offer to sell," by which alone the penalty was incurred, and "yet no sale be made;" "the offer to sell must *precede* the sale, and is a distinct and separate act. The sale might follow or might not. Why then, should the previous commission of the offence, by which the penalty is incurred, vitiate the subsequent sale?" The arguments in that case are the same now urged, that the introduction for sale must "precede the sale;" that is, the thing forbidden and that the "previous commission of this offence" does not "vitiate the subsequent sale," which is "a distinct and separate act." An actual sale is no more within the words "*offer to sell*," than it is within the words "introduce as merchandise and for sale;" and in both cases the offence, in a technical sense, may be completed, and no sale take place; but, although such technicalities and adherence to the letter against the spirit of the act, may be the rule on indictments for the penalty or offence, yet we have seen it is far otherwise, when the court acts upon the contract, which is always void, though not within the letter, if against the policy of the act.

And here let me examine the case on which the counsel rely on the other side of Toler v. Armstrong, 11 Wheat. 258. The facts were, that Toler, the plaintiff in the court below, paid a sum of money, for which the suit was brought, for Armstrong, namely, the appraised value of certain goods of Armstrong, in which, or the importation of which, Toler had no interest or concern, and which goods were condemned to the United States as illegally imported in time of war, by a pretended and collusive capture, and Toler paid the appraised value of the goods thus condemned, and other charges, and the expenses of the prosecution, for Armstrong. When the goods were libelled by the United States, they were delivered up by them to the claimant, De Koven, on a bond for the appraised value, Toler becoming responsible for the appraised value in case of condemnation; and they were delivered afterwards to Armstrong, on his agreeing to pay Toler such sums as he would be compelled to pay for Armstrong. By a reference to the Appendix to 2 Wheat. 51, it will be seen, that this sale for the appraised value on such bond as was given in this case is made by the marshal, and is the legal and proper method.

Now, if a man is the owner of certain goods illegally imported, is that any reason why a just and legal contract, to be refunded the money which he might have legally advanced on account of *other* goods of *another* person under a lawful contract, should not be fulfilled? Surely not; for the offence of Toler, *as to his goods*, was a distinct offence, and unconnected with the other offence committed by Armstrong in importing *his goods*, and with which latter offence, as the jury found, Toler had no connection whatever, direct or indirect. The case, then, was reduced simply to this; that A. illegally imports goods, and they are libelled by the United States, to whom B., at the request of A., pays the appraised value, and other charges and costs incident to the prosecution, having agreed to do so at the request of B. before the condemnation, and become liable to do so in the event of the condemnation. This was the contract to recover these advances, on which the court decided, and nothing more. The contract made by Toler "with the government," under which he paid the money, was, in the language of the court, "a substantive independent contract, entirely distinct from the unlawful importation;" "it is the payment of a debt due in good faith to the government;" and "if it may not constitute the consideration of a promise to repay it, the reason must be, that two persons, who are *separately* engaged in an unlawful trade, can make *no contract* with each other." "This would be to connect distinct and independent transactions which have no connection with each other." The court say—"It is laid down with great clearness, that if the importation was the result of a scheme between the plaintiff and defendant, or if the plaintiff *had any interest* in the goods, or if they were *consigned to him with his privity*, that he might protect and defend them for the owner, a bond or promise given to repay any advance made in pursuance of such understanding or agreement would be utterly void." The court add—"The point of law decided is, that a subsequent independent contract, founded on a new consideration, is not contaminated by the illegal importation, although such illegal importation was known to Toler when the contract was made; provided *he was not interested in the goods*, and had no *previous concern in their importation*." "*Provided* HE WAS NOT INTERESTED IN THE GOODS." A subsequent independent contract, founded on a new consideration, is not contaminated by the illegal importation." Had the plaintiff in this case no interest in these slaves? Why

c 2

he was the owner of them. Had he "no previous concern in their importation?" Why he was the guilty importer himself, and for a guilty purpose, which is to be consummated only by allowing the sale. And here let it be observed, that the whole charge of the court below was not reviewed by this court, but only that part quoted by the court in 11 Wheat. pages 268 and 269. The obiter dictum in arguendo by the court below, as to the validity of certain sales by an importer, had no necessary connection with the facts of the case, and could have no influence on the decision, and was not reviewed by this court, it not being necessary, as the court said, that all the arguments of the court below, in arriving at their conclusions, should be correct, but that "to entitle the plaintiff in error to a judgment of reversal, he must show that some one of these principles (of the charge) is erroneous *to his prejudice;*" and the court declared that it was "unnecessary to review" the charge further than was done in the case.

Now as to the obiter dictum in this case in 4 Wash. 297, found in the charge to the jury in the hurry of a trial at nisi prius and not affirmed by this tribunal, that dictum is: "So far as the rule operates to discourage the perpetration of an immoral or illegal act, it is founded in the strongest reason; but it cannot safely be pushed farther. If, for example, the man who imports goods for another, by means of a violation of the laws of his country, is disqualified from founding any action upon such illegal transaction for the value or freight of the goods, or for other advances made on them, he is justly punished for the immorality of the act, and a powerful discouragement from the perpetration of it is provided by the rule. But after the act is accomplished no new contract ought to be affected by it. It ought not to vitiate the contract of the retail merchant, who buys these goods from the importer; that of the tailor, who purchases from the merchant; or for the customers of the former, amongst whom the goods are distributed in clothing, although the illegality of the original act was known to each of those persons at the time he contracted." Now if the court designed to say that *upon the facts of that case* the importer, except under his subsequent repurchase from the United States at the appraised value, could recover on his contract of sale of goods imported as were these goods during war and against the war policy by a collusive capture, it is against the well established law of the land. These goods were "condemned to the United States upon the ground of a collusive capture by the Fly." They were then confiscable and confiscated goods, because "shipped at St. Johns," a town in a British colony, "in December, 1813," during the war with England, and shipped for this country for "the defendant," and attempted to be illegally introduced by a collusive capture. From the moment then of their importation, being property from an enemy's port, they were forfeited by the laws of war to the United States, and no sale of these goods by the importer, without a repurchase from the United States, would be valid. One case only I will cite on this subject, a decision of Justice Story, subsequently affirmed by this court. In the case of the Rapid, 1 Gallison, 295, in the case of the property of a "native citizen of the United States" owned by him previous to the war, and then in New Brunswick, and for which he sent, *immediately* after the war commenced, an *American* vessel to bring home for him to Boston, it was declared that even this was a trading with the enemy, and that the property on its way on the 7th July, 1812, to Boston, in an American vessel, was confiscated as being imported against the laws of war. The court said: "The contamination of *forfeiture is consummate* the moment that the property becomes the *medium,* or the object of illegal intercourse." In confirming this decision in 8th Cranch, 163, this court said: "We are aware that there may exist considerable hardship in this case; the owners both of vessel and cargo may have been *unconscious* that they were violating the duties which a state of war imposed on them." Nevertheless the property was forfeited. To speak then in the case of Toler and Armstrong of a valid sale by the importer of the goods in regard to which "the contamination of forfeiture was consummate," preceding any sale in Boston, never could have been the intention of Judge Washington, for he was one of the judges who concurred in the opinion of this court in the above cited case of the Rapid. But if we look at the facts of this case, and apply them to the sale by the *importer of the goods in this case,* we will see why such sale of these goods might be valid. They were, as is stated, "delivered to De Koven, the owner and commander of the Fly, who brought in the George (and these goods as part of her cargo) upon *admiralty stipulations* given by De Koven," and it was *after this* that De Koven, the importer, sold and delivered the goods for $5000 to Armstrong.

These admiralty stipulations are known to every admiralty lawyer, and described in the note quoted from 2d Wheaton, by which the claimant (DeKoven) receives the goods from the United States, to whom they are claimed to be forfeited, and with a right to sell them upon giving bonds with adequate security to the government, for the appraised value, in case of a decision against the claimant. But in any other case than this waiver and repurchase from the government, I call for the production of a single case in which a sale by the importer of prohibited goods has been held valid. And here I will state that our chancellor, Mr. Buckner, though a very able and upright judge, never has, I believe, tried or heard the trial of a single case in admiralty, and it is evident from a reference to his opinion as to the validity of this sale, that he was misled by the general phraseology of Judge Washington in this case as to the sale by De Koven, the importer in that case, without reflecting that this sale, thus held valid, was, after the importer had paid the penalty by his bond, and repurchased at the appraised value from the government.

The court say in regard to the rule which avoids the contract as unlawful, that "so far as the rule operates to discourage the perpetration of an immoral or illegal act, it is founded in the strongest reason." Now if the importer cannot sell the slaves, and in the language of Chief Justice Marshall, in 12 Wheat. 439, "no (slaves) would be imported if none could be sold" by the importer, would it not then "discourage the perpetration of the immoral or illegal act" of importation for sale? Would such a construction "extend the sale beyond the policy which introduced it?" Would it "lead to the most inconvenient consequences?" What inconvenience is it except to the violator of the law, that he cannot recover the price of the slaves unlawfully introduced for sale Judge Washington admits that the contract cannot be enforced where it "grows immediately out of, and is connected with an illegal or immoral act;" so also he says "if the contract be IN PART only connected with the illegal act, and growing immediately out of it, *though it be in fact a new contract,* it is equally tainted by it." Now, does the subsequent sale grow out of the importation for sale, or has it no connection with it? Chief Justice Marshall, in 12 Wheat. 447, says: "*Sale* is the object of importation, and it is an *essential ingredient* of that *intercourse* of which importation constitutes A PART. It is as essential an ingredient, as indispensable to the existence of the entire thing, then, as importation itself." Now, if the right of sale constitutes a part of the right of importation for sale, and is an essential ingredient of that right, how can it be said that the sale had no connection with the illegal introduction for sale, for though the sale *by the importer* "be in fact a new contract, it is equally tainted" by the unlawful importation *by him* for sale. And recollect, that Chief Justice Marshall was speaking in the case cited, of the introduction of foreign goods *for sale* by the *importer,* and that the decision was confined *to him only;* it being declared that the right of sale by the *importer* was considered "as a component part" of the right of importation. We may then safely consider it an established rule that wherever "sale is the object of importation," it is essentially connected with and grows immediately out of the importation; and that as a consequence, wherever the introduction for sale is prohibited, the sale by the importer will be unlawful.

In the case ex parte Bell, 1 Maule and Selw. 751, it was decided, that money advanced by S. to B. one of several partners, out of the partnership funds, on account of payments to be made (on unlawful insurances) in pursuance of a previous agreement between them to become sharers in profit and loss on such policies, was held not provable under the commission of S., who became bankrupt, by the surviving partners of B., "although the surviving partners were ignorant of the illegal character of the advances." In this case it was strongly contended that this was a contract collateral to and independent of the original transaction." But the court decided that there could be no recovery, and established the principle that "money advanced for the purpose of carrying on a smuggling transaction or any other illegal traffic," could not be recovered. And see 8 T. R. 715; 6 T. R. 132; and Sullivan v. Graves, 1 Park's Insu. S.

In Mitchell v. Cockburne, 2 H. Black. 336, the court decided that, where A. and B. are engaged in a partnership, in insuring ships, &c., which is carried on in the name of A., and A. pays the whole of the losses, such a partnership being illegal, A. cannot maintain an action against B. to recover a share of the money that has been so paid. The alleged illegality of the partnership was founded on the beforementioned statute, forbidding insurances by partnerships; but it was alleged that this only extended to public partnerships, and that the collateral contract might be valid by one partner to pay over to his co-partner his share of the profits recovered. The court said : " The cases which have been cited, were one step removed from the illegal contract itself, and did not arise immediately out of it." " Thus in Faikney v. Reynous, the bond was given to secure the repayment by a third person, of his proportion of the money paid by the plaintiff, in stock-jobbing; and in *Petrie v. Hannay*, the money had been paid to the broker by *Keeble*, and the action was brought to reimburse his executors for the defendant's share. In that case indeed, *Lord Kenyon* seemed to be of opinion that the action could not be maintained, and it was decided expressly on the authority of Faikney v. Reynous. But, perhaps, it would have been better if it had been decided otherwise ; for when the principle of a case is doubtful, I think it *better to overrule it at once*, than build upon it at all. But be that as it may, it is sufficient now to say, that those cases are one step short of the direct illegal transaction, but that the present case arises immediately out of it."

" *Heath, J.,* I am of the same opinion. It seems to me that the *object of the statute would be totally defeated,* if it were to extend only to those policies in which the names of all the partners were inserted."

" With respect to the case of *Petrie v. Hannay,* one judge there, (Ashhurst,) hinted that his opinion might have been different, if the question had been *res integra,* and Lord Kenyon dissented."

But, if this case of Petrie v. Hannay, were the law, it would only establish the principle, that an *innocent third person,* from whom a loan is made, to pay a debt in which he had no connection or participation, arising out of an illegal transaction, that this third person can recover, even although the borrowed money is applied by the borrower to pay a debt arising out of such unlawful transaction. There, the party whose right was upheld, had no participation in the illegal transaction ; here, the plaintiff is the guilty transgressor : there, the person, Fortis, through whose rights the recovery was had, in the language of Justice Ashhurst, " was not concerned in the use which the other made of the money, it was a fair and honest transaction, as between those parties." And Faikney v. Reynous, proceeds on the same principle. Was this a fair and honest transaction on the part of the plaintiff? Was it fair and honest for the slave trader in this case, with intent to sell, to introduce the slaves, in defiance of law, and consummate that unlawful intention by the sale ? The case, then, of Petrie and Hannay would prove nothing against us, but as it has been repeatedly disregarded, and the distinction between malum prohibitum and malum in se, exploded in England and America, the decision in such a case against the plaintiff, would go far beyond the present; for, if a broker, who, at the winding up of a partnership, paid debts due third persons, arising out of illegal transactions, in which he had no participation, interest, or concern, could not recover the money thus advanced after the conclusion of all these unlawful transactions, on the subsequent, new, distinct, and independent contract, on the part of an innocent third person, what hope could the slave trader plaintiff have of a recovery in this case ? And yet the English law is now settled, that such third person could not recover.

In the case of Booth v. Hodgson, 6 T. R. 409, it was expressly conceded, that under no case, not even that of Faikney v. Reynous, was it ever supposed " that one delinquent can maintain an action against another."

Difficulties arose as to the pleadings on the bond in the case of Faikney v. Reynous, upon the ground that the defence was not properly before the court, and therefore, in Petrie v. Hannay, Lord Kenyon, did not expressly overrule this case of Faikney v. Reynous, but if not determined on the form of the plea, he did most expressly dissent from it, especially the distinction between malum prohibitum and malum in se, saying, " if one of two partners advance money in a smuggling transaction, he cannot recover his proportion of it against his partner, because the transaction is prohibited ; and yet smuggling is not *malum in se as* contradistinguished from *malum prohibitum.*". The rest of the court who did not think Faikney and Reynous was decided on the pleadings, said, in that case, " Lord Mansfield and the whole court proceeded on the ground, that as it was not MALUM IN SE, but only *malum prohibitum,* and as the plaintiff was not concerned in the use which the other made of the money, it was a fair and honest transaction, as between those parties." 3 T. R. 422.

Now, if the distinction between malum prohibitum and malum in se, be now entirely exploded, as these two cases of Faikney and Petrie proceeded on that distinction, they must both fall to the ground.

In Aubert v. Maze, 2 Bos. & Pul. 370, it was decided, that " money paid by one of two parties for the other on account of losses incurred by them in partnership insurances, cannot be recovered in an action brought by him against the other partner. And, if this, with other causes of dispute be referred to an arbitrator, who awards a sum due from one to the other for money so paid, the court will set aside that part of the award." In deciding this case, Lord Eldon, Chief Justice, said : " Some of the cases on this subject, especially that of Petrie v. Hannay, have proceeded on a distinction, the soundness of which I very much doubt." Referring again to the two cases of Faikney v. Reynous and Petrie v. Hannay, Lord Eldon, after quoting the statement of C. J. Eyre, in Mitchell v. Cockburne, that " it would have been better if they had been decided otherwise," adds as his own opinion, " Indeed it seems to me, that if the principle of those cases is to be supported, *the act of parliament will be of very little use.*" After giving it as his opinion that the cases of Booth v. Hodgson, and Mitchell v. Cockburne, were opposed to those of Faikney v. Reynous, and Petrie v. Hannay, he states : " In addition to this, the cases of Steers v. Lashley, and Brown v. Turner, 7 T. R. 630, stand in opposition to Petrie v. Hannay, Faikney v. Reynous, and Watts v. Brooks. With respect to Petrie v. Hannay, very great weight is due to the opinion of Lord Kenyon, who dissented from the rest of the court."

Heath, Justice, concurred and disapproved the distinction between *malum in se* and *malum prohibitum.*

Yorke, Justice, said : " I perfectly agree with my brother, Heath, in reprobating any distinction between *malum prohibitum* and *malum in se,* and consider it pregnant with mischief. Every moral man is as much bound to obey the civil law of the land as the law of nature."

Chambre, Justice, concurred and expressed his dissent from the cases of Faikney and of Petrie. See 3d East, 222.

In Steers v. Lashley, 6 T. R. 61, " A. being employed as a broker for B. in stock-jobbing transactions, paid the differences for him ; a dispute arising between them as to the amount of A's. demand, the matter was referred to C. who awarded £300 to be due ; on which, A. drew on B. for £100, part of the above, and endorsed the bill to C. after B. had accepted it ; held, that C. could not recover on the bill." Lord Kenyon, being of opinion, that as " the bill *grew out of a stock-jobbing transaction,* which was known to the plaintiff, he could not recover." It was urged on the authority of Petrie v. Hannay, that " as the broker had actually paid the differences for his employer, the bill in question, which was to secure him *repayment* of what he had paid, was not vitiated by the *original transaction* between the *defendant* and *those with whom he dealt.*" It was said, that " This is not an action to recover the differences of the stock-jobbing, nor is it brought by *either of the parties to those transactions ;* but by an innocent person on a bill of exchange, drawn by the broker on his principal, for sums of money actually paid by the broker, and for the balance of his account ;" but the plaintiff was not permitted to recover. Here, the broker had no interest in the stock-jobbing transactions, but simply advanced the differences arising out of these transactions as due by the defendant, for which advances he received from the defendant the bill in question. In Brown v. Turner,

7 T. R. 626, it was ruled, that "if a broker draw on his employer for differences paid for him in stock-jobbing transactions, and the employer accept the bill, and then the broker endorse it to a third person after it is due, the latter cannot recover on the bill."

In Cannon v. Bryce, 3 Barn. & Alderson, 179; it was adjudged, that "*money lent* and applied by the *borrower,* for the express purpose of settling losses or illegal stock-jobbing transactions, to which *the lender was no party*, cannot be recovered back by him." In this case A., who was not a broker, and not *concerned in any of the illegal transactions,* after all these transactions *were closed,* loaned money to B., to enable him to pay the losses which he had sustained in those transactions, and B. gave his bond for repayment, and yet it was ruled that no recovery could be had on the bond. We had seen it decided in Langton v. Hughes, which is affirmed here, that however it may be as to sales *abroad,* where the parties know that the goods are bought with a view to evade the revenue laws of *another country,* which the courts decline to notice, yet that sales made *in England* of an innocent article, such as ginger to a brewer, to be used in making beer, against a prohibition of the use of ginger by brewers in making beer, is void. And here we find that money loaned by an innocent third person, to enable another to pay losses which he had sustained in illegal transactions, cannot be recovered. Here, when the money was loaned, the offence of stock-jobbing had been committed; the loan of the money to pay the losses was a new, subsequent, distinct, and independent contract, and yet even such contract was void, as against the policy of the law. The court said, "On the part of the plaintiff, it was contended, that, as he was not a party to the illegal transaction, the loan was not illegal." "The authorities principally *in favour of the plaintiff,* are those of Faikney v. Reynous, and Petrie v. Hannay. The propriety, however, of these decisions, has been questioned in the several subsequent cases, that were quoted on the part of the defendant; and the distinction taken in the former of them, between malum prohibitum and malum in se, was expressly disallowed in the case of Aubert v. Maze. Indeed, we think no such distinction can be allowed in a court of law: the court is bound in the administration of the law, to consider every act to be unlawful, which the law has prohibited to be done;" and the bond for the money loaned, was held void. It was not pretended that the statute in this case declared loans, or notes, or bonds for money loaned, to pay the losses in this case, unlawful, or that it inflicted any penalty on such loans, or that such tender could be fined or punished in any way; but to engage in such stock-jobbing transactions was illegal, and therefore to prevent the violation of the statute, even the lender could not recover money loaned to pay losses arising out of such transactions, even after these losses had all been incurred.

The case arising out of a bankruptcy, I have transposed the words, *plaintiff* and *defendant,* in the text, to avoid a periphrasis. And now since this case, decided in 1819, I call upon the opposing counsel to show a single case, in which the authority of either of these decisions of Faikney v. Petrie, have been recognised.

In Cambden v. Anderson, 6 T. R. 723, 1 Bos. & Pul. 271, it was adjudged that "the exclusive right of trading to the E. Indies, granted to the E. I. Company, by 9, 10 W. 3, has never been put an end to, and any infringement of it is a public wrong. Though such parts of that act as inflicted penalties, &c., were repealed by 33 G. 3, c. 52, and though the latter act says, that no acts or parts of acts thereby repealed, shall be pleaded or set up in bar of any action, &c., it is competent to underwriters who have subscribed policies on ships trading to the E. Indies in contravention of 9, 10 W. 3, to avail themselves of the illegality of such trading, in an action on the policies." The court in that case said these plaintiffs, "may still insist that the exclusive trade of the company is no more than their private right, the infringement of which may perhaps give a right of action to the company, as for a civil injury over and above the several parliamentary provisions which have been made for securing it, but can have no other effect, and particularly cannot taint with illegality, *transactions and contracts which are collateral to it.*" "When this point was suggested in the course of the argument, Mr. Rous answered, that the exclusive trade of the company was a *public regulation* of the *national commerce,* and this was a very good general answer, but I will enter a little further into the discussion of it. The exclusive trade of the E. I. Company, is now so interwoven with the general interests of the state, that it is no longer to be considered as the private right of a corporation, but is become a great national concern, and the infringement of it a *public mischief*, and as such is prohibited by the *common law*. The principle and the effect of that prohibition, as applied to the present case, may be collected from the case of a bond given to the sheriff, to indemnify him against the voluntary escape of his prisoner, which is pronounced to be void by the *common law*." Here then it was contended that the law "cannot taint with illegality, transactions and contracts which are collateral to it;" and the court deemed Rous's answer to this position good, that even the collateral contract was illegal " where it concerned a public regulation of the national commerce." Was not this " a public regulation," by the constitution itself of the *traffic in slaves?* But again, the court considered the collateral contract void, where it arose out of a prohibited traffic, and also that the infringement of the statute was "a public mischief and a public wrong." And was not the slave trade, as prohibited by the framers of the constitution of Mississippi, considered by them " a public mischief, and a public wrong," endangering, as they conceived, the welfare and security of the people of Mississippi: and if so, was the transgressor of such a fundamental law on such a subject permitted to say that the contract was collateral? The court add in this case, " If we find an action brought upon a contract for a few bags of tea, or a few tubs of foreign spirits, *bought* or *sold* in the course of a contraband trade, we say without hesitation, this is a contract against law, and no action can be maintained upon it." And in Farmer's case, Chief Justice Eyre went still further, and declared " that violating a prohibition of a species of commerce in which the interest of the country was concerned, was not merely *malum prohibitum*, but *malum in se*." Apply that principle to this case.

The high court of errors and appeals of our state, have said in regard to the case above cited, as to the inter-state slave trade, as follows: " The convention deemed that the time had arrived, when the traffic in this species of property as merchandise, should cease. They had seen and deplored the evils connected with it. The barbarities, the frauds, the scenes so shocking in many instances to our feelings of humanity, and the sensibilities of our nature, which generally grow out of it; they therefore determined to prohibit it in future. Another alarming evil grew out of it, which was highly dangerous to the moral and orderly condition of our own slaves, and that was the introduction of slaves from abroad of depraved character, which were imposed upon our unsuspecting citizens, by the artful and too often unscrupulous negro-trader. This was intended to be suppressed. Perhaps another object was to prevent a too rapid increase of the slave population in our state. The cardinal policy of the state was then to suppress this trade; and this is what is prohibited." And who will deny the truth of this statement? Did not the entire South, with perfect unanimity, unite with the North, in making the African slave trade PIRACY, and punishing those engaged in that trade with *death?* And this inter-state slave trade is prohibited as *highly criminal* by the slave holding states; and in Georgia the guilty transgressors of the law must take their place for years with felons in the cells of a penitentiary.

These traders have filled many of the states with insurgents and malefactors, and who will deny the "barbarities," " the frauds," the " shocking scenes," " the alarming evils," which grew out of this traffic? who will deny that the disproportionate augmentation of the slave over the white population, so rapidly progressing prior to this prohibition, was, if not arrested, endangering the lives of many of our citizens, and that to arrest this traffic, was " the cardinal policy of the state?" If then, the slave traders subjected the state to all these dangers, why was not this traffic malum in se? and if so, no collateral contract arising out of such a traffic shall be maintained by the guilty offender, much less the very contract of sale by the slave trader of the slaves thus illegally introduced for sale. If, as a consequence of the prosecution of this traffic, the scenes of Southampton had been re-enacted within our limits, would not the blood of every innocent victim have crimsoned the hands and stained the soul of the trader, whose prosecution of this prohibited traffic had produced these dreadful consequences. And, if the vigilance of the state and final enforcement of the prohibition have prevented these consequences, the trader was no more free from crime, than is he who throws the torch of insurrection among us, because it has not yet exploded any of the combustible materials within our limits. These traders have offended against the majesty of the laws and the sovereignty of the people of Mississippi; they have put in jeopardy the lives of our citizens, disregarded our cardinal policy, and trampled under their feet the sacred prohibitory enactments of the constitution. And shall such offenders come into a court of justice, and through its decrees, reap the fruits of their transgressions?

In Wilkinson v. Lousondack, 3 Maule & Sel. 117, it was decided, that "The stat. 47, G. 3. which repeals so much of the statute of Ann, as vests in the South Sea Company the exclusive privilege of trading to parts within certain limits, extends only to such places within those limits, as were at the time of passing the act, or at any time since, in the possession of, or under the dominion of his majesty; and therefore, an action was held not to lie against the defendant for not safely stowing and conveying goods of the plaintiff from London to Buenos Ayres, which place was captured by his majesty's forces, but afterwards recaptured before the passing of the act, and the shipment of the goods; although the goods were shipped *under the sanction of an order in council purporting to authorize the voyage,* and the recapture was unknown when the goods were shipped and the voyage commenced." The case states, that the goods were shipped at London, October 26, 1806, and the freight there paid, for transportation to Buenos Ayres, to which port the ship sailed. Buenos Ayres was recaptured from the British "by the Spaniards in August, 1806; but that fact was not known in England at the time of the shipment of the goods and commencement of the voyage." It was agreed "that his majesty's order in council, dated Sept. 17, 1806, purporting to legalize the trade, should be read as part of the case by either party." This order in council is given in the case, and reciting that Buenos Ayres had been conquered by the British, and "*was then in his majesty's possession,*" authorized full and free trade there by the plaintiff and all others. Immediately after the order, and with a view to legalize it, the stat. 47 Geo. 3, c. 23, was passed, repealing after the date of the order in council, (17th Sept. 1806,) as was conceded, every thing in that of Ann, making voyages illegal to all places to which it was heretofore forbidden, "which now are, or at any time hereafter shall, or may be belonging to, or in possession of his majesty." The intention of parliament was to confirm the order, the act going into effect at the date of the order. But the king in council were mistaken, and the parliament was mistaken, and the parties were mistaken, when they entered as was admitted bona fide into this contract; for in August, 1806, Buenos Ayres had been most unexpectedly taken by the Spaniards; and therefore the words of the act of parliament did not reach the case. Yet, the counsel in that case, did not venture to contend that even the royal mandate by the king in council could render nugatory a preceding prohibition of an act of parliament, as it seems to be urged upon the court in this case, and that the supposed tax law may render inoperative a provision of our constitution; but they did contend that the language of the act of parliament, of 47 G. 3, reciting, as it did, the very date of the order in council, and to go into effect from that date, did legalize and adopt that order. The plaintiff also contended, that the case arising out of a "collateral damage" to the goods by the negligence and improper conduct of the defendant, by having been "torn and perforated by iron bolts, and otherwise damaged and spoiled," that the illegality of the voyage, even were it illegal, did not affect his collateral claim, which was distinct and independent. But the court decided that the plaintiff did well to admit that an order of the king in council could not render inoperative a preceding act of parliament; that the claim for the damages to the injury of the goods grew out of the contract of freight; and that the contract was invalid, because it related to a voyage that was illegal. The court said: "The only remaining argument in favour of the plaintiff was, that there had been no *wilful* contravention of the law; *both parties thought they were acting legally;* but their misapprehension *of the fact,* or *the law* cannot alter the character of the contract, which the court is called upon by this action to enforce."

In the case of Griswold v. Waddington, 15 John. 37; 16 John. 438, it was decided, that where there was a partnership existing before the late war with England, one partner residing here and the other in England, and where a balance arose in a partnership account on bills upon England, remitted there from this country during the war, there could be no recovery, even after the peace, on such account; all trading between our citizens and British citizens being contrary to the war policy of the country, and although it was distinctly proved as part of the case, that such remittances were impliedly sanctioned by the executive branch of the government of the Union; that they were innocent in intention, being remittances not of money or specie, but of bills, and the government itself having remitted during the war bills drawn on England. But the practice or sanction of the executive, nor the innocence of the intention of the parties would avail, even after peace was declared, to induce the court to give validity to any contract, express or implied, repugnant to the policy of the law.

In deciding this case, Chancellor Kent said :

"An objection to the perfidious character of the defence is not to be endured." Lord Hardwicke disregarded it in the case in 7 Vesey, 317. "Several cases," says he, "at common law and in equity, have gone upon this, that if the *contract relates to an illicit subject*, the court will not so encourage an action as to give a remedy. Nor is it any answer, that the defendant knew of this illegality, for this answer would serve in all these cases." " The plaintiff must recover upon *his own merits;* and if he has none, or if he discloses a case *founded upon illegal dealing*, and *founded on an intercourse prohibited by law*, he ought not to be heard, whatever the demerits of the defendant may be. There is, to my mind, something monstrous in the proposition, that a court of law ought to carry into effect a contract founded upon a breach of law. It is *encouraging disobedience*, and *giving to disloyalty its unhallowed fruits*."

If the contract "arise from a transgression of a positive law of the country," or if it relates "*to an illicit subject*," to allow a recovery would be "encouraging disobedience" and giving it "its unhallowed fruits." And in these two cases there was no doubt of the sanction of the contracts by the king in council, in the one case, and the executive department of the government of the Union in the other ; but all this, nor "any misapprehension of the fact or law" could avail to maintain the contract.

In the case of the Bank of the U. States v. Owens, 2 Peters, 527, it was decided by this court, that as the bank charter "forbids the taking a greater interest than 6 per cent.," but does not declare the contract void; "such a contract is void upon general principles;" and there could be no recovery, not merely of the usurious excess of interest, or of six per cent. interest, but also no recovery of any part of the principal of the money loaned. In this case most of the authorities as to illegal contracts are reviewed by the court, and they settle the principle, that when the construction of a statute regards the policy of the law as to the validity of contracts, the statute is to receive a liberal construction so as to uphold the policy of the law, and that reserving interest beyond six per cent. may be considered as embraced within the spirit of a law rendering it illegal "to take more than six per cent. interest." They say "courts are instituted to carry into effect the law of a country, how, then, can they become auxiliary to the CONSUMMATION *of violations of law*." Is not this sale by the importer of the slave that he could not introduce for sale, a "*consummation* of the violation of the law?" They thus recognise the great case of Aubert and Maze, exploding the distinction between malum prohibitum and malum in so. " In the case of Aubert v. Maze, it is expressly affirmed, that there is no distinction, as to vitiating the contract, between malum in se and malum prohibitum. And that case is a strong one to this point, since the contract there *arose collaterally* out of transactions prohibited by statute." " And so in another case of great hardships, 3 B. and P. 35, where the insurance was upon a trading in the East Indies prohibited by an *obsolete statute*, the plaintiff could not even recover his premium, although admitted that the *risk never commenced*, because the policy was void in its inception on the ground of illegality," and the court say,

D

111

the principle extends to any other contract where the prohibition arises by the common statute or maritime law; and they add, "nor is the rule applicable only to contracts expressly forbidden, for it is extended to such as are *calculated to affect the general interest and policy* of the country." See also 1 Peters, 37, 4 Ib. 184.

In Thomson v. Thomson, 7 Vesey, 470, 473, it was held, that "a contract for the sale of the command of an East India ship is illegal, and therefore cannot be enforced by suit upon the equity, against the fund paid by the company as a compensation, under the regulation of 1796, to restrain *the practice in future.*" The court said, "the defence is very dishonest; but in all illegal contracts it is against good faith, as between the individuals, to take advantage of that. *A man procures smuggled goods and keeps them, and refuses to pay for them;* so in the underwriters' case, an insurance contrary to Act of Parliament, the brokers had received the money and refused to pay it over, and it could not be recovered." Here the illegality of a sale of *smuggled* goods retained by the vendee is recognised. In Amay v. Meryweather, 4 Dow. & Ry. 86; 2 B. and Cres. 573, it was ruled, that where W. as agent for defendant, voluntarily paid £500 to compound differences, that to secure to W. *repayment* of that sum, defendant gave his note to W., which W. endorsed to plaintiff after due, that on threat of suit by the plaintiff, defendant gave his bond in lieu of the note to plaintiff; held there could be no recovery on the bond, as it grew out of an illegal transaction. Here the doctrine of Faikney v. Reynous is overruled in form and substance, this being the case of a bond given to an innocent person wholly unconnected with the original transaction. It was decided, in the St. Iago de Cuba, 9 Wheat. 409, that no wages could be recovered by seamen, nor money for supplies by material men, when they knew that the voyage of the ship was unlawful. And the principle was extended in the case of a vessel engaged in the slave trade, to supplies furnished after her return to Baltimore, by those who knew of the illegal voyage, and that she was remaining in port under false colours.

We have then numerous cases here cited, declaring the distinction between *malum in se* and *malum prohibitum*, exploded; and such also is the opinion of all the elementary writers. 1 Leigh's Nisi Prius, 6, 7; Collyer on Partnerships, 28; Chitty on Contracts, 231; Paley on Agency, ch. 2, sec. 2, p. 103, 104; 1 Kaimes, 355: and Chancellor Kent says: "The distinction between statutory offences which are *mala prohibita* only, or *mala in se*, is now exploded, and a breach of the statute law in either case, is equally unlawful and equally a breach of duty." 1 Kent's Com. 467, 468. See 7 Wendall, 276, 280. Mather's Case, 3 Vesey, 372, has been before quoted, in which this distinction was denounced, and the cases of Faikney and of Petrie overruled; and subsequently, in the case ex parte Daniels, 14 Vesey, 192, Lord Chancellor Eldon "expressed his disapprobation of the doctrine of Faikney v. Reynous, and Petrie v. Hannay." Such is the law of the continent of Europe, of Scotland, of England, and of America, on this subject, and the decisions in Ireland are to the same effect. In Ottley v. Brown, 1 Bal. and Beatty, 360, the chancellor decided that a "bill by a banker for an account of shares held *in trust for him* in a mercantile establishment" could not be maintained, because the statute 29 Geo. 3d, c. 16, "prohibited bankers from being traders," though the statute does not avoid the contract, nor does it extend in terms to a trust; yet a recovery was refused, because to permit it would be against the policy of the law. In referring to the case of Petrie v. Hannay, he expressed his concurrence in the views of Lord Kenyon in that case and against the case itself; and also declared the strongest disapprobation of the case of Faikney v. Reynous, remarking that "Lord Kenyon, Lord Roslyn and Lord Ellenborough, all differ from Lord Mansfield, and I am quite satisfied with the principles laid down in ex parte Mather." To these he might have added Lord Loughborough, Lord Eldon, Chief Justice Eyre and many other distinguished British judges before quoted by me, as overruling these cases and disapproving the distinction between malum prohibitum and malum in se. In this case of Ottley v. Brown, the chancellor expressly declared that whether the illegal contract was the original transaction, or only collateral and resulting from it, was equally void "on principles of policy." And in Knowles v. Haughton, 11 Vesey, 168, the court refused proof of any items in an account growing out of an illegal partnership, and overruled Watts v. Brooks; and in Ruth v. Jackson, 6 Vesey, 30, 35, even when no guilt attached to plaintiff or defendant, the court declared that no contract could be enforced contrary to "considerations of general policy." The distinction between malum prohibitum and malum in se, is denounced by Emerigon, vol. 1, pages 210, 542, sec. 5 and 31. He says this doctrine of distinguishing between breaches of the law "is reproved by St. Paul in his Epistle to the Romans. *It is necessary, says the Apostle, to obey the laws; not merely through fear of punishment, but also as a duty of conscience.* A christian obeys the laws from a conscientious obligation and as an indispensable duty of religion." And as concurring with him he cites Pothier, Denisart, Burlamaqui, Wolff's, Vattell, Grotius, Guidon de la Mer; and Denisart denounces the introduction of articles into a country against its laws as a CRIME. Tom. 1, page 714. If it be then a *crime* as now recognised in England, and Ireland, and Scotland, and upon the continent of Europe, to introduce prohibited articles into a country, who can contend that the guilty criminal shall obtain for his offence the sanction and encouragement of courts of justice, by enabling him through its decrees, to sell the very article it is a crime for him to introduce for sale?

Our opponents have cited the following sentence from Chitty on Contracts, 217: "A doubtful matter of public policy is not sufficient to invalidate a contract. An agreement is not void on *this ground*, unless it *expressly* and unquestionably contravene public policy and be injurious beyond all doubt to the interests of the state." Now Mr. Chitty was here speaking, as the very preceding sentence shows, "of contracts void at *common law as affecting public policy*," and not of contracts repugnant to the policy of a statutory or constitutional provision. We have seen in the numerous cases already cited, where the question is whether a contract is repugnant to the policy of the statute, that so far from the rule being that the agreement must expressly contravene the statute, it must receive the most liberal construction to prevent a defeat of the policy of the statute, and that if it be within the spirit or scope, intention or object of the law, by implication or otherwise, the agreement is void. Did Mr. Chitty also mean to say that the contract must be "injurious *beyond all doubt* to the *interests of the state*," in order to declare it void, when the question arose upon a statute? Why, if the statute by any fair and just construction avoided the contract, we have seen the courts in repeated instances, some of which have been cited, declare the contract invalid as contrary to the policy of a statute, whilst at the same time they announced their disapprobation of the policy of the statutes, and declared that in their judgments the contract was not injurious to the interests of the state. It is then when in the absence of a statute or constitutional provision, a court, *upon its own judgment*, is refusing its aid to a contract upon the ground that it is against the public policy, and injurious to the interest of the state, that it must be a clear case, and not "a doubtful matter of public policy." That such was Mr. Chitty's meaning, is evident from the fact that in this chapter, which is headed "of contracts void at common law, as affecting public policy," he enumerates only cases void at *common law* as injurious to the public interest, and not cases depending upon the construction of a statute; and then in a separate chapter he speaks "of contracts void by statute," and enumerates many instances under which contracts not within the words of the statute, are declared void, as repugnant to its intention, scope and spirit. In his notes to this chapter he refers to a treatise on the same subject, in the third volume of his commercial law, page 83, from which I quote: "But a distinction has been introduced into our law books, under the two several denominations of *mala prohibita* and *mala in se*." He denies and denounces this distinction; and then says, where "an act is prohibited generally by statute, the punishment which the law annexes to the offence is in general by indictment, and this is that species of *crime* which our law writers usually understand by the term *malum in se*." "And the circumstance of both parties being ignorant of the law, and being innocent of any intention to violate, will not constitute any distinction." "And the illegality affects all contracts calculated to violate the law; and therefore, where a voyage has been declared illegal, a person cannot be sued for carelessly stowing goods to proceed upon it." The authority then of Chitty is in our favour on all the contested points. Here Mr.

Chitty says, when the introduction of slaves for sale, (to specify the case) is " prohibited generally by a statute," and not the implied prohibition by a penalty, " this is that species of crime which our law writers usually understand by the term *malum in se.*" The words here then are " the introduction of slaves as merchandise or for sale shall be prohibited from and after the first day of May, 1833." The prohibition then being general after the day fixed, and without a penalty, the introduction of the slaves in this case for sale was a *crime*, it was *malum in se*, it was punishable by indictment, with fine and imprisonment; and all the argument that has been made to show that this is not a prohibition, but merely directory to the legislature, because there is no penalty, falls to the ground. And now then I approach the grave subject really referred to in the quotation made by our opponents from Chitty, and that is, whether the introduction of these slaves for sale, and the subsequent sale, would be so clearly repugnant to the true policy of the state, and so injurious to its interests, that such a contract of sale would be void on general principles, had there been no provision on the subject in the constitution or statutes of Mississippi. The power and duty of the court to declare such contracts void in clear cases of repugnance to the policy or interest of a state, even where there is no statutory or constitutional enactment, is admitted in the clause quoted by our opponents from Chitty; and upon reading that chapter, numerous instances of the application of the principle will be found, in cases less clear in my judgment than the present, and to these cases I refer the court.

The same doctrine is thus laid down by Lord Mansfield, in 1st Cowper, 39: "It is admitted by the counsel for the defendant, that the contract is against no positive law. It is admitted, too, that there is no case to be found which says it is illegal : but it is argued, and rightly, that notwithstanding it is not prohibited by any positive law, nor adjudged illegal by any precedents, yet it may be decided to be so upon principles ; and the law of England would be a strange science indeed, if it were decided upon precedents only. Precedents serve to illustrate principles, and to give them a fixed certainty. But the law of England, which is exclusive of positive law, enacted by statute, depends upon principles ; and these principles run through all the cases, according as the particular circumstances of each have been found to fall within the one or other of them. The question then is, whether this wager is against *principles ?* If it be contrary to any, it must be contrary either to principles of *morality ;* for the law of England prohibits every thing which is *contra bonos mores ;* or it must be against principles of sound policy ; for many contracts which are *not against morality*, are still void as being against the maxims of sound policy." This doctrine has been repeatedly recognised as the law in England and America, and this very principle *is quoted* and recognised by the supreme court of New Jersey in 5th Halsted, 91, and by the supreme court of Pennsylvania in 1st Binney, 123 ; and in the concluding opinion in that case, as to a sale of lands, the court say—"Exercising jurisdiction, the state is bound to preserve the peace and aid contracts, but not such as militate against her own rights. It would be unnatural and against reason, which is a ground of the common law. It is against public policy. Self-preservation forbids it. So that, *independent of any act of the legislature,* I must hold the transfer illegal, and the obligation, given under such consideration, void." Does it then in this case, independently of any constitutional or statutory enactment, clearly appear to the court, that at the date of this contract, the introduction and sale of slaves, as merchandise, was against the true policy, was dangerous to " the peace" of the state, or " injurious to its interests," it was the duty of the court not to maintain the action on the contract. No court is called upon to lend its assistance to contracts encouraging a traffic detrimental to the interests, or repugnant to the policy, or dangerous to the peace of the state. It is true that this is a power of judicial tribunals, where they act merely on general principles without precedents, which must be exercised only in clear cases; but where the case is clear, it is a great protective and conservative power, which no court can refuse to exercise, without a gross dereliction of duty. Is this a clear case?

The views of our highest court, of the dreadful consequences of this traffic, have been already quoted; and if they are correct, as no reasonable man can doubt, then is, there not strong ground upon which to contend that this contract was void on general principles, in the absence of all provisions in the constitution or statutes of the state? But suppose it not to be, merely on general principles, a case sufficiently clear for the court to refuse its aid by enforcing the contract, who can doubt what was their duty, when there was a constitutional mandate on the subject, supposing it only to be a command of the constitution, that on the 1st of May, 1833, the traffic shall be prohibited, was it not the declared policy of the state that the traffic should cease on that day; was it not the will of the convention, as announced in the fundamental law, that it should then cease; and was the court, in defiance of this annunciation, in defiance of the mandate of the convention, in defiance of the will of the people declared in convention, and again at the polls in 1833, by refusing to change this mandate into a grant of discretionary power to the legislature, to maintain contracts repugnant to that policy, because the legislature had not acted on the subject? We have seen that, in clear cases, it *is the duty* of a court to refuse its aid to contracts repugnant to the policy or interest of the state, or dangerous to its peace even in the absence of all legislative or constitutional prohibitions; but where there is a mandate of the constitution on the subject announcing the will, or, if you please, merely the opinion of the people of the state. that the traffic shall be prohibited on a day certain, must not all doubt cease, and the duty of the court become clear and obvious?

But, if this clause of the constitution does not of itself render the sale unlawful, it is insisted that it does so when taken in connection with the preceding act of the legislature, of the 18th June, 1822, Rev. Code, 369. It is declared by the 1st section of that act, "That all persons lawfully held to service for life, and the descendants of the females of them, within this state, and such persons and their descendants, as hereafter may be brought into this state, pursuant to law, being held to service for life, by the laws of the state or territory from whence they were removed, and no other person or persons whatever, shall henceforth be deemed slaves."

Now, if this clause of the constitution prohibits the introduction for sale, would these slaves have been introduced "pursuant to law?" That will not be contended. Then this section declares that they shall not "be deemed slaves;" that is, they shall not be deemed so in Mississippi for the purpose of lawful sale there by the importer, because the subsequent sections of this act explain its meaning, by imposing a penalty on the sale or purchase of all slaves not imported pursuant to law; and it will not be denied, that a penalty on the sale implies a prohibition of the sale, and renders that sale unlawful. Dwaris on Stat. 678 ; Carth. 251; 1 Bin. 118 ; 3 Chit. C. L. 84. For the purposes then of a lawful sale by the importer, negroes not "brought into the state pursuant to law" cannot " be deemed slaves," and if so, the sale must be unlawful. What then, it is asked, becomes of these slaves? In reply, I answer, what became of the slaves introduced against the provisions of the act of 1808 or 1822, and what becomes of the slaves unlawfully introduced since the act of 1837? In all these cases it is conceded that the sale is invalid by the importer, although no further provision is made in any of these cases in regard to the future condition of the slaves. In all these cases, however, *as in this*, the sale by the importer was invalid, and *for that purpose* they could not " be deemed slaves." So in the numerous cases cited in this argument, the land in Pennsylvania, the ginger sold to make beer, the butter, corn, and coal vended by unlawful measures, the ribbands bought as presents for voters, the vessels transferred contrary to the policy of the navigation or registry laws, the horses purchased on Sunday ; in all these cases the property remained property, and a subject of lawful traffic, but *the sale by the violator of the law* was held invalid. Now, this first section of the act of 1822, was in full force at the date of the framing of the constitution of 1832, and the 4th section of the schedule of that instrument declares, " All laws now in force in this state, not repugnant to this constitution, *shall continue to operate* until they shall expire by their own limitation, or be altered or repealed by the legislature." Now this constitution prohibits the introduction of slaves as merchandise or for sale, and this section of the act of 1822, declares, that such slaves as shall be unlawfully introduced hereafter, shall not " be

D 2

deemed slaves," for the purpose of a lawful sale by the importer. There is no repugnance whatever in the law to this constitutional prohibition; on the contrary, it is, if not clearly implied in the prohibition itself, certainly not *repugnant to it,* and conformable to its expressed object. This section then, of that act, so far from being repealed, was re-enacted and continued in operation by the 4th section of the schedule of the constitution of 1832, and must be construed in conjunction with that instrument. This section then, of the act, must be regarded as within the view of the framers of the constitution of 1832; for it was then continued in operation by them; and that section having rendered illegal the sale by the importer of *all slaves* that should thereafter be unlawfully introduced, rendered it unnecessary for the convention to declare the sale illegal. This also is a strong argument to show that this clause of the constitution was a prohibition, when we see that this section of the act of 1822, was thus, by that instrument, connected with, and made a part, and continued in operation thereby: and, even if this were regarded as a new and distinct prohibition from that of the acts of 1808 and 1822, but only so far differing as this, that by these laws the prohibition of this traffic was special and partial, and here it was general and total, would it not be a most extraordinary construction to suppose, that whilst the convention substituted a total for a partial prohibition, it should intend to depart from the policy of a quarter of a century, by which, under the acts of 1808 and 1822, whenever the *importation* was illegal, the *sale* also by the importer was void?

Perceiving the force of these arguments, our opponents meet them by asking, would you emancipate all these slaves introduced from 1833 until 1837? Were they emancipated under the act of 1808, of 1822, and of 1837, when unlawfully imported? and if not, the question presents no difficulty. Under the early acts of congress prohibiting the introduction of slaves from Africa, they were not emancipated; yet the sale by the importer was absolutely void. Laws in pari materia are to be construed together, and as one code; and when a code of laws has been compiled by the legislature, and by an amendment of the constitution, that instrument, whilst it expressly continues in force every portion of that law not repugnant to the constitution, introduces any new provision or modification of the pre-existing system, the whole is to be construed together; and the new provision or modification is to be regarded as incorporated in the former system, as constituting a part of it, and as substituted for any particular section of that system to which the new provision may be repugnant, or in which it may affect a change. Now, this act of 1822 before cited, was a complete code of laws in regard to slaves, consisting of eighty-six sections, nearly every one of which is now in undisputed operation. Every section of that law which is repugnant to the constitution of 1832, is thereby repealed, and the new provision substituted in place of the repealed clauses as a part of the system. The doctrine is thus laid down in Dwaris, 699-700, and is sustained by numerous authorities. "As one part of a statute is properly called in, to help the construction of another part, and is fitly so expounded as to *support* and *give effect,* if possible, *to the whole,* so is the comparison of one law with other laws made by the same legislature, or upon the same subject, or relating expressly to the same point, enjoined for the same reason, and attended with a like advantage. In applying the maxims of interpretation, the object is throughout, first, to ascertain, and next to carry into effect, the intentions of the framer. It is to be inferred, that a *code of statutes* relating to *one subject* was governed by *one spirit and policy,* and was intended to be *consistent* and *harmonious* in its several parts and provisions. It is therefore an established rule of law, that all acts in pari materia are to be taken together, as if they were *one law;* and they are directed to be compared in the construction of statutes, because they are considered as framed upon *one system,* and having *one object* in view. If one statute *prohibit the doing of a thing,* and another statute be *afterwards* made, whereby a *forfeiture is inflicted* upon the person doing that thing, both are considered *as one statute.* When an action founded upon *one* statute, is given by a *subsequent* statute in a *new case,* every thing annexed to the action by the first statute is likewise given. Indeed, the LATTER act may be considered as *incorporated with the* FORMER."

Here, it is expressly declared that the latter provision is considered as "incorporated with the former." Now, in place of the 2d, 4th, and 5th sections of this act of 1822, read, as a part of that act, the provision of the constitution of 1832, declaring that, "the introduction of slaves as merchandise or for sale, shall be prohibited from and after the 1st of May, 1833." And then, by the 1st section of the act, no such negroes thus introduced shall, for the purposes of lawful sale, by the importer, be "deemed slaves," and this is enough to decide this question. But this is not all, for I contend, that as this provision was thus incorporated by the new constitution, in place of sections 2, 4 and 5, as part of the act of 1822, the other provisions remaining in force, then the penalties attaching upon the sale of slaves imported as merchandise, contrary to the provisions of the law under the 6th section of the act of 1822 would apply. That section was not repugnant to the clause in question of the constitution, but remained in force, and *in aid thereof*, until the legislature attached other penalties. This we have seen is the principle cited, that all acts in *pari materia* are to be taken together, "*as if they were one law.*" Thus, "if one statute prohibits the doing a thing, and another statute be *afterwards* made, whereby a forfeiture is inflicted on the person doing that thing, both are considered as one statute." Thus, a new forfeiture attaches to an old prohibition as part of it; so "when an action *founded upon one statute*, is given by a *subsequent* statute in a *new case*, every thing annexed to the action by the first statute is likewise given. Indeed, the *latter* act may be considered as *incorporated with the former.*"

Here, then, was a penalty on the sale of slaves unlawfully introduced as merchandise; a subsequent act of sovereign legislation extends this provision by forbidding the introduction of all slaves as merchandise; does not the penalty under the old law clearly attach under the new provision, especially when every thing not repugnant to that provision in the former law is expressly continued in force by the last enactment? If this were a second supplemental act, there could be no doubt; and is it not more important to apply the principle to modifications of the former system introduced by a prohibitory provision of a new constitution?

It has been decided that "if a statute *prohibit contraband goods* under a *penalty*, a subsequent statute declaring goods contraband, will draw the penalty after it." "The statute of Anne, c. 7, s. 17, imposing a penalty of treble the value on the importation of foreign goods prohibited to be imported into this country, extends to all such goods as have been or may be prohibited *subsequently* to that statute, as much as if they had been prohibited at the time of making that statute." "Dwaris on Stat. 706, 743, 744; Atty. Genl. v. Saggers, 1 Price, 182. Thus, by the 8th Anne, c. 7, certain penalties are imposed on the importation of such goods as were prohibited, foreign gloves not being among the articles then prohibited. The 6th of G. 3, c. 3, an independent, not a supplemental act, passed several years subsequently, prohibited the importation of foreign gloves, and inflicted penalties on the concealment of them. The stat. of Anne inflicted a different penalty on persons knowingly having possession of such goods as were then prohibited. And the question was, whether the double penalties under both statutes could be recovered. The court decided that they could. They say, "the two statutes may well stand together. The one requires merely a possession of the goods, with a knowledge of their prohibition; the other, a possession with intent to conceal from forfeiture or seizure." And both penalties were enforced, though these gloves were "not prohibited by the first act." This is a much stronger case than the present, where only one penalty would be exacted; but the principle applies, that where certain classes of goods (or slaves) are prohibited to be imported under a penalty, and by subsequent legislation the prohibition is extended to another class of goods (or slaves), the penalty under the first act attaches to the goods (or slaves) enumerated in the second, although it be not a supplemental act, and not referred to in the second act. And Lord Mansfield upholds the same principle of considering as one act, statutes in *pari materia*, although the first act is "*not referred to*" in the last statute: and in aid of the construction of a late statute, he declares it a proper rule "to look into the policy of a former act in pari materia, although that act may have expired." Dwaris, 700, 701; 1 Bur. 449; Bac. Ab. T. Stat. 1, 3; 1 Vent. 246; Wallis v. Hudson, Chan. Rep.

276. And it is even competent to call in aid a "repealed statute," to assist in the construction of another statute in pari materia.

Now, if under the strict construction given to penal statutes, the penalty of the first statute on the importation of certain prohibited goods, will be inflicted as to other goods prohibited by a second statute, and even double penalties will be exacted, can there be a doubt that where the same acts are most liberally expounded, when the penalty is not demanded, but the act is only asked to operate so as to render the contract unlawful, that the 1st section of the act of 1822, which had that effect on the sale of all slaves that should not "hereafter be brought into this state pursuant to law," must expressly apply to such slaves as were prohibited to be introduced by the constitution? And is it not incredible, that when the constitution of 1832 prohibited the introduction of slaves as merchandise, it was intended to change the settled policy of the state for a quarter of a century, by which, under all acts in pari materia, the *sale* was *always* made unlawful *whenever the importation was forbidden?* This act, then, of 1822, is a part of this provision of the constitution of 1832, expressly continued in force thereby, and demonstrates that this was a prohibition; for why, by implication, is this clause to be rendered merely directory for future legislation, when there was already legislation full and complete upon the subject, and expressly continued in force by the constitution?

I have before quoted the decision in our favour of the highest court of our state; and here I contend, that the decision of the highest court of a state, expounding its constitution, is obligatory on this court in all cases when that construction involves no repugnance to the constitution of the United States. Could congress give to this court an appeal from the decisions of state tribunals in questions not involving a repugnance to the constitution of the United States? Surely not. And because it has jurisdiction, not on account of the *question*, but of the *parties*, between citizens of different states, shall it therefore assume the power of disregarding the construction of their own constitution, and of their own statutes by the highest courts of a state? If so, and it possesses this power in one case and in one state, it possesses the same power in every state and in all cases, and may overrule any number of decisions upon all their statutes and all their constitutions by all their courts; and thus establish two rules of property under the same state statute or state constitution, and both to be enforced within the state, the one by the state, and the other by the federal tribunals. Let us take the case of Maryland, and suppose, that under their laws, their courts not only invalidate the sale of slaves introduced for sale, but declare the negro free. If, in a case between citizens of different states, this court should give a different construction to the laws of Maryland, and declare the sale valid, and the negro a slave, what would be the result? Why, whilst the slave trader of another state, aided by this court, should collect the money for the sale of the slave, that same slave might be declared, upon his petition, a freeman, by the courts of Maryland; and no one pretends that from that decision there could be any appeal to this court. And to reverse the picture, whilst the state courts held the sale valid and the negro a slave, as between their citizens in expounding their laws, this court, in a case in which a citizen of another state was a party, might pronounce such sales invalid and the negro free, and thus *emancipate the slaves of a state against her will.*

This is but one case out of a thousand, of conflicting decisions that would constantly occur, bringing the state courts and state officers into constant conflict; often as to the same money or property, real or personal, and yet neither bound to acquiesce in the decision of the other, and of course resulting in contests of force or anarchy. Under our form of government there must be some tribunal, in the last resort, to expound laws and constitutions. That tribunal, in cases involving the construction of the constitution of the Union, is this court; and in all other cases involving only a construction of a state constitution, the highest court of the state is the expounding power, to whose decisions all must submit, or two opposite and contradictory constructions and rules of property must prevail and be enforced in the same state. No powers are retained by any state, if this court in all cases, though not involving a construction of the constitution of the Union, may demand obedience in every state and from all their courts, to all their decisions upon questions merely local, and embracing only an exposition of state laws and state constitutions. Over these local questions, it is conceded, that this *government* has no control. The constitution itself declares that "the powers not delegated to the United States by the constitution, nor prohibited by it to the states, are reserved to the states respectively, or 'to the people." These local questions upon which congress cannot legislate, are conceded to be cases of power reserved to the states, and not delegated to the United States. And yet, upon all these local questions, over which the governments of the states have exclusive power, and this *government* has no power, it may, upon this principle, nay, it must sweep them all within the controlling sway of one of the departments of this government. Especially over slavery, or any other local question, the states would have no power, and it would all be concentrated in one of the departments of this government.

If, in construing in the last resort, the constitution of a state, this tribunal may decide that upon their construction of that instrument, all the slaves within the limits of the state are free men, in vain may all the state tribunals have decided differently; in vain may we urge, and the opposing counsel concede, that no power over the "question," was delegated by the constitution of the Union to this government, that it is a power admitted to be exclusively reserved to the states; but if the question arises on the construction of a state constitution, in a case between citizens of different states, and comes into this court, its construction of that constitution, (if the state interpretation be not binding,) is to be the supreme law of the land, and obligatory on the same question on all the state tribunals. There is no escape from these consequences, but in the concession, that the state tribunals are not bound by the construction placed on local questions arising under state laws, and state constitutions. And is there to be no final and peaceful arbiter of any such questions? Must the conflicting decisions of the state and federal courts, both be executed without the power of appeal from either tribunal, and force decide between the marshal on the one hand, and the sheriff on the other, in carrying into effect these contradictory decrees? Such a system would be the reign of anarchy and civil war. Are we to be told, change your state constitutions, and we will expound them differently? So you will the *constitution as changed;* but that will not recall or change the past decree as made, whether for emancipation or any other purpose under the old constitution. Besides, it is no easy matter to change the constitution of a state. In most of the states a majority of at least two-thirds is required to effect this change. In some states, for instance, in Maryland, as to slavery, it requires the unanimous consent of both branches of the legislature; and in many cases the proposed remedy of changing our state constitutions, might prove quite ineffectual, and in no case could it recall the past, or obliterate the rights accrued under your construction of the old constitution.

In the case of the Bank of Hamilton v. Dudley, 2 Peters, 492, the question was, whether the court of common pleas of Ohio had authority, as a court of probate under the *constitution of that state,* to order the probate sale of certain property. The case was argued at one term; but the court hearing that the same question was "depending before the highest judicial tribunal of the state," Chief Justice Marshall announced that "the case was held under advisement," to receive that opinion. The counsel opposed to the Ohio decision, contended, that "this court will never follow the law as decided by the local tribunals, unless it be settled by *a series of decisions,* and is acquiesced in by the profession. But it is asked in this case, to yield implicit obedience to an *isolated case,* in the decision of which the court was divided; a decision, too, as it is solemnly believed, fraught with the most pernicious and ruinous consequences; and which, unless the learning and justice of the profession are greatly mistaken, will never meet its approbation." The same counsel also contended, that the order of the court of common pleas, to sell the property, must be considered res judicata and conclusive, till reversed, and not to be reversed in a collateral issue. In reply to this last position, as to the order of this *inferior court* of common pleas, the court regarded it as to "be treated with great respect, but not as conclusive authority." In regard, however, to the decision of the highest court of the state, expounding their state constitution, Chief Justice Marshall thus announced the opinion of this court: "It is also contended, that the jurisdiction of the court of common pleas in testamentary matters, is established by the constitution; and that the *exclusive power* of the state courts, to construe legislative acts, does not extend to *the paramount law*, so as to enable them to give efficacy to an act which is contrary to the constitution. *We cannot admit* this distinction. The judicial department of *any government*, is the *rightful expositor* of its laws; and EMPHATICALLY *of its supreme law.* If in a case depending before any court, a legislative act shall conflict with the constitution, it is admitted that the court must exercise its judgment on both, and that the constitution must control the act. The court must determine whether a repugnancy does or does not exist, and in making this determination, must construe both instruments. That its construction of the one is authority, while its construction of the other is to be disregarded, is a proposition for which the court can perceive no reason." Such was the view of this court, of a decision of the highest court of a state expounding its state constitution; not a series of decisions, but a *single* decision *just pronounced* by a *divided* court. It was regarded as *conclusive*, because the final construction of its state laws was a question within " the exclusive power of the state courts;" they were " the rightful expositor of its laws, *and emphatically of its supreme law.*"

In Coates v. Muse, 1 Brock. 539, 543, in a case overruling a decree for money, not land, growing out of a construction of a state statute, Chief Justice Marshall said : " It is always with much reluctance that I break the way in expounding the statute of a state, for the exposition of the acts of *every legislature* is, I think, *the peculiar* and *appropriate duty* of the tribunals created by that legislature."

In Gardner v. Collins, 2 Peters, 89, this court say, in regard to the construction of an act of the legislature of Rhode Island, that " If this question had been settled by *any* JUDICIAL *decision* in the state where the land lies, we should, upon the uniform principles adopted by this court, recognise that decision as part of the local law."

In the case of the United States v. Morrison, 4 Peters, 124, where the question arose on the construction of a statute of a state, in regard to the interpretation of which it was admitted by the court, that " different opinions seem to have been entertained at different times;" under which state of the facts, the circuit court of the United States, for the east district of Virginia, made a decision and construction one way, (Chief Justice Marshall presiding,) subsequently to this, the same question was decided differently by the highest court of Virginia; and the case not yet reported, was quoted in manuscript, when this court, Chief Justice Marshall pronouncing the opinion, reversed his own judgment below, upon this single decision just made by the state court, on a construction of their statute in regard to which much difference of opinion had before prevailed. In delivering the opinion of the court, Chief Justice Marshall, after referring to the decision by the circuit court, said : " A case was soon afterwards decided in the court of appeals, in which this question on the *execution law of the state* was elaborately argued, and deliberately decided. That decision is, that the right to take out an elegit is not suspended by suing out a writ of fieri facias, and consequently that the lien of the judgment continues pending the proceedings on that writ. This court, according to its uniform course, adopts that construction of the act which is made by the highest court of the state."

In Green v. Neal, 6 Peters, 291, when this court had twice decided in a certain manner the construction of a law of Tennessee, and the highest court of that state, by a single decision, ruled the same point differently, this court, in 1832, overruled its own two former decisions of this question, and adopted the last and recent decision of the supreme court of Tennessee. The very question raised was whether the state decision was merely entitled to high consideration or was conclusive; and the court expressly decided that " where a question arises under a local law, the decision of this question by the highest judicial tribunal of a state should be considered *as final* by this court." This was a strong case, especially as the state decision adopted in that case, was a single decision and of recent date, and opposed to previous and contrary decisions of the same question by the same state tribunals. But the court recognised the obligatory character of the state decision, even in a case " where the state tribunals should change the construction," although in such a case of contradictory decisions by the same state court of the same question, they might possibly not consider a "single adjudication" as conclusive. In such a case, we have seen Chief Justice Marshall's course was to wait, if possible, for further proceedings in the state courts; but where, as in the cases in 4th and 2d Peters, there was a single decision on the construction of a state law by the highest court of a state, (conflicting with no previous adjudication of the same tribunal) and a decision just made and in one case not yet reported, and contrary to a previous decision of the same question by the Chief Justice himself, he at once adopted these single decisions of a state court, and one of them made by a divided court, *as settling* the law of the state, and as conclusive and obligatory, and "emphatically" so, as regards a construction by the highest court of a state of its state constitution. And here I would urge respectfully, although it is unnecessary to go so far in this case, is not the last decision of the supreme court of a state expounding a state law, absolutely obligatory, even although it may conflict with a previous decision of the same tribunal? The court in the above case say: "Are not the injurious effects on the interests of the citizens of a state, as great in refusing to adopt the *change of construction*, as in refusing to adopt the first construction. A refusal in the one case, as well as in the other, has the effect to establish in the state *two rules of property*. Would not a change in the construction of a law of the United States, by this tribunal, be obligatory on the state courts? The statute, as *last expounded*, would be the law of the Union; and why may not the same effect be given to the last exposition of a local law by the state court?" Chief Justice Marshall, in 10 Wheat. 159, says: "This court has uniformly professed its disposition, in cases depending on the laws of a particular state, to adopt the construction which the courts of the state have given to those laws. This course is founded on the principle, supposed to be *universally recognised*, that the judicial department of every government, where such department exists, is the appropriate organ for construing the legislative acts of that government. Thus, *no court in the universe*, which *professed to be governed by principle*, would, we presume, undertake to say that the courts of Great Britain, or of France, or of any other nation, had *misunderstood their own statutes*, and therefore erect itself into a tribunal which should correct such misunderstanding. We receive the construction given by the courts of the nation as the true sense of the law, and feel ourselves *no more at liberty to depart from that construction*, than to depart from the words of the statute. On this principle, the construction given by this court to the constitution and laws of the United States is received by all as the true construction; and on *the same principle* the construction given by the courts of the several states to the legislative acts of those states, *is received as true*, unless they come in conflict with the constitution, laws, or treaties of the United States." Why then should this court presume that the highest judicial tribunal of our state "had misunderstood" their own constitution, and therefore that this court "should correct that misunderstanding." Is this court more familiar than the highest court of our state with the policy of the state as regards the introduction of slaves as merchandise; are they as likely to know the true intention of the framers of the constitution of our state as regards the clause in controversy as the distinguished judge who delivered the opinion of the court in our favour in this case, and who may be said to have framed and moulded into its present form that very clause as a member of the convention which framed the constitution, and as chairman of the very committee to whom the clause was confided? Chief Justice Marshall did not feel himself "at liberty to depart" from the construction of the state courts, and surely that truly great man has never been accused of endeavouring to press too far the powers of the state authorities. Here too is a complete answer to the position that the federal court has jurisdiction of the case between citizens of different states, and therefore may disregard the state decisions; and have not the tribunals of all the states of the Union jurisdiction in the same manner where a contract made in one state, is sued on in another state, or even in another country, if the defendant or his property can be found there; yet in all these cases it is conceded that the construction of the state law or constitution, by the state court, is conclusive in all other state courts or courts of other nations. This, says Chief Justice Marshall, is an universal principle; and it is known to extend to all cases whether involving controversies as to real or only as to personal property; and Judge Marshall considers it as more " EMPHATICALLY" the rule in all cases of the construction of a state constitution. But if there be any one case more than all others in which the rule should be rigidly applied, it is in *local questions as to slavery,* a question in itself so peculiarly local, so entirely dependent upon state laws, and in regard to which to establish "two rules of property" in the same state, the one by this court and the other by the state tribunals, would be attended with such fatal consequences. See 6 Wheat. 127; 5 Peters, 280. And now for the first time, after the lapse of more than half a century, is a different rule asked to be applied to the highest judicial tribunal of Mississippi, and the state itself to be humiliated by a discrimination so odious and unjust.

But the decision upon which we rely is said to be extra-judicial. Is not this, as regards this case, a mere formal distinction? The chancellor, in the case cited by our opponents, and sent up to the supreme court, gave "briefly" his views on *this question,* for the express and important purpose as he declared, "to put it in train for ultimate decision." Such was his desire, such the wish of the profession, and the true interest of all parties, that an "ultimate decision" should be made by the highest court of the state, so as to settle the law upon the question. The court expressly declare, in their opinion, that this question was involved in that case, and presented by it "for their consideration." They did *hear, consider,* and *determine* it; and now such a decision is called extra-judicial! It is called so because the question arose in a case in chancery, and not at law, and one of the judges who delivered the opinion permitted the slave trader to reap the fruits of his unlawful contract, because the defence was not made at law; but he decided that it was a good defence at law. Chief Justice Sharkey pronounced it a good defence both in law and equity, as certified in this very case under the seal of the court; and so far then as he was concerned, his opinion was both in form and substance a decision of the very question, and against the trader both as a question of law and equity. Call it by what name you may, it is a solemn and deliberate exposition, unanimously made, upon the fullest consideration, by the highest court of the state, of this very clause of our constitution, for the express purpose of settling the law upon the question; and it has so settled it in Mississippi.

Chief Justice Marshall, in the case in Brockenbrough, expressed his deep regret that he was compelled from necessity to construe a state statute in advance of a state construction. In the case in 4th Peters, he revoked his own decision a few months after it was delivered, upon a single unreported case, decided in the meantime by the highest court of a state, expounding their own statute upon a monied and not a landed controversy. What said he in the case in 10th Wheaton, of the impropriety of accusing the judicial tribunals of a state of misunderstanding and misconstruing their own state laws? What said he in the case from 2 Peters? Hearing that the question in that case, of the construction of a clause of the constitution of Ohio was pending before the highest court of that state, he *waited for a year* to hear that decision; and then conformed to it, though delivered by a divided court. What would he do in this case? conform to the exposition of their own constitution by the highest court of the state. Desiring, as he did, not a formal, but an actual and bona fide compliance with the exposition of their own constitution by its rightful expositors, the highest court of the state, would he, in the face of so solemn and deliberate a decision, rush headlong, now, at this term, without a moment's delay, into certain conflict with the highest courts of a state, upon a question regarding the construction of their own constitution? And, if this great man, with all his learning, experience, and unsurpassed intellectual power, would make no such experiments, and enter into no such conflicts, what other judge will venture?

——Quis poreat; ubi non dux erit Achilles.

I approach now the final question raised by our opponents in their printed brief, as follows: "But, assuming that the constitution of Mississippi does contain a clear and incontestable prohibition of the introduction of slaves as merchandise within its limits; then there remains, in the last place, to be considered fourthly, a grave and important question, which this court will have to decide; and that is, whether it is competent to any state in the Union, by its separate authority, either in its constitution or its laws, to regulate commerce among the several states, by enacting and enforcing such a prohibition? The constitution of the United States vests in congress the power ' to regulate commerce with foreign nations, and among the several states, and with the Indian tribes.' That power must be regarded as exclusively possessed by congress. The municipal laws of a state may, perhaps, decide what shall be the subjects of property; but when they have so decided, when they have stamped the character of property on any particular movables, they cannot interdict the removal of similar movables as merchandise from any other state, whose laws also recognise them as property. Such an interdiction would be a regulation of commerce among the states; and if a state can make it, it may prohibit the introduction of any produce from another state. South Carolina may prohibit the introduction of live stock from Kentucky, and Kentucky may prohibit the introduction within her limits, of the cotton or rice of South Carolina. It is not intended to argue that a state, which does not tolerate slavery, is bound to admit the introduction of slaves, to be held as property, within its limits; and the reason for excluding them is, that, by the laws of the free states, slaves cannot be held in bondage. The case before the court is, that of the transportation of slaves from one slave state to another slave state."

I concur with our opponents, that this is indeed, " *a grave and important question;*" the most so in my judgment which has ever been brought up for the determination of this court. The power to regulate commerce among the states is "supreme and exclusive," it is vested in congress alone; and if under it congress may forbid or authorize the transportation of slaves from state to state, in defiance of state authority, then indeed, we shall have reached a crisis in the abolition controversy, most alarming and momentous.

In their petitions to congress by the abolitionists, they assert the power here claimed, and call upon that body to exercise it by legislative enactments, in regard to the sale and transportation of slaves from state to state. These petitions have been repeatedly rejected or laid on the table, as seeking an object beyond the constitutional power of congress, by overwhelming majorities of both houses; but if this court, as the interpreter of the constitution of the Union, in the last resort, now inform congress that this power is vested in congress alone, no one can predict the consequences. Let it be observed, also, that whilst all these laws of all the slave-holding states on this subject are asked to be pronounced unconstitutional, the laws on the same subject, of the " free states," as they are designated by our opponents, are sought to be placed above the power of congress on this question. A distinction is thus directly made, by our opponents, between the " free states" and the " slave states," as contradistinguished in their brief on this question; and the " free states" are asked to be regarded as sovereign, and the " slave states" as subject states, upon all the points involved in this controversy. Thus it follows, that the contract sought to be enforced in this case, could not be enforced if made in Massachusetts, because prohibited by her constitution; but that the same identical contract can be enforced if made in the state of Mississippi, although expressly prohibited by the constitution of that state. Massachusetts, then, possesses sovereign and absolute power over this subject, and Mississippi no power whatever.

The constitution is then not to have the same uniform effect throughout all the states, as regards the supreme and exclusive power of congress to regulate commerce among the states; but this power is to range undisturbed throughout all the "slave states," striking down all their laws and constitutions on this subject, whilst the same power is arrested at the limits of each one of the "free states" of this Union. Such is the degrading attitude in which every slave-holding state is placed by this position. But, let me ask, is not the admission of our opponents, that this power of congress cannot enter the limits of the " free states," conclusive? The history of the constitution of the Union shows that the want of *uniformity*, as regards regulations of commerce, was the great motive leading to the formation of

E

that instrument. It was the sole cause assigned in the resolutions of Virginia (of Mr. Madison) of 1785 and 1786, as a consequence of which was assembled the convention which framed the constitution of the Union. 9 Wheat, 225. To Mr. Madison and to Virginia belong the undisputed honour of assembling that convention; and the *sole object* avowed in the Virginia resolutions was, by the adoption of the constitution, to procure for all the states " *uniformity in their commercial regulations.*" Virginia had endeavoured, prior to the adoption of the constitution, to regulate commerce between her ports and those of other states and nations, but she found that these regulations only drove this commerce to the rival ports of Maryland. She negotiated with Maryland to adopt similar regulations; but Maryland ascertained that she could not adopt them without driving her commerce to Pennsylvania, nor Pennsylvania without New York, nor New York without New England. Absolute and perfect uniformity was required to give due effect to regulations of commerce among *all the states;* and hence the call of the convention which formed the constitution of the Union, at the instance of Virginia, to establish this uniformity. If, then, this power to regulate commerce among all the states upon the principle of perfect uniformity, cannot, as regards the transportation and sale of slaves, have the same uniform effect in all the states, but can be exerted in and between some states only, and not in others, it is a conclusive argument, that as regards this local and peculiar question of slaves, and their sale and transportation from state to state, was never designed to be embraced under the authority of congress to regulate commerce among the states. The power to regulate commerce among the states, is a power to regulate commerce among all the states; and by regulations of perfect uniformity, applying to all, and exempting none. But Massachusetts, it is conceded, may, as regards the transportation into, and sale of slaves in that state, exempt herself from the operation of the power of congress to regulate commerce, and from all laws of congress on that subject. Yet this power is not only to operate with perfect uniformity, but is declared by our opponents to be "supreme and exclusive." And may this power be thus struck down as regards a single state, by the operation of state laws and state authority? Does any one state possess the authority to exempt herself from a power vested in congress alone, and prohibited to the states? Is this the tenure, at the will of a state, by which congress holds its powers, and especially those which are " supreme and exclusive."

It is said, Massachusetts may exempt herself from the operation of this power, by declaring slaves not to be property within her limits. But is there any *way* in which a state may exempt itself from the operation of a power vested in congress alone; or does this exempting power depend *on the mode* in which it is exercised by a state? But Massachusetts, it is said, may exempt herself from the operation of this power of congress, by declaring slaves not to be property within her limits; and if so, may not Mississippi exempt herself in a similar manner, by declaring, as she has done, that the slaves of other states shall not be *merchandise* within her limits. Cannot the state say, you may take back these slaves from our limits, but they shall not be an article of merchandise here; or may she not say, your slaves in other states shall not be introduced for sale here, or if so, our laws will emancipate them; or as Maryland now does, send them to Africa, if they will go, and if not, continue them as slaves in the state, but annul the sale by the importer? And must the state have previously emancipated all negroes who had been slaves within her limits, in order that she may be permitted to emancipate or forbid the sale of other negroes introduced as slaves from other states? A certain number of negroes are now slaves in Mississippi, and articles of merchandise by virtue of state laws and state power, within her limits. Now it is conceded, that the state may declare all these not to be slaves, or not to be merchandise, within her limits. Yet it is contended she may not make the same declaration as to the negroes of other states when introduced into the state.

A state may, it is conceded, establish or abolish slavery within her limits; she may do it immediately, or gradually and prospectively; she may confine slavery to the slaves then born and living in the state, or to them and their descendants, or to those slaves in the state, and those introduced by emigrants, and not for sale, or to those to be introduced within a certain date. All these are exercises of the unquestionable power of a state, and over which congress has no control or supervision. Or may congress supervise the state laws in this respect, and say to Massachusetts, and the other six states, who with her have abolished slavery, slaves from other states shall not against your laws be sold within your limits; but in all the remaining nineteen states where slavery does still exist, your laws against the sale of slaves from other states, shall be nugatory. Or may congress again, as between these nineteen states, say to New Jersey, Pennsylvania, &c., you have confined slavery to the slaves already within your limits, and make all born after a certain date free; slaves from other states shall not therefore be sold in your states, but in all the other states, where the existing slaves, as well as their offspring, are held in bondage, all other slaves may be sold within your limits, from other states; if this be not so, slaves from other states may be sold in Pennsylvania, Connecticut, Rhode Island, and New Jersey. Negro men who are held as slaves elsewhere, cannot be imported and sold as slaves in these states; because although negro men now there, are held and may be sold as slaves, yet the descendants of the female slaves, if there be any born hereafter, are to be free. And can it be seriously contended that this is so, and that upon an examination of the various conflicting provisions of state laws in this respect, as to slavery within their limits, shall depend the question whether congress, against the consent of the states, shall force upon some states, and not upon others, the sale of slaves within their limits, under a general comprehensive, uniform, supreme, and exclusive power to regulate commerce among all the states. The power to declare whether men shall be held in slavery in a state, and whether those only of a certain colour, who are already there, shall be held in slavery, or be articles of merchandise, and none others, or whether others introduced from other states shall also be held in slavery, or be articles of merchandise within her limits is exclusively a state power, over which it never was designed by the constitution, that congress should have the slightest control, to increase or decrease the number who should be held as slaves within their limits, or to retard or postpone, or influence in any way, directly or indirectly, the question of abolition. Such a power in all its effects and consequences, is a power, not to regulate commerce among the states, but *to regulate slavery,* both in and among the states. It is abolition in its most dangerous form, under the mask of a power to regulate commerce. It is clearly a power in congress to add to the number of slaves in a state against her will, to increase, and to increase indefinitely, slavery and the number of slaves in a state, against her authority. And if congress possess the power to *increase* slavery in a state, why not also the power to *decrease* it, and to regulate it at pleasure? Now it is a power as conceded to *increase* slavery against the will of a state, within its limits, whence it would follow, that if a state desires more slaves, congress, under the same power, may forbid the transportation of slaves from any state to any other state, and thus decrease slavery as regards any state, against her will and pleasure. The truth is, if congress possess this power to "regulate" the transportation and sale of slaves, from state to state, as it may all other articles of commerce, and slaves are to be placed on the same basis, under this supreme and exclusive power to regulate commerce, authority over the whole subject of slavery between and in the states, would be delegated to congress. And yet how strangely inconsistent are the arguments of the abolitionists: they say men are not property, and cannot be property by virtue of any laws of congress or of the states; and yet that as such, *commerce* in them among the states may be regulated by congress, and by congress alone. We say, the character of merchandise, or property, is attached to negroes, not by any grant of power in the constitution of the United States, but by virtue of the positive law of the states in which they are found; and with these states alone rests the power to legislate over the whole subject, and to give to them, or take from them, either the whole or from any part or number of them, those already there, or those that may be introduced thereafter, in whole or in part, the character of merchandise or property, at their pleasure, and over all which state regulations congress has not the slightest power whatever.

That this is so, follows from the admission, that a state can abolish slavery, and make all the slaves within her limits cease to be property. Massachusetts, it is said, may do this; and may, when done, prevent the sale of slaves within her limits. But may she therefore declare that horses, or cattle, or cotton, or any other usual article of commerce, shall not be property within her limits, and thereby prevent the sale by the importer of similar articles, introduced from abroad, or from any state in the Union within her limits? Not unless she can abolish property and commerce, so far as she is concerned with all foreign nations, and with all her sister states, or regulate it at her pleasure, or prescribe the articles in regard to which it shall exist.

As to those universal articles of commerce, known and recognised in all the states, and bought and sold in all the states, and the importation or exportation of which could be prohibited by no state; it was right and proper that the power of congress to regulate commerce among the states should apply, operating as such regulations would, with perfect equality, and uniformity upon all. But as regards slavery, which was a local matter, existing only in some states, and not in others, regarded as property in some states, and not in others, it would have been most unjust, that that very majority which did not recognise slaves as property in their own states, should by acts of congress regulate the transfer of them, and sale in and among other states, which did regard them to a certain extent as property.

That the very states which refused within their limits to recognise slaves as property, should claim the power by their votes in congress, to regulate their transportation and sale in other states, is preposterous. They claim the power first to exempt themselves from the alleged power of congress, to authorize or forbid commerce in slaves, and then assume the authority to apply this very power to other states, which prohibit the traffic, because they have not emancipated all other slaves already within their limits. Nay, the claim is still more preposterous; it is, that this power may be thus applied, by these states in congress, in Mississippi, but negro male slaves shall not be imported or sold in Pennsylvania, or New Jersey, Connecticut, and Rhode Island, because although the negro male slaves already there are continued as slaves, and may be sold as such, yet the descendants, should there be any of the female slaves, are emancipated. Slavery exists, as shall be shown, and slaves are property and may be sold in these and other states, that are called "free states;" and if the law of Mississippi, prohibiting the introduction and sale of slaves *from* other states is void, so is a similar law in all the states above enumerated, and slaves may now be lawfully imported and sold there. Mississippi has said these slaves shall not be merchandise within her limits. Can congress say they shall be merchandise? Can congress create in any state, the relation of master and slave, not only in cases in which it does not exist, but in cases forbidden by the laws of the states? Can it make more masters and more slaves, than the state desires to have within her limits? And if it can create the relation of master and slave in a state, *in cases* forbidden by the state laws, why not in the same cases forbid the creation of the relation, or dissolve it, when it already exist? If congress can increase and extend slavery in a state, against its wishes, why not limit it or abolish it; or can it *create*, and not *destroy*, *enlarge*, but not diminish? The commerce to be regulated, was that universal commerce in articles of merchandise, regarded as such in all the states, and throughout the nation, and which existed in every state, and which commerce was not to be created or abolished by state laws, but was subject between all the states to the supreme, exclusive, and uniform regulation of congress. It was commerce in merchandise, and regarded as such by all the states, and not commerce in persons, that was thus designed to be regulated by congress. Commerce, if it may be so called, in persons, was not the thing intended to be regulated by congress, for it was local and peculiar, and not national; but commerce in the broad and comprehensive sense of that term, embracing all the states by uniform regulations, and designed not to depend on state laws, but to be as eternal as the existence of the Union, and coextensive with the operation of the constitution, which embraced in all its power the whole Union, and all its parts.

This power as to commerce being "supreme and exclusive," it could recognise no conflicting or concurrent state legislation, and being a power to authorize and enforce this commerce in and among all tho states, and from state to state, it could compel, as this court have decided, *every state* to permit the sale by the importer of all these articles of commerce within her limits. If slaves are articles of commerce, in view of this power, congress can force their sale by the importer in every state; for no state, if these be articles of commerce in view of this power, can remove them from this list, by declaring them not to be property within her limits. And if a state may so defeat this clause of the constitution, as to one class of articles embraced within the commercial power, by declaring them not to be property within her limits, she may make the same declaration as to any or all other articles embraced by this power of the constitution; forbid their importation or sale within her limits, and thus regulate at her pleasure, or annihilate the commerce between that state and all the other states. It follows then as a consequence, either that each state at its pleasure may, as to that state, annihilate the whole commercial power of congress, by declaring what shall or shall not be property within her limits, or that slaves were designated by the constitution as " persons," and as such, never designed to be embraced in the power of congress to regulate commerce among the states. The commerce to be regulated was among the several states. Among what states? Was it among all, or only some of the states? Was it a national or sectional commercial code, which congress was to adopt? Was it to operate between Virginia and Mississippi, but not between Virginia and Massachusetts? Was it a regulation that would operate only between two states; but not as between one of these states, and another remote or adjacent state? Was it a regulation confined to particular states, and to be changed by those states, as from time to time they might change their policy upon any local question, and was it a local or a general commerce? Could it regulate by compulsory enactments an inter-state commerce in particular articles between certain states, because those states permitted an *internal commerce* in similar articles; but be authorized to extend no similar regulations to other states forbidding such internal commerce? If so, congress must look to *state laws* to see what articles are vendible in a state, or what *internal commerce* is authorized by it within its limits, before it can apply a general regulation of commerce to that state. Or does the authority of congress to regulate the external or internal state commerce, depend upon the manner in which a state exercises its own power of regulating its internal commerce? If so, and this be the rule as to slaves as embraced in the commercial power, it must be the same as to all other articles embraced in the same power; and the power of congress in regulating commerce among the states will depend upon the permission of each state in regulating its internal commerce. But not only was this uniformity in regulations of commerce required by the nature and national object of the grant; but the constitution, in the same article in which the power is given to congress to regulate commerce among the states, expressly declares, that " *No* preference shall be given by *any regulation of commerce* or revenue, to the ports of one state over those of another." Now, if Massachusetts and Mississippi both forbid by law the introduction of slaves as merchandise, and congress enact a law, or this court make a decree, by virtue of which, slaves are forced into the ports of Mississippi for sale, but cannot be forced for the same purpose of sale into the ports of Massachusetts, a direct preference is given by a " regulation of commerce," to the ports of one state over those of another. *It is a preference,* if one state may be permitted to exclude from introduction for sale within her ports, what another state is compelled to receive for sale. It is a preference which is asked in this case, to follow as a "regulation of commerce," by virtue of this very provision in the constitution itself, and in the absence of all congressional enactments, as if the constitution created these very preferences as to commerce, which it was the very object of that instrument to prohibit.

. As, then, it is conceded by our opponents, that the laws of Massachusetts do prohibit the introduction of slaves in her ports, and are constitutional, the same admission must follow as to the laws of Mississippi, forbidding the introduction of slaves in her ports; or a preference will be given by the constitution

E 2

127

itself, by "a regulation of commerce," to the "ports of one state over those of another."

But these state laws are not regulations of commerce, but of slavery. They relate to the social relations which exist in a state; the relation of master and slave; they define the "persons" to whom that relation shall be extended, and how and under what circumstances it shall be further introduced into the state."

Each state has exclusive power over the social relations which shall exist, or be introduced within her limits, and upon what terms and conditions, and what persons or number of persons shall be embraced within these regulations. The condition of master and slave is a relation; it is universally designated as the relation of master and slave; and whether this relation shall be confined to the slaves already within the limits of the state, or be extended to others to be introduced in future, is a matter exclusively within the power of each state. The relation of master and slave, of master and apprentice, of owner and redemptioner, of purchaser and convict sold, of guardian and ward, husband and wife, parent and child, are all relations depending exclusively on the municipal regulations of each state; and over which, to create or abolish, limit or extend, introduce or exclude, or regulate in any manner whatever, congress has no authority; and congress can no more say that a state shall have forced upon her more slaves than she desires, because there are slaves there, than that a state shall have more apprentices than she desires, because there are apprentices within her limits. I speak as a question of law, and not as instituting any moral comparison between slaves and apprentices; for from the ranks of the latter have risen some of the greatest and best men, and purest patriots. The master has the right, not created by the constitution of the United States, or to be regulated by it, but created and regulated by state laws, to the services of the slave for life, *the time prescribed by the laws of the state.* The master has the right to the services of the apprentice for the time prescribed by the laws of the state; and both, if the state permits, may assign to others their right to these services under the directions of state laws. Can therefore the right to the services of an apprentice, assignable in one state, be assigned in another state against her will, with the introduction of the apprentice there, because the services of other apprentices already there are assignable in that state?

Under the laws introduced into at least two of the free states of this Union, malefactors might have been sold for a term as long as life, and their services might be assignable for life by the *purchaser* at public sale, to any third person whatever; these malefactors, in the language of the constitution of the Union in regard to slaves, were "persons bound to service" for life, and their services for life assignable by their masters; and yet could these malefactors, thus assignable, be introduced into and be lawfully transferred in any other state, against her laws, because other malefactors already there were there assignable; yet, a malefactor *bound to service for life,* purchased by his *master* at public *sale,* and liable to be sold by his *owner,* is as much *his property* in contemplation of law, as the slave can be of his master. He is in fact a slave, having forfeited his liberty, and subjected himself to perpetual services by his crimes; a manner in which the most rigid moralists admit that servitude may be justifiably established. Yet such slaves cannot be transported and sold from state to state; though by the very constitution of Ohio and other of the free states, "SLAVERY" is expressly authorized therein, "for the punishment of crimes." It does not exist in Mississippi as in the free states, only as a "punishment for crimes," but from a state necessity, equally strong and powerful; the necessity of self-government, and of self-protection, and as best for the security and welfare of both races.

Slavery in Mississippi is a relation of perpetual pupilage and minority, and of contented dependence on the one hand, and of guardian care and patriarchal power on the other, a power essential for the welfare of both parties. With us the slaves greatly preponderate in numbers, and it is simply a question whether they shall govern us, or we shall govern them; whether there shall be an African or Anglo-American government in the state; or whether there shall be a government of intelligent white free men, or of ignorant negro slaves, to emancipate whom would not be to endow them with the moral or intellectual power to govern themselves or others, but to sink into the same debasement and misery which marks their truly unhappy condition in the crowded and pestilent alleys of the great cities of the north, where they are *called free*, but they are in fact a degraded caste, subjected to the worst of servitude, the bondage of vice, of ignorance, of want and misery. And if such be their condition where they are few in number and surrounded by their sympathising friends, how would it be where there are hundreds of thousands of them, and how in states where they greatly preponderate in number? Their emancipation, where such is the condition of the country, would be to them the darkest abyss of debasement, misery, vice and anarchy. And yet to produce this very result, is the grand object of that party in the north that demands of congress to regulate the slave trade among the states, not really with the view to prohibit that traffic, for it is prohibited by the slave-holding states, but with an ultimate view to emancipation as an incidental consequence from the action of congress over this subject. And here let me observe, that an adherence by the south to the policy in which they are now united, in abolishing as states the inter-state slave trade, and the support of that power and of that policy on the part of the states, by the decree of this court, and the denial of the power of congress, will do much to secure the continuance of that policy and to silence the most powerful of the batteries of abolition.

Another great mistake, maintained in the north by this party, is the ground now assumed in claiming this regulating commercial power of congress, that by the law of the slave-holding states, slaves are merely chattels and not persons, and therefore are subjected to the power of congress to regulate commerce among the states.

If it be intended to convey the idea that slaves are designed to be deprived by the laws of the south of the qualities and character of persons, and of the rights of human beings, and to degrade them in all things to the level of chattels, of inanimate matter, or of the brutes that perish, it is a radical error, and one that has been too long circulated uncontradicted by the abolitionists. In some of the states, they are designated as *real*, as *immovable* property. Is it therefore designed to deprive them of the power of locomotion, or to convert them into a part of the land or soil of a state? Far otherwise. Nor does their designation as personal property convert them into mere chattels, and deprive them of the character of human beings. In the South this is well understood, and no such meaning is attached to these terms, but in the North they are seized on and perverted, as if slaves were regarded and treated by us as inanimate matter. No, they are, in every thing essential to their real welfare, regarded as *persons*; as such they are responsible and punishable for crimes; as such to kill them in cold blood is murder; to treat them with cruelty or refuse them comfortable clothing and food, is a highly penal offence; as such they are nursed in sickness and infancy, and even in old age, with care and tenderness, when the season of labour is past. To call them chattels or real estate, no more makes them in reality land or merely inanimate matter, than to call the blacks of the north freemen, makes them so in fact. When the constitution of Mississippi, and laws made in pursuance thereof, require that slaves *shall* be treated with humanity, commands that they shall be well clothed and fed, and that unreasonable labour shall not be exacted, are these provisions applicable to a mere chattel, which the owner may mutilate or destroy at pleasure? No. The master has no right to the flesh and blood, the bones and sinews of any man under the laws of the south; this is an abolition slander, and the right is to the services of the slave, so declared expressly in the laws of the south, and so recognised in the constitution of the United States, where slaves are described as "persons bound to service or labour," and so unanimously decided by the highest court of our state. Jones' Case, Walker's Miss. Rep. 83. The right of the master is to the services of the slave, a right accruing only by virtue of the law of the state, and upon the terms therein prescribed. The rights of the master and slave are *reciprocal* under the laws of the south; the right of the master is to the services of the slave for life, and the right of the slave as secured by law, to humane and proper treatment, to comfortable lodging, food and clothing, and to proper care in infancy, sickness and old age. These are the *wages* paid, and that must be paid by the master; and if the doctrine of the abolitionists be correct, that slave labour is dearer than free labour, then higher wages are thus paid in the south than in the north for the same amount of labour; and that it is much higher wages than is paid to the toiling and starving millions of Europe, no candid man will deny. Let me be accused of making no comparison between slaves and my countrymen, the free white labourers of all the states. No; they are fitted morally and intellectually for self-government, and the slaves are not so fitted; and therefore, even for their own benefit, must be controlled by others.

· In truth, then, slavery is a condition of things; it is a relation, the relation of master and slave, the *status servi* of the Roman and Grecian law, so designated and recognised as a relation in the days of the Jewish Theocracy, as well as under the Christian dispensation. By all these laws it was designated as a relation, and as such we have seen it is expressly recognised in the constitution of the United States, where slaves are called "*persons* held to service or labour." How far they shall be so bound is exclusively a question of state authority, and over which the congress of the Union possesses not the slightest authority. The states and the states only can say what persons shall be so bound to service, and when they shall be released, and to what persons this relation shall be extended, and whether it shall be confined to those slaves already within the limits of a state, or be enlarged so as to include all others who may be introduced within their limits; and it is the abolitionists who must wholly deprive the slaves of the character of persons, and reduce them in all respects to the level of merchandise, before they can apply to them the power of congress to regulate commerce among the states.

. If a state or states chose to degrade not malefactors only, but a large portion of the present white or coloured race to the name and condition of slaves, could they therefore force them as slaves upon other states of the Union, under the power of congress to regulate commerce? Has congress any right to say slavery shall or shall not exist within the limits of the state of Mississippi; that slaves from other states shall or shall not be introduced within her limits? Has Virginia, or Pennsylvania, or any other state, a right to say slavery shall be abolished or established within the limits of Mississippi, and slaves shall or shall not be imported by her citizens for sale within her limits? Each state must legislate for itself alone on this subject, nor has congress nor any other state a right to interfere—in any manner whatever. And if Virginia can call upon congress, or upon this court, to compel Mississippi to receive or reject any or all of her slaves for sale, the states of Rhode Island, Connecticut, Pennsylvania, New Jersey, Delaware, Indiana and Illinois, can compel the state to receive all their slaves; still amounting under the last census to many thousands, notwithstanding they may all have been indoctrinated for years on the principles of abolition, surrounded with its teachers and disciples, and driven by force into our state, would come there prepared by theory and stimulated by revenge, to diffuse their emancipating creed among our slave population; to render them forever dangerous, worthless, sullen and discontented, and to excite successive insurrections from time to time within our limits. And yet by the argument of our opponents, the state possesses no power to guard her citizens against these evils, for if we cannot exclude at our pleasure the slaves of all the states, we can exclude the slaves of no one of the states, and are deprived of the power of self-preservation. And, let me ask, are not the slaves whom the doctrines and principles of abolition have now reached, upon those counties of Maryland, Virginia and Kentucky, bordering for more than a thousand miles upon the adjacent states of Pennsylvania, Ohio, Indiana and Illinois, unfit for a residence as slaves in Mississippi; and would it not be most dangerous to permit slave traders to drive them also in any number within our limit? Would they not contaminate our slave population, and diffuse among them the same doctrines and principles, which, from these bordering counties, have already peopled Canada with a colony of thousands of runaway slaves. In every point of view, the power to prohibit this traffic, is vital to the security and welfare of the people of Mississippi, and cannot be abandoned without surrendering the right of self-preservation. And yet to deprive the state of this authority has been called by our opponents a great conservative power of the constitution. Conservative of what? Of the power of the traders in slaves to drive thousands and hundreds of thousands of dangerous and discontented slaves, from any or all of these states, as merchandise, within our limits. And what must follow? Who will dare predict the result, or write the prophetic history of that drama which would soon be enacted within our borders.

The only clauses under which congress can legislate as to slaves, are the 2d clause of 9 sect., 1 art. of the constitution, 2 sect. 4 art., and the taxing power; in each of which they are spoken of, not as merchandise, but as *persons*. It is as *persons* they are enumerated under the census, and as such taxation and representation apportioned according to three-fifths of their *numbers*, not their *value*. In that section they are described as " three-fifths of all other persons;" in the 9th section, they are designated only as "persons;" and in the 2d section of the 4th article, they are described as " persons held to service or labour in one state under the laws thereof." Yes, "*under the laws thereof;*" and not by virtue of any authority of congress to force them within the limits of a state. If slaves are merchandise merely, under the power of the constitution of the Union, why is it that merchandise taken, or horses or cattle escaping from any one state into any other state, cannot be surrendered under the laws of congress upon the "claim" of the owner? Are articles of merchandise persons, or persons articles of merchandise, in view of any of the powers granted to congress in these provisions? It is as "persons" they are surrendered in one state when fugitives from another; and it is as "persons" they are enumerated for apportioning taxation and representation. If the constitution had slaves in view, when power was granted to regulate commerce among the states, how is it that in none of the debates on that clause, either in the convention which framed the constitution of the Union, or in the state conventions which ratified it, is there the slightest allusion to the existence of any such power? The journal of the convention shows that this clause, to regulate commerce with foreign nations and among the states, was proposed by Charles Pinckney, of South Carolina, and that it was adopted as proposed by him, with the addition of the words, as to *the Indian Tribes*. Did South Carolina, and did Mr. Pinckney, intend to give thereby this supreme and exclusive power under this article to congress as to slaves? No! The votes of Mr. Pinckney and of South Carolina in that convention, show conclusively that, that state and Mr. Pinckney were opposed to granting to congress *any power*, even over the African slave trade, even under specified and limited provisions on that subject in a different article. Fortunately, Mr. Pinckney has lived to declare his meaning, and that of the convention, in a speech made by him in congress on the Missouri question, in 1820, and reported in 18th vol. Niles' Register, p. 352; when, as a surviving witness of the views and deliberations of the convention in which he had acted so prominent a part, he bears testimony, specifically, to this very point, that under no clause of the constitution was any such power granted to congress. He says: " I have, sir, smiled at the idea of some gentlemen in supposing that congress possessed the power to insert the amendment, from that which is given in the constitution *to regulate commerce between several states;* and some have asserted that, under it, they not only have the power to inhibit slavery in Missouri, but even *to prevent the migration of slaves from one state to another*—from *Maryland* to *Virginia*. The true and peculiarly ludicrous manner in which a gentleman from that state lately treated this part of the subject, will, no doubt, induce an abandonment of this *pretended right;* nor shall I stop to answer it, until gentlemen can convince me that migration does not mean change of residence from one country or climate to another; and that the United States are not one country, one nation, or one people: if the word does mean, as I contend, and we are one people, I will then ask, how is it possible to migrate from one part of a country to another part of the same country? Surely, sir, when such straws as these are caught at to support a right, the hopes of doing so must be slender indeed."

We have then, here, at least one positive and uncontradicted witness in our favour, and that the very man who proposed this clause in regard to this power of congress to regulate commerce. Did South Carolina intend, in proposing this power, to give to congress *immediate* authority to prevent the transportation of slaves from all other states to that state, when she was then even opposed to the specific and prospective power to be exercised, at the end of twenty years, as to slaves from Africa? South Carolina has *always* viewed such a power as is now claimed for congress in regard to slaves, with absolute abhorrence; yet, by a new interpretation, this power is given by implication from that very clause in the constitution of the Union, which was proposed in the convention by South Carolina, and adopted on her motion. The source from which the power emanated, independent of the uncontradicted testimony of Mr. Pinckney, who proposed this clause, ought to be conclusive with every unprejudiced mind, that no such authority was designed to be thereby vested in congress. No one can believe that South Carolina, or the other slave-holding states, would *ever* have consented to the constitution, if by that instrument this supreme and exclusive power had been therein granted to congress; and it would be a fraud on those states, a fraud upon the constitution, a fraud in morals as well as law, now to interpolate by a new construction, at the end of half a century, a power which we all know would never have been granted by at least six out of the twelve states which formed the constitution.

In 9 Wheat. 194, Chief Justice Marshall declares: "That commerce, as the word is used in the constitution, is a unit;" but it is a cipher, if dependent on state regulations as to *internal commerce*, or state regulations as to what is property or merchandise; or if not a cipher, and different regulations as to the same articles, or operating differently in the several states can be made by congress, it is not a *unit*, but separated into as many fractions as there are states or sections. Chief Justice Marshall tells us: That the commerce designed to be regulated by congress, extends to all "those internal concerns which affect the states *generally*," 9 Wheat. 195; but as viewed by our opponents, it is not confined to that commerce which affects the states generally, but extends to that which affects only particular states or sections, and not the states generally, and might extend only to two states out of twenty-six, if there were but two slave-holding states in the Union. But again, at page 196 of 9 Wheaton, Chief Justice Marshall expressly declares the power to regulate commerce among the states, to apply to the one state in which the voyage by land or water begins, through any other state, and into still another state, in which the voyage terminates; and he instances the regulation of transportation between Baltimore and Providence "by land," which must pass into and through at least seven states, and that the power, he says, is to *enforce* this passage of these articles of commerce *through all these states*. What then follows? That a trader in slaves purchased at Baltimore to be sold in Wheeling, Virginia, may transport them in chains through Pennsylvania, the only practicable route by land, to Wheeling, and no law of Pennsylvania can forbid it. Again, a trader in slaves, purchased in Wheeling, Virginia, for Missouri, may drive them through Ohio, Indiana, and Illinois; or from Maryland for Missouri, by taking them through New York and the Lake route across to that state; or he might take them by sea, from Baltimore for Missouri, to Boston, then to pass them through Massachusetts, by the rail road to Buffalo, for the western route. The slave trader might, in this way, if slaves are embraced in the commercial power, encamp them in chains at Boston, Lexington, Concord or Bunker Hill, and drive them on to their destined market, and no state law can prevent it; and this *can be done now*, without any act of congress, and the state could not prevent it. This the abolitionists would regard with horror and dismay; but to all this they subject their own states, nay, as will be shown, they establish not only the slave trade but slavery there, in their efforts to force their doctrines upon the southern states.

At page 196, 9th Wheaton, Chief Justice Marshall says: This power in congress as to commerce, is "supreme and exclusive;" and that the power to *regulate* "is to prescribe the rule by which commerce is to be governed." At page 197, he says the power to regulate "commerce with foreign nations, and among the several states, is vested in congress as absolutely as it would be in a *single government*." So far as regards then this commercial power, the court distinctly declare, that the government of the Union is to be viewed as a *single government*; that state boundaries, and state jurisdiction, and the states themselves disappear, so far as this power is concerned, and that so far, the nation is a " Unit."

The authority then of Massachusetts disappears as regards the exercise of this commercial power by this single government. She ceases to exist as a separate state, so far as this power is concerned, and stands *so far as regards the power* towards this single government, in the same relation in which a county stands towards a state. Such is the decision of the court in the very case upon which our opponents rely. As then the power to regulate the sale and transportation of slaves from state to state is insisted by our opponents to be a commercial power, the states, by this decision, so far cease to exist as states; their separate state jurisdiction and boundaries so far disappear ; the states become a " Unit," and this power operates in and among all the states, as much as if the state governments had ceased to exist. What then becomes of the law of Massachusetts prohibiting the slave trade there, or the introduction from other states of slaves for sale there as merchandise, when brought in conflict with this commercial power ?. Why, not only would the sale be valid, and transportation through the state valid, by authority of an act of congress; but *now*, at *this moment*, on the principle contended for by our opponents, and heretofore adopted by this court, that, that commerce which congress leaves free and unforbidden, it authorizes as much as by an express law; the statutes of Massachusetts are unconstitutional, and slaves can now be transported from any state into Massachusetts, and sold there, or carried through there, for sale in some other state to which they are destined, these laws of the state being expressly declared by Chief Justice Marshall to be void, *if the commercial power extends to this case;* because the state " is exercising the very power that is granted to congress, and is doing the very thing which congress is authorized to do." 9 Wheat. 199—200. And at page 209, the court say : " To regulate, implies in its nature, full power over the thing to be regulated ; it excludes, necessarily, the action of all others, that would perform the same operation, on the same thing. That regulation is designed for the entire result, applying to those parts which remain as they were, as well as to those which are altered. It produces a *uniform whole*, which is as much disturbed and deranged by changing what the regulating power designs to leave untouched, as that on which it has operated."

The exercise of this power then, as well as the failure to exercise it, by leaving free what is not regulated, " produces a *uniform whole*," which the state law cannot disturb ; and yet this uniformity, thus required in all the states by the mere absence of congressional legislation, is completely subverted as regards these slaves, which are embraced, it is said, in the commercial power, and that commerce in them, which congress alone could regulate, and which it does regulate by leaving free as to all the states where it does not legislate, is in point of fact regulated at its pleasure by each state of the Union, and is dependent entirely on state laws. This power, we are told, is not now asked to be called forth to oppress the slave-holding states of the Union ; but the authority once established, it will recoil upon the free states with a force and power which was little dreamed of by the abolitionists; and will avail to establish slavery and the sale of slaves from other states in every state, and the traffic in slaves in and through all the states by the mere inaction of congress. Nay, if the argument of our opponents be correct, it is established and exists at this moment.

At page 224, 9th Wheaton, the court declare, that the constitution originated in the Virginia resolutions, which they say were intended to produce among the states " an uniform system in the commercial regulations;" and Mr. Madison's resolutions, which led to that measure, declare the object to be, as regards all the states, " to require uniformity in the commercial regulations," and prevent the states adopting " partial and separate regulations." These regulations then must be uniform ; this was the very object in granting the power, and the total impossibility of such uniformity as to slaves, shows that the power was never intended to extend to them ; and surely Virginia never designed to include them in the commercial power.

By the constitution, the rights that were delegated to congress, were delegated by *all* the states; the rights that were prohibited to the states, were prohibited to *all* the states; and the rights that were not delegated or prohibited, were reserved to *all* the states : but by the position of our opponents, the right to regulate the transportation and sale of slaves from state to state, was granted to congress only by the slave-holding states; the prohibition to that regulation by a state, was a prohibition only to the slave-holding states, and the reserved power over the regulation, was a power reserved by the non-slave-holding and not by the slave-holding states : and yet they all entered the confederacy as equals, and sovereigns, in every respect; and all granted, surrendered, and retained the same power.   Upon these terms only of perfect equality, and of subjection, or exemption of all the states from the national power, was the constitution framed; and to maintain the distinction now assumed between the slave-holding and non-slave-holding states, by which the last are sovereign, and the first are subject states on this question, is to place the former in an attitude of degradation, to which no one of these states ever would have assented in forming the constitution.   No! The constitution of the Union was one constitution, with one uniform operation and construction in all the states, and all its powers were to be enforced in all or none of the states; and not two constitutions, with two constructions, one for the North, and the other for the South, changing with geographical limits, lines, and sections.   If it be a constitution to be enforced by the Northern against the Southern states, rendering nugatory their laws upon this question, unless they will abandon their local institutions, and conform their policy in this respect to the will of the North, whilst the same powers of the government are to have no operation within the limits of the Northern states; the constitution would be a memorial of fraud and treachery, and would soon be broken into as many fragments as there are states or sections of the Union.

The whole power as to regulations of commerce being granted by each and every state, and vested by them exclusively in congress; no state can legislate or exercise any authority over the subject; and there can be no discrimination between the relative powers in this respect of the several states or sections of the Union.

At page 227, 9 Wheaton, the court say, that this provision as to commerce "carries the *whole* power and leaves *nothing* for the state to act on ;" that it is "the *same* power which *previously* existed within the *states*," which included the power of prohibition; that it is an authority as to commerce, "to limit or restrain it at pleasure."   They expressly declared, that it extended to an "embargo," which they had previously defined to be a " prohibition," and as a " branch of the commercial power."   If then this power extends to this case, this very decision so much relied on by our opponents, proves that if congress may *regulate*, it may "limit or restrain at pleasure," "embargo," or "prohibit" this traffic ; this being the same power pre-existing in the states, and wholly taken from them, and vested exclusively in the nation as a " single government."   How then can any state exempt herself from the operation of this power, by declaring such " subjects of commerce" as were within this clause of the constitution, and traffic in which was left free by the only power which can regulate it, shall not be subjects of commerce within her limits, and shall not be imported or sold therein ?

At page 228, 9 Wheaton, the court say, speaking of acts of congress on this subject : " Were every law on the subject of commerce repealed to-morrow, all commerce would be lawful ;" and there being no act of congress declaring this traffic unlawful, from the argument of our opponents, it follows, that this commerce in slaves between the states is now lawful in *all the states of the Union*.   It follows also, that there being no power either in the government of the states or the Union to prohibit this slave trade between the states, it is consecrated and perpetuated by the constitution.

The whole difficulty is solved by Mr. Madison, who tells us in the 54th number of the Federalist, page 236, that the case of slaves under the constitution was " a peculiar one;" and that the constitution " regards them as *inhabitants*, but as debased by servitude below the equal level of free inhabitants."

Did then the constitution of the United States design to give to congress power to regulate commerce in "inhabitants," in and between the states? To *regulate*, this court said, means "to prescribe the rules by which commerce is to be governed," and that "to regulate implies *full power* over the thing to be regulated." Then the framers of the constitution, although a majority were said to have been so much opposed to slavery, that they would not and did not put the word slave in that instrument, yet, by the position on which our opponents rely, congress was to prescribe the rules and the only rules by which commerce in slaves between the states should be regulated; that they were to authorize and direct this traffic, and that they were to keep open the markets in all the slave-holding states against their consent for this traffic; or, in other words, that congress was to perpetuate the slave trade between the states, and render it eternal in all the slave-holding states of the Union. That congress were ever intended to take the charge, much less the exclusive charge of the slave trade between the states, and regulate it at their pleasure, was a power never intended to be granted in the constitution. But if it be a power to *perpetuate*, it must be a power to *destroy*, and if not to destroy, at least to prescribe all the rules upon which the trade is to be conducted. Who is to judge of these rules? Congress, and congress only, by the argument of our opponents, have the full, supreme, and exclusive power. They may then say, how and by whom slaves shall be taken from state to state, and in what numbers, and of what age and sex, and how and to whom they shall be sold by the importer, and on what conditions, and in fact regulate every thing that relates to the transportation and sale. The power, if it exists at all, is plenary; and in the language of this court, in 12 Wheaton, "The power does not depend on the degree to which it may be exercised, if it may be exercised at all, it must be at the will of those who held it." Who then shall set bounds to this unlimited power, who shall restrain it—the states? Why, we have seen that they have surrendered all power over the subject, and that it is vested as completely in congress as if this were a "*single government.*"

We are then a single government, by the argument of our opponents, as regards the slave trade between the states, and every vestige of state authority is abolished. On the 9th of January, 1838, our able and distinguished opponent (Mr. Clay), read in his place in the senate, and sustained by a speech, the following, among other resolutions: "Resolved, that no power is delegated by the constitution to congress, to prohibit, in or between the states tolerating slavery, the sale and removal of such persons as are held in slavery by the laws of those states."—Nat. Intelligencer, 18, January 7, 1838. Here it is conceded that this government cannot prohibit this traffic. But why not, upon the case so much relied on by our opponents? It is true congress can impose no tax on exports from any state, but this the court say, is an exception from the *taxing* power, and that the power to tax imports is entirely distinct from that to regulate commerce. Although then congress, may not tax exports from the states, by the authority of this case, they may prohibit without a tax. What is an embargo, but a prohibition, not a tax: and in this case the court say, that an embargo is an "universally acknowledged power" of congress; and they expressly declare, that it is a commercial power. As then the prohibition to tax exports from any state, is a limitation only on the taxing power, and affects and limits, as the court expressly declares, in no way the power to regulate commerce among the states, congress may, if the position of our opponents be sound, and this is a case within the commercial power, lay an embargo on this slave trade between the states, or in other words prohibit it altogether. Grant but the first position of our opponents, and the case on which they rely, and that the commercial power extends to the sale and transfer of slaves from state to state, and all the consequences above stated must follow. But if neither the governments of the states, nor of the Union, possess this power to prohibit this trade, the power must be annihilated, and this without any grant of the power to congress, or prohition to the states, and although it is admitted to have existed in every state, before the adoption of the constitution. But the concession that congress cannot prohibit this trade, admits the whole case, by conceding that it is not within the meaning of the clause, which authorizes congress to regulate commerce. Why

F

then may not the states exercise this power? They are no where prohibited to exercise it in any clause of the constitution, unless it be as an inference from the authority of congress to regulate commerce. Now, if that inference follows, it would be because, in the language of this court, 9 Wheat. 199, "the state is exercising the *very power* that is granted to congress;" but if this prohibition of the importation of slaves be neither the "very power" that is granted to congress, nor included in that power, how is the state prohibited from exercising it? It is not *prohibited to the state,* unless included in the commercial power of congress; it is not delegated to congress, unless in that clause; hence, then, being a power neither delegated to congress, nor prohibited to the states, it is by the constitution expressly reserved to the state in which it pre-existed before the constitution was framed.

But again, this power to regulate commerce is an active power, a power "to prescribe the rules" by which that commerce may be conducted, and to enforce those rules; but here it is said no rule can be prescribed by congress on this subject, or enforced, no law can be passed by congress, to regulate this trade, but nevertheless, that the states cannot regulate nor prohibit this trade, because congress has the exclusive power. This is a strange contradiction, congress cannot legislate as to this case, although it may as to all other commerce among the states; but, notwithstanding, the state law is void, because the power is vested in congress. The power is vested in congress, but nevertheless it has no power to pass any law on the subject. But who is it that has the power? The constitution says congress shall have the power to regulate; and yet it is contended congress have no power to regulate this trade, but nevertheless the state law is void, in the absence of all power in congress to legislate on the subject. It is rendered then a *judicial* power, to be put in force by this court, and not by legislation, and yet have the judiciary any power to regulate commerce among the states? It is a sullen, dog in the manger power, that can neither act itself, nor permit action by any other authority. In the 32d number of the Federalist, Mr. Hamilton, who was the boldest opponent of state power, tells us there are but three cases under the constitution, in which a state cannot exercise a power, "where the constitution in *express terms* granted an *exclusive* authority to the Union. Where it granted in one instance an authority to the Union, and in another, prohibited the states from exercising the like authority; and where it granted an authority to the Union, to which a similar authority in the states would be absolutely and totally *contradictory* and *repugnant.*" It is conceded that there is no *express* grant of *exclusive* power to congress, or *express* prohibition to the states; but it is contended that the prohibition of the state power follows in this case, because its exercise would be the exercise of the same power granted exclusively to congress; and, therefore, the possession of such a power by the state would be "absolutely and totally contradictory and repugnant" to the possession of the same power by congress.

This is the argument in favour of this implied prohibition on state authority; but how is the power of a state to prohibit this traffic, "absolutely and totally contradictory and repugnant" to the possession of the same power by congress, when congress can make no such prohibition? Congress cannot prohibit, then there is no repugnance in a state prohibition. It is conceded the power existed in each state, prior to the adoption of the constitution; that instrument, it is admitted, grants no such prohibitory authority to congress; it prohibits the power no where to the states; how then have the states lost or alienated the power? The power to prohibit, or limit, or restrain the admission of slaves into any state, is conceded not to be vested in congress, then it must be vested in the states, or the power is annihilated; not by a grant of the power to congress, not by a prohibition to the states, but by some new rule of interpretation, under which, by a conjectural implication, the power has disappeared, without a grant, or without a prohibition. But these are the only modes by which a pre-existing state power can be annihilated.

By the 10th article, Amendments of the Constitution, "the powers not delegated to the United States by the constitution, nor prohibited by it to the states, are reserved to the states respectively, or to the people." This power then never having been either delegated to the United States, or prohibited to the states, is one of the reserved powers of the states, unless this amendment can be rendered a dead letter, by a broader construction than any heretofore maintained, even by the boldest adversaries of state authority, and the most latitudinous interpreters of the constitution. Nor was there any necessity or propriety, that congress should have this power to regulate the sale and transportation of slaves from state to state. It was not one of the difficulties which Mr. Madison or Virginia had in view, when they proposed calling the convention to create this government, for the express and only purpose of adopting uniform regulations of commerce, operating alike in all the states. No one complained of the want of such a power as to slaves, as a reason for adopting the constitution; and no such uniform regulations on that subject, as between the states, were ever anticipated or proposed. The convention was called at the instance of a slave-holding state, Virginia, under Mr. Madison's resolution, for the only express purpose of giving to congress power to adopt "uniform regulations" as to commerce; and the power in question was inserted in the constitution, on the motion of South Carolina. But did either of those states, or any other state, complain of the non-existence of such a power as to slaves, or desire that it should be granted to the general government? The power which Virginia and South Carolina, and all the states desired to be vested in congress, concerned only that universal commerce, extending to foreign nations, and among all the states, and effecting all that Virginia and South Carolina, or any other state desired to be regulated by the general government, and not the local and delicate subject of slavery; and neither in the debates or proceedings and resolutions of the various states, when delegates were chosen to form their constitution, nor in the resolutions, proceedings and debates of the congress of the old confederacy, on the same subject, nor in the general convention which framed, or the various state conventions which ratified it, nor in the contemporaneous commentaries of the great men who expounded it at the period of its adoption, is there one word showing that the sale or transportation of slaves from state to state, was one of the grievances to be remedied by the convention, or that any power over that subject was to be delegated to congress. Nor is it less remarkable, that in the various publications of the day, and arguments in and out of the various conventions which ratified it, did any one of its able opponents imagine that such a power was conferred by this clause on congress. Where was the Argus-eyed vigilance of Patrick Henry, and George Mason of Virginia, who so ably opposed the adoption of the constitution? Where the watchfulness of the other great statesmen of the south, so many of whom, as well as George Mason, Luther Martin, and others, had been members of the convention which framed the constitution, and opposed its adoption, by so many arguments in the state conventions which ratified it, that they never discovered, that under this power, congress might regulate or prohibit the transportation and sale of slaves from state to state, and that all state power over that subject was annihilated? It is true some of them did fear that for want of a bill of rights, similar to that subsequently adopted by the ten amendments to the constitution, and especially the tenth, that implied powers might be exercised under the general welfare and other clauses, but all which apprehensions were forever removed afterwards by the adoption of these amendments, the want of which was the cause of their opposition.

We are asked to admit the following propositions—1st, that congress was vested with power supreme and exclusive, to authorize and enforce the slave trade among the states, against their prohibition. 2d, that congress was denied all power to prohibit the slave trade among the states. 3d, that the states themselves were prohibited from arresting or regulating this trade. If this be so, it follows as a consequence, that the framers of the constitution intended to perpetuate under their authority the slave trade among the states, and to annihilate all power, either in the states, or in the general government, to arrest this traffic. To prohibit the slave trade among the states, by the authority of congress, would be most dangerous; but how infinitely more dangerous is the power now claimed for congress, by our opponents, to force all the slaves of eight or ten states into two or three states, as merchandise, against the consent of those states, and thus accumulate the disproportion in those states, between the whites and the slaves, and thus force upon those states revolt and insurrection on the one hand, or emancipation upon the other, extorted by the superiority of numbers. Who believes that the framers of the constitution ever intended to force such an alternative upon any of the states of the Union; or that all, or any of the states, would ever have consented to the vesting of such powers in the government of the Union?

It may be contended, however, that this power to regulate the transportation of slaves from state to state, arises by implication, under the 9th section of the 1st article of the constitution. That section is in these words : " Sec. 9. The migration or importation of such persons as any of the states now existing shall think proper to admit, shall not be prohibited by the congress prior to the year one thousand eight hundred and eight, but a tax or duty may be imposed on such importation, not exceeding ten dollars for each person."

Now, if this section be only an exception to the power of congress to regulate commerce, and I have shown that that power does not apply to this case ; then this section would have no operation whatever upon the present question. As, however, it is impossible for me to anticipate the views of the court in regard to this section, it is my duty to consider it, which shall be done in the only two aspects in which it could apply. First, as a substantive power ; and secondly, as an exception to the power of congress to regulate commerce. This section has never received a construction from this court, although there are some obiter dicta in which it is regarded as an exception to the power to regulate commerce. Now, although it may not be material to the determination of this question, and probably will not be so considered by the court ; yet I do regard this clause of the 9th section as a substantive power, and not an exception to a power already granted. Exceptions to granted powers are usually inserted in a proviso to the grant of those powers. When a power is delegated, and the grantors desire to reserve from those powers something by way of exception, that otherwise would follow from the grant, it is done by a proviso, designating the exception, and declaring that it shall not be included in the granted power. If this is not done by a proviso, it is done by language to the same effect, following immediately the words of the granted power, and designating the exception to it ; and we might as well look to a subsequent section of a constitution to find an enlargement of a granted power, as exceptions to it. When the power is granted, there is the appropriate place to enlarge or diminish the sphere of its operation, and not in a different section of the constitution. Now, this clause is wholly unconnected with the granted power to regulate commerce. It is in a different section of the constitution, entirely separated from the clause or section in relation to commerce, and disconnected from it, not only by position, but by no less than fourteen distinct and substantive grants of power, wholly unconnected with the authority to regulate commerce. Such is the separation in position of these two powers in the constitution ; but when we look beyond that instrument, to the journal of the convention which formed the constitution, and the debates in that body, we will find the same separation in the order of time, when these two sections were adopted.

At page 746, volume 2d, of the Madison papers, we will find this commercial power first proposed in the following words : " To regulate commerce with all nations and among the several states." This clause was afterwards modified by inserting "foreign nations," instead of " all nations," and by enlarging the power by the addition of the words " and with the Indian tribes." Here then was the place and the time when the convention was modifying and enlarging this power, to designate the exceptions to it. The date of this original proposition in regard to the commercial power, was the 29th of May, 1787. I find that on the 6th of August, following, pages 1226, 1232, 1233, 1234, of the same book, that this commercial power was again proposed by the committee of detail, in the following words, in the 1st section of the 7th article of the constitution. " To regulate commerce with foreign nations, and among the several states." The 3d section fixes the proportions, in which " taxation shall be regulated," and the 4th section, which follows, is in the following words : Section 4. " No tax or duty shall be laid on articles exported from any state ; nor on the migration or importation of such persons as the several states shall think proper to admit ; nor shall such migration or importation be prohibited." Here, this clause first appears, in a distinct section, in relation to the *taxing power*, and with a declaratory proviso to that power.

On the 15th of August, 1787, (page 1343) we find the convention adopting *unanimously*, the clause for regulating commerce as before quoted. Now, if the power to prohibit the importation of slaves, had been considered as included in the power to regulate commerce, we know, and no one denies, that at least two states, instead of voting for this clause as they did, would have opposed it, as they did all power to prohibit this importation; finally yielding to a compromise, by which the importation should not be prohibited until 1808. Is it not then inconceivable, that this prohibition thus opposed by at least two states, should have been regarded as included in the clause to regulate commerce; thus *unanimously* adopted; when, if such a prohibition had been supposed to be included, these two states had declared that they could not become parties to the constitution. Mr. Pinckney of South Carolina, had proposed this very clause to regulate commerce, and he, and his state, and all the states we have seen voted for it; but, at page 1389, we find, Mr. Pinckney declaring, "South Carolina can never receive the plan, if it prohibits the slave trade;" in which he was joined by Georgia. Yet, Georgia and South Carolina had both voted for this very commercial power, which is now asked to be regarded as including by implication a prohibition to which they could not assent.

On the 21st of August, this section as to migration and importation as before quoted, was taken up, (page 1382) and it was discussed at length, in connexion with the taxing power.

At page 1388, " Mr. L. Martin proposed to vary article 7, section 4, so as to allow a " prohibition or tax on the importation of slaves." Mr. Ellsworth of Con. opposed it; he said, " Let every state import what it pleases." Mr. Pinckney and Mr. Rutledge of South Carolina, opposed it; Mr. Sherman opposed it, and Gen. Pinckney, Mr. Baldwin, Mr. Gerry, Mr. Williamson. Here, very many of the states opposed it; two states declared that such a prohibition would prevent their becoming parties to the constitution; and yet all had voted for this very clause as to commerce, from which the prohibitory power is now asked to follow by implication. Such is the history of this matter as now furnished by Mr. Madison, and it appears to me conclusive on the question.

We have seen the order in which this clause stood in the constitution as reported by the committee of detail; and after undergoing various modifications, we have seen the order in which it now stands in that instrument. Separated as it was by the committee from the clause in relation to commerce, why, in the transposition which took place afterwards, was it not connected with that clause as a proviso, or in some other manner, if it was adopted by the convention as an exception to the commercial power? But there are other reasons still stronger against this position. The clause in question, gives to congress power to tax the importation of negroes, not exceeding ten dollars for each person. Now, is this a modification of, or exception to the commercial power?

In 9 Wheaton, 200–201, Chief Justice Marshall, in delivering the opinion of this court, declares, that duties or taxes on importation, are branches of the *taxing* power, and wholly distinct and separate from the commercial power; and he expressly declares, that exceptions from or modifications of this power of imposing duties or taxes on importation and exportation, are exceptions to or modifications of the taxing, and not of the commercial power. But again, the whole of this clause applies to *persons;* and this court have decided, that in contemplation of the constitution of the Union, *persons* " are not the subject of commerce," so as to be included in the construction of a power given to congress, to regulate " commerce." 11 Peters, 136–137. Now this clause speaks of persons, and of persons only; and it includes negro freemen, as well as negro slaves, as is expressly declared by Chief Justice Marshall, in 9 Wheaton, 216–217; the term migration embracing the free, and the term importation, the slaves; and upon this principle, congress has legislated on the subject. However, then, it may have been disputed whether slaves as articles of commerce were embraced in the commercial power; no one can pretend that free negroes were articles of sale or commerce, and em-

F 2

braced in the commercial power. This appears to me conclusive against the position that this clause is an exception from the power of congress to regulate commerce. If then this clause be a substantive power, does it confer the authority claimed in this case to prohibit the transportation of slaves from state to state? It is conceded that the term *importation* applies only to slaves introduced from abroad; but it has been contended that the term *migration* does apply to the transportation of slaves from state to state. Now this is against the opinion of Chief Justice Marshall, on the point last quoted—upon the ground that migration applies to free negroes, and to voluntary removal, or change of residence by them, and therefore can have no application to slaves. But independent of this decision, is it not clear that the term migration applies to persons coming from abroad, and not a removal from state to state? This is the true grammatical meaning of the term, but there is still higher authority not heretofore referred to.

In the Declaration of American Independence, we find the following clause : " He has endeavoured to prevent the population of these states ; for that purpose, obstructing the laws for naturalization of foreigners ; refusing to pass others to encourage *their migration hither;* and raising the conditions of new appropriations of lands."

Here the term migration, in its true American sense as applicable to our peculiar position as states and as a nation, is used as embracing only persons coming from abroad, and no other. Now, when we reflect, that many of the persons who signed the Declaration of Independence, were also members of the convention which framed the constitution of the United States, did these same distinguished statesmen use the term in one instrument as applicable only to persons coming from abroad, and in the other as only applicable to persons passing from state to state : thus using the same term to express a totally different thing in the two cases? But when the great statesmen of that day designed to designate a passing or removing from state to state, they used very different and appropriate terms to express that object.

In the articles of confederation they say : " The people of each state shall have free ingress and regress to and from any other state." Here, where they intend to designate a passing or removing from state to state, the terms " ingress and regress" are used, and not the term migration. Now, very many of those who framed the articles of confederation, were also framers of the Declaration of Independence, and of the constitution of the United States ; and is it conceivable that had they designed to regulate the ingress or regress from state to state, they would not have used the language of the articles of confederation, and not a word to which they had given a very different meaning in the Declaration of Independence. When looking beyond the words themselves, to the debates in the convention which framed the constitution, we find the construction universally confined to persons from abroad, and Gouverneur Morris and Col. Mason, both stated without contradiction in the convention the fact, that the clause extended to " freemen," and no one suggested the possibility of its being extended to the transportation of slaves from state to state. If, then, this clause be a substantive grant of power, and not an exception to the commercial power, and if, as we have seen, it does not extend to the transportation of slaves from state to state, there is an end to the question ; for here, if any where, the power would have been given. But, suppose it to have been an exception or proviso to the commercial power, is it any thing more than a declaratory proviso to prevent by a provision, added to this power, ex abundanti cautela, any construction, by which congress could prohibit the migration or importation of certain persons? This was the form in which it was first introduced, and the designation of the year 1808, as well as the *taxing* authority, were added by subsequent amendments.

· The convention grant to congress the commercial and taxing powers ; but to prevent these powers being construed to extend to an authority to prohibit the introduction of certain persons, such a proviso is proposed, which, by a compromise as to time and taxation, is made to assume its present shape ; and this is all that was intended by the obiter dicta before referred to, in which this clause is spoken of as an exception to the commercial power. Such language cannot imply that the powers granted in this clause would have been included in the commercial power; for we have seen that this power did not embrace an authority to lay duties or taxes on importation, nor extend to *persons* of any description, much less to freemen as articles of commerce. But, even if this clause, as an exception to the commercial power, would, but for this proviso have been embraced in that power, then the extent of the power as thus indicated by implication, would not go beyond the exception itself; and this, we have seen, did not embrace the transportation of slaves from state to state. Such being the case, what would be the extraordinary implication to which we are asked to resort? Why, that although the clause in question does not extend to the transportation of slaves from state to state; yet, as it does extend after a certain date to the importation of slaves from abroad, and as but for this exception, congress, even prior to that date, would have possessed this power as to such importation from abroad under the authority to regulate commerce, therefore, congress always possessed the authority under the commercial power to prohibit the transportation of slaves from state to state. Hence, it would follow, that by this construction, congress, immediately on the adoption of the constitution, without waiting till 1808, could at once prohibit the introduction of slaves from state to state, and yet a power so tremendous, now extracted by implication, was never even alluded to in the convention, nor would the constitution ever have been formed, if such a power had been asked to be vested in congress. Would the slave-holding states have consented that congress should forbid the importation or exportation of slaves from state to state, and that congress alone should regulate their policy in this respect? Especially would Georgia and South Carolina, that would not join the Union unless the African slave trade were kept open from 1787 to 1808, ever have agreed to a constitution, by which, *immediately* on its adoption, they could not introduce either for sale or use slaves from an adjoining state; no, not even when acquired by gift, devise, or inheritance? And, now let be observed, that, as it is shown, the power to prohibit the transportation of slaves from state to state does not follow from this 9th section, and to commence in 1808; that if it existed at all, it was as an inference from the commercial power which went into effect immediately. No one then can believe that any such power was ever designed to be vested in congress. It never could have been directly granted, and now to interpolate it by implication would be a fraud on the parties to the constitution.

But there is another reason why this clause is not a mere exception to the commercial power. That power this court have declared is vested exclusively in congress, and no portion of it can be exercised by any state even though congress may not have legislated on the subject. Now, this clause of the 9th section was admitted in the convention to extend to the prohibition of the admission of *convicts* from abroad. Madison Papers, 1430, 1436. Yet this court have declared, that the states do possess the power to prohibit the introduction of foreign convicts. 11 Peters, 148, 149. If, then, the states possess this power, and it is also vested in the general government, it must be a case of concurrent powers, and of course is not embraced in the commercial power, which we have seen is not the case of a concurrent authority, but of an authority denied altogether to the states and vested in congress alone. When the constitution was formed we became as to all powers conferred exclusively on congress by that instrument, as this court have decided, one country; especially as regards this commercial power, we were in the strong language of this court, " a single government," recognising as regarding this power no state boundaries. And yet, in relation to this very power, migrate, which means a removal from one country to another country, is asked to be construed to mean a removal from one part of a country to another part of the same country; and that too, when, as to this clause considered as an exception to the commercial power, the whole country in that respect was as this court have declared, a "unit," a "single government," knowing no separate state jurisdiction or boundaries.

It has been shown that this law is not embraced within the power of congress to regulate commerce; and this would be sufficient; but I will go further, and prove that it is a power reserved to the states. The reserved powers of the states, comprise all those not delegated to the general government, or prohibited to the states. The states were the fountain springs of all the powers vested in congress, and this is a case, which goes to the source of all power, and never was, and perhaps never could be abandoned, without a total surrender of all sovereignty. It is the power of self-preservation; it is a matter of the police of a state, regarding its internal policy; a municipal regulation, to preserve the tranquillity, or promote the prosperity of the state, and guard the lives of its inhabitants. It is similar in principle to the quarantine and health laws of a state, its pauper and inspection laws, and many others of a similar character. It is a local provision for the internal peace and security of the state, growing out of the inherent and inalienable right of self-preservation, and operating exclusively within the limits of the state. It is a power to guard the state, "*against domestic violence,*" which not only was reserved to the state, but to the state exclusively, unless upon its "application" for aid to the government of the United States. The 4th sec. 4th art. of the constitution, declares: "The United States shall guaranty to every state in this Union a republican form of government, and shall protect each of them against invasion, and on *application of the legislature,* or of the executive, (when the legislature cannot be convened,) against *domestic violence.*" It is then within the clearly reserved power of a state to "protect" itself, "against domestic violence;" and it may do so by the means of the state itself; or congress, upon the application of the state, and *not otherwise,* may come to its aid in such an emergency. In the state then alone resides the power to pass all laws, designed to protect its people against domestic violence. It is not to wait until the apprehension of domestic violence shall have been realized, it is not to wait until that violence shall have assumed the form of an "insurrection," but looking forward to the possibility of such an event, it may enact all laws calculated to prevent such a catastrophe. It is true that congress, under the 8th section of the 1st article of the constitution, have power "to provide for calling forth the militia to execute the laws *of the Union,* suppress insurrections, and repel invasions." But this clause has no application to this case, and even if it had, could not interfere with the state law upon this subject. But what is this power of congress in this section? It is peculiar and specific—1st, it relates wholly to insurrections to subvert "the laws of the Union," an insurrection against the government and authority of the United States, and not a case of "*domestic* violence," which applies peculiarly to a movement against the laws and government of a state. 2d, it is a power only to call forth the militia, and the purpose is to "suppress" the insurrection. But it will not be contended that this power applies to a case of "domestic violence," confined to the limits of a state, and conflicting only with its own laws, and its own authority. Each state then possesses the sole power of protecting its citizens, "against domestic violence;" the general government protects a state against *invasion from abroad,* without waiting for any application from the state. But desirable as such protection might be, in case of domestic violence, the states were not willing that in such a case the government of the Union should act, except upon the "*application*" of the state. What then is a case of domestic violence? Can any one doubt, that a rising of the slaves to assume the government of a state, or to take the lives of its citizens, or oppose or subvert its laws, would be a case of "domestic violence," to guard against which before it occurred, as well as to suppress it afterwards, is one of the powers clearly reserved by every state. Now may not a state, as a means of accomplishing this object, prevent the introduction of dangerous, or convict, or insurgent slaves, whose importation might produce domestic violence? This court determined upon a construction cotemporaneous with the formation of the constitution, that a state may prevent the introduction of malefactors, 11 Peters, 1.8. This is permitted as a measure of internal police, to guard the peace of the state, and promote the tranquillity and happiness of its people. This, all the slave states have ever done, and in pursuance of such a policy and to effectuate the same object, might they not prevent the introduction of wicked or dangerous slaves, although not yet condemned as convicts by the tribunals of a sister state? Suppose insurgent slaves had been reserved as informers, and never tried or condemned within the limits of a sister state, none can doubt the power of any state to prevent their introduction, and especially as slaves within their limits. In carrying out the same policy of self-preservation, might not a state have said after the Southampton massacre, that no slaves from that region, whether witnesses or participators in that transaction, should be brought within their limits; or if particular classes of persons importing slaves for sale, had been in the habit of introducing into a state, wicked or dangerous, insurgent or convict slaves, might not a state prohibit the introduction of slaves for sale, by such person altogether, especially if the state had endeavoured, (as we have seen Mississippi had done for years,) to prevent, by various requisitions, the introduction, by negro traders, of slaves of this description, all which had proved unavailing; might not the state, as the most or the only effectual remedy, exclude the introduction of slaves, by such traders or classes of persons altogether, embracing thus, in the exclusion, all slaves introduced as merchandise? Engaged as these traders were in this inhuman traffic; transporting these slaves in chains from state to state, for the sole purpose of a sale for profit; desirous of increasing this profit by purchasing the cheapest slaves, which would always be the most wicked and dangerous, reckless of the moral qualities and character of the slaves whom they bought, not for their own use, but to sell for speculation; tempted to buy the most wicked slaves, because always to be purchased at the lowest price, and sold in a distant state at the highest price, to those who would be ignorant of their dangerous character; inured as these traders were to scenes of wretchedness and cruelty, and entirely regardless of the means by which they reaped a profit from this traffic, why might we not, as a means of self-protection, arrest this traffic by forbidding the introduction of slaves as merchandise? Especially when a state had tried all other means to arrest the introduction of dangerous slaves, and had found the state, notwithstanding her previous restrictions, inundated by these traders with the wicked and abandoned slaves, the insurgents and malefactors, the sweepings of the jails of other states, might they not wholly exclude the traffic, as the only effectual means of self-preservation?

If experience had demonstrated that it was unsafe to trust with slave traders the introduction for sale of slaves, why might not the state arrest the importation by them of slaves as merchandise? But even if they could repose for the character of the slaves upon the traders, there was that in the very mode and purpose of introduction which rendered nearly all such slaves most dangerous to the tranquillity of the state. The very manner in which these slaves were forced from one state and driven into another, would introduce them with hearts overflowing with bitterness, and stimulated to revenge the most deadly, against the seller and the purchaser. Such slaves would seek for vengeance, not only by their own deeds, but they would endeavour to inflame the passions of all other slaves in the state, who but for their contaminating influence would have remained useful and contented. Who can deny that there was danger arising from such transactions? *The legislation of all the slave-holding states demonstrates that it is so ;* and our own courts have so declared the fact; and did the state possess no adequate power to prevent these dangers by the exclusion of all such slaves, and the arresting of all such traffic? Nor was it only succeeding the sale, but whilst these negroes are encamped by thousands throughout the state for sale, that the danger was imminent. And if any state might, for her own safety, thus interfere to guard the state against these dangers, from wicked or convict slaves introduced for sale from other states, and stimulated to revenge by the mode of their introduction; why might not the state, in addition to these evils from the character of the slaves, perceive new and greater sources of alarm, in the overwhelming preponderance in numbers, thus inevitably given to the slave over the white population; and might not Mississippi, situated as she was, find in this rapidly increasing disproportion, a sufficient reason upon the same principles of self-protection, to prevent the introduction of slaves as merchandise? In looking at the condition of the state, it was obvious that the disproportion was increasing in an alarming ratio, that the slaves already outnumbered the whites of the whole state, and in many adjacent counties three to one; and in many patrol districts, more than twenty to one. Who will dare to say, that there was no danger in permitting this disproportion to go on rapidly augmenting, and that self-preservation might not demand the prohibition of the traffic? And who was to judge of this internal danger, and to guard against it, except the state in which it existed?

If a state cannot prevent its becoming a refuge of insurgents, the Botany Bay of the slave malefactors of other states; if it cannot prevent the introduction of slaves of a class, and under circumstances, and in a disproportion inviting the overthrow of its laws, and the massacre of its freemen; if it must become one vast negro quarter, with only great and extensive plantations, superintended by one overseer, and owned too often by absentee masters; it does not possess the power to guard the state against domestic violence or maintain internal tranquillity, and it is not a state and possesses no one reserved right, or attribute of sovereignty, if it is thus despoiled of the power of self-preservation. The cases of comparative danger, above cited, may differ in degree, but in degree only, and not in principle. If then, internal tranquillity; and self-protection be legitimate ends of state legislation, and if such prohibition of the introduction of slaves as merchandise, be one of the means to effect these ends and purpose, if the purpose is lawful as an object of state legislation, who can say that these means are not adapted to the end, and calculated to secure the object? Is it not, perhaps, the only means suitable to the case, or at all events, where there is a choice of means by the state, is it not one of those means within the range of state authority, to effect the legitimate purpose of guarding against domestic violence?

These principles are settled in our favour in Miln's Case, 11 Peters, 102, when this court decided, that an act of New York, excluding paupers, was constitutional. In giving the opinion of the court, Judge Barbour said: "But how can this apply to *persons?* They are not the subjects of commerce, and not being imported goods, cannot fall within a train of reasoning, founded on the construction of a power given to congress to regulate commerce, and the prohibition to the states from imposing a duty on imported goods." "The power to pass inspection laws involves the right to examine articles which are imported, and are therefore directly the subjects of commerce; and if any of them are found to be unsound or infectious, to cause them to be removed, or even destroyed." "We think it as competent, and as necessary, for a state to provide *precautionary measures* against the moral pestilence of paupers, vagabonds, and possibly convicts, as it is to guard against the physical pestilence which may arise from unsound and infectious articles imported, or from a ship, the crew of which may be labouring under an infectious disease." Judge Thomson said: "The power to direct the removal of gunpowder, is a branch of the police power, which unquestionably remains, and ought to remain, with the states. The state law here is brought to act directly on the article imported, and may even *prevent its landing*, because it might *endanger the public safety*." "Can any thing fall more directly within the police power, and internal regulation of a state, than that which concerns the care and management of paupers, or convicts, or any other class or description of persons, that may be thrown into the country, and *likely to endanger its safety?*" And, he adds, the state may exclude all persons whose admission would "*endanger its safety or security*." Judge Baldwin, in his concurring opinion (Baldwin's Views,) 181, says: "On the same principle, by which a state may prevent the introduction of infected persons, or goods, and articles dangerous to the persons or property of its citizens; it may exclude paupers, who will add to the burdens of taxation, or convicts, who will corrupt the morals of the people, threatening them with more evils than gunpowder or disease." He adds, "if there is any one case to which the following remark of this court is peculiarly applicable, it is this: "It does not appear to me a violent construction of the constitution, and is certainly a convenient one, to consider the power of the states as existing over such cases as *the laws of the Union may not reach*." (4 Wheat. 193.) "But if the state (inspection) law imposes no tax on imports or exports, the prohibition does not touch it, either by requiring the consent of congress, or making the law subject to its revision or control." "The state (in excluding paupers or convicts,) asserts a right of self-protection." "Poor laws are analogous to health; quarantine and inspection laws, all being parts of a system of internal police, to prevent the introduction of what is *dangerous to the safety* or health of the people."

Here are important principles established, and many of them cited from the previous opinions of Chief Justice Marshall. First, a state law, excluding the introduction of convicts or paupers from other states is constitutional; so are health laws, and inspection laws, and all laws of an analogous character, excluding dangerous articles or persons. The principles on which these laws are founded, are directly applicable to the case before us; and although the laws may have a " considerable influence on commerce," or " operate directly on the subjects of commerce," they do not spring from that, but from a higher source, the pre-existing and undelegated power of a state, and are not an exercise of the power to regulate commerce among the states. That they are founded on the right of " self-protection" in each state; the right to guard against " moral or physical pestilence"—to " destroy," " remove," or " prevent the landing" of gunpowder and other dangerous articles; to exclude any thing which " might endanger the public safety;" to prevent the introduction not only of paupers and convicts, but that " *the principle* involved in it, must embrace *every description* which may be thought to *endanger the safety* and security of the country," or that may " threaten" a state " with more evils than gunpowder or disease," and to " all regulations of internal police." We find too, that under the power of a state to " *regulate pauperism therein*," is embraced the power to exclude paupers from other states; and upon the same principle the right of a state to *regulate slavery therein*, would include the right to exclude slaves from other states; and if the power to exclude exists, it carries the power to prescribe the terms of admission. And the principle of the law is the same in all these cases.

We have seen too, that the power of congress to regulate commerce does not extend to " persons;" and it has been shown, that slaves are so regarded and described in the constitution. But even if they were " the subjects of commerce," if their introduction " might endanger the public safety," the state has the power to exclude them. Thus, infected articles or vessels can be excluded, even where it is only apprehended that there may be danger. So also, to exclude gunpowder or similar articles, yet they are certainly articles of commerce; but the power of the state to guard the public safety being a higher power than that of the government to regulate commerce, all such state laws are of paramount authority, although they may have a " considerable influence on commerce."

Here, too, it is established, that inspection laws, where *no tax is imposed*, although they may act both on *importation* and *exportation*, are not an exception from the power of congress to regulate commerce, but rights pre-existing in every state, and not granted by the constitution.

Here, too, the principle which Chief Justice Marshall conceded in 4 Wheaton, 195, that it is a proper rule " to consider the power of the states as existing over such cases as the laws of the Union may not reach," is quoted and affirmed by Justice Baldwin. If, then, as at least one of our opponents admits, the power to prohibit this transportation and sale of slaves from state to state does not exist in congress, it must remain in the states. If not, it is annihilated, and the slave trade perpetuated by the constitution.

No matter in what fearful numbers, the slaves of very many states may be in the course of introduction from many into one of the slave-holding states by the slave traders; no matter how imminent the danger, there is no power any where to prevent it, unless indeed a state where the slaves preponderate, rushes upon her own destruction, and emancipates at once all the slaves within her limits. And was such the provision made in the constitution of the Union, and assented to by the slave-holding states? Did they consent to the alternative, you must at once emancipate all your slaves, or perpetuate the slave trade within your limits; you must either have no slaves, or all that may be introduced by traders   No one would have dared to make such a proposition in the convention which framed the constitution; no one of the slave-holding states would have assented to it; and had such a proposition been seriously entertained, it would have dissolved the convention. Indeed, such an idea is now for the first time announced; for I have called in vain for the production of a single suggestion to that effect, by any one preceding the argument of this case. It is a discovery made by our opponents, and is even more preposterous and humiliating, and no less dangerous to the South, than the power of absolute prohibition claimed by the abolitionists to be vested in congress. Indeed, that is the consequence of this very extraordinary position, for if congress can thus nullify the state law under the power to regulate commerce among the states, we have seen it settled on the very authority relied on by our opponents, that this power is " supreme and exclusive," as " full and plenary" as if vested in " a single government;" that it is a power to " prescribe the rules" by which commerce shall be conducted, the power to " limit and restrain" it, and to " embargo," which is *to prohibit.*

If we will look at the nature of the institution of slavery, we will see conclusive reasons against the extension of the commercial power to this subject. Slavery is a local institution, existing not by virtue of the law of nations, or of nature, or of the common law, but only by the authority of the municipal law of the state in which it exists. It is secured by the supreme, exclusive, pre-existing and undelegated power of each state, and not by the feeble tenure of any dependence upon the authority of congress.

In the case of Harvey v. Decker & Hopkins, Walker's Reports, 36, the supreme court of Mississippi declare, that slavery does not exist by " the laws of nature ;" and they add, " it exists *and can only exist through municipal regulations.*" The same court, in Jones' Case, Walker's Reports, 83, say : " In the constitution of the United States slaves are expressly designated as *persons;*" and they add, " the right of the master exists, *not by force of the law of nature or nations,* but by virtue *only* of the *positive law of the state.*" Such is the settled law of Mississippi twice unanimously pronounced by her supreme tribunal.

The same doctrine has been pronounced by the supreme court of all the states where the question has been determined. Thus, in the case of Lunsford v. Coquillon, 14 Martin's Reports, 404, the supreme court of Louisiana declare, " the relation of owner and slave in the states of this Union, in which it has a legal existence, *is a creature of the municipal law.*" See Law of Slavery, 368 ; Story's Conflicts of Laws, 92, 97.

The supreme court of Kentucky have declared, that " slavery is sanctioned by the laws of this state, but we consider that as a right existing by a positive law of a municipal character, without foundation in the law of nature." Rankin v. Lydia, 3d Marsh. 470, and this is an acknowledged doctrine of the common law. 2 B. & Cres. 448 ; 3 D. & Ry. 679 ; 20 State T. 1 ; 10 Wh. 120 ; Com. v. Aves, 19 Pick. Law of Slavery, 357, 363, 367, 368. This court have said, that " The *sovereignty* of a state extends to *every thing* which *exists by its own authority,* or is *introduced by its permission.*" 6 Wh. 469 ; 4 Peters, 564 ; Bald. Const. Views, 14. Slavery exists only by the authority of a state, it is introduced only by its permission ; and to contend that it may not be introduced, but may be extended against the will of a state, is strangely incongruous. The principle here quoted has been applied in restriction of the commercial power.

In 1824, it was attempted to apply the commercial power of congress to the New York Canals, in relation to boats passing through them, or entering them from state to state, by requiring tonnage duties and entrance fees. That this power could have extended to voyages commencing in one state, and touching at, or terminating in another, is decided by this court; but it does not extend to canals created by the state authority. New York Leg. Res. 8th Nov. 1824 ; Debate U. S. Senate, 19th May, 1826 ; 3 Cowen, 755. Now, the only reason for this distinction is, that canals are, and rivers are not created by a state ; otherwise the power to regulate commerce, which embraces navigation as well as traffic, must have included them. Now, this power is " supreme and exclusive," and if it extends to slaves, made so only by state authority, it must embrace all the canals, and perhaps all the rail-roads of every state. Property in slaves, so far as it exists, is created, not by the law of nature or of nations, but solely by the power of the state, and may be abolished at its will ; differing in these essential particulars from other property. So as was said as to other property created by the authority of a state, in state or bank stocks, or bank notes, or lottery tickets. It is a principle recognised in all the states, and by this court, that their introduction from other states, for sale or circulation, may be prohibited by any state, notwithstanding she may have state or bank stocks, or bank notes, or lotteries of her own, and these may be the subjects of lawful ownership and commerce in the state.

This power being claimed under the authority of congress to regulate commerce, the first congress which assembled in 1789, as well as every subsequent congress, would have possessed plenary, supreme and exclusive power over the whole subject of regulating the transportation of slaves from state to state. Why, then, during the lapse of more than half a century, has congress never exercised this power, which was an exclusive and not a concurrent power? Many of the great men who formed the constitution, were members of congress for many years succeeding its adoption. Why, then, did they never exercise, or even propose to exercise the power in question? They were called upon by petitions, immediately after the organization of the government, to exercise, both as among the states and as to foreign nations, the entire power which they possessed on this subject. Why did they not then exercise this power? Because, it was then universally acknowledged that congress possessed no such power.

In 1794, petitions were again transmitted by the Quakers and others to congress, calling on that body to exercise all its constitutional powers over the subject; and these memorials were referred to a committee of the house, consisting of Mr. Trumbull, Mr. Ward, Mr. Giles, Mr. Talbot, and Mr. Groves, all members from non-slave-holding states, except Mr. Giles, of Virginia; the select committee, according to parliamentary rule, being favourable to the object of the memorialists to the extent of the powers vested in congress. This committee, thus composed, clearly repudiated the power now claimed by our opponents, but brought in an act " to prohibit the carrying on the slave trade from the United States to any foreign place or country," which act became a law on the 22d March, 1794. 2d Vol. Laws United States, 383.

These proceedings, corroborated by Mr. Giles's statement as a member of the committee, ought to be conclusive. In the debates of the Virginia convention of 1829, 1830, page 246, we find Mr. Giles using the following language on the 10th Nov. 1829 : " Mr. Giles then referred to a memorial, which was presented to congress by the representatives of several societies of Quakers. He happened to be a member of the committee to whom the subject was referred. He had relied on the declaratory resolution, in the negotiation which he had to carry on with the Quakers. *All the committee were, in principle, in favour of the measure;* but it was his duty to satisfy these persons, that congress had no right to interfere with the subject of slavery at all. He was fortunate enough to satisfy the Quakers, and they agreed, that if congress would pass a law, to prohibit the citizens of the United States from supplying foreign nations with slaves, they would pledge themselves, and the respective societies they represented, never again to trouble congress on the subject. The law did pass, and the Quakers adhered to their agreement. He did not know whether or not the documents, on the subject of this negotiation, were still in existence; but he believed they had been filed away with other papers.

" Subsequently, an act was passed prohibiting the introduction of slaves into the United States, in which this principle was again touched in a more specific, but a different form. It was again his fortune to be on the committee to whom that subject was referred, and he drew up two provisoes to a bill then pending before congress, for prohibiting the introduction of slaves into the United States after the year 1807 ; the object of which was to draw a distinct line of demarcation between the powers of congress, for prohibiting the introduction of slaves into the *United States,* and those of the *individual states* and territories. It was then decided, by an *unanimous vote,* that when slaves *were brought within the limits of any state,* the power of congress *over them ceased,* and the power of the *state began the moment* they became within those limits." Here is the clearest testimony on the subject, that as to the slaves "*brought within the limits* of any state," congress had no power whatever; and that such was the "unanimous" opinion of the House of Representatives in 1794 and 1807.

The act of the 10th of May, 1800, 3 L. U. S. 382, prohibits citizens or residents

G

of the United States from owning or serving in vessels engaged in the foreign slave trade, forbidden by the act of 1794. The act of 28th February, 1803, 3 L. U. S. 529, prohibits the bringing of any negroes, mulattoes, or other persons of colour, not being natives, citizens, or registered seamen of the United States, into any state where the laws of the state prohibited such importation. This act extended to free negroes as well as slaves, and was a practical construction of the 1st clause of the 9th section of the 1st article of the constitution, applying that clause to such states as did not " think proper to admit" the persons prohibited by that act, the term " migration" being applied to free negroes, and " importation" to slaves. Then came the act of 2d March, 1807, 4th L. U. S. 94, (to go into effect on the 1st of January, 1808, the time designated in the 9th section of the 1st article of the constitution,) which prohibits the introduction from abroad into the United States of slaves under various penalties. The act of 20th April, 1818, 6th L. U. S. 325, enforces the last act chiefly by devolving the proof on the party accused, that the coloured persons had not been brought in, in contradiction of that law. The act of 3d March, 1819, 6th L. U. S. 433, authorizes the employment of the armed vessels of the United States in enforcing the previous acts. The act of 15th May, 1820, 6th L. U. S. 529, makes the foreign slave trade, before prohibited, *piracy*, and inflicts upon all concerned in it the punishment of *death ;* and no less than nineteen various laws, enforcing or providing money to enforce this act, have been since passed by congress down to the present period. No less than thirty laws have been passed by congress on the subject of the slave trade, and no less than fifty reports made in the two houses of congress from 1791 to the present period ; yet no one act embraces the slave trade between the states, except such as acknowledge the binding force of state laws, and require conformity on the part of vessels of the United States and their owners to those laws, (as they do to the health laws of the states;) nor in any one of these numerous reports was it ever pretended, that congress possessed the power now claimed by our opponents, but in all these acts or reports, it is either repudiated directly, or by implication. And if congress did not act in 1791, or 1794, or 1803, on this subject, why not in 1807—8, or in 1818, 1819, 1820, or on the numerous occasions upon which they have since legislated on this subject? Not only why did they not act by the passage of laws regulating or prohibiting this slave trade between the states, but why no proposal by any member of congress to act, and this universal concession that the power was not vested in the general government? Such has been the negative action of congress in regard to a power which is claimed to be vested exclusively in the general government. But not only has congress declined the exercise of this power, now claimed to be vested exclusively in the government of the United States, but congress has repeatedly recognised the existence of this power as vested in the states alone.

On the 19th April, 1792, the constitution of the state of Kentucky was formed. On the 6th November, 1792, Gen. Washington, then President of the United States, delivered his annual address to the two houses of congress, in which he said : " The adoption of a constitution for the state of Kentucky has been notified to me. The legislature will share with me in the satisfaction which arises from an event interesting to the happiness of the part of the nation to which it relates, and conducive to the general order." And on the succeeding day he transmitted to the two houses of congress in a special message, " a copy of the constitution formed for the state of Kentucky."

On the 9th of November, 1792, the senate of the United States responded to the address of the President, in which they say, " The organization of the government of the state of Kentucky, being an event peculiarly interesting to a part of our fellow citizens, and conducive to the general order, affords us peculiar satisfaction." On the 10th of November, 1792, the house of representatives responded through a committee, of which Mr. Madison was chairman, to the address of the President, in which they say, " The adoption of a constitution for the state of Kentucky, is an event on which we join in all the satisfaction you have expressed. It may be considered as particularly interesting, since, besides the immediate benefits resulting from it, it is another auspicious demonstration of the facility and success, with which an enlightened people is capable of providing, by free and deliberate plans of government, for their own safety and happiness."

Such were the solemn forms and sanctions under which this constitution of the state of Kentucky, the first of the new states, was then received by the President and two houses of congress, and the two members subsequently admitted under it as representatives of the state. Now this very constitution contains provisions as to slaves precisely similar to those embodied in the constitution of Mississippi, and among others, after prohibiting emancipation of slaves by the legislature, they say, "they (the legislature) *shall have full power* to prevent slaves from being brought into this state as merchandise." 1 Littell's Laws of Kentucky, 52. Here is this constitution, with this clause, thus solemnly sanctioned at that early period, almost cotemporaneous with the organization of the government, by George Washington, the President of the convention which formed the constitution of the Union, and by John Langdon and Nicholas Gilman, of New Hampshire; Rufus King and Elbridge Gerry, of Massachusetts; Roger Sherman and Oliver Ellsworth, of Connecticut; Jonathan Dayton, of New Jersey; Robert Morris and Thomas Fitzsimmons, of Pennsylvania; George Read, John Dickinson and Richard Bassett, of Delaware; James Madison, of Virginia; Hugh Williamson, of North Carolina; Pierce Butler, of South Carolina; William Few and Abraham Baldwin, of Georgia; *all* members of the congress which received and sanctioned this constitution of Kentucky, and *all* members of the convention which framed the constitution of the Union; thus constituting, in *that congress,* a representation from *ten* of the *twelve* states which formed the constitution. And yet this constitution, thus received and sanctioned, contains a clause directly repugnant to the constitution of the United States, and authorizes that state to violate that instrument, by an authority, as maintained by our opponents, to exercise that commercial power as to slaves, which was vested exclusively in congress, and prohibited to the states. But no one entertained that opinion in 1792, when ten of the twelve states which formed the constitution of the Union were represented in congress. Suppose, in lieu of this clause to prohibit the introduction of slaves as merchandise, the constitution of Kentucky had contained a delegation of power to the legislature of that state, to "regulate commerce between that state and all other states," or "to coin money," or to "declare war," or to exercise any other power vested exclusively in congress; who believes that such a constitution could ever have received the sanction of Gen. Washington, Mr. Madison, James Monroe, and all the other great men of the congress of 1792, or that the state could ever have been admitted, prepared and organized, to subvert the constitution of the Union, by that very executive and congress which was solemnly sworn to preserve and maintain that instrument? And yet, by the argument of our opponents, this very constitution of Kentucky, in this clause as to slaves, contains a delegation to the state of the power vested exclusively in congress to regulate commerce among the states. To every unprejudiced mind this authority ought to be conclusive.

On the 1st March, 1817, an act of congress was passed to enable the people of the western part of the territory of Mississippi "to form a constitution and state government." 6 L. U. S. 175. By which act it was required, as a condition precedent of admission, that this constitution should not be "*repugnant*" to the "*constitution of the United States.*" On the 4th December, 1817, this constitution was *submitted to both houses of congress*—Sen. J. 21; House J. 21; and on the 10th December, 1817, this constitution being declared to be in "pursuance" of the act before quoted, was admitted not to be repugnant to the constitution of the United States, and the state received as a member of the Union; yet, this very constitution contained the clause, that "they (the legislature) shall have full power to prevent slaves from being brought into this state as merchandise." Here, then, the very power under which Mississippi now acts, was thus deliberately conceded by congress not to be "repugnant to the constitution of the United States."

On the 26th August, 1818, the constitution of the state of Illinois was formed, and although slaves and slavery were by the 6th article prohibited to be "hereafter introduced into the state"—yet the slaves already there were not emancipated, although it was provided, that their "children hereafter born shall be free," and the introduction of slaves from any other state, even "to be hired," was prohibited. By the official census of 1820, 907 slaves were enumerated and returned from the state of Illinois, and in 1840, 184 slaves are enumerated and returned from the same state. Illinois, then, under her constitution of 1818, was to a limited extent, a slave-holding state; the slaves already there not being emancipated, but the future importation being prohibited, and the post nati being liberated.

This subject is thus referred to in a speech delivered by the Hon. Henry Baldwin, then a representative in congress from the Pittsburg district of Pennsylvania, and now one of the judges of this court. In that speech, Judge Baldwin said: "When the constitution of Illinois was presented to us, it was found, not to conform to the ordinance of 1787, in the exclusion and abolition of slavery; on comparing their provisions, they were inconsistent: the gentleman from New York, who moved this amendment last year, objected to the admission of Illinois on this account; there was a short but an animated discussion; it was contended, that the ordinance did not extend *to states*, and was not binding on them, *and so this house decided by a majority* of 117 to 34 (54 from the non-slave-holding states). In the senate, there *was no objection*. Illinois was admitted; she and Indiana now have slaves, *and always have had them.* Here is a precedent in point, and I hope will not be without its weight in the body which made it, at least with those members whose names are recorded in the journal." Niles' Reg. vol. 19, page 30. In 1818, as well as at this moment, the prohibition of the introduction of slaves for sale, is void in that state, if it be void in Mississippi; for the validity of the prohibition as a question of power, surely cannot depend upon the number of slaves in a state.

On the 2d March, 1819, an act passed to enable the people of the territory of Alabama to form a constitution and state government, 6th L. U. S. 380. By this act, one of the conditions precedent, on which this constitution was authorized to be formed, was, that it should not be "repugnant" to the "constitution of the United States." On the 7th Dec. 1819, a copy of this constitution was submitted to the house, and referred to a select committee, H. J. 8; and on the 6th Dec. 1819, it was also presented to the senate of the Union, and referred to a select committee, S. J. 6; and by a joint resolution of both houses of congress, of the 14th Dec. 1819, the constitution of Alabama, being conceded to be "in pursuance" of the act before quoted, and of course "not repugnant to the constitution of the United States," Alabama was admitted as a member of the Union. Yet the constitution of that state contains the clause, that "they (the legislature) shall have full power to prevent slaves from being brought into the state as merchandise." And here again the constitutionality of this provision was distinctly admitted by the congress of the United States.

In the case of Missouri, the question was decided in our favour, after a severe conflict. But let it not be supposed, that all who opposed the admission of Missouri as a state of the Union, did it upon the ground, that as a slave-holding state, she could not prohibit the introduction of slaves as merchandise; for the number who maintained any such doctrine, did not exceed half a dozen members, at any period of this discussion, and it was eventually abandoned, and the objection was, 1st to admit Missouri as a slave-holding state at all, and 2d to that clause of the constitution, which prevented "free negroes, and mulattoes, from coming to, and settling in this state, under any pretext whatsoever." As to the first, it was contended that the authority to admit new states into the Union, was a discretionary power vested in congress; and that in the exercise of a sound discretion, congress might make it a condition of admission, that slavery should be abolished. As to the 2d point, it was urged that the power to exclude free blacks, some of whom might be citizens and voters in the several states, conflicted with that provision of the constitution of the Union, in the first clause of the 2d section of the 4th article, which declared, that "the citizens of each state shall have the same privileges and immunities as citizens in the several states." The first question was decided in favour of Missouri, by the congress of 1819, 1820, and the second question was not then decided.

By the act of congress of the 6th March, 1820, the people of the Missouri territory were authorized to "form a constitution and state government," 6th vol. L. U. S., 455. By this act slavery was to be prohibited in the territory ceded by France, under the name of Louisiana, north of lat. 36° 30', not included in the state of Missouri. By this act the people of the Missouri territory were authorized to form "a constitution and state government. *Provided*, that the same when formed shall be republican, and *not repugnant to the constitution of the United States*," and the 7th section of this act was as follows: "That in case a constitution and state government shall be formed for the people of the said territory of Missouri, the said convention or representatives, as soon thereafter as may be, shall cause a true and attested copy of such constitution, or frame of state government, as shall be adopted or provided, to be transmitted to congress." This constitution, "in pursuance of this act," was formed on the 19th of July, 1820, and contained the following, among other provisions:—

26. The general assembly shall not have power to pass laws:—

1st. For the emancipation of slaves, without the consent of their owners:— They shall have power to pass laws:—

"To prohibit the introduction of any slave for the purpose of speculation, or as an article of trade or merchandise."

It shall be their duty, as soon as may be, to pass such laws as may be necessary.

1. To prevent free negroes and mulattoes from coming to, and settling in this state, under any pretext whatever: and

The constitution thus formed, was submitted to both houses of congress, and referred, in Nov. 1820, to special committees, who reported in its favour, and that it was *not repugnant to the constitution of the United States*. And now, then, it is believed not a single member upon the discussion which had taken place, did suppose that this clause prohibiting the introduction of slaves as merchandise, was unconstitutional, but it was contended by many, that the 4th clause of the 26th section of the 3d article, preventing "free negroes" coming into the state, was repugnant to the 1st clause of the 2d section of the 4th article of the constitution of the Union before quoted, as to the reciprocal rights of citizens in all the states, it being contended that free negroes were citizens in some of the states. The great difficulty then arising out of this clause, the whole question on the 2d February, 1821, was on motion of Mr. Clay, of Kentucky, referred to a select committee of thirteen, of which he was chairman, but eight of whom were from non-slave-holding states. On the 10th of February, Mr. Clay reported from this committee, declaring that they had "limited their inquiry to the single question, whether the constitution which Missouri had formed for herself, contained any thing in it, which furnished a valid objection to her incorporation in the Union. And on that question they thought that there was *no other provision* in that constitution, to which congress could of right take exception, but that which makes it the duty of the legislature of Missouri to pass laws to prevent free negroes and mulattoes from going to, and settling in the said state." After stating, that part of the committee believed this clause "liable to an interpretation repugnant to the constitution of the United States, and the other thinking it not exposed to that objection," they proposed that Missouri should be admitted, on her passing a law exempting this clause from any supposed interpretation, which would prevent citizens of any of the states from settling in Missouri. On the 2d March, 1821, congress passed a joint resolution, providing for the admission of the state of Missouri into the Union "upon the fundamental condition, that the 4th clause of the 26th section of the 3d article of the constitution, submitted on the part of said state to congress, shall never be construed to authorize the passing of any law, and that no law shall be passed in conformity thereto, by which any citizens of either of the states in this Union, shall be excluded from the enjoyment of any of the privileges and immunities, to which such citizen is entitled under the constitution of the United States," 6 vol. L. U. S. 390. The assent of Missouri was required to this condition, which being afterwards given, the state was admitted into the Union.

Now the power to prohibit the introduction of slaves as merchandise, was just as clearly granted in the constitution of Missouri, as the power to prevent the ingress

G 2

of free negroes or mulattoes. It had been expressly provided by congress, that the constitution of Missouri should not be repugnant to the constitution of the United States. That constitution was discussed in three committees, and in the two houses of congress for more than three months, and the whole subject, from 1818, till 1821, and after this full discussion, with an ardent desire on the part of a portion of congress, approaching an actual majority, to exclude Missouri, if any clause in her constitution should be found repugnant to the constitution of the United States, this clause as to the introduction of slaves as merchandise, was distinctly, and it may be truly said, almost unanimously conceded to be constitutional, and the only proviso required by congress from the state, was in relation to the clause in regard to free negroes. Surely this ought to be conclusive, so far as the authority of the almost unanimous voice of congress, on full deliberation, can go to settle any question. Amongst those who stand most conspicuously committed on the record, in favour of the validity of this clause in the constitution of Missouri, is Mr. Clay, of Kentucky, now one of my distinguished opponents in this case, for whose opinion as a statesman and a jurist, as then recorded, I ask from this court all the consideration to which it is so justly entitled. Of all the members of that congress, which admitted Missouri as a state of the Union, no one contributed more to that result, than the Hon. Henry Baldwin, now one of the judges of this court, and then the representative from the district of Pittsburg, Pennsylvania. And here I trust that I may be indulged in stating that I was one of his constituents at that period, and as he well recollects, one of the most ardent and active of the supporters of his course on this great question. At first, public sentiment seemed to be almost overwhelmingly against him in his district; the Legislature of Pennsylvania had passed unanimous resolutions against the admission of Missouri as a slave-holding state, and but one member of congress from the state, had then dared to follow his bold and daring lead upon this subject, and that member was driven for a long time most unjustly into disgrace among his constituents. He was burnt in effigy, and it is said, barely escaped from violence? Well do I recollect that momentous crisis, and the obloquy to which Mr. Baldwin was doomed for a time at that period. But he stood on the rock of the constitution; he stood unmoved by the surges of popular commotion; he was a leader who fought in the advanced guard of that great conflict, and although for a time he seemed like Curtius taking the fatal leap for the salvation of his country, he was saved by the returning justice and intelligence of a magnanimous people, triumphantly re-elected to congress, and elevated to higher and higher honours. The constitution of the state of Missouri, which by his vote he thus declared not to be repugnant to the constitution of the United States, contained this very clause for the prohibition of the introduction of slaves as merchandise, and I claim the full influence of his vote under these imposing circumstances.

On the 30th January, 1836, the people of the territory of Arkansas formed a constitution which contained the following clause: "They (the legislature) shall have power to prevent slaves from being brought to this state as merchandise." On the 10th March, 1836, this constitution was "submitted to the consideration of congress," in a special message by the President. Senate Journal, 210. On motion of Mr. Buchanan, of Pennsylvania, in the senate, on the same day, it was referred to a select committee. On the 22d March, 1836, Mr. Buchanan, as chairman from the select committee, reported a bill for the admission of Arkansas as a state, under the constitution submitted by the President, and after considerable debate, the bill passed the senate by a vote of 31 to 6, fifteen of the ayes being from non-slave-holding states and from both political parties, and four of the noes being from non-slave-holding states; namely, Messrs. Knight, Prentiss, Robbins, Swift, and two from slave-holding states, namely, Messrs. Clay and Porter, both of whom placed their negative on this ground alone, that Arkansas had formed her constitution without asking, as was usual, the previous assent of congress. Having participated in that debate, and taken a deep interest as a senator from Mississippi, in the admission of Arkansas, and successfully opposed an adjournment till the bill was engrossed, I recollect well all the proceedings, and that but a single senator based his objection on the ground of the particular clause in question, as to slaves. Such, then, was the view of the senate as to the constitution of Arkansas; and that they felt constrained to oppose any clause in the constitution of a state, which they deemed repugnant to the constitution of the Union, is clearly proved by a reference to the proceedings and debates on the confirmation by the senate, at the same time, of the constitution of Michigan. On the 1st April, 1836, when the adoption of the constitution of Michigan, and the bill for the admission of that state (as well as of Arkansas,) was pending before the senate, the following proceedings will be found at page 259. "The motion by Mr. Clay, to amend the bill, by inserting 2 line 4 after "confirmed," except that provision of the said constitution, by which aliens are admitted to the right of suffrage," yeas 14, nays 22; a reference to these proceedings and debates will show that the senate considered it its duty not to confirm any clause of the constitution of a state, repugnant to the constitution of the United States, but to strike out such clause before the admission of the state; and the clause in question as I well recollect, and as the printed debates will show, was not stricken out, because, after a very prolonged argument, it was not considered repugnant to the constitution of the United States, the question as to the qualification of voters in a state being decided to be a matter exclusively belonging to the states. Arkansas was admitted at the same time with Michigan, and under this view of the subject, why was not the clause in question as to slaves stricken out? For the most obvious of all reasons, because but a single senator considered it repugnant to the constitution of the United States. Such were the proceedings in the senate; and in the house, the constitution of Arkansas was submitted, and she was admitted as a state, on the 13th June, 1836, by a vote of 143 to 50, (House Journal, 1003,) several of the members from the slave-holding states voting in the negative, on the same ground as that assumed in the senate. Nor was the matter passed by in silence, for whilst this bill was pending, Mr. Adams moved to strike out from the bill, that portion of it in regard to slaves and slavery, (page 997,) but it was not seconded; and the constitution of Arkansas was confirmed and accepted with this clause included.

Here, then, in 1792, 1817, 1818, 1819, 1821, and 1836, are six states whose constitutions were expressly regarded by congress, to be conformable to the constitution of the United States, admitted at all these periods with clauses in all of them, as to the exclusion of slaves as merchandise, precisely similar to that now under consideration. One of these was the state of Mississippi, whose right thus to prohibit the introduction of slaves as merchandise, was in the act of admission and confirmation of her constitution, expressly conceded by congress.

Such has been the uninterrupted, positive, as well as negative action of congress on this subject for half a century, from the organization of the government to the present period, repudiating their own power, and admitting again and again the possession of this power by the states, and by the slave-holding states proper, as well as in the case of Illinois, where slavery existed when it became a state, and still exists, but is disappearing on the death of the slaves now living. Now, let it never be forgotten, that the case upon which our opponents rely, establishes the doctrine, that this power to regulate commerce, is not a concurrent power, but one vested exclusively in congress; and therefore, to show that the clause in question embraces an authority that can constitutionally be exercised by a state, demonstrates that congress has no power over the subject.

Having examined the action of congress on this question, let us now investigate that of the states. We have before referred to the clause in the original constitution of the state of Kentucky, authorizing the legislature to prohibit the introduction of slaves as merchandise. At the November session, 1794, the legislature of Kentucky passed a law, declaring, "That no slave or slaves shall be imported into this state as merchandise." This act inflicted a penalty of $300 for each slave so illegally imported, but did *not emancipate the slave;* and it permitted emigrants and citizens to bring in slaves for their own use. The act then was almost precisely similar to the provisions in Mississippi. 1 Lit. Laws Kentucky, 216. By the amended constitution of the state of Kentucky, adopted August 17th, 1799, the clause authorizing the legislature to prohibit the introduction of slaves as merchandise, is retained and adopted. Con. 237. By the act of Feb. 8th, 1815, 5 Lit.

Laws Ky. 293, a penalty is inflicted on the importation of slaves as merchandise, but the slave is not emancipated. The act of 12th Feb. 1833, 2d vol. Stat. of Ky. 1482, continues the restriction as to importation for sale, and introduces further restrictions with special exceptions as to emigrants, but the slave is not emancipated. During this very session of the legislature of Kentucky, in 1840 and 1841, an attempt was made to repeal this act and failed. These laws have been invariably enforced by all the judicial tribunals in Kentucky. I will refer only to a few decisions. Commonwealth v. Griffin, Oct. 7, 1832, 7 J. J. Marshall's Rep. 588 ; Lane v. Greathouse, Ib. 590. It was decided in these cases that either the importation or sale of slaves introduced for sale, was an indictable offence. See further, 5 Marsh. 481 ; 1 Bibb, 615 ; Barrington v. Logan, Fall Term, 1834 ; 2 Dana, 432.

In Virginia there are numerous laws before and since the adoption of the constitution, prohibiting the introduction of slaves from other states, except under special exception, one of which was an *oath that the owner did not introduce them for sale*. Act of 1778, preventing further importation of slaves, chap. 1, Cha. Rev. p. 80 ; act of 1785, chap. 77, p. 60 ; act of 1788, chap. 53, p. 24 ; act of 1789, chap. 45, p. 26 ; act of 1790, p. 7, chap. 11 ; act 17th Dec. 1792 ; Pleas. & Pace, 1 Rev. Code, 186, sec. 13, 1794, 1800, 1803, 1814, 1805, 1810, 1812, 1816, 1819 ; see 1 vol. Rev. Code Va. 421, and notes. Generally, by these laws, the slaves introduced against their provisions were declared free, and these laws have been uniformly enforced by all the courts of Virginia, by the highly respectable court for the District of Columbia, and by the Supreme Court of the United States. 1 Leigh. 172 ; Gil. 143 ; 2 Munf. 393 ; 2 Marsh. 467 ; Law of Slavery, 329 ; 5 Call, 425 ; 6 Randolph, 612 ; 3 Cranch, 324. and note, 326 ; 8 Peters, 44. The acts of Virginia of 1788, 1789, 1790, and 1792, cotemporaneous with and shortly after the adoption of the constitution, and passed by some of the very men who had either been in the convention which formed the constitution of the United States, or in that of Virginia, which ratified it, are entitled to high respect.

Tennessee, it is understood, took with her, on the separation from North Carolina, laws of that state, restricting the introduction of slaves for sale, and on the 21st October, 1812, that state passed a law prohibiting the introduction of slaves as merchandise ; but permitting emigrants or citizens to bring in their own slaves for their own use. The penalty for the violation of the law was the seizure for the state of the slaves illegally introduced, and sale to the highest bidder. 2 Scott's Laws of Tennessee, 101.

In 1798, the legislature of Georgia passed a law, forbidding the importation of slaves from any other state into Georgia, except by persons removing into the state, or citizens who became owners of slaves in other states by last will or otherwise. Marbury & Crawford's Digest of Laws of Georgia, page 440 ; and see also, act to same effect, Dec. 1793, cited Prince's Digest Laws of Georgia, page 455. By act of 1817, Prince's Digest, 373, the importation of slaves from any state for sale in Georgia was made a high misdemeanor, and punished with imprisonment for three years in the penitentiary.

By act 3d February, 1789, S. & J. Adams' Laws of Del. p. 942, not only the importation of slaves into that state, but their exportation from Delaware to other states without license from five justices, was prohibited under a severe penalty. This act is referred to and confirmed by act June 24th, 1793, c. 22, p. 10, 94 ; June 14th, 1793, c. 20, and by act January 18th, 1797, L. Del. 13, 21. To forbid by a state law the exportation of slaves, if they be articles of merchandise under the commercial power, is still more clearly to violate the constitution, than to prohibit their importation ; yet such laws have been passed and enforced by Delaware and many other states.

By the act of Pennsylvania, of the 29th March, 1788, and the act of 1st March, 1780, explained and amended by the last act, all negroes born after the passage of the act were to be free ; but the slaves then born and living in the state were continued in slavery, and to be registered. No slaves could be introduced for sale or exported for sale, and all who were brought in, except by sojourners for six months, and members of congress for temporary residence during the session of congress, were declared free. Purdon's Dig. 595, 597; 1 Dal. L. 838; 1 Smith, 692; 2 Dal. L. 586; 2 Smith, 443. At an early period the question of the existence of slavery in Pennsylvania was considered, and that slaves were property there, was unanimously pronounced, after the most elaborate arguments by the highest judicial tribunals of that state. In January, 1795, a suit for freedom under the operation of the general provisions of the constitution of Pennsylvania, was instituted, in the case of Negro Flora v. Greensberry. On the 15th December, 1797, a special verdict was found, and at the March term, 1798, the case was sent to the supreme court, and by them decided, that slaves were property in Pennsylvania. It was then taken to the high court of errors and appeals of that state, and after four days argument, it was announced by the court "that it was their unanimous opinion, slavery was not inconsistent with any clause in the constitution of Pennsylvania," and conformably to this opinion the entry of record is, "the court is *unanimously* of opinion, that Negro Flora is a *slave*, and that she is the *property* of defendant in error, and the judgment of the supreme court is affirmed."

Pennsylvania, we have seen, had slaves in 1780, and in 1788, and in 1790, when the laws of 1780 and 1788, were continued in force by her constitution, and she still has slaves, recognised as such in the state, and returned under the present and every preceding census, and as to these slaves, they are as much the property of their owners, and the subject of sale within the state, as the slaves of Mississippi. On this subject, we have not only the decision of their highest tribunal before quoted, but an uninterrupted series of decisions to the same effect from the earliest date down to the present period. I will now cite a decision of the circuit court of the United States for the Eastern District of Pennsylvania, at April term, 1835. Judges Hopkinson (and Baldwin of the supreme court of the United States) presiding. The case is reported in 1st Bald. Rep. p. 571. At page 589, Judge Baldwin, in delivering the opinion of the court, says : " While the abolition act put free blacks on the footing of free white men, and abolished slavery for life, as to those *thereafter born*, it did not otherwise interfere with those born before, or slaves excepted from the operation of the law ; they were *then*, and *yet are*, considered as *property;* slavery yet exists in Pennsylvania, and the rights of the owners are now the same as before the abolition act ; though their *number is small*, their *condition is unchanged*." Now, we have seen that Pennsylvania prohibited both the importation and exportation of slaves for sale; and her supreme tribunals, as well as the circuit court of the United States, have uniformly maintained and enforced these laws, yet upon the position assumed by our opponents, they are null and void, and slaves can be both exported from Pennsylvania for sale into other states, and introduced from other states into Pennsylvania for sale, and the sale is valid ; and the purchasers may hold property in any number of slaves thus introduced and sold.

See the following decisions of the highest judicial tribunals of Pennsylvania, affirming the existence of slavery there, and the validity of the laws forbidding the exportation of slaves for sale in Pennsylvania, and their importation from other states into Pennsylvania for sale. 4 S. & R. 218, 425 : 4 Yates, 115, 109, 240 ; 1 Dal. 167, 475, 469 ; 2 Yates, 234, 449; Addison, 284 ; 7 S. & R. 386, 378; 3 S. & R. 4, 5, 6, 396 ; 6 Bin. 213, 204, 297 ; 1 Wash. C. C. R. 499 ; 1 Bro. 113 ; 5 S. & R. 62, 333 ; 2 S. & R. 305 ; 1 Yates, 365, 368, 235, 220, 480 ; 4 Bin. 186 ; 1 S. & R. 23 ; 3 Bin. 301 ; 2 Dal. 224, 227 ; 4 Dal. 258, 260 ; 4 Wash. C. C. R. 396 ; 1 Watts, 155.

I will call attention but to one of these cases decided in 1806, by the circuit court of the United States for the Pennsylvania district, by Judge Peters, of the district court, and Judge Washington, one of the Judges of the supreme court of the United States, both experienced and eminent jurists, and both familiar with the proceedings of the convention which formed the constitution of the United States, and both distinguished cotemporaries with, and associates of its framers. This was the case of a suit for freedom by a slave imported from South Carolina into Pennsylvania in 1794, contrary to the prohibitory act of that state. The facts were embraced in a special verdict, and time taken for the court to deliberate, when the decision was pronounced by Judge Washington, as follows : " To dispose at once of an objection to the validity of this law, which was slightly glanced at, I observe, that the 9th section of the 1st article of the constitution of the United States, which restrains congress from prohibiting the importation of slaves prior to the year 1808, does not, in its words or meaning, apply to the state governments. Neither does the 2d section of the 4th article ; which declares, that ' no person, held to labour or service in one state under the laws thereof, escaping into another, shall, in consequence of any law therein, be discharged from such service ;' extend to the case of a slave _voluntarily carried_ by his master into another state, and there leaving him under the protection of some law declaring him free. The exercise of this right, of _restraining the importation of slaves from the other states_, under different limitations, is not peculiar to Pennsylvania. Laws of this nature, but less rigid, exist in most of the states where slavery is tolerated." 1 Wash. C. C. R. 560, 561. Although the constitutional objection to the prohibitory law of Pennsylvania was but slightly glanced at in the _argument_, it seems to have been maturely considered by the court, and the very question decided, that the law was constitutional, and that the clause in the constitution of the United States, restraining congress until 1808 from prohibiting the introduction of slaves, " does not in its words or meaning _apply to the state governments ;_" when we recollect that this was the case of a slave imported from one state into another, the importance of the above decision becomes obvious, and especially as the court recognises in the same decision the constitutionality of the laws of other states, and of the _states where slavery is tolerated_, restraining the importation of slaves from other states, and this very case, and the doctrine contained in it, were solemnly reaffirmed by the same court, in the case ex parte Simmons, 4 Wash. C. C. R. 396, and applied to the case of a slave introduced from South Carolina into Pennsylvania _in the year_ 1822.

In Maryland, by acts of 1796, variously modified in 1797, 1798, 1802, 1804, 1805, 1806, 1807, 1809, 1812, 1819, 1820, 1821, 1822, 1823, 1824, 1828, 1831, 1832, 1833, 1834, 1836, 1837, (see 1 Dorsey's Laws of Maryland, page 334, &c.) the importation of slaves for sale into Maryland was prohibited ; and in most of the laws, the slaves so imported were declared free, and importation, except by emigrants, though not for sale, was generally prohibited. These laws have been invariably enforced by repeated decisions of the judicial tribunals of that state, as well as of the adjacent states, and by _the Supreme Court of the United States._ 5 Har. & John. 86, 99, 107, and note ; Law of Slavery, 381, 382, 388, 389 ; 5 Rand. 126 ; 4 Har. & M'Ilen. 418 ; 4 Har. & John. 282 ; 3 Har. & John. 564 ; 6 Cranch, 1 ; 1 Wheaton, 1 ; 8 Peters, 44.

In New York, slavery existed to the same extent, as regards the rights of the master, as in most of the slave-holding states proper, until very recently. By the colony laws of New York, prior to the revolution, slavery was as firmly established in that state as in any of the Southern states, and the importation of slaves into New York _encouraged by law._ See acts of 1730 and 1740, et al.; 1 Colony Laws, 72, 193, 199, 283, 284.

The act of 20th March, 1781, c. 32, 56, recognised slavery as in full force in New York, as also did the act of 1st May, 1786, c. 58, sec. 29, 30. The act of the 22d of February, 1788, c. 40, enacted cotemporaneously with the adoption of the constitution of the United States, recognised and continued the existence of slavery in New York, but prohibited the importation of slaves _for sale_, and the act was continued by subsequent laws. 1 Revised Stats. 656 ; K. & R. 1 ; R. L. 614, cited 14 John. 269.

By the act of 4th July, 1799, c. 62, slaves born in the state after that date were declared free at 28 years of age, but all others were continued as slaves. By act 30th March, 1810, the importation of slaves, except by the owner for nine months residence, was prohibited ; and most of the former laws were incorporated into the act of 9th April, 1813 ; and finally, on the 4th of July, 1827, slavery was in fact abolished ; except, perhaps, as to the very few slaves born before 4th July, 1799, and subsequently lawfully introduced as slaves.

By the official census by the United States, of the population of New York, the following slaves were returned from that state. In 1790, 21,324 slaves; in 1800, 20,613 slaves; in 1810, 15,017 slaves; in 1820, 10,088 slaves; in 1830, 76 slaves; in 1840, 3 slaves. Let it be remembered also, that, by the constitution of New York, the statutes of that state, enacted by the legislature, received the sanction of a council of revision before they became laws, which council consisted of the governor, the chancellor, and judges of the supreme court. Con. 181. These laws, forbidding the importation of slaves for sale, received a judicial sanction before their enactment; and let it be remembered, that many of them passed with the sanction of many of the distinguished statesmen of New York, who had participated either in the convention which formed, or which ratified the constitution of the United States. Whilst, by the act of 1788, and other laws of a subsequent date, slaves subsequently imported into the state could not be sold by the *master* or *owner*; yet, *even these slaves* were property in all other respects; they were assets for the payment of debts; they could be sold by a trustee or assignee of an insolvent; by an administrator or executor, or by a sheriff under an execution; and all *other slaves* were subject to sale by their owners as all other property. 2 John. Cases, 79, 488, 89; 11 John. 68, 415; 17 John. 296; 3 Caines, 325; 8 John. 41; 14 John. 263, 324; 9 John. 67; 15 John. 283; 19 John. 53. The first case, in which the law was settled under these statutes in New York, was decided in 1800, and will be found reported in 2 John. Cases, 79, 488.

In 1794, A. the owner of a slave in New Jersey, removed to New York with the slave, and put the slave to service with B. until they or their executors should annul their agreement. Held, that a sale of the slave was prohibited by act of February, 1788; but that a sale of the slave by executors, trustees, assignees, &c. would be valid. Chancellor Kent declared, "The act (of 1788) was hostile to the *importation* and to the *exportation* of slaves, as an *article of trade*, not to the *existence of slavery itself;* for it takes care to re-enact and establish the maxim of the civil law, that the children of every female slave shall follow the state and condition of their mother." And he adds, that "sales made in the ordinary course of the law, and which are free from any kind of collusion, are not within the provisions of the act." "By considering the sale mentioned in the act, as confined to a voluntary disposition of the slave for a valuable consideration, by the owner himself, we are enabled effectually to reach the mischief in view, *the importation of slaves for gain,* and we take away every such motive to import them."

In the same case, Beeson, Justice, says: "By the law of this state slavery may exist within it. One person can have property in another, and the slave is part of the *goods of the master,* and may be *sold,* or otherwise aliened by him: or remaining unaliened, is on his death *transmissable to his executors;* but, by the act under consideration, a slave imported, or brought in, is not to be sold," &c.—as to all other slaves in New York, the court decide:

1st. That they may be sold by the owner as other property, but as to imported slaves, that they cannot be sold by the owner; but 1st, that he may give them away, and the title of the donor be valid.

2d. That their issue may be sold even by the owner who imported their mother.

3d. That the imported slaves are liable to sale by sheriffs, assignees, trustees, executors or administrators, as all other property.

In these opinions the court was unanimous, and the case is in point in every particular, and was subsequently recognised in all succeeding cases.

The same court, in 2 John. Cases, 89, held, that as to a slave imported in 1795, from New Jersey to New York, the sale was void, under the act of 1788: and this case also was affirmed in 1802, and the principle of the two cases, and especially of the former, was expressly recognised by the supreme court of New York in 1820; and that a *note given* for the purchase of a slave so imported and sold, was void. 17 John. 295.

In 1803 the supreme court of New York enforced the act of 1788 as well as of 1801, rendering void the sale of imported slaves. 3 Caine's Rep. 325. Now, slaves already in the state of New York, stood on the same footing as slaves in

Mississippi, and it was only as to slaves imported into either state, after a certain date, that the sale is sought to be invalidated; and if the law is void in Mississippi, under the argument of our opponents, it must have been equally void in New York, during all this period, notwithstanding these repeated decisions to the contrary of the courts of that state, upholding the rights of property and of sale of all the slaves in New York, upholding the right of property and the sale for debts, or in course of distribution even of these imported slaves, but rendering void *the sale by the importer.*

By the law of North Carolina, of 1794, Haywood's Man. 533, 4, c. 2, the introduction of slaves *after the 1st of May next,* for sale or hire, was prohibited, and an oath was required that the slaves were not introduced for traffic, with an exception in favour of emigrants bringing in their own slaves for their own use, and an exception in favour of travellers. The penalty was one hundred pounds for each slave so illegally introduced. Upon the general revisal of the laws of this state, at the September session, 1836-7, the importation of slaves from certain states was altogether interdicted. 1 Turner & Hughes' Dig. 571 to 574.

The acts of South Carolina, of 1800 and of 1801, prohibited the importation into that state of slaves from any place "without the limits of this state," under penalty of $100 for each slave so illegally imported, and forfeiture of the negro to be sold by the state. The act of 1802, excepts from former act, persons bringing into or through the state any slaves, on taking oath that they were not intended for sale; and if imported contrary to the law, they were declared free.

By the act of Missouri, of 19th March, 1835, digesting former laws, various restrictions were imposed on the introduction of slaves, and nearly similar provisions were adopted by Arkansas, on the 24th of February, 1838. Rev. Stat. Missouri, 581, Ib. Arkansas, 730. In Missouri, the validity of laws restricting or totally prohibiting the importation of slaves, has been repeatedly affirmed by the supreme court of that state, 1 Missouri Rep. 472, 2 Ib. 214, 3 Ib. 270; and several of these decisions recognise and enforce the provision, before quoted, of the constitution of Illinois, prohibiting the introduction of slaves into that state.

By territorial laws, before referred to, adopted in 1808, restrictions were imposed in the territory embracing the present states of Mississippi and Alabama, on the introduction of slaves as merchandise. By the constitutions of each of these states, adopted in 1817 and 1819, full power is given to the legislatures to prohibit this traffic. By the amended constitution of Mississippi of 1832, this traffic was entirely prohibited, and by the act of 13th of May, 1837, such importation for sale into that state, is declared a high misdemeanor, punishable with imprisonment, with a fine of $500 for each slave so introduced, and the nullity of the contract of sale, and forfeiture of the purchase money.

In Louisiana, by the acts of 1826; of the 19th of November, 1831; 2d of April, 1832; before referred to, the introduction of slaves into that state for sale, was prohibited under severe penalties, and the slaves so illegally introduced declared free.

By the act of Rhode Island, of 1784, subsequently continued and still in force, so far as shown by their most recent digests, the importation of slaves into the state was forbidden, with the exception of domestic slaves of "citizens of other states travelling through the state or coming to reside therein," and the slaves illegally imported declared free. The slaves then in the state, or imported under the above exceptions, were *continued as slaves,* but their children born after the date of the law became free. Laws of Rhode Island, page 441.

By the laws of Connecticut, of 1774 and of 1784, since three times re-enacted, and revised and continued in 1797 and 1821, slavery was continued as to the slaves already in the state, but all born after the 1st of March, 1784, were declared free. See Stat. 423, 440; 1 Swif. Sys. 220; 12 Con. Reps. 45, 59, 60, 64. These laws declared "that no Indian, negro, or mulatto slave shall at any time hereafter be brought or imported into this state, by sea or land, from any place or places whatsoever, to be disposed of, left or sold within the state."

In the case of a slave brought from Georgia to Connecticut, in 1835, and left there for temporary purposes, as was contended, such slave was declared free, one judge only dissenting, and he upon the sole ground that the slave was not *left* within the meaning of the act of 1784. In this case, reported in 12 Conn. 38 to 67, and decided in 1837, it was held, first, that slavery did exist in Connecticut as to the slaves introduced prior to a certain date; that these slaves "still continued to be held *as property,* subject to the control of their *masters;* and that numbers of them still continue so to be held, as proved by the last census of the state." 2d. The doctrine of 8 Conn. 393, was affirmed, in which it was declared that a certain negro in Connecticut "was the *slave* and *personal property*" of his master in Connecticut. 3d. That "there is nothing in the constitution of the United States" forbidding any state from preventing slaves being *voluntarily* brought within their limits. 4th. That slavery is local, and *must be governed entirely* by the laws of the state in which it is attempted to be enforced. 5th. That the law of Connecticut, and of any other state preventing the importation of slaves from any other state for sale, are valid. 6th. That a state, retaining in servitude the slaves within its limits, may legislate "to prevent the increase of slavery by importation." This case was very elaborately argued, and the opinion prepared with great care and ability; and upon these points, evolved by me from the decision, the court was unanimous. The case is precisely in point on the principles decided; and if slaves can be imported, for sale, into Mississippi, they can be imported, for sale, into Connecticut; for the slaves already in the latter are just as much "the property of their masters" as in the former. See also similar decisions in Connecticut on most of these points. 2 Root. 335, 517; 2 Conn. 355; 3 Conn. 467; 8 Conn. 393.

By the act of New Jersey of 14th March, 1798, Elmer's Digest, 520, slaves already within the state, it is expressly enacted, *shall remain slaves for life;* and their sale by their owners is permitted, except collusive sales of decrepit slaves. The importation of slaves, for sale, is prohibited under a pecuniary penalty, but certain persons are permitted to bring in certain slaves for their own use. By the act of 27th of February, 1820, Elmer, 525, slaves born after 4th of July, 1804, are declared free; the males at 25, and the females at 21 years of age. The importation of slaves into the state for sale, or exportation for sale, is forbidden, and also generally, with some exceptions; and the slave unlawfully imported or exported is declared free. The law of New Jersey, of 1798, differs in no respect from the present provision in Mississippi, and these laws have been universally recognised in New Jersey. See 2 Halsted, 253; 3 Hal. 219, 275; 1 Penning. 10; 4 Hal. 167; 1 Hal. 374.

In Indiana, no slave can be imported under their laws. 1 Blackford's Indiana Reports, 60; 3 American Jurist, 404. Nor in Ohio, Maine, Massachusetts, New Hampshire, or Vermont, under their constitutions. See Book of Cons. pages 273, 19, 38, 62, 81. See Com. v. Aves, 19 Pick.; 4 Mass. 123, 128, 129; 2 Tyler, 192.

When the constitution of the Union was formed, all the states were slave-holding states, except Massachusetts; and by the doctrine of our opponents, none of them but that state could have prohibited the introduction of slaves, for sale, and yet they all exercised the power. That there may be no mistake on the subject, I refer the court to Senate Document, 505, containing the census of each state, compiled by the department of state, under the resolution of congress of February 26th, 1833 (and the supplement returned this year), showing the number of slaves in those states generally denominated free states.

	1790.	1800.	1810.	1820.	1830.	1840.
New Hampshire,	158	8				
Rhode Island,	952	381	108	48	17	5
Connecticut,	2,759	951	310	97	25	54
Vermont,	17					
New York,	21,324	20,343	15,017	10,088	75	3
New Jersey,	11,423	12,422	10,851	7,557	2,254	658
Pennsylvania,	3,737	1,706	795	211	403	31
Delaware,	8,887	6,153	4,177	4,509	3,292	2,613
Illinois,			168	917	747	184

II

And yet all these nine states, now denominated free states, did, so far as they existed in 1790, hold slaves, and acknowledge property in slaves, and the sale of slaves within their limits was valid; and according to the argument of our opponents, all their laws, prohibiting the importation of slaves for sale, then were, and still are, unconstitutional; and slaves always could, and now can be, lawfully imported and sold, and held as slaves there: for the doctrine is, that so long as a single slave is held as such in any state, any number of slaves may be imported into and sold and held as slaves within its limits, the alternative being between total, immediate, and absolute emancipation of all slaves on the one hand, and the perpetuity of the slave trade on the other.

But the acts of 1792, of Virginia, and of 1796, as well as previous laws of Maryland, prohibiting in effect the introduction of slaves from other states for sale, have been repeatedly and unanimously recognised as valid, and enforced by the supreme court of the United States, and also by the highly respectable court for the District of Columbia.

By act of congress, the laws *in force* in Virginia and Maryland, at the date of the cession by those states of their respective portions of the District of Columbia, were *continued* in force after the cession, meaning thereby of course, only such laws of those states as were not repugnant to the constitution of the United States, for such laws only could have been previously in force in those states, and such laws only could have been *continued* in force in the District. These laws then under the declaratory act of congress, as has been universally conceded, continued in force by virtue of their previous operations over those parts of the District formerly included in the ceding states, and not by virtue of any act of congress re-enacting their provisions; and here let it be remarked, that even as to those laws of any state adopted prior to the constitution of the United States, but which were repugnant to powers granted exclusively to congress by that instrument, it is an admitted principle, that all such laws became null and void, after the adoption of the constitution, and all subsequent decisions enforcing any laws of a state even prior to 1788, forbidding the introduction of slaves for sale, proclaim the consistency of those laws with the constitution of the United States, as fully as though they had been subsequently enacted.

In 1802, a claimant of a slave, without the consent of the true owner, brought him from Maryland into Alexandria, in the District of Columbia, (formerly Virginia,) where he remained more than a year, and the circuit court for the District of Columbia decided, that being a slave imported contrary to the law of Virginia, of 1792, manumitting slaves imported from any other state, and held for twelve months in that state, unless upon oath made within a certain time that the importer did not bring them in "with an intention of selling them"—and this oath not having been taken by the *claimant* who introduced the slave, he was free. Scott v. Negro London, 3 Cranch, 326. The decision was reversed by this court, *upon the ground*, that although the prescribed oath was not made in due time by the *claimant*, who introduced the slave as his, yet such oath having been made within the proper time by the *owner*, that on that ground the slave was not free; but the validity of the Virginia law was fully recognised. 3 Cranch, 324.

In 6 Cranch, 1, this court also admitted the validity of the law of Maryland, of 1788, prohibiting the introduction of slaves into that state.

In 1 Wheaton, 1, this court again unanimously admitted the validity of the Maryland act of 1796, before quoted, prohibiting the importation of slaves for *sale*, or also to reside, except as to emigrants. The court expressly declare that, that "act of the state of Maryland," "*is in force* in the county of Washington (District of Columbia)."

In 8 Peters, 44, Lee v. Lee, the case is thus stated by the reporter, and the *unanimous* decision of this court, as pronounced by Justice Thompson, is also given. "The plaintiffs in error filed a petition for freedom in the circuit court of the United States for the county of Washington, and they proved that they were born in the state of Virginia, as slaves of Richard B. Lee, now deceased, who moved with his family into the county of Washington, in the District of Columbia, about the year 1816, leaving the petitioners residing in Virginia as his slaves, until the year 1820, when the petitioner Barbara, was removed to the county of Alexandria, in the District of Columbia, where she was hired to Mrs. Muir, and continued with her thus hired for the period of one year. That the petitioner Sam, was in like manner removed to the county of Alexandria, and was hired to General Walter Jones, for a period of about five or six months. That after the expiration of the said periods of hiring, the petitioners were removed to the said county of Washington, where they continued to reside as the slaves of the said Richard B. Lee, until his death, and since as the slaves of his widow, the defendant." The court said:

" By the Maryland law of 1796, it is declared, that it shall not be lawful to import or bring into this state by land or water, any negro, mulatto, or other slave for sale, or to reside within this state. And any person brought into this state as a slave, contrary to this act, if a slave before, shall thereupon cease to be the property of the person so importing, and shall be free."

"And by the act of congress of the 27th of February, 1801, it is provided, that the laws of the state of Maryland, as they then existed, should be, and *continue in force* in that part of the district, which was ceded by that state to the United States."

" The Maryland law of 1796, is, therefore, *in force in the county of Washington,* and the petitioners, if brought directly from the state of Virginia into the county of Washington, would, under the provisions of that law, be entitled to their freedom."

Here, the law of Maryland, of 1796, prohibiting the introduction of slaves from other states into that state, was *enforced* by the unanimous opinion of the Supreme Court of the United States. This is not an extra-judicial opinion, but a decision directly in point, *enforcing* a law of Maryland, which involved this very question now to be decided by this court. And, here let me observe, that if it is lawful and must be permitted under the commercial power to introduce slaves from one state into another for sale, it cannot be lawful in any state to emancipate them as a consequence of such introduction, any more than to forbid the sale. And here let it be remarked, that, our opponents concede that each state may emancipate all the slaves within their limits by a state law, where there is no opposing provision of the state constitution, and where there is, then by an amendment of her state constitution, to be adopted by the state. Each state may dissolve at pleasure, or establish the relation of master and slave within her limits, and that congress can neither dissolve nor establish that relation in a state. But to add to the number of slaves in a state against her will by the authority of congress, is so far to establish and extend the relation of master and slave within her limits by the authority of congress. But, by the concession of our opponents, a state may emancipate all the slaves within her limits, by declaring them not to be property within her limits, and then this commercial power they say will not extend to that state. As, however, a state cannot do this as to goods and merchandise, by declaring them not to be property within her limits, so as to exempt them when imported from the operation of the commercial power, this very distinction shows, that goods and merchandise are, and slaves are not within the operation of the commercial power. But this admission of our opponents, that a state may emancipate all or any portion of the slaves within her limits, concedes, as it seems to me, the whole case, for if the state may emancipate, must she not have the power, *the moment the slaves are brought within her limits;* for they are then within her territory and jurisdiction, and subject to her exclusive power; and if a state may not thus emancipate as soon as the slaves are landed, must she wait for days or years, or who is to prescribe the time when the state laws shall begin to operate, or the number of slaves that shall be embraced within the provision, whether it shall include the anti nati or post nati, or extend only to those that may be hereafter introduced, or include also all those already in a state; and no one will deny, that if to emancipate slaves introduced for sale be not forbidden by the commercial power, it cannot be forbidden by that power to declare the sale unlawful.

We have seen in the course of this argument, that ten of the twelve states which framed the constitution, have passed laws, many of them cotemporaneous with the

161

formation of the constitution or almost immediately aft r, prohibiting the introduction from other states, of slaves for sale, and have enforced these laws. That similar provisions have been made in effect by all the states in their laws or constitutions, and that these provisions have all been enforced, that the supreme judicial tribunal of every state (where the question has been made,) have again and again, during a period of more than fifty years, declared these laws to be valid; and that the supreme court of the United States have, again and again, unanimously recognised their constitutionality, *and carried them into execution*; that at least six of the new states have affirmed in their constitutions the power to pass those laws, and that congress (sometimes by an unanimous vote) have on all these occasions, commencing in 1792, and terminating in 1836, conceded that these constitutions affirming this power, were "not repugnant to the constitution of the United States."

Does not all this settled action of all the departments of the governments of the states, and of the United States fix the construction of the constitution in this respect, and leave it no longer an open question for the investigation of this court. This court have declared that "a cotemporary exposition of the constitution practised and acquiesced under for a period of years, fixes the construction, and *the courts* will not shake or control it." 1 Cranch 299. And now, will this court, by a single decree, overthrow the law as settled for more than fifty years, by all the departments of the governments of the states, and of the Union? If so, it must sacrifice at once a hecatomb of acts and decisions, and change the structure of the government itself. It would be a judicial revolution, more sudden and overwhelming in its effects, than the last great revolutions in France and England, which were little more than changes of dynasty. I have called it a revolution, not a usurpation; but the most daring usurper never effected so sudden and extensive a change in the civil and political rights, and settled internal policy of a nation. These have been generally spared by conquerors and usurpers, or if not spared, they were not subverted by a single decree, to be at once proclaimed and executed. But here, the moment this decree shall be recorded, the revolution will have commenced and terminated, and this court will reassemble among the fragments of laws subverted, and decisions overthrown. The constitutions of six of the states: the laws of all upon this subject, and a series of uninterrupted judicial decisions for more than half a century, will be at once obliterated. With them will fall the acts of congress upon this question, from the admission of the first, to the last of the new states, and many confirmatory decisions of this tribunal. This decree affects the past, the present, and the future. Reaching back to 1788, it annuls all the state laws forbidding the introduction of slaves, and reinslaves all, and the descendants of all that were liberated by those statutes. And all this is to be effected by a single decree, no time allowed to prepare for the mighty change, but it is to be the work of an instant.

So much for the past and present, and now for that dark and gloomy future, when this court, having annulled all the state laws on this subject, shall announce that it is a question over which the power of congress is supreme and exclusive. Could the Union stand the mighty shock, and if it fell, shall we look upon the victims of anarchy and civil war, resting wearied for the night from the work of death and desolation, to renew in the morning the dreadful conflict? Throwing our eyes across the Atlantic, shall we behold the consequences, when the overthrow of this Union, this second fall of mankind, shall be there promulgated? Shall we there see those daring men, now pleading the cause of self-government around the thrones of monarchs, sink despairing from the conflict, amid the shouts of tyrants exulting over the prostrate liberties of man. And who can expect such a decree from this tribunal? No, this court will now prove, that however passion or prejudice may sway for a time any other department of this government, here the rights of every section of this Union are secure. And when, as I doubt not, all shall now be informed, that over the subject of slavery, congress possesses no jurisdiction; the power of agitators will expire, and this decree will be regarded as a re-signing and re-sealing of the constitution.

EXAMINATION

OF THE

DECISION OF THE SUPREME COURT OF THE UNITED STATES,

IN THE CASE OF

STRADER, GORMAN AND ARMSTRONG *vs.* CHRISTOPHER GRAHAM,

DELIVERED AT ITS DECEMBER TERM, 1850:

CONCLUDING WITH AN

ADDRESS TO THE FREE COLORED PEOPLE,

ADVISING THEM TO REMOVE TO LIBERIA.

———————

BY JAMES G. BIRNEY.

———————

CINCINNATI:
TRUMAN & SPOFFORD, PUBLISHERS, 111 MAIN STREET.
BEN FRANKLIN OFFICE PRINT, WALNUT ST.
1852.

163

PREFATORY NOTE.

THE opinions expressed in this pamphlet do not fall in with the views of any party among us. That the *Colonizationists* earnestly desire the free colored class to emigrate to Liberia, is beyond all doubt; and that they will use measures *adequate to that end*, appears to the writer equally undeniable. The Constitution has been violated over and over again, that these people might be more certainly and securely reached. Still there has been no complaint by those who have influence with the Government. It is not to be supposed, then, that they will come to a complete stop, after having done so much to circumscribe, and render of small value, the liberty that the fathers of the Constitution intended to bestow on the colored people, or that they will hesitate to take from their victims gems of inferior value.

That the colored people should look on the Colonizationists as their enemies, and as offering them perfidious, injurious advice, is not to be wondered at. But let them remember, that those whom they regard as *enemies* have power—*effectual* power. The case of the Cherokee Indians, removed *by force* by the military of the country, from their native land, and transplanted to one thought much less desirable, ought not to be forgotten. It is not the *person* offering the advice that is to be considered, but the *advice*. An enemy, without even intending it, may give advice that we may often advantageously pursue.

To some, the first chapter of this essay will appear too long, if not almost unnecessary. But further investigation will dispel this opinion. It will be seen that it contains statements showing the former and present condition of the country, essential to the entireness of the essay.

The second, third and fourth chapters require no elucidation. They speak for themselves.

The fifth and last continues to show the *persecutions*—as the writer deems them—of the free colored class; concluding with an address advising them, as far as they can, to escape from these persecutions—by removing to Liberia. We recommend Liberia, not as *independently* desirable to the colored people, but as the best *retreat* they can find from the oppression of the whites.

Whilst everything like *compulsory* emigration is disclaimed, it is warmly hoped for, that whatever course it is thought best to pursue, may be the result of calm and wise consideration.

165

It is no disgrace to the colored people, that, as a *class*, they are ignorant. It would be strange, indeed, if they were not; for those whose more especial business it is to attend to matters of education, have omitted the usual means—sometimes, indeed, *preventing* them—in reference to that part of our population. Admitting many very honorable exceptions among them—they ought therefore to be *much* reasoned with. Fully persuaded of this, the writer could not well leave out any of the facts which he has stated, or any of the arguments he has used: everything that is introduced, being introduced, to make very plain to the colored population that they ought to remove to Liberia.

SUPREME COURT OF THE UNITED STATES.

DECEMBER TERM, 1850.

JACOB STRADER, JAMES GORMAN, JOHN ARMSTRONG, PLAINTIFFS IN ERROR, *vs.* CHRISTOPHER GRAHAM. IN ERROR TO THE COURT OF APPEALS FROM THE STATE OF KENTUCKY.

CHAPTER I.

PRELIMINARY REMARKS.

The intent of a document to be taken, and not particular parts of it—The Judges of the Supreme Court disqualified to decide properly between Liberty and Slavery—The United States compared to the Roman Government, after the Conquest of the East—to England, after the Restoration—Consequences, if Slavery be true by the Bible.

WE propose to examine the decision of the case placed at the head of this article, that we may see how far it agrees or disagrees with the generally received principles of liberty current among us; with the Constitution of the United States, the embodiment of those principles, and from which the court derive all their authority, and which, by the highest sanction used among men, they are appointed to support. Our examination will be thought rigid—perhaps too much so—almost animadversion, by some; but how can it be otherwise, if we are honest with ourselves, and faithful to the race of which we are part, when we believe injustice has been done to the weakest and most defenseless portion of them, by the highest power known to us in such cases?

We do not intend confining ourselves to an examination of the case itself, but we shall try to ascertain what has been, and what is now, the condition of the race in this country: so that we may well understand, that, instead of gaining, at least, in the same proportion as *we* have, they, as a whole, have fewer privileges at this juncture, than they had when the constitution was made; that every new movement in their behalf, or in which they were concerned, has resulted in wresting from them their rights—if those can be called *rights* that are only *permissive*—which they had sixty or seventy years ago, and that, in fact, they are, in every way, more and more circumscribed than they formerly were. To this will be added our opinion, if we should consider it of sufficient value, as to what the colored people should do in their present circumstances.

But before proceeding to argue any of the questions connected with this matter, let us try to find out what the makers of the constitution had in view, with regard to the colored people, when they adopted it, and what is the fair interpretation of that instrument—applying to it the same rules that we do to others. This, indeed, is the only true way of gaining a proper understanding of *any* such instrument, That liberty was the main object of the constitution, in relation to the *white* man, we think is beyond all cavil. That it was, also, the main object in relation to the colored people, we are led to conclude is equally undeniable, since there is no limitation with respect to *them*, any more than with respect to the whites. Any interpretation, then, that counteracts *this* must be wrong—and wrong in proportion as it counteracts it. We would not do injustice to our Revolutionary fathers—an injustice which we are certain they do not deserve—by supposing that while they themselves were struggling for liberty, and in the struggle, doing all they *could* do with their own might, and as if not satisfied with this, drawing assistance from every quarter, (not forgetting even the free colored people), that, if they should be blessed in their attempt, they intended to adopt a constitution, or plan, which would enable their descendants, not only always to maintain slavery, but to make the condition of those who might, in any manner, get away from that sad lot, less and less desirable.* *Before* our separation from England, we enjoyed the liberty for which we contended. Finding ourselves without a form of government capable of securing it, we adopted the Constitution. *One* of our chief aims, if not the *chief* one, being to make *permanent* the liberty we had achieved and possessed.

Judging from the best and most authentic history of the Convention of 1787, it was well known then, that liberty and slavery could not permanently co-exist—that if liberty got the upper hand, slavery, its everlasting antagonist, in some form or other, must, in the same proportion, go down, and *vice versa.* Being incongruous elements, they cannot dwell peaceably together—for incongruous they ever have been, and ever must be, as sin and holiness; one *must,* in time, put the other down. But the ingenuity, or, rather, the lubricity of the human mind is very great; men, without much difficulty, are persuaded to think of themselves as belonging to a *clique* or section of society, rather than to the race, and prone to interpret or construe matters pertaining to that section according to the prepossessions, prejudices, or passions which prevail among those who are looked on as composing it.

We do not intend to say, that the judges who gave the opinion at the head of this paper, or those of our fellow-citizens who approve it, or even the "Friends of the Union"—as for distinction sake they call themselves—are dishonest and insincere. We do not think they are, with but few exceptions; these exceptions are to be found generally among the most intelligent and best informed of the class. But the opinions they hold—and we intend to include the judges and those who think with them—disqualify them, almost unconsciously, too, from judging correctly, where liberty and slavery are the litigants. There are many in the world who think, that, if *they* are safe and well provided for, every body else must be so too. So it is, no doubt, with most of those whose *main* object appears to be, to *save the Union.* If the Union, *as it is,* is beneficial to their various pursuits, it is to such persons, very naturally the highest interest of the government. They consider but as subordinate to the Union—as of less importance—the liberty it was intended to secure; or if that liberty consist with the Union, so much the better, but it must not interfere with their main design—one to which their various callings point—the preservation of it.

Here they judge by the law that usually prevails in the section of society with which they are connected—by the lower law of selfishness; their opponents by the "higher law" of their nature, or by the law which tells us to "do unto others as we would have others do unto us." They despise the slaves and blacks, because they see them below their *own* condition, and the condition of the class with which they mostly company. Their interest in them as human beings—as part of the race to which they themselves belong—seldom shows itself. They think the slaves are made and qualified only for the station they occupy, and that the best thing *they* can do in the premises, is to keep them in that station. They think, too, that the condition of slavery serves to sustain their own condition of liberty, and this latter they wish to see maintained at all hazards. They hear with much interest the cries and complaints of the slaveholder about relaxing his grasp or weakening his power over his victim, but are deaf to the cries and complaints of the sufferer. If slavery should be

---

* Mr. Madison, in a letter to Joseph Jones, dated November 28, 1780, says, "Would it not be as well to liberate and make soldiers at once of the blacks themselves, as to make them instruments for enlisting white soldiers ? It would certainly be more consonant to the principles of liberty, which ought never to be lost sight of in a contest for liberty ; and with white officers and a majority of white soldiers, no imaginable danger would be feared from themselves, as there would certainly be none from the effect of the example on those who should remain in bondage ; experience having shown that a freedman immediately loses all attachment and sympathy with his former fellow-slaves." [1 Vol. Madison Papers, 69.]

abolished, the slaveholder would be reduced below *them*, and below the *caste* in which he had moved. In fine, they do not take the time and trouble to think much about the evils of slavery, but only about the distress of the slaveholder. Such persons embrace liberty as a *feeling* applying to them, and to those with whom they are, in some . way, connected—not as a *principle*, which they wish the whole world to enjoy. As mind and heart, in their most comprehensive sense, are the greatest powers, and the most esteemed gifts that men have, the friend of liberty wishes them to be free from all embarrasment, well knowing that this mental freedom contributes much to the happiness of the race. Under the interpretation of the *sectional* philanthropist—and we will call by that name him whose regards are almost all confined to the exaltation of the class to which *he* belongs—the *race* would improve slowly, if at all. Should there be *any* improvement, it would, in all likelihood, be confined to this class, as it is in England and the governments of the old world generally : but the deterioration of the other parts of the human family, on whom this *clique* would look down with contempt, would probably outweigh it. The position with which we set out is well illustrated by the different religious persuasions throughout Christendom. The *main* object of the Bible, on which they all profess their sects are founded—especially of the New Testament—is to persuade men to feel kindly, and to act justly to one another—indeed, to be brethren. But, if this be lost sight of, and resort be had to interpretation or construction of particular passages, on which a religious persuasion or sect is to be founded, what different and contrary notions we have! How is God represented as the friend of a *part* of his family here on earth—*all* of whom he has brought into being—and the enemy of another. The Pope will justify the Roman Catholic religion, its mummeries, convents, monasteries, &c., &c., by the Bible, while he calls heretics, all who are not in his church, and consigns to everlasting destruction largely more than half of his fellow-creatures. By the same book, the Protestant will justify *his* religion in its various forms. Now we would as soon expect from the sincere, and of course, zealous Catholic, an intelligent and well-founded opinion on a strictly Protestant question, relating to the advancement of Protestantism, and *vice versa*, from a sincere Protestant, the same kind of answer to a purely Catholic question, relating to *its* advancement, as we would a correct opinion relating to liberty from the court, or from any of the persons above mentioned, as affiliated with it in sentiment. But with the guide before given—the *main object* of the Bible, and with the love of mankind stronger than the love of sect or party—the task is an easy one. We have before said, that any interpretation opposed to this *must* be wrong. We have now only to add, that it must ever heretofore have been wrong, that it must ever hereafter be wrong; for justice must always be substantially the same, though the subjects to which it is applied may be very different.

Prescott, in his conquest of Mexico, tells us that Cortes and his followers found the *cross* in that country. A Roman Catholic—for with that church the pictures or representations of the cross and other réligious objects are more especially emblematic than with others—a rigid one, having more zeal than knowledge, would say it was intended to show that the Catholic religion is true, and that it would easily and soou supercede the Mexican heathenism. 'Tis true, that symbol might have been accidental, and this would have been more probable, had it been the only one found. But the historian accounts not only for this, but for others of a similar kind, in a more philosophic and satisfactory manner, when he says, that nations or communities, in the same progress of development are very likely to have similar usages and symbols.

But are there no developments of national character to which ours, in times past, as well as now, may be likened? We know *two*, that seem to us very striking—Rome. before and after the subjugation of the East, and the English government from the Restoration in 1660, for nearly thirty years, till the accession of William of Orange. Perhaps, the exclamation will at once be made, impossible! we possess more knowledge than ancient Rome ever possessed, and much more than England did, during the time spoken of. Believing both positions, and that society is getting better, and this in proportion as it embraces principles that are more interesting and nearer the truth, we will not deny them. We well know, too, that a mere pigmy, in comparison with Newton, can have a larger view from Newton's shoulders, than Newton himself had. But we may well be compared in national developments with communities inferior to us—especially, in a knowledge of *duty;* and if the parallel be good, it makes the comparison so much the worse for us.

Rome, for a long time after she was founded, was simple in her manners and desires—particularly, if we compare her with the renown she obtained in after times. To be sure, even from the first, she was quarrelsome with her neighbors, and warlike in her temper; nor did her aggressions cease till their territory was added to her's, and made a part of the nation. But in being addicted to war, she is not peculiarly noticeable. War was the vice and fashion of the times, and every people that could, carried on wars against those who happened to be near by. But this in time would disappear. Good sense, or justice would, at last, put an end to this game of passionate or ambitious men. 'Tis true, the *ancient* Romans lived on the simplest fare. Their chief magistrates and most illustrious generals, when out of office, cultivated their land with their own hands; sat down at the same board and partook of the food with their slaves—as Curtius, the Censor. They sometimes prepared the dinner themselves—as Cato did; or had their wives to carry it to them in the field. But slavery—injustice—was there. It had thus early been incorporated in the very frame-work, in the constitution of her society. Every day—every night—all the time—they did to others what they would not have others do to them. They became accustomed to violate justice—of course, careless of observing it among themselves, where their equals were concerned. Might became Right, and Rome and all the other ancient nations in the same predicament, are now the monuments of the certain defeat of those who habitually violate a law of nature—of that God who made nature.

We are not about to say, that Rome would not have been destroyed, had Sylla and Pompey never poured into her the immense wealth of the East, or had her other generals never conquered that country. There is hardly a doubt that her original injustice would have brought about her downfall, but the conquest of the East only *hastened* that event. Whilst luxury and vice were gaining possession of the land, the leading Romans spoke of their early ancestors as great and good men for their time, but as rather primitive and old-fashioned for things as they *then* were—that the "march of mind" was not so rapid with their fathers as it was with *them,* but they applauded their deeds, at least, as far as to make them godfathers to their own guilty objects. In all this time—even in the worst of it—Rome was not deficient in what we called "great men" —in sophists that artfully misled, in poets that flatteringly applauded, and in orators and politicians that were guided by the "lower" law, denying that there was any "higher!" Indeed, at no time, had she been deficient in them. She had, from her very origin, been so much agitated and so active, that the animal and intellectual powers of men were greatly excited, and to such she generally confided the direction of her national affairs. What she most needed were greatness and goodness combined—great men, and at the same time, good men—not great and wicked like the Devil, but great and good like God.

How much in substance, in principle, does this resemble our own history! Whilst we were weak—contending for national independence—striving to arouse all the energies of our own country to meet the crisis, and rather uncertain how that crisis would end—and wishing to obtain the good will of the just and virtuous everywhere, we announced in our DECLARATION some important truths—in governments before unheard of. If we had not announced them *then,* we, probably, would not, afterwards, when the danger of re-subjugation had passed away, by the acknowledgment of our Independence. We would certainly not announce them *now,* in the absolute and unqualified sense, in which, at that time, they were understood. The fathers of the Revolution were ignorant of what would be the expansion of mind at the present day; or, that its ingenuity must be called in to explain these principles and reconcile them with our practice.

What we have just now said, is not said at random. When all uncertainty was removed, and our character as a separate nation acknowledged—a very short time afterwards, when the present Constitution was made, there was no direct affirmation in it, that all men are created free—entitled to their liberty, &c., but many important things are indirect and left to be explained, much was made to depend on memory; and that instrument, itself, in a most important feature, was to be interpreted, not by what was in it—by rights that are inalienable and declared by us to be so—but by what is outside of it. It is by no means difficult, too, to see, that in proportion as we acquire strength as a nation, we are the less inclined to be trammeled, as we call it, by truths published to the world in the time of our weakness and distress. We then relied more on justice—now, on power.

To make the resemblance still more complete between the effect produced on Roman manners by the sudden influx of wealth from Asia, and the effect on ours from the same cause, let us take California. We are far from saying, that the gold from California is, at this time, comparable in amount to what the Romans got from the East. As, however, the circulating medium of the world was then pretty much confined to the Roman Empire, the wealth of the East, concentrating at the city of Rome, or distributed from that capital, must have produced a great effect. But it becomes us, not to "despise the day of small things," as some perhaps would call it. There cannot, now, be much less than *two hundred millions of dollars*—about the cost of the Mexican war to *us*—added to the circulating medium of the world. Hardly a vessel sent off from San Francisco to this country, or to Europe, but that carries gold dust and bars, averaging in all likelihood, fully half a million of dollars. This, of course, goes into the general circulation. If the expectations of the Californians are at all realized, their country will greatly affect the world in this way. Already the discerning see, that it has raised the price of real estate in the old, if not in the extreme, parts of the country. Facts seem to sustain theory, and all sound theory is but the generalization of facts—for never was real estate more saleable at good prices than it now is, or money more easily obtained. And how are our public men? Are they stationary? Do they furnish no index to the popular feeling? The answer must be, that they are not stationary—that they do furnish some index to general opinion, and that they are more extravagant with the revenues of the government than they ever were before, and that they deal in more useless projects than they formerly did. Indeed, they seem to think that the money necessary to accomplish these projects is to be used at *their* pleasure and whim. They identify the country with themselves, and not themselves with the country. They possess a greater than common regard for the Union, as if it had been made for them and their subordinates, and for *their* interpretation of the Constitution, because it suits them and their adherents. Well, truly may it be said to them as Jesus said to the Pharisees—"ye compass sea and land to make one proselyte, and when he is made, ye make him ten-fold more the child of hell than yourselves."

We will now consider the other instance, for with many it will serve better to illustrate our present condition than the one just now noticed—we mean England under the reign of Charles II, and James II. Their father, Charles I, had been beheaded in 1649, and the name of a republic had been substituted for the royal government, and the management of it assumed by Oliver Cromwell till his death. Afterward it was conducted by one of his sons, but greatly inferior to the father in governing men. Charles was restored to the throne in 1660, at the age of thirty. Being heir to the throne, as it was then considered—at the head of his party—together with the vagabond life he had led on the continent, during his banishment—had greatly corrupted his naturally very good talents. During the Republic, manners had been too austere and sanctimonious. The leaders in the government were greatly to blame for giving their countenance to this austerity. On the restoration of Charles—in an uncommon degree popular—the very contrary took place. Not only was austerity out of place at court, but even sobriety, in a good measure, was discarded. Open effrontery and ill-concealed vice, were the order of the day. Charles was the Head of the English Church, as established by law—for the Reformation was then considered as pretty well set up in that country. Dissolute himself, he placed, of course, little confidence in saving himself by goodness and justice. He thought, as was too often supposed *then*, and as too many think *now*, that a belief in the mere formula of a church, and, consequently, that a church thus favored, and receiving the last and best evidence of his sincerity, could save him—for Charles died a Roman Catholic—though only strongly suspected during his life—confessing to a monk, and receiving from him the last rites of that Church.

Charles was succeeded by his brother James. He, as Charles had been, was the Head of the English Church; but he was an avowed Catholic — the great object with him being to make the religion of the Church of Rome, the religion of the State. The probability is, that he would have succeeded, had he prosecuted his design coolly and dispassionately; but instead of doing so, he suffered his passions too much to interfere—impelling him to seek the accomplishment of his object *too* speedily. The power he possessed as the first officer of the kingdom —particularly the power of removing from office and appointing to it—enabled him so to influence the two Houses of Parliament, that they passed such laws as he thought necessary for the promotion of his design. Such was his influence too, over the Courts of law, by the use of the power already mentioned, that they declared these laws constitutional—such as Parliament had a right to pass. If any one of the judges refused entire obedience to James' will, he was displaced, and one appointed in his stead, who would unflinchingly carry out his wishes.* The notorious Jeffreys, raised from a low condition as the reward of his subservience, was his Lord Chancellor. The vulgar violence of his character was manifested by the frequent abuse of the most worthy, and, that he might the more fully meet the expectations of his sovereign, often at the expense of life. But the string was pulled too quickly, and too violently. It snapped, when suddenly the nation broke away as from a spell, from a fascination that seemed almost mesmeric, and dissipating the faction that had enchanted it, it put to death whomever of it they could lay hands on.

The attempt of James, forcibly reminds us of the attempt of the slaveholders, to fix their institution, as they please to call slavery, as an established condition of the government; one that, from being temporary and allowed. is to be consid-

ered as constitutional and permanent: as permanent, indeed, as our government was intended to be. Let it not be said that James was insincere and hypocritical. He was not, and he gave the best proof that he was not; for he suffered banishment on account of his religion, and died in its rites. The nation, equally sincere, thought, however honest James might be, that he was trying to palm on them a great lie, and that nothing could make it a truth. They found they could not dwell together in peace, and they cast him out, sincere though he was.

Neither let it be supposed that *all* the slaveholders are insincere and hypocritical. We well remember when the most conscientious and intelligent among them acknowledged that slavery was wrong, when they bemoaned the *necessity* (?) of enslaving their brethren, and wished to see the time come when all persons would be free. But that time has passed away. We no more hear that wish or that moan. The allies they have made in the north, where the deciders, having no slaves, are supposed to be impartial, have given them distrust of their former opinion; have led them to think slavery is not so bad a thing as they once fanatically supposed it to be; in fine, have put to sleep their aroused consciences. Indeed, influenced by this cause, they have gone so far as to say, that slavery is not only an indispensable element in the *best* organization of society, but that it is a *good* thing. To convince their associates, as well as to confirm themselves, and keep up the courage of both—for almost all men, if not all, prefer truth to a lie—they resort to the Bible to prove that God sanctions slavery, and that he has determined, at least in this country, that a part of his children shall be held in slavery, as articles of merchandise, by another more favored part. Parasites of some mental or moral malformation, but who pretend to a superior knowledge of the profoundest mysteries, have been found who encouraged the idea. Admitting that their plan succeed. with what a God, the infinitely perfect Creator, do they present us! By our perceptions of justice, perceptions which he has implanted in us, we see that he is unjust, that he himself violates the rule on which it is said, hang all the law and the prophets, a rule given for the direction of man, and which all good men approve, "thou shall do to others as ye would

*How naturally this brings to mind the manner in which Chief Justice Taney came into his present situation. Mr. Duane, thinking that he, as Secretary of the Treasury, had not the power to remove the public moneys from the United States Bank, where the law had placed them, refused to do so. He was at once removed by General Jackson, the President, and Mr. Taney succeeded him. The public moneys were removed. In a short time he was elevated to the place he now occupies.

others should do to you." Every one feels, intuitively, perhaps, that it would be a gross wrong to make *him* a slave. If the rule be a true one, and slavery be right, we are presented with a Father, who has invested the race with noble powers, powers like his own, capable of making man the paragon of animals, of raising him to heaven, or sinking him to hell; with powers that in bondage must lie dormant, unimproved, almost valueless; at the same time, enabling the most cunning and powerful of their brethren to hold others of them in a condition which the sufferers try not to *improve*, but to escape from entirely; a condition, too, that sours the temper of the oppressors towards their uneasy victims, and weakens their confidence in men generally. All these things appear unsuitable to the character of God, the author of order and not of confusion.

With these preliminary remarks and statements designed to show us our true condition and the point we have arrived at, we proceed to consider the decision at the head of this article, and lest we may be supposed to misunderstand and misrepresent it, we give it in full.

CHAPTER II.

Decision of the Supreme Court, with the examination of the first part of it relating more directly to Slavery.

Jacob Strader, James Gorman and John Armstrong, plaintiffs in error vs. Christopher Graham. In error to the Court of Appeals for the State of Kentucky.

Mr. Chief Justice Taney delivered the opinion of the Court:—

"This case is brought here by writ of error directed to the Court of Appeals of the State of Kentucky.

The facts of the case so far as they are material to the decision of this court, are briefly as follows:

The defendant in error is a citizen of the State of Kentucky, and three negro men, whom he claimed and held as his slaves, were received on board the Steamboat Pike at Louisville, without his knowledge or consent, and transported to Cincinnati, and from that place escaped to Canada and were lost to him. The proceedings before us were instituted under a statute of Kentucky, in the Louisville Chancery Court against the plaintiffs in error, to recover the value of the slaves who had thus escaped; and in default of payment by them to charge the boat itself with the damages sustained. Strader and Gorman were the owners of the boat, and Armstrong the master.

The plaintiffs in error among other defences, insisted that the negroes claimed as slaves were free; averring that some time before they were taken on board the Steamboat, they had been sent by the permission of the defendant in error, to the State of Ohio, to perform service as slaves; and that in consequence thereof they had acquired their freedom, and were free when received on board the boat.

It appears by the evidence that these men were musicians, and had gone to Ohio on one or more occasions to perform at public entertainments; that they had been taken there for this purpose with the permission of the defendant in error by a man by the name of Williams, under whose care and direction he had, for a time, placed them; that they had always returned to Kentucky as soon as their brief service was over, and for the two years preceding their escape, they had not left the State of Kentucky, and had remained there in the service of the defendant in error as their lawful owner.

The Louisville Chancery Court finally decided that the negroes in question were his slaves; and that he was entitled to receive $3,000 for his damages. And if that sum was not paid by a certain day specified in the decree, it directed that the Steamboat should be sold for the purpose of raising it, together with the cost of the suit. This decree was afterwards affirmed in the Court of Appeals of Kentucky, and the case is brought here by writ of error upon that judgment.

Much of the argument on the part of the plaintiffs in error, has been offered for the purpose of showing, that the judgment of the State Court was erroneous in deciding that those negroes were slaves. And it is insisted that their previous employment in Ohio, has made them free when they returned to Kentucky.

But this question is not before us. Every State has an undoubted right to determine the *status*, or domestic and social condition of the person domiciled within its territory, except in so far as the powers of the State in this respect are restained, or duties and obligations imposed upon them by the Constitution of the United States. There is nothing in the Constitution of the United States, that can in any degree control the law of Kentucky upon this subject. And the condition of the negroes, therefore, as to freedom or slavery, after their return depended altogether upon the laws of that State, and could not be influenced by the laws of Ohio. It was exclusively in the power of Kentucky to determine for itself whether their employment in another State should or should not make them free on their return. The Court of

Appeals have determined that by the laws of the State they continued to be slaves. And their judgment upon this point is, upon this writ of error, conclusive upon this court, and we have no jurisdiction over it.

But it seems to be supposed in the argument that the laws of Ohio, upon this subject, has some peculiar force, by virtue of the ordinance of 1787, for the government of the North Western Territory—Ohio being one of the States carved out of it.

One of the articles of this ordinance provides that "there shall be neither slavery nor involuntary servitude in the said Territory, otherwise than in punishment for crimes whereof the party shall have been duly convicted; but that any person escaping into the same, from whom labor or service is lawfully claimed in any of the original States, such fugitive may be reclaimed and conveyed to the person claiming his or her labor and service as aforesaid." And this article is one of the six which the ordinance declares shall be "a compact between the original States and the people and States in the said Territory, and forever remain unalterable except by common consent."

The argument assumes that the six articles which that ordinance declares to be perpetual are still in force in the States since formed within the territory and admitted into the Union.

If this proposition could be maintained, it would not alter the question, for the regulations of Congress under the old confederation, or the present Constitution, for the government of a particular territory, could have no force beyond its limits. It certainly could not restrict the power of the States within their respective territories; nor in any manner interfere with their laws and institutions, nor give this court any control over them. The ordinance in question, if still in force, could have no more operation than the laws of Ohio in the State of Kentucky, and could not influence the decision upon the rights of the master on the slaves in that States, nor give this court jurisdiction upon that subject.

But it has been settled by judicial decision in this court, that this ordinance is not in force.

The case of Permoli vs. First Municipality 3 How, 589 depended upon the same principles as the case before us. It is true that the question in that case arose in Louisiana. But the Act of Congress, of April 7, 1798, Chapter 28 (4 Statutes at large 549) extended the ordinance of 1787 to the Territory of Mississippi with the exception of the Anti-Slavery clause, and declared that the people of that Territory should be entitled to and enjoy all the rights, privileges and advantages granted to the people of the Territory North-west of the Ohio. And by the Act of March 2, 1805 chapter 23 (2 statute at Large 322) it was enacted that the then Territory of New Orleans should be entitled to and enjoy all the rights, privileges and advantages secured by the ordinance of 1787, and at that time enjoyed by the people of the Mississippi Territory.

In the case above mentioned, Permoli claimed the protection of the clause in one of the six articles, which provides for the freedom of religion, alleging that it had been violated by the First Municipality. And he brought this question before this court on the ground that it had jurisdiction under the ordinance. But the court held that the ordinance ceased to be in force, when Louisiana became a State, and dismissed the case for want of jurisdiction. This opinion is indeed confined to the territory in which the case arose. But it is evident that the ordinance cannot be in force in the States formed in the North-western Territory to which it was extended by the present government. For the ordinance and the pledges of the Congress of the old Confederation cannot be more enduring and obligatory than those of the new Government, nor can there be any reason for giving a different interpretation to the same words used in similar instruments, because the one is by the old confederation and the other by the present Government. And when it is decided that this ordinance is not in force in Louisiana, it follows that it cannot be in force in Ohio.

But the whole question upon the ordinance of 1787, and the acts of Congress extending it to other territory afterwards acquired, was carefully considered in Pollard vs. Hagan, 3 How, 212. The subject is fully examined in the opinion pronounced in that case, with which we concur; and it is sufficient now to refer to the reasoning and principles by which that judgment is maintained, without entering again upon a full examination of the question. Indeed it is impossible to look at the six articles, which are supposed in the argument to be still in force, without seeing at once that many of the provisions contained in them are inconsistent with the present constitution. And, if they should be regarded as yet in operation in the States formed within the limits of the North-western territory, it would place them in an inferior condition as compared with the other States, and subject their domestic institutions and municipal regulations to the constant supervision and control of this court. The Constitution was, in the language of the ordinance, "adopted by common consent," and the people of the territories must necessarily be regarded as parties to it, and bound by it, and entitled to its benefits, as well as the people of the then existing States. It became the supreme law throughout the United States. And so far as any obligations of good faith had been previously incurred by the ordinance, they were faithfully carried into execution by the power and authority of the new government.

In fact, when the constitution was adopted, the settlement of the vast territory was hardly begun; and the people who filled it, and formed the new populous States that now cover it, became inhabitants of the territory after the constitution was adopted, and migrated upon the faith, that its protection and benefits would be extended to them, and that they would, in due time, according to its provisions and spirit, be admitted into the Union upon an equal footing with the old States. For the new government secured to them all the public rights of navigation and commerce which the ordinance did, or could provide for; and, moreover, extended to them, when they should become States, much greater power over their municipal regulations and domestic concerns than the confederation had agreed to concede. The six articles, said to be perpetual as a compact, are not made part of the new constitution. They certainly are not superior and paramount to the constitution, and cannot confer power and jurisdiction upon the court. The whole judicial authority of the courts of the United States is derived from the constitution itself, and the laws made under it.

It is undoubtedly true that most of the territorial provisions and principles of these six articles, not inconsistent with the Constitution of the United States, have been the established law within this territory ever since the ordinance was passed; and hence the ordinance is sometimes spoken of as still in force. But these provisions owed their legal validity and force, after the constitution was adopted, and while their territorial government continued, to the act of Congress of August 7, 1789, which adopted and continued the ordinance of 1787 and carried its provisions into execution, with some modifications, which were necessary to adapt its form of government to the new constitution. And in the States since formed in the Territory, these provisions, so far as they have been preserved, owe their validity and authority to the Constitution of the United States, and the constitutionality of the laws of the respective States, and not the authority of the ordinance of the old confederation. As we have already said, it ceased to be in force from the adoption of the constitution, and cannot now be the source of jurisdiction of any description in this court. In every view of the subject, therefore, this court had no jurisdiction over the case, and the writ of error on that ground, must be dismissed."

It is almost unnecessary to say---for they are very apparent---that here, only two matters are disposed of. That both should be maintained as they have been heretofore understood, and, as the social and civil States are built on them, is very important to the *white* man; but still, the difficulties of a decision, overturning the common belief, are not insupportable by him: but such a decision is disastrous, ruinous, to the *free colored* man. The opinion decides that the third clause of the fourth article of the constitution, "No person held to service or labor," &c., does not furnish even the protection it was supposed to furnish. We expect to make it very evident, that an important part of the decision, when taken in connection with the late Fugitive slave act, furnishes *none*. The other part of the decision declares that the ordinance of '87 had no validity any longer than the adoption of the Constitution of the United States, that whatever validity it had, it derived from its being adopted by Congress in 1789; and *then*, only as other laws of Congress, applying alone to the Northwestern Territory or territories, in which, as soon as they became *States*, it ceased to operate.

We think it needless to delay here, to prove that *any* thing is generally or universally received by the country or not, but we cannot mistake when we assert, that in virtue of the clause already referred to (3d clause of 4th art. of the Constitution), any slave brought into a free State, by the authority of his owner, is, to all intents and purposes, *free*. If the argument of counsel, as the court seem to think, was intended to add any thing to the constitutional provision, by urging the previous employment of the negroes in Ohio, it was useless, to say the least of it. They were free whether employed or not. The moment a slave, by the consent of the owner, touches the soil of a State where all are free, that moment he owes allegiance to her laws, and that moment his rights are meant to be protected as the rights of others are. From this opinion we have heard no dissentient one, either among the learned or unlearned. We entertain no doubt, that it was the intention of the Revolutionists of 1776, as well as of the framers of the Constitution,* to make free colored men just what other citizens are, and not to take their complexion, or former condition, at all, into the account. To make what we intend so plain that no person can mistake it—if a colored man were taken by his owner, or by his authority, into a free State, and there should be given to him, or bequeathed to him a sufficient amount of property—admitting that there was a property-qualification—so that, as far as that was concerned, he could vote, he could exercise this right, entirely independently of his color, as others could. Indeed, if we proceed on the supposition, that they intended, that slavery should not last long to mar and defile what they had said and done—a supposition that is not only maintainable by the best records we have of our independence and of the formation of the Constitution, but without it, all that is said in them about the equality of man, the blessings of liberty, &c., &c., is not only idle and unmeaning bluster, but meant to deceive others at a distance—then, we say, they had good reasons, nay

imperative ones, too, for doing and saying as they did. They would, of course, wish to diminish the number of slaves. And what could they do more promotive of that purpose, than so to operate on the same class, as to make them desire to be free? And how could they better operate on that class, than to make the condition of the liberated person as desirable as possible? And how could they more successfully accomplish this, than to place them at once among those who voted, and who performed all the duties, and took on them all the responsibilities of citizens? We should thus connect them, not so much with the persecutions as with the interests, of the country; make them its friends rather than its enemies, by throwing them back into a class, in spite of all their efforts to escape from it; a class which, from its ignorance and wrongs are very inflammable. We should certainly not judge of them by their complexion, or by the former condition of their ancestors—characteristics that they cannot help or wash out by any alchemy with which we are acquainted. To do this was to do wisely; and, in this way, our fathers of the Declaration of Independence and of the Constitution did. But it is not so now. We have verified the old adage, that, *"whom the gods intend to destroy they first make mad."* Where we should act most wisely we act most foolishly—for the free colored people, influencing the slaves, have the greatest power to do us harm. As long as we continue to keep the slaves as *slaves*, we ought to lead them, as far as we can, on the road to justice. It takes but little reflection to convince us of this. But our passions are too strong for these checks, and we have given way to them. And it may be always observed that, although the injured party may forgive, the injuring party rarely does—and never, whilst he perseveres in doing the injury.

If a foreigner, other than African, comes to settle among us, and is, in due time, *naturalized*, and takes up his residence, we will suppose, in South Carolina: as soon as he acquires the qualifications that other men possess, to vote, he does so. He is not classed with foreigners who have not been naturalized—for he has left that class—but with those who vote and assume all the duties and responsibilities of the citizen. In this case, we act as we ought to do,

---

* If they thought so, and embodied their opinion in the Constitution, the work of their hands, then all laws, primary or secondary, of the States, and made to keep the colored man, because he is colored, out of their limits, or so to oppress him, when he comes within them, that he will be compelled to leave them, are manifestly unconstitutional.

and attach him to the country by the strongest ties we can apply. But if a colored citizen, we will suppose, of Massachusetts, who is competent in that State to fill its highest office, if the people choose to put him in it,* emigrates to the south, with a view of settling there, he is, at once, classed with those who do *not* vote—with those who are free colored people, and whom, with the slaves, it may be, he resembles only in his complexion, or in the former condition of himself, or his ancestors.

Any other interpretation of the constitution than the one we contend for, would annul that portion of the instrument which declares, that the "the citizens of each State shall be entitled to all the privileges and immunities of citizens in the several States:" for we well know,† that a citizen of Massachusetts—by the strictest rule a citizen—when he goes to South Carolina, cannot exercise the same privileges he may in Massachusetts. This is owing solely to what he cannot change, or nobody for him, and which has in it no moral or intellectual quality—his complexion, or his former condition, or the condition of his ancestors.

We are not unaware that a different opinion has been delivered by one (the late Judge Kent) having high reputation as a jurist; but when he says that a colored citizen of Massachusetts who voted in the latter, and who emigrates to North Carolina, would have no right to vote in the latter State, he is, in our judgment, wrong in his construction of the Constitution. That instrument will not bear such a construction, and it would be doing wrong to the makers of it, to suppose that they ever intended, that a citizen, free colored or not, should lose his citizenship by the bare fact of emigrating from one State to another. And, would it not annul

* When we deny the competency of the colored man to fill any office, simply on account of his color, do we not, also, deny the sovereignty of the people?
† The writer believes that the interpretation now given to these words of the Constitution is only the *secondary* one. The *primary* one, as he thinks, relates to the "privileges and immunities" one may have on his trial for any offence. For example : suppose A., a citizen of New York, domiciled there, commits an act, charged to be treasonable, in Louisiana, in which State, of course, he is tried. On his trial, he shall have all the "privileges and immunities" that a citizen of Louisiana, domiciled there, would have. The secondary meaning now, one which, perhaps, it will always have, seems to have displaced the other, and doubtless is the most important. But if ever there should arise a necessity for a strict construction of the words, they will be found, it is thought, to have that which we suggest.

that article in the Constitution which requires of all judges, whether State or Federal, to support the Constitution in preference to supporting any State law opposed to it. We must here say, that we do not only not see the force of the reasoning, but, on the other hand, we are well convinced, that the framers of the Constitution and the ratifiers of it, never meant it should be so. The impression it makes on us is very deep, that they expected that the free colored man, who possessed the same qualifications that those did, who voted for *Representatives* in Congress, might, if he should so choose, vote for *them;* and that as the Constitution of the United States was declared to be the supreme law of the land, and therefore superior to any State Constitution, and as every major proposition includes the minor one relating to the same subject, it was not supposed that any State would wish to exclude them. To strengthen this view, we might instance the case of North Carolina herself, where free colored men had a right to vote, and did vote till the amendment of her Constitution in 1835, when they were deprived of it; the very men, perhaps, who may have assisted in electing the persons who made the amendment.

We have before said, if the counsel for the Plaintiffs in error insisted that the employment of the negroes in Ohio, under a law of that State, further than what we conceive is the fair meaning of the ordinance, made them free, it was, in our judgment at least, useless. "But this question," the court say, "is not before us." We have read the opinion again and again, to find out whether or not we had made any mistake, and whether there could be any important question except the one we are now examining. But we can find none. Had the Court condescended to give any reasons for its conclusions, we should, in all likelihood, have had no difficulty. But it has not; the opinion consisting only of *dicta* without arguments to rest them on, or to convince any one whether these *dicta* are true or not. For the most part, the opinion is plain and easily understood; but at this point, either we do not fully comprehend it, or the Court attempt to mystify the subject---to muddy the water and escape under the natural effect of their own efforts. But subsequent remarks in the same paragraph convince us that we labor under no misconception, but that the aim of the court was to make a clear and full impression that a State might do as it pleased with its colored population, and neither they nor the slaves had any right at all, under the Constitution of the United States, available against a State law. In the paragraph referred to, the opinion proceeds to say, that "Every State has an undoubted right to determine the *status* or domestic and social condition of the persons domiciled within its territory, except in so far as the powers of the State are restrained, or duties and obligations imposed upon them by the Constitution of the United States." This doctrine, though entirely groundless, is a very fanciful one, and by *itself* would lead us to distrust ourselves, and fear that we *had* fallen into some misapprehension of the meaning of the court. The Constitution of the United States, stronger, as the court admit, than any *State* constitution, does not attempt, further than, as, we think, it considers some among us as slaves, to define the *status*, or domestic or social condition of any one, but views all others who have been born in the country, or who have been *naturalized* as its citizens. The framers of the Constitution, if we can suppose them unwise enough to make so impossible an attempt, should have known that, although the legislature of a country, allowing it to be plenipotentiary in the premises, might declare one dollar should be called fifty cents, and have their mandate obeyed too, they could not, while the people remained at all free, make it purchase less than one hundred cents would buy. If then a State try to do it, let it not suppose that it can derive any authority from the Federal Constitution. We would sooner suppose there was some misapprehension in us, than that the court intended to set aside so plain and well understood a clause. But what follows must set all at rest on this head. The opinion says, "There is nothing in the Constitution of the United States that can, in any degree, control the law of Kentucky upon this subject. And the condition of the negroes, therefore, as to freedom or slavery, *after their return*, depended altogether upon the law of that State, and could not be influenced by the law of Ohio. It was *exclusively* in the power of Kentucky to determine for itself whether their employment in another State should or should not make

them free, *on their return*. The Court of Appeals have determined, that by the law of the State, they continued to be slaves."

Allowing this exposition of the Constitution to be the true one, and that there is really no conflict between it and the law of Kentucky, the consequence mentioned *must* follow. But the federal Constitution, as all persons heretofore believed it to be, declares, substantially, that any slave taken, for example, from Kentucky into Ohio by his owner or by his owner's permission. is free. On this event, there is no qualification or modification of the freedom bestowed, nor is there even a show of such qualification or modification in the Constitution, but the slave becomes free, and was to be free as any other citizen; has the right to go into any State of the Union, unmolested of course, wherever he wishes to go or wherever his business may call him—the Constitution by which he was manumitted protecting him every where. The law of Kentucky declares, that although a slave have gone from that State to Ohio, with the permission of his owner, and have returned, resuming the place and condition of a slave, that his former condition of freedom in Ohio, has no influence to keep him free in Kentucky, that State having, according to the court, an "*undoubted*" right to determine his *status*, or his domestic and social condition, whether he is at that time a visiter or domiciled among them. Freedom is, doubtless, of great value to the slave, or, indeed, to any one, although it may be limited to a certain State or States. But is it seriously and deliberately believed that this restricted freedom was the boon the framers of the Constitution intended to confer on the slave, when the condition on which he was to have it was fully performed? That they intended he should never revisit the scenes of his infancy, sad though they might be to him, lest the freedom he enjoyed might make others deprived of it less contented with their lot, or lest his doing so might be construed by the master, the only judge in the case, into a wish to return to slavery, and have wrested from him the very freedom which he most valued—for which, as things are commonly estimated, he may have paid an extravagant and extortionate price, and which he supposed the Constitution had fully secured to him? Can any one charge them—to use an

3

old adage—with thus "whipping the devil round the stump?"

Except the North Western Territory, there was no Territory belonging to the Union when the Constitution was made. With this exception all the territory was included in the *States*. If then any one State has an "undoubted right to determine the *status*, or domestic and social condition of those domiciled within her territory"—to reduce one part of her population to be the slaves of another part—any other State, the States being politically equal—has a right to do it. Where then, we ask, could the Constitutional provision, if it can at any time, be defeated by a State-law, operate? With this construction, it is a nullity, a mere *brutum fulmen*, a meteor not intended to extricate the unhappy follower, but to allure him into a more desperate situation.

Let us suppose, that Mr. Graham's negroes were put on board of the Pike by him, under the charge of Mr. Williams. While the slaves were in Kentucky, and while the Pike was there, too, we know that Mr. Graham had the power to do so. But when they reached Cincinnati, to which place Mr. Graham knew he was sending them, the matter was entirely changed. The steamboat and all on board were subject to Ohio laws. The authority of Mr. Williams, the representative of their master, ceased. There are no masters in the Kentucky sense, in Ohio. The negroes were freemen, under the Constitution of the United States, with all the responsibilities of freemen to the laws of Ohio. Their very migration with the consent of the master, into a State where all were free, had suddenly changed them from the unnatural condition of *things* into the natural condition of *men*. But these matters neither Mr. Graham nor his *charge* Mr. Williams, seem to have understood—hard as it is to suppose them ignorant of the Constitutional provision. In a short time, the negroes are summoned to go back to Kentucky. They decline the trip—but giving sufficient reasons to all for their determination—slaveholders and their minions excepted. By the aid of others, who care little for liberty, Mr. Williams gets possession of their persons, and is about taking them to Kentucky, whether or not. A writ of Habeas Corpus is sued out in their behalf, commanding that they should be brought forthwith before a judge. Here they prove even a negative—that

they had NOT ESCAPED. but that they were brought to Ohio without any consultation with them, and that Mr. Williams. who received his directions from their master in Kentucky, was told to bring them into Ohio. Under the provision of the Constitution of the United States, already quoted, they are at once discharged. But Mr. Williams, looking on them as always to be slaves and nothing else, does not comprehend how they can so soon be transformed into *men*—does not at all understand the *rationale* of so summary a proceeding. He communicates the result, so sad to him, and apparently so disastrous to his principal, Mr. Graham. Neither does Mr. Graham fully see the reason why he was so quickly deprived of his slaves—particularly as he had taken all necessary precautions as far as he knew, against it. No doubt he thought, once a slave, always a slave. Like the clown to whom fifteen shillings was shown, and he thought it all the money in the world, Mr. Graham may have set down Kentucky as the greatest of all States—that none could differ much from her, and that his slaves must be his slaves every where. In this dilemma he goes to his lawyer to see what can be done. He is told that any State has an undoubted right to determine the *status* or domestic and social condition of persons domiciled within her territory, so that there be no conflict in this respect with the United States; that there is nothing in the Constitution of the latter that can, in any degree, control the law of Kentucky in this matter; that the condition of the negroes, as to freedom or slavery, *after their return* depended altogether on the laws of Kentucky, in whose power it was exclusively to determine whether their employment in another State, and, of course, their being there, should or should not make them free, *on their return;* that the Court of Appeals, the highest *State* Court, had decided that, in such cases, the negroes continued to be slaves, and that the only difficulty in the way, was to get them back into Kentucky. Now, is not there enough here to bewilder *any* common man, if his prejudices and interests are *with* the lawyer! Indeed, there is enough to bewilder almost *any* man if he is seeking information from another to guide him, when that other, too, is set down as knowing more about such matters than the inquirer does—so much more that he makes a due understanding of them part of his profession.

The great aim now is, in some way, to get the negroes back into Kentucky. But how is this to be done? The lawyer thinks, that the Fugitive Slave Act, just now passed by Congress, can be made well to suit his, and Mr. Graham's purposes. They had been so long accustomed to consider the slaves as entitled to none of the rights of human beings, that were the negroes to be inveigled back by false pretenses, or even by a downright falsehood, it would be deemed a clever trick. With the slaveholders, the negroes are not taken into the account, and as for the Yankees, or sons of Yankees, at Cincinnati, who are trying, they say, not to uphold their own institutions, but to *cleal* their negroes from them, they get only what they deserve!

Now we are not going to say, that Mr Graham is, in any respect, more unjust than slaveholders generally are—for we know nothing about him personally—but we suppose he is as ignorant and uninformed, as we know most of them to be. Nor are we, at all unaware, that the price of a single slave, valued by slaveholders, is, at all times, a great temptation—but especially *now*; nor do we suppose any lawyer need be told, how decisive will be his influence on a mind, such as we have described particularly if his advice is directed to the recovery of property that his client considers somewhat doubtful, or a full equivalent for it. Nor need he be told how lavishly his professional advice is given to one, when the latter and not himself, is to pursue it. The Fugitive Slave Act, as a convenient mode, comes into his mind. It will be quite an easy matter f r Mr. Graham to say—for there is no one to examine *what* he says—without alluding in the remotest manner to the fact of his having formerly sent the slaves to Cincinnati—that he had three slaves who, without his consent, were taken on board the steamboat Pike, then in the limits of Kentucky, in a manner forbidden by the law; that they had thus escaped from him, and that he has reason to believe they are in Cincinnati. He gets these facts—for they are such—all thrown into the form required by the Fugitive Slave law—passes them duly through the Court, and he has all that is necessary to his *ex parte* case, cut and dried, prepared for use, without any one to question him. The negroes, relying on the liberty they had acquired under the Constitution of the General Government, are still in Cincinnati, pursuing their ordinary vocations, without the least suspicion that they can again be reduced to slavery. In this condition Mr. Graham arrests them as his slaves. That he may the more easily accomplish his purpose, he watches his opportunity when no Judge of the United States Court is at hand, and takes them before a *Commissioner*. Here nothing but the *identity* is inquired into. This is fully made out by Mr. Graham's neighbors, who saw the negroes that were arrested working for him a few days before. He proves, too, all that took place about the Pike receiving them on board without his consent—in fine, that, they are his fugitive slaves. To prevent all *molestation* from any one, during the transfer to Kentucky, he takes the certificate.

Now here is a case where a slave may be made a freeman by—as far as we know—the universally received construction of this part of the Constitution, since it was made and ratified, and be reduced to slavery again by the operation of a *State* law. The operation of this provision was partially annulled by the decision in the Prigg case. The quiet and submissive manner in which this was received by the country. emboldened the Court and the other friends of slavery, till, at last, by the late Fugitive Slave Act, and the decision in hand, they have proceeded to annul it completely. This act, notwithstanding its gross violation of the principles of liberty we have no doubt, the Court will declare constitutional; such as was justly due to the South, and such as Congress ought to have passed. If there be a decision of the first Court in the land calculated to sink us in our own respect—in the respect of nations advancing almost with perceptible rapidity, in the march of civilization—to reduce us to the level of Spain and Portugal and Brazil, the basest nations of the civilized world; or of the rude and barbarous tribes of heathen Africa, this is that decision. Let us no longer boast before the world that we are the freest goverument of it, for we not only carry on the slave trade, driving it with our characteristic energy by water and by land, but we suffer the poor and defenseless, who have become free in the manner pointed ont by our fathers, to be again brought into slavery. To the fugitives from the oppression of other nations who come among us, we almost *give* a share of the public domain, but to the African, that statesman would be looked on as a fanatic who would offer any of it, large as it is. We not only exclude him, though he may have bought his freedom at a high price*—from any gratuitous share of the public domain, and although his ancestors may have died as slaves in the service of ours, but we exclude him by our *power*, not by the *Constitution*, from coming within the limits of many of the States. Fugitives from other lands we welcome—our own fugitives we hunt with dog and gun.

Those of a faith sufficiently unscrupulous to credit any monstrous marvel that may be presented to it may believe with the Court, that the fathers of the Revolution intended to declare—that the fathers of the Constitution intended to insert into that instrument with their own hands, so detestable, so fraudulent a provision. But knowing their characters as we do, and having the register of what they did before us, we cannot believe it. The truth we know is to be preferred to all things—then let not their memories be traduced, but give them the honor to which they are entitled.

But supposing the slaves, when brought back to Kentucky are persuaded to try the effect of the writ of *Habeas Corpus*—for they may have learned that this writ cannot be suspended, unless on two contingencies, neither of which then existed. And they will try the least glimmering of hope when liberty is the prize. Application may be made to a State Judge, or to a Judge of the United States, the mere creature of the Supreme Court, and in either instance, a slaveholder. But it may be met, by his saying, the writ does not apply to one in slavery; that (although uncharged with crime) *they* (the slaves) are in the custody of their masters (who, to be sure, are neither officers themselves nor deputed by officers) and that Attorney-General Crittenden has declared, that the writ has no relation to slaves—that it is not even mentioned in the Fugitive Slave Act—that it *follows* the law—is only the law's servant, &c., &c.

Thus it may be seen that, what with the decision in the *Prigg* case, aided by the one before us, together with the Fugitive Slave act, and by the legislative act of a State, the free colored people can have no *feeling* of security any where, in the Union. On the contrary, that, in a government, made in our low estate, to secure the blessings of liberty; in a government (taking the Declaration of Independence as part of it) that possessed many noble truths—democratic in its character—and proclaiming itself the asylum of the oppressed of all nations, we not only debate in our highest legislature whether slavery may not be the will of God, and therefore right, but we therefore conclude, that it is, and practically demonstrate our conclusions, by enslaving three millions of our fellow-beings—subjecting them to an everlasting bondage of body and mind—while about one-sixth of that number, on whom, or on whose forefathers, the boon of freedom was conferred, and who have dwelt among us for many years, are exposed every day to be delivered up to the slaveholder, to be by him led away into interminable bondage.

—

NOTE.

It occurred to the writer, after he had prepared the last chapter, that the constitutional provision might have been construed as it was, because the slaves, after having been *once* in Ohio, *voluntarily*—as far as we know—returned to the condition of slavery to Mr. Graham. But as this can make no difference we would reluctantly attribute a decision on this ground to any respectable court, much less to one esteemed very enlightened.

The Conventionists thought—as all sensible men, who have reflected on the subject do—that freedom is the *natural* state of man, and slavery the exception, or an *unnatural* state. Knowing that the ignorance of the slave would render him incompetent to make any moral distinction, however plain to others,—and that the *interest* of the owner might lead him to interpret it too much in his own favor, they made the freedom of the slave depend on his crossing a certain line with the consent of the owner. This act is neither moral nor immoral of itself; indeed, it has no moral quality in it. If the slave cannot judge of *it* as well as the owner can, he can judge of it, at least, as well as he can of any thing else. After he has once crossed this line as we have said, and therefore acquired his freedom, if he should be again taken into slavery, it demonstrates, in a very prominent manner, the great ignorance of the slave, the superiority of the owner's intelligence, his unwillingness to grant the slave his liberty, and that he has no *princi-* ple to restrain him from kidnapping on the African coast, if the temptation and risk should be as they are here.

The employment or the non-employment of the slaves in Ohio can have nothing to do with the question, and the arguments in the text are as entirely applicable as if the matter had never been thought of.

CHAPTER III.

Ordinance of 7787.

We will now consider the ORDINANCE and the circumstances under which it was entered into, that every one may plainly see, why we cannot coincide with the court, when rhey say it expired at the time the present constitution was adopted; that it received all its efficacy from the law of 1789, passed by the first Congress under the present constitution, *adapting* it *formally* to that constitution, that, therefore, it is to be viewed as merely a secondary or derivative law having application only to a Territorial form; and that as Ohio, Indiana, Illinois, Michigan and Wisconsin, parts of the Northwestern Territory, have become STATES, it has no application to them, and that, not being a part of the Constitution of the United States, it furnishes no rule of decision for the court, having lost whatever validity it once had.[*]

We may say at least, as much of the Ordinance, as we have said of the provision of the constitution already discussed—never was popular interpretation—and this includes the gifted and intelligent as well as the unlearned—more harmonious as to its continuing validity. As far as we know—till the late decision of the United States courts—we never heard from any one, be he "Greek or Barbarian," that the ordinance was at all doubtful or questionable.

Congress have passed acts, on the application of "districts of the North-Western Territory about to become STATES, mentioned above, in which they have proceeded on the still binding efficacy of the ordinance; and as it gave to these "districts" of the Territory the right of admission as STATES into the Union, when they contained a certain population, they have uniformly claimed it. Thus it would appear, that in their Ter-

ritorial form there was conferred on them a right which they could use in their *transition state.* In all these instances, Congress not only considered the ordinance of unspent efficacy on *them*, but they charge the districts applying to them—for their admission into the Union depended on their compliance—not to violate, in their forthcoming constitution, any of the "articles" in the ordinance. The convention, too, considered themselves as bound by the ordinance, and carefully observed it.

We, by no means, intend to insist that children or descendants must think as their parents and ancestors did : far from it. Nor do we mention this matter but with the view of showing what, at these several times, and ever since, as we think, was the unbroken consent of Congress and the convention about forming constitutions for the States carved out of the Northwestern Territory.

The legislatures of these States, too—although the territorial form had been changed—have considered themselves bound by the ordinance. Nor have the courts thought differently. We do not wish to be understood as saying that the ordinance has never been violated. No doubt it has; but this does not make it less obligatory than the commission of murder makes the law for the punishment of that crime less obligatory. The Supreme Court of Ohio, for instance, does not hesitate to declare the articles of the compact—the ordinance—as not only equal to the constitution, but superaior to it, for it says, "The Constitution may be altered by the people of the State, while *these* cannot be altered without the assent of the people of this State and of the United States through their representatives. It is an article of *compact,* and until we assume the principle that the sovereign power of the State is not bound by the compact, this alone must be considered obligatory."[*] And

---

[*] For a convention called together to make a State Constitution, so to form it that the State wil on it be admitted into the Union, and then for a convention to meet and form another, which would have kept it out, is a base juggle that has never yet been tried, and for the honor of the country, it is to be hoped if never will. Should it, however, be tried, it is, also, to be hoped that the fraudulent attempt will be met by Congress in a becoming manner.

---

[*] Hogg v. Zanesville Canal and Manufacturing Company, 5 Ohio Rep. 414.

even Justice McLean (residing in Ohio), of the Supreme Court of the United States, referring to the possibility that a majority of the voters of Ohio might so alter the Constitution (of the State) as to admit slavery, observed, " But does not the compact prevent such an alteration without the consent of the original States? If this be not the effect of the compact, its import has been misconceived by the people of the State generally. They have looked upon the provision as a security against the introduction of slavery, *even beyond the provisions of the Constitution.* And this consideration has drawn masses of population into our State, who now repose under all the guaranties which are given on this subject by the Constitution and the Compact."* And Justice Story, in his notice of the Ordinance, in his work on the Constitution, does not intimate any doubt as to the permanent obligation of its articles of compact."†

We should be dealing unjustly with those witnesses not to suppose that they were fully aware that the compact, or ordinance, formed no part of the Constitution—was not inserted into it; but that there were some things not embodied in that instrument, which were at least as obligatory as *it* was. The ordinance was not intended to confer any power on the court, nor to take away any, nor indeed does it. Let us suppose a public debt—for instance, ours to Holland or France or to our own citizens—for money loaned to the confederation to forward the cause of our national independence. The obligation to pay this debt can never be obliterated, but by the extinction of the nation—a thing not looked for among the civilized communities of the present day—or by payment—no matter what change of government may come, or what phasis may be assumed. *It is the debt of the* NATION. Not paying the interest on it—and we were beginning not even to do this under the confederation—is no discharge of the debt. Insolvency may be borne with, till better times, but repudiation, the odious resort of an imperfectly civilized people, is no satisfactory adjustment of the claim—the obligation to pay it remaining as strong as ever. Among nations there is no statute

of limitations, as there may be, properly enough, among individuals. The republic of France is liable for any public or national debt that may have been contracted by her most despotic monarchs; and we, ourselves, not many years since, collected from Louis Philippe a debt for wrongs done to our commerce by Bonaparte.

But if payment is the only mode by which communities can be released from the obligation of a debt, where then was the use of engrafting on the present constitution the clause declaring that, all debts contracted by the confederation should be as valid against the United States under the new constitution as the old? It was not indispensable, not absolutely necessary, for this object. Minds conversant with these things will at once, see the force of the foregoing remarks; but in order to take away every ground of cavil—to make very clear what before was not altogether clear to all—out of abundant caution, too, and to commend the constitution to popular acceptance, as far as that matter went, the assumption was formally inserted. Now, many will be inclined to say, that a debt thus contracted and provided for, and unalterable, is more lasting than any constitution (for constitutions take measures for their own change), *can be,* and think with the Supreme Court of Ohio, that although the constitution may be altered by the people, the debt must always remain the same till discharged. In addition to the proofs we have offered, of the manner in which the ordinance was viewed, we add that of Mr. Webster, given at a time, too, when great confidence, especially by the free States, was attached to his construction of the constitution; when he was called in a peculiar manner, its EXPOUNDER, and when not the slightest suspicion was connected with him by any one. In his speech, in 1830, on Mr. Foote's Resolution, respecting the sale of the public lands, &c.. he says:

" I doubt whether any single law of any lawgiver, ancient or modern, has produced effects of more distinct, marked and lasting character, than the ordinance of '87. That instrument was drawn by Nathan Dane, then and now a citizen of Massachusetts. It was adopted, and I think I have understood, without the slightest alteration ; and certainly it has happened to few men to be the authors of a political measure of more large and

---

* Spooner *v.* McConnell, 1 McLean, 349.
† The above facts, respecting the courts, are from Senator Chase's Speech in the Van Zandt Case.

enduring consequence. It fixed, *forever*, the character of the population in the vast regions northwest of the Ohio, by excluding from them involuntary servitude. It impressed on the soil itself, an incapacity to bear up other than freemen. It laid the interdict against personal servitude, in original compact, not only deeper than all local laws, but deeper also, than all local constitution. Under the circumstances then existing, I look upon this original and reasonable provision as a real good attained. We see its consequence at this moment, and we shall never cease to see them, perhaps, while the Ohio shall flow." Further on in the same speech, Mr. W. says, "I spoke, sir, of the ordinance of 1789, which prohibited slavery *in all future times*, northwest of the Ohio, as a measure of great wisdom and foresight; and one which had been attended with highly beneficial and permanent consequences. I supposed, that, on this point, no two gentlemen of the Senate could entertain different opinions."

These proofs—and every one must know, they are but a drop of the ocean—would entitle us to all the benefits of "long acquiescence," as that doctrine was pronounced in the Prigg case. But did not we ourselves discard it in our examination of that case,* and did we not say it had no proper application to it—indeed, to no case where there was a *written* constitution, on the same subject? All this is freely admitted, but the two cases are widely different, as we will proceed to show. In the former, a clause was inserted into the constitution, making part of it, which had been interpreted differently in different parts of the country—each part acting on its own interpretation. As usual, the southern interpretation prevailed in Congress, as far as the south cared for it. Here, we say, the Supreme Court ought to have intervened, and said what the constitution *was*—for it required but *one* thing. But in the case before us there is—as far as we are aware—an unbroken chain of proofs from the institution of the government, till the Supreme Court have made the attempt of late to change it. We have Congress after Congress passing laws for the holding of conventions, with

a special view to making *constitutions* for parts of the Northwestern Territory, and requiring them—in order to secure their admission into the Union—to conform to the "unalterable" parts of the ordinance; the different conventions recognizing the right of Congress to do so, and conforming in all respects; the local legislatures basing their legislation on this; the highest State courts, their decisions; the people' every where recogniizng its validity, with no dissentient practice under it any where; orators of every grade expatiating on it, ascribing the great progress of the States formed under the ordinance to the effects of it, and to its enduring character, and all this without a single unharmonious note: surely, if any case is entitled to all the benefits of "long acquiescence," this seems to be that case. The doctrine is thus laid down by the court in page 87 of the Prigg case: "under such circumstances, if the question, were one of doubtful construction, such long acquiescence in it, such contemporaneous exposition of it, and such extensive and uniform recognition of its validity, would, in our judgment, entitle the question to be considered at rest, unless, indeed, the interpretation of the constitution is to be delivered over to interminable doubt throughout the whole progress of legislation of national operations. Congress, the executive, and the judiciary have upon various occasions acted upon this as a sound and reasonable doctrine. Especially did the court in the case of *Stewart* vs. *Laird*, 1 Cranch, Rep., 299, and *Martin* vs. *Hunter*, 1 Wheaton Rep., 364; and in *Cohen* vs. *The Commonwealth of Virginia*, 6 Wheaton Rep. 264, rely upon contemporaneous expositions of the constitution and long acquiescence in it with great confidence, in the discussions of questions of a highly interesting and important nature."

We would here leave this part of the subject did we not wish to examine some of the reasoning used by this court to sustain this part of their monstrous decision. Permit us then to ask *why*, if a public debt be as inviolable, as well-informed and sound-principled men believe it to be—*why*, we say, shall we not construe the expression which immediately follows, "and engagements entered into"* in the same manner? *Engagement* may be considerd the generic word,

---

* The writer has prepared an examination of the decision in the Prigg case, to which he here refers, but which he has not yet published.

* See 1st clause of 4th article of the constitution.

and *debt* as one of the species. Engagement includes debt, but debt not engagement. Debt being a thing by itself—whose characteristics are well understood by nations—being so much money granted on the one side and so much received on the other, to be repaid at a particular time, or times, with interest—it is usually spoken of by itself; just as in giving a history of lions, for instance, we speak of the *species*, but not a part of the *feline genus* to which they belong. The first meaning that Webster in his Dictionary attaches to engagement, is "making liable for debt,"—the second, "obligation by agreement or contract." Common parlance, too, and the best lexicographers will bear us out in saying, we may make *an engagement* to pay a debt. And if we were inclined to draw over any small auxiliary to this cause, we might well use the words, themselves, "all debts and engagements, &c. Now, here *debt* means the money advanced to the confederacy by foreign nations, and by our own citizens, to secure our independence. *Engagements* might be something else, for we might be in debt to others where money was not at all concerned, as in *services*.

Now it seems to us that a very important question arises here—if ever it could be made one—had the Congress of the confederacy, composed as it was of *entirely* sovereign States, any power to pay the debt necessary to be contracted for our independence—to enter into engagements that seemed to favor that purpose and to be for the good of the country! Whatever might have been said on the question when *introduced* into that Congress, we, by accepting the debts and engagements of the confederacy, have stopped ourselves from making it a question. Whatever *they* were bound to do, we bound ourselves to do.

That there was a perfectly harmonious understanding between the Congress which sat in New York and the Convention which sat at the same time in Philadelphia, and that they were fully aware of each other's proceedings we have no doubt. All the claims of the States to the Northwestern Territory had been relinquished to the confederacy—making it the sole owner, for the use of the league or Union, as it then existed. Proceedings in relation to governing it, were commenced as early as 1784, but were not perfected as they come to us till July, 1787.

4

We have said, it becomes us to know what the confederacy are bound to do. The great thing it was bound to do, was, to make some arrangements for paying the public debt; but will any one say they are less bound to keep their *engagements*, especially to their own citizens, from whom the means of paying the debt were to come? At this time, the government had *no* territory but the Northwestern, and this, with the exception of some scattered French settlements on the Kaskaskia, and some straggling American pioneers on the Ohio river—could not well be reached, for it was dangerous from the Indian, and almost impracticable from any then known mode of conveyance. Having no authority to abolish slavery in the States they represented, and seeing the evils of it there, these Representatives determined to begin its extinction in the first territorial region that came into their hands. They engaged, whilst the country was almost uninhabited, that there never should be slavery there, as it existed south of Mason and Dixon's line. This was the assurance and the encouragement given to every individual that settled in that country. Judge, then, what injustice would be done to the minority who had removed their all to this Territory—whose consciences were opposed to one human being making a slave of another, and whose reason and experience told them, that, to set up slavery was the worst curse that could be adopted for the improvement and colonization of any country:—judge, we repeat, what injustice would be done to a minority were slavery established by a majority. The government was also pledged, that whenever a *district*—Ohio, we will suppose—of this Territory attained a population of sixty thousand, it should be *entitled* to admission into the confederacy as one of the States of it, provided, that in making its constitution, the ordinance was conformed to. This was the promise—the engagement—of the government, and it contains the correlative promise and undertaking on the part of the inhabitants. Slavery was not only forbidden in future, but to show entire sincerity, the little that was already there—for some had at this time found its way there—was extinguished. No one could truly plead ignorance, for the Congress had taken all necessary means for diffusing the information—and as a matter of fact, it was fully known. This—leaving out the public debt—was the only engagement of importance entered into.

In taking possession of the country, as we did, after the new constitution went into operation, we assumed to do what the Congress of the Confederacy engaged to do—nothing more nor less. Now, supposing that from any cause, the people had not ratified the former, what would Congress have been bound to do, as far as the Northwestern Territory was concerned? Certainly, they would have been bound to keep their agreements, and there was no *money* in the matter; nothing but *services*—as the lawyer would say, *facio ut facias.* Suppose farther, that in order to enter the Union, as it then was, this district (Ohio) of the Northwestern Territory had formed a constitution in the contemplated manner. In doing this, she had performed *her* engagement, the *reciprocal* one was, then, on the part of Congress. It is performed, and the newly formed State (Ohio) is admitted into the Union. She gains admission only because her constitution conforms to certain principles.* If she abandoned them, the corresponding engagement on the part of the Confederacy, or Congress, would not exist, and she would *not* be admitted. Now, supposing still further, that after her object had been accomplished, she should immediately turn round—for if she can rightfully violate, at all, the principles that secured her admission, she can violate them when she chooses—and make a new constitution entirely subversive of them— What, then, ought Congress to have done? Eject her from the Union—reduce her again to a territorial condition, *if that can be done*—would be the spontaneous exclamation of all just persons. But, supposing still further, we well know that it cannot be done. In this dishonest event, those who are opposed to her remaining in the Union, must submit to the fraud, but we may be assured the objects of the device will adhere to the guilty State—though it be in the Union—as firmly as Repudiation adheres to the State of Mississippi; or, perhaps, as closely as the garment of the Centaur adhered to Hercules—till it was the occasion of his death.

---

* Senator Chase says, most of the principles established by the ordinance, for all time, as fundamental law, are nothing else than the principles of natural right and justice. There can be no *binding* law—indeed no law—primary or secondary—that opposes these.

CHAPTER IV

The Ordinance of 1787 *shortly Before and After the Institution of the Present Government.*

WE had expected—and we have done all that can be properly done toward it—that we should be able, in the historical part of this examination, to make *more* distinct what we did, with regard to the ordinance under the *confederacy,* and what was done with regard to it under the *government* that superseded the confederacy. But in approaching the boundaries which separate them — for the Congress of the Confederation managed the affairs of the country, till the 4th of March, 1789, when the present government was organized—we find the historic facts a good deal like vines—they paying no respect to the limit that divides the two governments, but running over it, and almost hiding it from the careless observer,—yet by one who will take the pains, it can be discovered, for it is *there,* and it only requires the foliage to be lifted up, in order to see it. This thing, however, is very certain—that when the *old* Congress handed over to the new government *all* the country, the latter undertook to pay *all* the debts it had contracted, and *all* the engagements it had entered into. But the performance of an engagement must, in the view of right-minded persons, be *substantially,* according to the mode in which it was promised to be done, unless the promissor be released from it by the promissee, or unless the terms of it be changed by the consent of both parties. The executive, the legislative, and, indeed, all that had any thing to do in the matter, did to the North western Territory *according* to the ordinance,—looking on that instrument as entirely valid. It is only the Judiciary that has given an opinion at variance with the commonly received one. That there is error in the departments mentioned, or in the Judiciary, there can be no doubt. The best way of resolving it is, to find out what the *Congress of the Confederation* bound itself to do in regard to engagements with the Northwestern Territory; for we suppose no one will pretend that *we* were not bound faithfully to carry out what had been promised by the party whose promise we assumed.

Let us again suppose that the present constitution, having failed to secure the popular ratification, went out entirely, and was of no avail,—that the confederation—at least as far as the Northwestern Territory was concerned—was still in existence; and that one of the "districts"—the eastern one, we will suppose—deeming itself, from population, *entitled* to admission to the Union, wished to form a State constitution preparative thereto: would not her obligation to conform to the ordinance be as complete as it ever was, and the obligation of Congress to admit her be as valid as it was in 1787, when the ordinance was passed? If Congress had the right to pass an ordinance for the government of a Territory, then fully belonging (politically) to the sovereignties represented in that body—and if they were empowered to govern it, as long as it remained a Territory, had they not power to say on what terms it should emerge from a territorial form, to assume a grade that would bring it into the Union of States? Could not Congress in 1787, when they had undisputed possession of the country, then almost a wilderness, as well say, what should be the "fundamental" principles of its government as a Territory, and the "basis" of all "constitutions" which "forever thereafter should be formed in the said Territory: to provide also for the future establishment of State and permanent governments therein, and their admission to a share of the federal councils," as well as they could do it afterward, when application should actually be made for admission? To make the application as strong and binding on both parties as possible, the Congress called it a *compact;* and, as if to put it beyond any moral power to alter it—indeed, to make it unchangeable, irrepealable—this compact is considered as "between the original State and the people and States in the said Territory, and forever [to] remain unalterable, excep by common consent."* But it may be said that *any compact* or mutual obligation was needless—indeed, that it could not exist as against the confederacy—the higher power—inasmuch as the confederacy could compel its Territory to adopt any form of government it might choose to impose. If this argument be admitted as a good one, it abrogates all capacity in any government—for instance, the United States—to make any binding contract with her Territory. We shall not stop here to prove the position unsound, and untenable, and tyrannical, if it should be attempted to be enforced—but we view it as no small thing to get the *principles* of any government cheerfully complied with, and to have all the institutions of a country founded on them. As far as the States represented in Congress were concerned, they, to be sure, were not bound as individuals may be bound to one another—for individuals acknowledge a superior power to enforce their obligations, should they fail to perform them—and States don't; but then *they* are bound by the highest obligation that can be imposed—to do what they have pledged themselves before the world to do—especially when the thing to be done is *right.*

But this reasoning, which appears so sound to us, and which, indeed, appears so sound to the whole country—not, in all likelihood, even excepting the court itself—the decision renders thoroughly inapplicable; but it asserts that the ordinance was completely annulled or repealed by the ratification of the present constitution; and that the organization under it, was a full *merger* of the "common consent," without which the articles were to be "forever unalterable."

We must here say, that no part of the decision has, so much as this, given us a distrust of the integrity of the court.†

It appears quite irreconcileable with the intelligence we have attributed to that body. Nor will we say that the court, even in this instance, intended to violate the constitution. Yet we know there are other motives by which persons are sometimes influenced, that equally lead to the same disastrous results. The court seem to think so fervently that no part of this wide country, however well it may suit all others, is the place for the free colored man; and so earnestly to desire his departure from it, that, instead of spreading over him that justice—so honorable to a court anywhere—and which the constitution so amply secures to all *white* freemen, and that kindness and benevolence which the wrongs we have, as a people, done to him, or to his ancestors, should make grateful to us, and which his weakness and helplessness constantly call for—instead of doing this, the court seem ready to do all they can do—even to the breaking of the constitution—to accomplish their purpose of driving the colored people from among us—they seem to care little where.

But we will examine this matter from another point of view. Suppose, again, a *district* of the Northwestern Territory —that part of it which soon became Ohio —wishes to omit, in the constitution she is about to form, the articles of the ordinance—especially the one relating to slavery—how shall she proceed to get the "common consent" to the change? In our judgment, the way is this: the matter ought to be distinctly submitted to the people of the Territory in such manner as would best gain their opinion, one way or the other. We say the consent of the *Territory,* for the whole of it is a party to the compact. There is very good reason for this—strange as it may seem to many—lying right on the surface; for it is a matter of no small importance to the residue of the Territory, whether it shall have adjoining it a free State or a slave State, with all the influence of the latter, too, on the States yet to be formed.* We here say nothing about her having a right virtually to repeal or annul what was only confirmative of the declaration by which we came

---

*The *wisdom* of fixing, at that time, what those fundamentals should be, is *now,* if it was not *then,* very apparent. It enabled that country, from the *first,* to mould its institutions in conformity with the ordinance—with the expectation of always remaining a free country—without the taint of slavery.

†This distrust is a good deal increased when the court say, the ordinance is "*sometimes*" spoken of as "still in force." We will not say what the court has heard, or what it has not heard; but this we are very certain of, that admitting they heard the ordinance "*sometimes*" spoken of as still in force, what they heard did not, in the slightest manner, affect the sentiment of the public at large.

*The correctness of the contest about California in Congress—whether she should be admitted as a free or slave State—is decisive proof of the importance attached to this matter.

into being as a nation, or about its acts being opposed to natural justice; but we will suppose that these subjects are indifferent, and (with regard to them) that she could do as she pleased. We will now suppose that the popular assent is gained. The next step is the assent of the Legislature of the Territory, if it has but one legislature, or the assent of the legislature of the district, if it has one. If there should be one, two or more legislatures in the Territory, the assent of them *all* should be obtained. This will probably agree with that of the people. If a *State* should desire it, the assent of the Legislature, after getting the assent of the people in the manner just now mentioned, is to be obtained. This completes what is to be done as far as the Territory, or a State, or a district is concerned.

After this, there must be obtained the consent of the "original States," to be procured in some satisfactory manner. It is not *necessary* to be done in Congress—for other States than the "original" ones have nothing whatever to do with it. They are, in no way, parties to the contract—no right to vote on the question was reserved to them, and it is no part of the sovereignty possessed by them, on being admitted into the Union. Although the "*new*" States heretofore have acted on the question conjointly with the original States,* we do not once think, that the latter have any right to transfer or assign to the former, on their admission, the privilege which was confined—as far as words can go toward such an object—to the "*original* States." Nor is it at *this* time, even required that *all* the original States should unite in granting the permission, for only a majority of the members present—and that majority may be made up *entirely* by members from the *new* States—is deemed necessary, just as in the enactment of any other law.

But many will be ready to exclaim—the process you recommend is too difficult; and if not physically impossible, it appears to be morally so. When, however, the object of Congress is considered—the ultimate, but quiet abolition of slavery in all the States—our surprise very much abates. That the process for which we contend is difficult—so much so as to be almost impossible, especially in a moral point of view—is fully admitted. But, up to this time, we had given to the world no proofs, that, as *one* people, we were sincere in announcing the truths contained in the Declaration of Independence. Indeed, the proofs we had furnished from the slave states were entirely contradictory of them. The convention had now the opportunity, in the very first territory which they got into their possession, of giving *some* evidence, at least, of their sincerity, and of the wish of the country to abolish a system which was at war not only with whet had been said and done during the strife for national independence, but which they might have thought could not successfully be attacked as a political measure.

This appears to be a sufficient reason for *enacting* the ordinance, but it would not have produced the effect it was calculated, and, in all probability, intended to produce, unless it was made *permanent*. But ought difficulty, of itself, to be an objection with *us?* There is not a State constitution in the land in which the majority-principle is not set aside; and, with nearly all persons these constitutions are popular. Indeed, they are often commended, chiefly on the ground of the difficulty of amending or changing them. The Constitution of the United States, so dear to a vast majority, according to their interpretation of it, as we have lately seen, furnishes no exception. It probably will never be changed again, unless in some matter of mere form and convenience: for the dominant party can so stretch it as to make it cover any measure they may wish to adopt: the opposing one think that some day *they* will come into power, and that the example of their adversaries will be a good precedent for *them*.

But the court say, that the ordinance, thus endued with a lasting character, as far as words could give it, has been repealed by the adoption of the present constitution; and that this adoption was a substantial and sufficient giving of "common consent." That there is great error here, and that it may be made, as

---

* We do not mean that Congress is not to decide on admitting a State into the Union, but we mean that the question of slavery in the States formed out of the Northwestern Territory is *first* to be consented to by all the *original* States. Whether slavery shall enter into the consideration of members, or not, will depend altogether on the manner in which it is viewed.

we think, more apparent, let A be considered as the CONFEDERATION, and B, as the Northwestern Territory, and that they have entered into a mutual compact, by which A promises to do certain things, and B will do certain other things. After making the agreement, A clothes himself anew and assumes additional responsibilities to his coadjutors. In assuming them, he is not unmindful of his engagement with B—determines to fulfill it, in his new character, and thinks it amply provided for by a clause in the new constitution. B, as far as we know, is satisfied with it, for he has no representative or delegate in the convention, and his opinion of the matter was unknown: for it is a historic fact of which it may be necessary only to remind our readers, that, at the time of holding the convention, no territory was attached to the country but the Northwestern, and that, with the exception mentioned, almost uninhabited; and that a clause exists in the constitution, providing that when a certain number of States ratify it by their subordinate conventions, it shall be adopted: Territories out of the question.

Both parties to the contract proceeded in good faith, for they both thought that what they had done had the force of a constitutional provision. But the court say, it has utterly expired, and that it was renewed by the acts of Congress of August 7, 1789, and that, whatever validity it has had was derived from that act.

It is true, that at the very first session of Congress, after the new government was organized, the act alluded to was passed, entitled " An act to provide for the government of the Territory northwest of the Ohio river." But this act has not the most distant reference to a change in the articles declared "forever unalterable by common consent." The reason for passing it—given to us in a "whereas"—was to adopt the ordinance in formal, and by no means, unalterable part, to the present constitution. Inasmuch as the ordinance had been begun and perfected by the Congress of the Confederation, the appointment of Governor and Secretary was to be made by that body, and there was no provision for any person's performing the duties of Governor, if that officer should die or be. in any way, disqualified. Had this turned out the case, the Territory would

have been without a head—a necessary head—of the Government. This omission—for it must have been one—was so supplied by the act, that the Secretary, in the event supposed, should execute ad interim the duties of Governor. The other alteration was, that the Governor and Secretary should be appointed by the President of the (now) United States, instead of by the old Congress, and that official communications should be addressed to the latter and not the former.

Now, if, as the Court say, the ordinance became extinct when the present Constitution was ratified by nine States—and New Hampshire, the last of the nine, ratified it in June, 1788—there must unavoidably have been a hiatus in the Territorial government from that time, till the 7th of August, when the law was enacted. But, perhaps, some will say, we must allow a reasonable time for the organization of the new government. But this relieves us from only a part of the difficulty—for the organization was completed on the 4th of March, 1789— so that the vacancy must, at all events, extend from that time till the 7th of August of the same year. A lapse like this all governments try to avoid. Nor is there in the act itself, the least sign of annulling the ordinance, unless we admit the diminutive cavil—a cavil altogether unworthy of the Court—that may be founded on its title. Otherwise, there is not the least proof that the Congress enacting the law, did not think that the ordinance was not, at least, as binding on them as the Constitution. The act gives as a reason for its existence, that it was to "continue" the ordinance. Now, if before this time, there had been a lapse, as we have endeavored to show there was by the Court's construction—would sensible men have used the word continue to describe a revivification of an expired law—a renewal of its life? Would they have been entirely silent as to the former repeal or nullification? We think not: and if there had been any lapse—any extinction—there is not the slightest evidence of the fact.

There was no substantial change in the ordinance on the change of the government. It was adapted, as we are told, to the new form of government: only formally changed, as is before said, to enable the present Constitution to lay hold of it, and give it the greater effect. This adaptation was made by men who lived when the ordinance was first formed; by men who lived at the time of the transfer and change of government, and who knew the import—the understanding, attached to it, what was meant by it, and what was expected would be done concerning it. If any of the "Articles" of the ordinance were thought inconsistent with the present Constitution, here was an apt occasion for saying so. But Congress did not say a word about any discrepancy; they adopted the whole ordinance simply by *referring* to it.

But the decision further asserts, that if the "Articles" could be regarded as yet in operation in the States formed within the limits of the Northwestern Territory, it would place them in an inferior condition as compared with the other States, and subject their domestic institutions and municipal regulations to the constant supervision and control of the Court." We hardly know how to answer an objection of this kind; it is, indeed, so puerile, that we did not expect it from such a source. To dispose of it, however, in as few words as we can:—does not the Court very well know, that to enslave our fellow-creatures is no part of sovereignty; that it is an abuse of power which humanity and the law have utterly banished from a large majority of the most civilized countries; and that the free States, even with this inequality, as the Court seem to consider it, are greatly superior in every good respect to those that have this advantage; that "domestic institutions," "municipal regulations," are terms gotten up at the South, to create a prejudice against those who are opposed to slavery, and that they include *all* the slaves, whether predial or domestic, and that the latter, the house slaves, are very few in number, when compared with those who prepare the cotton, sugar, rice, &c., &c., for exportation? And if we should, at last, come to the low pass that the decision seems to think we would sink to without slaves, what can be a more honorable or appropriate employment for a Court, than to see that no man's liberty is invaded or trampled on by his overreaching neighbor? It appears to be more important, too, than deciding whether one person shall pay another a few hundred dollars or not. What renders the objection more frivolous—if that can well be—is the fact that, although

Congress have acted on the idea that the ordinance was yet in force, a case of the kind—cases that the Court suppose would be multitudinous—has never yet occurred to occupy its time.

But if the ordinance expired on the ratification of the present Constitution, there is an inference to which the Court is inevitably shut up. It is one, too, which the slaveholders, loudly and boldly deny, and which the Court will probably reluctantly admit. It is that Congress *legislated* at its first session under the Constitution, on the subject of slavery, forbidding its future existence in a Territory, not only whilst it was dependant on the head-government, but when it was about to make a Constitution, and through *it* to prepare for a higher political condition, and to participate in the public counsels. This matter is deemed so plain, that no argument of ours can make it plainer.*

The Court, as we think, lay rather more than usual stress on the source of their authority—the *Constitution*. It is well known that the judicial power is one of the main divisions of that instrument, and that from it the Court derives all its authority. But the ordinance was not intended to confer any power on the Court, nor to take away any. With these objects it has no more relation than any other public debt or engagement had. The United States stood pledged to pay the debts and to perform the engagements into which she had entered by an obligation, at least, as strong as any judgment of a Court sustained by the government could be.

If the ordinance really expired, as the decision asserts, any consistency or inconsistency of it with the Constitution must be useless and unavailing. But if it has gone out from the incompatibility of *some* of its "Articles" with Constitutional provisions, we would inquire, if that is the case with the Slavery article, now under discussion, and by what authority the Court pronounce the *whole* ordinance extinct, when this incompatibil-

* We are of those who think that Congress have a right to legislate on slavery, as on any other vice—to *suppress* it. Congress have a right to legislate on murder, perjury, &c., but only in *one* way—to put those vices or crimes *down*. So on slavery. No legislation can put murder *up*—or perjury, &c., *up*—neither can slavery be put *up*,

ity does not, in any degree, apply to *some* of the articles.

Any recapitulation of our replies—for as far as argument is concerned, we are now done with the question—may be very short. We may truly say, and it includes the whole recapitulation, that all parts of the country, all its parties, all official men, and men not official, looked on the ordinance as still enduring. The only exception that we know of, are the Judges of the Supreme Court.

CHAPTER V.

Colonization—Address to the Colored People.

MANY of our readers will be ready to ask, if the foregoing remarks are made, only with the view of showing the present situation of the country, and of examining the decision of the Court, so that its incompetency to decide rightly between Liberty and Slavery, may be clearly seen by all. The most intelligent and far-seeing may say, they are not, and that they are only the stepping-stones to some other purpose deemed still more important.

We have been convinced, for a long time, that it was the wish of many of the leading men amongst us, both North and South—but principally at the South where the scheme originated—a wish deemed worthy by them to be unceasingly labored for—that the condition of the free colored people should be rendered so undesirable, that the feelings of humane and conscientious owners would be so quenched or turned back that they would not emancipate; that many of the slaves would not greatly desire to enter that class; that when compared with the other classes of our population, it would appear to decrease, and that it would really *increase* but slowly; and that should the planners succeed in this, they, the free colored people would, in the end, be compelled to emigrate from this country—already beginning to be called "the white man's home, and his exclusively, and that God had so appointed it,"*—and seek some other where they would be at peace, and where, in consequence of their emigration, and of their emigration alone, the usual stimulants of men would be open to them and unrestrained.

That the framers of the Constitution intended the free colored man should be really free, we have before stated, and that they expected slavery would be of short duration—and even South Carolina encouraged the expectation—we have little, if any, doubt. It never entered their minds, that he was to be removed

or exiled to a foreign land. When the Constitution was made, more than sixty years ago, cotton cannot be said to have been cultivated as an article of exportation. For the sugar-cane we had no congenial climate—at least none of any consequence. The rice, the indigo—the culture of which was unwholesome, and therefore given over to slaves—was not sufficient to overmaster the spirit of liberty then among us. But the cultivation of cotton commenced on a larger scale, soon after the adoption of the Constitution, and, with very few interruptions, it has risen to its present large amount. Not long afterwards, we purchased Louisiana, and in it acquired a great deal of territory on which sugar could be profitably produced. Since then we have acquired much more—enough, indeed, to employ, for a long time, all the slaves, including their natural increase—in the country. 'Tis true California has excluded slavery, but New Mexico and Utah are undefended from its introduction; and unless things very much change, *they*, when admitted as *States*, will be admitted as *slave* States, or capable of becoming such.* As far back as the the time just

---

*See the letter of Mr. Latrobe of Baltimore. It was published in many of the American newspapers in August last.

*Already do we hear that a proceeding is vigorously prosecuted to divide California, so that the southern part of it may be an independent State—doubtless a *slave State*. In New Mexico and Utah, the newspapers tell us there are now many slaves. It is in vain to say, as Mr. Webster has said, and many others were found to reiterate the sentiment, that the laws of the formation of the earth, and of physical geography, would successfully forbid the introduction of slavery into these Territories, allowing that otherwise they would fully fall under his rule. Especially is this notion contradicted by the evidence furnished by our present slave States. There is, probably, not one of them, in which much territory is not inhabited by non-slave-holding whites—the land *they* occupy being thought too poor for slave cultivation. The non-slaveholders, too, constitute the majority—a very large majority—of the people of every State, without a single exception. Notwithstanding this, the Legislatures are made up of slaveholders, or their dependants in some way or other. There are no free schools successfully set on foot and kept up in them for the education and advancement of the children of the poor, but the legislation is invariably of the slaveholding type. Missouri, which has only about one slave to six or seven whites, is as much a slave State—has as much of the *esprit du corps* of slavery as South Carolina, where there is a majority against the whites of more than one hundred thousand. The slaveholders make up the weal

mentioned—when we had much territory that could be profitably used for the cultivation of cotton, and saw that we could acquire other territory on which the sugar cane could be grown; when the nation, particularly the southern part of it, asserted (and the assertion seemed generally to have been well believed), that the slaveholders and *they* only, knew all about slavery and the questions connected with it, and that the main productions of the South could be properly cultivated by the blacks alone, then slavery began to be looked on as more permanent, and the *temporary* provisions of the Constitution to be interpreted as guaranties that the power of the government should be used to make it as lasting as the government. Some, and they stand high, too, go so far as to say that the Union would not have been formed as we have it, unless these guaranties had been given. Those who take this ground, seem unconscious of the inconsistent and insincere manner, in which they present the framers of the Constitution—many of whom were actors in the Revolutionary war—as striving for liberty themselves, yet fastening on others, many of whom had assisted them in their struggle, the manacles of slavery.

Up to this time may be fairly traced the oppressions of the colored man, and they have grown just in proportion as slavery has been thought to be fixed and ascendant. At this time, they are almost unendurable—quite so, as we think, for any one aiming to be a freeman; and proceeding as we have done for the last fifty years, we bid fair, well to qualify ourselves for enacting such atrocious scenes as the one described by the Abbe Gregoire, in his work entitled "*Sur La Literature des Negres.*" He tells us that on the arrival of the bloodhounds from Cuba in the island of St. Domingo, "On leur livra, par maniere d'essai, le premier negre qui se trouva sous le main."

He adds, "La promptitude avec laquelle ils devorerent cette curee rejouit les tigres blancs, a figure humaine." "Those who hold that the negro is a distinct species from ours, and of a different and inferior grade in the scale of organized beings, smile at the good Abbe's simplicity, and observe that it cannot be much more criminal to destroy such creatures when they annoy us, than to extirpate wolves and bears; nor do they strongly reprobate the conduct of some white people in our Australian colony, who are said to have shot occasionally the poor miserable savages of that country as food for their dogs."[*]

The presence of the free colored people among the slaves always disturbed and angered the slaveholder. He had not the wisdom of Mr. Madison—whose opinion is quoted in a previous note—to attach them to the whites by good treatment and kindness; but giving way to the dominion of his passions, he constantly suspects them, and, in his malignancy, he drives them from him, and almost compels them to make the slaves their associates. The ill treatment of the free colored people was early exhibited, not only by debarring them from privileges which, if allowed, would greatly have contributed to the effect we have supposed, but by making it absolutely impossible for them, by any industry or good conduct, to attain these privileges. The people of the North, thinking that their Southern neighbors knew all about slavery, and the matters connected with it—as harlots are supposed best to understand all the devices of courtezanship—for the most part imitated them. They formed no associations with the free colored people—not even in the way of business—looking on them as a degraded *caste*, that nothing could elevate. As, of course, they did not intermarry with them, they managed to make the belief a general one, that any class with whom the most favored *caste* in society would not intermarry, must *really* be a low and degraded one. It would seem that they had forgotten that the earnest *Christian* does not marry with the avowed infidel—nor with the Mahommedan—

thy class, and have more leisure than the poor to electioneer for office and station. However this may be, they, as a matter of fact, manage "by hook or crook," to get into the Legislatures. Kentucky furnishes in her social condition, no exception to the remark, that a large majority of the population in the slave states are non-slaveholders, and we will hazard the assertion, that there is not a member of her legislature who is not a slaveholder. If there is any good soil in New Mexico or in Utah, on the banks of the streams or elsewhere—especially if there is but a tolerable prospect only of mineral wealth, and slavery be not excluded by law, these territories will be managed by slaveholders, and, as we said will, in all probability, be admitted as slave States.

*The whole quotation is from the "Natural History of Man," a work by Dr. Prichard, of Bristol, England—page 7. The part in French may be thus translated: "They gave to them, (the bloodhounds,) by way of trial, the first negro who fell into their hands. The promptitude with which they dispatched this game rejoiced the white tigers in human form."

nor that the American does not often intermarry with a native of France, or with one that speaks a language entirely different from his own. Yet so little in these, and similar cases, is it thought intermarrying has to do with *rights*, that they are conceded without difficulty. We can account for this in but one way: that we hate the colored people, bond and free, because we have injured them, and we continue to hate them because we continue to injure them.

Although this hostile feeling among the whites was, for many years, so scattered that it had not come to a head, anywhere, yet, throughout the land, it was of the *same* nature; and it so unceasingly continued to grow that it required vent in some way—for nothing but a pure and exalted principle of justice can quench or overcome our tendency to do as others do. This vent was found in the institution of the Colonization Society.

This society, instituted about the beginning of 1817, was formed chiefly by men who were more conspicuous as politicians, than as members of any benevolent association. It was nothing more than the bringing together, the aggregation and embodiment of propensities, or dispositions, that existed almost every where. It proposed a *compromise*—ending as all compromises about slavery have—by the free States giving up some good, and taking, in place of it, some evil- by which the North and the South were to co-operate in the same plan. The slaveholding South generally—with the exception of those who aided in setting on foot the enterprize—looked on it *suspiciously*, thinking it best that slavery should not be at all discussed. The dislike, often the malignity, which slaveholders feel toward the free colored man, was much—and, as it turned out, *truly* —relied on. And when, in addition to this, it was made very clear, how well the scheme could be made to minister to the support of slavery, the slave States, for the most part, not only willingly, but earnestly and encouragingly, embraced it. But, speaking generally, the remark that the slave States, at *first*, looked on the whole matter suspiciously is true. South Carolina and Georgia—States which, at the holding of the Constitutional Convention, laid the foundation of our present troubles about slavery— have never altered their opinion. In

these States, then, little has been done in the colonization cause.

The greatest difficulty the Society had to encounter was with the North. Northern men had not yet "sufficiently conquered their prejudices" against human bondage, as to make them concur with alacrity in the plan. Many of them had seen—more of them had known—that their fathers had put an end to slavery —either immediately or prospectively— as the worst condition to which their fellow beings could be brought. From this they learned to detest it. They knew, too, that the free colored people among them were the descendants of the slaves; and it is altogether likely that the Northern men would, if entirely uninfluenced, have acted toward them more kindly and justly than they often have.* But they took their temper toward the colored people from the slaveholding South, where—especially in the *country*†—they were treated with so much contempt and dislike, that it might be said to amount to persecution.‡ Still, the North somewhat shrank from the revolting dose. To make it more palatable for them, it was covered over with the notion that the free people of color were to emigrate to Liberia, *with their own consent§*— but

*Not long after the organization of the Coloniza-tion Society, a meeting to approve it, and perhaps to form an *auxiliary*, was held in Boston, at which Mr. Webster was present. He was nominated as one of the committee to prepare suitable resolutions, &c., &c., but viewing the whole matter as a device of the slaveholders to protract slavery, he would have nothing to do with it.

†This accounts, in some measure, for the great comparative number of free colored people in towns and cities. They there get employment, which few, or none, of the whites wish, and in which, of course, the competition is small.

‡Some may excuse, or even try to justify, the North by the fact that it requires much more magnanimity than is ordinarily seen, to behave benevolently and justly toward those who are neglected, or treated scarcely with common attention, by those who are most bound to show them attention, and who are supposed to know them best. But granting they fully succeed, it would only show that the nation is nothing more than a common one—anything, but the "winnowed seed of a great people."

§If the free colored people were treated *here* with that kindness and justice which the framers of the Constitution intended they should be, and which they thought they had secured to them, and were *voluntarily* to go to Liberia, as other freemen go to new countries, with a view of settling there, we see no moral objection that could fairly be made to the colonizing plan; but to harrass them in this country, to *make* them consent to emigrate, is such consent as might be expected from one that—to use a common saying—"jumps out of the frying pan into the fire," and is altogether unworthy of a generous people. This *expression* of consent—not the consent of the mind —is wrung from the colored people by the most tyrannical abuse of our power.

there they could "*rise,*" while *here* they could not (though this latter fact was entirely unexplained), and that by keeping up the discussion of slavery it would, at last, lead to entire emancipation.

By such arguments the favorers of the society recommended it, and by such arguments were the North—with some very honorable exceptions—induced to enter heartily into the plan.* The consequences proved to be disastrous, insamuch as the most discerning saw that this, the land of their nativity, was not to be their continuing country, and that, therefore, all plans of improvement, that looked to permanency, were useless; and in proportion as their good demeanor fitted them for remaining here, the efforts to pursuade them to remove to an equatorial and, to them, an unaccustomed climate—to a country new and uncivilized, one in which man was rude and untaught, would be more untiring. Many that went were, no doubt, a good deal taken with the missionary spirit—with the notion of bringing the rude heathen under the dominion of the cross: but saying nothing here of their entire unfitness for this work—for we think it requires talents and learning of the highest order—reliance for settling a new country speedily, is not to be placed on this spirit. Many of those who remained, like branches of certain forest-trees, when severed from the stem, put out buds for a short time, but having no place among us to take root, they withered and died. Their worst anticipations were verified. Not only was their residence here rendered precarious, but they were vilified by the high vulgar and by the low vulgar; by "mongrel, puppy, whelp and hound of low degree," as long as it was thought they were *determined* on remaining in this country. The† advantage that the colored man would enjoy in Liberia, the disadvantages *here,* were exultingly dwelt on, by those who stood high in society generally, and in the church. We forbear to mention the cases particularly, since they are too well known to make it at all necessary: we shall only give specimens, but each of them may be regarded as a *class.* A person of no mean standing, recommended the support of the Colonization Society, and the formation of an auxiliary, by saying that the free people of color, ought to be removed from the presence of the slave, in order that the latter might not suppose that liberty was *ever* the birthright of the colored man; another, the President of a College in a free State, that the free colored men ought to have the most stringent laws passed against them, to compel them to consent to emigrate; another, also the President of a College and a preacher in a slave State, explained the golden rule, or the rule of "doing to others as we would they should do to us" in this manner,—if the master were a slave with the ignorance and inferiority of the slave, and the slave were the master, with the master's greater knowledge and mental superiority, the latter (the master in this case) *would* *choose* that the master (here the slave) should choose for him. The real master would, of course, choose for the slave to remain a slave. Another, the Secretary of the principal society, and a minister of the Gospel, contended that the degradation of the free colored man *here,* was an ORDINATION OF PROVIDENCE; consequently, one that ought not to be opposed, and that could not be successfully opposed permanently.

Those who opposed them, and who were the advocates of justice to the colored man *here,* were few in number and weak in influence, when compared with their adversaries. In vain they urged on the Colonizationists, *the principles contained in the Declaration of Independence,* and in the Constitution; in vain they plied them with the laws of humanity, and the duties of Christianity. To arguments of this kind, they were deaf. They appeared determined, in disregard of every thing on the adverse side, to rush to their project. Not only to colored people, were names of great opprobrium applied, but names equally opprobrious were applied to all, who, in any way, favored their cause here. But the latter were like a reed in the storm, presenting no impediment to their course, bending to their pressure, but not uprooted.

But, were not goodmen warmly interested in Colonization? That they were is not at all denied; but it is known that

---

* This reconciliation between the North and South cannot fail to remind us of another very important one, the most important of any in history, and attended by consequences of great moment to all, and apparently disastrous to many. We, of course, refer to the reconciliation of Herod and Pilate.

† No *expedition* of emigrants to Liberia has ever sailed, that were not spoken of by the press, generally, previously to their embarkation, as rather a superior body of people, whilst those of them that remained, and appeared to have made up their minds to remain, were most unsparingly defamed.

good men are often connected with a bad institution. There are many whom we respect highly, who are engaged in supporting the monarchies of Europe. They think that a republic is another name for disorder. No one will deny that there are many good men, many excellent men, in the Catholic Church; yet reflective and impartial persons look on it as an institution used to support a great hierarchy, compounded of pride, credulity, superstition and imposition; and that the good are so, in *spite* of its adverse influence.

It will not be supposed that an association, such as we have described the Colonization society to have been, ramified, too, as it was, throughout almost the whole country, would not produce a strong effect on the public mind. Some of them, we will now proceed to exhibit. To the intelligent and unbiassed reader, it will make but little difference, whether they originated after the organization of the society or not, inasmuch as the same state of feeling in the community, produced them both. Some of them may have existed *before* it was formed, but the boldest and most flagrant, *since*. In the former case, the society only strengthened and confirmed what had been previously done.

1. Slavery—or rather the discussion of it, produced *mobs*. These mobs—where they could effect their purpose, in this way—so interrupted free discussion, as to prevent the exercise of it. In many cases, they have beaten and maltreated him who disclosed any of the abuses of slavery, and insisted on his right: they have even gone so far as to put to death the victim of their passions.*

If the interruption and suppression of discussion had confined itself to mobs—for all countries are liable to these outbreaks, notwithstanding the laws for their punishment—the case would have been more tolerable. But it did not. It found its way into Congress, from whom calmness of deliberation, and observance of the Constitution, are expected. To secure both of them—especially, the latter—the members are sworn, or affirmed, to support the Constitution: yet, the House of Representatives made a rule, or passed a resolution, after hearing a concurrent report from a committee, the chairman of which was a slaveholder, that all petitions sent into them, should be laid, *unread*, on the table, and, of course, unacted on. This rule was made with the view of defeating the many petitions that had already been sent in for the abolition of slavery—being meant, of course, where Congress had the right and power to abolish it—and of meeting the many that were supposed *would* be sent in for the same purpose. It prevailed for several years, with various modifications, none of which made it less stringent or less obnoxious, at the end of which time, it was set aside, mainly by the efforts of the late John Quincy Adams, who, from the first, was a strenuous opposer of it as unconstitutional. Since it has been left out, but few petitions have been presented on the subject, and those few have been as effectually put to sleep by a vote of the majority, consigning them "to the table," as by the former measure. Some of the members, most active in pressing the rule, sought refuge under the

---

* The Constitution has inhibited the free discussion of no question, not even its own entire change. Indeed, when we consider the amendment intended to secure freedom of speech, and the provision the Constitution makes for its own change, we are of the impression that it rather invites discussion on the preliminary means of substituting better arrangements, or such as may be proved to be inferior. As its best condition, as its greatest security, it leaves the mind of man perfectly free, and never meant that any subject should be above examination.

We know it may be said, for it was been said, that the alleged compromise about delivering up fugitive slaves, cannot be so abrogated that Congress can act on the matter; that without it, the Southern States would not have entered the Union, and that now to abolish it, would be an instance of bad faith, and that it ought to be viewed as completely and forever unchangeable, as much so as the Judicial or Legislative or Executive departments. We well know, that when we are excited things may be said which will not bear the scrutiny of our calmer reason. Slavery, saying nothing of Christian principle, has been abol-

ished in the most civilized countries in the world as too expensive to be maintained. Still their Sovereignty is not at all impaired by it, for it constitutes no part of the sovereignty of any State, any more than any other vice or form of oppression. But did we ever hear of a civilized government, without a legislative, executive, or judicial department? Not one. Again, it is said, we cannot abolish slavery as long as THE SOUTH is unwilling it should be. There is no provision of this kind anywhere. But, independently of one, is it true—consistent with principles which we act on as true? Now, supposing an attempt was made to abolish Southern slavery, and the minority—very small—but one State, all the others having set free their slaves. Does not this bare statement show the utter unreasonableness of the question, for it leaves the majority on a most important point, too, and the interests of the whole community, to be entirely controlled by a minority. The South was much opposed in the convention, to taxing "exports." We do not tax them, but who supposes it would be a case of bad faith in the government, and a suitable cause for dissolving the Union, if it were to be seen that the taxing of them, or laying a duty on them, would be for the good of the great majority, and injure no one.

provision of the Constitution, which says, "Congress shall make no LAW &c."—and Congress had, as yet, made no law—the House of Representatives, alone, had put down the right by one of its rules of proceeding, or by concurring with a committee in one of its own reported resolutions. But the absurdity of this was too great, to be much or long relied on.

The Senate have long used the plan adopted of late by the House of Representatives. This is attempted to be covered up under one of its own rules of proceeding, made, we suppose, to facilitate business, (?) and it has been found so effectual for excluding all anti-slavery petitions, disagreeable to that body, that one of its members, from a free State too, boasted, not long ago, that since the commencement of the anti-slavery "excitement" not one petition, intended to promote it, had been received or acted on by the Senate.

II. The existence of slavery has induced the legislatures of many of the slave States—led to it, doubtless, by the cause before stated—the dislike of the free colored men by the slaveholder—to pass acts declaring that they must leave the limits of the respective States in a given time, or that the penalties of these enactments would be enforced against them. Should they, through fear, remove, the penalties for their returning were so stringent and severe, that it was thought they would be kept away. In this the slave States have been followed by several of the free—particularly by Indiana, in the late constitution—so great a desire have they to convince the slaveholder of their determination to fulfill, to the utmost, all constitutional stipulations respecting slavery.*

III. Colored citizens of the United States, residents of the free States, and possessing all the privileges of them, when driven accidentally—for we suppose that none go of purpose—into the harbors of those States of the South that border on the Atlantic, or on the Gulf of Mexico,

are put into jail, regardless of any charge of crime.* This inhuman law, intended chiefly to apply to colored mariners, includes the colored citizen not only of our own States, but of all foreign countries. On the arrival of a vessel from a free country, she is visited by a State officer, who takes all the colored persons he can find, ashore, where he confines them. There they are kept till the vessel is ready to sail, the cost of the whole proceeding being charged to the master.† The late Justice Johnson of the Supreme Court—a resident of South Carolina—pronounced the law altogether unconstitutional. England has complained of it, and now complains of it. However, it is still persisted in. It is thought to apply as well to our national vessels as to others, and indeed, we do not see why the alleged reason of the rule does not make it as fairly applicable to them as to others; nor are we, at all, prepared to admit, that there should be a general breach of the Constitution charged against our country, while its government should be made an exception. The facts of the case to which we particularly refer are—according to our recollection—as follows: A national vessel—the Georgia—had occasion, not long since, to enter the port of New Orleans, having a colored man on board. She was at once visited by a State officer, who was about taking him off to jail. The officer was remonstrated with by the commander on the ground, as we remember, that the vessel was national. The officer consulted the Attorney-General of the United States, for that district, who was of the opinion, that the law did not apply to national vessels. He also consulted the Attorney for the State, who thought differently—that it intended to include all vessels having colored men on board, and that as it had not, to any way, been declared unconstitutional,‡ it

---

* If our recollection does not much mislead us, a Representative in Congress from Illinois—in order to show that his State had the same determination attributed to others—stated in his place, that a colored man suspected of being a slave, but whose owner, if he had any, was not known, was arrested and confined in jail till his owner should, in some way, be found out and informed of it. If this be so, and we know of nothing to contradict it, the situation of the colored man in Illinois is even more precarious than we had supposed, and the presumption that every one is free till the contrary is proved, cannot exist there.

* If civilized people were to be driven in distress, into a port that they had never heard of or seen before, and if all the seamen of a certain description were to be taken away from the vessel and confined at their own costs till the vessel was ready to sail again, and those left on the vessel watched, in the meantime, quite narrowly, it would be looked on as pretty conclusive evidence of a barbarous, if not of a savage nation, into whose hands they had fallen.

† This is, in part, a device to get rid of dealing with a colored man, as if he was free. It is well known that the amount is deducted from the seaman's wages. If the imprisoned party is not duly taken away he is sold into slavery for his jail fees.

‡ A law being declared constitutional does not make it so. As well might the Louisiana attorney

was still valid and ought to be applied to them all. The matter, as well as we remember, was finally compromised by the vessel leaving the port as soon as she could get ready—the State thus maintaining its act against the Constitution of the United States.

IV. Within the last few years, several of the free States—among them Connecticut—have formed new Constitutions. It was supposed that in New England the opposition to slavery was as decided, at least, as any where else. There was another reason, too, which we would have supposed would have made Connecticut still stronger in her opposition. She was small, and considering her extent, had many churches and colleges—boasted of her great intelligence, and of being really the "land of steady habits." Yet strange to say, in the very precincts of these institutions where it might be thought a good influence would be exerted, the opposition to slavery is feebler than in other parts of the State.* We can account for it but in one way: the commercial class in Connecticut have large business transactions with the South—the South influences the commercial class, and they the other affairs of the Connecticut community. The conventions for forming these constitutions are made up of the Representatives of the people. They have their power, their voice, to be modulated as they judge proper. They can regulate the elective franchise as they think best; and it is cause of thankfulness, that so far as the whites are concerned, these constitutions are made more and more democratic—but never in a single instance, unless Rhode Island be considered one, have they had the courage to say, that the colored people should vote as the whites do. Having no heart in the matter, and desirous to shift all sorts of responsibility from themselves, they timidly referred it to their constituents. The result in every case was what might have been foreseen. No matter which political party—whig or democratic—had the ascendancy, the popular majority was not only decisive, but overwhelming against colored suffrage. We have not said unadvisedly, that the Conventions timidly referred this matter to their constituents. They had the full power to do right, and what every one, at all conversant with such subjects, knew to be right; and we have always observed, that when *leading men* do right —when they suppose that in so doing, they assume a good deal of responsibil-

say, that all the laws passed against the free colored people in the several States—even the provision in the late Constitution of Indiana—keeping them out of the limits of her territory—are constitutional. They never have been declared otherwise, and probably never will. One may have various satisfactory reasons for submitting to what he knows is an unconstitutional enactment, rather than proving it to be one, before a competent court. He may think that he will never visit the State again, and, of course, never another time, be subject to its operation—or that he is too ignorant, or of too little note—too poor to undergo the expense. Suppose, by way of illustration, the colored man on board the Georgia, had made up his mind to try the constitutionality of the law, and had suffered himself to be led away to jail—intending to sue out a writ of *Habeas Corpus*, on which his whole case should be examined. He would almost certainly be unknown, a man of no figure in New Orleans. What lawyer there, would so endanger his reputation, as to undertake his case without a fee which the colored man would be wholly unable to give ? Who then, would present or prepare his petition, or speak to it. But supposing all this done, the Judge replies that the Habeas Corpus was never intended to relieve those who were in custody of the law, and that a law had been passed by the ! Legislature of Louisiana, on which the petitioner was in custody. In support of his position, he might cite the opinion of Attorney General Crittenden. He refuses granting the writ, saying he would only have to remand the applicant on his own showing. Here, in our judgment, is an end of the case. But we will suppose that judgment is given against him, and that he intends to take it up, if he can, to the Supreme Court, by writ of error or appeal. Who is to prepare the papers for him ? to be his surety in the bond, if only *one* should be required ? Who will attend to his case in the Supreme Court ? What lawyer practising there will he employ ? What fee will this lawyer ask, &c., &c. The whole matter is not only unprecedented, but it will never be seen, and is utterly out of the question. To ask mariners or seamen—whose means are usually small—to do these things, is to ask of them impossibilities. We will mention here, as most properly belonging to this place, that even now, and for many years back, the colored citizens of Massachusetts, without any allegation of crime, were, on their arrival at Charleston or New Orleans, put into the jails of those cities, *according to law.* Such was the state of public feeling about slavery that no resident lawyer could be gotten to attend to their cause. For the purpose of giving them all necessary aid, according to the Constitution of the United States, Massachusetts deputed two of her trustworthy white citizens to visit these places respectively. The one that went to Charleston was met by a mob. The Legislature was in session and resolutions were passed of a most inflammatory character—resolutions adapted to excite, as they did excite, the mob to greater extremity. This deputy was escorted by the rabble from his lodgings in Charleston to the steamboat which was to convey him back to Massachusetts. The other deputy went to New Orleans, where, to be sure, the Legislature was not in session, but his bare arrival at that city caused such a popular ferment, that, for fear of being mobbed, he made his way back to Massachusetts as soon as he well could. Neither of them accomplished any thing in relation to his mission. Nothing more of a public nature was done about it.

*We have with a great deal of uniformity found, that the most independent thinkers—the most self-relying men, are the most opposed to slavery. The ignorant and immoral—where they think about emancipation at all, are opposed to it.

ity, the great body of the people are ready to follow them—they are pleased that it is done already by those in whom they confide. We have said, too, that the issue might have been foreseen, for when the Conventions declined exercising the power conferred on them, the very act of declining, was tantamount to advising the people not to allow it. Beside all this, it gave ample time for party machinery to be brought into play, and to have its full effect.

We meant to say nothing, further than to mention them, of the riding of the colored people with the whites in the same coach, in the same steamboat—of their exclusion from the militia, from serving on juries—of the negro pew, &c., &c. Sometimes straws show better than heavier substances which way the wind blows—as these do the direction of public sentiment.*

We have been rummaging our historical recollections, to find out if there ever has been a case—especially in modern times, when we think we know all about Christianity—parallel to the one before us. So far as we know, there was but one—the EXPULSION of the Jews from Spain, then governed by Ferdinand and Isabella; and *that* has been condemned for its unchristian atrocity by all people in any good degree refined. Its *object* was the EXPULSION of the Jews, but we would not say this was the object of the Fugitive act, as regards the colored people. Its effects, however, rather have been to persuade them to leave the country—chiefly to migrate to Canada.

The same year [1492] that was made illustrious by the discovery of the New World, was also signalized by the expulsion of the Jews. The act was so irreligious—so inhuman—that even Prescott—with whom Isabella was a great favorite, and from whose history these

incidents are gathered—does not attempt to justify it. The sufferings the Jews underwent—and they were fomented by the Clergy—were very great; indeed, enough to appal any but the stoutest heart. Some of them had become rich. Their wealth had brought about alliauces, in the way of marriage with noble families, who, in acts of extravagance, had pretty well exhausted their own means. The sudden exposure to sale of so much property as the Jews possessed, brought the price of it down to almost nothing. That we may not be supposed to deal in exaggeration, "a chronicler of the day," Prescott tells us, "mentions that he had seen a house exchanged for an ass, and a vineyard for a suit of clothes." In the midst of their distress the Rabbis, or leading men, exhorted them to persevere—comparing their present afflictions to those that had been suffered by their fathers—to be crowned with a like happy result. The more wealthy among them enforced their exhortations by liberal contributions for the relief of their indigent brethren. When the period of their departure arrived, the principal routes were filled with them. The old and the young, the sick and the helpless, men, women, and children—some on horses or mules, but far the greater part on foot —were to be seen undertaking the tyrannous emigration from the land of their ancestors, a land, too, in which *they* had been born. Every precaution has been taken by them against suffering; but in spite of this—for they had only from the 30th of March to the end of the next July to prepare—their afflictions were so great, that the sight of so much misery touched even the Spaniards with pity. But none would succor or relieve them, for Torquemada, the Grand Inquisitor, had denounced all relief to them by heavy ecclesiastical censures.

A considerable number found their way into the parts of Santa Maria and Cadiz, where, after lingering some time, they embarked on board of a Spanish fleet for the Barbary coast. Having landed, they were assaulted on their route by the roving tribes of the desert, in quest of plunder. Notwithstanding the interdict, the Jews had contrived to secrete small sums of money, sewed up in their garments or the linings of their saddles. The spoilers even ripped open the bodies of their victims in search of gold, which they were supposed to have

---

*Some who have not had the opportunity of seeing the *practical* working of this thing, or, perhaps, do not give it as much thought as they do other things, are inclined to think there is less prejudice against the colored people at the South than at the North. This they generally ascribe to the greater number of colored people at the South, and the more frequent mingling of the whites with them. But, on closer examination, this will be found incorrect. At the North the seat in the public coach is taken by the colored man, paid for out of his own money, and he feels that he has as much right to it as others have to theirs. At the South, it is true, the free colored man takes and pays for the seat. To ride together with white people is, in both cases, considered as a *favor*. The violent feelings of the Southerner would be more fully shown, if the seat were demanded as a *right*.

swallowed. The lawless barbarians, mingling lust with avarice, abandoned themselves to still more frightful excesses, violating the wives and daughters of the unresisting Jews, or massacreing in cold blood such as offered resistance. They were driven even to such extremity of famine, that they were glad to force nourishment from the grass which grew scantily among the sands of the desert, until, at length, great numbers of them, wasted by disease, and broken in spirit, retraced their steps to Ercilla, a Christian settlement, and consented to be baptised in the hope of being permitted to revisit their native land.

Many of the emigrants took the direction of Italy. Those who landed at Naples brought with them an infectious disorder, contracted by long confinement in small, crowded, and ill-provisioned vessels. The disorder was so malignant, and spread with such frightful celerity, as to sweep off more than twenty thousand inhabitants of the city, whence it extended its ravages over the whole Italian Peninsula.

Others of them went to Genoa. Some of them were massacred by the captains of the vessels for their effects. Some had to sell their children for the expenses of the passage. They arrived in Genoa in crowds, but were not suffered to tarry there long, by reason of the ancient law, which interdicted the Jewish traveler from a longer residence than three days. They were allowed, however, to refit the vessels, and recruit themselves for some days from the fatigues of the voyage. One might have taken them for specters, so emaciated were they, so cadaverous in their aspect, and with eyes so sunken; they differed in nothing from the dead, except in the power of motion, which indeed they scarcely retained. Many fainted and expired on the mole, which being completely surrounded by the sea, was the only quarter vouchsafed to the wretched emigrants. The infection, bred by such a swarm of dead and dying persons, was not at once perceived; but when the winter broke up, ulcers began to make their appearance, and the malady, which lurked for a long time in the city, broke out into the plague the following year. Prescott supposes—as we think, correctly—that the number of exiles was about one hundred and sixty thousand, though it has been computed

as high as eight hundred thousand. Three years afterward, the Jews were prohibited from going to the New World. The consequences were disastrous in every way :—for the sufferers of a wrong, whether they suffer much or little, or, even if the matter end, so far as we can see, in something good for them, is of small account—none indeed—in considering the effect of the wrong on those who *perpetrate* it. *They* must always suffer, it being a part of our natures, and unavoidable.

Judging from the following extract from a Detroit newspaper, as also from the one from a Montreal paper, the resemblance of the case in hand to the one cited, is closer than we had at first supposed. The one from Detroit, of October 18, 1850, says, "Much excitement exists in this city in reference to the Fugitive slave Bill. Every steamer, propeller and vessel, from the ports in Ohio to this place, has a large number of fugitive slaves, that have resided for some time in various parts of Ohio, on their way to Canada.* Some bring their families with them. Fear of the slave catcher, and of a return to bondage at the South, nearly distracts them; consequently, they are flocking to free Canada for protection. The cars from the West also bring a great number to the city, and they go over the ferry to Canada in double quick time. The numbers now gathering in the villages of Malden, Sandwich and Windsor, is now estimated at near two thousand. The commandants of the British garrisons at Sandwich and Malden, have given up the barracks to lodge them in. The barns and vacant houses all up and down the river are full of them. *Some are suffering for food.* The Canadians are very hospitable to them, and much has been done for them in this city [Detroit]. The lower ports on lake Ontario are represented as being full of them. The Canadian back settlements have more than they can feed."

The other extract is from Montreal, October 31, 1850. It says: "A number of fugitives arrived here and at Toronto yesterday. It is estimated that nearly one

* It must appear to many an odd turn of things, that people should *escape* from this country to Canada, a Province of the British Empire, to secure their liberty, when we formerly went to war with that empire, because we had not liberty enough. But times are much changed, and slavery produces strange anomalies.

6

housand have reached Canada since the commencement of the agitation, many of whom have passed into the interior, where they intend abiding. There appears to be less sympathy shown for them than formerly, and many seem actually in want of the *necessaries of life*.*

This paper, which was written chiefly with the view of benefiting the free colored people, is now drawing to a close. The writer wishes to address his remaining remarks particularly to them.

MY FRIENDS:—According to my ability, and with entire candor, I have endeavored to make plain to you your condition, as a class, at the *Revolution*—at the *making of the Constitution* in '87; how the formers of it felt towards you, and how they impressed on that instrument, their feelings—your condition *since*, in the main, getting worse;—the *situation of the country*,—all leading to, and ending in, the present consummation of your uncertainty and distress—the decision of the Supreme Court, at its last term in the case I have presented to my readers in the second chapter.

It is evident to me, and, I think it must be so to you, too, that the decision, as far as it goes, not only overthrows the Constitution, but greatly disparages it; for the Constitution was not made to favor slavery, as under its influence it was

---

* The Colonial Secretary in England, Lord Grey, in August, 1850, saying that under certain circumstances the emigration of the black and colored population of this country, to the British West Indies, might be had, closes his letter thus,—" Before taking those steps, however, it would be necessary to ascertain, officially, that there would be no objection on the part of the United States Government, as it must of course be understood that otherwise her Majesty's Government could not countenance any attempt of the kind proposed." That is, the *Government* of England will not attempt this thing, without the full concurrence of *this* Government.

This government having passed an act of great injustice to the free colored population: the effect of which has been to drive many of them to Canada. She has gone as far as she can according to the forms of the constitution, or with any regard to them, substantially to drive them out. This government, it is true, cannot prevent their crossing the line into Canada, but by a successful negotiation with England, she may persuade her not to let the colored people enter Canada.

It would hardly be supposed that any hindrance would be interposed by this country to the departure of the free colored people from it. But we have a New York journal, the Spectator, that would not only carry the persecution of them into other lands, by reiterating with some praise and exultation, Lord Grey's sentiment, but in finding fault with the formation of an anti-slavery society at Toronto—a society which supports the policy of its own government respecting slavery, and gives the colored people the aid and comfort which they could not get at home.

---

supposed it would go out, but to establish and confirm and extend liberty. However: after all that may be said in favor of temporizing with an acknowledged evil, it shows the ill effects of it, or of passing it by in forming a government without routing it *entirely* from it.

The territory that composed the Union in '87, it was thought, would be free from the curse of slavery before very long. Other lands on which Americans settled, or which they might acquire, were to be sacred to freedom—they were to demonstrate the sincerity of the country in the professions it had made, through our fathers, to the world. Knowing how much the people love even the name of their Constitution, the doctrine of the decision has been trumped up and called *Constitutional*. Far be it from me to attribute this to ignorance, for I have too high an opinion of the court to suppose so. But their prejudice—pliancy—subserviency—has blinded them. Having no great and universal principles by which to test their decissions, they imitate the chamelion, generally supposed to take its color from surrounding objects. They saw the highest influences in the Church and in the State—the local legislatures, in Congress, in the Administration, *all*, indeed, with only rare exceptions, entertain but one and the same opinion. Desirous of avoiding singularity, they followed their inclinations, leading them, in all likelihood, to suppose that these influences, so many from such good men, could not be wrong: therefore we look on it as not at all improbable, nay, almost certain, that they *think themselves right*. Hence, their very sincerity in wrong, makes them more determined against truth and justice, whilst their ignorance, and defiance of instruction, except from their own books makes the case almost, if not utterly, hopeless. The decision, however, ought not to be regarded as deficient in forecast and deliberation: but as shewing the great solicitude of the court to conform to, what they *believed*, was public sentiment. You have, then, lived among us long enough, and truely, it is long enough, to see us disregard the Constitution,* when it was

---

*The newspapers inform us, that the highest judicial authority of Oregon has decided that the free people of color can be kept out of it, and expelled from it, by an act of the Legislature. In the case alluded to, the defendant, a colored man, was allowed thirty days to go out of it.

The prevailing opinion is, that Congress has control

in the way to an injurious scheme, one that we had much at heart, and by which you were to be removed from among us.

Be this as it may, you will soon have to make an election—an inevitable one, too,—depending on the open deeds of your class, rather than on their more secret thoughts. The election to which I refer is contained in this question, which each of you may ask himself—"*shall I, if I am able, emigrate from this country?*" If you have made up your minds *not* to emigrate, there will be no use in your determining to what country you should go. I am not unaware of the noble resolution passed in your meetings some years ago—that you would remain here, and abide the destiny of your colored friends in slavery. Neither am I unaware, that when this resolution was made known, your presence and good conduct among us were thought might be made serviceable in gaining liberty for the enslaved. But that day is passed by—that expectation—apparently so well founded—is vain. The state of case that rendered your resolution magnanimous has changed. Your presence here, now, can be of no service to your enslaved brethren. By remaining, you only destroy yourselves. Your submitting, suffering, ultimately dying here can effect nothing on the hearts and determination of your oppressors and the oppressors of your brethren. The nobleness of your conduct may extract the remark that "*such a fellow ought to have gone to Liberia—he would have been a great acquisition there.*" But no more influence on those who could serve him than the last gasp of a worn out German would, on the petty despots of his oppressed countrymen, or, of an Irishman, on the tyrannous rulers of his brethren. We think more highly of them, *coming over to this country*, than of their wilting, and at length sinking down ingloriously at home:—especially do we, if, by their self-restraint they *save* something, and send to their friends to get *them* away too. A plan is prepared by your enemies,—it is this, *they are deter-*

mined *to get you away that they may maintain slavery* more undisturbed.[*] As parts of this plan, they are resolved—(and when did they fail in any project to support slavery)—to extend it—to bring more persons to be interested and implicated in it, and thus to make all the mighty power of the government subservient to its existence and confirmation.

Superiority on the part of the whites will always be vaunted over you—*as a class, inferiority* will always be acknowledged by you. There are *individuals* who will be exceptions, but they will be rare, and *exceptions* only. But the frame of mind that these tempers are well qualified to beget, will, as a general thing, and in the long run, become habitual. To this, I know of no exception. We are told that *white* Americans, with all their high democratic notions, become the most listless and degraded beings, when reduced to slavery—as they formerly were by the corsairs of the Mediterranean. It would seem, indeed—as if to show how odious a thing slavery is—that, just in proportion as the feelings and honor of men are elevated in freedom, they become low and abject in slavery.

As long as there was any well-founded hope that the principles of our government would prevail, and that they would in the end exterminate slavery, I wished you to remain here. While I feel still convinced that—should we advance in population and wealth as we have done for the last fifty years—slavery will finally disappear, as it now has in almost all European countries, its abolition will not be brought about by the *principles* of the government, but by the causes mentioned and others united with them. Slavery is a most expensive thing, in a dense state of population. When this is the case, freeman will perform, and perform better than slaves, the offices to which the latter are often called. Should it ever be submitted to me, for instance, whether a friend should go to purgatory—from which, it is said he *may* be gotten out—or to hell, from which they say no one can get out—I should have no hesitation in advising him to try the former.

---

over the legislation of a Territory, and that it may annul any law passed by it. But it is to be apprehended this will not be; for some years ago, when a member of the H. of R. moved to take up for consideration an act of the Territory of Florida, by which the free colored man, merely for visiting that country, or remaining in it, might be reduced to slavery, it was voted down. It still remains a disgrace to our Statute book, and a denial of our professions as a people.

---

[*]Some one in the House of Representatives in Congress—Mr. Pickens, from South Carolina, I believe—in a speech in favor of Slavery, remarked, that it *must be free from constant molestation, or it was not worth maintaining at all.*

Or, had I lived in the time of Troy, and had she been able to beat off and defeat the invading Greeks, it is very certain, that I would not have advised Æneas and his few friends, to seek a new country, through all their perils; but as Troy was burned down, her defenders slain, but few of the inhabitants left, Æneas broken up in his private affairs by death, and loss, and utter discomfiture, the best thing that he and his faithful followers could do, was, to seek a new country, where, undisturbed, and under more favorable auspices, they could re-establish the government and laws which they preferred.

But let us suppose that you have answered the first question in the affirmative, and that you have fully made up your minds to remove. The next that naturally arises is, 'to what country shall I go?' There are three countries, Canada, the British West Indies, and Liberia, to which you can go, and to the last two you may be said to be invited.

Canada, at best, is a cold and wintry country, with a climate farther north and colder than those in which most of you have been brought up. The most desirable part of it, too, the southern, is already occupied by the whites, and the lands are at a higher price than you could afford to pay. Almost of necessity, you will be pushed into the bleak and hyperborean regions of it. Besides, a spirit of contempt and hostility against the colored man, akin to our own, prevails much in Canada. They have their Provincial legislature in which white men, mostly of the Anglo-Saxon race, bear sway. While I would say, go anywhere to get rid of this country, go not there, if you can help it. If you do, you go as an inferior class, and many of the ills you suffer here, you will continue to suffer there. Nor do we know—and such a thing is not to my mind more improbable, than was, two or three years ago, the passing of the Fugitive Slave Act in Congress—that a negotiation may not be successfully made by this country with Great Britain, in which may be contained a provision for your being delivered up to this government, or to its proxy, the slave-catcher. Remember, too, that you are to assist in building up the the nation into which you go, and of which you and your descendants are to constitute a part. On that account if you do not think you owe it to yourselves,

you certainly do to them, not to emigrate to any land where you will, by caste, be an inferior portion of it, and always remain such. And it may be, too—and if I read the signs of the times right, it will be—that before very long Canada will be separated from Great Britain, and constitute, in all likelihood, a part of this government.

Many of our remarks about Canada, will also apply to the British West Indies. They too, have their Provincial legislatures, though they are not so inaccessible to the colored man as the one in Canada. But the whites there, once were slaveholders, and when compelled to relinquish slavery, they did not relinquish the unjust and domineering spirit of the master. This spirit is seen in their multifarious oppressions of the emancipated people under color of law. They seem to be mad at being forced to give up their dominion over the slaves, and, in this cowardly way, to take their revenge, as far as they can. The climate is sultry, warm, tropical—warmer, indeed, than many of you have been accustomed to. But it is one of the kind providences of God, that our physical constitutions become more and more adapted to the climate in which we live —especially if it be a warm one. [See Appendix.]

But I have said, you were invited there. 'Tis true, it may be so said. But why? To labor for them. That you may assist them in making more sugar than they now have, and in giving new value to old and neglected estates. It is very true that all the honors that can be bestowed there are accessible to the colored man, and that public opinion against him is not so prevalent as it is in Canada. In this respect they may be superior to Canada —but you are invited, because they expect you will be inferior, as a class. If you were not to be laborers for the planters, you would occasion disappointment. So you would, too, should you emigrate to those islands solely for the sake of bettering your own condition, or of setting up for yourselves. The British West Indies will gain but little distinction till the majority rule there, and till they of that majority show themselves, also, friends of popular rights, and qualified in every way to bear office and transact business.

There is another reason which ought not to be omitted, and which would, probably, have some influence in dissuading you from settling down in the British West Indies. Like other old slave holding colonies, they are much in debt and the taxes are high. Taxes, to be sure, are paid, as we all know, by different interests; but every where, and under all governments, they are paid by *labor*, in some form. I know of no exemption that you could claim, were you to fix your residence there.

Of Liberia, I intend to say but little. She is now, and she has been for the last four years, politically detached from this government. She is entirely free and her national independence has been recognized by France and Great Britain. What is true of it, has been as well said as I could say it—perhaps, much better. It would be strange, indeed, if its warm advocates had not, in commending it, gone a good deal beyond the truth. That Liberia is no *elysium* is very clear to my mind. Should you conclude to emigrate to it, I would not have you to imagine that you are going to any such place. In saying this, I intend no disparagement of Liberia, below other *new* countries, but they all testify to the truth of the remark. In going there you are going to a land—rich and fertile I believe it to be—in which much *work*—particularly of the rough kind—is to be done, before the conveniences and advantages you leave behind, can be had; where *labor* of the right kind is scarce and hard to be obtained; where society is rude and uncouth, and where, after struggling with difficulties for a life-time, you will die, leaving things, it is to be hoped, better than you found them. There may be some exceptions, but I speak not of them, but of the general social condition.

Lastly, having seen the miseries and evils of slavery, here, in every way, it is to be supposed that you will exercise restraint enough, not only *not* to engage in it yourselves, but to discountenance any approach to it in others. This should be done, on the first and least attempt that way—for although the secondary law, and even *constitutions*, may forbid slavery—as is the case in some of our free States—yet slavery may, substantially, be *practiced;* and you here see "what a great matter a little fire kindleth." And yet I must say,—considering who are at the head of the Colonization cause in this country, many of them being themselves slaveholders, or the friends of

slavery here,—it would not much surprise me, if you were to become somewhat implicated in it; especially too, when I remember, that some of our early settlers fled from their own country to avoid persecution, and became a good deal remarkable as persecutors here. But be assured, if you tolerate slavery among you, the foundation will be laid of much trouble; of a superstructure that will be weak and unstable, and that will not stand a heavy blow. But putting aside all this—notwithstanding reports, which I must say are not favorable, have been set on foot, but which, although they have been re-iterated, I trust, have been amply disproved from the most reliable sources—what recommends Liberia to me for you, and what ought to recommend it to you, is, that the germs of civilization are there, and the white man does not rule. *

It would not much surprise me, if the counsel I have thought it well to offer were, *at first* rejected by you all. Indeed, it would more surprise me, if it were not—although you must see that it is offered for *your* good—that it springs from the oppressive principle that gave birth to the Colonization Society, and from the wrongs inflicted on you by the whites—wrongs that you are unable to resist. I am fully prepared, too, for *permanent* opposition on the part of two classes of the colored people. 1. Those who have made money, however small in amount, it must be when compared with the whites, and wish to enjoy it here, content that they and their families suffer all the impositions they now suffer, impositions that, if the belief I entertain is true, will be aggravated in future. 2. Those who have not more energy or force of character than will suffice them to run their chance of getting enough in this country to eat and wear.

To these two classes—knowing it would be useless—I have nothing to say. But to the more noble-minded—to those who wish to get from under the pressure of irresistible, unjust power—to those who wish to give full sweep to the faculties which God has given to all his children—to those who wish to make MEN

*For more particular information, see a pamphlet (published in 1850), by I. W. Lugenbeel, formerly Colonial physician, and United States agent in Liberia. Whilst we see no reason for distrusting the facts as related, we do not agree with him in some of his inferences.

of themselves—to those, the sooner the idea is proposed the better.*

I have said that, at first, my counsel will be rejected by all of you. There may, however, be a few who will not reject it—such as have had rather a dim or obscure view of the plan proposed, and who would not even mention what they knew for fear of incurring an odium which they could not meet, or of separating from a class of which they still wished to form a part.

With these exceptions, and only as exceptions ought they to be considered, the colored people have fallen into the nation—a notion in which, perhaps, they have been trained—that it is a point of honor for them to remain in this country as long as their colored brethren are enslaved, and that it will gratify their enemies—the Colonizationists—should they go to Liberia. Admitting that the Colonizationists are all they are supposed to be—a thing I feel no inclination to controvert—it is an unworthy motive, and it will be as sure to injure you, as any other unworthy motive is sure to injure him, who entertains it. It matters not how small the thing may be, or whether he against whom the wrong may be done knows of it or not.

But ought the whole matter of your emigration to be thought of thus? It is too important to be committed to the direction of feeling and passion. It ought to be submitted to our best judgment—to our most deliberate reason—the highest faculty of our nature, and therefore well adapted for deciding such questions. A fair appeal to this power will enable you to determine, whether, on the whole, you should leave this country, and what other you should seek.

But you will no doubt say, that this counsel coming from an old and reputed friend will precipitate on you evils which you are unprepared for, and which otherwise you would not suffer. I would be very far from aiding, in any way, in bringing about such a state of things, nor do I think that what I have said will do so. But it must be remembered that the "oppressor" here has "power," and that he has all the effective and official departments of the government on his side; that the whites have already explained away and overlooked the provisions of their Constitution; that they have forgotten and disregarded the humanity we owe all our fellow-beings, and that they will proceed as far as they may think necessary to accomplish their purpose—no matter what may be the extremity.

But some of you, in your dejection and in your oppugnation to injustice, may say we can suffer it. That may be. I will not dispute it. But to be cast down, discouraged, becomes no one whose constant aim is to do right, least of all, him who aspires to lead others by perilous paths to safe places.

Whilst it must be almost needless to say to you that the counsel I have offered is only the expression of my opinion; that it can be disproved of if unsound, and that if unsound, it has no binding force on any one; I trust it is equally needless to say, that its fair and candid consideration will be very gratifying, and that this gratification will be much increased, if it should lead to happy results.

*Governor Roberts, of Liberia, in a late letter to some one in this country inviting the people of it to emigrate, says, however it may be protracted, it will come to this at last.

APPENDIX.

It is a belief almost universally entertained, both by the friends of the black and colored people, and by those who are not so considered, that they are better fitted *constitutionally* to be exposed in a Southern climate than the whites. But I apprehend this opinion when it comes to be more closely examined will be much modified, if not entirely given up. It is supposed, that our Creator gave to MAN a physical constitution of such pliability as to fit him for *any* climate. It is not intended to deny, that particular classes of people and their ancestors, from having long resided in the same climate, acquire, in a good degree, a physical or constitutional fitness for it. The black people, as far as we can trace them back, were originally the inhabitants of warm climates, and no doubt is entertained, that their physical constitutions are much affected by that fact. But take any large number of blacks—say fifty or more, and the same number of whites—they and their ancestors being brought up nearly, or quite alike, and in the same climate—and they will, under the same circumstances stand any change of latitude, however great, pretty much alike. That the descendants of the Liberians will, in two or three generations, become acclimated, we have no doubt.

CORRECTIONS.

Page.	Column.	Line from top.	
8	2	11	for *called* read *call.*
12	2	32	for *person* read *persons.*
12	1	41	for *it* read *its.*
13	2	31	for *io* read *in.*
17	1	36	supply *that* between *declare* and *one.*
19	1	19	for *cteal* read *steal.*
20	2	13	for *possessed* read *professed.*
22	1	5	for *rhey* read *they.*
24	1	18	for 1789 read 1787.
26	1	14	for *agreements* read *engagements.*
28	2		In a Note read *earnestness* for *correctness.*
30	1	35	for *acts* read *act.*
30	1	49	for *adopt* read *adapt.*
30	1	49	supply *a* before *formal.*
37	1		In the 6th line of the Note read *as* for *on.*

If other errors are discovered by the reader, it is thought they are not of sufficient consequence to lead him into any mistake of the writer's meaning.

[From the November number of the American Law Register, Volume IV.]

DISTRICT COURT OF THE UNITED STATES FOR THE EASTERN DISTRICT OF PENNSYLVANIA:

UNITED STATES OF AMERICA, EX RELATIONE WHEELER, VS. WILLIAMSON.

OPINION OF JUDGE KANE

ON THE SUGGESTION OF JANE JOHNSON.

OCTOBER 12, 1855.

PHILADELPHIA:

CRISSY & MARKLEY, PRINTERS, GOLDSMITHS HALL, LIBRARY STREET.

1855.

UNITED STATES OF AMERICA, EX RELATIONE WHEELER, vs. WILLIAMSON.

OPINION OF JUDGE KANE.

[From the November number of the American Law Register, Volume IV.]

IN THE DISTRICT COURT OF THE UNITED STATES FOR THE EASTERN DISTRICT OF PENNSYLVANIA.

On Wednesday, the 3d October, 1855, Mr. Townsend and Mr. Read presented to the court a paper purporting to be "The Suggestion and Petition of Jane Johnson;" on which they moved for a rule to show cause why the writ of habeas corpus heretofore issued against Passmore Williamson, on the relation of John H. Wheeler, should not be quashed.

On Friday, October 12th, Judge Kane delivered his opinion:—

KANE, J.—Before entering upon the question immediately before me at this time, it is proper that I should advert to the past action of this court in the case of Passmore Williamson, and to the considerations that led to it. I do this the rather, because in some of the judicial reviews to which it has been submitted collaterally, after an ex parte argument, it does not seem to me to have been fully apprehended.

I begin with the writ which originated the proceeding.

The writ of habeas corpus is of immemorial antiquity. It is deduced by the standard writers on the English law from the great charter of King John. It is unquestionable, however, that it is substantially of much earlier date; and it may be referred without improbability, to the period of the Roman invasion. Like the trial by jury, it entered into the institutions of Rome before the Christian era, if not as early as the times of the republic. Through the long series of political struggles which gave form to the British Constitution, it was claimed as the birthright of every Englishman, and our ancestors brought it with them as such to this country.

215

At the common law, it issued whenever a citizen was denied the exercise of his personal liberty, or was deprived of his rightful control over any member of his household, his wife, his child, his ward, or his servant. It issued from the courts of the sovereign, and in his name, at the instance of any one who invoked it, either for himself or another. It commanded, almost in the words of the Roman edict,[1] that the party under detention should be produced before the court, there to await its decree. It left no discretion with the party to whom it was addressed. He was not to constitute himself the judge of his own rights or of his own conduct; but to bring in the body, and to declare the cause wherefore he had detained it; and the judge was then to determine whether that cause was sufficient in law or not. Such in America, as well as England, was the well known, universally recognized writ of habeas corpus.

When the Federal Convention was engaged in framing a constitution for the United States, a proposition was submitted to it by one of the members, that "the privileges and benefits of the writ of habeas corpus shall be enjoyed in this government in the most expeditious and ample manner; and shall not be suspended by the legislature except upon the most urgent and pressing occasions."[2] The committee to whom this was referred for consideration, would seem to have regarded the privilege in question as too definitely implied in the idea of free government to need formal assertion or confirmation; for they struck out that part of the proposed article in which it was affirmed, and retained only so much as excluded the question of its suspension from the ordinary range of congressional legislation.

The convention itself must have concurred in their views; for in the Constitution, as digested, and finally ratified, and as it stands now, there is neither enactment nor recognition of the privilege of this writ, except as it is implied in the provision that it shall not be suspended. It stands then under the Constitution of the United

---

[1] "De libero homine exhibendo" D. 43. T. 29.

[2] See the Madison papers, Vol. III. p. 1365.

States, as it was under the common law of English America, an indefeasible privilege, above the sphere of ordinary legislation.[1]

I do not think it necessary to argue from the words of this article, that the Congress was denied the power of limiting or restricting or qualifying the right, which it was thus forbidden to suspend. I do not, indeed, see that there can be a restriction or limitation of a privilege which may not be essentially a suspension of it, to some extent at least, or under some circumstances, or in reference to some of the parties who might otherwise have enjoyed it. And it has appeared to me, that if Congress had undertaken to deny altogether the exercise of this writ by the federal courts, or to limit its exercise to the few and rare cases that might per-adventure find their way to some one particular court, or to declare that the writ should only issue in this or that class of cases, to the exclusion of others in which it might have issued at the common law, it would be difficult to escape the conclusion, that the ancient and venerated privilege of the writ of habeas corpus had not been in some degree suspended, if not annulled.

But there has been no legislation or attempted legislation by Congress, that could call for an expansion of this train of reasoning.

There was one other writ, which, in the more recent contests between the people and the king, had contributed signally to the maintenance of popular right. It was the writ of scire facias, which had been employed to vindicate the rights of property, by vacating the monopolies of the crown. Like the writ of habeas corpus, it founded itself on the concessions of Magna Charta ; and the two were the proper and natural complements of each other.

The first Congress so regarded them. The protection of the citizen against arbitrary exaction and unlawful restraint, as it is the essential object of all rightful government, would present itself as the first great duty of the courts of justice that were about to be

---

[1] "The privilege of the writ of *habeas corpus* shall not be suspended unless when in cases of rebellion or invasion the public safety may require it." Const. U. S. Art. 1, § 9, par. 1.

constituted. And if, in defining their jurisdiction, it were thought proper to signalize two writs, out of the many known to the English law, as within the unqualified competency of the new tribunals, it would seem natural that those two should be selected, which boasted their origin from the charter of English liberties, and had been consecrated for ages in the affectionate memories of the people as their safeguard against oppression.

This consideration has interpreted for me the terms of the statute, which define my jurisdiction on this subject. Very soon after I had been advanced to the Bench, I was called upon to issue the writ of habeas corpus, at the instance of a negro, who had been arrested as a fugitive from labor. It was upon the force of the argument, to which I now advert, that I then awarded the process ; and from that day to this, often as it has been invoked and awarded in similar cases that have been before me, my authority to award it has never been questioned.

The language of the act of Congress reflects the history of the constitutional provision. It enacts (*First Congr.*, *Sess.* 1, *ch.* 20, *sec.* 14) " that all the before mentioned courts of the United States" (the Supreme, Circuit and District,) " shall have power to issue writs of scire facias habeas corpus and all other writs not specially provided for by statute which may be necessary for the exercise of their respective jurisdictions and agreeable to the principles and usages of law."

I am aware that it has sometimes been contended or assumed, without, as it seems to me, a just regard to the grammatical construction of these words, that the concluding limitation applies to all the process of the courts, the two writs specially named among the rest ; and that the federal courts can only issue the writ of habeas corpus, when it has become necessary to the exercise of an otherwise delegated jurisdiction ; in other words, that it is subsidiary to some original process or pending suit.

It is obvious, that if such had been the intention of the lawmakers, it was unnecessary to name the writ of habeas corpus at all ; for the simpler phrase, " *all writs* necessary, &c." would in that case have covered their meaning. But there are objections to this reading more important than any that found themselves on grammatical rules.

The words that immediately follow in the section, give the power of issuing the writ to every judge, for the purpose of inquiring into the causes of a commitment. Now, a commitment presupposes judicial action, and this action it is the object of the writ to review. Can it be, that a single judge, sitting as such, can re-examine the causes of a detainer, which has resulted from judicial action, and is therefore *prima facie* a lawful one; and yet that the court, of which he is a member, cannot inquire into the causes of a detainer, made without judicial sanction, and therefore *prima facie* unlawful?

Besides, if this were the meaning of the act, it might be difficult to find the cases to which it should apply. I speak of the writ of *habeas corpus ad subjiciendum*, the great writ of personal liberty, referred to in the constitution; not that modification of it which applies specially to the case of a commitment, nor the less important forms of habeas corpus, *ad respondendum, ad faciendum*, &c., which are foreign to the question. I do not remember to have met a case, either in practice or in the books, where the writ *ad subjiciendum* could have performed any pertinent office in a pending suit. There may be such, but they do not occur to me; and I incline very strongly to the opinion, that if the power to issue the writ of habeas corpus applies only to cases of statutory jurisdiction, outrages upon the rights of a citizen can never invoke its exercise by a federal court.

If such were indeed the law of the United States, I do not see how I could escape the conclusion, that the jealousy of local interests and prejudice, which led to the constitution of federal courts, regarded only disputes about property; and that the liberty of a citizen, when beyond the State of his domicil, was not deemed worthy of equal protection. From an absurdity so gross as this, I relieve myself by repeating the words of Chief Justice Marshall, in *ex parte Watkins*, 3 Pet. 201: "No law of the United States prescribes the cases in which this great writ shall be issued, nor the power of the court over the party brought up on it."

Whether, then, I look to the constitution, and its history, or to the words or the policy of the act of Congress, I believe that it was

meant to require of the Courts of the United States, that they should
dispense the privileges of the writ of habeas corpus to all parties
lawfully asserting them, as other courts of similar functions and
dignity had immemorially dispensed them at the common law.   The
Congress of 1789 made no definition of the writ, or of its conditions, or effects.   They left it as the constitution left it, and as it
required them to leave it, the birthright of every man within the
borders of the States ; like the right to air, and water, and motion,
and thought, rights imprescriptible, and above all legislative discretion or caprice.

And so it ought to be.   There is no writ so important for good,
and so little liable to be abused.   At the worst, in the hands of a
corrupt or ignorant judge, it may release some one from restraint
who should justly have remained bound.   But it deprives no one
of freedom, and devests no right.   It could not give to Mr. Wheeler
the possession of his slaves, but it might release them from the
custody of a wrong-doer.   Freemen or bondsmen, they had rights ;
and the foremost of these was the right to have their other rights
adjudicated openly and by the tribunals of the land.   And this
right at least, Mr. Wheeler shared with them ; he also could claim
a hearing.

Unless these views are incorrect throughout, the District Court
had jurisdiction of the case, which came before it at the instance of
Mr. Wheeler.   He represented in substance, by his petition under
oath, that three human beings had been forcibly taken possession of
by Passmore Williamson, without authority of law, within the
Eastern District of Pennsylvania; and he prayed, that by force
of the writ of habeas corpus, Mr. Williamson might be required
to produce their bodies before the court, and to declare what was
the right or pretext of right, under which he claimed to detain
them.

Whether Mr. Wheeler was in fact entitled to demand this writ,
or whether upon a full discussion of the law the court might have
felt justified in refusing it to him, is a question of little moment.
Every day and in every court, writs issue at the instance of parties
asserting a grievance, and very often when in truth no grievance

has been sustained. The party assailed comes before the court in obedience to its process. He perhaps questions the jurisdiction of the court. Perhaps he denies the fact charged. Perhaps he explains that the fact, as charged, was by reason of circumstances a lawful one. The judge is not presumed to know beforehand, all the merits of the thousand and one causes that come before him: he decides when he has heard. But the first duty of a defendant, in all cases, is obedience to the writ which calls him into court. Till he has rendered this, the judge cannot hear the cause, still less pass upon its merits.

Mr. Williamson came before the court; but he did not bring forth the bodies of his alleged prisoners, as the writ had commanded him. He did not question the jurisdiction of the court : he did not assert that the negroes were free, and that the writ had been applied for without their authority or consent : but he simply denied that they had ever been in his custody, power or possession, as Mr. Wheeler asserted.

Witnesses were heard, and, with one consent, they supported the allegations of Mr. Wheeler, and contradicted the denial of Mr. Williamson.

Mr. Williamson's counsel then asked time to enable them to produce witnesses who were material on his behalf; remarking that their client might desire to bring the negroes into court, to prove that they had not been abducted. The judge informed them, in reply, that upon Mr. Williamson making the customary affidavit that there were material witnesses whom he wished to adduce, the cause would be continued, as of course, till a future day. Mr. Williamson declined making the affidavit.

He however asked leave to declare for himself what he had done, and why. He was heard, and, speaking under solemn affirmation, he not only verified all the important facts that had been sworn to by Mr. Wheeler and the witnesses, but added that immediately before coming into court with his return, he had called upon a negro who had been his principal associate in the transaction, to ascertain whether the negroes were " safe," and had been informed by him that they were " all safe."

Two motions were then made by Mr. Wheeler's counsel; the first, that Mr. Williamson should be committed for a contempt of process, in that he had made a false return to the writ; the second, that he should be held to answer to a charge of perjury. He summed up the evidence, and referred to authorities in support of these motions. The counsel of Mr. Williamson then asked leave to consult together as to their appropriate course of action; and this being assented to by the Court, they retired with their client for the purpose, from the court room. Returning after some time, they informed the court that they declined making any argument upon the questions which were before it.

The case, which was in this manner thrown upon the court for its unaided adjudication, had assumed an aspect of grave responsibility on the part of Mr. Williamson. It was clearly in proof that the negroes had been removed by persons acting under his counsel, in his presence, and with his co-operation : his return to the writ denied that they had ever been within his possession, custody, or control. Under ordinary circumstances, this denial would have been conclusive; but being controverted by the facts in evidence, it lost that character. "The court," said Judge Story, in a case singularly analogous in its circumstances, (*U. S.* vs. *Green*, 3 Mas. 483,) "will not discharge the defendant, simply because he declares that the infant is not in his power, possession, control or custody, if the conscience of the court is not satisfied that all the material facts are fully disclosed. That would be to listen to mere forms, against the claims of substantial justice, and the rights of personal liberty in the citizen. In ordinary cases, indeed, such a declaration is satisfactory and ought to be decisive, because there is nothing before the court upon which it can ground a doubt of its entire verity, and that in a real and legal sense the import of the words "possession, power, or custody," is fully understood and met by the party. The cases of the *King* vs. *Vinton*, 5 T. R., 89, and of *Stacey*, 10 Johns. 328, show with what jealousy, courts regard returns of this nature. In these cases, there was enough on the face of the returns to excite suspicions that more was behind, and that the party was really within the constructive control of the defendant. Upon examining the circumstances of this case, I am not satisfied that the return contains all those facts within the knowledge of the defendant, which are necessary to be brought before the court, to enable it to decide, whether he is entitled to a discharge; or in other words, whether he has not now the power to produce the infant, and control those in whose custody she is."

"There is no doubt," he adds, "that an attachment is the proper process to bring the defendant into court."

Anxious that this resort to the inherent and indispensable powers of the court might be avoided, the judge, in adjourning the case for advisement until the following week, urged upon Mr. Williamson and his associates, that if practicable, the negroes should, in the meantime, be brought before the court.

But the negroes were not produced. They came forward afterwards, some of them, as it is said, before a justice in New York; and by a process of a Pennsylvania State court, they or some of them were brought forward again in this city, to testify for Mr. Williamson or some of his confederates. But before the Court of the United States, sitting within the same curtilage, at the distance of perhaps a hundred yards, it was not thought necessary or expedient or practicable to produce them. Their evidence, whatever might have been its import or value, was never before the court, and could have no bearing upon its action.

The decision was announced at the end of the week. It was, that Mr. Williamson's answer was evasive and untrue; that he, therefore, had not obeyed the writ of habeas corpus, and must consequently stand committed as for a contempt of it. The order to that effect having been made, a discussion arose between the counsel as to the propriety of certain motions, which on one side and the other they invited the court to consider.

It was apparent, that the learned gentleman[1] who at this time addressed the court on behalf of Mr. Williamson, as his senior counsel, was imperfectly prepared to suggest any specific action either for the bench, or for his client. His remarks were discur-

---

[1] Mr. Charles Gilpin.

sive; and when invited to reduce his motion to writing, according to the rules of practice, he found difficulty in defining its terms. This led to an intimation on the part of the judge, that, inasmuch as the opinion was in writing, and would be printed in the newspapers of the afternoon, it might be best for the counsel to examine its positions before submitting their motion. The intimation was received courteously. The question was asked whether the court would be in session on one or another of days that were named; and the reply was given, that upon a note being left at the Clerk's office at any time, the judge would be in attendance to hear and consider whatever motions the counsel might see proper to lay before him.

This was the last of the case. No motion was made; no further intimation given on the part of Mr. Williamson or his counsel, of a wish to make one.

Commitments for contempt, like the contempts themselves, may be properly distributed in two classes. Either they are the punishment for an act of misconduct, or it is their object to enforce the performance of a duty. The confinement in the one case is for a fixed time, supposed to be commensurate with the offending; in the other, it is without prescribed limitation, and is determined by the willingness of the party to submit himself to the law.

In the case of Mr. Williamson, the commitment is for a refusal to answer; that is to say, to make a full and lawful answer to the writ of habeas corpus, an answer setting forth all the facts within his knowledge, which are necessary to a decision by the court, "whether he had not the power to produce the negroes, and control those in whose custody they were." He is now undergoing restraint, not punishment. Immediately after the opinion was read, he was informed, in answer to a remark from his counsel, that the commitment was "*during the contempt:*" the contempt of the party and the order of the court consequent upon it, determine together.

This is all that I conceive it necessary to say of the strictly judicial action in the case. The opinions, announced by the judge upon other points, may perhaps be regarded as merely *dicta*. But it had appeared from the defendant's declarations when upon the stand, that he supposed Mr. Wheeler's slaves to have become free, and that this consideration justified his acting towards them as he had done. It seemed due to him, that the court, believing as it did those views to be incorrect, should not withhold an expression of its dissent from them. Several succinct positions were accordingly asserted by the judge: two of which may invite a few additional remarks at this time.

"I know of no statute of Pennsylvania," the judge said, "which affects to devest the rights of property of a citizen of North Carolina, acquired and asserted under the laws of that State, because he has found it needful or convenient to pass through the territory of Pennsylvania; and I am not aware that any such statute, if such a one were shown, could be recognized as valid in a court of the United States."

The first of these propositions may be vindicated easily. By the common law, as it came to Pennsylvania, slavery was a familiar institution. Only six days after the first legislative assembly met in Philadelphia, and thirteen days before the great charter was signed, the council was engaged in discussing a law " to prevent the escape of runaways;" and four days later, it sat judicially, William Penn himself presiding, to enforce a contract for the sale of a slave, 1 *Colonial Records*, 63.[1] The counties of New Castle, Kent, and Sussex, which were at that time and for many years after annexed to Pennsylvania, and governed by the same law, continue to recognize slavery up to the present hour. It survived in our Commonwealth, as a legally protected institution, until some time after the census of 1840; so cautiously did the act of 1780, for its gradual abolition among us, operate upon the vested interests of our own slave owners.

---

[1] "At a council, held at Philadelphia, yᵉ 29th 1st mo., 1683. Present, William Penn, Proprietary, and Governor of Pennsylvania and counties annexed, Thos. Holmes, John Richardson, William Clarke, John Simcox, James Harrison, (and eight others.)

"The petition of Nathaniel Allen was read, shewing that he had sould a servant to Henry Bowman, for six hundred weight of beefe, with yᵉ hide and tallow, and six pounds sterling, which yᵉ said Bowman delayed to pay yᵉ said petitioner, shewing

That act excepted from the operation of its provisions the domestic slaves of delegates in Congress, of foreign ministers, of persons passing through, or *sojourning* in the State, and *not becoming residents* therein, provided such slaves were not *retained* in the State longer than six months. The act of 1847 repealed so much of the act of 1780 as authorized masters and owners of slaves to bring and *retain* their slaves within the Commonwealth for the period of six months, or for any period of time whatever. But it did not affect to vary or rescind the rights of slave owners *passing through* our territory. It applied to persons *resident* and persons *sojourning*, who brought and sought to *retain* their slaves here; for over such persons and their rights of property the State had lawful dominion: but it left the right of transit for property and person, over which it had no jurisdiction, just as it was before, and as it stood under the constitution of the United States and the Law of Nations.

This brings me to the second part of the position affirmed in the court's opinion, namely: the right of a citizen of one State to pass freely with his slaves through the territory of another State, in which the institution of slavery is not recognized.

I need not say, that before the compact of union was formed between the States, each of them was an absolutely sovereign and independent community; and that, except so far as their relations to each other and to foreign nations have been qualified by the Federal Constitution, each of them remain so. As such, it is bound

---

likewise that yᵉ said Henry Bowman and Walter Humphrey hired a boat of the said petitioner only for one month, and kept the same boat 18 weeks from the petitioner to his great prejudice: Then it was ordered, that William Clarke, John Simcox and James Harrison should speak to Henry Bowman concerning this matter."—p. 62.

The Great Charter was signed by William Penn, 2d day, 2d mo., 1683, (see p. 72.)

A practice analogous to the Fugitive Slave Law of modern times seems to be referred to in the following minute, at p. 147 of the same volume.

"24th 5 mo., 1685. William Hague requests the secretary, that an hue and cry from East Jersey after a servant of Mr. John White's, a merchant at New York, might have some force and authority to pass this province and territories: the secretary indorsed it, and sealed it with yᵉ seal of this province."

by that great moral code, which, because of its universal obligation, is called the Law of Nations. What it could not do if freed from federative restrictions, it cannot do now: every restraint upon its policy, which duty to other States would in that case involve, binds it still, just as if the union had been dissolved or had never been formed.

All the statists unite in regarding the right of transit for person and property through the territory of a friendly State, as among those which cannot, under ordinary circumstances, be denied. Vattel, B. 2, ch. 10, §132, 3, 4; Puffendorf, B. 2, ch. 3, § 5, 67; Rutherf. Inst. B. 2, ch. 9; 1 Kent Com. 33, 35. It is true that the right is not an unqualified one. The State may impose reasonable conditions upon its exercise, and exact guaranties against its abuse. But subject to these limitations, it is the right of every citizen of a friendly State.

The right is the same, and admits just the same qualifications, as to person and to property. The same argument, that denies the right of peacefully transmitting one's property through the territories of a State, refuses the right of passage to its owner. And the question, what is to be deemed property in such a case, refers itself necessarily to the law of the State from which the citizen brings it: a different test would sanction the confiscation of property at the will of the sovereign through whose territory it seeks to pass. If one State may decree that there shall be no property, no right of ownership in human beings; another, in a spirit of practical philanthropy only a little more energetic, may deny the protection of law to the products of slave labor; and a third may denounce a similar outlawry against all intoxicating liquids: And if the laws of a State can control the rights of property of strangers passing through its territory; then the sugar of New Orleans, the cotton of Carolina, the wines of Ohio, and the rum of New England may have their markets bounded by the States in which they are produced; and without any change of reasoning, New Jersey may refuse to citizens of Pennsylvania the right of passing along her railroads to New York. The doctrine is one that was exploded in Europe more than four hundred and fifty years ago, and finds now, or found very lately, its parting illustration in the politics of Japan.

It was because, and only because, this right was acknowledged by all civilized nations, and had never been doubted among the American colonies—because each colony had at all times tendered its hospitalities freely to the rest, cherishing that liberal commerce which makes a brotherhood of interest even among alien States; it was because of this, that no man in the convention or country thought of making the right of transit a subject of Constitutional guaranty. Everything in and about the Constitution implies it. It is found in the object, "to establish a more perfect union," in the denial to the States of the power to lay duties on imports, and in the reservation to Congress of the exclusive right to regulate commerce among the States.

This last power of the general government according to the repeated and well considered decisions of the Supreme Court of the United States, from *Gibbons* vs. *Ogden*, 9 Peters, to the *passenger cases*, 7 Howard, applies to intercourse as well as navigation, to the transportation of men as well as goods, of men who pass from State to State involuntarily, as of men who pass voluntarily; and it excludes the right of any State to pass laws regulating, controlling, or *a fortiori*, prohibiting such intercourse or transportation. I do not quote the words of the eminent judges who have affirmed this exposition of the Constitution; but it is impossible to read their elaborate opinions, as they are found in the reports, without recognizing this as the fixed law of the United States.

It needs no reference to disputable annals, to show that when the Constitution was formed in 1787, slaves were recognized as property, throughout the United States. The Constitution made them a distinct element in the distribution of the representative power and in the assessment of direct taxes. They were known and returned by the census, three years afterwards, in sixteen out of the seventeen States then embraced in the Union; and as late as the year 1830, they were found in every State of the original thirteen. How is it possible then, while we assert the binding force of the constitution by claiming rights under it, to regard slave property as less effectively secured by the provisions of that instrument than any other property which is recognized as such by the law of the owner's domicil? How can it be, that a State may single out this one sort of property from among all the rest, and deny to it the right of passing over its soil—passing with its owner, parcel of his travelling equipment, as much so as the horse he rides on, his great coat, or his carpet bag?

We revolt in Pennsylvania, and honestly no doubt, at this association of men with things as the subjects of property; for we have accustomed ourselves for some years—now nearly fifteen—to regard men as men, and things as things: *sub modo*, however; for we distinguish against the negro much as our forefathers did; and not perhaps, with quite as much reason. They denied him civil rights, as a slave: we exclude him from political rights, though a freeman.

Yet no stranger may complain of this. Our constitutions and statutes are for ourselves, not for others. They reflect our sympathies, and define our rights. But as to all the rest of the world; those portions, especially, towards whom we are bound by the "supreme law" of the federal constitution; they are independent of our legislation, however wise or virtuous it may be; for they were not represented in our conventions and assemblies, and we do not permit them to legislate for us.

Whether any redress is provided by the existing laws of Pennsylvania for the citizen of another State, whose slaves have escaped from him while he was passing through our territory, it is not my province to inquire. It is quite probable that he may be denied recourse to the courts, as much so as the husband, or father, or guardian, whose wife, or child, or ward, has run away. He may find himself referred back to those rights, which annex themselves inseparably to the relation he occupies, the rights of manucaption and detainer. These, I apprehend that he may assert and exercise anywhere, and with such reasonable force as circumstances render necessary. And I do not suppose that the employment of such reasonable force could be regarded as a breach of the peace, or the right to employ it as less directly incident to his character of master than it might be to the corresponding character in either of the analogous relations.   In a word, I adopt fully on this point the views so well enforced by Judge Baldwin, in the case of *Johnson* vs. *Tompkins*, Baldw., 578, 9 :

"The right of the master to arrest his fugitive slave, is not a solitary case in the law.   It may be exercised towards a fugitive apprentice or redemptioner to the same extent, and is done daily without producing any excitement.   An apprentice is a servant, a slave is no more : though his servitude is for life, the nature of it is the same as apprenticeship or by redemption, which, though terminated by time, is during its continuance as severe a servitude as that for life.   Of the same nature is the right of a parent to the services of his minor children, which gives the custody of their persons.   So, where a man enters bail for the appearance of a defendant in a civil action, he may seize his person at his pleasure, and commit him to prison ; or, if the principal escapes, the bail may pursue him to another state, arrest, and bring him back, by the use of all necessary force and means of preventing an escape. The lawful exercise of this authority in such cases is calculated to excite no sympathy : the law takes its course in peace, and unnoticed.   Yet it is the same power, and used in the same manner, as by a master over his slave.   The right in such case is from the same source, the law of the land.   If the enforcement of the right excites more feeling in one case than the other, it is not from the manner in which it is done, but the nature of the right which is enforced, property in a human being for life.   If this is unjust and oppressive, the sin is on the makers of laws which tolerate slavery : to visit it on those, who have honestly acquired, and lawfully hold property under the guarantee and protection of the laws, is the worst of all oppression, and the rankest injustice towards our fellow men.   It is the indulgence of a spirit of persecution against our neighbors, for no offence against society or its laws, but simply for the assertion of their own in a lawful manner.

"If this spirit pervades the country," he goes on to say : "if public opinion is suffered to prostrate the laws which protect one species of property, those who lead the crusade against slavery, may at no distant day find a new one directed against their lands, their stores, and their debts.   If a master cannot retain the custody of his slave, apprentice, or redemptioner, a parent must give up the guardianship of his children, bail have no hold upon their principal, the creditor cannot arrest his debtor by lawful means, and he, who keeps the rightful owner of lands or chattels out of possession, will be protected in his trespasses.

"When the law ceases to be the test of right and remedy ; when individuals undertake to be its administrators, by rules of their own adoption ; the bands of society are broken as effectually by the severance of one link from the chain of justice which binds man to the laws, as if the whole was dissolved.   The more specious and seductive the pretexts are, under which the law is violated, the greater ought to be the vigilance of courts and juries in their detection.   Public opinion is a security against acts of open and avowed infringements of acknowledged rights ; from such combinations there is no danger ; they will fall by their own violence, as the blast expends its force by its own fury.   The only permanent danger is in the indulgence of the humane and benevolent feelings of our nature, at what we feel to be acts of oppression towards human beings, endowed with the same qualities and attributes as ourselves, and brought into being by the same power which created us all; without reflecting, that in suffering these feelings to come into action against rights secured by the laws, we forget the first duty of citizens of a government of laws, obedience to its ordinances."

There was one other legal proposition affirmed in the opinion of this court, but it cannot need argument. It was, that the question, whether the negroes were or were not freed by their arrival in Pennsylvania, was irrelevant to the issue; inasmuch as whether they were freed or not, they were equally under the protection of the law, and the same obligation rested on Mr. Williamson to make a true and full return to the writ of habeas corpus. Simple and obvious as this proposition is, it covers all the judicial action in the case. The writ required him to produce the negroes, that the court might pass upon his legal right to carry them off or detain them. What questions might arise afterwards, or how they might be determined, was not for him to consider. His duty then, as now, was and is to bring in the bodies; or, if they had passed beyond his control, to declare under oath or affirmation, so far as he knew, what had become of them: And from this duty, or from the constraint that seeks to enforce it, there can be no escape.

(*See the argument of Sergeant Glynn, and the remarks of Mr. Justice Gould, in the case of Mr. Wilkes, 2 Wils. 154.*)

The application immediately before me, hardly calls for these expanded remarks; though, rightly considered, they bear upon most of the points that were elaborated in the argument upon the question of its reception. It purports to be a suggestion and petition from a person now in Massachusetts, who informs the court that she is one of the negroes who escaped from Mr. Wheeler, that she did so by Mr. Williamson's counsel, and with the sanction of his presence and approval, but that he never detained her, nor has any one since, and that she has never authorized an application for the writ of habeas corpus in her behalf. Thereupon, she presents to me certain reasons, founded as she supposes in law, wherefore I

2

ought to quash the writ heretofore issued at the relation of Mr. Wheeler.

When application was made to me for leave to file this paper, I invited the learned counsel to advise me upon the question, whether I could lawfully admit the intervention of their client. My thanks are due to them for the ability and courteous bearing with which they have discussed it. But I remain unconvinced.

The very name of the person who authenticates the paper is a stranger to any proceeding that is or has been before me.[1] She asks no judicial action for herself, and does not profess to have any right to solicit action in behalf of another: on the contrary, her counsel here assure me expressly, that Mr. Williamson has not sanctioned her application. She has therefore no status whatever in this court.

Were she here as a party, to abide its action, she would have a right to be heard according to the forms of law; were she here as a witness, called by a party, her identity ascertained, she might be examined as to all facts supposed to be within her knowledge. But our records cannot be opened to every stranger who volunteers to us a suggestion, as to what may have been our errors, and how we may repair them.

I know that the writ of habeas corpus can only be invoked by the party who is restrained of liberty, or by some one in his behalf. I know, too, that it has been the reproach of the English courts, that they have too sternly exacted proof, that the application was authorized by the aggrieved party, before permitting the writ to issue. But, as yet, the courts of the United States have, I think, avoided this error. The writ issues here, as it did in Rome,[2] whenever it is shown by affidavit that its beneficent agency is needed. It would lose its best efficiency, if it could not issue without a petition from the party himself, or some one whom he had delegated to represent him. His very presence in court to demand the writ would, in

---

[1] Neither the petition for the writ of habeas corpus, nor the writ itself, names Jane *Johnson*.

[2] "Interdictum omnibus competit.—*Nemo* enim prohibendus est libertati favere."—*Dig. B.* 43, *T.* 29, ≥ 9.

some sort, negative the restraint which his petition must allege. In the most urgent cases, those in which delay would be disastrous, forcible abduction, secret imprisonment, and the like, the very grievance under which he is suffering, precludes the possibility of his applying in person or constituting a representative. The American books are full of cases,—they are within the experience of every practitioner at the bar,—in which the writ has issued at the instance of third persons, who had no other interest or right in the matter than what every man concedes to sympathy with the oppressed. I need only to refer to the case I have quoted from in 3 Mason, and the case of Stacy, in 10 Johnson, for illustrations of this practice.

Of course, if it appears to the court at any time, that the writ was asked for by an intermeddling stranger, one who had no authority to intervene, and whose intervention is repudiated, the writ will be quashed. But it is for the defendant, to whom the writ is addressed, to allege a want of authority in the relator. The motion to quash cannot be the act of a volunteer. Still less can it come to us by written suggestion, from without our jurisdiction, in the name of the party who is alleged to be under constraint, and whose very denial that she is so may be only a proof that the constraint is effectual.

I may add, that I have examined all the authorities which were brought before me by the learned counsel: with most of them I was familiar before. But there is not one among them, which in my judgment conflicts with the views I have expressed.

The application to enter this paper among the records of the court, must therefore be refused.

———

Upon the reading of the above opinion, Mr. Cadwalader, as a member of the bar of the court not counsel or attorney in the original or subsequent proceedings, asked leave as amicus curiæ to suggest that, in the Opinion of the court, an incident of the original proceeding, which has been publicly misrepresented, was not noticed.

"It has been publicly reported," Mr. Cadwalader said, "that after the opinion of the court, which resulted in Mr. Williamson's commitment, had been read, his counsel applied to the court for leave to amend his return, which leave was refused. The present suggestion is made under the belief of the member of the bar who makes it, that this report was erroneous, and that what occurred was as follows. When the opinion in the original proceeding was read, the counsel of Mr. Williamson asked if a motion to amend the return would be received, and the court replied, that the motion must be reduced to writing, and that it could not be received until the court's order should be filed with the Clerk and recorded; adding that the court would then receive any motion which the counsel for Mr. Williamson might desire to make. The court's order was then filed by the Clerk, and entered on record; but no motion to amend was then or afterwards made, although the court paused to give an opportunity for making it, and invited the counsel then or afterwards, to make any motion which their client might be advised to make."

Judge Kane said:—The recollections of Mr. Cadwalader concur substantially with my own. There certainly was no motion made by the counsel of Mr. Williamson, for leave to amend his return. A wish was expressed to make such a motion, and the judge asked that the motion might be reduced to writing and filed. But the motion was not drawn out or presented for the court's consideration, and the court never-expressed any purpose to overrule such a motion, if one should be presented.

CASE OF PASSMORE WILLIAMSON.

REPORT OF THE PROCEEDINGS

ON THE

WRIT OF HABEAS CORPUS,

ISSUED BY

THE HON. JOHN K. KANE,

JUDGE OF THE DISTRICT COURT OF THE UNITED STATES FOR THE
EASTERN DISTRICT OF PENNSYLVANIA,

IN THE CASE OF

THE UNITED STATES OF AMERICA EX REL.

JOHN H. WHEELER vs. PASSMORE WILLIAMSON,

INCLUDING

THE SEVERAL OPINIONS DELIVERED;

AND

The Arguments of Counsel, Reported by Arthur Cannon, Esq., Phonographer.

PHILADELPHIA:
URIAH HUNT & SON, N. FOURTH STREET.
1856.

CASE OF PASSMORE WILLIAMSON.

In the matter of the U. S ex rel. J. H. WHEELER vs. PASSMORE WILLIAMSON, the proceedings were begun by petition presented to the Hon. J. K. Kane, Judge of the District Court of the U. S. at Chambers, on the 18th day of July, 1855. The petition is in the following words, viz:

To the Honorable John K. Kane, Judge of the District Court of the United States, in and for the Eastern District of Pennsylvania.

The Petition of JOHN H. WHEELER, respectfully represents:

That your Petitioner is the owner of three persons held to service or labor by the laws of the State of Virginia, said persons being respectively named Jane, aged about thirty-five years, Daniel, aged about twelve years, and Isaiah, aged about seven years, persons of color; and that they are detained from the possession of your Petitioner by one Passmore Williamson, resident of the City of Philadelphia, and that they are not detained for any criminal or supposed criminal matter.

Your Petitioner, therefore, prays your Honor to grant a writ of habeas corpus to be directed to the said Passmore Williamson, commanding him to bring before your Honor the bodies of the said Jane, Daniel and Isaiah, to do and abide such order as your Honor may direct.

JOHN H. WHEELER.

Sworn to and subscribed, July 18, 1855.

CHAS. F. HEAZLITT, U. S. Com.

Thereupon, a writ of *habeas corpus* as prayed for, was allowed, returnable the next day at 3 o'clock P. M., at the U. S. Court room, before the Hon. J. K. Kane.

At the appointed time and place, viz: Thursday, July 19, at 3 o'clock P. M., EDWARD HOPPER, Esq., appeared before Judge Kane, (Col. Wheeler being present, accompanied by his counsel,) and stated:

That he had been called upon by Thomas Williamson, father of the respondent, who brought with him the writ of *habeas corpus*, which he now had in his hand. That Passmore Williamson was absent from the city, having gone to Harrisburg on private business. That said writ was left at the office of Thomas Williamson & Son; the respondent was absent, and it could not be considered as a service of the writ; but he (Mr. H.) appeared at the instance of Thomas Williamson, out of respect to the process of the Court, and would say, that the respondent was expected home that night, and would, on his return, doubtless respond to the writ.

J. C. VANDYKE, Esq., for relator, then moved the Court for an alias writ of *habeas corpus*, returnable at the earliest convenient time.

The Court allowed the alias writ, returnable the next morning at 10 o'clock; which was issued as follows, viz:

UNITED STATES,
Eastern District of Pennsylvania, } SS.

[SEAL]   }   *The President of the United States*
J. K. KANE.   }   TO
                     Passmore Williamson.

Greeting: We command you, as before we commanded you, that the bodies of Jane Daniel and Isaiah, persons of color, under your custody, as it is said, detained, by whatsoever names the said Jane Daniel or Isaiah, or either of them, may be detained, together with the day and cause of their being taken and detained, you have before the Honorable John K. Kane, Judge of the District Court of the United States in and for the Eastern District of Pennsylvania, at the Room of the District Court of the United States in the City of Philadelphia, immediately, then and there to do submit to and receive, whatsoever the said Judge shall then and there consider in that behalf.

Witness the Honorable John K. Kane, Judge of said Court at Philadelphia, this nineteenth day of July A.D. 1855 and in the eightieth year of the Independence of the said United States.

CHAS. F. HEAZLITT, for Clerk Dist. Ct.

On Friday, July 20th, at 10 o'clock A. M., the respondent Passmore Williamson, accompanied by his counsel EDWARD HOPPER, ESQ., appeared in Court and made return to the alias writ, under affirmation, in the following words:

To the Honorable J. K. Kane, the Judge within named:

Passmore Williamson, the defendant in the within writ mentioned, for return thereto, respectfully submits that the within named Jane

Daniel and Isaiah, or by whatsoever names they may be called, nor either of them, are not now, nor was, at the time of the issuing of said writ or the original writ, or at any other time, in the custody power or possession of, nor confined nor restrained their liberty by him the said Passmore Williamson. Therefore he cannot have the bodies of the said Jane Daniel and Isaiah, or either of them, before your Honor, as by the said writ he is commanded.

P. WILLIAMSON.

The above named Passmore Williamson being duly affirmed, says that the facts in the above return set forth are true.

P. WILLIAMSON.

Affirmed and subscribed before me this 20th day of July, A. D. 1855.

CHAS. F. HEAZLITT,
U. S. Commissioner.

Mr. VANDYKE, counsel for Mr. Wheeler, asked the Court to permit him to offer testimony to rebut the statements of the respondent in his return.

Mr. HOPPER for respondent, contended that the return was sufficient and conclusive, and, as it was a complete denial of the custody, power or control, they could not go behind it.

Mr. VANDYKE replied by stating what he was prepared to prove.

Mr. HOPPER said, that if testimony was to be heard in the case, he would ask for time to prepare; that the course which the case had taken was certainly a surprise; that his client had returned the night before after one o'clock, which had given him a very meagre opportunity for consultation; that he had seen him but for a few minutes while the return was being prepared.

Judge KANE remarked, that if the bodies of the three servants were produced in Court, the question of time for preparation could be considered. The conduct of those who interfered with Mr. Wheeler's rights, was a criminal, wanton and cruel outrage. If the testimony would show that the defendant had been guilty of contempt in the return made to the *habeas corpus*, he might, as a committing magistrate, feel it to be his duty to hold the defendant to answer for perjury, without hearing testimony in defence. It would be sufficient to have a *prima facie* case made out.

Messrs. VANDYKE and WEBSTER for Col. Wheeler stated, that if the servants were produced in Court, no objection would be made to giving time to the defendant

Judge KANE overruled the motion for time and said he would now hear testimony.

C. GILPIN, Esq. came into the case just at this moment, as counsel for the respondent, and said that they had complied with the usual form in making a return to the habeas corpus, and that they had denied the custody now or at any time. If not deemed sufficient it would be necessary to take other steps or proceedings. The prosecutor had his remedy in a civil action for damages against the offending parties. The defendant desired to put in a complete return, and then be permitted to go without day as having made sufficient answer.

After some further remarks by respondent's counsel on technical points, Judge Kane said : A return has been made to the writ, and the counsel for the relator ask permission to traverse that return, having presented to the Court a certain state of facts, in opening, as a ground for the traverse. It has been settled by this Court, that the relator, where the truthfulness of the return is denied, and a different state of facts alleged to exist, may show those facts to the Court ; that a person who has the possession or control of property will not be permitted, by an evasion or a manufactured return, to destroy the effect of this writ and render it powerless. In this case, a state of facts totally different from the return were alleged. Under these circumstances, the Court would hear the evidence traversing the return : and, second, the Court thought it its duty to ascertain and satisfy its conscience whether, if a different state of facts were established, it was not matter for the judicial notice of the Court sitting as a Committing Magistrate, if a *prima facie* case were made out, to bind the defendant over to answer on a charge of perjury.

Mr. WHEELER was then called.

Mr. GILPIN said that he should object to the examination of the witness, but there being no direct issues for trial before the Court, specific objections could not be made. He therefore left the matter with the Court, under a general objection.

John H. Wheeler, sworn. I am a native of the State of North Carolina, and a citizen thereof ; I am the owner of three colored persons, named Jane Dan and Isaiah, and have been for some time ; I hold them to labor under the laws of the State of N. Carolina, and of my country ; I left Washington on Wednesday the 18th ; I was under orders from my Government to proceed to the republic of Nicaragua forthwith ; I have been the Minister for one year, and had returned with a couple of treaties, and was upon my return to take passage from New York, in company with my three servants, whom I was taking to their mistress, who is now in Nicaragua; my wife is a native of Philadelphia, where I married her; I stopped at Bloodgood's to dine, having missed the 2 o'clock boat; I was sitting on the verandah talking to a friend.

I took the five o'clock boat, and proceeded to the hurricane deck, accompanied by my servants; there were a few persons only there; several ladies; while there the defendant, Passmore Williamson, stepped up to me, and asked me to allow him to have some conversation with my servants; I told him if he had anything to say he could say it to me; he laid his hands on the woman's shoulder very pointedly, and said, "Do you know that you are in a free State, and have only to go ashore to be free;" I told him they knew where they were going and with whom; the defendant said to me that he did not want to hear me talk, but would hear the woman; he asked her if she was a slave; she replied, yes; he said just step on shore and you are free; he pulled her by the arm, when she and her boys began to cry, and said they wanted to go with their master; several gentlemen stepped up and interfered; two negroes caught me by the collar, one on each side; one of them said to me, if you draw a weapon or make any resistance, I will cut your throat from ear to ear. A gentleman, who appeared to be a traveller, stepped up and told the negroes to release me; they did so; the defendant and they forced my servants on shore, and hurried them away; when the gentleman interfered I told him that I was in a country of laws, and that it could protect me in my person and property; I followed after them; they took my servants around into a street with a broad space, (Dock st.) where a hack was in waiting, and they forced them into it; I asked the defendant what they were going to do with my servants; he replied, that he would be responsible for any claim that I might have for the servants; he gave me his name as Passmore Williamson. I saw a policeman standing near, and I stepped up to him and asked him to take notice what was doing and who were the persons; the defendant stepped up to the officer and whispered something in his ear, when the officer replied, that he would have nothing to do with catching slaves; I told him that I did'nt want him to catch slaves, but only wanted him to take notice.

Thos. Wallace sworn. I am an officer; I saw the occurrence on the Avenue, but not on the boat; a crowd was coming down towards Dock street; I thought it was a fight, and went up; saw several negroes forcing along a colored woman who was holding back with all her strength, and two boys who were also struggling; they were all crying; four or five black fellows had the boys; they said they were slaves, whom they were taking away; the defendant was following the crowd; saw him do nothing but follow after the negroes; the negroes were pushing the woman and boys along; they all pulled back; I followed to Dock street, and saw the negroes put the woman and boys in a carriage; I knew the negroes; the defendant whispered to me, and said that they were slave —they were getting away—and asked me to protect them; I said that I would have nothing to do with the matter.

Robert T. Tumbleston, sworn. I am a travelling agent between Philadelphia and New York; I was standing on the forward part of the boat, and saw a crowd; I went forward, and saw a colored woman and two boys being forced ashore by some colored men; I know two of the men, Custiss and Ballard, who were very busy; they said the persons they had were slaves; Custiss said to Mr. Wheeler, that if he interfered he would cut his throat from ear to ear; Custiss had one of the boys by the arm; I followed a short distance and then returned.

Mr. Edwards, sworn. I take messages to the line and from it; I was on the wharf when this thing occurred; I saw two boys forced away by two colored men; the boy cried, and was struggling very hard to get away from those who held him; there were ten or fifteen negroes in the crowd.

Capt. Andrew Heath, sworn. Am in the employ of the Camden and Amboy Railroad Company; was on board the boat; saw a negro bringing a small boy down the stairs of the boat; the boy cried murder; there were twelve or fifteen negroes forcing the woman and two boys along in a crowd; the boys kicked and cried to get away; they said they wanted to go with their master; I saw the defendant walking along with them.

The testimony here closed, when Mr. VANDYKE said, that he had two motions to make; first, for an attachment against the defendant for making an insufficient return; and second, that he be held to answer for wilful and malicious perjury. Mr. VANDYKE urged his motion with argument, after quoting the act of Congress of 1825.

Mr. GILPIN asked for time.

Judge KANE said he would hear anything on the question of contempt, as that would cover the whole ground.

Mr. GILPIN thought they could put a different face upon the matter, as to the absconding or escaping of the servants.

Judge KANE said he would hear an argument now upon the evidence as it stands, or he would hear testimony for the defence.

Mr. HOPPER said that the defendant was not now prepared to say that he had testimony to show a different state of facts. There was one witness that he might be able to get, but this was uncertain. Counsel would, therefore, ask until to-morrow, with a view of consultation and the examination of authorities.

Judge KANE said, that he had decided no question before him. There were two motions pending, and if the defendant was prepared to say what testimony he would be able to adduce, he could take the witness stand and state it under oath. If he would do this then it became a question for a continuance until to-morrow.

Mr. VANDYKE said, that the act of Congress provided for but one condition of things for a continuance.

The application for further time having been refused, Judge KANE said, that the respondent might now purge himself, but if he did not do so now, he would not have the opportunity afterwards.

After some consultation the counsel for respondent put him on the stand to purge himself of contempt.

Passmore Williamson, affirmed. I was informed that three slaves were at Bloodgood's Hotel, who wished to assert their right to freedom; I went to the hotel and saw a yellow boy on the steps fronting on Walnut Street; I made enquiry of him and he stated that such was the case, but referred me up stairs to one of the waiters for further information; the latter informed me that the slaves, with their master, had just gone on board the steamboat at the end of Walnut street wharf for the purpose of going to New York in the 5 o'clock line. I went on board the boat, looked through the cabin and then went up on the promenade deck; I saw that man, (pointing to Mr. Wheeler,) sitting sideways on the bench on the farther side; Jane was sitting next to and three or four feet from him,—the two children were sitting close to her; I approached her and said, " you are the person I am looking for I presume;" Wheeler turned towards me and asked what I wanted with him; I replied nothing, that my business was entirely with this woman; he said she is my slave, and any-thing you have to say to her you can say to me; I then said to her you may have been his slave, but you are now free, he brought you here into Pennsylvania, and you are now as free as either of us,—you cannot be compelled to go with him unless you choose; if you wish your liberty all you have to do is to walk ashore with your children. Some five minutes were consumed in conversation with Wheeler, Jane and a stranger, when the bell rang, and I told her if she wished to be free she would have to act at once, as the boat was about starting; she took one of her children by the hand and attempted to rise from her seat; Wheeler placed his hands upon her shoulders and prevented her; I then for the first time took hold of her arm and assisted her to rise; the colored people who had collected around us, seized hold of the two children, and the whole party commenced a movement towards the head of the stairs leading to the lower deck, Mr. Wheeler having at the start clinched Jane, and during the progress repeatedly and earnestly entreated her to say she wished to stay with him; at the head of the stairway I took Wheeler by the collar and held him to one side; the whole company passed down and left the boat, proceeding peacefully and quietly to Dock and Front streets, where Jane and her children with some of her friends entered a carriage and were driven down Front street; I returned to my office. After the colored people left Dock street in the carriage, I saw no more of them,—have had no control of them, and do not know where they are. My whole connection with the affair was this.

Cross-examined. I heard of their being at the wharf at 4½ o'clock; Wm. Still, a colored man, informed me; he laid before me on my desk, at my office S. W. corner of 7th and Arch streets, a note stating the fact; I told him to go down and get such information as might be necessary to telegraph to New York, as it was too late to obtain a writ of habeas corpus here, and I was too busy preparing to leave home that evening on important business to attend to it; as he left, he enquired what there was to hinder them from leaving their master without the aid of legal process. After he had gone, I changed my mind and started for the wharf; I got there first, but saw him coming down Walnut street as I left the hotel; he came on board the boat and joined in the conversation with Wheeler, Jane and myself; he was the sole person I knew there; I saw him this morning; we had some conversation about this case; I asked him if they were safe and satisfied with what had been done; he said they were, and would not return under any circumstances; I did not enquire where they were, nor did he tell me. He is a clerk at the Anti-Slavery Office, in 5th street above Arch: I am Secretary of the acting committee of the Pennsylvania Abolition Society, as it is usually called.

At the conclusion of the cross-examination Mr. WILLIAMSON declared to the Court that in the proceedings he had not designed to do violence to any law, but supposed that he had acted throughout in accordance with the law, and the legal rights of the respective parties.

Mr. VANDYKE then addressed the Court.

After the conclusion of Mr. VANDYKE's remarks, a short delay took place in consequence of a momentary and unavoidable absence of the respondent from the court-room. Upon his return, his counsel remarked to the Court, that they declined making any argument at this time, and must leave the matter with the Court.

Judge KANE said the case was so grave, and its consequences might be so very grave to the respondent, who might even pass into the condition of a prisoner, that he was desirous, before passing upon the two motions, to have time for reflection. In the mean time, bail might be taken in $5,000. for a further hearing on the second motion, (on the charge of perjury,) and the motion for contempt could go over.

He would also say at the risk of its being considered extra-judicial, that if it is in the power of the defendant to produce the bodies of the three persons, it would be better for him to do so. Judge KANE said in conclusion, that he would hold Mr. WILLIAMSON in $5,000 for a further hearing on this day week.

Bail was entered accordingly.

On July 27, 1855, Judge KANE delivered the following opinion :

The U. S. A. ex rel. Wheeler vs. Passmore Williamson.—Sur. habeas corpus, 27th July, 1855.

Colonel John H. Wheeler, of North Carolina, the United States Minister to Nicaragua, was on board a steamboat at one of the Delaware wharves, on his way from Washington, to embark at New York for his post of duty. Three slaves belonging to him were sitting at his side on the upper deck.

Just as the last signal bell was ringing, Passmore Williamson came up to the party, declared to the slaves that they were free, and, forcibly pressing Mr. Wheeler aside, urged them to go ashore. He was followed by some dozen or twenty negroes, who, by muscular strength, carried the slaves to the adjoining pier; two of the slaves at least, if not all three, struggling to release themselves, and protesting their wish to remain with their master; two of the negro mob in the mean time grasping Col. Wheeler by the collar, and threatening to cut his throat if he made any resistance.

The slaves were borne along to a hackney coach that was in waiting, and were conveyed to some place of concealment; Mr. Williamson following and urging forward the mob, and giving his name and address to Col. Wheeler, with the declaration that he held himself responsible towards him for whatever might be his legal rights, but taking no personally active part in the abduction after he had left the deck.

I allowed a writ of *habeas corpus* at the instance of Col. Wheeler, and subsequently an *alias;* and to this last Mr. Williamson made return that the persons named in the writ, "nor either of them, are not now, nor was at the time of issuing of the writ, or the original writ or at any other time, in the custody, power or possession of the respondent, nor by him confined or restrained; wherefore he cannot have the bodies," etc.

At the hearing I allowed the relator to traverse this return; and several witnesses, who were asked by him, testified to the facts as I have recited them. The district attorney, upon this state of facts, moved for Williamson's commitment: 1, for contempt in making a false return: 2, to take his trial for perjury.

Mr. Williamson then took the stand to purge himself of contempt. He admitted the facts substantially as in proof before, made it plain that he had been an adviser of the project, and had given it his confederate sanction throughout. He renewed his denial that he had control at any time over the movements of the slaves, or knew their present whereabouts. Such is the case as it was before me on the hearing.

I cannot look upon this return otherwise than as illusory—in legal phrase, as evasive, if not false. It sets out that the alleged prisoners are not now, and have not been since the issue of the *habeas corpus*, in the custody, power or possession of the respondent; and in so far it uses legally appropriate language for such a return.—But it goes further, and by added words, gives an interpretation to that language essentially variant from its legal import.

It denies that the prisoners were within his power, custody, or possession *at any time whatever*. Now, the evidence of respectable, uncontradicted witnesses, and the admission of the respondent himself, establish the fact beyond controversy that the prisoners were at one time within his power and control. He was the person by whose counsel the so-called rescue was devised. He gave the directions, and hastened to the pier to stimulate and supervise their execution. He was the spokesman and first actor after arriving there. Of all the parties to the act of violence, he was the only white man, the only citizen, the only individual having recognized political rights, the only person whose social training could certainly interpret either his own duties or the rights of others under the constitution of the land.

It would be futile, and worse, to argue that he who has organized and guided and headed a mob to effect the abduction and imprisonment of others—he in whose presence and by whose active influence the abduction and imprisonment have been brought about, might excuse himself from responsibility by the assertion that it was not his hand that made the unlawful assault, or that he never acted as the gaoler.

He who unites with others to commit a crime, shares with them all the legal liabilities that attend on its commission. He chooses his company and adopts their acts.

This is the retributive law of all concerted crimes; and its argument applies with peculiar force to those cases in which redress and prevention of wrong are sought through the writ of *habeas corpus*. This, the great remedial process by which liberty is vindicated and restored, tolerates no language in the response which it calls for that can mask a subterfuge. The dearest interests of life, personal safety, domestic peace, social repose, all that man can value, or that is worth living for, are involved in this principle. The institutions of society would lose more than half their value, and courts of justice become impotent for protection, if the writ of *habeas corpus* could not compel the truth, full, direct and unequivocal, in answer to its mandate.

It will not do to say to the man whose wife or whose daughter has been abducted, " I did not abduct her; she is not in my possession; I do not detain her, inasmuch as the assault was made by the hand of my subordinates, and I have forborne to ask where they propose consummating the wrong."

It is clear, then, as it seems to me, that in legal acceptance the parties whom this writ called on Mr. Williamson to produce were at one time within his power and control; and his answer, so far as it relates to his power over them, makes no distinction between that time and the present. I cannot give a different interpretation to his language from that which he has practically given himself, and cannot regard him as denying his power over the prisoners now, when he does not aver that he has lost the power which he formerly had.

He has thus refused, or at least he has failed, to answer to the command of the law. He has chosen to decide for himself upon the lawfulness as well as the moral propriety of his act, and to withhold the ascertainment and vindication of the rights of others from that same forum of arbitrament on which all his own rights repose. In a word, he has put himself in contempt of the process of this Court, and challenges it action.

That action can have no alternative form. It is one too clearly defined by ancient and honored precedent, too indispensable to the administration of social justice and the protection of human right, and too potentially invoked by the special exigency of the case now before the Court, to excuse even a doubt of my duty or an apology for its immediate performance.

The cause was submitted to me by the learned counsel for the respondent, without argument, and I have therefore found myself at some loss to understand the grounds on which, if there be any such, they would claim the discharge of their client. One only has occurred to me as perhaps within this view; and on this I think it right to express my opinion. I will frankly reconsider it, however, if any future aspect of the case shall invite the review.

It is this: that the persons named in this writ as detained by the respondent were not legally slaves, inasmuch as they were within the territory of Pennsylvania when they were abducted.

Waiving the inquiry whether for the purposes of this question they were within the territorial jurisdiction of Pennsylvania while passing from one State to another upon the navigable waters of the United States —a point on which my first impressions are adverse to the argument— I have to say—

1. That I know of no statute, either of the United States, or of Pennsylvania, or of New Jersey, the only other State that has a qualified jurisdiction over this part of the Delaware, that authorizes the forcible abduction of any person or anything whatsoever, without claim of property, unless in aid of legal process.

2. That I know of no statute of Pennsylvania which affects to divest the rights of property of a citizen of North Carolina, acquired and asserted under the laws of that State, because he has found it needful or convenient to pass through the territory of Pennsylvania.

3. That I am not aware that any such statute, if such a one were shown, could be recognized as valid in a Court of the United States.

4. That it seems to me altogether unimportant whether they were slaves or not. It would be the mockery of philanthropy to assert that, because men had become free, they might therefore be forcibly abducted.

I have said nothing of the motives by which the respondent has been governed; I have nothing to do with them; they may give him support and comfort before an infinitely higher tribunal; I do not impugn them here.

Nor do I allude, on the other hand, to those special claims upon our hospitable courtesy which the diplomatic character of Mr. Wheeler might seem to assert for him. I am doubtful whether the acts of Congress give to him, and his retinue, and his property, that protection as a representative of the sovereignty of the United States which they concede to all sovereignties besides. Whether, under the general law of nations, he could not ask a broader privilege than some judicial precedents might seem to admit, is not necessarily involved in the cause before me.

It is enough that I find, as the case stands now, the plain and simple grounds of adjudication that Mr. Williamson has not returned truthfully and fully to the writ of habeas corpus. He must, therefore, stand committed for a contempt of the legal process of the Court.

As to the second motion of the district attorney, that which looks to a committal for perjury, I withhold an expression of opinion in regard to it. It is unnecessary, because Mr. Williamson being under arrest, he may be charged at any time by the grand jury; and I apprehend that there may be doubts whether the affidavit should not be regarded as extra-judicial and voluntary.

Let Mr. Williamson, the respondent, be committed to the custody of the marshal without bail or mainprize, as for a contempt of the Court in refusing to answer to the writ of habeas corpus, heretofore awarded against him at the relation of Mr. Wheeler.

After the opinion had been delivered, Mr. GILPIN rose and addressed the Court, stating the propositions and conclusions of the Court in the opinion as he understood them from listening to the delivery of the opinion, and suggesting a motion to amend the return so as to conform to the views of the Court, and to preclude the argumentative conclusions deduced from the alleged surplusage, viz., the added words "*or at any other time.*" While he was addressing the Court, Mr. VANDYKE rose and made a motion for a commitment, under the seal of the Court. As he began to speak, the Court remarked, "*the District Attorney has precedence;*" and requested respondent's counsel, if they had any motion to make, to reduce it to writing. Mr. Gilpin proceeded, remarking that the motion of the District Attorney was not in writing, when the Court said, that his motion was already granted; and as there might be misapprehension as to some of the positions of the opinion, it would be best for respondent's counsel to wait until they could read and examine the opinion, which would be in print in the afternoon papers, before offering any motion to the Court.

Respondent's counsel regarded the intimation of the Court as conclusive against any immediate relief by the amendment suggested, and did not persist in it.

On the 31st day of July, 1855, a petition was presented by Messrs. GILPIN and BIRNEY to the Hon. ELLIS LEWIS, Chief Justice of the Supreme Court of Pennsylvania, praying for a writ of Habeas Corpus, as follows :—

*To the Honorable Ellis Lewis, Chief Justice of the Supreme Court
of Pennsylvania.*

The petition of PASSMORE WILLIAMSON respectfully sheweth :

That your Petitioner is confined in the jail of the City and County of
Philadelphia under certain warrants of commitment, copies of which are
hereunto annexed. He also annexes hereunto a copy of the record of
the proceedings upon which such warrant was issued. To be relieved
from which imprisonment, your petitioner now applies, praying that a
writ of habeas corpus, directed to the Keeper of the said prison and
the said Marshal, may be issued according to the Act of Assembly in
such case made and provided, so that your Petitioner may be brought before your Honor to do, submit to and receive what the laws may require.

P. WILLIAMSON.

County Prison, July 31st, 1855

The next day, to wit, on the 1st day of August, Chief Justice LEWIS
filed the following opinion :

*Commonwealth ex rel. P. Williamson vs. F. M. Wynkoop, U. S.
Marshal, and Chas. Hortz, Keeper of the Philadelphia County Prison.*

This is an application for a writ of habeas corpus. It appears by the
copies of the warrants annexed to the petition, that the prisoner is
confined for a contempt of the District Court of the United States, "in
refusing to answer a writ of habeas corpus, awarded by that Court
against him at the relation of John H. Wheeler."

The counsel of Mr. Williamson very frankly stated, in answer to an
interrogatory on the subject, that they did not desire the useless
formality of the issuing of the writ of habeas corpus, if, on view of the
cause of detainer exhibited, I should be of opinion that the adjudication
of the U. S. District Court was conclusive. The habeas corpus act does
not require the writ to be granted in all cases whatever. Whenever it
appears upon the face of the petition, or, which is the same thing, by
the detainer annexed to it and forming part of it, that the prisoner is
" detained upon legal process, order or warrant, for such matter or
offences for which by the law the said prisoner is not bailable," the case
is excepted out of the act ; see act 18th of Feb., 1785, sec. 1. In like
manner, where the case has been already heard upon the same evidence
by another court, the act of Assembly does not oblige the Judges to
grant a habeas corpus for the purpose of rehearing it, although, perhaps,
they may deem it expedient to do so in some extraordinary instances.
Ex. parte Lawrence, 5 Bin. 304.

We come, therefore, at once to the cause of the detainer Is it a " legal

process, order or warrant for an offence which by law is not bailable?"
Mr. Justice Blakstone, in Brass Crossby's case, 3 Wilson, 188, declared
that "all Courts are uncontrolled in matters of contempt. The *sole*
adjudication of contempts, and the punishment thereof in any manner,
belongs *exclusively*, and *without interfering*, to each *respective Court*.
Infinite confusion and disorder would follow if Courts could by writ of
habeas corpus examine and determine the contempts of others. This
power to commit results from the first principles of justice; for if they
have the power to decide they ought to have the power to punish."
"It would occasion the utmost confusion if every Court of this State
should have the power to examine the commitments of the other Courts
of the State for contempts; so that the judgment and commitment of
each respective Court *as to contempts, must be final and without control.*"
3 Wilson, 304. This doctrine was fully recognized by the Court of
Common Pleas in England, in the case referred to. It has since been
approved of in numerous other cases in that country and in this.

In ex parte Kearney, 7 Wheaton, 38, it was affirmed by the Supreme
Court of the United States, in accordance with the decision in Brass
Crossby's case, 3 Wilson, 188, that, "when a Court commits a party
for contempt, their adjudication is a conviction, and their commitment
in consequence is execution." 7 Wheaton, 38, 5 Cond. Rep. 227. In
the case last cited, it was also expressly decided, that "a writ of habeas
corpus was not deemed a proper remedy where a party was committed
for a contempt by a Court of competent jurisdiction; and that if
granted, the Court could not inquire into the sufficiency of the cause of
commitment." 7 Wheaton 38. Many authorities to the same effect
are cited by Chief Justice Cranch, in Nugent's case, 1 American Law
Journal 111.

But it is alleged that the District Court had no jurisdiction. It does
not appear that its jurisdiction was questioned on the hearing before it.
The Act of Congress of 24th September, 1789, gives it power to issue,
"writs of *habeas corpus* which may be necessary for its jurisdiction, and
agreeably to the principles and usages of law;" and the same act
expressly authorizes the Judge of that Court to grant writs of *habeas
corpus* "for the purpose of inquiry into the cause of commitment;
provided, that writs of *habeas corpus* shall in no case extend to persons
in goal, unless where they are in custody under the authority of the
United States or committed for trial before some Court of the same, or
are necessary to be brought into Court to testify. Other acts of Congress give the United States Judges jurisdiction in writs of *habeas corpus*
in cases therein specified. It does not appear that the writ issued for

2

persons in goal, or in disregard of State process or State authority. It may be that in an action at law, where the judgment of a United States Court is relied on as a justification, the jurisdiction should be affirmatively shown. But in a writ of *habeas corpus*, issued by a Judge having no appellate power over the tribunal whose judgment is shown as the cause of detainer, where the jurisdiction of the latter depends upon the existence of certain facts, and no objections to its authority are made on the hearing, the jurisdiction ought to be presumed, as against the party who might have raised the question at the proper time, but failed to do so. It is true that if the jurisdiction be not alleged in the proceedings, the judgments and decrees of the United States Courts are erroneous, and may, upon writ of error or appeal, be reversed for that cause. But they are not absolute nullities. If other parties who had no opportunity to object to their proceedings, and who could not have writs of error, may disregard them as nullities, it does not follow that the parties themselves may so treat them. Kempe's lessee vs. Kennedy, 5 Cr. 185; Skillern's Exec's., vs. May's Exec'r., 6 Cranch 267; McCormick vs. Sullivan, 10 Wheat. 192.

It is alleged that the right of property cannot be determined on *habeas corpus*. It is true that the *habeas corpus* act was not intended to decide rights of property; but the writ *at common law* may be issued to deliver an infant to a parent, or an apprentice to a master. Com. vs. Robinson, 1 S. & R., 35 B. On the same principle, I see no reason why the writ at common law may not be used to deliver a slave from illegal restraint, and to restore him to the custody of his master. But granting, for the purpose of the argument, (which I am far from intimating) that the District Judge made an improper use of the writ; that he erred in deciding that the prisoner refused to answer it—that he also erred in the construction of the answer which was given, and that he otherwise violated the rights of the prisoner; it is certainly not in my power to reverse his decision.

If a writ of *habeas corpus* had issued from a State Court to the United States Marshal, and that Court had adjudicated that the Marshal was guilty of a contempt in refusing to answer it, and committed him to prison, the District Court of the United States would have no power to reverse that decision, or to release the Marshal from imprisonment. No Court would tolerate such an interference with its judgments. The respect which we claim for our own adjudications, we cheerfully extend to those of other Courts within their respective jurisdictions.

For these reasons the writ of *habeas corpus* is refused.

August 1st, 1855.   ELLIS LEWIS.

APPLICATION FOR A WRIT OF *HABEAS CORPUS*, TO THE SUPREME COURT, SITTING IN BANK, AT A SPECIAL* SESSION HELD AT BEDFORD, BEDFORD COUNTY, PENNSYLVANIA.

On Monday, the 13th day of August, 1855, Messrs. HOPPER and GILPIN appeared before the Supreme Court at Bedford, and presented the following petition; Chief Justice LEWIS and Justices LOWRIE, WOODWARD, KNOX and BLACK, being present:—

To the Honorable the Judges of the Supreme Court of Pennsylvania.

The petition of Passmore Williamson respectfully sheweth,—That your Petitioner is a citizen of Pennsylvania, and a resident of Philadelphia; that he is a member of "The Pennsylvania Society for Promoting the Abolition of Slavery, and for the Relief of Free Negroes Unlawfully held in Bondage, and for Improving the Condition of the African Race," incorporated by Act of Assembly passed the 8th day of December, A. D. 1789, of which Dr. Benjamin Franklin was the first President, and that he is Secretary of the Acting Committee of said Society.

That, on Wednesday, the 18th day of July last past, your Petitioner was informed that certain negroes, held as slaves, were then at Bloodgood's hotel in the city of Philadelphia, having been brought by their master into the State of Pennsylvania, with the intention of passing through to other parts. Believing that the persons thus held as slaves were entitled to their freedom by reason of their having been so brought by their master voluntarily into the State of Pennsylvania, the Petitioner, in the fulfilment of the official duty imposed upon him by the practice and regulations of the said Society, went to Bloodgood's hotel for the purpose of apprising the alleged slaves that they were free; and finding that they with their master had left said hotel, and gone on board the steamboat of the New York Line, then lying near Walnut street wharf, your Petitioner went on board the same, found the party, consisting of a woman named Jane, about 35 years of age, and her two sons, Daniel, aged about 12, and Isaiah, aged about 7, and, in the presence of the master, informed the said Jane that she was free by the laws of Pennsylvania; upon which she expressed her desire to have her

* By an Act of Assembly of 26th April, 1855, authority was given to the Supreme Court to order special terms to be holden at the seat of Justice of any County within the Commonwealth, for the purpose of hearing arguments, &c. See Pamphlet Laws, 1855, p. 305. Under this act a special term was held at Bedford, August 13th, 1855.

freedom, and finally, with her children, left the boat of her own free will and accord, and without any coercion or compulsion of any kind; and having seen her in possession of her liberty with her children, your Petitioner returned to his place of business, and has never since seen the said Jane, Daniel and Isaiah, or either of them; nor does he know where they are, nor has he had any connexion of any kind with the subject.

Your Petitioner used no violence whatever, except simply holding back Col. Wheeler, their former master, when he attempted by force to prevent the said Jane from leaving the boat. Some half dozen negroes, employed, as your Petitioner is informed, as porters and otherwise, at the wharf, and in the immediate neighborhood, of their own accord and without any invitation of the Petitioner, but probably observing or understanding the state of affairs, followed the Petitioner when he went on board the boat. An allegation has been made that they were guilty of violence and disorder in the transaction; your Petitioner observed no acts of violence committed by them, nor any other disorder than the natural expression of some feeling at the attempt of Col. Wheeler to detain the woman by force; that there was not any violence or disorder amounting to a breach of the peace, is also fairly to be inferred from the fact that two police officers were present, who were subsequently examined as witnesses, and stated that they did not see anything requiring or justifying their interference to preserve the peace. And your Petitioner desires to state explicitly that he had no pre-concert or connexion of any kind with them or with their conduct, and considers that he is in no way responsible therefor. Your Petitioner gave to Col. Wheeler at the time, his name and address, with the assurance that he would be responsible if he had injured any right which he had; fully believing at the time, as he does still believe, that he had committed no injury whatever to any right of Col. Wheeler.

On the night of the same day, your Petitioner was obliged to leave the city to attend an election of the Atlantic and Ohio Telegraph Company at Harrisburg, and returned to Philadelphia on Friday, the 20th of July, between 1 and 2 o'clock A. M. Upon his return, an *alias* writ of habeas corpus was handed to him, issued from the District Court of the United States, for the Eastern District of Pennsylvania, upon the petition of the said John H. Wheeler, commanding him that the bodies of the said Jane, Daniel and Isaiah he should have before the Hon. John K. Kane, Judge of the said District Court, forthwith. To the said writ your Petitioner, the same day, viz., the 20th day of July last past, made return, that the said Jane, Daniel and Isaiah, or by whatever name they may be called, nor either of them, were not then, nor at the time of issuing said writ, or the original writ, or at any other time, in the custody, power, or possession of, nor confined nor restrained of their liberty, by your Petitioner ; therefore he could not have the bodies of the said Jane, Daniel and Isaiah before the said Judge, as by the said writ he was commanded.

Whereupon and afterwards, to wit, on the 27th day of July aforesaid, it was ordered and adjudged by the Court, that your Petition r be committed to the custody of the Marshal, without bail or mainprize, as for a contempt in refusing to make return to a writ of habeas corpus theretofore issued against him at the instance of Mr. John H. Wheeler ; all which appears by the record and proceedings in the said case, which your Petitioner begs leave to produce, and a copy of an exemplification of which is annexed to this petition. Thereupon, on the same day, a warrant was issued, commanding that the Marshal of the United States, in and for the Eastern District of Pennsylvania, forthwith take into custody the body of your Petitioner for a contempt of the Honorable the Judge of the said District Court, in refusing to answer to the said writ of habeas corpus, theretofore awarded against him the said Petitioner, at the relation of Mr. John H. Wheeler ; a copy of which is hereto annexed, and also a warrant, by and from the Marshal of the United States, to the keeper of the Moyamensing Prison, a copy of which is also hereto annexed ; under which warrants your Petitioner was committed to the said prison, and is now there detained, without bail or mainprize.

Notwithstanding the record is silent on the subject, your Petitioner thinks it proper to state that, on the return of the writ of habeas corpus, the Judge allowed the relator to traverse the said return by parol, under which permission the relator gave his own testimony, in which he stated that he held the said Jane, Daniel and Isaiah as slaves, under the laws of Virginia, and had voluntarily brought them with him, by railroad, from the city of Baltimore to the city of Philadelphia, where he had been accidentally detained at Bloodgood's hotel about three hours ; and certain other witnesses were examined ; from the testimony thus given, though not at all warranted by it or by the facts, the said Judge decided that your Petitioner had been concerned in a forcible abduction of the said Jane, Daniel and Isaiah, against their will and consent, upon the deck of the said steamboat, but admitting that your Petitioner took no personally active part in such supposed abduction after he had left the deck.

The hearing took place on the morning of Friday, the 20th of July, at 10 o'clock, your Petitioner having had the first knowledge of the existence of any writ of habeas corpus between 1 and 2 o'clock, on the same morning. Under these circumstances, before the said testimony was gone into, and afterwards, the counsel of your Petitioner asked for time, until the next morning, for consultation and preparation for the argument of the questions which might arise in the case, which applications were refused by the Court, and the hearing went on, and closed on the same morning between 12 and 1 o'clock.

On Tuesday, the 31st of July, 1855, your Petitioner presented to the Hon. Chief Justice of this Court, a petition for a habeas corpus, which was refused.

Inasmuch as your Petitioner is thus deprived of his liberty for an indefinite time, and possibly for his life, as he believes, illegally ; inasmuch as he is a native citizen of Pennsylvania, and claims that he has a right to the protection of the Commonwealth, and to have recourse to her Courts for enlargement and redress, he begs leave respectfully to state some of the grounds on which he conceives that he is entitled to the relief which he now prays.

Whatever may be the view of the Court as to the probability of his discharge on a hearing, your Petitioner respectfully represents that he is clearly entitled to have a writ of habeas corpus granted, and to be thereupon brought before the Court. Upon this subject the Pennsylvania Habeas Corpus Act is imperative. Indeed, as the question of the sufficiency of the cause of his detention directly concerns his personal liberty, any law which should fail to secure to him the right of being personally present at its argument and decision, would be frightfully inconsistent with the principles of the Common Law, the provisions of our Bill of Rights, and the very basis of our government.

It is believed that no case, prior to that of your Petitioner, is reported in Pennsylvania, of a refusal of this writ to a party restrained of his liberty, except the case of *ex parte Lawrence*, 5 Binn, 304, in which it was decided that it was not obligatory on the Court to issue a *second* writ of habeas corpus where the case had been already heard on the same evidence upon a first writ of habeas corpus granted by another Court of the petitioner's own selection : in other words, that the statutory right to the writ was exhausted by the impetration and hearing of the first writ, and that the granting of a second writ was at the discretion of the Court. This case, therefore, appears to confirm strongly the position of your Petitioner that he is absolutely entitled at law to the writ for which he now prays.

On the hearing there will be endeavored to be established on behalf of your Petitioner, on abundant grounds of reason and authority, the following propositions, viz:—

1. That it is the right and duty of the Courts, and especially of the Supreme Court, of this Commonwealth, to relieve any citizen of the same from illegal imprisonment.

2. That imprisonment under an order of a Court or Judge not having jurisdiction over the subject matter, and whose order is therefore void, is an illegal imprisonment.

3. That the party subjected to such imprisonment has a right to be relieved from it on habeas corpus, whether he did or did not make the objection of the want of jurisdiction before the Court or Judge inflicting such imprisonment; and that if he did not make such objection, it is immaterial whether he were prevented from making it by ignorance of the law, or by the want of extraordinary presence of mind, or by whatever other cause.

4. That the Courts and Judges of the United States, are Courts and Judges of limited jurisdiction, created by a government of enumerated powers, and in proceedings before them the record must show the case to be within their jurisdiction, otherwise they can have none.

5 That if the record of any proceeding before them show affirmatively that the case was clearly without their jurisdiction, there can no presumption of fact be raised against such record for the purpose of validating their jurisdiction.

6. That no writ of habeas corpus can be issued to produce the body of a person not in custody under legal process, unless it be issued in behalf, and with the consent, of said person.

7. That at common law, the return to a writ of habeas corpus, if it be unevasive, full and complete, is conclusive and cannot be traversed.

8. That a person held as a slave under the laws of one State, and voluntarily carried by his owner for any purpose into another State, is not a fugitive from labor or service within the true intent and meaning of the Constitution of the United States, but is subject to the laws of the State into which he has been thus carried, and that by the law of Pennsylvania, a slave so brought into this State, whether for the purpose of passing through the same or otherwise, is free.

9. That the District Court of the United States has no jurisdiction whatever over the question of the freedom or slavery of such person, or of an alleged abduction of him, nor any jurisdiction to award a writ of habeas corpus commanding an alleged abductor or any citizen by whom he may be assumed to be detained, to produce him.

10. That in case of a fugitive from service or labor from another State, the District Court of the United States has jurisdiction to issue a warrant for the apprehension of such fugitive, and, in case he be rescued and abducted from his claimant, to proceed by indictment and trial by jury, against such abductor, and on conviction to punish him by limited fine and imprisonment; but even in the case of a fugitive slave, said Court nor the Judge thereof, has no jurisdiction to issue a writ of habeas corpus commanding the alleged abductor to produce such fugitive; or to enforce a return of such writ, or allow a traverse of the return thereof if made, or upon such traverse in effect convict the respondent without indictment or trial by jury, of such abduction, and thereupon punish him therefor by unlimited imprisonment, in the name of a commitment as for a contempt in refusing to return such writ of habeas corpus.

11. That generally, it is true, that one Court will not go behind a commitment by another Court for contempt; but that is only where the committing Court has jurisdiction of the subject-matter; and your Petitioner submits that where the circumstances of the supposed contempt are set forth upon the record of commitment, and it further appears thereupon that the whole proceedings were *coram non judice*, and that for that and other reasons, the commitment was arbitrary, illegal and void,—it is the right and duty of a Court of competent jurisdiction by writ of habeas corpus to relieve a citizen from imprisonment under such void commitment.

12. That neither the District Court of the United States nor the Judge thereof, had any shadow or color of jurisdiction to award the writ of habeas corpus directed to your Petitioner, commanding him to produce the bodies of the said Jane, Daniel and Isaiah, and that such writ was void:—that your Petitioner was in no wise bound to make return thereto:—that the return which he did make thereto was unevasive, full and complete, and was conclusive and not traversable:—that the commitment of your Petitioner as for a contempt in refusing to return said writ, was arbitrary, illegal, and utterly null and void:—that the whole proceedings, including the commitment for contempt were absolutely *coram non judice.*

13. That in such oppression of one of her citizens, a subordinate Judge of the United States has usurped upon the authority, violated the peace, and derogated from the sovereign dignity of the Commonwealth of Pennsylvania; that all are hurt in the person of your Petitioner; and that he is justified in looking with confidence to the authorities of his native State to vindicate her rights by restoring his liberty.

To be relieved, therefore, from the imprisonment aforesaid, your Petitioner now applies, praying that a writ of habeas corpus may be issued according to the Act of Assembly in such case made and provided, directed to Charles Hortz, the said Keeper of the said prison, commanding him to bring before your Honorable Court, the body of your Petitioner, to do and abide such order as your Honorable Court may direct.

And your Petitioner will ever pray, &c.

PASSMORE WILLIAMSON.

Moyamensing Prison, August 9th, 1855.

COPY OF RECORD.

To the Honorable John K. Kane, Judge of the District Court of the United States, in and for the Eastern District of Pennsylvania.

The Petition of John H. Wheeler, respectfully represents:

That your Petitioner is the owner of three persons held to service or labor by the laws of the State of Virginia, said persons being respectively named Jane, aged about thirty-five years, Daniel, aged about twelve years, and Isaiah, aged about seven years, persons of color; and that they are detained from the possession of your Petitioner by one Passmore Williamson, resident of the City of Philadelphia, and that they are not detained for any criminal or supposed criminal matter.

Your Petitioner, therefore, prays your Honor to grant a writ of habeas corpus to be directed to the said Passmore Williamson, commanding him to bring before your Honor the bodies of the said Jane, Daniel and Isaiah, to do and abide such order as your Honor may direct.

JOHN H. WHEELER.

Sworn to and subscribed, July 18, 1855.

CHAS. F. HEAZLITT, U. S. Com.

And thereupon it is ordered by the Court, that a Writ of Habeas Corpus issue, directed to the said Passmore Williamson, commanding him to bring the bodies of the said Jane, Daniel and Isaiah, forthwith before the Honorable John K. Kane, Judge of said Court, the hearing thereof to be on the 19th day of July at 3 o'clock P. M., and thereupon, a Writ is issued in the words following to wit:

The President of the United States

[SEAL.]   TO

Passmore Williamson.

We command you that the bodies of Jane, Daniel and Isaiah, persons of color, in your custody detained (as it is said) by whatsoever names they or each of them may be charged, together with the cause of their and each of their detention, you have before the Honorable John K. Kane, Judge of the District Court of the United States, at the room of the said Court in the City of Philadelphia, forthwith, then and there to do and be subject to whatever the said Judge shall consider in that behalf; and have you then and there this writ.

Witness the Honorable John K. Kane, Judge of said Court at Philadelphia, this Eighteenth day of July A. D. 1855, and in the Eightieth year of the Independence of the said United States.

Signed,   CHAS. F. HEAZLITT,
                                   for Clerk District Court.

ENDORSED.

U. S. A. Ex. Rel. John H. Wheeler

vs.

Passmore Williamson.

Habeas Corpus, Ret. 19 July, 1855, at 3 P. M.

On which said 19th day of July A. D. 1855, Mr. J. C. Van Dyke, for Petitioner, presents the affidavit of William H. Miller, Deputy Marshal, setting forth the manner of service of said writ, to wit, that it was left at the corner of 7th and Arch Sts., and no return being made to the said writ, Mr. Van Dyke moves for an alias writ to be directed to the said Passmore Williamson, and thereupon it is ordered that an alias writ do issue, returnable to-morrow morning at 10 o'clock, said writ to be served upon defendant at his place of residence. Which said writ is in the words following to wit.

UNITED STATES,   ⎫
Eastern District of Pennsylvania, ⎬ *S.S.*
                      ⎭

[SEAL]   ⎫   *The President of the United States*
J. K. KANE. ⎬   TO
             ⎭   *Passmore Williamson.*

Greeting: We command you, as before we commanded you, that the bodies of Jane Daniel and Isaiah, persons of color, under your custody, as it is said, detained, by whatsoever names the said Jane Danie. or Isaiah, or either of them, may be detained, together with the day and cause of their being taken and detained, you have before the Honorable John K. Kane, Judge of the District Court of the United States in and for the Eastern District of Pennsylvania, at the Room of the District Court of the United States in the City of Philadelphia, immediately, then and there to do submit to and receive, whatsoever the said Judge shall then and there consider in that behalf.

Witness the Honorable John K. Kane, Judge of said Court at Philadelphia, this nineteenth day of July A.D. 1855 and in the eightieth year of the Independence of the said United States.

CHAS. F. HEAZLITT, for Clerk Dist. Ct.

ENDORSED.

U. S. A. ex. rel. John H. Wheeler *vs.* Passmore Williamson, alias writ of habeas corpus. Returnable Friday 20th July, 1855, at 10 A. M. On which said 20th day of·July, A. D. 1855, return is made to the said writ in the following words, to wit:

To the Honorable J. K. Kane, the Judge within named:

Passmore Williamson, the defendant in the within writ mentioned, for return thereto, respectfully submits that the within named Jane Daniel and Isaiah, or by whatsoever names they may be called, nor either of them, are not now, nor was, at the time of the issuing of said writ or the original writ, or at any other time, in the custody power or possession of, nor confined nor restrained their liberty by him the said Passmore Williamson. Therefore he cannot have the bodies of the said Jane Daniel and Isaiah, or either of them, before your Honor, as by the said writ he is commanded.

P. WILLIAMSON.

The above named Passmore Williamson being duly affirmed, says that the facts in the above return set forth are true.

P. WILLIAMSON.

Affirmed and subscribed before me this 20th day of July, A. D 1855.

CHAS. F. HEAZLITT,
U. S. Commissioner.

Whereupon, afterwards, to wit, on the 27th day of July, A.D. 1855, the Counsel for the several parties having been heard, and the said return having been duly considered, it is ordered and adjudged by the Court that the said Passmore Williamson be committed to the custody of the Marshal, without bail or mainprize, as for a contempt in refusing

261

to make return to the writ of Habeas Corpus heretofore issued against him at the instance of Mr. John H. Wheeler.

UNITED STATES,
Eastern District of Pennsylvania.

I certify the foregoing to be a true and faithful copy of the record and proceedings of the District Court of the United States in and for the Eastern District of Pennsylvania, in a certain matter therein lately depending between the United States of America ex. rel. John H. Wheeler and Passmore Williamson.

In testimony whereof I have hereunto subscribed my name and affixed the seal of the said Court at Philadelphia this thirtieth day of July, A. D. 1855, and in the eightieth year of the Independence of the said United States.

Seal of the Court.

CHAS. F. HEAZLITT,
for *Clerk Dist. Court.*

I certify the foregoing attestation to be in due form, and by the proper officer.

J. K. KANE,
Dist. Judge.

After the reading of the petition the following motion was entered upon the minutes of the Court :—

Commonwealth ex rel.
PASSMORE WILLIAMSON
vs.
CHARLES HORTZ, *Keeper of Moyamensing Prison.*

S. C.
Sur Petition for Habeas Corpus.

And now, to wit, on the 13th day of August, 1855, upon the reading of the said petition, this day filed, HOPPER, C. GILPIN and MEREDITH moved the Court to award a writ of habeas corpus, agreeably to the prayer of the said Petitioner.

The Court then assigned Thursday, the 17th day of August, 1855, for hearing the argument upon the motion.

Bedford, August 17th, 1855. Supreme Court. All the Judges present. The Hon. CHARLES GILPIN addressed the Court as follows :—

May it please your honors, I rise to the argument of this cause with some embarrassment, and a deep sense of the responsibility of my position. I shall endeavor to consume, however, as little time as possible, and in that little time it shall be my effort rather to prepare the way for one who, coming after me, is preferred before me, whose place I feel that I cannot fill on this occasion, to the satisfaction of the honorable Court, or of the intelligent audience which this important case has called together.

I am impressed on rising with a sense of want of preparation, for which the peculiar circumstances of the case must be my apology. I am impressed, also, with the peculiar feature presented by this case in its present stage, a feature most apparent, and made more apparent when this application for the writ of habeas corpus is contrasted with the recent application of Col. John H. Wheeler, of North Carolina.

I am the more impressed, too, with the importance of this discussion at this time, as it involves not only questions arising under the habeas corpus Act of Pennsylvania, and its imperative injunctions, and under the discretionary power of the Court to grant the writ at common law without the statute; but imposes on us the necessity of travelling beyond that through all the ramifications of the case, that nothing may be omitted which is deemed essential to the interests of our client, Passmore Williamson, who is now suffering imprisonment in the city of Philadelphia, who is not here, and who cannot be here, or before this Court, unless this writ be granted, to listen to what his counsel may say for him, to what his accusers may say against him, and to what the Court may consider and decree in his behalf.

I have said that this case presents, at this stage of it, a peculiar and somewhat startling feature—startling to the mind of the Pennsylvania lawyer. What is it? Why is it? This is a hearing upon an application for a *habeas corpus*. It is not a hearing upon a writ where the prisoner is brought before the Court in the free air, where he may hear and be heard, as is provided by our Bill of Rights; but it is a case of argument upon an application, and, to say the least of it, an application made under circumstances of uncommon hardship, for the *allowance* of the writ of *habeas corpus*.

How many writs of *habeas corpus* are granted in this great Commonwealth under the imperative injunctions of the act—how many under the discretionary power of the Court—as a matter of course, upon the application of any felon, of any pickpocket, and of any scurvy knave arrested within the limits of a great city, although no great principles are involved; that the prisoners may have a hearing; that they may be

brought before the Court to hear what is to be said touching their rights
before their case is determined, and that they may be admitted to bail,
if the case be bailable, or discharged if a *prima facie* case be not made
out against them. But in a case of this importance, in which the
sovereign power of the State has been usurped by the Federal Court,
where the powers of the Pennsylvania judiciary have been invaded, and
the trial by jury virtually superseded, where the proceedings and practice under the writ of *habeas corpus* at common law have been departed
from, where unusual and most oppressive means have been adopted to
incarcerate an individual who is still restrained of his liberty—in a case
of this pressing moment, a man of undoubted character and high re-
spectability now appears here by his counsel, before a full Court, presenting and pressing his application for this writ. The necessity for this
is a somewhat startling feature to my mind, and to the mind of every
Pennsylvania lawyer. Is it not rendered still more so, when we contrast it with the application of Col. John H. Wheeler, of North Carolina,
to the Federal Court for a similar writ, which was granted without a
hearing by a Court of limited jurisdiction, without any statutory obligation ; as we allege, without any jurisdiction of the subject matter ? Nay,
more, this contrast renders this feature of the case still more remarkable.
We have been taught to believe always that a *habeas corpus cum
causa* is a writ *in favorem libertatis*. It is a writ which is supposed to
emanate from the sovereign, for the enlargement and redress of his subject.

This is the theory and foundation of the writ, and the ground upon
which it is claimed by Passmore Williamson. But the Federal Court
has converted it into a writ *in favorem servitudinis*. Does not this stage
of the case, then, present a somewhat startling feature to the mind of the
Pennsylvania lawyer ? Such an extension and perversion of the law of
habeas corpus by a Judge of one of the Federal Courts, and the
possibility of a refusal of this great writ by the Supreme Court of Pennsylvania to a citizen of Pennsylvania, actually restrained of his liberty,
who appeals to his sovereign, the Commonwealth of Pennsylvania.
through her Courts for enlargement and redress .

Let us turn to the petition of Col. John H. Wheeler, to see if I am
right in making this contrast. I need not go over the petition of Passmore Williamson, for there stands upon the record a certified copy of his
jailor, that he is restrained of his liberty ; and he asks you here that he
may have the writ of *habeas corpus* granted to him according to the act
of Assembly. Whether his case meets the requirements of that act or
not, we are yet to conisder.

What does Col. Wheeler say when he applies for this high prerogative writ to the Federal Court? Not a word which should bring his application within the act of Assembly of Pennsylvania, if that had been necessary. There is not a word in it that any party is restrained of his liberty. He alleges that certain persons, whom he claims to be his slaves, under the laws of another State, are detained from him by Passmore Williamson, but how, his petition does not say; there is not one word to indicate that any party is suffering from incarceration or deprivation of liberty. My conclusion, therefore is, that in the Federal Court every facility is afforded, even in doubtful cases, for the granting of the writ, and if there be doubt or danger, those matters are to be discussed at the time the writ is made returnable on the hearing. But in our State Courts, although there is an act imperative upon them to issue the writ, we are compelled to proceed slowly, cautiously and laboriously, beset with difficulties, and met with opposition at every stage of our proceedings. Permit me to allude to one of those obstacles, which I see in my path, before I proceed to discuss the principles that are involved in the case. I allude now to the opinion of the learned Chief Justice of this Court upon an application to him to award this writ. It is my purpose, if I can, to remove the impression which that opinion is calculated to make unfavorable to our case; an erroneous impression, permit me to say, with all respect, misleading the legal as well as the popular mind of the country. In doing so, it shall be with all respect and deference to the learned and estimable gentleman who occupies that place; and if, in the hurry of argument, anything shall escape me which may not be becoming the occasion, his position or my own, I am sure that it will be attributed to the zeal which I feel in behalf of one who is placed *in salva et arcta custodia*, rather than to any intentional disrespect to the Court which I now address.

We are told, may it please your honors, by the learned Chief Justice, that the issuing of this writ is not imperative upon the Court. It is not my purpose to read this opinion throughout, but there is one startling objection made by the learned Chief Justice which meets me almost upon the threshold, which, if it be valid, might be conclusive against the statutory right of the relator to the writ, and leave it discretionary with the Court as at common law. The Chief Justice remarks:

" The *habeas corpus* act does not require the writ to be granted in all cases whatever. Whenever it appears upon the face of the petition, or, which is the same thing, by the detainer annexed to it and forming part of it, that the prisoner is ' detained upon legal process, order, or warrant, for such matter or offences for which by the law the said prisoner is not bailable,' the case is excepted out of the act. See Act 18th February, 1785, Sec. 1."

If this position be correct, I shall have to abandon the ground that it was *obligatory* to issue the writ, and to admit that it was discretionary with the Court. But we contend that this application of this quotation from the act is a mistake and misapplication, and that those words used in the *habeas corpus* act are exclusively applicable to the regulation of the proceedings under the writ *after* it has been granted, and in no wise to the *granting* of the writ, or to the cases in which it is to be granted.

There are exceptions in this act of Assembly, and I want to allude to them. The act says : " If any person stand committed for any criminal or supposed criminal matter, unless for treason or felony." These are the only exceptions in the act, and they are in the first section. What is the reason of the exception ? Our act is mainly a transcript of the act of 31 Charles 2d, chap. 2, which was intended to remedy certain great and crying evils. The writ had been in existence as a prerogative writ for a long time before ; but judges at that time were dependent on the "powers that be." There was a great distinction between the commonalty and the judiciary, and Courts reposed very much on the bosom of the appointing power. They were very apt in cases of general warrants, to refuse the writ of habeas corpus under the discretion which they had. The case of Sir John Elliot, I think, was one of them, and the case of Jenks was another, the charges being contempt and inflammatory speeches derogatory to the government. There was no statutory provision compelling the judge to issue the writ, nor any means by which a prisoner so committed upon general warrant from the King in Council, or Secretary of State could be heard. The Judges neglected their duty, and hence the passage of the habeas corpus act ; these exceptions, treason and felony, were made, as is stated by Blackstone, because in all cases, excepting treason and felony, the general grant of the writ under the statute could not result in any inconvenience or detriment to the public or the government. There is no particular reason, perhaps, why these exceptions should have been put in our act, though perhaps there may be in the case of treason. But all felonies, except homicide, are now bailable ; and the scurviest knave, the lowest pickpocket, and the meanest pilferer, though charged with felony, looks upon the grant of this writ, as a matter of course, while we, who are not within those exceptions, who are not charged with treason or felony, but within that large class embraced in the act, being all cases except treason and felony, are made to rest a long while before we are allowed to enter the portal of justice. Now if your honors will look at the first section of this act, you will see that it applies to the allowance of the writ. It is in these words :—

" 1. If any person shall be, or stand committed or detained for any criminal, or supposed criminal matter, unless for treason or felony, the species whereof is plainly and fully set forth in the warrant of commitment in vacation time, and out of term, it shall and may be lawful to and for the person so committed or detained, or any one on his or her behalf, to appeal or complain to any Judge of the Supreme Court, or to the President of the Court of Common Pleas for the county within which the person is so committed or detained ; and such Judge or Justice, upon a view of the copy or copies of the warrant or warrants of commitment or detainer, or otherwise, upon oath or affirmation legally made, that such copy or copies were denied to be given by the person or persons in whose custody the prisoner is detained, is hereby authorized and required, upon request made in writing by such prisoner, or any person on his or her behalf, attested and subscribed by two witnesses, who were present at the delivery of the same, to award and grant a *habeas corpus* under the seal of the Court whereof he shall then be a Judge or Justice, to be directed to the person or persons in whose custody the prisoner is detained, returnable immediately before the said Judge or Justice; and to the intent, and that no officer, sheriff, jailor, keeper or other person, to whom such writ shall be directed, may pretend ignorance of the import thereof, every such writ shall be made in this manner : ' By Act of Assembly, one thousand seven hundred and eighty-five,' and shall be signed by the Judge or Justice who awards the same."

This section, though referred to for the words of exception which the Chief Justice has quoted and I have read to you from his opinion, does not contain them.

The precise words of the quotation are in the second section, which is as follows :—

" 2. And whenever the said writ shall by any person be served upon the officer, sheriff, jailor, keeper, or other person whatsoever to whom the same shall be directed, by being brought to him, or by being left with any of his under officers or deputies, at the jail or place where the prisoner is detained, he, or some of his under officers or deputies shall, within three days after the service thereof, as aforesaid, upon payment or tender of the charges of bringing the said prisoner, to be ascertained by the Judge or Justice who awarded the writ, and thereon endorsed, not exceeding twelve pence per mile, and upon security given by his own bond to pay the charges of carrying him back, if he shall be remanded, and not to escape by the way, make return of such writ, and bring, or cause to be brought, the body of the prisoner unto or before the Judge or Justice before whom the said writ is made returnable, and, in case of his absence, before any other of the Judges or Justices aforesaid, and shall then likewise specifically and fully certify the true cause or causes of the commitment and detainer of the said prisoner, and when he was committed, unless the commitment be in any place beyond or twenty miles from the place where such Judge or Justice shall be residing ; and if beyond the distance of twenty miles and not above one hundred

3

miles, then within ten days, and if beyond the distance of one hundred miles, then within twenty days. And thereupon, the Judge or Justice before whom the prisoner shall be so brought shall, within two days, discharge the prisoner from imprisonment, taking his or her recognizance, with one or more surety or sureties, in any sum, according to his discretion, having regard to the circumstances of the prisoner and the nature of the offence, for his or her appearance at the next Court of Oyer and Terminer, general jail delivery, or general quarter sessions, of or for the county, city or place where the offence was committed, or in such other Court where it may be properly cognizable, as the case shall require, and then shall certify the said writ, with the return thereof, and the said recognizances, into the Court where such appearance is to be made, unless it shall appear to the said Judge or Justice that the party so committed is *detained upon legal process, order, or warrant for such matter or offences for which, by the law, the said prisoner is not bailable;* and that the said Judge or Justice may, according to the intent and meaning of this act, be enabled, by investigating the truth of the circumstances of the case, to determine whether, according to law, the said prisoner ought to be bailed, remanded, or discharged, the return may, before or after it is filed, by leave of the said Judge or Justice, be amended, and also suggestions made against it, so that, thereby, material facts may be ascertained."

The perusal of the two sections makes it plain; the first relates exclusively to the issue of the writ; the second exclusively to the service, proceedings and hearing; the pith of it all is that the second section requires on hearing that the prisoner, though a case may be presented, requiring that he shall be held for trial, shall be admitted to bail and so held for trial, unless the charge be not bailable. If the prisoner be held, without sufficient cause, illegally, the Judge must discharge him; if cause be shown, the Judge must hold him for trial in prison or by bail.

The second section does not come into operation until the first has been complied with, and the writ allowed and issued; then the requirements of the second section begin.

But the writ has gone forth and penetrated the doors of the prison.

What we ask for here, the allowance and issue of the writ, must be granted, before the words or directions of the second section can be invoked either for the benefit or to the prejudice of the prisoner or relator.

Is not the application of this quotation by the Chief Justice a plain mistake?

Now, I do ask in candor, does it mean that this is a case excepted by the *habeas corpus* act? It is only a case excepted out of the duty imposed on the Judge in the second section, who is directed to take bail only in such cases as are bailable. It is easily understood in that connection. When the opinion first met my eye I confess that it almost confounded me, for it was not in accordance with any previous opinion that I had formed.   I think that my view of the matter cannot be wrong, and if it be not wrong it is an answer, and a full one, to the objection that an offence not bailable is excepted out of the injunction to the Court, in the first section, to issue the writ.

In the same opinion the case of *ex parte* Lawrence, 5 Binn. 304, is cited.   Reference is also made to this case in the petition of the relator. Our version of the case is, that it does not conflict at all with the right of the prisoner to the writ.   It only decides that the hearing of the case before a Court of competent jurisdiction, of the prisoner's own selection, after the granting of the writ, satisfies the demand of the statute.   In this case we have had no writ; we have not been heard; the requirements of the statute in our behalf have not been satisfied.   The case of *ex parte* Lawrence is not applicable farther than, as we think, to enforce the position we take,'that the act and its injunctions are imperative upon the Court, and require the allowance of the writ to the relator.

We next meet, in the opinion of the Chief Justice, a reference to the case of Brass Crossby, 3 Wilson, 188.   What was that case? It was a commitment for contempt of the privileges of the House of Commons; neither the Judges nor the people of that day ventured to question the jurisdiction of the House, either in matters of contempt or matters of privilege, in violation of which contempts were committed.   It is, therefore, an authority not applicable to the present case, as, I think, your honors will see.   We allege that there is no jurisdiction to authorize the writ asked for by Col. Wheeler.   In every case of refusal of the writ cited by the Chief Justice, and especially in the cases of contempt cited by him, indeed, in every case that has come under my eye, there has been, without exception, an admission that the subject matter before the tribunal, Court or Judge, in connection with which the commitment was made, was *within its jurisdiction.*   That is our position.   Besides, Brass Crossby's case was suited to other times rather than the present.

In the case of *ex parte* Kearney, cited by the Chief Justice, (7 Wheaton, 38) the committing Court had undoubted jurisdiction of the subject matter, and so in Nugent's case, (1 Am. Law Reg., p. 111,) the jurisdiction of the Senate was not doubted but alleged by Judge Cranch. The honorable Judge of the District Court of the United States, while holding a session of the Court, if interrupted in the course of the proceedings by some flagrant violation of decency and propriety, may commit for contempt, whether the guilty person be party, spectator, or casual visitor in the Court.   The commitment may be general in its terms. I would not be here to argue such a case and say that there was a power of revision here.   That, I admit, is a case of summary conviction with in the legitimate powers of any Court, and it matters not what might be the business before the Court at the moment, so that the Court was in session, and the act was an invasion of its rights and dignity. But it would be a vastly different case if a Judge of a Federal Court should commit for contempt, in open violation of the act of Congress, prohibiting jurisdiction of contempts for matters done out of Court. If any Federal Judge should undertake to bring the publisher of a newspaper before him for having refused to comply with an order of the Court in reference to business before the Court, or for having used disrespectful language concerning the Court, and if, on the commitment, it should appear that he was so committed for such contempt, there very clearly, any State Court of general jurisdiction would have a right to interfere and be bound to grant relief. And why? Because by the act of Congress itself, all jurisdiction of such offences and such contempts is taken away from the Federal Courts, although they have limited jurisdiction in commitments for contempt.

The whole stress and weight of the authorities cited by his Honor, the Chief Justice, will be removed if we can establish that Col. Wheeler's application for the habeas corpus is a case without the jurisdiction of the Federal Court; that once established, the want of such jurisdiction makes the proceedings *coram non judice*, renders them a nullity and utterly void, and of no effect in law. We can satisfy your honors, by precedent and authority, that in cases of contempt there have been instances of interference by Courts under similar circumstances, and of writs granted for the relief of the persons in jail, under which the relators have been relieved.

Now, may it please your Honors, had the Judge of the District Court of the United States jurisdiction in this case? The Federal Courts are not *inferior*, but they are *limited* in their jurisdiction. Their jurisdiction is obtained from the Constitution and from the acts of Congress passed in pursuance thereof. There are three classes of cases into which I have looked in vain to find anything that can sustain the jurisdiction exercised in this case. The first is the jurisdiction as to that class of cases arising between citizens of different States. This application for the writ of *habeas corpus* could not, by any forced construction, be within it. The writ of *habeas corpus* is not a proceeding *inter partes*. It is a proceeding *ex parte* and *in personam*, and that provision, as far as litigation is concerned, is intended to be applicable to proceedings *inter partes*, where the parties are citizens of different States. It would be a monstrous construction to say that, because the relator, Col. Wheeler, was a citizen of North Carolina, and the respondent was a citizen of the State of Pennsylvania, that this difference of citizenship should give jurisdiction to the United States Court. If that could be pretended for a moment, it would give jurisdiction in all criminal matters, in every case in which an informer or relator might not happen to be a citizen of the State in which the proceedings are instituted. There can be no reason, there can be no authority, there can be no case shown, which will bring an *ex parte* application or a petition for a *habeas corpus* within the law on this head

The next class of cases is that of fugitives from justice. Is there any pretence that this is such a case? We have to look into these matters before your honors that the interests of our client may not be disregarded, for the learned Judge who delivered the opinion of the U. S. District Court has not deigned to tell us where, in the written or unwritten law, he finds authority for the assumption of jurisdiction by him. We must speculate upon it, in order that we may not be charged with neglect of duty towards our client. Such authority certainly cannot be found. Can it be said that Jane, the alleged slave, had escaped or was a fugitive from justice? No. Can there be any law of North Carolina or Virginia by which a desire, if she entertained one, a dream, if she ever had one, or a wish or intention to be free, if she ever expressed one, can be construed into a crime against the laws of North Carolina or Virginia, so that she could be pursued here, or any proceedings be instituted here which could be styled a *habeas corpus cum causa*, and sustained under the clause applicable to fugitives from justice? I cannot imagine such a case coming within that class. If the Federal judiciary, or rather our brethren in any of our sister States, by any such forced construction, should ever attempt to raise questions of that kind upon such feeble and frail grounds, I think that they will do much —and they have done something in this case—to weaken if not to snap asunder, the bonds which have united us in this powerful sisterhood of States.

Judge LOWRIE.—I believe our neighbors immediately south of us did pass an act of assembly declaring it criminal for slaves to escape across the line into this State. I think they have repealed it, however.

Mr. GILPIN.—I know that there have been enormities—I use the term in no offensive sense—enormities in the eye of the law, committed in that way; and I have been trying to find what one could be suggested, for the purpose of bringing this within the jurisdiction of the United States Court. I hope the day will never come when it will be attempted to stretch the authority of the law for that purpose.

The next class is that of fugitives from service or labor. Does this case come within that class ? There is no allegation here that this party came otherwise than with the voluntary consent of the alleged master, from the State where they belonged to the State of Pennsylvania. There are two cases which I think proper to cite to your honors in this connection. One is a case decided by a Southern Judge, an upright and learned man, Judge Washington. The case is *ex parte* Simmou's in 4 Washington Circuit Court Reports, 396. In that case, before the repeal of any portion of the proviso or exemption of the abolition act of 1780, a citizen of South Carolina came voluntarily with his slave into Pennsylvania, and resided in Philadelphia. Wishing to return to South Carolina, he appeared before the Judge, (whether with or without his slave, the case does not say, the alleged slave being evidently within his power and control,) and asked from Judge Washington a certificate of removal. But Judge Washington said, no; that case is not within the act of 1793, and I cannot help you.

This is the syllabus :—

"The Act of Congress respecting fugitives owing labor does not apply to slaves brought by their masters from one State to another, who afterwards escape or refuse to return."

And these are the words of the Judge :—

"The slave in this case having been voluntarily brought by the master into this State, I have no cognizance of the case so far as respects this application, and the master must abide by the laws of the State so far as they may affect his rights. If the man claimed as a slave be not entitled to his freedom under the laws of this State, the master must pursue such remedy for his recovery as the laws of the State have provided for him."

Judge BLACK. Have you a copy of the record in the case now before us ?

Mr. GILPIN. It is printed in the paper-book, and your honors have it all, and all the p oceedings *except that portion which is omitted in the certified copy procured from the office,* and to which we can only allude in our petition. *The traverse of the return to the habeas corpus does not appear upon the record.* We have to take the record as it is given to us, as importing verity, it being signed by the clerk and certified by the Judge. If it be within the course of their procedure to traverse a return, not by the verdict of a jury, but by the opinion of the Court on parol proofs, and not to certify the traverse on the exemplification at all, it is an irregularity that has never before crept into the most irregular proceedings of any Court of Pennsylvania.

I confess that the hearing before Judge Kane was a case of unusual hardship upon the professional gentlemen engaged, hardship of a kind which I never before experienced in my professional life. I never, when

called into court, upon the spur of the moment, without an instant for
consideration, was met with a refusal of time to consider, as we were
there met with the refusal of the learned Judge, who, after hearing the
argument on one side, and after the counsel on the other side had declined to speak on account of a want of time for preparation, said to the
counsel to whom he denied time, that he must take a week to prepare
his opinion.

I have given your honors the syllabus of *ex parte* Simmons, and the
words of Judge Washington's opinion. Here is high authority. Here
is—not using the term in an invidious or obnoxious sense—Southern
authority, though the opinion was delivered, it is true, within the
borders of a free State.

I will refer to another case to show that this matter has been before
the Courts of Pennsylvania, and that they have extended to the utmost
the free and liberal construction of the act of 1793, and of the provision
in the Constitution for the relief and benefit of the master. The case
to which I allude is, Butler vs. Delaplaine, 7 S. & R., 385. This was
a case of *homine replegiando ;* the alleged slave had been brought into
this State, not by or with the consent of the owner, but by a bailee for
hire ; in other words, the owner resided in Maryland, the slave was
hired out, and, without the knowledge or consent of the master, brought
into Pennsylvania. When in Pennsylvania the slave claimed his or
her freedom, and the writ of *homine replegiando* was used to try the
question. Judge Duncan, with the spirit that has always prevailed in
our judiciary to do full and ample justice to our Southern brethren,
said :—

"The slave who is removed into this State without the consent or connivance
of the master, may be considered as a slave absenting himself, absconding, or
clandestinely carried away under the 11th section of the Pennsylvania Abolition
Act of 1st March, 1780."

And : "Such removal under the 4th art. 2d section of the Constitution of the
United States, would be an escaping into another State."

"And the slave coming into the State in any other way than by the consent
of the owner, whether he comes in as a fugitive or run-away, or is brought in
by those who have no authority so to do, cannot be discharged under any law of
this State, but must be delivered up on claim of the party to whom his service
or labor may be due."

But in this case the Judge admits, in the course of his opinion, that
if the master had connived at, or had consented in any way to the bringing into this State of the alleged slave, the law would have been entirely different.

There is another case to which I wish to call attention in this connection, as it throws some light upon the question before us. It is the case of Choteau vs. Marguerite, 12 Peters' Reports, page 361. This was a contest for freedom, under the laws of Missouri, in the State Court, I believe. It was a writ of error to the Supreme Court of the United States. The question of freedom or slavery was involved in the decision of the Court below: an application was made to dismiss the writ of error to the Supreme Court of the United States, and it was dismissed. And why? For want of jurisdiction. And why? Because the case was not within the appellate jurisdiction of the Supreme Court of the United States, given in the Judiciary act, no law of the United States or treaty being in question. Jurisdiction is not to be inferred or presumed because a question of freedom or slavery is involved, though exclusively cognizable in the case of fugitives from service or labor, by the United States Courts and Judges, or because such question was raised and decided in a State Court, the person not being a fugitive.

I cannot, therefore, see that there is anything in either of these three classes of cases, from which it can be inferred that jurisdiction was given to the District Court of the United States in the matter now before you. I do not want to dwell long upon the Judiciary act of 1789 ; mainly upon it, all the Courts of the United States depend for their powers. The 9th section of the act is the one upon which the District Court of the United States chiefly depends for its powers. There are other sections giving it jurisdiction, in other matters foreign to this question. The 14th section of the act prescribes that the Courts of the United States shall have power to issue the writ of *habeas corpus* in certain cases. The right to issue the writ of *habeas corpus*, given in the first part of the fourteenth section, is in aid of the jurisdiction of the Court, not in favor of liberty. The fourteenth section has two divisions. The former being a grant of power in aid of proceedings within the jurisdiction theretofore conferred ; the latter in favor of the liberty of the citizen. Unless, therefore, something can be found in the ninth section to sustain the jurisdiction of the Federal Court, the fourteenth section, and the power given under it, is utterly at fault in any support that it can give. I need not allude to the latter part of the fourteenth section, which gives power to inquire into commitments, because that is expressly limited to commitments and bindings over by and to the *Federal* Court and the power in cases of commitment by the *State* Court is expressly excluded. This view has been sustained by case after case, the most prominent of which is Dorr's case, with which your honors are all familiar.

I will not dwell longer upon this matter, for I cannot find, as I before said, any precedent upon which the jurisdiction can be sustained ; the cases before Judges Grier and Kane in the Federal Court arising out of certain occurrences in Luzerne county, and their doctrines, have been repudiated by this Court, and do not seem to me to apply.

The position we first take, and upon which we hope to obtain this writ and the discharge of the prisoner, is the entire want of jurisdiction in the Federal Court upon the petition as presented by Col. John H. Wheeler, of North Carolina. The next question that comes up is, if the court had no jurisdiction, are not its proceedings *coram non judice*, *nullities, utterly null and void?* I know that there is a distinction between Courts of inferior and Courts of limited jurisdiction in regard to the character of their proceedings and how they are to be treated ; but there are cases, and very pointed ones, of very good authority, in which the proceedings of Courts not inferior, but of record, and of limited jurisdiction, have been held and treated as nullities for want of jurisdiction of the subject-matter. Let me put a case, may it please your honors. We have had with us a very estimable gentleman, who presides over a Court of Philadelphia City and County, of limited jurisdiction, with power to entertain civil, but not criminal pleas. We might imagine a case—but certainly not under the administration of the President Judge or either of his associates, in which, by an usurpation and assumption of power, that Court of limited jurisdiction, but not an *inferior* Court—might undertake by indictment, by trial by jury, or by any other means which might suit the capricious fancy of the man at its head to oppress an individual, to try him for larceny. Such a case might result in a conviction, and the accused might be, with a certificate to that effect, lodged with the warden at the penitentiary. A commitment being thus issued by the District Court of the City and County of Philadelphia, a Court without criminal jurisdiction, not an *inferior* Court, but of *limited* jurisdiction, will any one say to me, that you would not interfere? it *cannot* be. There is *something* in the liberty and in the protection of the liberty of the citizen, there is *something* in the powers of Courts of concurrent and co-ordinate jurisdiction, and *something* in the power of the Supreme Court of the land that will justify interference in a case like that. What difference is there between the case which I have just supposed and the case decided by he District Court of the United States? The District Court of the United States had no jurisdiction, but acted under an assumed and usurped power ; and with all deference to the learned federal judge who pronounced the opinion, I must say, that I do not think my supposed case would be a much more flagrant assumption of power and jurisdiction than the real one is, in which Passmore Williamson is the the respondent and victim, and the Hon. Judge of the District Court of the United States for the Eastern District of Pennsylvania, the actor.

I will now refer to several cases which I have upon my notes, upon this point of proceedings *coram non judice*. Kemp vs. Kennedy, 1 Peters' Circuit Court Reports, page 36; also to be found reported in 5 Cranch, 172. The proceedings of any tribunal not having jurisdiction of the subject matter which it professes to decide are void. Wickes vs. Caulk, 5 Harr. & J., 42. Griffith v. Frazier, 8th Cranch, 9 Den vs. Harnden, Peirce, 55.

The next case to which I will refer, is in Wharton's Digest, 1850, 1st volume, page 321, s. 282. The Com. vs. Smith, Esq. Sup. Ct. Penn. Oct. 1809, Pamphlet, p. 47-8. A State Court has a right to discharge a prisoner, committed under process from a Federal Court, if it clearly appears that the Federal Court had no jurisdiction of the case."

The next is Olmstead's case.

Judge BLACK.—In what year was that case decided?

Mr. GILPIN.—Com. vs. Smith, was in 1809, the year in which I was born; a pretty old case, but if it has kept as well as I have, I hope it will be good law yet.

Chief Justice LEWIS.—That principle does not need authority. It is certainly law.

Mr. GILPIN.—Am I to understand his honor, the Chief Justice, to say that if the proceedings before the District Court of the United States were not within its jurisdiction that they are *coram non judice, null and void?* for it is a great step in our argument if we can reach that point.

Chief Justice LEWIS.—I concede the very words of the decision you have just cited to be undoubted law.

Judge BLACK.—I suppose the decision settles that as far as it goes.

Mr. MEREDITH.—This is precisely our point.

Chief Justice LEWIS.—And you should have the benefit of it, if it *clearly* appears that the District Court of the United States had not jurisdiction. In such case I think that the State Court would have power to discharge; in fact, I have no doubt of it, if it *clearly* appears upon the face of the record.

Mr. GILPIN.—Then it will be necessary for me to fall back upon the record, perhaps, but I should like to give the authorities upon that point. Olmstead's case is cited in Wharton's Digest, and also in Brightley's Reports, page 9.   It was there decided that the State Court has a right to discharge a prisoner under process of a Federal Court, when it clearly appears that the Federal Court has no jurisdiction.   Brightley has gathered up cases not before published in any book of reports.

In the case of Holden vs. Smith, 14 Adolphus & Ellis, N. S. 841, the Court held that in the absence of jurisdiction the proceedings were to be treated as a nullity.

Judge LOWRIE.—We frequently go a little further than that in relation to soldiers.   We send the writ of *habeas corpus* to the United States officer, directing him to relieve them from custody and discharge them.

Mr. MEREDITH.—Nobody ever doubted your jurisdiction, may it please your honor.

Mr. GILPIN.—I have just mentioned the case of Holden vs. Smith, which I want to give in brief, to be found in 14 Adolphus & Ellis, new series, page 841.   It is remarkable in some of its features.   It was a case of commitment for contempt, not by an inferior Court, but by a Court of record.   Proceedings at law for damages were instituted against the judge of the Court committing, by the party so committed, and the Court sustained the action, deciding that the proceedings of the Court below, in the absence of jurisdiction of the subject matter, were a nullity, and that the judge was responsible.

We take Col. Wheeler's petition as presented to the Court, we give the judge the full benefit of the facts set forth upon the face of the record, and we say that there was no jurisdiction.

There is another case to which I would direct attention, supposing jurisdiction to exist, to show the arbitrary and oppressive nature of these proceedings.   I have also a number of other cases under the head of *habeas corpus, the return* and *the traverse of the return*.   But I want particularly to allude to one case, cited by his honor, the Chief Justice of this Court, in the case of Thomas vs. Crosson, and relied upon as authority on one point, which is fully and substantially authority on another point, establishing that the whole proceedings upon the traverse of the return before the Federal Judge were wilfully wrong and unjust to the defendant.

The case of Renney vs. Mayfield, in 4 Hayw. 166, cited by the Chief Justice, decides that the return being full and complete, and not evasive, was not traversable; but the case decided more than that.   The *habeas corpus* was granted in favor of liberty to produce the body of a person who was alleged, by the respondent in his return, to be a slave.   The respondent made return that he held the person, who was thus in his custody, as a slave. The relator, or the friends of the relator, offered a bill of exceptions to the return, in the way of traverse, alleging that it was untrue, and that the party was free. The judges not only decided that the return could not be traversed, but also, that in those proceedings by habeas corpus the question of freedom could not be decided at all. If in a slave State the question of freedom cannot be tested under a writ of *habeas corpus*, and if this be good law in a slave State, where a bill of exceptions is not allowed to traverse the return in favor of freedom, shall it be said that in a free State where a free citizen, a respondent in a habeas corpus, makes a full, complete and unevasive return, that the party who asks to enforce the claim of property—not to relieve a party from unjust imprisonment—shall be permitted to traverse the return, when the result of the traverse is presumptions and conclusions by the Judge, which end in a commitment for contempt without bail or mainprize? Let us have equal law all around. This ought to be good law for us as well as for them. I know his honor. the Chief Justice, so viewed it, or he would not have cited and relied on it in Thomas vs. Cros-on.

I wish, before taking my seat, to call the attention of the Court to the case of Thomas vs. Crosson, to the very contradictory results which are to follow, and the very absurd relations in which we are to be placed hereafter, if the writ of *habeas corpus* be now refused. In that case (Thomas vs. Crosson,) on motion for attachment against the Sheriff, he not bringing in the body, he was held to be in contempt, because he had not brought in the body. What was the justification set up by the Sheriff? That the defendant had been discharged on habeas corpus by the District Court of the United States. It is alleged that he was not justified by that discharge. Be it so. That was the law in Thomas vs. Crosson. The whole proceedings before the Federal Court were regarded and treated as nullities. Why? Because the Federal Court had no jurisdiction. It was so alleged and ably argued, by counsel, before the Chief Justice and rightly decided by his honor, the Chief Justice and his associates. It is said that in this case we cannot avail ourselves of the want of jurisdiction, because the question was not raised in the District Court. Look at the arguments before Judges Grier and Kane, and the proceedings in Crosson's case, as reported in Wallace, Jr., and the American Law Journal. No question of jurisdiction was raised, so far as appears by the report of the several cases.

If, in Thomas vs. Crosson, the proceedings were held nullities, why should not the proceedings in Williamson's case, before Judge Kane, be held null and void?

If null and void when Crosson was discharged, the order being *coram non judice*, why not null and void when Williamson is incarcerated by an order and commitment *coram non judice?*

Suppose to-morrow this alleged slave (Jane) is found walking in the streets or highways of the Commonwealth of Pennsylvania, and she is abused, as was alleged in the case of Thomas, an affidavit is made under like circumstances, as in the case of Thomas vs. Crosson, and process, a *capias ad respondendum* is allowed by one of the Judges of this Court, upon which the officer is arrested, as in Thomas vs. Crosson. The District Court of the United States issues a *habeas corpus* to the Sheriff, who has arrested on the *capias ad respondendum*, and the Sheriff takes his instructions from the opinion in Thomas vs. Crosson. He appears with his prisoner before the honorable Judge Kane, and says: "Sir, I have been instructed by the Supreme Court of Pennsylvania not to discharge the prisoner under such circumstances, and I have him in custody under the writ." His Honor says: "I do not care for the writ. Mr. Marshal, take the Sheriff below, as for contempt in not obeying our order, and let the prisoner go free." The Sheriff is then required to answer a rule in this Court because he has not produced the body which he had under arrest; and when he comes to answer this rule for an attachment, he says in one breath, by his counsel, for he is below for contempt, that the prisoner was discharged by the interference of the District Court of the United States, on *habeas corpus*, and in the next breath he presents to your honors a petition for a *habeas corpus* to relieve himself from prison; and you tell him that you cannot relieve him, the commitment being for contempt, and not bailable, and not within the *habeas corpus act.* It is true that he has acted under the instructions and the authority of the case of Thomas vs. Crosson. He did right to say to the honorable Judge of the Federal Court, "you have no jurisdiction; I will not discharge the prisoner." He did right in submitting to commitment for contempt of Court. You sustain him in it, in Thomas vs. Crosson, and yet will not relieve him on his petition for *habeas corpus.* This is a case which may at any time come to pass.

Chief Justice LEWIS—Why will not the Court relieve him?

Mr. GILPIN—Unless Passmore Williamson is relieved, I do not see how the Court could relieve him.

Chief Justice LEWIS—The difference between the case of Thomas vs. Crosson and the one now before us, is that Crosson and others were in arrest under the custody of a State officer, in pursuance of a process issued by a sovereign State, and that the act of 1789, giving jurisdiction to the United States Courts to issue writs of *habeas corpus*, expressly prohibits them from relieving persons in prison under State process. The act, therefore, cited here did not give them any jurisdiction in that case; it appearing, through the whole record, that the District Court had undertaken to nullify the process of the State, and to relieve a man from imprisonment under that process, in defiance of the act of Congress giving jurisdiction. Then they put forward the allegation that they claimed jurisdiction under the force bill of 1833, which allowed them to relieve a United States officer, who was imprisoned by the State for any act done under, and in pursuance of an act of Congress, and the decision in that case was that it did not appear on the record that Crosson was imprisoned for anything done under any act of Congress, but for an outrage committed against all law.

Mr. GILPIN—I should be very glad if I could see the distinction drawn by your honor; but it seems to me that the circumstances in the two cases necessarily involve the same consequences.

I wish to cite two other cases before I close my argument. One is a decision of Judge Betts, and the other of Judge McLean. The decision of Judge Betts, in the case of Barry vs. Mercein, is referred to in 5th Howard, 103, S. C.

In that case the question to be adjudicated was the claim of two contending parties to the guardianship and custody of a child.

Judge Betts refused the writ of *habeas corpus* for want of jurisdiction, and the Supreme Court, in 5th Howard, decided they had no appellate jurisdiction.

The other, and a most important case, is reported in a newspaper; it was decided by Judge McLean, of the Supreme Court of the United States, who interfered by *habeas corpus*, where a party was in custody for contempt under an order of a State Judge, and discharged the party so committed for contempt. All the authorities which we have previously adduced to your honors, are those from which this right to hear and determine on *habeas corpus* is to be deduced and inferred. We now come to *the* authority, a case exactly in point. If the right of the citizen of Pennsylvania is invaded, as in this case, and his body incarcerated, the State Court will not hesitate certainly to follow in the footsteps of the Federal Court, where it proceeds for the purpose of liberating the prisoner. This case of *ex parte* Robinson, is to be found in the Cincinnati Gazette, of Thursday morning April 5, 1855, headed, "An important decision of Judge McLean in the case of the U. S. Marshal," &c.

Proceedings were begun before a United States Commissioner under the fugitive slave act, and while they were pending the State judge issued a *habeas corpus*, which the marshal refused to obey, for which refusal he was attached forthwith and committed for contempt by the State judge. An affidavit and petition for *habeas corpus* were presented by him to Judge McLean of the Supreme Court of the United States. The *habeas corpus* was issued, and the Judge decided that the State Court had, under the circumstances, no jurisdiction, treated the whole procee·ling as a nullity, and interfering, discharged the prisoner, which is all that we ask your honors to do here.

May it please your honors, apologizing for the time which I have al. ready occupied in the discussion of this case, I am not disposed to dwell any longer upon it, although I leave it without a proper arrangement of the authorities. I desire to make way for a gentleman who will very ably and fully supply all my omissions and neglects.

The Hon. WM. M. MEREDITH succeeded Mr. Gilpin in the following argument in favor of the prayer of the petitioner:

Mr. MEREDITH.—The petition shows that Passmore Williamson •tands committed and detained for a criminal, or supposed criminal matter, *other than* treason or felony, and in due form he prays for the writ of *habeas corpus*. The *habeas corpus* act of 1785 imperatively requires that the writ shall be issued upon such petition, and imposes a penalty upon any judge who shall refuse or neglect to award the same. Instead of awarding the writ upon the presentation of the petition and the usual motion, the Court has directed that a preliminary *ex parte* argument shall be submitted on the questions which would arise upon the return of the writ if it had been awarded.

With all the respect which I habitually pay to all tribunals of justice, and which for every reason, public and personal, I most habitually pay to this, I enter my protest, as a citizen of Pennsylvania, against the establishment of such a precedent. We find none such, that I am aware of, heretofore reported in this State. In one case, where a *second* writ of *habeas corpus* was applied for on the same commitment, Chief Justice Tilghman held the statutory right to be exhausted by the issuing of the first writ and hearing thereon, and that the issuing of a second writ was therefore discretionary, and he refused to issue the second writ in that case, because, as he stated, it was to be heard upon the same evidence that had been given on the first writ, before a judge of the party's own selection. But by whatever authority, whether United States or other, and whether judicial or executive, a citizen of Pennsylvania has been detained in custody within the State for a criminal or supposed criminal matter, (unless for treason or felony) the Supreme Court has never hitherto failed, in the discharge of the duty imposed upon it, to award a *habeas corpus* to inquire into the cause of his commitment.

Olmsted's case and *Lockington's case*, both decided before Chief Justice Tilghman, and in fact every case of the kind that has hitherto been presented to the Court, or to a judge in vacation, is clear to this point.

I protest, therefore, against the course pursued upon this occasion:

First, Because it is directly contrary to the express requirements of the great statute of *habeas corpus*—the act of 1785   It is, in fact, *pro tanto* a suspending of a law—the power of suspending which the twelfth section of the Bill of Rights provides shall not be exercised unless by the Legislature or its authority—and further, it is a suspending of the privilege of the writ of *habeas corpus*, which the fourteenth section provides shall not be suspended (even by the Legislature) unless when, in cases of rebellion or invasion, public safety may require it.

Secondly, Because by the course pursued, the Petitioner, now incarcerated in the city of Philadelphia, is deprived of the right which the common law gave him, (and which the spirit or letter of every constitution in this country has assured to him,) of being present at the discussion of the question of his personal liberty, and of participating in that discussion at his option.

Thirdly, Because the counsel of the Petitioner are here required to argue *ex parte* questions, on which, before their decision, the respondent has the right to be heard on his return, and are thus necessarily trammelled and embarrassed at every step.

For these reasons, and I will not further dwell upon them, I have felt myself bound to make the protest which I have respectfully submitted to the Court, and having done so, will now proceed, under the express direction of the Court, to offer some considerations upon the question of Passmore Williamson's right to a discharge by this Court from his present imprisonment.

It appears from the petition and papers annexed, that the petitioner is in custody under process of the District Court of the United States as for a contempt of that Court, and I am to establish three principal positions

First, That it is the right and duty of this Court to discharge him, if the District Court of the United States has exceeded its jurisdiction in committing him.

Second, That the proceedings in that Court, which resulted in his commitment, were wholly and absolutely *coram non judice*, and were therefore null and void.

Third, That the fact that the commitment is as for a contempt, does not preclude this Court from inquiring into the jurisdiction upon which such commitment professes to be founded.

First, The Supreme Court of the Commonwealth of Pennsylvania is a Court, not of limited, but general jurisdiction, and established by a government, not of enumerated, but of general powers. Those who deny your jurisdiction must show by what statute or by what constitutional provision it has been taken from you, and if such cannot be shown, you are bound to inquire into the legality of the imprisonment of any citizen of Pennsylvania, under whatever pretended authority. I speak as a citizen of Pennsylvania and as a citizen of the United States, sincerely attached to the Constitutions of both, when I say that I believe neither can be ultimately preserved upon any other principle or by any other course than the exercise, whenever the occasion shall arise, of the just authority of the State Courts which is now invoked.

In *Olmsted's case*, (*Brightley's Reports*, 9,) in which Chief Justice Tilghman awarded a writ of *habeas corpus* to bring up a prisoner in custody under an attachment for contempt issued from the District Court of the U. S., the counsel of the respondent on the hearing upon the return brought forward directly the question whether the Chief Justice had a right to discharge the prisoner, even if he should be clearly of opinion that the District Court had no jurisdiction. That learned, wise, and excellent judge said:

"I am aware of the magnitude of this question, and have given it the consideration it deserves. My opinion is, with great deference to those who may entertain different sentiments, that in the case supposed, I should have a right, and it would be my duty, to discharge the prisoner. This right flows from the nature of our federal constitution, which leaves to the several States absolute supremacy in all cases in which it is not yielded to the United States. This sufficiently appears from the general scope and spirit of the instrument. The United States have no power, legislative or judicial, except what is derived from the Constitution. WHEN THESE POWERS ARE CLEARLY EXCEEDED, THE INDEPENDENCE OF THE STATES, AND THE PEACE OF THE UNION, DEMAND THAT THE STATE COURTS SHOULD, IN CASES BROUGHT PROPERLY BEFORE THEM, GIVE REDRESS. THERE IS NO LAW WHICH FORBIDS IT; THEIR OATH OF OFFICE EXACTS IT, AND IF THEY DO NOT, WHAT COURSE IS TO BE TAKEN? WE MUST BE REDUCED TO THE MISERABLE EXTREMITY OF OPPOSING FORCE TO FORCE, AND OF ARRAYING CITIZEN AGAINST CITIZEN, FOR IT IS IN VAIN TO EXPECT THAT THE STATES WILL SUBMIT TO MANIFEST AND FLAGRANT USURPATIONS OF POWER BY THE UNITED STATES, IF (WHICH GOD FORBID) THEY SHOULD EVER ATTEMPT THEM."

The Courts of the United States have a similar authority in any case in which the State Courts may trench upon the rightful jurisdiction of the federal courts or authorities, and the only mode of securing permanently the peace, union, and constitutions of the country, is by the calm and firm performance of their respective duties in this regard, by the State and Federal Courts, as occasions shall arise. If it be said that this may produce a *dead lock* in case those courts directly differ, there being no common arbiter to decide between them, I answer that the common arbiters are immediately the representatives of the States and of the people of the respective States, and, ultimately, the good sense of the people themselves; and, being a republican myself, and believing the continuance of a republican government to be practicable, I do not doubt the sufficiency of such arbitrament. If the People were not competent to feel where the right is, upon the broad and great principles of our Constitutions, State and Federal, and of the essential divisions of powers between them, we should have, indeed, reason to despair of the republic.

Secondly, I am to establish that the proceedings in the District Court of the United States, of which the Petitioner complains, were absolutely *coram non judice*, and therefore null and void.

I put the case upon this ground distinctly. I am to show this clearly.

The record of that Court shows that a *habeas corpus* was issued on the petition of Mr. Wheeler, directed to Mr. Williamson, for the bodies of certain persons alleged by the Petitioner to be owned by him, and held to service or labor by the laws of the State of Virginia, and to be detained from his possession by the said Passmore Williamson. The record does not allege that they were *fugitives* from service, or had *escaped* from the State of Virginia or any other State to the State of Pennsylvania, and the parole evidence taken in the case, as well as the opinion of the learned Judge of the District Court, show that in fact they had not so escaped, but had been voluntarily brought by Mr. Wheeler, their owner, into the State of Pennsylvania. The learned Judge, in his opinion, speaks of their being upon the navigable waters of the Delaware. In point of fact, as shown clearly by the evidence, they had been brought by Mr. Wheeler, by land, through a portion of the State of Pennsylvania, and at the time of their alleged abduction, were on board a steamboat lying at a wharf on the river Delaware. The present petitioner states these facts in his petition, and is ready to prove them, on a traverse, according to the Act of Assembly, if they should be denied in the return, or if they should be otherwise questioned.

The record itself, however, does *not* show that they were "fugitives from service or labor" within the provisions of the Constitution of the United States, and therefore they are to be taken *not* to have been so.

I. It is scarcely necessary to show by authority that a slave voluntarily brought by his owner into the State of Pennsylvania is not a *fugitive* who has *escaped* from another State within the provisions of the Constitution. But without dwelling on other cases, I will remind the Court of the cases of Simmons, (4 Washington Circuit Court Reports, 390.) and Butler vs. Hopper, (1 Washington Circuit Court Reports, 499;) which are express to this point.

II. Not being fugitives within the provisions of the Constitution of the United States, these alleged slaves, as well as their master, while within this State, were subject to the laws of this Commonwealth. Judge Washington says, in *Simmons' case*, which was an application for a warrant under the act of 1793 :

"THE SLAVE IN THIS CASE HAVING BEEN VOLUNTARILY BROUGHT BY HIS MASTER INTO THIS STATE, I HAVE NO COGNIZANCE OF THE CASE, SO FAR AS RESPECTS THIS APPLICATION, AND THE MASTER MUST ABIDE BY THE LAWS OF THIS STATE SO FAR AS THEY MAY AFFECT HIS RIGHTS. IF THE MAN CLAIMED AS A SLAVE BE NOT ENTITLED TO HIS FREEDOM UNDER THE LAWS OF THIS STATE, THE MASTER MUST PURSUE SUCH REMEDY FOR HIS RECOVERY AS THE LAWS OF THE STATE HAVE PROVIDED FOR HIM."

In affirming this principle, Judge WASHINGTON merely conformed to the law of every country on earth which has any law, for it is impossible that the *status* of an individual within the jurisdiction of any government can be regulated otherwise than by the law of that government. It is said that in this case, Mr. Wheeler was merely *in transitu* with his slaves—passing through the State of Pennsylvania, and that, therefore, they had not become free by being voluntarily brought into it. If that were so, it would still be so by the law of Pennsylvania, for no other law exists in the case, no clause in the constitution of the United States applies to it. The domestic institutions of each State, including the rights of personal property, the *status* of individuals and the relations of husband and wife, parent and child, master and apprentice, master and slave, etc., are subject to the regulations which the State itself may choose to adopt, and those who voluntarily come upon her soil or within her jurisdiction, must, while there, abide by them.. The Constitution of the United States provides that the citizens of each State shall be entitled to all the privileges and immunities of citizens in the several States, and under that clause, a citizen of another State who comes to Pennsylvania is entitled to all the immunities and privileges of a citizen of Pennsylvania, but to no others. To those, and those only, was Mr. Wheeler entitled under that clause. I am not aware that, until within some two or three years past, it has ever been seriously contended any where that the *status* of an individual is not to be governed by the law of the jurisdiction in which he actually is for the time, whether for the purpose of transit or any other purpose. In fact, no such principle would be practicable or possible to be carried into effect consistently with the provision of any law, without creating utter confusion. Take, for instance, the case of a master and slave. The Constitution of the United States is part of the law of Pennsylvania, and provides that a fugitive from service, escaping from another State, shall be delivered up to his claimant. While such fugitive is in custody within the State of Pennsylvania, it is for the purpose of being so delivered up, and carried out of the State, and the same law applies to him as to other prisoners lawfully in custody. But as the Constitution of the United States does not provide for the case of a slave voluntarily brought by his owner into Pennsylvania, suppose that by the law of Pennsylvania, the relation of master and slave has been absolutely abolished, and that, notwithstanding, it should be determined that the relation shall continue to exist between master and slave in transit through the State, what will follow ? The relation of master and slave, like every other relation, consists in their reciprocal rights and duties, and their sanctions. In the case supposed, the law of Pennsylvania recognizes no rights or duties or sanctions. Is the law of another State to be superinduced upon the soil of Pennsylvania ? And if so, how is it to be enforced ? If the tribunals of Pennsylvania be appealed to, they have no jurisdiction but what has been conferred by her constitution and laws ; and in the case supposed, none would have been conferred over the subject. If the tribunals of the United States be appealed to, the constitution of the United States has no provision on the subject.

How then are the rights of the master to be enforced ? Is he to be left to execute the laws of his own State upon the slave at his own pleasure, and according to his own understanding ? If so, suppose a citizen of Pennsylvania seduces or abducts his slave, is the master also to execute the law, as he understands it, upon such citizen ? That would be clearly not to be tolerated ; and yet in the case supposed, no Court or tribunal exists that would have any jurisdiction in the case, or any law applicable to it.

The same obstacles would exist to the introduction of the principle, in the case of any other relations, whether of person or property. It is impossible even to conceive, much less to establish, the practicability of any such system. In this case, therefore, the question of the right of the master and his alleged slaves, voluntarily brought into Pennsylvania, whether in transit or otherwise, depended on the law of Pennsylvania and on nothing else. The legislature of Pennsylvania, from comity or courtesy, might provide that the relation should continue in such case, and certainly did so provide in the act of 1780, under which the relation in such a case was governed and regulated by our own previously existing Slave Laws, which were continued in force for that purpose. But such comity or courtesy is to be exercised by the legislative authorities, and if they have repealed that provision, no judicial tribunal has a right to re-establish it.

III. I shall not discuss the question whether these alleged slaves did by the law of Pennsylvania become free or not. I think it wholly immaterial to the matter now before the Court. That question, if it be a question, is no doubt interesting to the parties concerned in it, and it may become highly material to Mr. Williamson, if Mr. Wheeler should proceed against him civilly or criminally in an appropriate forum. As a citizen of another State, he has, of course, a right to a civil action against Mr. Williamson, being a citizen of Pennsylvania, in the Circuit Court of the United States, by reason of the *parties*, and not of the *subject matter*, and if such an action should be brought, it would be the duty of that Court to administer in this regard the law of Pennsylvania, and no doubt they would do so. If he should choose to proceed to enforce any alleged right against Mr. Williamson, or to punish any alleged offence of his, the Courts of Pennsylvania are also open to him. But that is not the question. Therefore, I repeat, that I will not argue the question whether these persons are by law free or not; though after reading the act of 1780, and the act of 1847, it may admit of no doubt that they were in fact, by our law, as free as any other persons upon our soil, and that the comity or courtesy which had been extended by the former act, was (whether for sufficient reasons or not, it is not for me or the Court to decide,) withdrawn by the latter. We are all bound to respect the lawful exercise of the legislative power by the constituted authorities of our own Commonwealth, and it is our duty to obey their acts. Forced into an *ex parte* argument, I shall not ask the Court, in the absence of Mr. Wheeler, to express an opinion upon a question which I conceive to be not material to the matter in hand, and on which he certainly has a right to be heard.

IV. On this state of the case I submit that the District Court of the United States, nor the Judge thereof, had no authority whatever to issue the writ of *habeas corpus* under which the present petitioner was committed. Congress could not, under the provisions of the Constitution, have conferred such authority upon any tribunal of the United States, and, even if they could, they have not done so. It is clearly and absolutely a direct usurpation without color or right. I am not dealing with the motives of the learned Judge of the District Court, for every man is subject to error of judgment, and besides the esteem and personal regard which I entertain for that learned Judge, my respect for this Court would prevent me from the discourtesy of making it an arena in which to assail unnecessarily the motives of a Judge sitting in another tribunal.

Still the question remains, in what clause of the Constitution, or in what act of Congress, is to be found a word or syllable that can be so construed as to validate the jurisdiction which he has assumed in this case? And the answer is, *in none.*

The writ of *habeas corpus* is not a proceeding *inter partes*, and if it were, and the parties were considered to be Mr. Wheeler and Mr. Williamson, the Circuit Court of the U. S. would have jurisdiction in a civil action by reason of their respective citizenship, not because of the subject matter; but even in that case the District Court of the U. S. could have none

But the *habeas corpus cum causa* is not at all a proceeding *inter partes.* It is the inquisition of the Crown into the cause of the imprisonment of one of its subjects:—it is the inquisition of the Commonwealth into the cause of the imprisonment of one of her citizens, or of any human being on her soil:—and it can be prosecuted only in the courts of the government upon whom the protection of the liberty of the individual, in the particular case devolves.

Judge BETTS' opinion in the case of *Barry* vs. *Mercien*, contains so clear and lucid an explanation of the law on this subject, that it is not necessary to do more than to refer to it.

Now, under the Constitution of the United States, what interest has the government of the United States in the question of the domestic relations of individuals on the soil of Pennsylvania, or of the domestic institutions of this or any other State, or how has the protection of such relations or such institutions been devolved upon any branch of that government? Not only is there nothing in the letter of the Constitution of the United States to sanction such a claim, but it is inconsistent with, and subversive of, the whole spirit, intent and meaning of that instrument, and of the inherent and essential rights of the several States. It goes to the root of our frame of government, and it would be destructive of all its principles.

Even if this were not so, no act of Congress has conferred the power to issue a *habeas corpus* in such case.

The powers of the District Court to issue writs of *habeas corpus* are three-fold.

1. Under the act of 1789, to issue that writ in cases necessary for the exercise of its jurisdiction, and agreeable to the principles and usages of law. But in this case that Court had no jurisdiction for the exercise of which this *habeas corpus* was either necessary or agreeable to the principles and usages of law.

2. A judge of the District Court (by the same Act) may grant a writ of *habeas corpus* for the purpose of inquiring into the cause of commitment (*that is to say, commitment under process*) provided such writs shall in no case extend to prisoners in jail (*that is, so committed*) unless they are in custody under or by color of the authority of the United States, or are committed for trial before some Court of the same, or are necessary to be brought into Court to testify. This case cannot be pretended to be within any of those clauses.

3. Under the " Force Bill " the District Court of the United States may issue a *habeas corpus* in certain cases of persons committed under a State authority by reason of acts done in pursuance of an act of Congress of the United States. This case does clearly not fall within that clause. The opinion of Judge Betts, in *Barry* vs. *Mercein*, above mentioned, shows conclusively that in this case no jurisdiction whatever to award a *habeas corpus* existed in the District Court. It is clear, therefore, that the District Court had, neither under any clause in the Constitution, nor under any act of Congress, jurisdiction over the subject matter, or to award the writ of *habeas corpus* under the proceedings in which Mr. Williamson was committed, and that all those proceedings, including his commitment, were null and void, as if a private person without any judicial authority had assumed to conduct and enforce them.

V. I have thus far considered the case as it stands upon the record, and as the facts are known to exist, and to be undisputed. But it has been suggested, that in some way or other, a presumption may be raised of a fact, not appearing on the record, and well known not to be true, viz : (*that the alleged slaves were fugitives, and had escaped from Virginia or North Carolina into Pennsylvania,*) by which presumption, the jurisdiction of the District Court may be endeavored to be bolstered.

1. I deny that any such presumption can lawfully be made. The Courts of the United States, being courts of limited jurisdiction, the circumstances necessary to give them jurisdiction, ought to appear affirmatively on their record, and if they do not so appear they cannot be presumed.

2. If the Court had the discretion, in any case, to raise such a presumption, they would not raise it against what they know to be the real truth and verity of the case.

3. This record shows no finding of any fact, or proof of any fact or decision of the Judge of the Court upon any fact necessary to give jurisdiction. Suppose the Court were to raise the presumption that the petitioner in the District Court stated in his petition that these were fugitives, and had escaped from the State of Virginia, which he has not stated, still, for all that appears upon the record, it would remain merely as the statement of his petition. For, though the record shows that there was a return, yet it does not show that there was a traverse, though no doubt what was called a traverse was admitted by parole against law, as I consider it, yet the commitment is as for a contempt in refusing to make any return, and upon this record the presumption referred to would be to supply a defect in the mere statement of the petitioner himself, and not a presumption of *omnia rite acta* by the Judge.

In the *habeas corpus* under which the Judge of the same District Court discharged the defendants in Thomas vs. Crosson, who were held under a *capias* specially allowed by a Judge of this Court upon affidavits in a case in which the jurisdiction of this Court was undoubted, he held himself so far from being bound to raise presumptions in favor of the decision which had been made by the Judge of this Court, or to supply any defects in the affidavits on which that decision was grounded, that on a very critical examination of the affidavits, he arrived at the conclusion that the judge had been wrong in allowing the *capias*, and therefore discharged the prisoners.

4. Even if this record had shown these persons to be fugitives from service, having escaped from another State, and therefore within the provisions of the constitution of the United States, and if that fact had been undisputed, still the District Court would have had no jurisdiction to award the writ of *habeas corpus* now complained of. The act of 1850, purports to give that Court, as well as the Commissioners of the United States, jurisdiction to issue a warrant for the arrest of the fugitive, and also in case of rescue or abduction to give the District Court jurisdiction to proceed by indictment against the rescuer or abductor, and on conviction, after trial by jury, to inflict an imprisonment not exceeding six months, and a fine not exceeding a certain sum. But it cannot be pretended that that act gives any right to issue a *habeas corpus* against any citizen of Pennsylvania in whose custody the alleged fugitive might be alleged to be. The warrant would take the fu-

gitive from any private custody. The writ of *habeas corpus* is unne
cessary for the exercise of his jurisdiction in this case.

The Commissioners of the United States, mere officers appointed by
the Judges, and removable at their pleasure, have the same jurisdiction in regard to the issuing of warrants for fugitives, that the Judges
of the Courts themselves have, and have all the powers necessary to the
exercise of that jurisdiction, but of course they would have no power to
issue a writ of *habeas corpus*. Nor can it be conceived in any case
that the writ of *habeas corpus* is necessary to the exercise of the jurisdiction of granting a warrant immediately for the arrest of the fugitive. It is equally clear that the issuing and proceedings on a writ of
habeas corpus, such as have occurred in this case, are not only not authorized by the act of 1850, but are implicitly prohibited by that statute; for when it provides for the indictment trial, and ultimate punishment of a rescuer or abductor, it does in effect provide that he shall
not be in any shape convicted of such abduction without a trial by jury,
or in case he be guilty of it, be coerced by an imprisonment for contempt on a *habeas corpus*, or in any other mode to restore the fugitive. The restitution of the fugitive is no part of the judgment provided for against him. The common law proceeding *de homine replegiando* (which is by no means unfamiliar in our practice,) or an action
for damages remain open to the party claimant, in which also the trial
is to be by jury. Congress has authorized a summary decision without jury, upon the claim to the fugitive slave, but has not given the
shadow of authority to any Judge, Court, or Commissioner of the United States, without jury, summarily to decide upon the fact of the abduction of the slave by a citizen, and having found that, to coerce
the restitution of the fugitive by the indefinite imprisonment of the
alleged abductor. The proceedings here complained of would have
been glaringly and clearly beyond the jurisdiction of the District
Court, even if these persons had been fugitives. The proceedings
would have been just as null and void as they are now.

Third. In every case in which one Court has refused to inquire
into the causes of commitment for contempt by another Court, the ground
is clearly stated that the refusal was because the committing Court
was a Court of competent jurisdiction over the subject matter on which
the contempt was alleged to have arisen. It follows, therefore, from all
these cases, which I need not repeat, that if the Court be not a Court
of such competent jurisdiction, a commitment for contempt is no more beyond remedy than any other commitment.

In Holden vs. Smith, 14 Ad. and Ell. N. S. 8 41, already referred to, not only does it appear that the party was discharged on a habeas corpus, but afterwards judgment was obtained in an action for trespass for false imprisonment against the judge of a Court of record who had gone beyond his jurisdiction in committing the plaintiff for a contempt, in disobeying illegal process. The cases cited in that report are referred to.

It has been suggested that in some mode the present Petitioner is to be injured or his rights affected, because he did not object to the want of jurisdiction of the District Court before that Court itself. I would observe upon this,

1. That it does not appear by the record that he had any reason to raise the objection there, for as his return was that he had not, and never had, the possession or custody of the parties named in the writ, and as that return was by law conclusive, it was surely not incumbent on him to raise the abstract question whether, if he had them, he would have been bound to produce them.

2. It appears from the statement of the Petitioner as to the course of the proceedings and the time that was occupied by them, and the suddenness with which the whole matter was pressed upon him, that it would have required extraordinary presence of mind to raise any objection. Perhaps few men would have been able to collect their thoughts. The traverse of the return—the evidence upon that—the question of his commitment for perjury—the question of his commitment for contempt in refusing to make any return—would appear to have been all going on simultaneously, and the hearing upon all to have been concluded within the space of something more than two hours. I can have no personal knowledge of the facts, (not having been present at or concerned in that hearing,) but, taking the Petitioner's statement of them, he would appear rather to have been *hustled* than heard.

3. It is believed to be the first time that the proposition has been advanced, that a party unlawfully summoned in judgment before a tribunal that has no jurisdiction, is bound to make the objection of the want of it. In the case of *Holden vs. Smith* it did not appear that any objection to the want of jurisdiction was made in the Court whose acts were complained of. In the case of *Thomas vs. Crosson,* decided by three Judges of this Court, it did not appear that any such objection was made. Yet in both these cases the proceedings were held to be null and void. In no case that I am aware of, where the question has been of the nullity of the proceedings for want of jurisdiction, has it been deemed material to inquire whether such objection was made, unless where *motive* becomes material to inflame

damages. Indeed, if there be no jurisdiction, there is as little to decide the question of jurisdiction as any other. How is it that a party can lose his rights, by refusing to submit the question of jurisdiction to a Court that is incompetent to decide it? In certain civil cases in the Supreme Court of the United States, referred to by the Chief Justice, in his recent opinion, it has, indeed, been held that where the jurisdiction of Courts of the United States did not appear affirmatively on the record, they would not hold the proceedings absolutely null and void, as regarded the parties, as they might be reversed upon writ of error. But I do not understand that in these cases the party lost his right to object to the want of jurisdiction, by omitting to make the objection in the Court below. On the contrary, I gather from them that the decision would have been the same, even if that objection had been so made.

I speak of the opinion recently delivered by the learned Chief Justice of this Court in this case, without any reserve, because I know that if from the haste with which it was necessarily prepared, he has fallen into error, no man living will be so anxious to correct that error as himself.

I observe upon these cases—

1. That they were merely civil actions *inter partes*.

2. That it is probable that the defects in the averments there were merely formal and accidental, and that, according to the real truth of the facts, the Courts had jurisdiction.

3. That no offer was made to go behind the record of a Court of limited jurisdiction, and show, as is offered to be done here, that in truth the fact necessary to give jurisdiction did not exist.

4. That in these cases there was a fact consistent with the record, a presumption of which might be raised, that would give the Courts jurisdiction; whereas, in the present case, as I have endeavored to show, there is no fact consistent with the record which, even if the presumption of it be raised, would bring the case within the jurisdiction of the District Court. If the Court of Common Pleas of Philadelphia were to entertain an action of ejectment for land in Allegheny county, can it be supposed for a moment that the Sheriff would be justified in executing an *habere facias* under its judgment, or that the defendant would be bound to defend the action, or reverse the judgment on error? No man can maintain that to be the law.

5. That the reason upon which those decisions appear to be founded, to wit: that a party in the suit has another remedy, by reversing the judgment on a writ of error, does not exist here, the Supreme Court of

the United States having decided, in the case of *Barry* vs. *Mercein*, in 5 *Howard*, that no writ of error lies to the decision of an inferior Court of the United States on a *habeas corpus*.

6. I will observe further that if a writ of error did lie from the decision of the District Court, it would only be to another Court of the United States, and the case of the Petitioner here would be as strong as it is now, even if the Supreme Court of the United States had affirmed the decision of the District Court. Where the question is of a direct usurpation by the Courts of the United States upon the rights of the State, it is immaterial by which of such Courts that usurpation is made, and though none such can be anticipated from so august a tribunal as the Supreme Court of the United States, still, in point of law, if it were attempted, the duty of checking it would devolve upon the State tribunals. In *Olmsted's case*, already cited, in which Chief Justice Tilghman expressed clearly the extent and ground of that duty, the proceeding was in fact under a decision of the Supreme Court of the United States, who had awarded a *mandamus* to the District Court to issue the process complained of. In fact every proceeding by which the Courts of one Government do in fact usurp upon the rights of another, is null and void as against the Government usurped upon, and is to be so held in her Courts, who, where the substantial fact of usurpation exists, have no right to resort to fictitious presumptions against the truth, for the purpose of supporting the usurpation which it is their duty to resist.

I have endeavored to establish my positions. As regards the proceedings of the District Court, I have argued the question of jurisdiction only. The errors in law in other respects of these proceedings I shall not enter upon. The odd use of the writ of habeas corpus in applying it to the purpose of depriving a party of liberty, instead of restoring it; —the allowing a traverse of the return, which can only be allowed by statute, and which no statute allows in the Courts of the United States —the taking that traverse by parole merely—the assuming to decide upon it the fact of abduction upon insufficient evidence, and from that to deduce a continuance of custody on no evidence at all—the absolute inconsistency of the record, which, after setting out a full, complete, and unevasive return, proceeds to a commitment for a supposed refusal to make any return,—I do not know that all these and other errors, would of themselves enable this Court to interfere, if the District Court had jurisdiction of the case. But as that Court had no jurisdiction, these circumstances, all of them operating oppressively on a citizen entitled to your protection, do greatly aggravate the case, and enhance, if that be possible, your just obligation to relieve him. They do indeed tend to show a want of jurisdiction, for surely Providence would never have permitted a court of competent jurisdiction to fall into so many errors in one case.

Nor shall I say anything of the official position of Mr. Wheeler. I regard him as a citizen of another State, and entitled, while here, to all the immunities and privileges of a citizen of Pennsylvania. His position as a minister of the United States to a foreign country, neither diminishes nor enhances his privileges in this.

This argument is necessarily summary and incomplete, both as regards the illustrations and the authorities. Of the latter, the few to which I have referred have been principally the decisions of highly esteemed judges of the Courts of the United States and of this State. We desire only that those safe and reasonable views of their own powers which they have heretofore expressed, shall continue to be acted on by the successors of both.

We do not ask this Court to trench in any way upon the just authority of the United States. They have a large scope in the construction of the constitution and statutes under which they act. It is right that great deference should be always paid to their construction of the meaning of any clause in the constitution of the United States, or in any act of Congress, and that as a general rule such construction should be left very much to them ; but where (as in this case) there is no clause in the constitution, or in any act of Congress, which upon any construction can be held even to refer to the subject matter over which a Court of the United States undertakes to assume jurisdiction—where the usurpation therefore is obvious and palpable—the citizen can have no recourse for relief but to the Courts of his own State.

I now leave the matter in the hands of the Court. It is impossible to conceal from ourselves the fact that the essential rights of this Commonwealth are invaded. This position of things is inauspicious. To correct it nothing is wanted but the firm and temperate discharge of your duties as magistrates and ministers of the law.

Pennsylvania has always truly performed her duties to her sister States. If it were justifiable to occupy the time with matter not directly pertinent to this case, I would go into the details and show how clear of just reproach her career has been. Whatever may happen, she will never be mean enough to enjoy the benefits of the Constitution, and at the same time refuse to fulfil in good faith her obligations under it. She deserves all our love and affection. Yet there may be some—sons, too, of her soil—who ignore the assault upon her liberties —who affect not to see that she is struck at and hurt—who, in the fervency of their superserviceable protestations of fealty to the domestic laws and institutions of other States, have no time nor thought to bestow upon the question of the invasion or even overthrow of their own.

The question here has nothing to do with the rights or wrongs, the conduct or misconduct of the North or the South. It concerns principles upon which all are agreed. *That each State has the right to regulate her own domestic relations and institutions—that the Courts of the United States have no right to interfere with or control them—that citizens of other States who come upon her soil are, while there, bound to respect and obey her laws:—these,* I say, are the principles involved here, and they are quite as dear to the SOUTH as to the NORTH, they ought to be quite as dear to the NORTH as to the SOUTH.

It has come to the point that, failing your aid, they are no longer safe in Pennsylvania. I invoke that aid with confidence, and, if it be granted, the rights of the commonwealth will have been vindicated, and the affair from which these questions have originated—untoward in all its aspects—will be left to be determined by the laws of the State in some appropriate forum.

On the 8th day of September, 1855, the Supreme Court (all the Judges present) met at Philadelphia, when the decision of the Court was pronounced by Justice BLACK in the following opinion, Justice KNOX dissenting.

OPINION OF JUSTICE BLACK.

This is an application by Passmore Williamson for habeas corpus.— He complains that he is held in custody under a commitment of the District Court of the United States for a contempt of that Court in refusing to obey its process. The process which he is confined for disobeying, was a habeas corpus commanding him to produce the bodies of certain colored persons claimed as slaves under the laws of Virginia.

Is he entitled to the writ he has asked for? In considering what answer we shall give to this question, we are, of course, expected to be influenced, as in other cases, by the Law and the Constitution alone. The gentlemen who appeared as counsel for the petitioner, and who argued the motion in a way which did them great honor, pressed upon us no considerations, except those which were founded upon their *legal* views of the subject.

It is argued with much earnestness, and no doubt with perfect sincerity, that we are bound to allow the writ, without stopping to consider whether the Petitioner has or has not laid before us any probable cause for supposing that he is illegally detained—that every man confined in prison, except for treason or felony, is entitled to it *ex debito justitiæ*— and that we cannot refuse it without a frightful violation of the Petitioner's rights, no matter how plainly it may appear on his own showing that he is held in custody for a just cause. If this be true, the case of ex parte Lawrence, (5 Binn. 304,) is not law. There the writ was refused, because the applicant had been previously heard before another Court. But if every man who applies for a habeas corpus must have it, as a matter of right, and without regard to anything but the mere fact that he demands it, then a Court or a Judge has no more power to refuse a second than a first application.

Is it really true that the special application, which must be made for every writ of habeas corpus, and the examination of the commitment, which we are bound to make before it can issue, are mere hollow and unsubstantial forms? Can it be possible that the Law and the Courts are so completely under the control of their natural enemies that every class of offenders against the Union, the State, except traitors and felons, may be brought before us as often as they please, though we know beforehand, by their own admissions, that we cannot help but remand them immediately? If these questions must be answered in the affirmative, then we are compelled, against our will and contrary to our convictions of duty, to wage a constant warfare against the federal tribunals by firing off writs of habeas corpus upon them all the time. The punitive justice of the State would suffer still more seriously. The half of the Western Penitentiary would be before us at Philadelphia, and a similar proportion from Cherry Hill and Moyamensing would attend our sittings at Pittsburgh.

To remand them would do very little good, for a new set of writs would bring them all back again. A sentence to solitary confinement would be a sentence that the convict should travel for a limited term up and down the State, in company with the officers who might have him in charge. By the same means the inmates of the lunatic asylums might be temporarily enlarged, much to their own detriment; and every soldier or seaman in the service of the country could compel their commanders to bring them before the Court six times a week.

But the habeas corpus act has never received such a construction. It is a writ of right, and may not be refused to one who shows a *prima facie* case, entitling him to be discharged or bailed. But he has no right to demand it who admits that he is in legal custody for an offence not bailable : and he does make what is equivalent to such an admission when his own application, and the commitment referred to in it, show that he is lawfully detained. A complaint must be made, and the cause of detainer submitted to a judge, before the writ can go. The very object and purpose of this is to prevent it from being trifled with by those who have manifestly no right to be set at liberty. It is like a writ of error in a criminal case, which the Court or Judge is bound to allow, if there be reason to suppose that an error has been committed, and equally bound to refuse it, if it be clear that the judgment must be affirmed.

We are not aware that any application to this Court for a writ of habeas corpus has ever been successful, where the Judges, at the time of the allowance, were satisfied that the prisoner must be remanded. The petitioner's counsel say that there is but one reported case in which it was refused, (5 Binn. 304 ;) and this is urged in the argument as a reason for supposing that, in all other cases, the writ was issued without examination. But no such inference can be fairly drawn from the scarcity of judicial decisions on a point like this. We do not expect to find in reports so recent as ours those long established rules of law which the student learns from his elementary books, and which are constantly acted upon without being disputed.

The habeas corpus is a common law writ, and has been used in England from time immemorial, just as it is now. The statute of 31 Charles II. c. 2, made no alteration in the practice of the courts in granting these writs. (3 Barn. and Ald. 420—2 Chitty's Reps., 207.) It merely provided, that the Judges in vacation should have the power which the courts had previously exercised in term time, (1 Chitty's Gen. Prac. 686,) and inflicted penalties upon those who should defeat its operation. The common law upon this subject was brought to America by the colonists ; and most, if not all of the States, have since enacted laws resembling the English statute of Charles II., in every principal feature. The Constitution of the United States declares that " the privilege of a writ of habeas corpus shall not be suspended unless when, in cases of rebellion or invasion, the public safety may require it." Congress has conferred upon the federal judges the power to issue such writs according to the principles and rules regulating them in other Courts. Seeing that the same general principles of common law on this subject prevailed in England and America, and seeing also the similarity of the statutory regulations in both countries, the decisions of the English judges as well as of the American Courts, both State and Federal, are entitled to our fullest respect as settling and defining our powers and duties.

Blackstone (3 Com. 132) says the writ of habeas corpus should be allowed only when the Court or Judge is satisfied that the party hath probable cause to be delivered. He gives cogent reasons why it should not be allowed in any other case, and cites with unqualified approbation the precedent set by Sir Edward Coke and Chief Justice Vaughan in cases where they had refused it. Chitty lays down the same rule. (1 Cr. Law, 101 ; 1 Gen'l Prac., 686–7). It seems to have been acted upon by all the Judges. The writ was refused in Rex vs. Schiever, (1 Burr 765,) and in the case of the three Spanish Sailors (2 Blacks. R. 1324.) In Hobhouse's case (3 Barn. and Ald., 420,) it was fully settled by an unanimous Court, as the true construction of the statute, that the writ is never to be allowed, if upon view of the commitment it be manifest that the prisoner must be remanded. In New York, when the statute in force there was precisely like ours, (so far I mean as this question is concerned,) it was decided by the Supreme Court (5 Johns. 282) that the allowance of the writ was a matter within the discretion of the Court, depending on the grounds laid in the application. It was refused in Huster's case (1 Johns. C. 136,) and in ex parte Ferguson (9 Johns. R. 139.)

In addition to this, we have the opinion of Chief Justice Marshall in Watkin's case, (3 Peters, 202,) that the writ ought not to be awarded if the Court is satisfied that the prisoner must be remanded. It was accordingly refused by the Supreme Court of the United States in that case, as it had been before in Kearney's case.

On the whole, we are thoroughly satisfied that our duty requires us to view, and examine the cause of detainer *now*, and to make an end of the business at once, if it appears that we have no power to discharge him on the return of the writ.

This prisoner, as already said, is confined on a sentence of the District Court of the United States for a contempt. A habeas corpus is not a writ of error. It cannot bring a case before us in such a manner that we can exercise any kind of appellate jurisdiction in it.

On a habeas corpus, the judgment even of a subordinate State Court cannot be disregarded, reversed or set aside, however clearly we may perceive it to be erroneous, and however plain it may be that we ought to reverse it, if it were before us on appeal or writ of error. We can only look at the record to see whether a judgment exists, and have no power to say whether it is right or wrong. It is conclusively presumed to be right until it is regularly brought up for revision.

We decided this three years ago, at Sunbury, in a case which we all thought one of much hardship. But the rule is so familiar, so universally acknowledged, and so reasonable in itself, that it requires only to be stated. It applies with still greater force, or at least for much stronger reasons, to the decisions of the Federal Courts.

Over them we have no control at all under any circumstances, or by any process that could be devised. Those tribunals belong to a different judicial system from ours. They administer a different code of laws, and are responsible to a different sovereignty.

The District Court of the U. S. is as independent of us as we are of it—as independent as the Supreme Court of the U. S. is of either. What the law and the Constitution have forbidden us to do directly on writ of error, we of course, cannot do indirectly by habeas corpus.

But the petitioner's counsel have put his case on the ground that the whole proceeding against him in the District Court was *coram non judice*, null and void.

It is certainly true that a void judgment may be regarded as no judgment at all; and every judgment is void, which clearly appears on its own face to have been pronounced by a Court having no jurisdiction or authority in the subject matter.

For instance, if a Federal Court should convict and sentence a citizen for libel ; or if a State Court, having no jurisdiction except in civil pleas should try an indictment for a crime and convict the party—in these cases the judgments would be wholly void.

If the Petitioner can bring himself within this principle, then there is no judgment against him ; he is wrongfully imprisoned, and we must order him to be brought out and discharged.

What is he detained for? The answer is easy and simple. The commitment shows that he was tried, found guilty, and sentenced for *contempt of Court*, and nothing else. He is now confined *in execution of that sentence*, and for no other cause. This was a distinct and substantive offence against the authority and government of the United States. Does anybody doubt the jurisdiction of the District Court to punish the contempt of one who disobeys its process? Certainly not. All courts have this power, and must necessarily have it. Without it they would be utterly powerless. The authority to deal with an offender of this class belongs exclusively to the Court in which the offence is committed, and no other Court, not even the highest, can interfere with its exercise, either by writ of error, mandamus, or habeas corpus. If the power be abused, there is no remedy but impeachment. The law was so held by this Court in McLoughlin's Case, (5 W. & S. 275,) and by the Supreme Court of the U. S., in Kearney's Case, (7 Wheaton, 38.) It was solemnly settled, as part of the common law, in Brass Crossby's

Case, (3 Wilson, 183) by a Court in which sat two of the foremost jurists that England ever produced. We have not the smallest doubt that it is the law; and we must administer it as we find it. The only attempt ever made to disregard it was by a New York Judge, (4 Johns. R. 345,) who was not supported by his brethren. This attempt was followed by all the evil and confusion which Blackstone and Kent and Story declared to be its necessary consequence. Whoever will trace that singular controversy to its termination will see that the Chancellor and the majority of the Supreme Court, though once outvoted in the Senate, were never answered.

The Senate itself yielded to the force of the truths which the Supreme Court had laid down so clearly, and the judgment of the Court of Errors in Yate's case, (6 Johns. 503) was overruled by the same Court the year afterwards, in Yates vs. Lansing, (9 Johns. R. 423,) which grew out of the very same transaction. and depended on the same principles. Still further reflection, at a later period, induced the Senate to join the popular branch of the Legislature in passing a statute which effectually prevents one Judge from interfering by habeas corpus with the judgment of another, on a question of contempt.

These principles being settled, it follows irresistibly that the District Court of the United States had power and jurisdiction to decide what acts constitute a contempt against it; to determine whether the petitioner had been guilty of contempt, and to inflict upon him the punishment which, in its opinion, he ought to suffer. If we fully believed the Petitioner to be innocent—if we were sure that the Court which convicted him misunderstood the facts or misapplied the law—still we could not reexamine the evidence, or re-judge the justice of the case, without grossly disregarding what we know to be the law of the land. The Judge of the District Court decided the question on his own constitutional responsibility. Even if he could be shown to have acted tyrannically or corruptly, he could be called to answer for it only in the Senate of the United States.

But the counsel of the Petitioner go behind the proceeding in which he was convicted, and argue that the sentence for contempt is void, because the Court had no jurisdiction of a certain other matter, which it was investigating, or attempting to investigate, when the contempt was committed. We find a judgment against him in one case; and he complains about another, in which there is no judgment. He is suffering for an offence against the United States; and he says he is innocent of any wrong to a particular individual. He is conclusively adjudged guilty of contempt; and he tells us that the Court had no jurisdiction to restore Mr. Wheeler's slaves.

It must be remembered that contempt of Court is a specific criminal offence. It is punished sometimes by indictment and sometimes in a summary proceeding, as it was in this case. In either mode of trial, the adjudication against the offender is a conviction, and the commitment in consequence is execution. (7 Wheat. 38.) This is well settled, and, I believe, has never been doubted. Certainly the learned counsel for the Petitioner has not denied it. The contempt may be connected with some particular cause, or it may consist in misbehavior, which has a tendency to obstruct the administration of justice generally. When it is committed in a pending cause, the proceeding to punish it is a proceeding by itself. It is not entitled in the cause pending, but on the criminal side (Wall, 134.)

The record of a conviction for contempt is as distinct from the matter under investigation when it was committed, as an indictment for perjury is from the cause in which the false oath was taken. Can a person, convicted of perjury, ask us to deliver him from the penitentiary, on showing that the oath on which the perjury is assigned, was taken in a cause of which the Court and no jurisdiction? Would any Judge in the Commonwealth listen to such reasons for treating the sentence as void? If, instead of swearing falsely, he refuses to be sworn at all, and he is convicted not of perjury, but of contempt, the same rule applies, and with a force precisely equal. If it be really true that no contempt can be committed against a Court while it is inquiring into a matter beyond its jurisdiction, and if the fact was so in this case, then the Petitioner had a good defence, and he ought to have made it on his trial. To make it after conviction is too late. To make it here is to produce it before the wrong tribunal.

Every judgment *must* be conclusive until reversed. Such is the character, nature and essence of all judgments. If it be not conclusive it is not a judgment. A Court must either have power to settle a given question finally and forever, so as to preclude all further inquiry upon it, or else it has no power to make any decision at all. To say that a Court may determine a matter, and that another Court may regard the same matter afterwards as open and undetermined, is an absurdity in terms.

It is most especially necessary that convictions for contempt in one Court should be final, conclusive and free from re-examination by other Courts on habeas corpus. If the law were not so, our judicial system would break to pieces in a month. Courts totally unconnected with each other would be coming in constant collision. The inferior Courts would revise all the decisions of the Judges placed over and above them. A party unwilling to be tried in this Court need only defy our authority, and if we commit him, take out his habeas corpus before an Associate Judge of his own choosing, and if that Judge be of opinion that we ought not to try him, there is an end of the case.

This doctrine is so plainly against the reason of the thing that it would be wonderful, indeed, if any authority for it could be found in the books. There is none, except the overruled decision of Mr. Justice Spencer, of New York, and some efforts of the same kind to control the other courts, made by Sir Edward Coke, in the King's Bench, which are now universally admitted to have been illegal, as well as rude and intemperate. On the other hand, we have all the English judges, and all our own, disclaiming their power to interfere with, or control, one another in this way. I will content myself by simply referring to some of the books in which it is established that the conviction of contempt is a separate proceeding, and is conclusive of every fact which might have been urged on the trial for contempt, and among others want of jurisdiction to try the cause in which the contempt was committed. 4 Johns. R. 325, et sequ. The opinion of Ch. J. Kent, on pages 370 to 375. 6 Johns. 563. 9 Johns. 423. 1 Hill, 170. 5 Iredell, 199. ib. 153. 2 Sandf. 724. 1 Carter, 160. 1 Blackf. 166. 25 Miss., 886. 2 Wheeler's Criminal Cases, p. 1. 43 Ad. and Ellis, 558.

These cases will speak for themselves, but I may remark as to the last one that the very same objection was made there as here. The party was convicted of contempt in not obeying a decree. He claimed his discharge on habeas corpus, because the Chancellor had no jurisdiction to make the decree, being interested in the cause himself. But the Court of Queen's Bench held that if that was a defence it should have been made on the trial for contempt, and the conviction was conclusive. We cannot choose but hold the same rule here. Any other would be a violation of the law which is established and sustained by all authority and all reason.

But certainly the want of jurisdiction alleged in this case would not even have been a defence on the trial. The proposition that a Court is powerless to punish for disorderly conduct or disobedience of its process in a case which it ought ultimately to dismiss for want of jurisdiction, is not only unsupported by judicial authority, but we think it is new even as an argument at the bar. We ourselves have heard many cases through and through before we became convinced that it was our duty to remit the parties to another tribunal. But we never thought that our process could be defied in such cases more than in others.

There are some proceedings in which the want of jurisdiction would be seen at the first blush; but there are others in which the Court must inquire into all the facts before it can possibly know whether it has jurisdiction or not. Any one who obstructs or baffles a judicial investigation for that purpose is unquestionably guilty of a crime for which he may and ought to be tried, convicted and punished. Suppose a local action to be brought in the wrong county ; this is a defence to the action, but a defence which must be made out like any other. While it is pending neither a party nor an officer, nor any other person can safely insult the Court or resist its order. The Court may not have power to decide upon the merits of the case ; but it has undoubted power to try whether the wrong was done within its jurisdiction or not.

Suppose Mr. Williamson to be called before the Circuit Court of the United States as a witness in a trial for murder, alleged to be committed on the high seas ; can he refuse to be sworn, and at his trial for contempt; justify himself on the ground that the murder was in fact committed within the limits of a State, and therefore triable only in a State Court ? If he can, he can justify perjury for the same reason. But such a defence for either crime has never been heard of since the beginning of the world. Much less can it be shown, after conviction, as a ground for declaring the sentence void.

The writ which the Petitioner is convicted of disobeying, was legal on its face. It enjoined upon him a simple duty, which he ought to have understood and performed without hesitation. That he did not do so, is a fact conclusively established by the adjudication which the Court made upon it. I say the writ was legal, because the act of Congress gives to all the Courts of the United States the power " to issue writs of habeas corpus when necessary for the exercise of their jurisdiction, and agreeable to the principles and usages of Law. " Chief Justice Marshall decided, in Burr's trial, that the principles and usages referred to in this act were those of the common law. A part of the jurisdiction of the District Court consists in restoring fugitive slaves; and the habeas corpus may be used in aid of it when necessary. It was awarded here upon the application of a person who complained that his slaves were detained from him. Unless they were fugitive slaves, they could not be slaves at all, according to the Petitioner's own doctrine, and if the Judge took that view of the subject, he was bound to award the writ.

If the persons mentioned in it had turned out, on the hearing, to be fugitives from labor, the duty of the District Judge to restore them, or his power to bring them before him on a habeas corpus, would have been disputed by none except the very few who think that the Constitution and laws on that subject ought not to be obeyed. The duty of the Court to inquire into the facts on which its jurisdiction depends is as plain as its duty not to exceed it when its duty is ascertained.

But Mr. Williamson stopped the investigation *in limine;* and the consequence is, that everything in the case remains unsettled—whether the persons named in the writ were slaves or free—whether Mr. Wheeler was the owner of them—whether they were unlawfully taken from him —whether the Court had jurisdiction to restore them—all these points are left open for want of a proper return.   It is not our business to say how they ought to be decided; but we do not doubt that the learned and upright magistrate who presides in the District Court would have decided them as rightly as any judge in all the country.   Mr. Williamson had no right to arrest the inquiry because he supposed that an error would be committed on the question of jurisdiction, or any other question. If the assertions which his counsel now make on the law and the facts be correct, he prevented an adjudication in favor of his proteges, and thus did them a wrong, which is probably a greater offence in his own eyes than anything he could do against Mr. Wheeler's rights.   There is no reason to believe that any trouble whatever would have come out of the case if he had made a true, full, and special return of all the facts; for then the rights of all parties, black and white, could have been settled, or the matter dismissed for want of jurisdiction, if the law so required.

It is argued that the Court had no jurisdiction, because it was not averred that the slaves were fugitives, but merely that they owed service by the laws of Virginia. Conceding, for the argument's sake, that this was the only ground on which the Court could have interfered—conceding, also, that it is not substantially alleged in the petition of Mr. Wheeler—the proceeding was, nevertheless, not void for that reason. The Federal tribunals, though Courts of limited jurisdiction, are not *inferior* Courts.   Their judgments, until reversed by the proper appellate Court, are valid and conclusive upon the parties, though the jurisdiction be not alleged in the pleadings nor on any part of the record, (10 Wheaton, 192).   Even if this were not settled and clear law, it would still be certain that the fact on which jurisdiction depends need not be stated *in the process.*   The want of such a statement in the body of the habeas corpus, or in the petition on which it was awarded, did not give Mr. Williamson a right to treat it with contempt.   If it did, then the Courts of the United States must set out the ground of their jurisdiction, in every supœna for a witness: a defective or untrue averment will authorize the witness to be as contumacious as he sees fit.

But all that was said in the argument about the petition, the writ, and the facts which were proved, or could be proved, refers to the *evidence* on which the conviction took place. This had passed *in rem judicatam*. We cannot go one step behind the conviction itself. We could not reverse it if there had been no evidence at all. We have no more authority in law to come between the prisoner and the Court to free him from a sentence like this, than we would have to countermand an order issued by the commander-in-chief to the United States army. We have no authority or jurisdiction to decide anything here, except the simple fact that the District Court had power to punish for contempt a person who disobeys its process—that the Petitioner is convicted of such contempt—and that the conviction is conclusive upon us. The jurisdiction of the Court on the case which had been before it, and everything else which preceded the conviction, are out of our reach; they are not examinable by us, and, of course, not now intended to be decided.

There may be cases in which we ought to check usurpation of power by the Federal Courts. If one of them would presume, upon any pretence whatever, to take out of our hands a prisoner convicted of contempt in this Court, we would resist by all proper and legal means. What we would not permit them to do against us, we will not do against them. We must maintain the rights of the State and its Courts, for to them alone can the people look for a competent administration of their domestic concerns; but we will do nothing to impair the constitutional vigor of the general government, which is "the sheet anchor of our peace at home and our safety abroad."

Some complaint was made in the argument about the sentence being for an indefinite time. If this were erroneous, it would not avail here; since we have as little power to revise the judgment for that reason, as for any other. But it is not illegal, nor contrary to the usual rule in such cases. It means commitment until the party shall make proper submission. (3 Lord Raymond 1103. 4 Johns. R. 375.) The law will not bargain with anybody to let its Courts be defied for a specified term of imprisonment. There are many persons who would gladly purchase the honors of martyrdom in a popular cause at almost any given price, while others are deterred by a mere show of punishment. Each is detained until he finds himself willing to conform.

This is merciful to the submissive and not too severe upon the refractory. The Petitioner, therefore, carries the key of his prison in his own pocket. He can come out when he will, by making terms with the Court that sent him there. But if he choose to struggle for a triumph, if nothing will content him but a clean victory or a clean defeat—he cannot expect us to aid him. Our duties are of a widely different kind. They consist in discouraging as much as in us lies all such contests with the legal authorities of the country. *The writ of Habeas Corpus is refused.*

The following opinion was then delivered by Justice KNOX :

OPINION OF JUSTICE KNOX.

I do not concur in the opinion of the majority of this Court refusing the writ of habeas corpus, and shall state the reasons why, in my judgment, the writ should be granted.

This application was made to the Court whilst holding a special session in Bedford, on the 13th day of August, and upon an intimation from the counsel that in case the Court had any difficulty upon the question of awarding the writ, they would like to be heard. Thursday, the 16th of August, was fixed for the hearing. On that day an argument was made by Messrs. Meredith and Gilpin, in favor of the allowance of the writ.

I may as well remark here, that upon the presentation of the petition I was in favor of awarding a habeas corpus, greatly preferring that the right of the Petitioner to his discharge should be determined upon the return of the writ. If this course had been adopted, we should have had the views of counsel in opposition to the discharge, and, moreover, if necessary, we could, after the return, have examined into the facts of the case.

I am in favor of granting this writ, first, because I believe the Petitioner has the right to demand it at our hands. From the time of Magna Charta the writ of habeas corpus has been considered a writ of right, which every person is entitled to *ex merito justiciæ.* "But the benefit of it (says Chancellor Kent) was in a great degree eluded in England prior to the statute of Charles II., as the Judges only awarded it in term time, and they assumed a discretionary *power of awarding or refusing it.*" 2 Kent's Commentaries, 26. And Bacon says, "Notwithstanding the writ of habeas corpus be a writ of right, and what the subject is entitled to, yet the provision of the law herein being in a great measure eluded by the Judges being only enabled to award it in term time, as also by an *imagined notion of the Judges* that they had a discretionary power of granting or refusing it," the act of 31 Charles II. was made for remedy thereof.

I am aware that, both in England and in this country, since the passage of the statute of Charles II., it has been held that where it clearly appeared that the prisoner must be remanded, it was improper to grant the writ, but I know of no such construction upon our act of 18th February,

1785. The people of these United States have ever regarded the privilege of the habeas corpus as a most invaluable right, to secure which an interdiction against its suspension, " unless when in cases of rebellion or invasion the public safety may require it," is inserted in the organic law of the Union, and, in addition to our act of 1785, which is broader and more comprehensive than the English statute, a provision in terms like that in the Constitution of the United States is to be found in the Constitution of this State.

It is difficult to conceive how words could be more imperative in their character than those to be found in the statute of 1785. The Judges named are authorized and required, either in vacation or in term time, upon the due application of any person committed or detained, for any criminal or supposed criminal matter, except for treason or felony, or confined or restrained of his or her liberty under any color or pretence whatsoever, to award and grant a habeas corpus, directed to the person or persons in whose custody the prisoner is detained, returnable immediately. And the refusal or neglect to grant the writ required by the Act to be granted, renders the Judge so neglecting or refusing, liable to the penalty of three hundred pounds.

I suppose no one will doubt the power of the Legislature to require this writ to be issued by the Judges of the Commonwealth. And it is tolerably plain that where, in express words, a certain thing is directed to be done, to which is added a penalty for not doing it, no discretion is to be used in obeying the mandate.

The English statute confined the penalty to a neglect or refusal to grant the writ in vacation time, and from this a discretionary power to refuse it in term time was inferred, but our act of Assembly does not limit the penalty to a refusal in vacation, but is sufficiently comprehensive to embrace neglect or refusal in vacation or in term time.

I have looked in vain through the numerous cases reported in this State, to find that the writ was ever denied to one whose application was in due form, and whose case was within the purview of the act of Assembly.

In Respublica vs. Arnold, 3 Yates, 263, the writ was refused because the Petitioner was not restrained of his liberty, and therefore not within the terms of the statute; and in ex parte Lawrence, 5th Binney, 304, it was held that the act of Assembly did not oblige the Court to grant a habeas corpus, where the case had already been heard upon the same evidence by another Court. Without going into an examination of the numerous cases where the writ has been allowed, I believe it can be safely affirmed that the denial of the writ in a case like the present is without a precedent, and contrary to the uniform practice of the bench, and against the universal understanding of the profession and the people; but what is worse still, it appears to me to be in direct violation of the law itself.

It may be said that the law never requires a useless thing to be done. Grant it. But how can it be determined to be useless until the case is heard? Whether there is ground for the writ is to be determined according to law, and the law requires that the determination should follow, not precede the return.

An application was made to the Chief Justice of this Court for a writ of habeas corpus previous to the application now being considered. The writ was refused, and it was stated in the Opinion that the counsel for the Petitioner waived the right to the writ, or did not desire it to be issued if the Chief Justice should be of the opinion that there was not sufficient cause set forth in the petition for the prisoner's discharge. But this can in no wise prejudice the Petitioner's right to the writ which he now demands. Even had the writ been awarded and the case heard, and the discharge refused, it would not be within the decision in ex parte Lawrence, for there the hearing was before a Court in term time, upon a full examination of the case upon evidence adduced, and not at chambers; but the more obvious distinction here is, that the writ has never been awarded. And the agreement of counsel that it should not be in a certain event, even if binding upon the client there, would not affect him here.

Now, whilst I aver that the writ of habeas corpus, *ad sub jiciendum*, is a writ of right, I do not wish to be understood that it should issue, as matter of course. Undoubtedly the petition must be in due form, and it must show upon its face that the Petitioner is entitled to relief. It may be refused if, upon the application itself, it appears that, if admitted to be true, the applicant is not entitled to relief; but where, as in the case before us, the petition alleges an illegal restraint of the Petitioner's liberty, under an order from a Judge beyond his jurisdiction, we are bound in the first place to take the allegation as true; and so taking it, a probable cause is made out, and there is no longer a discretionary power to refuse the writ. Whether the allegation of want of jurisdiction is true or not, is determinable only upon the return of the writ.

If one has averred in his petition what, if true, would afford him relief, it is his constitutional right to be present when the truth of his allegations is inquired into; and it is also his undoubted right, under our habeas corpus act, to establish his allegations by evidence, to be introduced and heard upon the return of the writ. To deny him the writ, is virtually to condemn him unheard; and as I can see nothing in this case which requires at our hands an extraordinary resistance against the prayer of the Petitioner to be permitted to show that his imprisonment is illegal, that he is deprived of his liberty without due course of law, I am in favor of treating him as like cases have uniformly been treated in this Commonwealth, by awarding the writ of habeas corpus, and reserving the inquiry as to his right to be discharged until the return of the writ; but as a majority of my brethren have come to a different conclusion, we must inquire next into the right of the applicant to be discharged as the case is now presented.

I suppose it to be undoubted law that, in a case where a Court acting beyond its jurisdiction has committed a person to prison, the prisoner, under our habeas corpus act, is entitled to his discharge, and that it makes no difference whether the Court thus transcending its jurisdiction assumes to act as a Court of the Union or of the Commonwealth. If a principle, apparently so just and clear, needs for its support adjudicated cases, reference can be had to Wise vs. Withers, 3d Cranch, 331; 1st Peters' Condensed Reports, 552; Rose vs. Hinely, 4th Cranch, 241, 268; Don vs. Harden, 1st Paine's Reports, 55, 58 and 59; 3d Cranch, 448; Bollman vs. Swartwout, 4th Cranch, 75; Kearney's case, 7th Wheaton, 38; Kemp vs. Kennedy, 1st Peters' C. C. R. 36; Wickes vs. Caulk, 5 Har. and J., 42; Griffith vs. Frazier, 8 Cranch, 9; Com. vs. Smith, Sup. Ct. Penn., 1st Wharton's Digest, 321; Com. ex. relatione Lockington vs. the Jailor, &c., Sup. Ct. manuscript, 1814, Wharton's Digest, vol. 1st, 321; Albee vs. Ward, 8 Mass. 86.

Some of these cases decide that the act of a Court without jurisdiction, is void: some, that the proper remedy for an imprisonment by a Court having no jurisdiction, is the writ of habeas corpus; and others, that it may issue from a State Court to discharge a prisoner committed under process from a Federal Court, if it clearly appear that the Federal Court had no jurisdiction of the case; altogether they establish the point that the Petitioner is entitled to relief, if he is restrained of his liberty by a Court acting beyond its jurisdiction.

Neither do I concieve it to be correct to say that the applicant cannot now question the jurisdiction of the Judge of the District Court, because he did not challenge it upon the hearing. There are many rights and privileges which a party to a judical controversy may lose if not claimed in due time, but not so the question of Jurisdiction; this cannot be given by express consent, much less with acquiescence for a time waive an objection to it. (See U. S. Digest, vol. 1st, p. 639, Pl. 62, and cases there cited.)   It would be a harsh rule to apply to one who is in prison, "without bail or mainprise," that his omission to speak upon the first opportunity, forever closed his mouth from denying the power of the Court to deprive him of his liberty.   I deny that the law is a trap for the feet of the unwary.   Where personal liberty is concerned, it is a shield for the protection of the citizen, and it will answer his call even if made after the prison door is closed upon him.

If, then, the want of jurisdiction is fatal, and the inquiry as to its existence is still open, the only question that remains to be considered is this.   Had the Judge of the District Court for the Eastern District of the United States, power to issue the writ of habeas corpus, directed to Passmore Williamson, upon the petition of John H. Wheeler.   The power of that Court to commit for a contempt is not denied, and I understand it to be conceded as a general rule by the Petitioner's counsel that one Court will not re-examine commitment for contempt by another Court of competent jurisdiction, but if the Court has no authority to issue the writ, the respondent was not bound to answer it, and his neglect or refusal to do so would not authorise his punishment for contempt.

The first position which I shall take in considering the question of jurisdiction, is that the Courts of the United States have no power to award the writ of habeas corpus, except such as is given to them by the acts of Congress.

"Courts which orginate in the common law possess a jurisdiction which must be regulated by the common law; but the Courts which are created by written law, and whose jurisdiction is defined by written law, cannot transcend their jurisdiction.   The power to award the writ by any of the Courts of the United States must be given by written law." Ex parte Swartwout, 4th Cranch, 75.   Ex parte Barry, 2 Howard, 65. The power of the Courts of the United States to issue writs of habeas corpus is derived either from the 14th section of the Act of 24th September, 1789, or from the 7th section of the Act of March 2d, 1833.

The section from the Act of 1789 provides that "all the Courts of the United States may issue writs of scire facias, habeas corpus, and all other writs not specially provided for by statute which may be necessary for the exercise of their respective jurisdictions, and agreeable to the principles and usages of law.   And either of the Justices of the Supreme Court, as well as the Judges of the District Courts, may grant writs of habeas corpus for the purpose of inquiry into the cause of commitment but writs of habeas corpus shall in no case extend to prisoners in jail, unless they are in custody under or by color of the authority of the

United States, or are committed for trial before some Court of the same, or are necessary to be brought into Court to testify." The 7th section of the Act of 2d March, 1833, authorises " either of the Justices of the Supreme Court, or a Judge of any District Court of, the United States, in addition to the authority already conferred by law, to grant writs of habeas corpus in all cases of a prisoner or prisoners in jail or confinement, where he or they shall be committed or confined on or by authority of law for any act done or omitted to be done in pursuance of a law of the United States, or any order, process, or decree of any Judge or Court thereof, anything in any Act of Congress to the contrary notwithstanding."

Now unless the writ of habeas corpus issued by the Judge of the District Court was necessary for the exercise of the jurisdiction of the said Court, or was to inquire into a commitment under, or by color of the authority of the United States, or to relieve some one imprisoned for an act done, or omitted to be done, in pursuance of a law of the United States, the District Court had no power to issue it, and a commitment for contempt in refusing to answer it, is an illegal imprisonment, which, under our habeas corpus act, we are imperatively required to set aside.

It cannot be pretended that the writ was either asked for or granted to inquire into any commitment made under, or by color of the authority of the United States, or to relieve from imprisonment for an act done or omitted to be done in pursuance of a law of the United States, and, therefore, we may confine our inquiry solely to the question whether it was necessary for the exercise of any jurisdiction given to the District Court of the United States for the Eastern District of Pennsylvania.

This brings us to the question of the jurisdiction of the Courts of the United States, and more particularly that of the District Court. And here, without desiring or intending to discuss at large the nature and powers of the Federal Government, it is proper to repeat what has been so often said, and what has never been denied, that it is a government of enumerated powers delegated to it by the several States, or the people thereof, without capacity to enlarge or extend the powers so delegated and enumerated, and that its Courts of Justice are Courts of limited jurisdiction, deriving their authority from the Constitution of the United States, and the acts of Congress under the Constitution. Let us see what judicial power was given by the people to the Federal Government, for that alone can be rightly exercised by its Courts.

" The judicial power," (says the second section of the third article) " shall extend to all cases in law and equity arising under this Constitution, the laws of the United States, and treaties made or which shall be made under their authority, to all cases affecting ambassadors, other public ministers and consuls, to all cases of admiralty and maritime jurisdiction; to controversies to which the United States shall be a party, to controversies between two or more States, between a State and a citizen of another State, between citizens of different States, between citizens of the same State claiming lands under grants of different States, and between a State or the citizens thereof and foreign States, citizens or subjects."

The amendments subsequently made to this article have no bearing upon the question under consideration, nor is it necessary to examine the various acts of Congress conferring jurisdiction upon the Courts of the United States, for no act of Congress can be found extending the jurisdiction beyond what is given by the Constitution, so far as relates to the question we are now considering. And if such an act should be passed, it would be in direct conflict with the 10th amended article of the Constitution, which declares that "the powers not delegated to the United States by the Constitution, nor prohibited by it to the States, are reserved to the States respectively or to the people."

If this case can be brought within the judicial power of the Courts of United States, it must be either

1st, Because it arises under the Constitution or the laws of the United States.

Or, 2d, Because it is a controversy between citizens of different States, for it is very plain that there is no other clause in the Constitution which, by the most latitudinarian construction, could be made to include it.

Did it arise under the Constitution or the laws of the United States? In order to give a satisfactory answer to this question, it is necessary to see what the case was.

If we confine ourselves strictly to the record from the District Court, we learn from it that on the 18th day of July last, John H. Wheeler presented his petition to the Hon. John K. Kane, Judge of the District Court for the Eastern District of Pennsylvania, setting forth that he was the owner of three persons held to service or labor, by the laws of the State of Virginia, said persons being respectively named Jane, aged about thirty-five years; Daniel, aged about twelve years, and Isaiah, aged about seven years; persons of color; and that they were detained from his possession by Passmore Williamson, but not for any criminal or supposed criminal matter. In accordance with the prayer of the petition, a writ of habeas corpus was awarded, commanding Passmore Williamson to bring the bodies of the said Jane, Daniel and Isaiah, before the Judge of the District Court forthwith. To this writ Passmore

Williamson made a return, verified by his affirmation, that the said Jane, Daniel and Isaiah, nor either of them, were at the time of the issuing of the writ, nor at the time of the return, nor at any other time, in the custody, power or possession of, nor confined, nor restrained their liberty by him ; and that, therefore, he could not produce the bodies as he was commanded.

This return was made on the 20th day of July, A. D. 1855. "Whereupon, afterwards, to wit : on the 27th day of July, A. D. 1855, (says the record,) the counsel for the several parties having been heard, and the said return having been duly considered, it is ordered and adjudged by the Court, that the said Passmore Williamson be committed to the custody of the Marshal, without bail or mainprize, as for a contempt in refusing to make return to the writ of habeas corpus, heretofore issued against him, at the instance of Mr. John H. Wheeler."

Such is the record. Now whilst I am willing to admit that the want of jurisdiction should be made clear, I deny that in a case under our habeas corpus act the party averring want of jurisdiction cannot go behind the record to establish its non-existence. Jurisdiction, or the absence thereof, is a mixed question of law and fact. It is the province of fact to ascertain what the case is, and of law to determine whether the jurisdiction attaches to the case so ascertained. And says the 2d section of our act of 1785, "and that the said judge or justice may, according to the intent and meaning of this act, be enabled by investigating the truth of the circumstances of the case, to determine whether, according to law, the said prisoner ought to be bailed, remanded or discharged, the return may, before or after it is filed, by leave of the said judge or justice, be amended, and also suggestions made against it, so that thereby material facts may be ascertained."

This provision applies to cases of commitment or detainer for any criminal or supposed criminal matter, but the 14th section, which applies to cases of restraint of liberty "under any color or pretence whatsoever," provides that "the court, judge or justice, before whom the party so confined or restrained shall be brought, shall, after the return made proceed in the same manner as is hereinbefore prescribed to examine into the facts relating to the case, and into the cause of such confinement or restraint, and thereupon either bail, remand, or discharge the party so brought, as to justice shall appertain."

The right and duty of the Supreme Court of a State to protect a citizen thereof from imprisonment by a Judge of a United States Court having no jurisdiction over the cause of complaint, is so manifest and so essentially necessary under our dual system of government, that I cannot believe that this right will ever be abandoned or the duty avoided; but, if we concede, what appears to be the law of the later cases in the Federal Courts, that the jurisdiction need not appear affirmatively, and add to it that the want of jurisdiction shall not be proved by evidence outside of the record, we do virtually deny to the people of the State the right to question the validity of an order by a Federal Judge consigning them to the walls of a prison "without bail or mainprize."

What mockery to say to one restrained of his liberty, "True, if the Judge or Court under whose order you are in prison, acted without jurisdiction, you are entitled to be discharged, but the burthen is upon you to show that there was no jurisdiction, and in showing this we will not permit you to go beyond the record made up by the party against whom you complain."

As the Petitioner would be legally entitled, upon the return of the writ, to establish the truth of the facts set forth in his petition, so far as they bear upon the question of jurisdiction, we are bound, before the return, to assume that the facts are true as stated, and so taking them, the case is this:

John H. Wheeler voluntarily brought into the State of Pennsylvania three persons of color, held by him, in the State of Virginia, as slaves, with the intention of passing through this State. Whilst on board of a steamboat, near Walnut street wharf, in the city of Philadelphia, the Petitioner, Passmore Williamson, informed the mother that she was free by the laws of Pennsylvania, who, in the language of the petition, "expressed her desire to have her freedom, and finally, with her children, left the boat of her own free will and accord, and without coercion or compulsion of any kind; and having seen her in possession of her liberty with her children, your Petitioner (says the petition) returned to his place of business, and has never since seen the said Jane, Daniel and Isaiah, or either of them, nor does he know where they are, nor has he had any connection of any kind with the subject."

One owning slaves in a slave State voluntarily brings them into a free State with the intention of passing through the free State. Whilst there, upon being told that they are free, the slaves leave their master. Can a Judge of the District Court of the United States compel their restoration through the medium of habeas corpus directed to the person by whom they were informed of their freedom? Or, in other words, is it a case arising under the Constitution of the United States?

What article or section of the Constitution has any bearing upon the right of a master to pass through a free State with his slave or slaves? Or, when has Congress ever attempted to legislate upon this question?

6

I most unhesitatingly aver that neither in the Constitution of the United States nor in the acts of Congress can there be found a sentence which has any effect upon this question whatever. It is a question to be decided by the laws of the State where the person is for the time being, and that law must be determined by the Judges of the State, who have sworn to support the Constitution of the State as well as that of the United States—an oath which is never taken by a Federal Judge.

Upon this question of jurisdiction it is wholly immaterial whether by the law of Pennsylvania a slaveholder has or has not the right of passing through our State with his slaves. If he has the right, it is not in virtue of the Constitution or laws of the United States, but by the law of the State, and if no such right exists, it is because the State law has forbidden it, or has failed to recognise it. It is for the State alone to legislate upon this subject, and there is no power on earth to call her to an account for her acts of omission or commission in this behalf.

If this case could, by any reasonable construction, be brought within the terms of the third clause of the second section of Article Four of the Constitution of the United States, jurisdiction might be claimed for the Federal Courts, as then it would be a case arising under the Constitution of the United States, although I believe the writ of habeas corpus is no part of the machinery designed by Congress for the rendition of fugitives from labor.

"No person (says the clause above mentioned) held to service or labor in one State, under the laws thereof, escaping into another, shall, in consequence of any law or regulation therein, be discharged from such service or labor, but shall be delivered up on claim of the party to whom such service or labor may be due." By reference to the debates in the Convention it will be seen that this clause was inserted at the request of delegates from Southern States, and upon the declaration that in the absence of a constitutional provision the right of reclamation would not exist, unless given by State authority. If it had been intended to cover the right of transit, words would have been used evidencing such intention. Happily, there is no contrariety in the construction which has been placed upon this clause of the Constitution. No Judge has ever so manifestly disregarded its plain and unequivocal language as to hold that it applies to a slave voluntarily brought into a free State by his master. Upon the contrary, there is abundant authority that such a case is not within either the letter or the spirit of the constitutional provision for the rendition of fugitives from labor. Mr. Justice Washington, in ex parte Simmons, 6 W. C. C. Reports, 396, said:

"The slave in this case having been voluntarily brought by his master into this State, I have no cognizance of the case, so far as respects this application, and the master must abide by the laws of this State, so far as they may affect his right. If the man claimed as a slave be not entitled to his freedom under the laws of this State, the master must pursue such remedy for his recovery as the laws of the State have provided for him."

In Jones vs. Vanzandt, 5 Howard, 229, Mr. Justice Woodbury uses language equally expressive : " But the power of national law (said that eminent jurist) to pursue and regain most kinds of property in the limits of a foreign government is rather an act of comity than strict right, and hence as property in persons might not thus be recognised in some of the States in the Union, and its reclamation not be allowed through either courtesy or right, this clause was undoubtedly introduced into the Constitution as one of its compromises for the safety of that portion of the Union which did permit such property, and which otherwise might often be deprived of it entirely by its merely crossing the line of an adjoining State ; this was thought to be too harsh a doctrine in respect to any title to property of a friendly neighbor, not brought nor placed in another State under State laws by the owner himself, but escaping there against his consent, and often forthwith pursued in order to be reclaimed."

Other authorities might be quoted to the same effect, but it is unnecessary, for if it be not clear that one voluntarily brought into a State is not a fugitive, no judicial language can ever make it so. Will we then, for the sake of sustaining this jurisdiction, presume that these slaves of Mr. Wheeler escaped from Virginia into Pennsylvania, when no such allegation was made in his petition ; when it is expressly stated in the petition of Mr. Williamson, verified by his affirmation, that they were brought here voluntarily by their master; and when this fact is virtually conceded by the Judge of the District Court in his Opinion ? Great as is my respect for the judicial authority of the Federal Government, I cannot consent to stultify myself in order to sustain their unauthorised judgments, and more particularly where, as in the case before us, it would be at the expense of the liberty of a citizen of this Commonwealth.

The only remaining ground upon which this jurisdiction can be claimed, is that it was in a controversy between citizens of different States, and I shall dismiss this branch of the case simply by affirming, first, that the proceeding by habeas corpus is, in no legal sense, a controversy between private parties ; and 2d, if it were, to the Circuit Court alone is given this jurisdiction. For the correctness of the first position I refer to the opinion of Mr. Justice Baldwin, in Holmes vs. Jennifer, published

in the appendix to 14 Peters, and to that of Judge Betts, of the Circuit
Court of New York, in Barry vs. Mercein et al., reported in 5th Howard,
103. And for the second, to the 11th section of the Judiciary Act,
passed on the 24th of September, 1789.

My view of this case had been committed to writing before I had seen
or heard the·opinion of the majority of the Court. Having heard it
hastily read but once, I may mistake its purport, but if I do not, it places
the refusal of the habeas corpus mainly upon the ground that the conviction for contempt was a separate proceeding, and that, as the District
Court had jurisdiction to punish for contempts, we have no power to review its decision. Or, as it appears from the record that the prisoner
is in custody upon a conviction for contempt, we are powerless to grant
him relief.

Notwithstanding the numerous cases that are cited to sustain this position, it appears to me to be as novel as it is dangerous. Every court of
justice in this country has, in some degree, the power to commit for contempt. Can it be possible that a citizen once committed for contempt
is beyond the hope of relief, even although the record shows that the
alleged contempt was not within the power of the Court to punish summarily? Suppose that the Judge of the District Court should send to
prison an editor of a newspaper for a contempt of his Court in commenting upon his decision in this very case; would the prisoner be beyond
the reach of our writ of habeas corpus? If he would, our boasted
security of personal liberty is in truth an idle boast; and our constitutional guaranties and writs of right are as ropes of sand. But in the
name of the law, I aver that no such power exists with any Court or
Judge, State or Federal, and if it is attempted to be exercised, there are
modes of relief, full and ample, for the exigency of the occasion.

I have not had either time or opportunity to examine all of the cases
cited, but, as far as I have examined them, they decide this and nothing
more—that where a Court of competent jurisdiction convicts one of a
contempt, another Court, without appellate power, will not re-examine
the case to determine whether a contempt was really committed or not.
The history of punishments for contempts of Court, and the legislative
action thereon, both in our State and Union, in an unmistakeable manner
teaches, first, the liability of this power to be abused; and second, the
promptness with which its unguarded use has been followed by legislative restrictions. It is no longer an undefined, unlimited power of a star
chamber character, to be used for the oppression of the citizen at the
mere caprice of the Judge, or Court, but it has its boundaries so dis-

tinctly defined that there is no mistaking the extent to which our tribunals of law may go in punishing for this offence.

In the words of the act of Congress of 3d March, 1831, "The power of the several Courts of the United States to issue attachments and inflict summary punishment for contempts of Court, shall not be construed toe xtend to any cases except the misbehaviour of any person or persons in the presence of said Courts, or so near thereto as to obstruct the administration of justice, the misbehaviour of any of the officers of the said Courts in their official transactions, and the disobedience or resistance by any officer of the said Courts, party, juror, witness or any other person or persons, to any *lawful* writ, process, order, rule, decree, or command of said Courts."

Now Passmore Williamson was convicted of a contempt for disobeying a writ of habeas corpus commanding him to produce before the District Court certain persons claimed by Mr. Wheeler as slaves. Was it a lawful writ? Clearly not, if the Court had no jurisdiction to issue it; and that it had not, I think is very plain. If it was unlawful, the person to whom it was directed was not bound to obey it; and, in the very words of the statute, the power for contempt "shall not be construed to extend to it."

But, says the opinion of the majority, he was convicted of a contempt of Court, and we will not look into the record to see how the contempt was committed. I answer this by asserting that you cannot see the conviction without seeing the cause, for it is a part of the same record which consists, 1st, of the petition; 2d, the writ and alias writ of habeas corpus; 3d, the return, and 4th, the judgment. "It is ordered and adjudged by the Court that the said Passmore Williamson be committed to the custody of the Marshal without bail or mainprize, as for a contempt in refusing to make return to the writ of habeas corpus heretofore issued against him at the instance of Mr. John H. Wheeler." As I understand the opinion of a majority of my brethren, as soon as we get to the word contempt the book must be closed, and it becomes instantly sealed as to the residue of the record. To sustain this commitment we must, it seems, first presume, in the very teeth of the admitted fact, that these were runaway slaves; and second, we must be careful to read only portions of the record, lest we should find that the prisoner was committed for refusing to obey an unlawful writ.

I cannot forbear the expression of the opinion that the rule laid down in this case, by the majority, is fraught with great danger to the most cherished rights of the citizens of the State. Whilst in contests involving the right of property merely, I presume we may still treat the judg-

ments of the United States Courts in cases not within their jurisdiction,
as nullities, yet, if a single Judge thinks proper to determine that one
of our citizens has been guilty of contempt, even if such determination
had its foundation in a case upon which the Judge had no power to pronounce judgment, and was most manifestly in direct violation of the
solemn act of the very legislative authority that created the Court over
which the Judge presides, it seems that such determination is to have
all the force and effect of a judgment pronounced by a Court of competent jurisdiction, acting within the admitted sphere of its constitutional
power. Nay, more. We confess ourselves powerless to protect our
citizens from the aggressions of a Court, as foreign from our State
government in matters not committed to its jurisdiction as the Court of
Queen's Bench, in England, and this upon the authority of decisions
pronounced in cases not at all analogous to the one now under consideration. I believe this to be the first recorded case where the Supreme
Court of a State has refused the prayer of a citizen for the writ of habeas
corpus, to inquire into the legality of an imprisonment by a Judge of a
Federal Court for contempt, in refusing obedience to a writ void for want
of jurisdiction.

I will conclude by recapitulating the grounds upon which I think this
writ should be awarded.

1st. At common law, and by our statute of 1785, the writ of habeas
corpus *ad subjiciendum* is a writ of right demandable whenever a petition in due form asserts what, if true, would entitle the party to relief.

2d. That an allegation in a petition that the Petitioner is restrained
of his liberty by an order of a Judge or Court without jurisdiction, shows
such probable cause as to leave it no longer discretionary with the Court
or Judge to whom application is made, whether the writ shall or shall
not issue.

3d. That where a person is imprisoned by an order of a Judge of the
District Court of the United States, for refusing to answer a writ of
habeas corpus, he is entitled to be discharged from such imprisonment,
if the judge of the District Court had no authority to issue the writ

4th. That the power to issue writs of habeas corpus by the judges of
the Federal Courts is a mere auxiliary power, and that no such writ can
be issued by such judges where the cause of complaint intended to be
remedied by it is beyond their jurisdiction.

5th. That the Courts of the Federal Government are Courts of limited
jurisdiction, derived from the Constitution of the United States, and the
acts of Congress under the Constitution, and that, where the jurisdiction

is not given by the Constitution, or by Congress in pursuance of the Constitution, it does not exist.

6th. That when it does not appear by the record, that the Court had jurisdiction in a proceeding under our habeas corpus act to relieve from an illegal imprisonment, want of jurisdiction may be shown by proving the facts of the case.

7th. That where the inquiry as to the jurisdiction of a Court arises upon a rule for a habeas corpus, all the facts set forth in the petition tending to show the want of jurisdiction are to be considered as true, unless they contradict the record.

8th. That when the owner of a slave voluntarily brings his slave from a slave to a free State, without any intention of remaining therein, the right of the slave to his freedom depends upon the law of the State into which he is thus brought.

9th. That if a slave so brought into a free State escapes from the custody of his master while in said State, the right of the master to reclaim him is not a question arising under the Constitution of the United States or the laws thereof, and therefore a Judge of the United States cannot issue a writ of habeas corpus directed to one who, it is alleged, withholds the possession of the slave from the master, commanding him to produce the body of the slave before the said Judge.

10th. That the District Court of the United States for the Eastern District of Pennsylvania has no jurisdiction, because a controversy is between citizens of different States, and that a proceeding by habeas corpus is, in no legal sense, a controversy between private parties.

11th. That the power of the several courts of the United States to inflict summary punishment for contempt of Court in disobeying a writ of the Court, is expressly confined to cases of disobedience to lawful writs.

12th. That where it appears from the record that the conviction was for disobeying a writ of habeas corpus, which writ the Court had no jurisdiction to issue, the conviction is *coram non judice*, and void.

For these reasons I do most respectfully but most earnestly dissent from the judgment of the majority of my brethren, refusing the writ applied for.

On the 20th day of September, 1855, the following opinion of Justice Lowrie appeared in the Philadelphia newspapers as having been filed in Court.

OPINION OF JUSTICE LOWRIE.

After the argument of this motion for a habeas corpus, I wrote an opinion which I expected to deliver; but, on further consultation with my brethren, and fuller reflection on the subject, I became convinced that it was partly erroneous. This prevented me from delivering my views when the case was decided, and I do it now, avoiding as much as possible any unnecessary repetition of what has already been said by others.

I have not been able to doubt that this Court is, in many cases, bound to exercise its judgment as to the propriety of granting the writ before allowing it to issue. Notwithstanding the words of the act which impose a penalty for refusing the writ, we are not forbidden to interpret the law; and the necessity of presenting a petition to the Court or to a Judge thereof, of stating therein whether the prisoner was detained on criminal or on civil process, or neither, of producing the warrant of committal or accounting for not doing so, and the fact that traitors and murderers, and fugitives from the justice of other States, are excluded from the benefit of the act, and that the writ was not intended for the relief of convict criminals, (Cro. Car. 168. 1 Salk. 348,) and was not extended to them by our act; all these matters show plainly enough that the judge or Court is not exercising a mere ministerial function in granting the writ. On any other supposition, there is no reason at all for applying to the Court, for the prothonotary could grant it as well.

And no one can examine the provisions of magna charta, the petition of right, 3 Charles 1, the statute repealing the Starchamber Court, 16 Ch. 1, c. 10; the habeas corpus act of 31 Ch. 1, and ours of 1785, and the numerous kindred statutes to which that investigation will lead him, without perceiving that a free and open Court, and a full and open trial before the superior judges by due course of law, have always been regarded as the best guaranty of the liberty of the citizen. He will see, moreover, very plainly, that the habeas corpus is only a means by which this end is to be secured, so that no ignorance or tyranny of king, or king's council or minister, or of mere local and inferior Courts, dependent on and governed by local customs, or of justices of the peace, shall imprison a man without a chance of bail, or a hope of obtaining a speedy trial by the law of the land.

The habeas corpus was not intended, and could not be intended, to authorize the superior judges, being substantially those of the higher Courts of record, to interfere with the jurisdiction of each other. The purpose of the writ was satisfied when the jurisdiction of the superior Courts attached, for the State could not know any better means of securing a fair and impartial trial. If that, with the ordinary provisions for the correction of errors, was not sufficient, then humanity has only to acknowledge its incapacity to provide entirely against error and injustice. Certainly the habeas corpus was not intended to provide a remedy against the unjust judgments or sentences of the higher Courts, and when it is asked for, for such a purpose, it ought to be refused; unless, possibly, when it is asked from a Court that may officially revise and correct the proceedings, 7 Pet. 572. Cro. Car. 175. 1 Mod. 119. 11 Queen's B. 566. 5 Com. B. 418. 1 B. & C. 655.

But even if our habeas corpus act of 1785 did mean to say that the writ shall always be granted when prayed for, it could not be obeyed so far as to conflict with the new order of things introduced in 1787 by the Constitution of the United States. Hence originated other and independent jurisdictions, with which our habeas corpus act was not intended to interfere, for when it was passed it could have no reference to them. How far it can be used in paralyzing those jurisdictions, or subjecting them to those of the States, is proper matter to be decided on the presentation of the petition, or on the return of the writ, as the Court may think proper. We saw such difficulties as led us to hear an argument from the Petitioner's counsel on the presentation of the petition, and still our difficulties have not been removed.

But I have a very strong impression, that no Court is justified in issuing a habeas corpus for the purpose of restoring a slave to his master; and that is very plainly the purpose for which the writ was issued out of the District Court. I do not think that our writ has any such purpose, or ever had. It was intended to secure the liberty of the subject, and not to try rights of property. It is sometimes used to obtain the custody of children; but then it proceeds upon the principle that children are restrained of their liberty who are in a custody that is disapproved of by their lawful guardians. Arrived at years of discretion, the writ is not used to retain them in an unwilling subjection. It is not usually allowed in order to recover the possession of an apprentice, as such; 5 East, 38; 6 Term R., 497; 7 Id., 741; 11 Mass., 63.

The common law of England, as it was when Pennsylvania was settled, could not have allowed a habeas corpus for the purpose of enforcing slavery, for it did not recognise such an institution. The common law remedy, for trying the title to a feudal villein, was the writ *de homine repligiando*, and that was the writ used by us in slave cases;

323

2 Dall., 56; 3 Binn., 101; 3 S. & R., 396; 7 Id., 299. And this application of the habeas corpus is, to my mind, seriously startling.

I have, moreover, a very strong impression that there is no way in which the case before the District Judge can be regarded that would entitle the Federal Judiciary to take cognizance of it; but I will not trouble any one with my reasons for this.

Regarding the matter thus, it seemed to me that there was real merit in the claim that the Petitioner should be discharged; and I did not see any very satisfactory reason in opposition to our hearing and deciding the case; and therefore I was willing to grant the writ and hear the other side. I was very strongly impressed by the argument that the District Judge exceeded his authority in entertaining the case; and that the Supreme Court of the State has power, on a habeas corpus, to discharge the prisoner; especially considering that this Court is one of general jurisdiction, and part of a government of general powers; whereas the District Court belongs to a government of limited powers, and necessarily partakes of the same character. But this proposition involves consequences so grave, in theory at least, and principles so essential to political order, that it ought not to be readily admitted.

We may first set aside the consideration that the Federal Courts are of limited jurisdiction; for even conceding that they are, it does not follow that we may review and restrain them in the exercise of it. To use this as a reason for treating their acts as void, when we think them unauthorized, is to apply an English reason to an American institution, without any resemblances sufficient to make the application legitimate. The English superior Courts might have had very good reasons for treating all the unauthorized acts of their inferior tribunals as void, in order to keep them within their proper limits. But we cannot so treat the United States Courts; for, in the English sense, they, too, are superior Courts, and especially they are not subordinate to us.

The proposition then remains that, whenever any of the public tribunals of the United States exceed the jurisdiction, which, under the Constitution, can be given to them, and, in doing so, a citizen is arrested or imprisoned, then our habeas corpus is a proper and effectual remedy.

If this is so, then certainly there are places where the Courts of the United States can have but little power for any purpose. Any man, arrested or imprisoned by warrant, or execution, or sentence from District, Circuit, or Supreme Court, or either House of Congress, may have relief from any friendly County Judge wielding the power of the habeas corpus. A Judge impeached, convicted and sentenced, a traitor tried and condemned, may still have hopes from the habeas corpus, if a Judge can be found, ignorant, or insubordinate, or degraded enough to declare that his superiors acted without jurisdiction.

And since the force of the argument does not at all depend upon any peculiar virtue in the habeas corpus, but simply on the supposed want of jurisdiction in the federal tribunals, we may apply it to all cases. Then we may have summary replevins and ejectments, and prohibitions, and injunctions, and attachments to support them, heard and decided by single judges, or even commissioners or justices of the peace, everywhere and without review, for the purpose of testing the validity of the judgments of the United States tribunals, and the constitutionality of federal tax laws and tariffs, and the frustration of disagreeable laws, become perfectly simple and regular.

And if we should do this in any honest belief in its political rightness, we should, of course, be willing to have the same principle applied in reference to our own official system. Then habeas corpus would stand as a writ designed to set aside all official order, and to place single judges above the very tribunals of which they are members.

On one occasion the laws of the United States were attempted to be thus summarily set aside, and to prevent it the force bill, 2 Mar., 1833, s. 7, P. Laws, p. 51, declared that habeas corpus out of the U. S. Courts, shall relieve any person confined by any authority, for acts done in pursuance of any order or decree of a U. S. Court. This is not a strange way of protecting one court against the encroachments of another; 1 Rolle, 315, 2 Chit. G. Pr., 317, 1 Mad. Ch. Pr., 135. And it is certainly most effectual, for it would protect the Marshal in disobeying an order by us to discharge the prisoner; and thus, it very plainly forbids us to discharge him. If, in this law, there is any encroachment upon State rights, it is no more than might have been expected at the time, for the cause of freedom always suffers from the restrictions that become necessary, in order to suppress disorder, whether that disorder arises from mere vice or from an over-zealous urging of principles and institutions that are supposed to be good.

If it be meant that the Supreme Court has a peculiar authority to interfere in such cases, I have failed to discover whence it arises. The habeas corpus act makes no distinction between the different Courts and Judges who may exercise the powers given, and I do not see how we can make any, except that which is necessarily involved in the principle of subordination.

All the institutions of the same government, however complex, are intended to be in harmony with each other, and unitedly to aid in the preservation of order. It is therefore the duty of all public officers to avoid, if possible, all conflict of functions in the execution of their offices, and to follow the principles that provide for this result. The most obvious of these is, that co-ordinate tribunals cannot interfere with each other, nor inferior with superior ones. Without this rule, government would be a mere mob of officials, wanting an essential element of unity, and would soon fall to pieces. Without this, the habeas corpus law would set aside all order, by allowing the lowest of all subordinate Judges to annul, on constitutional grounds, the judgments of every Court in the State, even the very highest; and such apparently gross insubordination would be a mere error in judgment, and not an impeachable offence.

The Supreme Court of the State is in no sense the official superior of any of the United States Courts, but co-ordinate with them all. We are not set as checks upon each other, and cannot directly review each other's decisions in any matter. Each of us occupies a different position in our compound system of government, and each of us must answer to our official or political superiors. This Court is not set to watch over the Federal Courts and suspect them of excess of jurisdiction; and we should be ourselves disorderly, if we should assume any control over them, set as co-ordinate tribunals upon an entirely separate foundation. No one will pretend that our writ of prohibition would be of any value there, and hence it is plain that we cannot interfere without disorder.

Like most other writs, habeas corpus must be more efficacious in the hands of a superior Court than of any subordinate one; for the law of order requires that those who are officially equal, shall not sit in review of each other's acts. The cases that illustrate this are very numerous, declaring that the superior Courts of law and equity cannot interfere with each other; that the regular Courts cannot interfere with the sentences for contempt and breach of privilege, by the Senate or House of Representatives, House of Lords, or House of Commons. Where the duty of final decision, and the whole control of any matter is given to one set of officers, the interference of others is mere usurpation. And here I may remark, that a sentence for contempt is not essentially different from any other judgment, decree or sentence. It is a matter adjudicated, and it belongs to the very essence of governmental order, that it cannot be reviewed except by the Court that pronounced it, or by its official superiors; and, therefore, in this instance, not by us.

It is insisted that this sentence, being in excess of authority, is void, and we are asked to declare it so. Without stopping to notice the habitual misapplication of this word, *void*, to all acts of public authority which are made the subject of an opposing criticism, I may say that it is a plain solecism thus to qualify any act that is so efficient of results. A sentence, by which a man is committed to prison and held there, cannot be void. If we wish to treat the subject profitably, we must speak of it more accurately.

Is it meant to say that we must, on habeas corpus, inquire whether a Court legitimately established has rightly decided the question of its jurisdiction? Substantially this is the same objection that we have already considered. If it is well founded, then it applies to all sorts of cases; for the question of jurisdiction is involved in them all; every judgment rendered is an assertion of the jurisdiction of the Court that renders it. If the allegation of want of jurisdiction entitles us to review it, then there are but few cases in the Federal Courts that are beyond the interference of the State Courts, if a defendant desires to have it.

The superior Courts in England may treat as void the unauthorized acts of *their* inferiors, and be justified by the peculiarities of their system and the fact of their superiority; but they could not, with propriety, so treat each other. Their practice relative to each other never contained such an element of disorder. A party summoned to answer, is bound to obey, or give a good reason for not doing so. He cannot treat public authority with contempt. If he thinks that the Court lacks jurisdiction, a decent respect for public order requires him to appear and raise the question, so that it may be decided in an orderly way. He need not raise it in order to insure his right to the objection in a Court of error, but it may be necessary in order to stop the unauthorized process. Judges cannot keep all the law in their minds, and parties are heard in order that they may insist upon every principle that is in their favor. It would be very disorderly for defendants to hold back an objection to the jurisdiction of the Court, and then raise it by rebellion against the public authorities when the writ of the Commonwealth comes to be executed; and habeas corpus would be a most disorderly writ, if it could be thus used in contempt of authority.

Government consists of fallible men, who do not always know their duty; and parties may lose some of their rights, if they do not aid the public officers, by notifying them of their views, and urging them; and questions of jurisdiction are very often as difficult to decide as any other. It is an essential element of Government that it must be the judge of its own jurisdiction; and I do not know that this rule is pecu liarly applicable to the higher Courts. The lowest must act upon it, subject to the higher social law that is involved in official subordina tion. Often the question may be erroneously decided. Often such decisions may result in great injury to the citizen : but it is the lot of Government to err, because it is human, and a man of well-trained mind will think it no great hardship to submit to authority even in error.   In the name of order, the country demands, and has a right to demand it.

It is usual to say, even of foreign judgments, that, if pronounced by a competent tribunal and carried into effect without our assistance, they are conclusive of the question decided.   And here " competent tribunal" means one of the regularly established Courts of the country and in it.   If its government could, according to the law of nations, have jurisdiction of such a case, we concede to the Court itself to decide upon its own jurisdiction; 4 Cranch, 276; 1 Rawle, 389; for we are not interested in the manner in which other States distribute their civil functions among their different departments.

Applying this principle here, our interference is certainly excluded. Not that the United States is a foreign country, but that its Courts belong to a different system from the State Courts, and thus these respective authorities are, as authorities, foreign to each other.   Each must respond to its own superiors; neither can call the other officially to account.   I speak not here of the action for damages for excess of authority.   True enough, we do thus leave the Federal Government at liberty to make continual encroachments upon State rights, without being responsible therefor to any organized power; but this cannot be avoided.   There can be no organized authority superior to government itself.   However we may define its functions, itself must interpret them, subject only to the right of the people to give new instructions.   It must be so with every government.   Manufacture and repair constitutions and bills of rights as we may ; multiply checks and restrictions upon official functions as we may, we cannot shut out human error and its consequences, which are sometimes distressing—while we may carry our suspicions of government so far as to take away its real efficiency, as a means of preserving social order; and then we shall reject it as totally worthless, and the circumstances of its rejection must give the form to its successor.

In civil matters there can be no moral principle of higher importance than the one that is most deeply involved in this case—the principle of social order.   It is a principle of action that is as binding on the conscience as any other.   It is the great moral principle of social man. Without it we must endanger and retard our social progress.   Without it we confound all official subordination, and infect with disease the very organs of social life.   This principle expresses itself, as best it can, in our civil institutions, and thus originating, they are morally entitled to our respect and obedience, imperfect as we may suppose them to be. He that rejects this principle from his moral code, or gives it a low place there, can hardly be an orderly citizen; but must be dangerous to the public peace and progress, in proportion as he is otherwise intelligent, influential and active. If the Supreme Court, as the highest impersonation of the judicial order of the State, should set aside this principle, there can be no guaranty for the healthy administration of our social system. In the name of the order which we represent and enforce, I decline any and every usurpation of power or control over the United States Judiciary; it being a system, collateral to ours, as complete and efficient in its organization, and as legitimate and final an authority as any other. I concur in refusing the writ.

Afterwards to wit on the 17th of October, 1855, the following motion was made and affidavit presented to the Court.

> *U. S. ex rel. Wheeler*
> vs.
> *Williamson.*
> } District Court U. S.

Oct. 17, 1855. E. HOPPER and C. GILPIN move the Court for leave to file of record in this case an affidavit of respondent.

COPY OF AFFIDAVIT.

> *United States ex rel. John II. Wheeler*
> vs.
> *Williamson.*
> } In the D. C. of the U. States for the E. D. of Pa. Habeas Corpus.

Passmore Williamson being duly affirmed, saith, that on the eighteenth day of July last past, at or about five o'clock in the afternoon, the said Jane, Daniel and Isaiah in the writ mentioned, left Dock Street, in a carriage, but affirmant did not then know in whose company, nor has he any knowledge now of the persons who accompanied them, other than from newspaper publications. That since the said time when the said Jane, Daniel and Isaiah left Dock Street in a carriage as aforesaid, this affirmant has not seen them or either of them; nor has he communicated or corresponded with them or either of them directly or indirectly; nor has he had the custody or possession of, or had or exercised any power or control over them or either of them directly or indirectly; nor has he confined or restrained them or either of them of their liberty directly or indirectly; nor has he known that any person has had the custody, power over or possession of them or of either of them, or confined or restrained them or either of them of their liberty; nor has he had any knowledge of what became of them after the time before stated, other than from the newspapers and statements therein read by him, or reported orally to him. This affirmant further saith that the facts stated are just and true to the best of his knowledge, recollection, information and belief, and further this affirmant knoweth not and saith not.

P. WILLIAMSON.

Affirmed and subscribed before me the 16th day of October, A. D. 1855.

CHAS. F. HEAZLITT,
U. S. Commissioner.

Judge KANE said: "It seems to us that this should come in the form of a petition; but we will grant a rule to show cause why the affidavit should not be read and filed."

Mr. GILPIN. After the intimation from the Court as to the form the application should take, counsel do not desire a rule to show cause, but ask the Court to act on the motion as presented.

The Court did not act on the motion, but virtually and substantially refused it, by turning to the Court officer and directing him to call the Jury in another case.

On the 22d of Oct. 1855, the following motion was made and petition presented to Judge Kane.

U. S. ex rel. Wheeler
    vs.   } Dist. Court, U. S. E. D. Pa.
Williamson.

Oct. 22d 1855   E. HOPPER, C. GILPIN and MEREDITH move the Court for leave to present and file of record in the case a petition of the respondent.

COPY OF PETITION.

U. S. ex rel. Wheeler } District Court, U. S. East District of Pa.
    vs.   Habeas Corpus.
Williamson.

The petition of Passmore Williamson respectfully represents, that on the eighteenth day of July last past, at or about five o'clock in the afternoon, the said Jane, Daniel and Isaiah in the writ mentioned, left Dock Street in a carriage, but the Petitioner did not then know in whose company, nor has he any knowledge now of the persons who accompanied them, other than from newspaper publications. That since the said time when the said Jane, Daniel and Isaiah left Dock Street in a carriage as aforesaid, the Petitioner has not seen them or either of them; nor has he communicated or corresponded with them or either of them directly or indirectly; nor has he had the custody and possession of or had or exercised any power or control over them or either of them directly or indirectly; nor has he confined or restrained them or either of them of their liberty directly or indirectly; nor has he known that any person has had the custody, power over or possession of them or of either of them, or confined or restrained them or either of them of their liberty; nor has he had any knowledge of what became of them after the time before stated, other than from the newspapers and statements therein read by him or reported orally to him; and further the Petitioner knoweth not.

That the Petitioner has been imprisoned in Moyamensing Prison under an order of this Honorable Court, as for a contempt, in this case, since the twenty seventh day of July last past; and while he respectfully protests against the proceedings of the Court in the premises, and against the jurisdiction of the Court in the case, or of the subject matter thereof, he prays to be discharged from the further custody of the marshal.

P. WILLIAMSON.

Eastern District of Pennsylvania.

Passmore Williamson being duly affirmed says that the facts stated in the foregoing petition are just and true to the best of his knowledge, recollection, information and belief.

P. WILLIAMSON.

Affirmed and subscribed before me the 19th day of October A. D. 1855.

CHAS. F. HEAZLITT.
U. S. Commissioner.

On the 26th of October, 1855, upon notice to J. A. VANDYKE, Esq., an argument was heard on the foregoing motion and petition.

DISTRICT COURT OF THE UNITED STATES.

In and for the Eastern District of Pennsylvania, October 26th, 1855.

JUDGE KANE PRESIDING.

The Crier opened Court at 10 o'clock, A. M.

Mr. HOPPER. If the Court please, I expect my colleague, Mr. MEREDITH, here in a moment.

In order to comply with strict form, we have made an application to

7

the Marshal for the bill of costs in the present case, which we are prepared to pay ; and the Marshal has informed us that whatever the counsel for the Petitioner shall consider proper will be perfectly satisfactory to him.

Judge KANE. Does that connect itself in any way with the motion you propose making?

Mr. HOPPER. It may form part of the case, and we wish to conform strictly to the precedents.

Judge KANE. But that is not the question I wish to have argued. ·I do not wish to hear that.

(Judge KANE to Mr. GILPIN who had arrived at this moment.) I was about remarking to Mr. Hopper that it is not the right of petition that I request to have argued : I have no doubt on that subject at all. The question is, whether I can receive any communication from a party who is in contempt, which does not, primarily, seek to absolve him from the contempt. That is the simple question.

Mr. HOPPER. That is the petition which we moved, and we will present the specific paper which will bring up the matters upon which the Court desires to hear argument.

Judge KANE. I know nothing of the petition, but the simple question; but, (irrespective of the paper which I do not wish to see unless upon the announcement of counsel as to its tenor and effect,) I put myself in the position of a Court that cannot hear an application from a party in contempt, except to absolve himself from that contempt. That is the question.

Mr. HOPPER. I understand that to be the question, and it is for the counsel to narrow themselves to that point.

(Mr. MEREDITH arrives at this moment.)

Mr. GILPIN (to the Court.) Is your honor ready to proceed ?

Judge KANE. I am ready Sir, but Mr. Meredith was not here when I last spoke.

I understand that there is an application, by petition to me, in the name of Passmore Williamson, and in his behalf, which petition is not an application to relieve himself from contempt.

Mr. MEREDITH. Well, Sir, I feel at a loss to assent to that proposition or to say what it is ; because it is rather a delicate matter to put a construction on a petition before it is heard.

Judge KANE. I have a right to ask, as it seems to me, Mr. Meredith. that counsel, before presenting a petition, shall announce its import.

Mr. MEREDITH. Undoubtedly, Sir, and I did, the other day, announce its import, and the view which I take of the subject ; and I think th..:

I am prepared to show that it is the kind of petition that you speak of.

Judge KANE. That it is a petition to relieve himself from the contempt, and submit himself to the Court?

Mr. MEREDITH. I conceive it to be of that import, but I understood your honor somewhat differently the other day.

Judge KANE. On the contrary. Let us not be misunderstood. I am sure that we misunderstand each other unintentionally, and with an anxious wish to understand each other.

Mr. MEREDITH. I am sure of that, Sir.

Judge KANE. I am prepared to receive an application from Passmore Williamson, the party in contempt of this Court, to relieve himself from the contempt by purgation. I am of opinion, until otherwise instructed, that that is the indispensable preliminary to any other application from him. If, therefore, the learned counsel rise before me to present an application from Mr. Williamson to admit him to purge his contempt, I have no difficulty, at all, in hearing the application. If the learned counsel do not inform me that they are here, from Mr. Williamson, with an application to purge the contempt, as at present advised, I have no power to hear their application, whatever it may be.

Mr. MEREDITH. I do not know Sir, how it is possible that you should make such a decision, as I am sure you would desire to make, upon an application like the present, without hearing the petition read, or reading it yourself. But, may it please the Court, I do consider, and I think and hope that I am prepared to show, according to the best precedents that I can find, that this is such an application, as in cases of similar contempt, as near as I can find such, have been received and are perfectly proper to be received. But, at the same time if you mean to put it whether there are the words that "he prays to be admitted to his purgation," they are not in his petition. I do not know how it is possible to get on, however, without your reading the petition or hearing it read, because the argument must apply itself to that petition.

Judge KANE. All I ask is this, if gentlemen, whom I respect so much as I do the one who addresses me, tell me that the object is to purge the contempt I will go on and hear the argument.

Mr. MEREDITH. I should like your honor to decide because upon this depends the character of the argument. I cannot undertake to affirm what it may be, or what it may not be, as there are, very possibly, differences of opinion, on the part of counsel, in relation to it.

Judge KANE. Is it intended to be a petition to purge the contempt?

Mr. MEREDITH. It is intended for the purpose of obtaining his relief from imprisonment for contempt in a manner consistent, as I understand it, with the practice and precedents which we find in the books.

Judge KANE.   Without a purgation?

Mr. MEREDITH.   With, or without, it as you may think fit to order.

Mr. VAN DYKE, (who had been in Court during its morning's proceedings.) I understood that the learned counsel on the other side admitted that this was not a petition to come before the Court to purge from contempt.   It is not for me to say what is in that petition, but my understanding of it is, that it is not a petition to purge from contempt; on the contrary,—that it is a direct protestation against the action of the Court, and, on the part of the Government I protest against any such paper being received.

Mr. MEREDITH.   On the part of the Government?

Mr. VAN DYKE.   Yes, sir.

Mr. MEREDITH.   I had supposed that Mr. Van Dyke appeared as the Counsel for Mr. Wheeler, in this case.

Mr. VAN DYKE.   I object to the reception of a paper, which will be an additional insult to the Court.

Mr. MEREDITH.   May it please your honor, I am quite as incapable of presenting such a paper as is the learned gentleman who has objected to it.

Mr. VAN DYKE.   My remark did not apply to Mr. Meredith at all.

Mr. MEREDITH.   It ought not to have been put in this way.   In regard to Mr. Van Dyke appearing for the Government, I respectfully ask your honor to prohibit his so doing.

If Mr. Van Dyke appears as the counsel for Mr. Wheeler, he is entitled to be heard; and it is the more evident from what he has said, that the ground on which I have asked your honor to receive the petition is a sound one, for he avowedly takes a different view of it from myself.

Now:—how are you to decide between us?   When a member of the bar differs from me, I have no right to assume the correctness of my views in opposition to his.   I, therefore, ask the Court to decide upon the paper and to allow us to be heard.

Mr. VAN DYKE.   I do not understand my learned friend, in his capacity as a member of the bar, to say that this is an application from Passmore Williamson to allow him to purge his contempt.   If he does, there will be an end to this preliminary question.

If he asserts, in his professional capacity, that this is a petition from Passmore Williamson for leave of this Court to purge his contempt, that assertion must be taken. But neither at the last hearing, nor now, do I understand my learned friend to say that such is the case.

Mr. MEREDITH. I will not say what is the legal effect of the paper, particularly when I find there is a difference of opinion in regard to it. Your honor knows, very well, that the very question on which you invited an argument was:—whether this petition was such a one, as, in conformity to the practice governing such cases, would be received as a petition to purge from the contempt; and for me to come into Court, and, upon my bare assertion to say that it is so, I cannot do it. I find that Mr. Van Dyke thinks differently of it; and he has as good a right to his opinion as I have to mine. It is for the Court, therefore, to decide between us. I do not know that any harm can result, and if you please I can state, very briefly, its contents, as I did the other day.

Judge KANE. I beg the gentleman's pardon. There is no gentleman at the bar for whom I have a higher regard, or with whom I have been more agreeably associated under every circumstance.

Mr. MEREDITH. I am happy to know and feel it, sir.

Judge KANE. But the only question before me, is one absolutely of an entirely abstract character.

I have been under the impression, derived from the authorities of Lord Mansfield on the common law side, and Lord Eldon on the chancery side, that I cannot, in the present state of the relations of the Court towards Passmore Williamson, and his relations towards the Court, hear from him, as a Judge, except by an application to purge his contempt. The particular paper which was before the Court some days since, I have never seen a copy of, nor do I know its contents.

I understood the learned counsel, when presenting that paper some days ago, to speak of it, not as an application to purge a contempt, but, as a petition setting forth facts upon which the Court had, heretofore, been called to act, protesting against the jurisdiction which the Court had exercised, and asking, thereupon, to be discharged.

Taking that as the substance of the instrument, I was of the opinion that it was not such an instrument as the Court could receive at that time, and I invited counsel not to argue the question whether this particular paper had, or had not, one character or another, but, whether I could hear from a party in contempt, except upon an application to purge his contempt. That is the question that I desire to hear an argument upon.

I am perfectly satisfied that any paper which the respectable counsel will present to me, will be one appropriate for me to listen to. If I cannot properly listen to an application from Mr. Williamson, that is not an application to purge from contempt, then my course is a simple one, viz: to refuse to hear a paper which does not propose to be offered to purge from the contempt.   And I will intimate to the counsel why I suppose that rule to be proper to be observed in this case.   Whether with sufficient reason, or otherwise, it is obvious that there has been feeling excited in regard to the action of this Court: feeling, almost necessarily, on the side of the party who has been the subject of the Court's action. The only protection that this Court can have, or any Court has, against renewed contempt, is the punishment, the action, the restraint, whatever you call it, which the Court has already exercised.

The action of the Court has been expended.   If it be in the power of a party, still under contempt, to renew applications to the Court, what security can the Court have that there will not be accumulated contempts from the objects of the punishment, because the entire action of the Court has been expended upon the first.   Such I understand to have been the argument which has influenced other Courts, and it was in the view of that argument, as well as of the present one, that I invited the counsel to argue before me the simple question : whether I can hear an application from Passmore Williamson, other than an application to purge his contempt.   That is the question.

Mr. Meredith.   Well, Sir—it still comes down to this; because, as I understand it, there are two kinds of contempts, differing entirely in substance and character.   One : a contempt consisting in personal disrespect of the Court; the other: in some disobedience or omission in regard to obeying the process of the Court.

The first kind is that with which this of Mr. Williamson's is not concerned.

I have not understood, so far as I have heard, that there was anything in his deportment before the Court disrespectful to the Court, or involving a punishment for a contempt of that kind.

The punishment of a contempt of that kind, as I understand it, is by a limited term of imprisonment, and this being not for a limited time shows, further, that this offence is not of that nature. . It is the mere offence of not making a sufficient return, or rather (as the record shows) of refusing to make a return to a writ of habeas corpus.

Now, Sir, the nearest contempt that I can find, is the contempt of a party in a Court of Chancery who does not answer or appear, or, in some other particular, does not obey the process of the Court, as by violating an injunction; or, in any other way disobeying its process.

Now, Sir, I find that, in such cases, the form in which a party applies is simply to show the Court that he is ready to comply with its requisitions.

In this case, to go back to the petition, as I understand it, (as it was only read over to me, and I bear in mind, particularly, its import on this point, and it was one to which my attention was turned) in this case I understand that the petition does not go back to the original transactions at all, further than to make a starting point, since which the Petitioner states that he has known nothing of these people, except what he has heard from public rumor and the newspapers, and that he has had no information about them up to the present time. It is submitted to satisfy your honor that it is not in the Petitioner's power to produce these people before the Court. Now, Sir, under these circumstances, I do find that the practice, as to contempts of this nature in the Courts of Chancery is this: Nine times out of ten an answer is filed without asking leave if the contempt be in not answering. It is held, however, that in strictness the answer ought not to be filed without leave of the Court, and that, therefore, the more rigorous mode of practice is, to apply to the Court for leave to put in the answer.

If the petition be presented, as I understand it, the party is entitled to his discharge on payment of costs. *Strictly* speaking he is to get leave, but, in *ordinary* practice, he presents his petition to the Court, saying that he has filed his answer, and that he is ready, or has tendered, to pay the costs, and *thereupon*, he is entitled to his discharge.

Now, Sir, this petition cannot be *precisely* in that form, but it combines both, and I think is fully within the principles of each. Instead of his undertaking to make a further return to the writ of habeas corpus, which it would not be wise for him to do, this petition corroborates his *statement* under oath on this subject, not going back to the origin of the affair, but taking it up from the time that he saw the woman in a carriage in Dock street, and bringing it down to the present time, overlapping the matters before only so far as is essential to show your honor the state of the case, and to connect the chain of events from that time to the present; and the essence of which I understand to be, that from that hour to the present it has been, and is, utterly out of his power to obey the mandate of the Court. Now, Sir, in addition to that, he tenders in Court here, the payment of the bill of costs, which the officers have been kind enough, I understand, to say shall be considered paid; (but he is ready to pay all the costs that may have accrued) and I am prepared to endeavor to show to your honor, respectfully, by precedents, that in this course we are clearly within the established rules of the Courts of Chancery, in which that species of contempt is most

common, and whose books therefore afford the greatest body of precedents.   The petition does refer to another matter, and respectfully protests against the jurisdiction of this Court.   I had no scruple in allowing
the petition to pass with that protest; in the first place, because as that
ground had been taken by him elsewhere, I considered it due in candor
by him to present it here, and in the second place, because I have not
the most remote conception of the belief that a respectful protest of that
kind, which every party has a right to make, is going to affect your
decision in his regard one iota.

I know very little of you, Sir, if I can suppose that that circumstance
is going to affect you.   I had, therefore, no scruple in allowing it.   It
is due to candor on his part.   If the question of jurisdiction were open
for argument, I would with cheerfulness present my views to you; but,
that not being so, I will not urge it upon you at this time.

Now, sir, if you will allow me, I will go one step further in the
practice.   When everything has been done that can be done, as this
petition shows in the present case, the order of the Court is, frequently,
conditional, and a party is put, precisely, in the knowledge of what he
has to do.

The order may be, for instance, that a party is to be discharged on
filing his answer and paying costs; or, if the answer be already filed,
that he be discharged on tender of the costs.

A conditional order of that kind, sir, if you will make it, is open for
you to make when the petition has been carefully considered, if you
will receive it; and if you should find that, in the body of the petition
there is not sufficient ground to discharge the petitioner, it will be for
you to enter upon the record that the party be discharged upon doing
so and so, whatever it may be.

Now, sir, I do not find, (if you will pardon me for going a little further,) I have not been able to find, that upon a contempt, not consisting,
or supposed to consist, in anything but a mere non-compliance with the
process of the Court—I do not find, sir, that the Chancellor—I was
going to say—allows, (but I will not say that, although I think it probable that he ought not to allow—but he does not call for) that sort of
expression which is required where the contempt is of a different kind.

If Mr. Williamson had been guilty of personal disrespect to the Court,
of course, there would be required a different mode of procedure.   He
would then have been committed for a limited time, and there would be
an end of it, unless he did what ought to be done under the circumstances, and which I should be sorry to think that he would have any
reluctance to do, if he had permitted himself to fall into the grave

error of personal disrespect to the Court. But where he is simply in custody for omitting to do something which he was directed to do, I can find nothing in the books which I am aware of, (and I trust that this argument will lead to some information to be derived from the Court,) but I do not find that form in the books or in the cases.

I do find in one case, where a party was in contempt for a direct breach of an injunction, and for doing, wilfully, the very thing that he had been ordered not to do; I do find, after he had lain for some time in contempt,—(long enough, as the Court supposed, to operate as a warning to him in the future,)—that he was discharged on mere motion, without petition, and that the Court of Exchequer had consulted with the highest authority before rendering their decision on the subject. This case is to be found in 6th Price, 321, and is one which I intended to present to your honor.

On the subject of interrogatories, I find that the party in contempt is ordered to come in and answer interrogatories, and is held bound by recognizance to do so, and then interrogatories are propounded to him. That is the uniform practice in cases proper for interrogatories, so far as I can find, in the English books. One or two cases, not in accordance with this practice, are to be found in Pennsylvania.

Now, I do not know whether, in this case, Passmore Williamson was subjected to interrogatories or not; but I understood that he was sworn upon the original hearing of the case.

JUDGE KANE.—At his own request.

MR. MEREDITH.—But whether considered as upon interrogatories or not, I do not know.

MR. GILPIN.—My recollection, may it please your Honor,—and I would like to state it here, so that we may agree upon that point,—I was in Court, and my recollection was this.

MR. MEREDITH.—Will Mr. Gilpin be so good as to defer his remarks for a short time.

MR. GILPIN.—My recollection is different, and if the Court will allow me, I will state it.

JUDGE KANE.—I do not know that it is necessary that the Court should have your recollection on the subject; it was merely in answer to a suggestion thrown out by Mr. Meredith, that I made the remark.

MR. GILPIN.—My recollection is different.

MR. MEREDITH. I wanted to know if he were considered to be in course of purgation when he was examined.

JUDGE KANE. He was not. He proffered himself as a witness.

Mr. MEREDITH.   Then I am to understand that he was not examined in purgation.

Now, sir, if this be a case in which you will put interrogatories to him, which you may do on receiving this petition, though I do not think that there is any ground for it, for I think that the statement is full and clear; but if you think that interrogatories should be filed, and that he should answer, you can make any order that the practice in such cases leads to.

I find in the English books, sir, so far as I have been able to trace, no trace that these interrogatories are voluntary on the part of the party in contempt. I do find, and I am bound to say so, in some of our books something of a different kind; I mean in the Pennsylvania books. But in the English books I find the principles laid down entirely different.

In the first place, upon the attachment, the Sheriff is allowed to take bail; and the condition of that recognizance is, that the party shall appear at a certain time and place and answer the interrogatories.

I find also, sir, in the English Courts of Common Law, cases in which a party has come in, being guilty of gross contempts, such as beating an officer of the Court, or using offensive or improper language to the Court, (in cases of gross contempts, not of the kind that I am upon now,)—I find, sir, there that a party coming into Court and offering to confess his guilt and submit to punishment, is not permitted to do so, until the interrogatories are filed and are put to him.

I find also, sir, that the rule, as laid down in Hawkins' Pleas of the Crown, is, that the interrogatories *must* be propounded to the party in contempt within four days after the attachment, or if he is under recognizance; and if not filed within those four days, so that he may come in and answer them, he is entitled to be discharged on that ground, whatever may have been the violent contempt of which he was guilty.

Now, sir, I do not mean to say, looking to the cause of commitment in this case, as set out upon your record, that this course is necessary to be pursued, because I am aware that in the class of cases that I speak of, it is a class of cases of a different kind to that which is upon the record. It is a class involving actual personal disrespect, something like a mutinous or contumacious disrespect of the Court; and not where the contempt consisted of a mere non-compliance with the mandate of the Court in its process.

Therefore I do not feel that I have a right to say, as the record stands, that, as the interrogatories have not been administered, the party is for that reason absolutely entitled to his immediate discharge.

At the same time, sir, I find that this interrogatory principle (viz: that interrogatories, where necessary at all, are to be propounded by the Court, and not petitioned for by the defendant) applies itself to this case, and that we have nothing to do with them unless—(as you have entire right to do, and which is done in Chancery)—unless you do find occasion, on the reception of the petition, to submit the party to interrogatories for the purpose of assuring yourself, by his further examination,—(which is final,)—of the correctness and bona fide truth of the statement. And if, upon hearing the petition, you should so decide, it would be an easy matter to make the order that he be heard upon interrogatories.

Will your honor allow me trespass upon your time one moment more in regard to the feeling which has arisen in this case?

Judge KANE. Certainly, sir.

Mr. MEREDITH. Which we all know to have been great, where it has prevailed, and which is, perhaps, widely extended.

I do not know, sir, that I should exactly agree with you in regard to the question in whose behalf that feeling has been most eminently exhibited; but I most certainly do heartily agree in the sincere deploring of the fact that there should have been in the proceedings of a Court of justice, or bearing upon the proceedings of a Court of justice, an occasion for any of this excitement out of doors; because I do not conceive that excitements of that kind, or of any sort, tend at all to promote the administration of justice.

I need not say, therefore, that I have looked with regret upon all the excitement outside of the Court-House; and I have regretted it, and could have wished that it could have been avoided; and I could have desired that whatever efforts may have been used to prevent it entirely might have been more successful.

I have the misfortune, on this occasion, as you know very well, to differ very materially from the views which have occurred to you, sir, and which, in the discharge of your duty, you have announced as the law in this case. That is a difference which, at the Bar and between the Bar and the Bench, we are accustomed to every day. But this is the arena (I will not say arena, sir, but this is the place) in which these differences are to be discussed, respectfully, by the Bar—in Courts of justice themselves, and not elsewhere,—and I should be sorry to see the day at which these discussions shall come to be held,—while a case is pending in a Court of justice,—anywhere but in the walls of a Court from which redress is sought; whether the Court in which the proceedings originated, or any other Court, which the party may believe he is entitled to look to.

I know that I agree with you in this sentiment, and I have thus given a public expression to my views that my feelings may be known and understood.

Judge KANE. I would take occasion to say, that from the first, up to this moment, there has been on the part of the individual to whom the functions of a Court of justice have been delegated, and by whom they have been exercised in this matter, not one particle of conscious excitement. I do not believe that it would be in the power of the entire press of the United States, after I had honestly and, according to my best ability, administered justice, to give me a pang or produce an excited feeling. I therefore, now, as heretofore, look upon the question as a question that has no feeling on the bench.

If I understood an observation of Mr. Meredith, he meant to say to the Court that Passmore Williamson was desirous of testifying, now, his willingness to obey the exigency of the writ of habeas corpus. If so, he has a simple, straightforward, honorable course to pursue; it is: so to advise this Court by his petition to this Court. He has no need of making a narrative of facts, an argument or a protest. Now, as heretofore, let him come forward into Court, declaring that he is now willing to obey the writ which was issued from this Court, and he has done that which, in the estimation of the Judge, is a purgation of his contempt.

There has been nothing, on his part, of personal offence to the Judge, as his demeanor in Court, so far as was observed by the Judge, was entirely respectful. He has failed to obey the writ which the law issued to him, and when he is willing to obey that writ, it will become the duty of the Court to hear him. What is understood by a purgation is very simple. I need not explain it to the learned counsel. I suppose that it is, (whatever may be its form of words,—I am not jealous about words,—I care not what the form of words may be,—provided I receive from the party who is in contempt for having disobeyed the process of the Court,) the assurance that he is now prepared to obey it, and I will gladly receive it.

There is no form of words necessary; but, as it seems to me, while I should be very glad indeed to hear the arguments which the learned counsel have sketched, it seems to me that until he is prepared and so announces himself to obey the process of the Court, I cannot hear from him on any other subject. I cannot hear from him that the Court has erred either in point of fact, or in point of law; that the Court has exercised a jurisdiction which did not belong to it. The adjudication of the Court under which, up to the present moment, the party is in the custody of the Marshal, cannot be reviewed at his instance, from the fact that he is not in Court, and cannot come into Court except by means of that which the law calls a purgation, as it seems to me. I will hear the argument of counsel, if they be willing, upon this point.

Mr. MEREDITH. I wish your honor to understand clearly the point to which I refer. I have had myself, very little, or scarcely any, personal communication with Mr. Williamson. I have seen him but about three times since he has been in prison. I meant to speak of what was in the ·petition. I do not speak of his desires or willingness, beyond what is in the petition itself. It appears to me to be a real compliance with the exigency of the writ of habeas corpus, by satisfying your honor that it is impossible for him to obey it, otherwise than to return his inability to comply with its mandate.

Judge KANE. Then let him simply say that to the Court. Let him not combine it with other things. If he be prepared to submit to the jurisdiction of the Court and to obey its writ, let him merely say that, then he is reinstated. The words are simple; they are unequivocal; they admit of no argument; they can lead to no excitement;—the simple declaration.

Mr. MEREDITH. I really believe sir, that if you will allow me, privately as it were, to read this petition to you, or if you will take it and read it for yourself, that you will find that the statement of facts is, precisely to that point; that down to this time he is utterly unable, and has no knowledge of the whereabouts, or locality of these parties, except that which everybody else has from the newspapers and what is said out of doors, and that, of his own knowledge, he knows nothing about them.

Judge KANE. That, it seems to me, is the supplementary return; the answer upon interrogatories which follows the purgation.

Mr. MEREDITH. The purgation, as I understand it, if it be a case for interrogatories, is by the answer to the interrogatories.

Judge KANE. I do not so understand it. I understand that a party in contempt, in order that he may be heard in Court comes forward by purgation, and he submits himself to interrogatories touching all the matters which should have been embraced in his return. Mr. Williamson coming forward declaring to the Court that he has meant no disrespect, (and there are words of mere form, because we know that there was none,) but that he is now prepared to submit himself to the exigency of the writ, passes, at once, into the condition of an ordinary suitor,—and the Court hears him. If he does thus comply with the exigency of the writ, he is discharged as a matter of course.

Mr. MEREDITH. There is exactly the point on which I have been unable to find anything which I should call direct authority; although I have been enabled to find some cases very much like this.

Judge KANE. I shall be very glad to hear Mr. Meredith upon that point.

Mr. MEREDITH. I find in Smith's Chancery Practice, which is a modern book, but which contains the practice of the Court very well—but if your honor intends to hear an argument, perhaps it will be better that Mr. Gilpin should go on.

Judge KANE. In whatever order you please.

Mr. GILPIN. May it please your honor.

Judge KANE. Let me just notice, first, the motion.

Mr. GILPIN. I will present it to your honor in the form which we thought appropriate.

U. S. ex rel. Wheeler vs. *Williamson.*	District Court, U. S., Eastern District of Pennsylvania, Oct. 22, 1855

HOPPER, C. GILPIN and MEREDITH, move the Court for leave to present and file of Record in the case, a Petition of the Respondent.

This is the form of the motion. The petition speaking for itself, it was not deemed necesary to say what was contained in it.

Judge KANE. That our notes may stand correct sir, I understand, simply, that the Court asks whether this petition is a petition to make purgation.

Mr. GILPIN. I can only answer by referring to the paper and the conversations which have taken place between yourself and the senior counsel. It is the paper which has been the subject of remark, and, perhaps I may say, conversation between him and the Court.

Judge KANE. So I understand. I simply wish our notes to stand regularly.

I ask the question whether it is a petition to make purgation; and I invite argument whether I can receive any other.

Mr. GILPIN. I will endeavor to define that petition; perhaps in not so clear and terse a manner as my learned colleague; but in a way to give the Court to understand that it is my intention to refer to this one *dry* point, if I may so call it, in the case, to show by reason and authority that there is ground for sustaining the present motion *modo et forma*.

Judge KANE. I ask the counsel, whether I can receive any application from Mr. Williamson other than an application to purge himself of the contempt, and I desire counsel to confine themselves to that point.

Mr GILPIN. Your honor desires us to address ourselves to that point.

Judge KANE. To that question, yes, Sir.

Mr. GILPIN. May it please your honor.

After the very lucid exposition of the law of contempt of different classes, and the mode of being relieved from them, by my colleague, I shall feel myself very much relieved from making any general statements, or propositions, upon that head, and shall proceed as speedily, and as briefly, as possible to the statement of a few facts, connecting themselves, necessarily, with the law of the case, in order to make my remarks, directed to the particular point to which the Court calls our attention, more easily and better understood.

The substance of this application first assumed the shape of a motion, on the 17th of this month, for leave to file an affidavit; the Court expressed the opinion that *petition* was the proper mode to approach it, with anything that ought to be communicated to it, and, with that suggestion, said that it was open to counsel to take a rule to show cause why that affidavit should not be filed.

But as the Court was more likely to be correct, as to the mode of approach that was lawful, or, at least, as to the mode of approach which it desired to be adopted, and as the argument was simply on a question of form and would have been of no benefit to the respondent, it was not deemed advisable to ask or argue a rule to show cause, hence, the substance of that application took the shape of the petition which is now before you.

There was, therefore, at that time, an impression on the mind of the counsel, that it was rather a matter of form than of substance, and, that being the impression, your honor will understand that counsel were somewhat disappointed, when the suggestion fell from the Court, on the presentation of the petition, that the Court could only be approached, where a party was in contempt, by direct application, in terms, to purge from contempt.

This, naturally, induced counsel to cast their eyes over the whole field of the case, to learn what had occurred during its progress to raise their expectations, that the Court was open to an application other than the one then suggested by the Court.

I will now call your honor's attention to the opinion of the Court which was delivered in the matter—I may call it,—*In re Johnson;* a matter of which I knew nothing and heard nothing, either as an application, or intended application, to your honor, until I saw the public announcement of it in the daily afternoon newspaper, the Bulletin.

It surprised me. I do not find fault with the gentleman who made it at all, for that was all proper and right,—but it surprised me quite as much as, when seated in the Court of Quarter Session, as a listener to its proceedings, the name of "Jane Johnson" was called, and she appeared on the witness stand. My surprise was alike in both cases.

In this opinion your honor says, in alluding to a legal proposition which you had advanced in a former opinion:

"His (the respondent's) duty then, as now, was and is, to bring in the bodies; or, if they passed beyond his control, to declare under oath or affirmation, so far as he knew, what had become of them; and from this duty, or from the restraint that seeks to enforce it, there can be no escape."

This remark in your honor's opinion, as you may well suppose, struck the counsel of Mr. Williamson with some force.

They had reason to believe it was expected of their client, that he should set out and present, in some respectful form, to your honor, his full knowledge upon this subject, and reason to believe that the form of affidavit would be acceptable to the Court. Perhaps, that was a hasty conclusion made by them at the time; but certainly with this opinion before them, they had ground to suppose that the Court was open and ready for such an application; they had reason to think so, for when the opinion of the Court was delivered, the attention of the Court was called by an *amicus curiæ*, to a supposed inaccuracy in the report of the former proceedings. The report runs thus:—Judge Kane said * * *—"A wish was expressed," (by the counsel of Mr. W.,) "to make such a motion" (to amend,) "and the Judge asked, that the motion might be reduced to writing and filed. But the motion was not drawn out or presented for the Court's consideration, and the Court never expressed any purpose to overrule such a motion, if one should be presented." This was said after Mr. Williamson was in custody for contempt.

There was that said both by your honor, and the gentleman who acted as *amicus curiæ*, which created the impression, that the Court was open to Mr. Williamson by motion; that it did not require the presentation of a petition in the form which your honor has intimated to us now. Hence the counsel have been, if they are wrong, mislead in this matter.

I do not intend to allude to the recollections of the different parties:

it is of no consequence here; but I intended to call the attention of the Court to it, to show what leads to the application now before your honor.

Then, again, when the application was made to this Court for leave to file this petition, counsel were at a loss for precedents, and so intimated to the Court; your honor alluded to a case which had occurred not long ago, and cited and quoted it as a precedent, as I understood it, which we would be justified in relying upon in this case, although the character of the contempt was somewhat different. I allude to the case of the Commonwealth *vs.* Wynkoop;—the habeas corpus in the case of Bill Fisher. Your honor stated that the Marshal acted under your advice, and we presumed that the same course ought to be followed here.

As it is intimated that the application must be by petition, counsel, naturally, looked to that case to find form and precedent to guide them. But I find, in that case, no such form and no such precedent. The defendant in that habeas corpus admitted that he had possession of the *bodies*, and set up his right to detain *them* by the process of another tribunal, a United States Commissioner. The Court said that it was his duty to produce them, and, as he declined to do so, committed him for that contempt. He was in the custody of the Sheriff as clearly and fully, for contempt, as Mr. Williamson has ever been, although I do not know that he was ever confined within the walls of Moyamensing— at least, I hope *not*—as to the fact, I did not inquire.

The contempt continued for several days; and what occurred during its continuance I will not state, particularly as there is no record of it; but I do find that on the 25th day of July, two days, certainly, after the contempt was committed, Marshal Wynkoop appeared in person, in Court, without any petition, without any purgation, so far as the record gives light upon the subject, and moved to amend his return, so as to comply with the order of the Court by producing the body, and set up, in connection with that production, his right to retain it under other process.

The contempt is immediately purged, Marshal Wynkoop is discharged, Bill Fisher is placed, by order of the Court, in the joint custody of the Marshal and the keeper of the county prison, until further order, and the next day, upon consideration, the Court order Bill Fisher to be remanded to the exclusive custody and control of the Marshal, under the process that he held for his removal. Now, if precedent, to which we have been referred, is to guide us, then after respectful application to this Court, either by motion as Wynkoop made

8

in person—(as our client cannot do)—or by counsel, or by petition to the Court, setting forth, substantially, what Wynkoop stated on that motion, and in his amended return, a compliance with the original order of the Court, or his inability to comply, we are entitled to relief.

Upon this point your honor has also said something in re *Johnson*.

Judge KANE. I would say to you, Mr. Gilpin, that the precedent to which you refer includes facts which do not appear upon the record as you have it in your hands. They are important facts.

Mr. GILPIN. There was no written communication to the Court that I am aware of. I have not alluded to all the facts, as some of them are private. And if there was any purgation other than the motion in Court, I presume it must have been made at the residence of the Judge when the Deputy Sheriff accompanied Wynkoop there during the time he was under contempt. Further than that it is not, perhaps, necessary to remark.

I should think that this case would not constitute a precedent in law, to establish that in all cases parties should file a petition in Court, in order to do what Wynkoop did, under the circumstances, by motion.

Judge KANE. I presume that you are aware of the facts bearing upon the case. There was a purgation, which you are aware of.

Mr. GILPIN. There was a visit to the residence of the Judge.

Judge KANE. There was a purgation in formal terms, and the individual who speaks to you at this moment was an agent in making it.

Mr. GILPIN. Nothing was done in Court. I have referred to the report of proceedings in Court.

Judge KANE. The first and last steps are correct as you have stated them.

Mr. GILPIN. It would have been, perhaps, an intrusion into private relations, to have alluded to it in any other way.

Therefore that case, as a judicial precedent, affords no ground for an application, by petition, to the Court. Nor can I conceive anything further, that could have been asked of Marshal Wynkoop than what he did when he went into Court. He was guilty of no personal disrespect.

It has never been laid down, as a principle, that a party who disobeys the process of the Court, is guilty of personal disrespect to the Court. But I will leave that branch of the subject.

Now, there are two classes of contempts; the one may be called *ordinary* and the other *extraordinary*. The ordinary contempts are those which relate to the proceedings of the Court, disobedience of the orders of the Court, whether upon mesue process, interlocutory proceedings, or final process of the Court.

Extraordinary contempts are those flagrant acts in the presence of, or against the Court and its officers, its peace, its dignity and the conduct of its business.

It is within the former class, I think, that the case of our client comes; an ordinary contempt being a disobedience, as your honor has decided,—and I am not going to review that decision,—to the original order of the Court when it issued the habeas corpus requiring the production of the body of Jane Johnson. I am assuming that as the platform from which we start.

I find the practice laid down in several elementary books into which I have looked, that the party can take, as a general rule, no step in the case in which the contempt has been incurred until he purge his contempt, except: That he is allowed, either by petition, or by motion, to do any act which has a connection with his contempt, either in the way of showing the original order for it was irregular or void, that it has been satisfied, or that he is unable to perform the order of the Court;—and I can find no authority against that position. I can find cases in which it has been allowed.

In Daniel's Chancery Practice, the position which I have stated, the unquestionable right to proceed in any respectful application to the Court, either by motion or by petition, to relieve himself from the contempt, is not questioned; but it is stated as an elementary principle, and cases referred to sustain it.

If the door were effectually closed against a man imprisoned for contempt, it would be a very hard matter, under some circumstances, for counsel to know how, in the case of an ordinary contempt, to advise their client to proceed. There are even other applications which do not relate to the primary case in which the contempt was committed, in which the Court would be fully justified in allowing it without compromising its own dignity; and yet, if the door were shut to a petition like this, it would effectually shut the door to all such applications.

I want, respectfully, to call your attention to a little matter that occurred pending this case in which I was not concerned. An application was made to you, I have understood, without the knowledge of Mr. Williamson, for some relief or change, in the arrangements connected with his imprisonment. That application was not made, perhaps —(though your honor knows precisely and exactly how it was made,) —in open Court; the answer to it was, however, given by you in open Court. I saw it in the newspaper, and I have, therefore, alluded to it

I think I may say that that application was entertained by the Court; although the decision was against it.

Judge KANE.   What application do you refer to?

Mr. GILPIN.   Relative to a change of the place of his confinement.

Judge KANE.   It has, perhaps, very little connection with the present case, but as it was thought advisable to introduce it into argument, I will correct the counsel as to the facts.

An application was presented to the Judge by two very respectable gentlemen of the medical profession, that Mr. Williamson should be removed from the prison where he then was into another prison, in as much as his health was suffering.

The Judge intimating, on the instant, that he would take care that such a removal was made, was told by the gentleman who made the application that it was not an application sanctioned by Mr. Williamson.

The Judge then said, I care not with whose sanction, or without whose sanction, the information is brought to me, that any one who is in confinement under the process of this Court is suffering in health, it is my office to see that he is relieved. Be good enough to place, said the Judge, that it may appear on paper, merely the physician's certificate to that effect.

And immediately after this and while these respectable gentlemen were preparing a certificate, it was mentioned to the Judge, by some of the members of the bar, that the place to which these medical gentlemen solicited that Mr. Williamson might be removed, was much less comfortable, and much less salubrious than the place where he then was.

Upon the gentlemen returning with their certificate, the Court so said to them, and said that Mr. Williamson should not be removed to a place which was less comfortable and less salubrious, without his sanction. They had no authority to give his sanction, and, thereupon, the Court, to guard against the possibility of Mr. Williamson's health suffering, endorsed, upon the application, authority to the Marshal to procure such accommodations as might be required by the health of the prisoner, the Court having authority to provide a special place of imprisonment where the present place of confinement is, by any means, unsuited to the prisoner's health.

From that day the Judge has heard nothing further of it, and knows only by common fame, what action was had on the part of Mr. Williamson. The Marshal had informed the Court, but it is unnecessary that the Court should mention to the counsel what was done.

Mr. GILPIN.   I am very much obliged to your honor for giving all the facts of the case, but it was not with a view to find fault, or to make a partial statement of facts, because I was, and my client was, perfectly satisfied with the action of the Court in that matter; and, as I stated, he had never made a complaint upon the subject, or a request.

I only made the application to show that there are circumstances under which a party might be very peculiarly situated, and if the doctrine were laid down so narrowly that, while in contempt, he can do nothing but apply by a naked and simple petition to purge that contempt, a prisoner might be in a peculiar predicament.

I will now state a case or two, to show you that in cases of ordinary contempt, committed by parties, they have been allowed to make application to the Court for relief, application less formal than the application which we now make to your honor

It is not necessary, I take it, to show cases where the application, or the prayer of the Petitioner, has been granted. That is not what we are now to argue, nor the sufficiency of this petition, and the disclosures in it, to entitle the respondent to his discharge; but it is the reception of it, the reading of it, and the filing of it that we are to discuss.

Judge KANE. Simply that one question.

Mr. GILPIN. There is one case to which I want to refer you as it occurred in one of the United States Courts. It is not quite to the point of the very matter under discussion before the Court, but it, at least, gives the views of one of the Justices of the Supreme Court of the United States, on the subject of contempt; and it throws some light upon the subject of contempt under the Act of Congress, of 1831, the conclusiveness of answers or allegations under oath, submitted to the Court in aid of the answer, where the Court requires the party to travel further than the answer which was put in.

I allude to the case in 1 Curtis' Circuit Court Reps. p. 190, in re Pitman.

I will now call your attention to the case in 4 Henning and Mumford; the case of Fisher vs. Fisher, a party in contempt for failure to answer.

He came into Court without any petition, and asked leave, and was allowed to file his answer, he only being put upon terms that he should not avail himself of the delay which the Statutes of the State would have allowed him, of not filing his answer until six months had elapsed. This was a case of flat contempt. In the same book, p. 504, Lane vs. Elvey, a plea was allowed where the defendant was in contempt. In Palmer vs. Kelly, 4 Sanford's Chancery Reps., p. 575, a defendant committed for contempt, for violating an injunction by selling property equitably belonging to the complainant, after two months' imprisonment, applied for his discharge, on the ground that he had no means of paying the fine imposed upon him by the Court, which fine was equivalent to the value of the property which he had sold. The prayer was refused; that is, his discharge was refused, but the application was entertained, and argued on the merits; his discharge was refused on other grounds, so that you will perceive that this case is, exactly, in point. Mr. Williamson now moves, may it please your honor,—upon the ground stated in the petition—showing an utter inability to comply with the original order of the Court.

It is not for me to say whether the court will believe that statement or give it full credence; that is not what we are here to discuss, but that the Court ought to entertain it, under this authority, it seems to me very clear, and it ought to allow him to have a hearing upon the merits.

Your honor has said in an opinion to which I have referred several times, *in re Johnson :* " In the case of Mr. Williamson, the commitment is for a refusal to answer, that is to say, to make a full and lawful answer to the writ of habeas corpus, an answer setting forth all the facts within his knowledge, which are necessary to a decision by the Court, whether we have not the power to procure the negroes and control those in whose custody they were."

If I may be permitted, without going beyond the limit which the Court has assigned, I would say that petition is intended to show that Mr. Williamson had not the power to produce the alleged slaves, and that he had no control over the parties in whose custody they were.

There are many other cases to which I might refer, to show that applications for relief, in a respectful manner, in any shape, have not been refused. Indeed I cannot find any instance in which it has been refused. Not one ; and the absence of all authority, to the contrary is, it seems to me, something in our favor.

There is a case, referred to by my colleague, in 6 Price's Rep., which I will not read ; and as I do not wish to go further into the law on this head, I will leave these authorities with you, and trust that you will, upon a calm consideration of this matter, allow the Petitioner to apply, by petition in a respectful way, that you will hear it, and decide upon its merits afterwards.

If Mr. Meredith has any authorities, I will cite them for him before Mr. Vandyke speaks.

Mr. MEREDITH. I would say, Sir, with regard to the authorities which I shall have occasion to refer to, that I never like the habit of merely handing the counsel about to speak, a list of authorities, as it has a tendency to confuse him, although I think it quite fair that Mr. Van Dyke, should have a right to reply to any authorities that I may cite.

Judge KANE. Perhaps the better plan will be for you to open your views at once.

Mr. MEREDITH. That would amount to my not having a reply.

Judge KANE. In any way most agreeable to you. You may give and receive the same opportunity on both sides.

Mr. MEREDITH. I have no objection to Mr. Van Dyke having reference to the authorities.

Mr. VAN DYKE. I suppose it right for the learned counsel to present all their authorities upon the case, as it may not be necessary for me to say a word, as is often the case; and therefore, I think that all the views of the gentlemen on the other side ought to be, first, presented to the Court.

Judge KANE, (to Mr. MEREDITH.) I will hear you Sir. I would rather hear all the views that are on one side, and then I can call upon the counsel opposed to you.

Mr. MEREDITH. That will make a double opening.

Judge KANE. Unless you do not confine yourself to the remarks of your colleague; the usual course is, that one side presents all the points to which the attention of the other is to be called.

Mr. MEREDITH. I do not know that I shall present any different points from my colleague, because, from the nature of the case, it can hardly be said to have points, as it involves a general view of the whole subject.

Judge KANE. The only thing which I gathered from Mr. Gilpin's argument is a question of form. His view, as presented to me, simply makes it a question of form.

Mr. MEREDITH. I will say sir, in regard to this petition, that I should be exceedingly sorry, in the view that I take of the subject, for a great many reasons, if it should be found impossible to be entertained. Because, Sir, my own feelings, from the beginning of this very untoward affair have been, that there was no benefit or advantage to be derived in any respect, either to the party or to the administration of justice, or in any aspect that you can take of the matter, by a repetition of applications; causing, undoubtedly, more or less irritation, I mean out of doors, sir, and beyond the walls of a Court of justice.

I have, therefore, felt it to be my duty, both to the party, and to the administration of justice, to endeavor, when we come before the Court, to come with an application that will lead to some distinct and specific result, and I shall be exceedingly sorry to find that the result is, simply, that to which I have alluded, of additional excitement and disturbance; further applications necessary, and all this sort of thing.

While absent from the city, as the origin of this petition has been gone into, I will observe that during a temporary absence of mine from the city, an affidavit was prepared and presented to your honor, the ideas contained in which, as I understood afterwards, were founded upon expressions in the opinion delivered by you, in the matter of Jane Johnson, as reported in the newspapers. With the application of Jane Johnson I had nothing to do, nor had I any knowledge of it until I heard it casually spoken of as an item of intelligence, of what had been done in Court. Your opinion was directed to the nature and character of this contempt; and it was substantially understood to be announced, that the prisoner would be held until he should satisfy the Court by his oath or affirmation, that it was out of his power to produce the bodies, or, in default of which, he should produce the bodies. Founded upon this,—and I have no doubt with a full belief that it would meet the views of the Court,—my learned colleagues, during my absence, had taken the affidavit of Mr. Williamson to that effect, covering a period of time, posterior to that to which the former opinion of the Court was understood to refer, and beginning at the time when he lost sight of the woman in the carriage at Dock street.

As I understood the opinion of the Court, in Mr. Williamson's case, there was no evidence, whatever, that, at any moment, posterior to that time, he had control of the woman,—direct evidence I mean, sir; but, —if I understood the opinion of the Court upon this subject,—that there was conceived by the Court to be direct evidence of some control previous to that time, which would, by inference, draw down a subsequent control; and I believe that I understood it rightly

Judge KANE. That is correct, sir.

Mr. MEREDITH. This affidavit took up the transaction at that point of time where, in the opinion of the Court, the direct evidence ceased. It then, in the most direct terms, assures the Court that neither directly nor indirectly, had he any knowledge, other than that which was derived from the newspapers, or reports of public occurrences, of the whereabouts or of the situation of the party.

Now, sir, I regretted, very much, to find that that was not the view which the Court had intended to express; because I could have desired, as I have said, that any application presented to you should be one that you could entertain.

My learned colleagues who presented that paper, I have no doubt, were perfectly sincere in the belief that the form of the paper which was required by the Court,—(under the view which they had taken of the opinion of the Court, on refusing leave to file this affidavit,)—was that of a petition instead of an affidavit; and that that was the only difficulty with the case.

They, therefore acted, I have no doubt, in perfect good faith, in preparing this petition, believing it to be in conformity with the wish of the Court. It appears, now, that they misunderstood what transpired, to a certain extent at least. They prepared, one of them, a short petition, praying that the affidavit might be permitted to be filed; and it was at my suggestion, that instead of this the substance of the affidavit was embodied in the petition. The petition as originally prepared, also contained a respectful protest against the jurisdiction of the Court, which I did not consider as objectionable, my reasons for which I have already stated, as to its being, in my opinion, more candid on the part of Mr. Williamson, and because I had no reason to believe that it would have the slightest unfavorable effect upon the decision of the case.

Now, sir, under these circumstances, in presenting not merely a petition to file an affidavit, but in presenting a petition for the discharge of the Petitioner, I was in the hope and expectation that, upon this petition you would do one of two things. The non-reception of the petition I did not look to as a probable result, I must confess, but I did hope that you would do one of two things.

Either, that being satisfied with the statements in the petition as to the absolute inability to produce the bodies, that you would, thereupon, discharge the Petitioner; or that, if you did not think that that was a sufficient information to your conscience of the fact that he was unable to obey the writ, that you would make a conditional order that upon the answering of interrogatories, or upon the doing of some positive thing, placed upon the record, so that he might know exactly where he was, that he should be, thereupon, discharged. Now, sir, it is with great sorrow, not on my own account, because, after all, it does not affect us if we have been so unfortunate as to misunderstand the desire of the Court, and to present facts in a manner not acceptable to the judgment of the Court, but it is on various accounts—

Judge KANE. The views which you express, Mr. Meredith, strike me with very great force. I have no wish at all, that a mere form, however I may consider it is required by precedent, shall be adhered to where, substantially, what I suppose to be due course of law is observed.

It may be, that upon a view of this petition, that I may find in it that which might influence my judicial action; and while there is a difference of opinion between counsel on the two sides as to what may be its contents, it may be that I may be misled upon any adjudication which I am to make upon this preliminary motion.

I am not sure whether it is not best that I should, as an individual, take that paper that I may examine it for myself. If there is nothing in it but what I would esteem a formal variance from the regular course of procedure, I should entertain it. If, on the other hand, there were objections of a more serious character, I should indicate it perhaps with more clearness, than when listening to an argument which, necessarily, takes an abstract form.

Unless there is, apparent to the counsel who are before me, any objection to such a course, I will receive from you a copy of it, not as a paper filed, but as a paper which you offer to argue from; if that will facilitate in any way the discussion or the result.

Mr. MEREDITH. I was about to press, as seriously as I was able, the absolute necessity of your reading the contents of this petition, because the proprieties of feeling which I have already expressed upon the subject forbid us to affirm positively that it is what we suppose it to be; and where we differ in opinion I cannot say that my opinion is the correct one, according to the views of the Court.

Mr. VAN DYKE. I differ in opinion.

Mr. MEREDITH. (Handing an instrument in writing to the Court.) Here is the petition, sir, or a copy of it.

Judge KANE. I will take the copy and will meet you, if agreeable, to-morrow morning at 10 o'clock.

Mr. VAN DYKE. Will your honor hear me on that point.

Judge KANE. Certainly, sir.

Mr. VAN DYKE. I take it, sir, upon the present aspect of the cause, and under the call of the learned counsel, by the Court, to state the substance of that petition, and they having failed to state that the character of that petition is such as comes within the ruling of the Court, it is not competent for that petition to be presented.

The Judge of a Court may see a paper, as an individual, but I take it that it cannot be presented, except it is of a certain character to the Court, in open Court. And I support my view, sir, with this simple argument.

I am enabled, I think, to show to the satisfaction of the Court, that a party in contempt, whether it be a contempt arising from a refusal to obey some remedial process of the Court, or a contempt arising out of a direct and positive insult to the Court, that a party in such contempt has no status in Court to present any paper until he is clear of his contempt. That he has no right to ask the Court to receive a paper, even for the purpose of taking a rule to show cause why the paper should not be filed.

Such papers have been presented in Courts, but they have been presented, whenever they have been, under an assertion and belief that it was a paper to purge the contempt. And, until the Court sees the paper, that allegation having been made by the party presenting the petition, the Court has to take it for granted that it is such a paper. But the learned gentlemen, on the day of the first hearing, when the last motion was made, and also to-day, have yet failed to state to this Court, in their professional capacity, that they consider this petition a petition from Mr. Williamson to purge his contempt.

I will read to your honor, in support of this, a single authority or two, simply upon the question whether this paper should go to the Court at all ; and I think they are clear.

The first case to which I will refer is that of Lott vs. Burrow, 2 Con. Court Rep. 167.—"If a witness in Court refuse to answer questions touching his interest in the cause, he may be committed as for a contempt," (this is not a direct insult to the Court, but arising out of a refusal to do justice to a party in litigation) "and closely confined without bail or mainprize until he purge his contempt and answer."

I read the case, as I have not been able to get the book, from the digest, and it may not be the exact words of the report.

In Johnson vs. Pinny 1, page, 646.—"Where a party is in contempt, the Court will grant no application of his which is not a matter of right. He must first purge his contempt by complying with the order of the Court which he has not obeyed. An evasive answer or an insufficient return to a *habeas corpus*," &c., which refers to a matter which is not in dispute.

Grant vs. Grant, 10 Humphrey's Tennessee Rep. p. 464.—"No answer can be received from a defendant in Chancery who stands in contempt, until he is discharged from such contempt by order of the Chancellor. The clerk has no power to discharge the contempt or receive the answer."

In Wallace Rep. 134, U. S. vs. Wayne.—"Where a defendant is brought in he may submit his contempt,"—this is an answer to the suggestion of Mr. Meredith, with regard to interrogatories,—" or he may demand of the Court to have interrogatories put."

Mr. MEREDITH. That is the case to which I referred ; and the one in which, as I mentioned, the rule had been held differently. There is another case in 9 Watts.

Judge KANE. That same question occurred in the case of a party whose name resembles the party here, Passmore's case.

Mr. MEREDITH. There the question did not exactly arise. I think that interrogatories were propounded there, according to the English practice; but there is a case in 9 Watts in which the Supreme Court have said something like what was said in U. S. vs. Wayne.

Judge KANE. I speak of Passmore's case; the case that led to the impeachment of the Judges.

Mr. MEREDITH. I intended to refer to the same case.

Mr. VAN DYKE. The case in Wallace is, that a party need not be submitted to interrogatories where he had an opportunity of answering, as Mr. Williamson had, at his own suggestion. There is another case in 2 Brown's Par. Rep. 277. Oswald vs. Disson. It is also quoted in 5 Viner's abridgement 450.

In 1 Simons and Stewart, 121, Green vs. Thompson.—"The defendant, in order to clear his contempt, must not only tender the costs, but if they are refused, must also obtain the order for discharging his contempt."

In Jones's Case, 2 Strange.—" One guilty of contempt cannot have the benefit of rules."

The same is laid down in Smith's Chancery, the book to which my friend has referred.

Now, sir, I take it, if these authorities are law, that Mr. Williamson has no position in Court, except upon a petition to purge his contempt. And, upon a petition to purge his contempt—which petition is an admission of the contempt—upon a petition to purge his contempt drawn in due form; then, if the Court is satisfied of the sincerity of that petition, and of the sincerity of his allegation in that petition, it reinstates him just in the position that he was immediately before the contempt.

The only question, therefore, to which I direct the attention of the Court, (and I have only referred to the few authorities which I have just cited for the purpose of discharging my duty in protecting the Court from a further insult which might take place,) the simple question is: Whether this paper can be presented to the Court except it is accompanied at the time with the prima facie allegation on the part of the counsel present presenting it, that it is a petition to purge his contempt.

The learned gentlemen might assert that, and it might turn out afterwards not to be such a petition; but upon the allegation of the learned gentlemen,—counsel familiar with the rules of practice,—that it is such a petition, I take it that not only myself, that the Court would be bound to receive it; and then it would be for the Judge to decide whether or not it is a petition to purge the contempt. But the party having no standing in Court, except upon a prayer in due form to purge the contempt that he has already been guilty of, no paper can be presented to this learned Court, except accompanied with the allegation of that party that it is a paper for that purpose.

With these simple remarks I leave that question with the Court at the present stage.

Mr. MEREDITH. If your honor please, it seems that a part of that protection which the learned counsel on the other side feels it to be his duty to extend to the Court, consists in endeavoring to prevent you from knowing the contents of the paper,—of which he is advised,—in order that you may judge whether it contains any further insult to the Court, as he contends it does, or not.

Judge KANE. I do not so understand it.

Mr. VAN DYKE. I do not object to the Court taking the paper.

Judge KANE. I do not understand Mr. Van Dyke as objecting to the Judge taking the paper.

Mr. MEREDITH. Then to what did the remarks of the gentleman apply? I understood that to be his whole argument.

Mr. VAN DYKE. I object to its being presented in that way. A paper presented to the Court becomes part of the records of the Court, if presented in argument. I object to its being presented in that way.

Judge KANE. That is what I understood to be the import of the gentleman's remarks.

Mr. VAN DYKE. I object to its being presented in such a phase. If, in argument, counsel rise and present a paper to the Court, it becomes part of the record, and I say, therefore, that it must be accompanied with the allegation, that it is a petition to purge from contempt.

Mr. MEREDITH. Our learned opponent has felt it to be his duty to deliver an address in opposition to that which your honor proposed doing; and I must beg your patience, because I do not wish to be misundrstood in this matter, to say a few words in reply.

I was about to represent to you, before I came to argue upon the point as to the contents of this petition, that it was utterly impossible to form a conception of its receivability,—to coin a word for the occasion,—without knowing the contents of it; and, that the only mode of knowing them was, by allowing the Court to have them read, or read them for itself. I do not agree, on the contrary, I have never heard, that by reading a paper to the Court in argument, it becomes, ipso facto, part of the record. It was not so understood by me; and I presumed, that if the paper had been received it would be filed, but if not received it cannot, possibly, be filed. However, I am better satisfied that you should read it privately, as you will have a better opportunity of digesting it. But, sir, I must say that the idea of putting it to counsel to affirm that it is, in point of law, a certain thing, particularly when the opposite counsel, having read it, affirms that, as far as he understands it, it is no such thing,—would be to reduce the administration of justice to such a point, as it never will be while you preside; that, to wit, of calling upon counsel, before their clients shall be heard, to pledge their veracity as to a point of law.

Now, sir, we are so far from admitting that this paper is not a purgation of the kind that I have mentioned, by showing the real state of facts, that, on the contrary, what we have tendered to demonstrate is, that it is, substantially, in accordance with the precedents upon that very subject.

Every case cited by Mr. Van Dyke, (except the case in Brown's Parl. Reports, which, as he states it, contains nothing that we should quarrel with;)—I say that upon almost every case which he has cited, we intend to rely.

The question is, what is a clearance of contempt? and I offer to show that upon the principles of these adjudications, that this is a clearing of the contempt.

In regard to interrogatories,—and I was going further into the cases if necessary,—as I stated, I cannot find any case in England, where they have been put at the instance of the party defendant.

In the case decided by Judge Griffith and Judge Tilghman, Wallace's Reports, it was, certainly, left to the option of the party, whether he should be placed upon interrogatories. In 9 Watts, the Court did, undoubtedly, say that the absence of interrogatories is not fatal. It is an opinion of Judge Sergeant's, that it was pretty much at the option of either party or the Court, whether the interrogatories should be propounded. But all these matters will be properly heard if you will take the petition and read it.

Judge KANE. Well, gentlemen, I will meet you to morrow morning, at 10 o'clock.

The Court was then adjourned accordingly.

DISTRICT COURT OF THE UNITED STATES.

October 27th, 1855.

BEFORE JUDGE KANE.

Court opens at 10 o'clock, A. M.

Judge KANE. I have looked through, gentlemen, the paper submitted to my inspection by the counsel of Mr. Williamson yesterday. I do not find that it contains a purgation of his contempt or the expression of any wish, on his part, to make such purgation. I, therefore, will hear the counsel further if they see fit to go on.

Mr. MEREDITH. I was in hopes, sir, that your examination of that paper would have had a different result. I will now, briefly proceed to lay before you the authorities which have occured to me on this subject, bearing in mind, throughout, what I stated yesterday about the different kinds of contempt.

The contempt here, sir, consists in nothing but an alleged want of compliance with the writ issued by the Court, or the process of the Court. Now, sir, I have not been able to find any precisely such cases in the books either English or American ; i. e. I have not been able to find a case in which a party has been in custody as a respondent on a *habeas corpus* for any other purpose than to answer interrogatories propounded to him by the Court, or even for that purpose unless there were something on the face of the return itself, evasive. For that reason, it will not be easy to find the precise mode in which this particular matter is to be treated, but I take it, by analogy, to be like an ordinary case of a non-compliance with the process of the Court.

In the first place I would observe that wherever, in such cases, interrogatories have been administered, it has not been, technically, for the purpose of obtaining a disavowal of any personal disrespect to the Court, for that is not involved in the question, but they have been administered for the purpose of sifting the conscience of the party making the return, or who is called upon for the answers ; in either case, the return, or answer, being *prima facia* conclusive, the return absolutely so, and the answer remaining so, until contradicted, as the rules of equity require.

Now, sir, the question that I am considering is,—whether it lies

on the party to pray to be submitted to interrogatories or whether
it is a matter for the Court to administer to him if deemed necessary,
and which, when administered, he is to answer. As I understand
it, Judge Story says, upon the state of facts adduced in the case in
3 Mason, to which I wish to refer, although you are no doubt well
acquainted with it, that the regular course of practice was to propound interrogatories and compel the party in that way to disclose,
more fully, the matters within his knowledge for the satisfaction of
the Court.

Judge KANE. I am very familiar with the case.

Mr. MEREDITH. I should like to call your attention to what
Judge Story said on that occasion. (The book not being in Court
at the time, it was sent for and Mr. M. proceeded with his remarks.)

Now, sir, I have looked as carefully as I could into the English
books, and as I have had no authority produced by the other side
differing from what I myself have found, I am left to assume that
there is none; and as I understand them, I cannot find a case of any
other practice whatever, than that of which Judge Story speaks.
In those Courts where the process of interrogatories commenced, it
was exactly the compulsory process of the Court in compelling
answers to them which was most complained of by the subjects.
When that principle was, from necessity, adopted in the common
law, and in the Court of Chancery in common law proceedings,
which a habeas corpus is, and which the Chancellor, though it has
been denied that he could issue a writ of habeas corpus, before the
Stat. Charles 2, yet, undoubtedly, under that statute, has the same
right to do as the other Judges; when this came to be adopted in
these Courts, sir, this proceeding by interrogatory accompanied
it as a necessary accompaniment.

At what precise period it became necessary to resort to process
of this kind I cannot state; it, probably, was pretty early, but it was
after the commencement of the reports of the common law.

The common law generally executed its own process; that is to
say, when it first began to be complained that men were unlawfully
deprived of personal liberty, the writ of homine replegiando was the
writ of common law which the Sheriff executed. The defendant in
the writ was commanded to do nothing. The Sheriff was ordered to
replevy the man that was unlawfully in custody if he could find him,

and, thereupon, the defendant must either produce the party or submit to the due process of law.

But the writ of *habeas corpus* being found more convenient, the process of homine replegiando fell into comparative disuse, and then when a case arose that a party absolutely disobeyed the mandate of the Court, he committed that species of contempt of which I have spoken, viz., a contempt in disobeying process.

The interrogatories were therefore put upon him by the Court, as in the case in 3 Mason. I need scarcely say that I cite this case for this point only. I do not admit its authority on the question of jurisdiction.

This case, U. S. vs. Green, (3d Mason Rep. p. 484,) was of a *habeas corpus*, where the judge was not satisfied with the return. Judge Story says:

"I am not satisfied that the return contains all those facts within the knowledge of the defendant, which are necessary to be brought before the Court, to enable it to decide, whether he is entitled to a discharge, or, in other words, whether he has not now a power to produce the infant, and control those in whose custody she is.

"There is no doubt that an attachment is the proper process to bring the defendant into Court. But suppose he were here, the next step would be to require him to purge his contempt, and to answer interrogatories. That is the very object of the present motion."

Judge KANE. I do not know whether I have misconceived, but I think that under the Pennsylvania practice,—I speak from my general recollection,—it has been asserted to be the right of the defendant to claim that interrogatories be administered to him. I have never doubted that the Court had the right to require them.

Mr. MEREDITH. But this case (in 3 Mason) as I understand it, is in conformity with all the English cases that I have been able to find, not that the Court has a right to require them, but that it is the course of the Court, and it is the duty of the Court to administer those interrogatories, if the case be one requiring interrogatories, which upon the record this case is not, or to discharge the party.

I will now present, sir, what perhaps I should have presented sooner, an English authority, although it is not my purpose to trouble you with a numerous list of cases, because I find none inconsistent with the one that I have already cited, and as none have been produced by the other side differing therefrom, I am at liberty to presume that Sergeant Hawkins states the matter correctly.

9

Now, sir, this is a work of so much authority, that, as I have said, I do not feel myself justified in toiling with you through a considerable number of English cases, and I shall merely say, as I did at first, that I find none contradicting it; and if there be any such I should be glad to have them presented that I may have an opportunity of making my observations and answers by other cases. I take the authorities that I have already cited, therefore, upon this subject, as a true statement of the course of the Court upon contempts, namely, that interrogatories are to be administered, where the contempt does not consist in a mere refusal to make a sufficient return; as for instance, where the object of the interrogatories is to ascertain the fact whether the party has used opprobrious language to the Court, or done violence to the officers of the Court or in presence of the Court. Under these circumstances and in this connection he is called upon to answer interrogatories, and he is bound over to do so; and the Court compels him to do so, because he stands charged with contempt; and if he be convicted, he is sentenced to imprisonment for a limited time. But still more is this course necessary where the whole object of the process of contempt is to enforce his answer. That is the very thing which he has failed to do sufficiently, or which it is assumed he has failed to do. The whole object of the Court is not to punish a personal disrespect of the Court, or its officers or process, because none such has been committed, in this case, but it is to enforce an answer in order to do away with that constructive disrespect which consists in the mere disobedience of process, in not complying with it in a complete and full manner. It does not involve any other kind of disrespect than that constructive kind. The whole object, therefore, in such case is to force the party to answer interrogatories. He is to be compelled to do it. He ought to be committed or held to bail to answer interrogatories. I find that the common law rule laid down, as I say, clearly and fully upon this point, is, that if the practice of the King's Bench were to be understood as prevailing here, and this party had been so committed, he could now claim to be entitled to a discharge on the ground that interrogatories had not been administered within the four days. I ought to add, however, that upon reference to the cases which Sergeant Hawkins relies upon, I do find that in some of them the Court require, that notice should be given to the other side, so that he may not be taken by surprise, and then he is to file his interrogatories within the time above mentioned.

Now, sir, this shows, I think, clearly :—that in a Court of common law upon the worst kind of contempt, upon that kind which is between the Court or the public and the party, and not that between party and party merely, as it is in cases where the defendant has not made a full return to the process of the Court, which might happen by inadvertence, or a thousand causes not at all leading to any intention to disobey its process,—that even in the worst kind of cases, and still more in the more favorable kind, so far there is no necessity for the presentation of a petition, praying to be allowed to purge contempt ; but that the contempt is actually purged, *ipso facto*, by the neglect of the crown or of the opposite party to file interrogatories within four days, and the defendant is entitled to be discharged upon mere motion on the ground of that default.

Now, sir, when we look to Chancery, we find there what amounts substantially to the same thing. The nearest that I can come to the position of this case in point of principle in Chancery, (and I shall be exceedingly obliged, if you know of anything which approaches nearer in analogy, that you will mention it so that I may refer to it,) the nearest position to which I can come is a refusal to appear or a refusal to answer. Upon these points I find the practice of the English Chancery to be, as I understand it, very clear, and for that practice I shall not refer so much to the cases now, because they speak in general terms of clearing contempt, and they leave open the question as to what is considered a clearing of contempt. We find here in Hawkins what is considered a clearing of contempt at common law, and here I must make another reservation. I do not understand that in every possible case the answer of a defendant is to clear himself of contempt. I admit that I can find cases in which it is laid down in the common law Courts that where a party has beaten an officer, for instance, in an attempt to serve process, that the Court is not tied down to his mere answers as to the fact, because that fact may be ascertained otherwise; but if the body of testimony be not entirely overwhelming but a mere balance between the statement of the respondent in his answer and another witness, the Court have given credence to the answer of a party even in such a case as that. But on the other hand I do affirm with entire confidence that where the contempt consists in the mere want of a sufficient return to a writ, that there the Court *must* take the answer of the party as final and conclusive, and therefore the sole object is to administer interrogatories in order to purge the conscience of the defendant, and they can be administered only where the return is on its face evasive.

On page 206, Sergeant Hawkins, in his Pleas of the Crown, says:

" And if the offence be of a heinous nature, and the person attending the Court upon such a rule to answer it, or appearing upon an attachment, be apparently guilty, the Court will generally commit him immediately, in order to answer interrogatories to be exhibited against him in relation to such contempt. But if there be any favorable circumstances to extenuate or excuse the offence, or if it appears doubtful whether the party be guilty of it or not, the court will generally in their discretion suffer the party, having first given notice of his intention to the prosecutor, to enter into a recognizance to answer such interrogatories; and if no such interrogatories be exhibited within four days after such recognizance, will discharge the recognizance upon motion. but if the party do not make such motion, and the interrogatories be exhibited after the four days, the Court will compel him to answer them."

Well, sir, I have shown by Hawkins in the English common law that the defendant is purged by answering the interrogatories that the Court command him to answer. That is a purgation of contempt. There is no disavowal of disrespect to the Court, because it would be a constructive disrespect to make a disavowal of the kind, and it would be drawing into the case that which thus far had not existed, to wit: an intentional disrespect; and therefore I cannot find in the common law books, on a failure to make a sufficient answer to a writ, that there ever has been in the books of practice, or forms, or anywhere else, anything like an approach to a petition, praying to purge him from disrespect to the Court, which indeed, would consist in an unnecessary disavowal of that which never existed. The purgation of that contempt is, by making full that answer which the Court found on the face of it not to be full, or by making that return which had not been made, or by obeying that writ which had not been obeyed; and when that is done, the record is sufficient and the contempt is purged. And so much does the purgation of such a contempt depend upon that, that as I have shown by the authority already cited, if these interrogatories be not propounded within four days, such default of the opposite party is a purgation of the contempt, and the party is entitled to his discharge.

I find, sir, in Chancery, the forms and proceedings are of the same character. For instance, I refer to the forms in Smith's Chancery Practice, which is a recent book, and although not of so high authority as the one which I have just cited, yet as to the forms themselves, of course, must be supposed to follow the course of the Court; and, as to the substance of the treatise itself, it is subject to correction by the authorities referred to. (Referring to Smith's Practice, Mr. M. here remarks:) Here are forms, sir, of notices of motion, and one of them is a notice of a motion to commit the defendant and to examine him *viva voce* before the master, the third answer being regarded as insufficient, that is, he having for the third time made an evasive answer to the process of the Court, which commanded him to make a full answer the first time. I will read this notice, sir, which is, I think clear proof for the course of the Court.

In 2d Smith's Chancery Practice, page 562, I find the following form of notice.

"Notice of motion to commit the defendant, and to examine him *viva voce* before the Master, his third answer being reported insufficient

IN CHANCERY.—*Between, &c.*

Take notice, &c., that the said defendant may be examined upon interrogatories before the said Master to the points wherein the said defendant's answers are reported insufficient, and that he may stand committed to his Majesty's Prison of the Fleet, until he shall perfectly answer the said interrogatories, or this Court make other order to the contrary. Dated, &c.

Yours, &c.
To &c."

I will now read the petition from Smith, p. 577.

"*Petition to discharge a Defendant out of Custody.*

IN CHANCERY.—*Between, &c.*

To the Right Honorable, &c., the humble petition of the defendant showeth, that the plaintiff having filed his bill against your petitioner, he appeared thereto. That your petitioner being in contempt for want of his answer, an attachment was issued against him, and your petitioner was taken thereon, (or gave bail:) that your petitioner has filed his answer, and is willing to pay the costs of his contempt

Your petitioner, therefore, &c., that your petitioner upon his paying or tendering his costs of contempt, may be discharged out of the custody of ———, as to his said contempt.

And your petitioner, &c."

Now, sir, that is all; that is the form in which the contempt is cleared. But, although this be the usual form, I presume, used in Chancery now, yet in strict practice I admit that it is proper and right to get leave from the Court first to file his answer.

I will now read from Newland's Chancery Practice and Forms, 2d vol. as to a like petition, which is a book of more authority than that of Smith's.

I find on page 187, as follows:

"Petition to be discharged out of custody of the Sergeant-at-arms.

Between, &c.

To the Right Honorable, the Master of the Rolls, the humble petition of the defendant showeth, That your petitioners are and have been (for above a fortnight) in custody of the Sergeant-at-arms attending this Court, for not answering to the plaintiff's bill, which your petitioners have since answered, and paid the cost of the contempts, and the Clerk of the other side, who consents to your petitioner's discharge, as by the certificate annexed appears: your petitioners, therefore, humbly pray your Honors that your petitioners may be discharged out of the custody of the Sergeant-at-arms, paying their fees,

And your petitioner shall ever pray, &c."

Upon that petition the party had filed his answer and paid the costs, and the opposite party consenting, he is discharged, which shows that when the thing ordered by the Court to be done, is done, there is an end of it;—there is nothing further to purge. That is the clearing of the contempt. Now, sir, in the text of these books, you will find the same principles laid down. I shall not detain you, however, by reading it, and with your permission, you will consider me as having referred to the text which relates to this matter.

Now, sir, so much as to what is the purgation of a contempt of this kind. It consists in giving to the Court in full that information which the Court thought was not given to it in full by the original answer or return, or by making such a statement as satisfies the Court, that the original return or answer so far as appertains to any question pending in the case itself, was really and truly full and correct. Taking the case of an insufficient return to a *habeas corpus*, sir, where the insufficiency consisted in the belief on the part of the judge, that there had been a custody or control of some kind, of the party whose body is required to be produced, before the issuing of the writ, and upon that founding the inference, that

that control or custody continued at the time of the service of the writ, and that therefore that part of the return which had unnecessarily stated anything about the control or custody, before the service of the writ, being untrue, the inference carried to the subsequent part of the return, is such as to require further clearing up on the part of the respondent,—taking it in that connection, which I suppose to be this case as nearly as I can state it, what ought the commitment to be for? To coerce; it is not as a punishment, or else it would be for a limited time. It should be on its face, simply to coerce a fuller answer by the party, because the return of the respondent to these prerogative writs is conclusive, and all the Court can do is to require it to be made more full, and to sift and purge his conscience in any mode that it may think necessary to the administration of justice.

The whole purpose and intent, therefore, of this commitment, should have been like that mentioned in the petition which I read from Smith. The Petitioner is—he can only be, in due course of law—committed until he shall make response to such interrogatories as the Court shall command him to answer. Now, sir, why have they not been filed, if this is the purpose of the commitment? This Petitioner has now already lain in prison three months this day, I think, because his answer to the writ of habeas corpus was believed by your honor not to be sufficiently full. He should have been committed, therefore, until he should answer such interrogatories as you might think fit to put to him, or to allow the other party to put to him. Now, I shall be glad if the learned counsel on the other side will show me a case in which, under such circumstances, the party has been compelled to remain in custody until he presents a prayer that he may be submitted to interrogatories. If he can, I shall be exceedingly glad to see it. And this is not answered by saying what we all admit, and what I am as ready to concede as the opposite side to advance and your honor to decide, to wit: that when a party is in contempt his first step is to clear himself of contempt. That is very true: but what is the clearance of his contempt? For that we are to look to the law, and we find in this connection, that the clearance is in the answer to the interrogatories put to him. How is he to answer when none are put? Here is the prayer of the opposite party in the Chancery books, praying that the respondent be committed until he shall answer

interrogatories, or the Court shall direct that he need not do it
That is the term of his commitment. In common law courts, we
find when he is taken on attachment he is held to bail—to do what?
To answer interrogatories. That is the end which the law proposes.

How is he to do it until they be put, and where is the case to be
found in which a party committed for an insufficient return or
answer to any process of the Court—nay, for refusing to answer
at all the process of the Court, which is a much higher contempt
than that of merely an insufficient answer, because it involves a
sort of absolute disregard of the Court;—where is the case to be
found, I ask, in which a party so committed, has been left to lie for
three months without ever having interrogatories propounded in
writing or orally, or anything being put upon the record for him to
answer? Sir, I have not been able to find such a case. I do find,
as I say, and I admit, that he is first to clear his contempt, that is
to say, that he is not to be at liberty to disregard the step in which
he has disobeyed the process of the Court, and to come into Court
and move in other respects like a common suitor. He cannot do it.
Therefore, in Chancery, if he be committed for a contempt in filing an
in sufficient answer, or in refusing to answer the bill, he is not at
liberty until that contempt has been cleared, to come in and file a
demurrer to the bill, thus declining to answer altogether, and going
back a step in the cause. I believe in such a case, that he may
file a plea to the bill, because that goes to matter of fact material
to the case. But he lies there in that case until he comes forward
to make his answer, the order of the Court being that he shall
answer, in the case just mentioned, the bill, or in another case
the interrogatories, because there is nothing else for him to answer.
And in fact, this party stands as if he were committed for not
answering a bill which has never been filed; for the original
writ of habeas corpus simply commands him to bring in the body.
It assumes the fact, that he has the body in his possession, and his
return that he has not the body, if not sufficiently clear to satisfy
the conscience of the Court, puts the Court, which has for the first
time heard of it, under the necessity of examining him in regard
to that fact; and that examination I take to be by the interrogatories,
which are in fact the bill which he is called upon to answer, and if he
refuses, he is to be committed until he answers it. So that this petitioner has been imprisoned for three months, and may be for life, for

370

not answering interrogatories which have never been propounded to
him, or put upon the record :—which, in fact, have no existence.

In Daniel's Chancery Practice I find this passage :

(1 Dan. p. 559,) "It is to be observed, that where process of contempt has been issued against a defendant for want of an answer, he is
entitled to be discharged from his contempt immediately upon his putting in an answer, and paying or tendering the costs of his contempt;
and the Court will not detain him in custody till the sufficiency of his
answer has been decided upon, unless he has already put in three answers
which have been reported insufficient. For by the 10th order of 1828,
upon a third answer being reported insufficient, the defendant shall be
examined upon interrogatories to the points reported insufficient, and
shall stand committed until such defendant shall have perfectly answered
such interrogatories. An order for the defendant's discharge may be
obtained by motion, *ex parte*, upon production of the certificate of answer
filed, and proof of the tender of costs."

You will find in that passage, I think, the law clearly stated, to
wit: that the clearance of the contempt consists in presenting himself to the Court, upon such a ground as shows a compliance with
the order of the Court. My colleague also yesterday, sir, gave you
a case in Sandford's Reports, in which a motion was received for
the discharge of a party, on the ground of his inability to obey
the mandate of the Court.

In 6 Price's Reports is a case to which I wish to call your attention, where a party who was in contempt was discharged upon
motion, although he had been committed for disobeying an injunction of the Court, which is a very high grade of contempt. Being
thus in contempt and having lain some time, he was discharged on
motion simply, and without any petition. Now, sir, that was a
contempt of a somewhat higher nature than this, although it belonged to the same general class, to wit : disobedience to the process
of the Court.

Judge KANE. You refer to the case in 6 Price; do you not ?

Mr. MEREDITH. Yes, sir. The book will be here in a moment.

Now, sir, that is a contempt of a higher nature, although it belongs to the same general class, but it consists in an absolute refusal
to obey, whereas, *this* consists of a believed want of a full obedience,
and that want to be tested, if required, by a further examination on
interrogatories. Yet, even in that case, sir, after the party had lain
in prison for a time, which was conceived to be long enough to operate
as a punishment, he was discharged, upon motion, and that in a very

solemn way.   The practice was not a common one ; it was, perhaps new, and the Court held the matter under consideration for the purpose of consulting with the highest authority, and, after that consultation, discharged him.

Mr. Meredith here asked again for 6 Price, and not obtaining it, he remarked :

It is very unpleasant to me, sir, not to have the books ; not so much, because it disorders the train of my own ideas, as because the fact of my being obliged for want of them to pass from point to point, in a somewhat disconnected way, must necessarily tax your mind.

Judge KANE.   Not at all, sir.

Mr. MEREDITH.   I will therefore, for a few moments, go back and say a few words as to its being the duty of the Court to propound interrogatories, as I have shown you by the English practice, the commitment tends to that end solely.

Judge KANE.   A case to my mind more closely analogous than that to which you have referred, is where a party refuses to answer interrogatories, and who is in contempt for thus refusing to answer.

Mr. MEREDITH.   There he is to pray, because he cannot otherwise get out to answer : but then he must have refused to answer before he was committed.   This Petitioner has never refused to answer any thing.

Judge KANE.   I speak of it as a case more nearly analogous when he prays that he may come in to make the answer.   By the analogy, the party who is in contempt for not answering fully to the writ of habeas corpus, prays that he may come in to make a full answer.

Mr. MEREDITH.   I will come to that presently ; but I will say, respectfully in the meanwhile, that I do not consider the case of a refusal to answer interrogatories analogous, because in that instance, you have got to the end of the thing.

Judge KANE.   On an interrogatory in cases of contempt, or an interrogatory administered before the master or in Court, where there is a refusal to make a response and the party is in contempt for refusal and has been so adjudged, the party desiring to make the answer applies to the Court, if I understand the practice, for permission *now* to answer, and thereupon he is permitted to come into Court to make the answer.

Mr. MEREDITH. He has had something put to him to answer, and he has refused to answer it.

Judge KANE. That is the *former* interrogatory put to him. The analogy, too, of his having refused to answer to the demands of the writ of habeas corpus, he asks now to come in and to make that answer which should have been made before—this is the analogy which to my mind is more direct than any cases to which you have referred.

Mr. MEREDITH. I am happy that you have mentioned it, as I consider it perfectly analogous to the case of a Bill, and I will show why, presently. In the meanwhile, I will say a word in regard to the course which has been pursued in one or two cases that have occurred in this district. One is the case from Wallace, in which undoubtedly Judge Griffith and Judge Tilghman did lay down the rule to be, that it was at the option of the party, to pray to be submitted to interrogatories. There the other side had asked the Court to propound them; and although the Court spoke of the English practice, as in accordance with the course which they adopted, no authorities were given, and I am totally unable to find on what they relied. In Passmore's case, (3 Yates, 438,) the party submitted to answer interrogatories; that is to say, being brought before the Court to answer them, he did so; but there is no petition praying that interrogatories might be propounded; and it simply amounts to this, that upon the interrogatories being put to him he answered them.

Judge KANE. I find in the arguments of Mr. Dallas and Mr. Ingersoll, which followed the impeachment of the Chief Justice, that this is spoken of as the established Pennsylvania practice; but upon what basis I do not know.

Mr. MEREDITH. That is so:—and in fact there is nothing which goes to show that the Pennsylvania practice differed from the English.

In the case in 9 Watts, the County Commissioners had disobeyed the order of the Court, and it was decided to be a contempt, and they were committed without interrogatories. The case was taken up by *certiorari* to the Supreme Court—and it was decided that the mere want of interrogatories was not a fatal defect. As far as I can understand the Court, they seem to think that if the interrogatories were not required by the defendant to be filed, the omission to file them could not be taken advantage of after conviction. I do not think that the case throws a great deal of light upon the subject, other than that the omission to file the interrogatories, was not .fatal to the commitment in the appellate Court; and I am sorry to say that I do not find any reference to any English or any other authority upon that point. It therefore does not amount to anything, and we have against it the whole body of the English authorities, and, as I understand it, the Supreme Court, under the lead of Judge Shippen, in Passmore's case, the simple *dictum* of Judges Griffith and Tilghman, in Wayne's case in Wallace's Reports. These judges were men for whom we all entertain the highest respect, but where their opinion purports to be based upon something in the English books and not upon any peculiarity of practice here, and when the English books are searched in vain to find the authority on which alone they gave their judgement, the necessary presumption is, that they were mistaken in gathering the purport of the precedents to which they had referred. I can come to no other conclusion.

Judge KANE. Do you remember who were the counsel in that case of Wallace?

Mr. MEREDITH. I think Mr. Dallas and Mr. Ingersoll on one side, and Mr. Chauncey and Mr. Wallace on the other side. There were two sets of cases going on at the same time. They were both of a political cast; one against the editor of the "United States Gazette," and the other against the editor of the "Aurora;" and they seemed to go on neck and neck at the same time.

Now, sir, under this view of this part of the case, what analogy can we find between a case like this and the case of the refusal to answer an interrogatory? As in the case of a refusal to answer a bill, the object of commitment is to compel an answer to the interrogatory, a thing which is on the record. I consider the refusal to answer the interrogatory exactly like the refusal to answer the bill, because the bill is an interrogatory propounded by the authority of the Court, and the exigency of the writ of subpœna is, that the defendant shall come in and answer that bill; so that I look upon it to be the same case precisely. But the difficulty here is, sir, that there is nothing on the record for him to answer. Now, this is not merely formal, as you will perceive in a moment. Here is a writ of habeas corpus, which assumes that the party is in the custody of the respondent. There is nothing propounded to him on that subject in the writ. He is commanded to produce the body. On the return of the writ, instead of producing the body, he presents the excuse that he cannot produce it, because the body is not in his custody, and has not been since the time that the writ was served. Now, sir, he has made his statement directly to the fact. Upon that statement the learned judge, before whom these proceedings are pending, arrives at the conclusion, that his conscience is not satisfied that that statement of the fact is true. It desires therefore, to sift the conscience of the party. How is he to do this? By interrogatories. Now, if it be said, let him go on and make a fuller answer, how is he to do it? A fuller answer he cannot make, because, when he answered that he has not now the custody, &c. of the parties, and that he never had, that is as full an answer as it is possible for human ingenuity to conceive. But you have thought fit to commit him, for the purpose as I gather, that he may be, in the way of a cross-examination, sifted as to the circumstances. Now, sir, how is he to foresee what that examination may be?

Judge KANE. You have named the precise difficulty that rests upon my mind. How can he make a response in advance by any instrument that he files? Not knowing what is the interrogatory which will be administered to him, I apprehend that the answer precludes that part of the argument. It is impossible that he can know beforehand what will be the character of the interrogatory, and it does not seem to me clear that he can file a paper which shall be responsive to, he knows not what, and thus relieve himself from contempt. It seems to me that the argument you are kind enough to address to me, would carry us to this: that the party having been committed for refusing to make the full answer, must declare that he is willing to make the full answer when thereto interrogated, whereupon the Court interrogates him. The first step, inasmuch as there is no definite interrogatory to which he can file his answer, must be, as it strikes me from the necessities of the case, a protestation on his part, that he is now prepared to make an answer to such interrogatories as shall be administered to him, touching the proper return to the writ of habeas corpus.

Mr. MEREDITH. That relieves me from this part of the argument, because it shows that the propounding of interrogatories is the thing to which he can alone answer, and therefore he has no mode of purging the contempt or showing that he is not guilty of it, but by answering those interrogatories ; and here none have been propounded.

Judge KANE. And the Court cannot administer the interrogatories to a party who has already placed himself in contempt, until he proffers himself as willing to do so.

Mr. MEREDITH. These cases all show that on the contrary, the very commitment of the party ought to be until he shall answer interrogatories, and these are required to be promptly filed, that he may know what he has to answer and prepare his answer accordingly.

Judge KANE. In that class of cases which must have been distinguished in your mind, the business of the party who prosecutes, that is to say, upon whose motion the commitment for contempt is made, undoubtedly is to file his interrogatories. It is undoubtedly competent, however, to the defendant to remain in prison as long as he chooses, unless he will avail himself of the laches of the party prosecuting, and make a motion for his discharge, because there has been a failure on the part of the other side to file his interrogatories. No doubt, in that class of cases, such is the fact. The one party is bound to file interrogatories. If he does not file interrogatories, the other party gives him notice that he will move the Court for a discharge, because of the default of the party prosecuting in not filing interrogatories within the four days ; and thereupon, as a matter of course, the party is discharged upon simply proving that he has given notice of the motion, and upon inspection of the record of the Court, finding there no interrogatories.

Mr. MEREDITH. Then I need not argue further the point which I was upon, that he is not called upon, nor is it possible for him to make further answer to the writ of habeas corpus ; and as it stands now, he must wait until he is cross-examined. So far there is no difference of opinion between us, as that is the point I was about to prove. This alters the aspect of the case as it stands on the record. Now, sir, I would respectfully ask the learned counsel on the opposite side to produce any case in England or this country, from the beginning of the recorded decisions of either down to the present time, in which a party has been kept in prison for not answering that which has never been propounded to him or is not filed upon the record of the Court. He cannot do it, sir, because the case does not exist. If a party refuses to answer a bill, the bill is filed ; he knows what it is he has to answer. If he refuses to answer an interrogatory, whether a party or a witness, the interrogatory is upon the records of the Court, or has been put to him orally, and he knows what he has to answer. But where, I would like to see, is the case in which a party has been held in restraint not only for three months, but for the shortest space of time, for not answering interrogatories which are not filed? How can he answer them? He would be discharged under the four day rule, and he is now restrained in custody for an unlimited time by the default of the opposite party in not doing that which it is their duty to do. On this ground, there is not, certainly, a non-compliance, on his part, with the order of the Court.

Judge KANE. It is not so, by any means. He is committed because he has made an evasive return which the Court has held to be not a legal return. It is competent to him to declare his willingness to make a full return. Whenever he does so the Court indicates to him, by interrogatories, the points as to which his return or his answer must be other than as it is. The only difficulty which seems to me to pervade the argument, (perhaps because I have not correctly followed you) is merely in that there is no interrogatory filed. It seems to me there could be none filed addressed to a party who is at the time in contempt. I mean that it would be in vain for the Court to direct a party to answer, the party having refused. I will not interrupt you further.

Mr. MEREDITH. I think that we agree upon the question of the return. If he amends his return without interrogatories, who knows that it will be better than the original? It cannot be done. If, on the other hand, it be upon interrogatories, it cannot be by an amendment of his return. The amendment of his return cannot be by answers to interrogatories. Your honor may, after interrogatories have been answered, if you think fit, give him leave to amend his return in accordance with those answers, (though I know of no such practice,) but the two things are essentially distinct. The return is his own. It must be hit or miss when he is in trouble, the conscience of the Court not being satisfied with his original return, because it is not for him to assume in regard to what particular matters the Court may desire to be further informed. Therefore, it is impossible for him to say, " I will amend my return," because his answer may not be what is required, and he is left in the dark to grope his way about until he happen to hit that which will satisfy the conscience of the Court. But the moment you come to interrogatories, you have done with the possibility of an amendment to the return, because he cannot amend his return by answers to interrogatories.

Judge KANE. My remark was, return or answer. They are clearly distinguishable. I do not mean to say that a man's answers in Court can be considered an amendment of his return. It is merely a question of phraseology, in which I am anxious to stand corrected.

Mr. MEREDITH. I will confine myself, therefore, to the question of interrogatories. I say, then, the party is in the situation of one who is committed for cross-examination for the purpose of sifting his conscience. Now, sir, in such a case, the practice is to propound to him the interrogatories which he is called upon to answer, the purpose of his committment being to make him answer,—the recognizance being that he will appear to answer—the prayer in Chancery being that he may be committed until he shall answer—answer what? Answer something which is on the record of the Court after four days, during which time he is bailed or is under an attachment. That is the practice in all the cases which I have been able to find. The thing on the record is what he is to come forward and answer. Now, sir, I again request that if there be found in the books a case in which a party is held for refusing to answer interrogatories, to submit to a cross-examination, when there are no interrogatories filed during the short interval which the common law rule allows for the purpose of filing them, I should be very glad if the opposite side would furnish it. I think that there is no such case; for in all the cases which I have found there has been something filed on the records of the Court for the party to answer, and then he can answer and then he can be discharged.

Now, sir, under these circumstances, let me say a word as to the real scope, as I understand it, of this petition. The Petitioner shows his readiness to answer. There are no interrogatories filed. He shows his readiness to answer, and his desire to give full information to the Court by making a clear, distinct, positive averment, so far as he is able by the exercise of his intellect to make it full and complete; that in point of fact since the time when he saw the parties in the carriage in Dock street, he has had no communication, direct or indirect, and no knowledge, direct or indirect, further than everybody has had through the public press or rumors of public events, of the whereabouts or situation or position of these people at all.

Now, sir, suppose you are satisfied, upon this averment, of the utter impossibility of his obeying the writ or producing the bodies; and suppose, moreover, that you should be of opinion that the statement ought to be made in answer to interrogatories, or that the return ought to be amended. If so, make the order that interrogatories shall be filed and command him, for the first time, to answer, which he either does, or remains as he is if he refuses. He then has propounded to him that which I find from the cases he is entitled to have, namely, something on the record of the Court which he is called upon to answer. Now, sir, if you are satisfied that his suggestion in the petition shows the impossibility of his obeying the writ by producing the bodies, discharge him upon that; but if you think that the stricter forms of proceeding would require an amendment of the return, by stating these facts, or if you think that interrogatories are wanting, let the interrogatories be propounded to him, and he will then be in contempt if he refuses to answer them; but that has not yet come. He has never yet failed to answer everything that has been propounded to him. Now, sir, I was not, as I have already explained to you, in Court, nor had I any personal knowledge of what occurred at the time when the affidavit was presented out of which this petition grew, but from the information which I derived of what transpired before the presentation of this petition from the only one of my learned colleagues with whom I had an opportunity of consulting, the other being absent in Mifflin county, I had not the slightest doubt on my mind that the real and *bona fide* belief of my colleague was and is that this petition was in accordance with the suggestion of your honor. It seems, however, that you were misunderstood, and it is very unfortunate that it is so.

Judge KANE. I am sorry to think so, for I have taken great pains upon a great many occasions to indicate what was the opinion of·the judge upon this subject. I think that neither counsel—I do not speak of yourself, sir, because I have not had the honor of communicating with you—I think that neither counsel nor client has had, for months past, any doubt as to what was considered by the judge the appropriate course of proceeding.

Mr. MEREDITH. Now let me ask you to do that which the Chancellor has done a thousand times, and which he does every day, because it is, after all, hard measure, perhaps, that by the misapprehension of counsel of what passes verbally at the bar, or by the still easier misapprehension of a party, who, being in custody, has no knowledge of what is passing, that through these misapprehensions a citizen should be detained an hour beyond the time when he is entitled to his discharge; and let me, under these circumstances, ask you, as I was about to do before, that if you find that this answer contained in his petition does not satisfy your demands, and are of opinion that in point of form it ought to be by answering interrogatories or by amending his return,—let me ask you to do as the Chancellor does every day, as precedents show,—make an order specifying what is to be done, that is, that he be discharged upon answering interrogatories, or on such other condition as you may deem proper. If you are not satis-

10

fied in point of fact that the statement in his petition is true, order interrogatories to be filed in a certain time, and that he be discharged on making satisfactory answer to them, although this would not be required in the English practice, because he would be entitled to his discharge, though the answer be insufficient, if interrogatories be not filed within four days.

Judge KANE. I have no difficulty at all upon the point suggested by Mr. Meredith, and there never has been a difficulty in my mind of indicating in any form most acceptable.

Mr. MEREDITH. If your honor will make on this petition an order that he shall be discharged upon satisfactorily answering the interrogatories that shall be filed in a certain time, or if you are satisfied that he may be discharged by amending his return in accordance with his petition, give him leave to do so.

Judge KANE. The proper course, as it seems to me, is simply this: The party adjudicated to be in contempt submits himself by writing to the jurisdiction of the Court to answer interrogatories. I speak of the particular case. That is what I understand to be technical purgation, the clearing of the contempt. The party declares that he is now willing to answer interrogatories upon the subject matter. The Court then proceeds, either by the aid of counsel or directly, to interrogate him in writing or orally (both forms, I believe, are practised in precedents,) and he is discharged or not, as the case may be. I see no difficulty in indicating this in the form of an order upon the mere suggestion of the learned counsel who stands before me, that upon his filing what I have called a purgation, a declaration that he is now prepared to answer interrogatories, and to submit himself to examination touching matters which, in the judgment of the Court, should have been embraced in his return, that he then be submitted to those interrogatories or subjected to that examination. I see no difficulty in it. All that seems to me to be necessary now, or which has been necessary heretofore, is a distinct declaration by the party in contempt that he is prepared to answer when called upon to answer by the Court. That seems to me to be the practice. And I will say this: the research which the gentlemen have been kind enough to submit themselves to, which they have found necessary to do, and which I have found necessary to precede them in, has satisfied them, I have no doubt, as it has satisfied me, that the precedents are not clear; but one thing has seemed to me perfectly certain, that it was in the power of the party, even supposing the Court had erred as to the proper form, to present himself before the Court from the very hour in which he was committed and onward up to the present time, as one willing to answer touching the subjects which should have been embraced in the return to the writ. That has been, in my view, a course so simple, so free from all embarrassment, that I have felt some surprise that after the repeated intimations that have fallen from the bench that such was the course, that it has never been pursued. There seems to have been misapprehension on the part of the counsel, and it may possibly be that their client himself has not been advised of what was the declared view of the Court. If so, it is a regret to me.

Mr. MEREDITH. The apprehension of counsel concerned at the time when the case was first before your honor, and of which I knew nothing, was that on that occasion the Petitioner was submitted to an examination under the contempt, and of course you perceive that that was a misapprehension of a very grave character and productive of peculiar consequences. At a later period in the proceedings you stated that there had been a misunderstanding, and that you had not then so looked upon it. But such was the understanding of counsel present, and from what transpired they of course were of the opinion that it was impossible for him to present himself in the shape you speak of without being guilty of a further contempt. Now, sir, the want of precedents as to matters of this kind of course shows why the petition is in such a shape; but I do find cases constantly, and almost uniformly, in the books, that upon petition to be discharged from contempt, the Chancellor refusing to discharge upon that petition, makes an order that the party shall be discharged upon doing so and so, that is upon answering interrogatories or on some other condition. I do not see why the Petitioner should be required to make a petition stating that he is willing to answer, but let the Court first file the interrogatories and then let him answer them or not.

Judge KANE. It may be that I am in error, but forms have *sometimes* meaning and I think that in this case the form is not without meaning. I am not aware that it would be exactly right for a Court, after a party has for three months remained in contempt, when committed for an omission or refusal to make a full and true return to the writ of habeas corpus, for the Court to speak on its records of interrogatories to be administered to him, he being already recusant. It seems to me that the party should declare his willingness. It seems to me that we have such cases constantly occurring where witnesses refuse to answer at the bar, who are parties in contempt, and when the witnesses announce that they are now ready to answer, the Court addresses questions to them.

Mr. MEREDITH. I am so far from questioning the fact that forms have meaning, that I should enlarge your observation and say, not only that they *sometimes* have meaning, but that they *always* have meaning. Now, my difficulty is that I cannot find a form anywhere in which a party professes his willingness to answer something which has never been propounded to him. I can find abundance of forms where the parties are in custody for refusing to answer something that has been propounded, a point on which I agree with your honor; but I most respectfully affirm that I cannot find a form in which a party expresses his willingness to answer that which has never been propounded, neither do I think that such a form can be found. There is always in all the cases which have come within my observation something upon the record which has been propounded by the Court for him to answer, some question or interrogatory that he is called upon to answer.

Judge KANE. There is one case which I remember in which the party in contempt requested that the questions should be propounded to him before he was required to say that he would answer.

Mr. MEREDITH. And that was an objection.

Judge KANE. Yes, sir, and the Court held that he must engage to answer the questions before they were propounded.

Mr. MEREDITH. Do you remember where it is?

Judge KANE. I think that I can find it. It has occurred to me since this case began.

Mr. MEREDITH. I think that there must be something peculiar in that case, because the general class is not of that kind. Where a party is bailed on the attachment, the condition of the recognisance is that he will appear and answer interrogatories to be filed. Perhaps in the case you refer to, the defendant may have refused to give such a recognisance, in which case he would of course be committed to answer.

Now, sir, here is this case in 6 Price's Exchequer Reports, page 321. It was decided thus—I will read the syllabus:

"The Court will order a person who has been in custody for any given time under an attachment for a contempt of its authority in disobeying an injunction, to be discharged on motion, if the portion of his imprisonment be shewn to its satisfaction to be commensurate with the degree of the offence, on the terms of paying the costs of his contempt; notwithstanding the application be opposed on the part of the plaintiff."

That is to say, although the Petitioner did not make an offer to do the thing which the Court thought necessary, before he could be discharged, yet the Court made an order directing that upon the doing of a certain thing he should be discharged.

Judge KANE. The case to which you have referred was that of an irreparable injury, and it was not in the power of the party to restore the land to pasture.

Mr. MEREDITH. Without a petition, or an affidavit declaring any willingness on the part of the party to do anything, but simply an affidavit stating certain facts, and the motion being thereupon that he should be discharged on certain grounds, the Court made an order that he should be discharged on complying with certain conditions which they set down and which were not mentioned before. That seems to tally with all the other precedents, even in instances of the worst kinds of contempt, such as disrespect to the Court itself by a turbulent deportment or by the use of ill language, under which circumstances the punishment is by imprisonment for a limited time; but where the contempt consists in the mere disobedience of the process of the Court, or of the want of a full answer, an insufficient answer being filed, in such cases I find always, so far as I can see, that when a petition is presented praying for a discharge, the Court does not tell the Petitioner that he must put something additional in his petition; they take the fact of his presenting himself by petition, or, (as in the case referred to in in 6 Price) by affidavit, as sufficient, and thereupon order him to be discharged on condition that he do so and so,—that he answer interrogatories if they be filed, or if it be for not answering a bill, that on answering the bill and paying costs he shall be discharged. So in this case I ask your honor to make a similar order.

Mr. VAN DYKE. I shall not detain your honor more than five minutes, I think, in replying to what Mr. Meredith has said, because, in addition to the cases and authorities which I offered your honor yesterday, it seems to me that the reply to the learned gentleman's argument may be contained in a few words. His argument has taken a wide scope, sir, and it appears to have been more an argument that Mr. Williamson should be discharged by the Court as the case now stands, than an argument upon the question whether a person in contempt has any standing in Court whatever. It is an argument, sir, whether a party is properly in contempt, and not an argument whether a party by a solemn adjudication of a Court of justice being in contempt has a standing in Court. Now, I did not understand this learned Court, when the case was heard on a prayer to file an affidavit or a motion to file an affidavit, to intimate to the learned counsel that it would hear an argument as to whether Mr. Williamson was in contempt. I have taken it, may it please the Court, that you have solemnly adjudicated that fact, that such a judgment of the Court stands upon the records of the Court, and so far as Mr. Williamson is concerned, before this honorable Court he is to take it as law and verity. I say then that the argument of the learned gentleman of the other side has taken a very wide scope when he undertakes to question the propriety of the Court in committing a person for contempt, when there have been no interrogatories filed, and when he undertakes to say that the commitment for contempt was wrong because it was a commitment of contempt for not answering something which was not upon the records of the Court for him to answer. That whole matter has been adjudicated by this learned Court, and the counsel on the other side as well as myself, the Court and the respondent, will take it as law that he is in contempt. Now the only question which your honor suggested to the learned gentleman is this, can a party confessedly in contempt come into Court and ask to be discharged when he still remains in contempt; and if he can, how is he to get clear of his contempt? The learned gentleman has farther, as it appears to me, forgotten the distinction, or at least not adverted to the distinction between a party under attachment prior to an adjudication of contempt, and a party after the judgment of the Court is past. The case referred to in 3 Mason was that of a party under an attachment, no official judgment upon the question of contempt having passed. An attachment is not a commitment, except of a temporary character. It may be a commitment from day to day until the Court adjudges the question of contempt, and so long as the party is in confinement under the attachment, it being but a temporary judgment of the Court, or an interlocutory decree of the Court, it is perfectly competent for the party to come in and say that he wants interrogatories propounded to him, or, as in 9 Watts, he may do otherwise, or the Court may order that interrogatories be put, and so long as the judgment of the Court upon the contempt is not rendered, although the defendant be in confinement under an attachment, he may do so, because it is interlocutory. That was the case in 3 Mason; but after a solemn judgment passed by the Court upon reviewing the return that the party has made which is stated to be contemptuous, after hearing all the facts of the case, and the party is by a solemn decree of the Court said to be in contempt, then it is too late for the defendant, so long as he thus remains in contempt, to ask this Court or any other Court in contempt of which he remains, to do anything until there be an order of the Court showing that that contempt is purged and that he is reinstated as he was in the Court immediately previous to the decree of the Court by which he was adjudged to be in contempt.

Now, the learned gentleman has said that there is nothing upon the record for him to answer. That is not the question. The Court has adjudged that there was something upon the records for him to answer; and they have further adjudged, after hearing the facts of the case from the lips of the witness, as in the Circuit Court of the District of Columbia, in the case of Davis, which was an application of some negroes to be discharged from the custody of a party who held them as slaves— they have adjudged so as in the case of Davis before Judge Cranch, upon his voluntarily submitting himself, that not only was there something for him to answer, but that he has not answered it. What was there for him to answer? There was nothing in the shape of interrogatories put to a witness brought before a commissioner or before the Court to procure testimony; there was not an injunction with which he refused to comply, which is not something for the party to answer, but something for him to obey; but there was a writ of this Court, ordering him to bring certain persons before this honorable Court, which he answered by stating certain facts, which the Court adjudged to be evasive and illusory, and that was the contempt. I say, then, that the learned gentleman appears to have wandered from the main question here, and to have argued questions he was not called upon to argue; because, in the second place, there is nothing for the party to answer, when the Court has solemnly adjudged that there was something to answer and he has not done it. Now, it will be said that it is hard that a party cannot make this objection. Why, it is not pretended—at least I do not pretend—that he has not an opportunity, and cannot have an opportunity, of making it. But how is he to do it? Why, he must first get rid of that difficulty which stands in his way, and which, so long as it stands there, he can take no step before the Court, and he must be reinstated by submitting to the judgment of this Court solemnly made, and in a collateral question solemnly reaffirmed, offer a review of all the facts in the case; he must first submit to the judgment of the Court by coming in and asking to be relieved by purgation of his contempt, whereupon he is reinstated in the position he formerly occupied in Court, and interrogatories are submitted or not, as the case may afterwards shape itself in its different phases. Now, this is the law, and why is it so? The Court has adjudicated that the return made by Mr. Passmore Williamson is a contempt, and he asks now to come in and file a petition. I will not undertake to say (because I object to its being read in Court) what it contains, although we know as individuals and not as part of this case, the Court has seen it. It is perfectly proper, therefore, for me to presume what is contained therein. It may be a petition reiterating the return already made. If so, he commits a second contempt, and how is the Court to punish him for it while he is in contempt now? It may be a petition reiterating part of the return already made, and, by implication, confessing the falsity of another part. If so, he comes into Court, and in the very petition praying for his discharge, because he has not committed a contempt, admits the falsity of his former return, which the Court has adjudged to be a contempt. If so, he commits an additional contempt, and how is the Court to punish him for it? He is already in confinement for contempt of Court, and if he is to be permitted to file a petition which may contain these things, he commits an additional contempt and the Court has no power over him; and if he can do it once, he can do it fifty times, and as often as there are days in the year

Now, in reference to the request of the learned gentleman, that the Court shall make a written decree as to what Mr. Williamson must do, I have a single word to suggest to your honor, and I think it is a proper one.

It strikes me that if this Court, or the counsel who are opposed to Mr. Williamson, treat him in any way as a party not in contempt, the contempt is waived; and I take it that an order from this Court requesting Mr. Williamson, or telling him upon the records of this Court that he shall do this or that, or any order except it be an order merely propounding what the law is, is a waiver on the part of the Court of the contempt in which he now stands. If a defendant refuse to answer to a bill in equity and he is committed for a contempt in not answering, and the complainant subsequently receives his answer, the contempt is waived, upon the principle that he is dealing with him as a party not in contempt; and I therefore most respectfully object to the suggestion of my learned friend that this Court shall say to Mr. Williamson, " You may do this," or "you may do that;" and I respectfully suggest to your honor that the only step which this Court can take under the present aspect of the case in delivering its opinion to propound what the law is, that you neither can tell him what he may do any more than this learned Court can call him before the bar now and ask him the question whether he intended to evade the writ, or whether he was connected with certain persons for the purpose of evading just such a process as this was which issued from this Court, and which certainly, if I were now to come into Court and ask an order that Mr. Williamson be allowed to answer such a question, your honor would say, " Mr. Williamson is in contempt; I cannot permit this question to be answered until he gets rid of it." The learned gentleman asks the Court to go still further; that is, to call upon him, or to say that he must do this or that, directed to him as an order, thus preparing the petition for him to get rid of the contempt, which it is his duty to do himself. I do not think, may it please the Court, that there is anything else in the argument of the learned gentleman, or anything that has been said to which I have occasion to reply. The case of Davis in 5 Cranch, to which I have referred, your honor, as well as the learned counsel, are aware of, and I do not think that there is anything else unanswered. I have not quite kept my pledge in regard to the time which I would consume. I hope your honor will excuse me for not doing so.

Mr. MEREDITH. I have very little to reply to the learned counsel who has just spoken. The manner in which this present application originated is quite familiar to your honor. Some days ago this very petition was offered to be presented to the Court, and you expressed, I will not say a disinclination to receive it, but that it was not such a one as ought to be received; and you were good enough, sir, to invite an argument on that subject. In obedience to that invitation, with notice to the counsel of Col. Wheeler in order that he might appear upon the argument, we have presented ourselves to argue the case. Now, sir, it seems that the learned counsel of Mr. Wheeler understands me to have gone beyond the precise point to which you invited, and beyond which you declined to hear this argument. I inquired pretty particularly at the commencement of it what was the point to which you intended to confine us, and I understood it was to the point as to whether this was a proper petition to be received upon this occasion or not. Now, the learned counsel of Mr. Wheeler unfortunately—

Mr. VAN DYKE. I do not appear as such. At the commencement of the case, as I stated, I appeared as the counsel for the U. S.

Mr. MEREDITH. Then I decline taking any notice of the District Attorney, as I consider that he has nothing to do with the matter at all, and I shall consider Mr. Van Dyke in the remarks which he has made as acting as an *amicus curiæ.*

Mr. VAN DYKE. The gentleman may consider me as acting in any position he pleases; it makes no difference, one way or the other.

Mr. MEREDITH. That may be, sir; but I cannot admit that Mr. Passmore Williamson is in contest with the United States, or that the District Attorney, or the law officer of the United States, has anything to do with it. I will not admit it unless your honor says that I am bound to do so. In whatever light I am to consider this matter, I cannot stop to argue the point; and as I was about to observe, in whatever capacity our learned opponent appears, I must regret that he has so entirely misunderstood my argument as I had intended to make it, as to be under the impression that I had gone beyond the limits which the Court had assigned me. The objection being to the petition that it does not pray to be allowed to answer interrogatories, I conceived it to apply directly to the point to show that so far from a party being called upon to ask for them, that it was the duty of the Court to propound them at the time of his commitment or afterwards, and I thought that that was clear, sir. I intended to go no further, because if any other questions were open I should have much to say, but I thought that you limited us to this one point.

Now, sir, I should have been glad if the District Attorney, or the counsel for Col. Wheeler, or the *amicus curiæ*, or in whatever capacity the learned gentleman acted, if he had shown me what I asked him for.

Mr. Van Dyke. What is that, sir?

Mr. Meredith. An authority or a case in which a party committed, has been committed for refusing to answer an interrogatory not propounded to him.

Mr. Van Dyke. I have cited the case of Davis as one in point.

Mr. Meredith. Will you read it?

Mr. Van Dyke reads from the case in 5 Cranch, as follows:

(5 Cranch. CC. Rep. page 623.) "The Court having examined and considered the return of Thomas M. Davis to the writ of *habeas corpus* aforesaid, and having heard Counsel thereupon, do adjudge the said answer to be evasive and insufficient, and that the said Davis is bound to produce the bodies of the said negroes, mentioned in the said writs, before the Court; and the said Davis being now present in Court, and refusing to produce the said negroes, it is therefore, this sixteenth day of January, 1840, ordered that the said Davis be committed to the custody of the Marshal, until he shall produce the said negroes, or be otherwise discharged in due course of law.

On the eighteenth day of January, 1840, it was further ordered by the Court, that in case the said Emanuel Price and Maria Course shall be surrendered by the said Thomas N. Davis, or by any other person for him, to the Marshal, he shall take the said negroes into his custody, subject to the further order of the Court, and that he then discharge the said Davis from jail."

The negroes afterwards came in and voluntarily submitted themselves, and were afterwards discharged as free negroes.

Mr. Meredith (taking the book). Now, sir, you will observe that the party was not committed there for the purpose of further sifting his conscience, was not merely attached, but convicted and adjudged in contempt for refusing to produce the bodies, and there was therefore no interrogatory put to him. And in addition to that, on the the 18th of January, 1840, without statement that it was upon petition and therefore assumed to be on motion, it was further ordered by the Court, "That in case the said Emanuel Rice and Maria Course shall be surrendered by the said Thomas N. Davis, or by any other person for him, to the Marshal, he shall take the said negroes into his custody, subject to the further order of the Court, and that he then discharge the said Davis from jail."

Judge KANE. The same action that Chief Justice Kent took in the case of Stacey,

Mr. VAN DYKE. If Mr. Williamson does that there is no difficulty about it.

Mr. MEREDITH. If the Court do the same thing, Mr. Williamson will be discharged upon the propounding of interrogatories.

Mr. VAN DYKE. The Court ordered that if Davis did a certain thing he should be discharged.

Mr. MEREDITH. Your honor understands what I mean, and I will not further detain you, because I have detained you too long already; and I simply ask you either to discharge the party or to do what the Chancellor does every day, that is, to say what the party shall do as the condition of his discharge.

Now, sir, the commitment before Judge Story, in 3 Mason, was just such a one as you have stated this was intended to be. There was no final adjudication of the Court at all, and, as I need not say, after what has fallen from your honor, there has been nothing of the kind here.

Judge KANE. It is an interlocutory order.

Mr. MEREDITH. It stands, therefore, *ex confesso*, as such, notwithstanding the view of our Cerberean opponent. Now, sir, in regard to my opponent's argument, I have shown by all the authorities that it is a clearance of his contempt if he comply with the order of the Court when it has filed interrogatories, upon his doing which to the satisfaction of the Court he is to be discharged. I do not find, as I have said, (and I have asked Mr. Van Dyke to furnish me, if he could, and he has not done so) a case in which a form of petition of this kind has been rejected. In addition to this, I have shown a case in which, on bare motion, without petition, a party has been discharged; and I find always, where a party is committed upon interlocutory commitment, that the party is discharged where he complies with the order of the Court and answers the interrogatories which have been put to him.

Judge KANE. I will endeavor, gentlemen, either to file or deliver my opinion in open Court, on Monday next, or it may perhaps occupy me until Tuesday.

On Monday, Oct. 29th, 1855, a paper, of which the following is a copy, was filed of record :—

In the District Court of the United States, in and for the Eastern District of Pennsylvania.

U. S. A.   } Sur motion for leave to file among the
vs.   } Records a certain paper.
WILLIAMSON. }

And now, October 29th, 1855, the Court having heard argument upon the motion for leave to read and file among the records in this case, a certain paper writing, purporting to be the petition of Passmore Williamson, and having considered thereof, do refuse the leave moved for ; inasmuch as it appears that the said Passmore Williamson is now remaining in contempt of this Court, and that by the said paper writing he doth in no wise make purgation of his said contempt, nor doth he thereby pray that he may be admitted to make such purgation ; wherefore the said Passmore Williamson hath not, at this time, a standing in this Court.

To the end, however, that the said Passmore Williamson may, when thereto minded, the more readily relieve himself of his said contempt, it is ordered, that, whenever by petition in writing to be filed with the clerk, Passmore Williamson shall set forth under his oath or solemn affirmation, that he " desires to purge himself of the contempt, because of which he is now attached, and to that end is willing to make true answers to such interrogatories as may be addressed to him by the Court, touching the matters heretofore legally inquired of by the writ of habeas corpus to him directed, at the relation of John H. Wheeler," then the marshal do bring the said Passmore Williamson before the Court, if in session, or if the Court be not in session, then before the Judge at his chambers, to abide the further order of the Court in his behalf. And it is further ordered, that the clerk do furnish copies of this order to the said Passmore Williamson, and to the Attorney of the United States, and to the Marshal.

On Friday, Nov. 2d, 1855, Messrs. HOPPER, GILPIN and MEREDITH presented the following petition :—

U. S. A.   }   District Court U. S ,
vs.   } Eastern District of Pennsylvania.
WILLIAMSON. }

To the Honorable the Judge of the District Court of the United States for the Eastern District of Pennsylvania.

The petition of Passmore Williamson respectfully showeth :—
That he desires to purge himself of the contempt because of which

he is now attached, and to that end is willing to make true answers to such interrogatories as may be addressed to him by the Court touching the matter heretofore inquired of by the writ of habeas corpus to him directed at the relation of John H. Wheeler.

Wherefore he prays that he may be permitted to purge himself of said contempt, in making true answers to such interrogatories as may be addressed to him by the Hon. Court touching the premises.

P. WILLIAMSON.

Affirmed and subscribed before me, Nov. 2d, 1855.

CHAS. F. HEAZLITT,
U. S. Commissioner.

Some conversation took place between the Judge and Counsel in relation to the omission of the word "legally" in the petition. The petition was received on Saturday, Nov. 3d. Mr. WILLIAMSON, his counsel, and JAMES C. VAN DYKE, Esq. appeared in Court, when the following proceedings took place :—

The Court addressed the defendant as follows :—

" Passmore Williamson—The Court has received your petition, and, upon consideration thereof, have thought right to grant the prayer thereof. You will, therefore, make here, in open Court, your solemn affirmation, that in the return heretofore made by you to the writ of habeas corpus which was issued from this Court at the relation of John H. Wheeler, and to the proceedings consequent thereupon, you have not intended a contempt of this Court, or of its process. Moreover, that you are now willing to make true answers to such interrogatories as may be addressed to you by the Court, touching the premises inquired of in the said writ of habeas corpus."

The required affirmation was then made in the form indicated by the Judge.

Judge KANE then inquired of Mr. VAN DYKE, if he had any suggestions to make to the Court.

Mr. VAN DYKE replied, that for the United States in the case of the United States vs. Passmore Williamson, he desired to propound a question he had drawn up.

The Judge directed Mr. Van Dyke to submit the interrogatory to respondent's counsel, which was accordingly done.

This interrogatory was submitted in writing.

Mr. GILPIN said Mr. Williamson was perfectly willing to answer the interrogatory submitted by the District Attorney, but as he did not know what other interrogatories might follow this, he thought it best that it and its answer should be filed.

Mr. Van Dyke said he was willing to file the interrogatory, or to submit it for immediate reply.

Mr. Gilpin and Judge Kane both remarked that they had understood the District Attorney to intimate that if the question was answered in the affirmative, he would be satisfied. The Court further said, that it was for the Petitioner to make his election whether or not the interrogatories and the replies should be filed.

After consultation, the counsel of Mr. Williamson elected to have the interrogatories and answers filed, and Mr. Van Dyke accordingly filed the interrogatory, which was as follows :—

INTERROGATORY.

United States *vs.* Passmore Williamson, Nov. 3d, 1855. And now, James C. Van Dyke, attorney for the United States, by leave granted, files the following interrogatory :—

Interrogatory.—Did you, at the time of the service of the writ of habeas corpus, at the relation of John H. Wheeler, or at any time during the period intervening between the service of said writ and the making of your return thereto, seek to obey the mandate of said writ, by bringing before this Honorable Court the persons of the slaves therein mentioned ?

If to this interrogatory you answer in the affirmative, state fully and particularly the mode in which you sought so to obey said writ, and all that you did tending to that end.

And therefore, it is ordered that the defendant, Passmore Williamson, do make true answers to said interrogatories.

Mr. Williamson and his counsel then retired. After a brief absence from the Court room, they returned, and Mr. Gilpin read a reply.

Mr. Van Dyke objected to the form of the answer. It was evasive, he contended, and was not a simple positive "yea" or "nay" to the query propounded.

Judge Kane said the answer was liable to exceptions, but he thought the same matter might be so expressed as to relieve the answer from all objections.

That the answer to the first clause was a distinct negative, but the party had a perfect right to expand the answer, and make such explanations as he deemed necessary.

The Judge was of opinion that the answer to the second clause might also be coupled with an explanation. If the defendant were to reply simply "No," to the second clause, he then might be charged with contempt in not seeking to obey the mandate of the Court, and he had a right to explain that he thought it useless to make such search.

The counsel of Mr. Williamson then amended the answer so as to read as follows :—

ANSWER OF DEFENDANT.

I did not seek to obey the writ by producing the persons therein mentioned before the Court, because I had not, at the time of the service of the writ, the power over, the custody or control of them, and therefore it was impossible for me to do so. I first heard of the writ of habeas corpus on Friday, July 20th, between 1 and 2 o'clock, A. M., on my return from Harrisburg. After breakfast, about 9 o'clock, I went from my house to Mr. Hopper's office, when and where the return was prepared.

At 10 o'clock I came into Court as commanded by the writ. I sought to obey the writ by answering it truly ; the parties not being in my possession or control, it was impossible for me to obey the writ by producing them. Since the service of the writ I have not had the custody, possession or power over them ; nor have I known where they were, except from common rumor or the newspaper reports in regard to their public appearance in the city or elsewhere.

Mr. VAN DYKE objected to this reply, as it was in his opinion evasive. The respondent is asked to state whether at any time since the service of the writ and the return thereto, he has sought to obey its mandates, and then to state, too, in what manner he did seek to obey it. That the answer was defective. That the answer was not in the terms of the interrogatory, and is, therefore, not a clear, full, and unevasive answer. He asked that the interrogatory be again propounded to the respondent to answer it directly, one way or the other, in the terms of the interrogatory ; first, whether he did seek to obey the mandate of the writ, and if so, then to state to the Court the manner in which he sought to obey its mandates. That there can be no misapprehension as to the meaning of the terms he had used in the interrogatory. The answer should be yea or nay ; if yea, then how ; if nay, there is an end to the question. If the terms of the interrogatory were not definite, it was the duty of the defendant's counsel to object to them and let them be amended.

Mr. GILPIN said, he did not understand that where an interrogatory was put to a party before the Court, with a view to purge himself, or elicit further information, the contents of the return were to be answered simply yea or nay, without being permitted, in connection with the answer, to give facts explanatory of the yea or nay, and to inform the Court of the facts ; and if, therefore, a defective form of inquiry be used in the interrogatory, it is not for the respondent, placed in a very peculiar position, to correct the terms of the interrogatory. If the interrogatory be defective, by the ordinary rule of pleading, the party first in default must go back again, and correct his error.

Mr. VAN DYKE offered to alter the form of the interrogatory, but Mr. Gilpin said it had not yet been objected to.

Mr. GILPIN continued, and said that two questions had been propounded.

First, as to whether the defendant had sought to obey the writ; and secondly, *how*. If the answer was full, it was only such as was necessary to explanation. If the reply was not responsive, it was not for the want of an honest effort to make it so. The desire not to evade was at least evident.

The Judge said that his impression was that a direct answer could be given thus:—"I did not, at the time indicated in the first branch of the question, seek to obey the mandate of the writ by bringing into Court the persons of the slaves therein mentioned, *because*, &c." And "I did not so seek, *because*, &c."

Mr. MEREDITH said the difficulty arose from the ambiguity about the word "seek." He could not see what answer the defendant could make other than that offered. He had no control over the slaves. He explains so, and gives a direct answer to the question asked him.

The Judge said he was as anxious as any one to throw no unnecessary difficulty in the way of the settlement of this matter. The District Attorney had a right to explain his meaning for the word as he had applied it.

Mr. MEREDITH said he would suppose a case. Suppose a person were commanded to produce the body of a person he never saw. How could he reply to the question, "Did you seek for him?"

Judge KANE said the reply proper in such a case would be, "I did not seek, because," &c.

Mr. VAN DYKE said he took the dictionary meaning of the word "seek." If it were necessary to add the definitions of Walker and other lexicographers, he would do so. He defined the word as he understood its meaning.

Judge KANE again repeated the opinion that if there is anything equivocal about the interrogatory the defendant should say so. If it was not equivocal, he should answer directly in the affirmative or negative, and add his reasons for doing so.

The Judge said the difficulty, he thought, could be easily overcome by amending the answer, and at the suggestion of the Court it was amended in the following manner:

"I did not seek to obey the writ by producing the persons in the writ mentioned before this Court.

"I did not so seek, because I verily believed that it was entirely impossible for me to produce the said persons agreeably to the command of the Court."

The answer was then accepted by the Court, and ordered to be filed.

Mr. VAN DYKE then submitted another interrogatory, the effect of which was to inquire of Mr. Williamson whether or not he had made any mental reservation in the answer already made to the interrogatory propounded.

The Judge, without waiting for any objection to this interrogatory, overruled it, saying he considered it objectionable. The answer of the defendant must be taken as a matter of course, and no inquiry could be made such as that contemplated by the interrogatory.

Mr. VAN DYKE then withdrew the interrogatory.

Mr. V. then offered another interrogatory, which was also overruled, as it tended to elicit such replies as had already been objected to by the District Attorney.

Mr. VAN DYKE also withdrew this question.

Judge KANE then remarked that the District Attorney had been invited to aid the Court in this case, but that he would bear in mind that nis relation to Mr. Wheeler was now suspended. This was only an inquiry as to what injury had been done the process of the Court.

Mr. VAN DYKE said he was aware of the position he occupied.

Judge KANE then said :—"The contempt is now regarded as purged and the party is released from custody. He is now reinstated to the position he occupied before the contempt was committed. Mr. Williamson is now before me on the return to the writ."

Mr. VAN DYKE then stated that suit had been brought in the United States Circuit Court by his client against Passmore Williamson, and as he (Mr. Van Dyke) appeared in a different character, he would read from a paper (which he drew from his pocket) the remarks he had to make in reference to the habeas corpus.

In the case of the United States *ex relatione* John H. Wheeler *vs.* Passmore Williamson.

Mr. Williamson being now, by his purgation, reinstated in the standing before this Honorable Court which he occupied immediately preceding the time when he was guilty of the contempt, for which he was committed on the 27th of July last, I have, in connection with my colleague, Mr. Webster, to suggest, that Mr. Wheeler, at whose relation this writ of habeas corpus had been issued, was, at the time he filed his petition,

11

in hopes that the remedial process of this Court would not have been evaded or disregarded by Mr. Williamson, but that he would have cheerfully, by an endeavor to obey that writ, sought an adjudication of the highest judicial tribunal of the country, of the questions, Whether Mr. Wheeler was entitled to pass over the soil of Peensylvania with his property? and whether or not a wrong had been committed in the forcible abduction thereof? He also, for some time subsequent to the return to said writ, indulged the hope that, upon reflection, Mr. Williamson would yield a proper submission to the constitutional sovereignty of existing law by rendering obedience to the orders of this Court, and submitting in proper form to legally constituted authority, all matters of dispute between the parties.

But in this hope he has been deluded. His remedy was, at an early period of the proceedings in this case, arrested by the contumacious disregard on the part of the defendant of the lawful process of this Court, and having waited for a reasonable time for him to ask leave to purge his contempt, in order that he might further pursue the remedies afforded by reason of the writ of habeas corpus, and finding that the defendant was controlled, as this relator believed, by a pertinacity in violation of his duty, and injurious to the rights of the relator, he determined to institute a suit in another branch of the Courts of the United States, for the recovery of damages which have accrued by the tortious acts of the defendant towards his person and property, and a suit for this purpose has been commenced in the Circuit Court of the United States for this Circuit, and will be duly prosecuted, with the hope that it may afford a more ample remedy to Mr. Wheeler than he has been enabled to obtain by the present proceeding. It was instituted as soon as it became apparent that owing to the evasion of the process of this Honorable Court it was impossible for Mr. Wheeler to repossess himself of his property by the aid afforded by the writ of habeas corpus, which he had invoked. He determined from that time to take no further part in these proceedings, leaving Mr. Williamson to atone to the Government of the United States, where such atonement properly belonged, for his offence against the sovereign majesty of her laws, and from that time neither he nor his counsel have had any part in the proceedings in the case of the United States vs. Passmore Williamson.

Mr. Wheeler regrets that the neglect and refusal of the defendant, which has induced him for so long a time to refuse obedience and a proper submission to this Court, has been a barrier to a previous announcement of his determination.

In addition to this, Mr. Wheeler will be able to prove all the important points of his case in the Circuit Court, which renders unnecessary any information that he might at this stage of the proceedings gain by true answers to such interrogatories as by law he is allowed to propound. He, therefore, respectfully waives his right in this respect, placing a firm reliance on the laws of the land and a jury of his country to repair the injury which he has suffered at the hands of the defendant and his confederates.

After Mr. Van Dyke had concluded, Mr. Meredith inquired—" Is Mr. Williamson discharged ?"

Judge KANE replied—" He is.   I understand from the remarks of the District Attorney that a *nolle prosequi* has been entered in the case, n this Court."

The Court then adjourned.   Mr. Williamson was congratulated by his friends on his restoration to liberty.

APPENDIX.

PROCEEDINGS UPON THE PETITION OF JANE JOHNSON.

United States District Court, Eastern District of Pennsylvania.

On the third day of October, 1855, JANE JOHNSON, by her attorneys, JOSEPH B. TOWNSEND and JOHN M. READ, Esqs., presented the following petition :

The United States of America,
Ex rel. JOHN H. WHEELER, } *Alias Habeas Corpus.*
vs.
PASSMORE WILLIAMSON.

To the Honorable John K. Kane, Judge of the aforesaid Court.

The suggestion and petition of Jane Johnson, respectfully showeth, that she is one of the three parties named in the aforesaid writ of habeas corpus, and the mother of the two children, Daniel and Isaiah, also named therein, and thereby required to be produced. That before the occurrences hereinafter stated, this petitioner and her said two children lived in Washington, in the District of Columbia, and were claimed and held by the said John H. Wheeler as his slaves, according to the laws and usages of that District. That on the 18th day of July, 1855, the said John H. Wheeler voluntarily brought your petitioner and her two children from the City of Washington to the City of Philadelphia, passing through Baltimore and reaching Philadelphia by way of the Philadelphia, Wilmington and Baltimore Railroad. Mr. Wheeler stopped at Bloodgood's Hotel, in Philadelphia, at the foot of Walnut street, and fronting on the Delaware River, and remained there with your petitioner and her said two children, from about two o'clock, P.M., until shortly before 5 o'clock, P.M., when he directed your petitioner to bring her children and accompany him on board a steamboat belonging to the railroad line to New York, which boat was then being attached to the pier in front of the said hotel, which direction was complied with, and your petitioner seated herself with her said two children on the upper deck of the said boat, near Mr. Wheeler. Your petitioner was very desirous of procuring the freedom of herself and her children, and before she left Washington determined to make an effort to do so, if said

Wheeler should take her North. While stopping at the hotel as aforesaid, Mr. Wheeler went to dinner, and while your petitioner was absent from his presence, she informed one of the waiters at the said hotel (a colored woman) that she and her children were slaves. A few minutes before 5 o'clock, while said Wheeler, your petitioner and her children were on the upper deck of the steamboat as aforesaid, a white gentleman, whose name your petitioner has since been informed is Passmore Williamson, approached your petitioner and informed her that she was free if she chose to claim her liberty, and asked her if she desired to be free. Your petitioner replied that she did wish to be free, as in truth and in fact she did; and said Williamson then further informed your petitioner that if she wished her liberty, she could go ashore and take her children with her, and that no one had a right to prevent her doing so; but that she must decide promptly whether she would go or stay, as the boat would soon start.

Your petitioner being desirous to go on shore, rose to go, and was taken hold of by said Wheeler, who urged her to stay with him, but your petitioner refused to stay, and voluntarily and most willingly left the boat, aided in the departure by several colored persons, who took her children, with her consent, and led or carried them off the boat, and conducted your petitioner and her said children to a carriage, a short distance from the boat, which carriage they entered and went away. Mr. Williamson did not accompany the colored persons who were assisting your petitioner to get away, but remained some distance behind, and your petitioner has never seen him since she left the steamboat as aforesaid.

Your petitioner further states that she was not, at the time of her leaving Mr. Wheeler, as aforesaid, or at any time since, in any way or manner whatever, in the custody, power, possession or control of Mr. Williamson, nor has she received from him any directions or instructions, directly or indirectly, whither she should go. But claiming and believing that she and her children are free, your petitioner has, ever since her leaving said Wheeler, exercised her right as a free woman to go whither she pleased, and to take her said children, and has not since that time been restrained of her liberty by any person whatever.

Your petitioner is advised, and respectfully submits to your Honor, that the said writ of habeas corpus ought to be quashed under the facts above stated, and for the following among other reasons : First,—The said Wheeler had no control over or right to the possession of your petitioner or her said children at the issuing of the aforesaid writ, they being then free. Second,—Because the said writ was issued without the knowledge or consent of your petitioner and against her wish. Third,—Because, in truth and in fact, at the issuing of the said writ, and at all times since your petitioner left the company of said Wheeler as aforesaid, neither she nor her said children have been detained or restrained of their liberty by said Williamson or any other person whatever. Fourth,—Because, under the writ of habeas corpus, which is a writ devised and intended to restore freemen to liberty when unduly restrained thereof, the said John H. Wheeler seeks to reclaim and recover your petitioner and her said children, and reduce them again into slavery.

Wherefore, your petitioner respectfully prays this honorable Court, that the said writ of habeas corpus and all proceedings under it, may be quashed, and especially that the said Passmore Williamson may be discharged from his imprisonment.

her
JANE ✕ JOHNSON.
mark.

United States of America, District of Massachusetts. On this twenty-sixth day of September, A. D., 1855, the above named Jane Johnson personally appearing, made solemn oath that the facts stated in the foregoing petition, so far as they are within her own knowledge, are true, and all other facts therein stated she believes to be true, before me.

C. W. LORING,
Commissioner U. S. Court for the District of Massachusetts.

Upon the presentation of the petition, the Court intimated a doubt of the petitioner's having such *status* as would entitle her to be heard, and directed the counsel to address their remarks to that point. At the request of the counsel, Monday, Oct. 6th, was fixed by the Court for the argument, at which time, J. B. TOWNSEND, Esq., on behalf of the petitioner, addressed the Court as follows:

This application is on behalf of Jane Johnson, a party named in the writ and thereby required to be produced. The sole question now to be considered is, has she such *status* as will entitle her to intervene and ask the Court to quash the writ and the proceedings had under it?

As the record stands, the writ issued on the petition of John H. Wheeler, who avers that Jane and her children were his slaves according to the laws of Virginia, and that they were detained from his possession by Passmore Williamson, and that they were not detained for any criminal or supposed criminal matter.

The alias writ was served, and to it a return has been made by Mr Williamson denying wholly and in general terms, any detention or re straint by him of the parties required by the writ, or either of them, or any custody or possession of, or control over them or either of them.

This return, ordinarily considered conclusive, this Court has permitted to be traversed, and has heard oral testimony both from Mr. Wheeler and Mr. Williamson, as also from other parties, as to its truth and sufficiency, and on the testimony *then* adduced, and as the case then stood, the Court has committed Mr. Williamson "as for a contempt of Court in refusing to make return to the writ," which, so far as I can gather it, means that, because the Court considered that the return was, by the testimony adduced, shown to be untrue, it must be considered as no return.

With the conclusion arrived at by the Court with the light *then* before it I have nothing to do. I do not in any way represent Mr. Williamson, nor has he, his friends or his counsel been consulted in regard to the present application. But the action of the Court was based upon certain facts which were considered as established by the evidence then before Court.

What I now ask is, that a party to the proceeding—the party most interested in it—the very party who was sought to be relieved from the alleged illegal custody or detention of Mr. Williamson, shall intervene in the manner allowed by courts of justice, that is, by petition, verified under oath, to declare her knowledge of the subject matter, to disclaim and repudiate this proceeding, which Mr. Wheeler can only maintain with her consent, and to deny all custody, detention or restraint over her on the part of Mr. W. or any other person, in order, if the Court shall receive her statement, that it may consider and decide as to whether it does not conclusively show the propriety of the return, and refute the truth of the supposed facts upon which the former action of the Court was based; because, I assume that neither the writ nor the commitment would be sustained if the matters set up by way of traverse to the return can be disproved by any party to the proceeding.

In this habeas corpus there are three parties : 1st, the relator ; 2d, the party to whom the writ was addressed; and 3d, the party required by the writ to be produced.

The sole object of the writ of habeas corpus *ad subjiciendum* (which this is) is to relieve the party required to be produced, from alleged illegal and improper custody or restraint exercised by the party to whom the writ is addressed. The proceeding is an inquisition or examination on the part of the sovereign power through the judges of its courts, as to any restraint of the liberty of any human being against the will of the party restrained. It is a great prerogative writ in aid of the personal

401

liberty and freedom of the subject, and I submit, as a proposition which cannot be questioned, that the aim, object and end of the writ is the personal relief, favor and protection of the party alleged to be detained; it is in substance the writ of the party detained, and never issued or maintained without the consent of such party when of years of discretion.

It cannot be used as a means of trying a title or right of possession of persons, especially where there is no custody, actual or potential, by the party to whom addressed.

Is it to be supposed that every man to whom such a writ is addressed is bound, in answer to the writ, to bring in the body or make an effort to do so, when there is no actual or potential custody on his part, even though he might happen to know where the required party was at the time? No doctrine so unreasonable has ever been broached in a court of justice.; if it were so, then the writ of habeas corpus would be a command to commit an assault and battery. See Linda *vs.* Hudson, 1 Cushing's Rep. 385.

I propose to cite some authorities to show how far the Courts in England have gone in recognizing that this writ requires for its support that there should be custody or restraint over the party required to be produced, and that such custody or restraint should be exercised *contrary to the will of such party;* and if the party required to be produced disclaims such custody, the writ cannot be maintained.

In Rex *vs.* Roddam, Cowp. 672, Lord Mansfield denied a habeas corpus because it was claimed without the consent of the parties who were sought to be produced, saying, "they can never be brought up as prisoners against their consent."

In the King *vs.* Reynolds, 6 Tenn. Rep. 497, an apprentice, eighteen years old, left his master and entered the sea service. His master petitioned for a habeas corpus to bring him up. Lord Kenyon denied the master's right to it, saying that the master had his remedy by action, but could not maintain a habeas corpus. The apprentice, who is of sufficient age to judge for himself, can apply for it if he wishes it.

To the same point is The King *vs.* Edwards, 7 Tenn. Rep. 741, which was a petition by a master for a habeas corpus to bring up his apprentice. The Court say that the distinction was properly taken in the last case, that the apprentice might obtain the writ, but the master could not, "for its object is the protection of the liberty of the party;" that the master was not without his remedy, but not in this form.

Exparte Lansdown, 5 East. 38, also an application by a master to bring up by habeas corpus an apprentice alleged to have been improperly taken from him, per Lord Ellenborough: "The writ of habeas corpus is for be protection of the personal liberty of the subject. If the party him self, being of competent years of discretion, do not complain, we cannot issue the writ on the prayer of the master, who has remedy by action, if his apprentice be improperly taken from him.

Ex parte Sandilands, 12 Eng. Com. Law and Eq. Reps. 463, where a wife is voluntarily and without any restraint absent from her husband, a Court of common law has no jurisdiction, upon his application, to issue a habeas corpus to bring her up.

The King *vs.* Wiseman, 2 Smith's Reps. 617, is to the same effect.

I cite these cases to show that it is the rights and liberties of Jane Johnson and her children that this Court is charged with protecting in this proceeding, and not the rights of Mr. Wheeler. If he has suffered injury, the law is open to him for redress, but not in this form.

It being therefore virtually her proceeding, why cannot she terminate it and declare that it was vicious from its inception for want of her assent to it? Why cannot she be heard? Have not both the other parties had their hearing? – Mr. Wheeler in support of his claim, Mr. Williamson in support of his return. It seems to me that if any party to the proceeding can be heard, my colleague and myself represent that very party, the sole question being whether there is any detention or restraint of this woman against her will. Surely no one is so competent to satisfy the Court upon that point as the woman herself; her declaration is the best evidence attainable, all others being but secondary.

There is a long and uninterrupted current of decisions, both in England and this country, establishing that it is the practice of Courts to learn from the parties required to be brought up, whether there is any detention of or restraint over their persons contrary to their wish, and to receive for this purpose either their affidavits or oral testimony ; and if this element be wanting, the writ and all proceedings under it must be quashed. Some of these cases are:

Rex *vs.* Viner, 2 Levinz, 128 ; Rex *vs.* Clarkson, 1 Strange, 444 ; Rex *vs.* Smith, 2 Strange, 982 ; Rex *vs.* Clark, 1 Burr., 606 ; Rex *vs.* Mead, 1 Burr. 542 ; Rex *vs.* Delaval, 3 Burr. 1434 ; Anne Gregory's case, 4 Burr. 1991 ; Ex parte Hopkins, 2 Peere Wms. 152 ; in re Spence, 2 Phillips, Ch. cases, 253 ; in re Parker, the Canadian prisoner's case, 5 Mees and Wel. 32 ; ex parte Woolstoncraft, 4 John Ch. Rep. 80 ; and the Pennsylvania cases of Com. *vs.* Robinson, 1 Sergt. and R. 353, and Com. *vs.* Addicks, 5 Binney, 520.

The practice of the Court of Common Pleas of this County I am sure has always conformed to this rule, and if the Court can learn from the party whose body is required to be produced, that he or she is ex-

ercising a free will in the disposal of himself or herself, there is an en
of all proceeding under the writ, the only exception to this rule bein
the case of infants of such tender years that they cannot exercise
choice in the matter.   But in the case of ex parte Woolstoncraft above
cited, the Court received the declaration of the infant, who was only fourteen years of age.

It is this declaration that we now present, and ask the Court to receive
and consider ; and I submit that the precedents for this course are uniform and abundant.

Whether the Court shall consider that the freedom or slavery of Jane
Johnson is to affect her right to be heard here, I do not know ; but if it
is to have any bearing upon the matter now before the Court, we contend
that being brought here by her former master of his own free will, she
became a free woman within the territory of Pennsylvania ; but by arrangement between my colleague and myself, and that we may not travel
wholly over the same ground, the discussion of this question is to be left
with him, and I leave it with the simple statement of the position we
take on this question.

There are two cases which I wish to furnish to this Court which are
well worthy of consideration upon the question of the right of possession of an alleged slave being considered or decided upon in a habeas
corpus.   The first is, the State vs. Frazer, Dudley's Reps. (Georgia) p.
42, and the second is Nations vs. Alois, 5 Smede and Marsh, (Mississippi) p. 338.   In the first case the Superior Court of Georgia refused to
pass upon or decide the right to the possession of a negro woman claimed
as a slave, under habeas corpus, on the ground that this writ was for
the personal liberty of the subject, and the only question to be considered
was whether there existed any detention or restraint of the negro against
her will.

In the second case, the question arose upon an act of the Legislature
of Mississippi, which allowed, at the instance of the master, a writ of
habeas corpus, when his slaves had been taken from him by fraud, force
or violence.   Certain slaves had been fraudulently taken from their
owner in Tennessee and brought into the State of Mississippi.   A habeas
corpus was taken out by their master, and the Court held that the acts
which the statute required as necessary to the maintenance of the writ
having occurred in another State, the writ could not lie.   The case was
ably argued and well considered by the Court, and I cite it to show that
it was never suggested, either by Court or counsel, that the writ could
be supported at common law for the recapture or restitution of the slaves
to their master.

It is not now the time to discuss the questions which may arise if the Petition shall be received by the Court, but I earnestly desire that the Court should understand that I am here, not on behalf of Mr. Williamson, nor by his means or procurement in any way; he is represented by counsel much better able than I am to protect his interests. But having received this petition from the party whose rights and interests are mainly involved in the proceeding, and believing that under the authorities and practice of the Courts it was proper to be presented to the Court, we claim the right to do so, and to ask the redress it prays for, and we respectfully submit that in receiving and entertaining this application, the Court will be administering justice according to the due course of law.

Mr. TOWNSEND was then followed by Mr. READ.

Mr. READ said that the question was upon the reception of the petition. He only asked that it should be filed, so that the party could be heard at this stage of the proceedings. It is a general principle that the writ of habeas corpus must always be *issued by or on behalf of the party whose liberty is restrained*. It was known that there were three kinds of writs of habeas corpus in England—one under the statute of Charles I., one of 56th Stat. of George III., and one at the Common Law. That the writ in this case must be one at common law, not specially restrained by any statute.

Mr. R. referred then to the case of ex parte Siriderlisi, 12 En. L & E., page 63, and to 29 Law and Equity 259—in the case of a lunatic, wherein the rule to show cause why a habeas corpus should not issue to bring up his body was dismissed because the party had not made any application to the Court, nor was it shown that he was so coerced as to prevent his doing so.

The law is clearly stated by Chitty, vol. 1, pages 684 and 687, English edition. He then read the law as laid down and compiled by the commentator. He argued from the synopsis in the books that the principle laid down was a fair and legal one. All the acts tend only to protect the liberty of the subject—and the title of the acts absolutely prove it. The writ is one of privilege; it is for a party restrained to issue it, and not for a party wishing to restrain another, and Mr. R. cited the Constitution of the United States and the Bill of Rights of the State of Pennsylvania to sustain the position.

The case of an infant to whose custody the father was entitled, was referred to. In the case of an apprentice, he said that against his will no master can call him on a writ of habeas corpus. The master has another remedy—he cannot use the habeas corpus to decide a question of property. Mr. R. referred to the case decided by Judge Rogers in 1848, in Com. vs. Roberts, and to 7 Pa. Law Journal, Com. against Harris, which was a habeas corpus to bring up the body of a minor who had been an apprentice, and had enlisted. The Court would not remand the apprentice to the custody of the master, leaving him to his suit for damages against the officer who enlisted the apprentice.

The writ issued by this Court in Williamson's case, was a writ of habeas corpus at common law, and must be so regarded. He cited from the discussions of the Law Reformation Society, of which Lord Brougham is the head, and handed the book of the proceedings of the Society to the Court—not endorsing all the sentiments therein contained, but only using it for the purpose of the present case. He then read at some length from the book referred to, the essay upon the writ of habeas corpus. He cited the case decided by Lord Chancellor Cottingham, *in re* Spence, 2 Phillips' Chancery cases, page 252, and followed and quoted from 3 Stephens' Black. 756, and 7 Barr 336; to the same purpose 3d Hallam was cited and commented on, and the act of 18th September, 1850, the fugitive slave law.

Another important branch of the case worthy of special notice is, that Jane Johnson claims that her children are free. That was a matter for the determination of the Court.

That from some causes or other, necessity, and sometimes from a much smaller reason, these States had made it an offence to bring a free colored man into the slave States, or to keep one there.

He cited the laws of South Carolina, 7th vol., under the head of Acts relating to the State, 20th Dec. 1800, which was "An Act to prevent the introduction of any slaves or keeping them in the State." One section of this act allows the right of migration under certain limits. On the 19th Dec. 1801, another act of the same Legislature, bearing on the case, was passed. It provided that any negro coming into the State should be sold, and that persons bringing such negroes into the State must exculpate themselves.

The act of 18th December, 1802, provided for the migration of slaves and the allowance of their transit through the State, upon the deposit of a declaration of intention to that effect in the County Clerk's office, by the person wishing to so transport them.

He then read the act of 17th December, 1803, and the act of 19th Dec. 1816, entitled "An act to prohibit the importation of slaves from any State," &c., and the act of Dec. 19th, 1835. Passing, then, from the State of South Carolina, he quoted the Act of Assembly of the

State of Georgia of the same date, almost the same in terms as the act of the former State. In North Carolina, an act was passed which was almost unintelligible—he read from the digest the law in relation to the introduction of any colored person into that State and the punishments attached to doing so. It was a prohibitory statute, and a penalty was also attached to it. He then read the habeas corpus act of North Carolina, and spoke of the laws of Maryland and Virginia.

The policy of these States was entirely to exclude negro slaves brought there unless under the restrictions mentioned. In 1840, the people of Kentucky held a convention and reiterated the conditions of the Constitution of 1793. The remarks of some of the distinguished Kentuckians at that convention were quoted.

The Southern States have always assumed plenary power; they have stood for the doctrine of State rights, that what is not given is withheld; that the powers not delegated to the Union are withheld by the State itself, and are by it to be exercised. This brings me to the question of the *status* of Jane Johnson. The State of Pennsylvania, like other States, formerly held slaves within her borders—an unchristian practice as many of her citizens have always regarded it. There were but few slaves here in comparison to the resources or population of our State. In 1780 the act for the gradual abolition of slavery was passed. It was passed in spite of opposition from those who doubted its policy.

This act, (or the 10th section of it,) to which the attention of the Court was specially directed, was read, and at much length and with great force of reasoning commented on by the learned counsel. He stated that he never yet had felt (unless when travelling with children) the necessity of having a personal servant with him. He believed that a man, if put to it, might even brush his own coat or black his own boots—or he might procure those services to be done for him by persons employed for the purpose at any hotel. Where, then, was the necessity of having a personal attendant to travel with you?

In 1786, the Legislature chose to amend the act, fearing its abuse—in this State the law remained until the year 1847—certainly with great benefit to the persons of color, for the mere making a man free may not make him better ;—this takes time. Here the benefit which has been derived from the act is manifest to every one who can recollect the condition of the negroes then and compare that with their present situation.

He spoke of the unanimous feeling occasioned by the application of Missouri for admission to the Union in the years 1817 and 1818. In 1846, the admission of Texas, resolved on by two administrations, came up for its consideration. It was the first time we were called upon to admit to the Union an organized body of men as a State. True, we had purchased territory from France and Spain, but then we could do what we pleased with it. The line of 36 deg. 30 min. was run through Texas; all north of that line was to be free.

That Jane Johnson never consented to the issuing of the habeas corpus in this case. He then cited the case of Straighter and Graham, 10 Howard, U. S. Supreme Court Reports. It decides that the Courts of the State (Kentucky) had the right to decide the *status* of a person on its own territory, and remarked that—

"If a man allows his slave to go to a free State and reside there, and then takes him back to a slave State, he places himself in the position of introducing a free person of color to that State, and is liable to be mulcted under the laws of the State."

He adverted to the correspondence between Mr. Webster and Lord Ashburton—in which Mr. W. admits that a slave escaping into Canada is free—and the present position of England was adverted to. In the revolutionary war, England did not cause a servile insurrection in this country, because then she was committed to the policy of slavery. She is not so now, and what would be the consequence were a war to occur between the two countries?

If Jane Johnson was a free woman, she should have been a party to the writ. She was not so—she now petitions, as a free woman, and we ask that the petition shall be filed. After so filing, the disposition of it is a matter of argument.

He said that under any aspect, the name of Jane Johnson having been introduced in the writ of habeas corpus, she has a right to be heard in this Court.

On Friday, October 12th, Judge KANE delivered his opinion :—

KANE, J.—Before entering upon the question immediately before me at this time, it is proper that I should advert to the past action of this Court in the case of Passmore Williamson, and to the considerations that led to it. I do this the rather, because in some of the judicial reviews to which it has been submitted collaterally, after an ex parte argument, it does not seem to me to have been fully apprehended.

I begin with the writ which originated the proceeding.

The writ of habeas corpus is of immemorial antiquity. It is deduced by the standard writers on the English law from the great charter of King John. It is unquestionable, however, that it is substantially of much earlier date; and it may be referred, without improbability, to the period of the Roman invasion. Like the trial by jury, it entered into the institutions of Rome before the Christian era, if not as early as the times of the republic. Through the long series of political struggles which gave form to the British Constitution, it was claimed as the birthright of every Englishman, and our ancestors brought it with them as such to this country.

At the common law, it issued whenever a citizen was denied the exercise of his personal liberty, or was deprived of his rightful control over any member of his household, his wife, his child, his ward, or his servant. It issued from the Courts of the sovereign, and in his name, at the instance of any one who invoked it, either for himself or another. It commanded, almost in the words of the Roman edict,* that the party under detention should be produced before the Court, there to await its decree. It left no discretion with the party to whom it was addressed. He was not to constitute himself the judge of his own rights or of his own conduct; but to bring in the body, and to declare the cause wherefore he had detained it; and the judge was then to determine whether that cause was sufficient in law or not. Such in America, as well as England, was the well known, universally recognized writ of habeas corpus.

When the Federal Convention was engaged in framing a constitution for the United States, a proposition was submitted to it by one of the members, that "the privileges and benefits of the writ of habeas corpus shall be enjoyed in this government in the most expeditious and ample manner; and shall not be suspended by the legislature except upon the most urgent and pressing occasions."† The committee to whom this was referred for consideration, would seem to have regarded the privilege in question as too definitely implied in the idea of free government to need formal assertion or confirmation; for they struck out that part of the proposed article in which it was affirmed, and retained only so much as excluded the question of its suspension from the ordinary range of congressional legislation.

The convention itself must have concurred in their views; for in the Constitution, as digested, and finally ratified, and as it stands now, there is neither enactment nor recognition of the privilege of this writ, except as it is implied in the provision that it shall not be suspended. It stands then under the Constitution of the United States, as it was under the

---

* "De libero homine exhibendo" D. 43. T. 29.
† See the Madison papers, Vol. I.

common law of English America, an indefeasible privilege, above the sphere of ordinary legislation.[*]

I do not think it necessary to argue from the words of this article, that the Congress was denied the power of limiting or restricting or qualifying the right, which it was thus forbidden to suspend. I do not, indeed, see that there can be a restriction or limitation of a privilege which may not be essentially a suspension of it, to some extent at least, or under some circumstances, or in reference to some of the parties who might otherwise have enjoyed it. And it has appeared to me, that if Congress had undertaken to deny altogether the exercise of this writ by the federal courts, or to limit its exercise to the few and rare cases that might per-adventure find their way to some one particular Court, or to declare that the writ should only issue in this or that class of cases, to the exclusion of others in which it might have issued at the common law, it would be difficult to escape the conclusion, that the ancient and venerated privilege of the writ of habeas corpus had not been in some degree suspended, if not annulled.

But there has been no legislation or attempted legislation by Congress, that could call for an expansion of this train of reasoning.

There was one other writ, which, in the more recent contests between the people and the king, had contributed signally to the maintenance of popular right. It was the writ of scire facias, which had been employed to vindicate the rights of property, by vacating the monopolies of the crown. Like the writ of habeas corpus, it founded itself on the concessions of Magna Charta ; and the two were the proper and natural complements of each other.

The first Congress so regarded them. The protection of the citizen against arbitrary exaction and unlawful restraint, as it is the essential object of all rightful government, would present itself as the first great duty of the courts of justice that were about to be constituted. And if, in defining their jurisdiction, it were thought proper to signalize two writs, out of the many known to the English law, as within the unqualified competency of the new tribunals, it would seem natural that those two should be selected, which boasted their origin from the charter of English liberties, and had been consecrated for ages in the affectionate memories of the people as their safeguard against oppression.

This consideration has interpreted for me the terms of the statute,

---

[*] " The privilege of the writ of *habeas corpus* shall not be suspended unless when in cases of rebellion or invasion the public safety may require it." Const. U S. Art. 1, § 9, par. 1.

which define my jurisdiction on this subject. Very soon after I had been advanced to the Bench, I was called upon to issue the writ of habeas corpus, at the instance of a negro, who had been arrested as a fugitive from labor. It was upon the force of the argument, to which I now advert, that I then awarded the process; and from that day to this, often as it has been invoked and awarded in similar cases that have been before me, my authority to award it has never been questioned.

The language of the act of Congress reflects the history of the constitutional provision. It enacts (*First Congr., Sess.* 1, *ch.* 20, *sec.* 14) "that all the before mentioned Courts of the United States" (the Supreme, Circuit and District,) " shall have power to issue writs of scire facias, habeas corpus and all other writs not specially provided for by statute, which may be necessary for the exercise of their respective jurisdictions and agreeable to the principles and usages of law."

I am aware that it has sometimes been contended or assumed, without, as it seems to me, a just regard to the grammatical construction of these words, that the concluding limitation applies to all the process of the Courts, the two writs specially named among the rest; and that the federal Courts can only issue the writ of habeas corpus, when it has become necessary to the exercise of an otherwise delegated jurisdiction; in other words, that it is subsidiary to some original process or pending suit.

It is obvious, that if such had been the intention of the law-makers, it was unnecessary to name the writ of habeas corpus at all, for the simpler phrase, "*all writs* necessary, &c." would in that case have covered their meaning. But there are objections to this reading more important than any that found themselves on grammatical rules.

The words that immediately follow in the section, give the power of issuing the writ to every judge, for the purpose of inquiring into the causes of a commitment. Now, a commitment presupposes judicial action, and this action it is the object of the writ to review. Can it be, that a single judge, sitting as such, can re-examine the causes of a detainer, which has resulted from judicial action, and is therefore *prima facie* a lawful one; and yet that the Court, of which he is a member, cannot inquire into the causes of a detainer, made without judicial sanction, and therefore *prima facie* unlawful?

Besides, if this were the meaning of the act, it might be difficult to find the cases to which it should apply. I speak of the writ of *habeas corpus ad subjiciendum*, the great writ of personal liberty, referred to in the constitution; not that modification of it which applies specially to the case of a commitment, nor the less important forms of habeas

12

corpus, *ad respondendum, ad faciendum,* &c., which are foreign to the question. I do not remember to have met a case, either in practice or in the books, where the writ *ad subjiciendum* could have performed any pertinent office in a pending suit. There may be such, but they do not occur to me : and I incline very strongly to the opinion, that if the power to issue the writ of habeas corpus applies only to cases of statutory jurisdiction, outrages upon the rights of a citizen can never invoke its exercise by a federal court.

If such were indeed the law of the United States, I do not see how I could escape the conclusion, that the jealousy of local interests and prejudice, which led to the constitution of federal Courts, regarded only disputes about property; and that the liberty of a citizen, when beyond the State of his domicil, was not deemed worthy of equal protection. From an absurdity so gross as this, I relieve myself by repeating the words of Chief Justice Marshal, in *ex parte Watkins,* 3 Pet. 201 : "No law of the United States prescribes the cases in which this great writ shall be issued, nor the power of the Court over the party brought up on it."

Whether, then, I look to the constitution, and its history, or to the words or the policy of the act of Congress, I believe that it was meant to require of the Courts of the United States, that they should dispense the privileges of the writ of habeas corpus to all parties lawfully asserting them, as other Courts of similar functions and dignity had immemorially dispensed them at the common law. The Congress of 1789 made no definition of the writ, or of its conditions, or effects. They left it as the constitution left it, and as it required them to leave it, the birthright of every man within the borders of the States ; like the right to air, and water, and motion, and thought, rights imprescriptible, and above all legislative discretion or caprice.

And so it ought to be. There is no writ so important for good, and so little liable to be abused. At the worst, in the hands of a corrupt or ignorant judge, it may release some one from restraint who should justly have remained bound. But it deprives no one of freedom, and divests no right. It could not give to Mr. Wheeler the possession of his slaves, but it might release them from the custody of a wrong-doer. Freemen or bondsmen, they had rights ; and the foremost of these was the right to have their other rights adjudicated openly and by the tribunals of the land. And this right, at least, Mr. Wheeler shared with them ; he also could claim a hearing.

Unless these views are incorrect throughout, the District Court had jurisdiction of the case, which came before it at the instance of Mr. Wheeler. He represented in substance, by his petition under oath, that three human beings had been forcibly taken possession of by Passmore Williamson, without authority of law, within the Eastern District of Pennsylvania ; and he prayed, that by force of the writ of habeas corpus, Mr. Williamson might be required to produce their bodies before the Court, and to declare what was the right or pretext of right, under which he claimed to detain them.

Whether Mr. Wheeler was in fact entitled to demand this writ, or whether upon a full discussion of the law the Court might have felt justified in refusing it to him, is a question of little moment. Every day and in every Court, writs issue at the instance of parties asserting a grievance, and very often when in truth no grievance has been sustained. The party assailed comes before the Court in obedience to its process. He perhaps questions the jurisdiction of the Court. Perhaps he denies the fact charged. Perhaps he explains that the fact, as charged, was by reason of circumstances a lawful one. The judge is not presumed to know beforehand all the merits of the thousand and one causes that come before him : he decides when he has heard. But the first duty of a defendant, in all cases, is obedience to the writ which calls him into Court. Till he has rendered this, the judge cannot hear the cause, still less pass upon its merits.

Mr. Williamson came before the Court ; but he did not bring forth the bodies of his alleged prisoners, as the writ had commanded him. He did not question the jurisdiction of the Court : he did not assert that the negroes were free, and that the writ had been applied for without their authority or consent : but he simply denied that they had ever been in his custody, power or possession, as Mr. Wheeler asserted.

Witnesses were heard, and, with one consent, they supported the allegation of Mr. Wheeler, and contradicted the denial of Mr. Williamson.

Mr. Williamson's counsel then asked time to enable them to produce witnesses who were material on his behalf ; remarking that their client might desire to bring the negroes into Court, to prove that they had not been abducted. The judge informed them, in reply, that upon Mr. Williamson making the customary affidavit that there were material witnesses whom he wished to adduce, the cause would be continued, as of course, till a future day. Mr. Williamson declined making the affidavit.

He however asked leave to declare for himself what he had done, and why. He was heard, and, speaking under solemn affirmation, he not only verified all the important facts that had been sworn to by Mr. Wheeler and the witnesses, but added that immediately before coming into Court with his return, he had called upon a negro who had been his principal associate in the transaction, to ascertain whether the negroes were "safe," and had been informed by him that they were "all safe."

Two motions were then made by Mr. Wheeler's counsel; the first, that Mr. Williamson should be committed for a contempt of process, in that he had made a false return to the writ; the second, that he should be held to answer to a charge of perjury. He summed up the evidence, and referred to authorities in support of these motions. The counsel of Mr. Williamson then asked leave to consult together as to their appropriate course of action; and this being assented to by the Court, they retired with their client for the purpose, from the Court room. Returning after some time, they informed the Court that they declined making any argument upon the questions which were before it.

The case, which was in this manner thrown upon the Court for its unaided adjudication, had assumed an aspect of grave responsibility on the part of Mr. Williamson. It was clearly in proof that the negroes had been removed by persons acting under his counsel, in his presence, and with his co-operation : his return to the writ denied that they had ever been within his possession, custody, or control. Under ordinary circumstances, this denial would have been conclusive; but being controverted by the facts in evidence, it lost that character. "The Court," said Judge Story, in a case singularly analogous in its circumstances, (U. S. vs. Green, 3 Mas. 483,) " will not discharge the defendant, simply because he declares that the infant is not in his power, possession, control or custody, if the conscience of the Court is not satisfied that all the material facts are fully disclosed. That would be to listen to mere forms, against the claims of substantial justice, and the rights of personal liberty in the citizen. In ordinary cases, indeed, such a declaration is satisfactory and ought to be decisive, because there is nothing before the Court upon which it can ground a doubt of its entire verity, and that in a real and legal sense the import of the words " possession, power, or custody," is fully understood and met by the party. The cases of the King vs. Vinton, 5 T. R., 89, and of Stacey, 10 Johns. 328, show with what jealousy, Courts regard returns of this nature. In these cases, there was enough on the face of the returns to excite suspicions that more was behind, and that the party was really within the constructive control of the defendant. Upon examining the circumstances of this case, I am not satisfied that the return contains all those facts within the knowledge of the defendant, which are necessary to be brought before the Court, to enable it to decide, whether he is entitled to a discharge ; or in other words, whether he has not now the power to produce the infant, and control those in whose custody she is."

"There is no doubt," he adds, "that an attachment is the proper process to bring the defendant into court."

. Anxious that this resort to the inherent and indispensable powers of the Court might be avoided, the judge, in adjourning the case for advisement until the following week, urged upon Mr. Williamson and his associates, that if practicable, the negroes should, in the meantime, be brought before the court.

But the negroes were not produced. They came forward afterwards, some of them, as it is said, before a justice in New York; and by a process of a Pennsylvania State Court, they or some of them were brought forward again in this city, to testify for Mr. Williamson or some of his confederates. But before the Court of the United States, sitting within the same curtilage, at the distance of perhaps a hundred yards, it was not thought necessary or expedient or practicable to produce them. Their evidence, whatever might have been its import or value, was never before the Court, and could have no bearing upon its action.

The decision was announced at the end of the week. It was, that Mr. Williamson's answer was evasive and untrue; that he, therefore, had not obeyed the writ of habeas corpus, and must consequently stand committed as for a contempt of it. The order to that effect having been made, a discussion arose between the counsel as to the propriety of certain motions, which on one side and the other they invited the Court to consider.

It was apparent, that the learned gentleman* who at this time addressed the Court on behalf of Mr. Williamson, as his senior counsel, was imperfectly prepared to suggest any specific action either for the bench, or for his client. His remarks were discursive; and when invited to reduce his motion to writing, according to the rules of practice, he found difficulty in defining its terms. This led to an intimation on the part of the judge, that, inasmuch as the opinion was in writing, and would be printed in the newspapers of the afternoon, it might be best for the counsel to examine its positions before submitting their motion. The intimation was received courteously. The question was asked whether the Court would be in session on one or another of days that were named; and the reply was given, that upon a note being left at the Clerk's office at any time, the judge would be in attendance to hear and consider whatever motion the counsel might see proper to lay before him.

* Mr. Charles Gilpin.

This was the last of the case. No motion was made; no further intimation given on the part of Mr. Williamson or his counsel, of a wish to make one.

Commitments for contempt, like the contempts themselves, may be properly distributed in two classes. Either they are the punishment for an act of misconduct, or it is their object to enforce the performance of a duty. The confinement in the one case is for a fixed time, supposed to be commensurate with the offending; in the other, it is without prescribed limitation, and is determined by the willingness of the party to submit himself to the law.

In the case of Mr. Williamson, the commitment is for a refusal to answer; that is to say, to make a full and lawful answer to the writ of habeas corpus, an answer setting forth all the facts within his knowledge, which are necessary to a decision by the Court, "whether he had not the power to produce the negroes, and control those in whose custody they were." He is now undergoing restraint, not punishment. Immediately after the opinion was read, he was informed, in answer to a remark from his counsel, that the commitment was "*during the contempt:*" the contempt of the party and the order of the Court consequent upon it, determine together.

This is all that I conceive it necessary to say of the strictly judicial action in the case. The opinions, announced by the judge upon other points, may perhaps be regarded as merely *dicta*. But it had appeared from the defendant's declarations when upon the stand, that he supposed Mr. Wheeler's slaves to have become free, and that this consideration justified his acting towards them as he had done. It seemed due to him, that the Court, believing as it did those views to be incorrect, should not withhold an expression of its dissent from them. Several succinct positions were accordingly asserted by the judge: two of which may invite a few additional remarks at this time.

"I know of no statute of Pennsylvania," the judge said, "which affects to divest the rights of property of a citizen of North Carolina, acquired and asserted under the laws of that State, because he has found it needful or convenient to pass through the territory of Pennsylvania; and I am not aware that any such statute, if such a one were shown, could be recognized as valid in a Court of the United States."

The first of these propositions may be vindicated easily. By the common law, as it came to Pennsylvania, slavery was a familiar institution. Only six days after the first legislative assembly met in Philadelphia, and thirteen days before the great charter was signed, the council was engaged in discussing a law "to prevent the escape of run-aways;" and four days later, it sat judicially, William Penn himself presiding, to enforce a contract for the sale of a slave, 1 *Colonial Records*, 63.* The counties of New Castle, Kent, and Sussex, which were at that time and for many years after annexed to Pennsylvania, and governed by the same law, continue to recognize slavery up to the present hour. It survived in our Commonwealth, as a legally protected institution, until some time after the census of 1840; so cautiously did the act of 1780, for its gradual abolition among us, operate upon the vested interests of our own slave owners.

That act excepted from the operation of its provisions the domestic slaves of delegates in Congress, of foreign ministers, of persons passing through, or *sojourning* in the State, and *not becoming residents* therein, provided such slaves were not *retained* in the State longer than six months. The act of 1847 repealed so much of the act of 1780 as authorized masters and owners of slaves to bring and *retain* their slaves within the Commonwealth for the period of six months, or for any period of time whatever. But it did not affect to vary or rescind the rights of slave owners *passing through* our territory. It applied to persons *resident* and persons *sojourning*, who brought and sought to *retain* their slaves here; for over such persons and their rights of property the State had lawful dominion: but it left the right of transit for property and person, over which it had no jurisdiction, just as it was before, and as it stood under the constitution of the United States and the Law of Nations.

This brings me to the second part of the position affirmed in the court's opinion, namely: the right of a citizen of one State to pass freely with his slaves through the territory of another State, in which the institution of slavery is not recognized.

I need not say, that before the compact of union was formed between the States, each of them was an absolutely sovereign and independent community; and that, except so far as their relations to each other and to foreign nations have been qualified by the Federal Constitution, each of them remain so. As such, it is bound by that great moral code, which, because of its universal obligation, is called the Law of Nations. What it could not do if freed from federative restrictions, it cannot do now: every restraint upon its policy, which duty to other States would in that case involve, binds it still, just as if the union had been dissolved or had never been formed.

* "At a council, held at Philadelphia, ye 29th 1st mo., 1683. Present, William Penn, Proprietary, and Governor of Pennsylvania and counties annexed,

All the statists unite in regarding the right of transit for person and property through the territory of a friendly State, as among those which cannot, under ordinary circumstances, be denied.   Vattel, B. 2, ch. 10, § 132, 3, 4; Puffendorf, B. 2, ch. 3, § 5, 67; Rutherf. Inst. B. 2, ch. 9; 1 Kent Com. 33, 35.   It is true that the right is not an unqualified one.   The State may impose reasonable conditions upon its exercise, and exact guaranties against its abuse.   But subject to these limitations, it is the right of every citizen of a friendly State.

The right is the same, and admits just the same qualifications, as to person and to property.   The same argument, that denies the right of peacefully transmitting one's property through the territories of a State, refuses the right of passage to its owner.   And the question, what is to be deemed property in such a case, refers itself necessarily to the law of the State from which the citizen brings it: a different test would sanction the confiscation of property at the will of the sovereign through whose territory it seeks to pass.   If one State may decree that there shall be no property, no right of ownership in human beings; another, in a spirit of practical philanthropy only a little more energetic, may deny the protection of law to the products of slave labor; and a third may denounce a similar outlawry against all intoxicating liquids: And if the laws of a State can control the rights of property of strangers passing through its territory; then the sugar of New Orleans, the cotton of Carolina, the wines of Ohio, and the rum of New England may have their markets bounded by the States in which they are produced; and without any change of reasoning, New Jersey may refuse to citizens of

Thos. Holmes, John Richardson, William Clarke, John Simcox, James Harrison, (and eight others.)

"The petition of Nathaniel Allen was read, shewing that he had sould a servant to Henry Bowman, for six hundred weight of beefe, with yᵉ hide and tallow, and six pounds sterling, which yᵉ said Bowman delayed to pay yᵉ said petitioner, shewing likewise that yᵉ said Henry Bowman and Walter Humphrey hired a boat of the said petitioner only for one month, and kept the same boat 18 weeks from the petitioner to his great prejudice: Then it was ordered, that William Clarke, John Simcox and James Harrison should speak to Henry Bowman concerning this matter."—p. 62.

The Great Charter was signed by William Penn. 2d day, 2d mo., 1683, (see p. 72.)

A practice analogous to the Fugitive Slave Law of modern times seems to be referred to in the following minute, at p. 147 of the same volume.

"24th 5 mo., 1685. William Hague requests the secretary, that an hue and cry from East Jersey after a servant of Mr. John White's, a merchant at New York, might have some force and authority to pass this province and territories: the secretary indorsed it, and sealed it with yᵉ seal of this province."

Pennsylvania the right of passing along her railroads to New York. The doctrine is one that was exploded in Europe more than four hundred and fifty years ago, and finds now, or found very lately, its parting illustration in the politics of Japan.

It was because, and only because, this right was acknowledged by all civilized nations, and had never been doubted among the American colonies—because each colony had at all times tendered its hospitalities freely to the rest, cherishing that liberal commerce which makes a brotherhood of interest even among alien States; it was because of this that no man in the convention or country thought of making the right of transit a subject of Constitutional guaranty. Everything in and about the Constitution implies it. It is found in the object, "to establish a more perfect union," in the denial to the States of the power to lay duties on imports, and in the reservation to Congress of the exclusive right to regulate commerce among the States.

This last power of the general government according to the repeated and well considered decisions of the Supreme Court of the United States, from *Gibbons* vs. *Ogden*, 9 Peters, to the *passenger cases*, 7 Howard, applies to intercourse as well as navigation, to the transportation of men as well as goods, of men who pass from State to State involuntary, as of men who pass voluntary; and it excludes the right of any State to pass laws regulating, controling, or *a fortiori*, prohibiting such intercourse or transportation. I do not quote the words of the eminent judges who have affirmed this exposition of the Constitution; but it is impossible to read their elaborate opinions, as they are found in the reports, without recognizing this as the fixed law of the United States.

It needs no reference to disputable annals, to show that when the Constitution was formed in 1787, slaves were recognized as property, throughout the United States. The Constitution made them a distinct element in the distribution of the representative power and in the assessment of direct taxes. They were known and returned by the census, three years afterwards, in sixteen out of the seventeen States then embraced in the Union; and as late as the year 1830, they were found in every State of the original thirteen. How is it possible then, while we assert the binding force of the constitution by claiming rights under it, to regard slave property as less effectively secured by the provisions of that instrument than any other property which is recognized as such by the law of the owner's domicil? How can it be, that a State may single out this one sort of property from among all the rest, and deny to it the right of passing over its soil—passing with its owner, parcel of his travelling equipment, as much so as the horse he rides on, his great coat, or his carpet bag?

We revolt in Pennsylvania, and honestly no doubt, at this association of men with things as the subjects of property; for we have accustomed ourselves for some years—now nearly fifteen—to regard men as men, and things as things: *sub modo*, however; for we distinguish against the negro much as our forefathers did; and not perhaps, with quite as much reason. They denied him civil rights as a slave: we exclude him from political rights, though a freeman.

Yet no stranger may complain of this. Our constitutions and statutes are for ourselves, not for others. They reflect our sympathies, and define our rights. But as to all the rest of the world; those portions especially, towards whom we are bound by the "supreme law" of the federal constitution; they are independent of our legislation, however wise or virtuous it may be; for they were not represented in our conventions and assemblies, and we do not permit them to legislate for us.

Whether any redress is provided by the existing laws of Pennsylvania for the citizen of another State, whose slaves have escaped from him while he was passing through our territory, it is not my province to inquire. It is quite probable that he may be denied recourse to the Courts, as much so as the husband, or father, or guardian, whose wife, or child, or ward, has run away. He may find himself referred back to those rights, which annex themselves inseparably to the relation he occupies, the rights of manucaption and detainer. These, I apprehend that he may assert and exercise anywhere, and with such reasonable force as circumstances render necessary. And I do not suppose that the employment of such reasonable force could be regarded as a breach of the peace, or the right to employ it as less directly incident to his character of master, than it might be to the corresponding character in either of the analogous relations. In a word, I adopt fully on this point the views so well enforced by Judge Baldwin, in the case of *Johnson* vs. *Tompkins*, Baldw., 578, 9:

" The right of the master to arrest his fugitive slave, is not a solitary case in the law. It may be exercised towards a fugitive apprentice or redemptioner to the same extent, and is done daily without producing any excitement. An apprentice is a servant, a slave is no more: though his servitude is for life, the nature of it is the same as apprenticeship or by redemption, which, though terminated by time, is during its continuance as severe a servitude as that for life. Of the same nature is the right of a parent to the services of his minor children, which gives the custody of their persons. So, where a man enters bail for the appearance of a defendant in a civil action, he may seize his person at his pleasure, and commit him to prison; or, if the principal escapes, the bail may pursue him to another State, arrest, and bring him back, by the use of all necessary force and means of preventing an escape. The lawful exercise of this authority in such cases is calculated to excite no sympathy: the law takes its course in peace, and unnoticed. Yet it is the same power, and used in the same manner, as by a master over his slave. The right in such case is from the same source, the law of the land. If the enforcement of the right excites more feeling in one case than the other, it is not from the manner in which it is done, but the nature of the right which is enforced, property in a human being for life. If this is unjust and oppressive, the sin is on the makers of laws which tolerate slavery: to visit it on those who have honestly acquired, and lawfully hold property under the guarantee and protection of the laws, is the worst of all oppression, and the rankest injustice towards our fellow men. It is the indulgence of a spirit of persecution against our neighbors, for no offence against society or its laws, but simply for the assertion of their own in a lawful manner.

"If this spirit pervades the country," he goes on to say, "if public opinion is suffered to prostrate the laws which protect one species of property, those who lead the crusade against slavery, may at no distant day find a new one directed against their lands, their stores, and their debts. If a master cannot retain the custody of his slave, apprentice or redemptioner, a parent must give up the guardianship of his children, bail have no hold upon their principal, the creditor cannot arrest his debtor by lawful means, and he, who keeps the rightful owner of lands or chattels out of possession, will be protected in his trespasses.

"When the law ceases to be the test of right and remedy; when individuals undertake to be its administrators, by rules of their own adoption; the bands of society are broken as effectually by the severance of one link from the chain of justice which binds man to the laws, as if the whole was dissolved. The more specious and seductive the pretexts are, under which the law is violated, the greater ought to be the vigilance of courts and juries in their detection. Public opinion is a security against acts of open and avowed infringements of acknowledged rights; from such combinations there is no danger; they will fall by their own violence, as the blast expends its force by its own fury. The only permanent danger is in the indulgence of the humane and benevolent feelings of our nature, at what we feel to be acts of oppression towards human beings, endowed with the same qualities and attributes as ourselves, and brought into being by the same power which created us all; without reflecting, that in suffering these feelings to come into action against rights secured by the laws, we forget the first duty of citizens of a government of laws, obedience to its ordinances."

There was one other legal proposition affirmed in the opinion of this Court, but it cannot need argument. It was, that the question, whether the negroes were or were not freed by their arrival in Pennsylvania, was irrelevant to the issue; inasmuch as whether they were freed or not, they were equally under the protection of the law, and the same obligation rested on Mr. Williamson to make a true and full return to the writ of habeas corpus. Simple and obvious as this proposition is, it covers all the judicial action in the case. The writ required him to produce the negroes, that the Court might pass upon his legal right to carry them off or detain them. What questions might arise afterwards, or how they might be determined, was not for him to consider. His duty then, as now, was and is to bring in the bodies; or, if they had passed beyond his control, to declare under oath or affirmation, so far as he knew, what had become of them: And from this duty, or from the constraint that seeks to enforce it, there can be no escape. (See the argument of Sergeant Glynn, and the remarks of Mr. Justice Gould, in the case of Mr. Wilkes, 2 Wils. 154.)

The application immediately before me, hardly calls for these expanded remarks; though, rightly considered, they bear upon most of the points that were elaborated in the argument upon the question of its reception. It purports to be a suggestion and petition from a person now in Massachusetts, who informs the Court that she is one of the negroes who escaped from Mr. Wheeler, that she did so by Mr. Williamson's counsel, and with the sanction of his presence and approval, but that he never detained her, nor has any one since, and that she has never authorized an application for the writ of habeas corpus in her behalf. Thereupon, she presents to me certain reasons, founded as she supposes in law, wherefore I ought to quash the writ heretofore issued at the relation of Mr. Wheeler.

When application was made to me for leave to file this paper, I invited the learned cousel to advise me upon the question, whether I could lawfully admit the intervention of their client. My thanks are due to them for the ability and courteous bearing with which they have discussed it. But I remain unconvinced.

The very name of the person who authenticates the prayer is a stranger to any proceeding that is or has been before me.* She asks no judicial action for herself, and does not profess to have any right to solicit action in behalf of another: on the contrary, her counsel here assure me ex-

---

* Neither the petition for the writ of habeas corpus, nor the writ itself, names Jane *Johnson*.

pressly, that Mr. Williamson has not sanctioned her application. She has therefore no status whatever in this Court.

Were she here as a party, to abide its action, she would have a right to be heard according to the forms of law; were she here as a witness, called by a party, her identity ascertained, she might be examined as to all facts supposed to be within her knowledge. But our records cannot be opened to every stranger who volunteers to us a suggestion, as to what may have been our errors, and how we may repair them.

I know that the writ of habeas corpus can only be invoked by the party who is restrained of liberty; or by some one in his behalf. I know, too, that it has been the reproach of the English Courts, that they have too sternly exacted proof, that the application was authorized by the aggrieved party, before permitting the writ to issue. But, as yet, the Courts of the United States have, I think, avoided this error. The writ issues here, as it did in Rome,* whenever it is shown by affidavit that its beneficent agency is needed. It would lose its best efficiency, if it could not issue without a petition from the party himself, or some one whom he had delegated to represent him. His very presence in Court to demand the writ would, in some sort, negative the restraint which his petition must allege. In the most urgent cases, those in which delay would be disastrous, forcible abduction, secret imprisonment, and the like, the very grievance under which he is suffering, precludes the possibility of his applying in person or constituting a representative. The American books are full of cases,—they are within the experience of every practitioner at the bar,—in which the writ has issued at the instance of third persons, who had no other interest or right in the matter than what every man concedes to sympathy with the oppressed. In need only to refer to the case I have quoted from in 3 Mason, and the case of Stacy, in 10 Johnson, for illustrations of this practice.

Of course, if it appears to the Court at any time, that the writ was asked for by an intermeddling stranger, one who had no authority to intervene, and whose intervention is repudiated, the writ will be quashed. But it is for the defendant, to whom the writ is addressed, to allege a want of authority in the relator. The mo-

---

* "Interdictum omnibus competit.—*Nemo* enim prohibendus est libertati favere."—*Dig. B.* 43, *T.* 29, § 9.

tion to quash cannot be the act of a volunteer. Still less can it come to us by written suggestion, from without our jurisdiction, in the name of the party who is alleged to be under constraint, and whose very denial that she is so may be only a proof that the constraint is effectual.

I may add, that I have examined all the authorities which were brought before me by the learned counsel: with most of them I was familiar before. But there is not one among them, which in my judgment conflicts with the views I have expressed.

The application to enter this paper among the records of the Court, must therefore be refused.

——————

Upon the reading of the above opinion, Mr. Cadwalader, as a member of the bar of the Court, not counsel or attorney in the original or subsequent proceedings, asked leave as amicus curiæ to suggest that, in the Opinion of the Court, an incident of the original proceeding, which has been publicly misrepresented, was not noticed.

"It has been publicly reported," Mr. Cadwalader said, "that after the opinion of the Court, which resulted in Mr. Williamson's commitment, had been read, his counsel applied to the Court for leave to amend his return, which leave was refused. The present suggestion is made under the belief of the member of the bar who makes it, that this report was erroneous, and that what occurred was as follows. When the opinion in the original proceeding was read, the counsel of Mr. Williamson asked if a motion to amend the return would be received, and the Court replied, that the motion must be reduced to writing, and that it could not be received until the Court's order should be filed with the Clerk and recorded; adding that the Court would then receive any motion which the counsel for Mr. Williamson might desire to make. The Court's order was then filed by the Clerk, and entered on record; but no motion to amend was then or afterwards made, although the Court paused to give an opportunity for making it, and invited the counsel then or afterwards, to make any motion which their client might be advised to make."

Judge KANE said:—The recollections of Mr. Cadwalader concur substantially with my own. There certainly was no motion made by the counsel of Mr. Williamson, for leave to amend his return. A wish was expressed to make such a motion, and the judge asked that the motion might be reduced to writing and filed. But the motion was not drawn out or presented for the Court's consideration, and the Court never expressed any purpose to overrule such a motion, if one should be presented.

NARRATIVE

OF

FACTS IN THE CASE

OF

Passmore Williamson.

———————

PHILADELPHIA:

Published by The Pennsylvania Anti-Slavery Society,

No. 31 NORTH FIFTH STREET.

MERRIHEW & THOMPSON, PRS., MERCHANT ST., ABOVE FOURTH.

1855.

NARRATIVE.

John H. Wheeler, of North Carolina, the accredited Minister of the United States to Nicaragua, arrived in the city of Philadelphia, on his way from Washington to Nicaragua, on Wednesday the 18th of July, 1855. He brought with him Jane Johnson, a woman whom he had purchased as a slave, some two years before, at Richmond, Virginia, and her two children, both sons, one between 6 and 7, and the other between 11 and 12 years of age. His professed design was to hold them as slaves, not only in the free States of Pennsylvania, New Jersey and New York, but also in the free country of Nicaragua. Lawyer by profession, and Diplomatist by occupation, he must have been fully aware that none of the States named tolerated the existence of slavery for a moment within their limits, excepting in the case of slaves escaping from other States. He seems to have relied for immunity upon the respect inspired by his representative character and upon his personal vigilance in guarding Jane and her children.

Upon his arrival at the Baltimore Railroad Depot, corner of Broad and Prime streets, in this city, he conveyed them to Bloodgood's hotel, near Walnut street wharf, stopping on the way at the house of a relative. During the two and a half hours of their stay at Bloodgood's, he lost sight but once of his companions. Jane's intention to assert her freedom at the earliest opportunity, had been fully formed before starting from the South. She is a remarkably intelligent woman for one wholly without education. When Mr. Wheeler was called to dinner, she feared to move, thinking his eye was upon her. It was well she did so, for in a few minutes he left the dining hall to see whether she was still there; and being satisfied on that point, returned to finish a hasty repast. At this time she spoke to a colored woman who was passing, and told her that she was a slave, and to a colored man she said the same thing, afterwards adding, that she wished to be free. An hour afterwards, William Still, an active member of the Vigilance Committee, and clerk at the Philadelphia Anti-Slavery Office, received a note asking him to come down to Bloodgood's hotel as soon as possible, as there were three slaves there

429

who wanted liberty, and that their master was with them, on his way to New York.

With this note in his hand, Mr. Still called upon the Secretary of the Acting Committee of " The Pennsylvania Society for Promoting the Abolition of Slavery, and *for the Relief of Free Negroes unlawfully held in Bondage*, and for improving the condition of the African Race." This Society, whose objects are sufficiently indicated by its name, was incorporated by Legislative Act in 1789 ; Benjamin Franklin was its first President, and it has ever since been an efficient aid to Freedom in Pennsylvania. Mr. Williamson, the present Secretary, is every way worthy to fill his post. Well educated, intelligent, of active habits and sound judgment, he has long enjoyed the respect, and unlimited confidence of a large circle of acquaintances and friends.

Ever active at their important posts, Mr. Williamson and Mr. Still hastened to the hotel. Mr. Williamson, who arrived first, found that the party had gone on board the boat then at the wharf, designing to take the five o'clock Camden and Amboy train for New York.— Thither he followed them, and found Jane and her children seated upon the upper deck. He went up to her and said, " You are the person I am looking for, I presume." Mr. Wheeler, who was sitting on the same bench, three or four feet from her, asked what Mr. Williamson wanted with him. The answer was, " Nothing, my business is entirely with this woman." Amid repeated interruptions from Mr. Wheeler, Mr. Williamson calmly explained to Jane that she was free under the laws of Pennsylvania, and could either go with Mr. Wheeler, or enjoy her freedom by going on shore. The conversation between Williamson, Wheeler, Still and a by-stander, was kept up for several minutes, the same ideas being frequently repeated. A few persons gathered about them to hear. Wheeler begged Jane, in the most hurried and earnest manner, to say that she wanted to go with him to her children in Virginia. She made answer that she wanted to see her children, but she wanted to be free. At last the bell rang, and Mr. Williamson, supposing the boat was about to start, turned to Jane and said, " The time has come when you must act; if you wish to exercise your right of freedom, you will have to come ashore immediately." She looked round at her two children, grasped the hand or arm of the one next her, and attempted to rise from her seat. Wheeler pushed her back, saying, " Now don't go, Jane." She renewed her effort to get up, and did so, with the aid of Mr. Williamson. Wheeler's first movement had been to push Jane back, but he soon clasped her tightly round the body. Mr. Williamson pulled him back and held him till she was out of danger from his grasp. Jane moved steadily forward towards the stairway leading to the lower deck. It was at the head of the stairway, if we may believe Mr. Wheeler, that he was seized by two colored men and threatened by one of them; but the most careful and repeated examination of witnesses has failed to elicit any testimony to a threat except one made on the lower deck. She was led down the stairs of the boat and her children picked up and carried after her; one of them cried vociferously. She and her children were conducted ashore, and put into a carriage, and, amid the huzzas of the spectators, were driven off to a place of safety. There was a crowd of persons, including some police officers, on and about the boat at the time, but no one offered any resistance. All seemed to regard it as a work proper to be done, and to approve of the manner in which it was executed. Mr. Williamson behaved very judiciously in the affair, and discharged the duty imposed on him, by his office, in a manner becoming its importance. To the threats of Mr. Wheeler, he replied by giving him his card, indicating where he was to be found, if wanted, and saying that he would be responsible for the legal consequences of his action.

In order to judge respecting the legal consequences or character of Passmore Williamson's action in this case, it is necessary to recall certain facts in the legislation of Pennsylvania. On the 1st of March, 1780, the Legislature of Pennsylvania passed an Act providing for the gradual abolition of Slavery within the State. The following is the Preamble of that Act:

"When we contemplate our abhorrence of that condition to which the arms and tyranny of Great Britain were exerted to reduce us, when we look back on the variety of dangers to which we have been exposed, and how miraculously our wants in many instances have been supplied, and our deliverances wrought, when even hope and human fortitude have become unequal to the conflict, we are unavoidably led to a serious and grateful sense of the manifold blessings, which we have undeservedly received from the hand of that Being, from whom every good and perfect gift cometh. Impressed with these ideas, we conceive that it is our duty, and we rejoice that it is in our power, to extend a portion of that freedon to others which hath been extended to us, and release them from that state of thraldrom to which we ourselves were tyranically doomed, and from which we have now every prospect of being delivered. It is not for us to enquire why, in the creation of mankind, the inhabitants of the several parts of the earth were distinguished by the difference in feature or complexion. It is sufficient to know that all are the work of an Almighty Hand. We find, in the distribution of the human species, that the most fertile as well as the most barren parts of the earth are inhabited by men of complexions different from ours, and from each other ; from whence we may reasonably, as well as religiously, infer, that He who placed them in their various situations, hath extended equally his care and protection to all, and that it becometh not us to counteract his mercies. We esteem it a peculiar blessing granted to us, that we are enabled this day to add one more step to universal civilization, by removing, as much as possible, the sorrows of those who have lived in undeserved bondage, and from which, by the assumed authority of the Kings of Great Britain, no effectual legal relief could be obtained. Weaned by a long course of experience from those narrow prejudices and partialities we had imbibed, we find our hearts enlarged with kindness and benevolence towards men of all conditions and nations ; and we conceive ourselves at this particular period extraordinarily called upon by the blessings which we have received, to manifest the sincerity of our profession, and to give a substantial proof of our gratitude.

"II. And whereas, the condition of those persons who have heretofore been denominated Negro and Mulatto slaves, has been attended with circumstances, which not only deprived them of the common blessing that they were by nature entitled to, but has cast them into the deepest afflictions by an unnatural separation and sale of husband and wife from each other and from their children, an injury, the greatness of which can only be conceived by supposing that we were in the same unhappy case. In justice, therefore, to persons so unhappily circumstanced, and who, having no prospect before them whereon they may rest their sorrows and their hopes, have no reasonable inducement to render their services to society, which they otherwise might, and also in grateful commemoration of our own happy deliverance from that state of unconditional submission to which we were doomed by the tyranny of Britain :

"III. Be it enacted, and it is hereby enacted," &c.

This Act declares that "no man or woman of any nation or color," (excepting the slaves then living in the State and registered as required by law,) "shall at any time hereafter be deemed, adjudged or holden, within the territories of this commonwealth, as slaves or servants for life, but as free men and free women, except the domestic slaves attending upon delegates in Congress from the other American States, foreign ministers and consuls, and persons passing through and sojourning in this State, and not becoming residents therein, and seamen employed in ships not belonging to any inhabitant of this State, nor employed in any ship owned by any such inhabitant: *Provided,* Such domestic slaves shall not be alienated nor sold to any inhabitant, nor (except in the case of members of Congress, foreign ministers and consuls) retained in this State longer than six months."

On the 3d of March, 1847, the Legislature of Pennsylvania passed a statute, repealing this permission to hold slaves even temporarily in this State. The language of the statute is as follows:

"So much of the Act of the General Assembly, entitled 'An Act for the gradual abolition of Slavery,' passed the 1st day of March, 1780, as authorizes the masters or owners of slaves to bring or retain such slaves within this commonwealth, for the period of six months, in involuntary servitude, or for any period of time whatsoever, and so much of said act as prevents a slave from giving testimony against any person whatsoever, be and the same is hereby repealed."

Thus was freedom established as the rule for the Courts, absolute and unlimited, in all cases of slaves brought into the State by their owners.

The Pennsylvania law on this subject is given with great clearness in 1849, by the Supreme Court, in *Kauffman vs. Oliver*, 10 Barr's Reports:

"The principle sprung fresh, and beautiful, and perfect from the mind of Lord Mansfield, in the great case of the negro Somerset, that, by the common law, a slave, of whatever country or color, the moment he was on English ground, became free—endowed with the sanctity of reason. This case was decided before the revolution, and became the common law of this State, always saving and excepting the inroad of the compact and compromise. This action, then, professes to be founded on the principles of the common law; but by the principles of law, the fugitives *were free the moment when they touched the soil of Pennsylvania.* All the incidents, accompaniments and attributes of bondage fell from around them."

Immediately after he had been left by his travelling companions Mr. Wheeler sought the potential assistance of John K. Kane, Judge of the District Court of the United States. It seems to have been decided by these gentlemen that a warrant, under the Fugitive Slave Act, could not be sustained—that warrant applying only to cases of slaves escaping from another State into Pennsylvania. The ingenious device was hit upon of making the writ of Habeas Corpus—that glorious old bulwark of personal liberty—an instrument for getting possession of the mother and her children. Mr. Wheeler made the following affidavit:—

"To the Honorable John K. Kane, Judge of the District Court of the United States, in and for the Eastern District of Pennsylvania:

"The petition of John H. Wheeler respectfully represents:

"That your petitioner is *the owner of three persons* held to labor by the laws of the State of Virginia, said persons being respectively named Jane, aged about 35 years, Daniel, aged about 12 years, and Isaiah, aged about 7 years, persons of color; and that they are detained from the possession of your petitioner by one Passmore Williamson, resident of the city of Philadelphia, and that they are not detained for any criminal or supposed criminal matter.

"Your petitioner therefore prays your Honor to grant a writ of habeas corpus to be directed to the said Passmore Williamson, commanding him to bring before your Honor the bodies of the said Jane, Daniel and Isaiah, to do and abide such order as your Honor may direct.

[Signed]   JOHN H. WHEELER."

"Sworn to and subscribed, July 18, 1855.

CHAS. F. HEAZLITT, U. S. Com."

It will be observed that the benefit of the writ is not solicited in behalf of Jane and her children; Mr. Wheeler does not allege that they are his wife, children, or wards, but that they are slaves; he does not bring the case within the Fugitive Slave Act, by asserting their escape from another State into Pennsylvania, but rests his claim upon the naked fact that they are his slaves by Virginia law. Instead of promptly rejecting this application, on the ground of want of jurisdiction, Judge Kane granted the writ, returnable on the 18th instant, the next day, at 3 o'clock. All the facts—the sudden departure of Jane, the visit of Mr. Wheeler to Judge Kane, the affidavit, the application, the granting and issuing of the writ—seem to have been crowded into an incredibly short space of time after five o'clock P. M. on the 18th. On the 19th, a Deputy Marshal made affidavit that he had served the writ at the residence of Passmore Williamson. This was a mistake, as he had served it at the residence of his father, corner of Seventh and Arch streets. On its discovery the affidavit was changed in accordance with the fact. An alias writ was issued, returnable at 10 o'clock, A. M. on the 20th.

Mr. Williamson, though under no legal obligation to obey or to notice a writ thus illegally issued, made the following return:

"To the Honorable J. K. Kane, the Judge within named :

Passmore Williamson, the defendant in the within writ mentioned, for return thereto respectfully submits, that the within named Jane, Daniel, and Isaiah, or by whatsoever names they may be called, nor either of them, are not now, nor were at the time of issuing the said writ, or the original writ, *or at any other time*, in the custody, power, or possession of, nor confined, nor restrained their liberty by him, the said Passmore Williamson. Therefore he cannot have the bodies of the said Jane, Daniel and Isaiah, or either of them, before your Honor, as by the said writ he is commanded.   (Signed,)

P. WILLIAMSON.

The above named Passmore Williamson, being duly affirmed, says that the facts set forth in the above return are true.

(Signed,)   P. WILLIAMSON.

Affirmed and subscribed before me, this 20th day of July, A. D., 1855.
(Signed,)   CHAS. F. HEAZLETT,
                                  U. S. Commissioner."

The return is in the ordinary form, with the addition of the words in italics.

Mr. Vandyke, the United States District Attorney and counsel for Mr. Wheeler, objected to the return as insufficient and untrue. Mr. Williamson's counsel contended that the return was complete, that it was not competent to go behind it, and that if the charge of untruth were brought, it should be made the subject of another hearing and of a separate and substantial allegation. Judge Kane said that the testimony offered by Mr. Vandyke should be admitted, and might be such as to make out a prima facie case of perjury, in which event it might be his duty as committing magistrate to bind Passmore Williamson over for perjury. This revelation of the feelings of the Judge changed in a moment the whole aspect of the case. The Judge had become the prosecutor, and before hearing evidence had allowed his feelings to betray him into a violation of the decency of the Bench, and an outrage upon the personal character of one of the most respectable of our citizens.

Mr. W.'s counsel asked for time to examine the case and prepare a proper defense, which was refused by Judge Kane, unless the persons named in the writ were brought into Court. Mr. Vandyke moved for an attachment against Passmore Williamson for contempt, and that he be held to answer a charge of perjury. Mr. W., took the stand, and, under affirmation, made a full and clear statement of the whole transaction, so far as his knowledge of it, and connection with it, extended. His counsel, at the opening, stated that they rested their case upon the fact of entire negation of possession, and were

1*

ready to amend the return in any manner directed by the Court, compatible with that position. But at this stage of the proceedings, they declined an argument, submitting the case to the judgment of the Court. Judge Kane said that in view of the gravity of the case, he would take time to consider it, and in the mean time, the respondent must enter bail, in the sum of $5000, for his appearance on Friday morning, the 27th of July, to answer the charge of perjury; that the motion in relation to contempt would go over till that day, when he would deliver his written opinion on the whole subject. He added, that "he would also say, at the risk of being considered extra judicial, that if it is really in the power of the defendant to produce the bodies of the three persons, it would be better for him to do so," thus leaving little room to doubt that his foregone determination had been to obtain Jane and her children, for the purpose of their re-enslavement, or, failing to do that, to inflict vengeance on the man who had enabled them to assert their legal rights.

These proceedings occupied little time. Nothing further was done until the morning of the 27th, when the Judge took his seat upon the Bench, and, to the surprise of the counsel, abandoned the charge of perjury, and committed the prisoner for contempt. Probably, during the week in which he considered the case, visions of a jury came between him and the man whom he would willingly condemn for perjury, and therefore he chose to construct a case where this troublesome element of American jurisprudence would not interfere with his plans. And thus was an innocent citizen sentenced to indefinite imprisonment, without a hearing, without a trial, without the verdict of a jury of his peers, after having been brow-beaten and charged with crime of a deep dye, by a Judge who should have presumed him innocent until he was proved guilty.

The decision delivered by Judge Kane on this occasion is perhaps the most remarkable legal document of our times. It will certainly be regarded as a barbarism of the nineteenth century, should it be preserved for the criticism of a wiser and better generation. Among its monstrous features it is difficult to decide whether it is most strongly marked by its perversion of the facts, its quibbling ingenuity on the question of constructive custody, or the arrogance with which it nullifies the statute law of Pennsylvania. It is wholly based on a double falsehood, *viz:* that Jane Johnson did not desire her freedom and was forcibly abducted by Passmore Williamson. It asserts facts in contradiction to the plainest testimony of respectable witnesses, and even contradicts the statement of the Judge's friend,

Mr. Wheeler. It represents Passmore Williamson as heading a riotous mob, the object of which was "*to effect the abduction and imprisonment*" of unoffending citizens. It insists that Jane Johnson and her children were within his custody and control because he told the woman that she was free by Pennsylvania law, and offered to lead her off the boat if she desired to go.

Not the least remarkable passage in this strange document is the following:

"The cause was submitted to me by the learned counsel for the respondent without argument, and I have therefore found myself at some loss to understand the grounds on which, if there be any such, they would claim the discharge of their client."

The reader who recollects that Judge Kane *refused to allow the counsel time for preparation for the argument*, though he took a week to prepare his decision, will not hesitate to characterize this statement as an insult to Mr. Williamson and to his counsel.

Another striking point is the profession of ignorance, on the part of its author, respecting Pennsylvania law. He says that he knows "of no statute of Pennsylvania which affects to divest the right of property of a citizen of North Carolina, acquired and asserted under the laws of that State, because he had found it needful or convenient to pass through the territory of Pennsylvania." By this circumlocution he means that he knows of no law in force in Pennsylvania which would deprive a slaveholder of his power to hold his slaves on her soil, after he had voluntarily brought them hither on his passage to another place. If this is not his meaning, his remark is irrelevant to his argument. Such a defence of his course is, certainly, made at an expense of his reputation for legal knowledge which one would scarcely have expected in a lawyer and judge. Yet, in the very next sentence, he incautiously permits the truth to appear that, after all, he has some idea of the existence of such a law, by expressing his doubt of its recognized validity by a United States' Court. What is this but an insult to Pennsylvania,—an intimation that, as a sovereign State, she has no right to determine whether or not slavery shall be transplanted by Southern masters to her own soil, and the laws of Virginia be dominant here. Again, this law-defying Judge says that he waives the inquiry whether, for the purposes of this question, they (Jane Johnson and her children) were in the territorial jurisdiction of Pennsylvania, while passing from one State to another, upon the navigable waters of the United States;" but adds, that his first impressions, upon this point, are adverse to the argument. One might fairly infer from this clause that Judge Kane had not the slightest idea that these persons had ever set foot on Pennsylvania soil; notwithstanding Wheeler's statement before the Court, that they spent some hours at Bloodgood's Hotel, in Walnut street, and notwithstanding the fact, well known to the Judge, that their route from Washington to New York lay through the heart of the City of Philadelphia. And the utterer of these contemptible quibbles dares to charge Passmore Williamson with falsehood and evasion, and to read to his auditors a homily on the importance of speaking "full, direct, and unequivocal" truth. After the decision was pronounced, Mr. Williamson's counsel, Hon. Charles Gilpin, rose and addressed the Court in some remarks preliminary to a motion which he intended to make. He had contended that Williamson had not possession or custody of the persons whom he was commanded to produce, and he now suggested that the return should be amended to express this, in a manner conformatory to the views of the Court. *While he was speaking*, Mr. Vandyke rose and moved that a commitment, under the seal of the Court, be issued, and the defendant, Passmore Williamson, be placed in the custody of the Marshal. Mr. Gilpin proceeded, when Judge Kane remarked that the District Attorney had precedence, and that any motion of defendant's counsel must be reduced to writing. Mr. Gilpin was about to reply to the motion of the District Attorney, saying that it had not been reduced to writing, when the Judge announced that it had been already granted. Such conduct on the part of a judicial officer needs no comment.

While these scenes, so disgraceful to Pennsylvania, were transpiring in the city of Philadelphia, another plot of the minions of slavery was in process of execution. On the 19th of July, Mr. Wheeler entered complaint before James B. Freeman, Alderman, who issued a warrant for the arrest of Isaiah Moore, Wm. Custis, John Ballard, James Martin, and James S. Braddock, (colored men.) They were arrested and thrown into the "lock up" of a station-house, where they were left until the afternoon of the next day, suffering from *intense heat*, without food, and without permission to see their friends. They were then brought before the magistrate, exhausted with fatigue, want of sleep, excitement and hunger, and held to bail in the excessive sum of $7000 each, to answer to the charges of highway robbery! inciting to riot! riot! and assault and battery. In default of bail, they were committed to prison.

Passmore Williamson was also arrested on the last three charges.

He had a hearing before Alderman Freeman, and was held to answer in the sum of $6000.

On the 28th of July, Isaiah Moore, Wm. Custis, John Ballard, James Martin, and James S. Braddock were brought before Judge Kelley, on a writ of habeas corpus, and an application made for reduction of bail. Mr. Wheeler was again present, and testified against them. District Attorney Mann abandoned at once the charge of highway robbery, characterizing it as "absurd," and again as "ridiculous." Judge Kelley, after inflicting a reprimand upon the Alderman, reduced the bail to $1000, in the cases of Ballard and Custis, and $500 in the others. On the 7th of August, Mr. Wheeler went before the Grand Jury. The result was an indictment for riot and assault and battery against these five persons, and also against Passmore Williamson, and William Still, the well-known clerk at the Anti-Slavery office. The case was called for hearing on the 9th inst., but the parties, not being ready for trial, showed cause for a continuance, which was granted.

On Wednesday morning, August 29th, they were all, excepting Passmore Williamson, put upon their trial, upon the charge of riot and assault and battery, in the Court of Quarter Sessions, in the city of Philadelphia, Judge Kelley presiding.

Wheeler appeared as the principal witness against the defendants. His testimony was substantially the same that he gave before Judge Kane. He swore that the "defendants came on board the boat, headed by Mr. Williamson; that Williamson, and the defendant, Still, talked to the woman Jane, and endeavored to persuade her to go off the boat; both Still and Williamson telling her that she was free and urging her to go ashore; she was asked by them if she did not wish to be free; she replied that she did, but *did not want to leave her master;* during the ringing of the last bell, *she was seized and carried down the gangway and on shore;* the two children were also seized and carried after her by the defendants."

On the cross-examination he said he did not remember whether he told her on the boat that she was free to go if she wished; but he declared that he "had said so before, had always felt so; did not want to have any one about him who did not wish to stay; had exercised no restraint or control over her; she knew perfectly well where she was going, and was satisfied to go."

Believing that all the persons who could contradict their testimony were included in the indictment, Wheeler and the other witnesses for the prosecution were emboldened to swear in the strongest manner to such points as they thought could not fail to secure a conviction. There amazement and confusion can be better conceived than described, when Jane Johnson suddenly appeared on the witness stand. Her testimony utterly destroyed that of Mr. Wheeler and his witnesses. It was as follows:

"I can't tell my exact age; I guess I am about 25; I was born in Washington City; lived there this New-Year's, if I shall live to see it, two years; I came to Philadelphia about two months ago.

I came with Col. Wheeler; I brought my two children, one aged 10, and the other a year or so younger; we went to Mr. Sully's and got something to eat; we then went to the wharf, then into the hotel.

Col. Wheeler told me to stay on the upper porch and did not let me go to dinner, and sent by the servants some dinner to me, but I did not desire any; after dinner he asked me if I had dinner; I told him I wanted none; while he was at dinner I saw a colored woman, and went to her and told her I was a slave woman traveling with a very curious gentleman, who did not want me to have anything to do or say to colored persons; she said she was sorry for me; I said nothing more; then I went back and took my seat where I had been ordered by Col. Wheeler; he had told me not to talk to colored persons; to tell everybody I was traveling with a minister going to Nicaragua; he seemed to think I might be led off; he did not tell me I could be free if I wanted to when I got to Philadelphia; on the boat he said he would give me my freedom; he never said so before; I had made preparations before leaving Washington to get my freedom in New York; I made a suit to disguise myself in—they had never seen me wear it—to escape in when I got to New York; Mr. Wheeler has that suit in his possession, in my trunk; I wasn't willing to come without my children; for I wanted to free them; I have been in Col. Wheeler's family nearly two years; he bought me from a gentleman of Richmond—a Mr. Crew; he was not a member of Col. Wheeler's family; Col. Wheeler was not more than half an hour at dinner; he came to look at me from the dinner-table, and found me where he had left me; I did not ask leave of absence at Bloodgood's Hotel; while Col. Wheeler went on board the boat a colored man asked me did I want to go with Col. W.; I told him "No, I do not;" at 9 o'clock that night he said he would touch the telegraph for me and some one would meet me at New York; I said I was obliged to him; no more was said then; I had never seen the man before; when Col. Wheeler took me on board he took me on the upper deck and sat us down alongside of him. While sitting there I saw a colored man and a white one; the white man beckoned me to come to him; the colored man asked did I desire my freedom; the white man approached Mr. W. and said he desired to tell me my rights; Mr. W. said, "My woman knows her rights;" they told me to go with them; he held out his hand but did not touch mine, and I immediately arose to go with him; I took my oldest boy by the hand; the youngest was picked up by some people and became very much alarmed, and I proceeded off the boat as quickly as I could, being perfectly willing and desirous to go; Mr. Wheeler tried to stop me, no one else; he tried to get before me as though he wanted to talk to me; I wanted to get off the boat, and didn't listen to what he had to say. I did not say I did not want my freedom; I have always wanted it; I did not say I wanted to go with my master; I went very willingly to the carriage, I was very glad to go; the little boy said he wanted to go to his massa, he was frightened; I did not say I wanted to go to Col. Wheeler; there was no outcry of any kind, my little boy made all the noise that was made."

The presentation of Jane as a witness, in the Court-room, was a bold and perilous act on the part of her friends, and one in which they would not have felt justified, had they not been assured that a strong force should be provided for her protection by the State authorities. Although they had this assurance, serious apprehensions were felt for the result. The United States officers were there with an extra force, evidently determined to arrest her. The officers of the Court and other State officers were there to protect the witness and vindicate the laws of the State. Vandyke, the United States District Attorney, swore he would take her. The State officers swore he should not, and for awhile it seemed that nothing could avert a bloody scene. It was expected that the conflict would take place outside of the door when she should leave the room, so that when she and her friends went out, and for some time after, the most intense anxiety pervaded the Court-Room. The way to the carriage was lined by a strong body of policemen, placed there by order of District Attorney Mann and Judge Kelley.

The courage of Vandyke and his allies seemed to pale before the stern determination of Judge Kelley and District Attorney Mann, to vindicate the dignity of the Courts and to enforce the laws of Pennsylvania, and Jane Johnson entered the carriage which was in waiting for her without disturbance. She was accompanied by an intrepid police officer, and the carriage was borne away in safety, and State sovereignty triumphed over the insolent invasion of usurped authority on the part of Federal officers.

Judge Kelley, in his charge to the Jury, a document honorable to him as a man and as a judge, explicitly asserted "that when Col. Wheeler and his servants crossed the border of Pennsylvania, Jane Johnson and her two sons became as free as he."

The jury returned a verdict of "not guilty" as to all the parties on the count charging them with riot. On the second count, charging them with an assault upon Col. Wheeler, Ballard and Custis were found "guilty"—the rest "not guilty." Ballard and Custis were sentenced by Judge Kelley to pay a fine of ten dollars each and the costs of prosecution, and to be imprisoned during one week. Measures were taken to relieve these unfortunate men, who were doubtless sufferers from perjury, of the pecuniary part of their burden. Thus ended one act of this strange drama.

When Passmore Williamson was committed to prison, every learned and upright lawyer, of our city, and every citizen capable of appreciating and respecting the rights and true liberties of the people under a free government, was shocked and alarmed by the outrage upon the plainest principle of law and of justice, of which Judge Kane had been guilty. But the people of Pennsylvania never imagined that a sovereign State was impotent to redress the wrong, and to protect against judicial error, folly, or wickedness, the personal liberty of her own citizens. Their thoughts instantly and naturally turned to the *habeas corpus;* that dear-bought right of a free people, that sacred palladium of their liberty, in which our nation glories. To this Passmore Williamson might confidently appeal. The aid of this he might demand, by undoubted right. He did demand it. Application was made by his counsel to Chief Justice Lewis, of the Supreme Court of Pennsylvania, for a writ of *habeas corpus,* with a view to his liberation if the commitment of Judge Kane should be found to be illegal. Judge Lewis, though bound, by virtue of his office, to issue this writ upon such application, assumed the responsibility of refusing to do so, on the ground that one Court should yield to another the respect which it claims for its own adjudications!

Failing to obtain justice where it should have been promptly awarded him, Mr. Williamson, by his counsel, renewed his application to the Supreme Court *in banc,* sitting at Bedford on the 13th of August. His application was fully and ably argued by Messrs. Charles Gilpin and Wm. M. Meredith. These gentlemen asserted the petitioner's *right* to the writ, and earnestly protested against being called upon to argue the question, in face of the imperative requisition of the act of 1785 ; that the writ shall be issued upon such petition, and its imposition of a penalty upon any judge who shall refuse to award it. Mr. Meredith concluded his eloquent and impressive argument with the following language :

" As regards the proceedings of the District Court, I have argued the question of jurisdiction only. The errors in law in other respects of these proceedings I shall not enter upon. The odd use of the writ of Habeas Corpus in applying it to the purpose of depriving a party of liberty, instead of restoring it ;—the allowing a traverse of the return, which can only be allowed by statute, and which no statute allows in the Courts of the United States—the taking that traverse by parol merely—the assuming to decide upon it the fact of abduction upon insufficient evidence, and from that to deduce a continuance of custody on no evidence at all — the absolute inconsistency of the record, which, after setting out a full, complete, and unevasive return, proceeds to a commitment for a supposed refusal to make any return,—I do not know that all these and other errors would of themselves enable this Court to interfere, if the District Court had jurisdiction of the case. But as the Court had no jurisdiction, these circumstances, all of them operating oppressively on a citizen entitled to your protection, do greatly aggravate the case, and enhance, if that be possible, your just obligation to relieve him. They do indeed tend to show a want of jurisdiction, for surely Providence would never have permitted a Court of competent jurisdiction to fall into so many errors in one case." .   .   .   .   .

" I now leave the matter in the hands of the Court. It is impossible to conceal from ourselves the fact that the essential rights of this Commonwealth are invaded. This condition of things is inauspicious. To correct it, nothing is wanted but the firm and temperate discharge of your duties as magistrates and ministers of the law." .   .   .

" The question here has nothing to do with the rights or wrongs, the conduct or misconduct of the North or the South. It concerns principles on which all are agreed. THAT EACH STATE HAS THE RIGHT TO REGULATE HER OWN DOMESTIC RELATIONS AND INSTITUTIONS —THAT THE COURTS OF THE UNITED STATES HAVE NO RIGHT TO INTERFERE WITH OR CONTROL THEM—THAT CITIZENS OF OTHER STATES THAT COME UPON HER SOIL ARE, WHILE THERE, BOUND TO RESPECT AND OBEY HER LAWS :—THESE, I say, are the principles involved here, and they are quite as dear to the SOUTH as to the NORTH: they ought to be quite as dear to the NORTH as to the SOUTH.

It has come to the point that, failing your aid, they are no longer safe in Pennsylvania. I invoke that aid with confidence, and, if it be granted the rights of the Commonwealth will have been vindicated, and the affair from which these questions have originated—untoward in all its aspects—will be left to be determined by the laws of the State, in some appropriate forum."   .   .   .   .   .   .

Posterity will scarcely believe that Pennsylvania, boasting of her democracy, and her tenacious respect for State Rights, could have had a Supreme Bench of Judges, all of whom, *with one exception*, united in refusing to grant a writ of *habeas corpus* upon this application. Yet such was the fact, and long will it be remembered, to the shame of the Commonwealth, and the disgrace of those judicial officers who perverted justice, and sought to establish iniquity by their interpretations of law. Judge Black pronounced the opinion of the Court, which was concurred in by Judges Lewis, Woodward and Lowrie. The writ was refused for the following reason, expressed in the language of Judge Black :

" We have no authority, jurisdiction or power to decide anything here except the simple fact that the District Court had power to punish for contempt a person who disobeys its process—that the petitioner is convicted of such contempt—and that the conviction is conclusive upon us. The jurisdiction of the Court on the case which had been before it and everything which preceded the conviction are out of our reach, and they are not examinable by us—and, of course, not now intended to be decided."

Thus it has been determined, by the highest judicial authority of Pennsylvania, that the etiquette of courts towards each other, is of greater value, and its maintenance of more importance, than the dearest rights and the personal liberties of the citizens. However unworthy or illegally a Federal Judge may imprison any man or woman of this commonwealth, though his decision may be the result of stupid ignorance, personal dislike, or desire for revenge, (and the world's history furnishes abundant proof that judges may be guilty of all these,) there is no redress for the outraged citizen ; the officers of the State, who were appointed by the people to protect him against such outrage deliberately connive with his persecutor, and even the right of a free people to the *habeas corpus is sacrificed to the etiquette of Courts!*

The Court, in this case of Passmore Williamson, not only denied to him that which was his by legal right, but, it stooped to insult a prisoner with taunts worthy of the judicial bench of England in the days of James the Second. Incapable of comprehending the moral heroism which suffers imprisonment and death, for the sake of a *principle*, these judges sneeringly intimate that he is covetous of the honors of martyrdom : and, then, with the heartless sarcasm of an Inquisitor over his tortured victim, they coolly tell him that he "carries the key of his prison in his own pocket," and "can come out when he will, by making terms with the Court that sent him there." The terms which he must make, are, of course, the disavowal of what he believes to be truth, and the utterance of what he believes to be a lie, and *they* cannot imagine why he does not make them ; the key which would open his prison door, is the stain of perjury on his soul, and they cannot imagine why he does not use it.

From this decision, which will be remembered, with that of Judge Kane, long after the authors of both will wish them forgotten, Judge Knox emphatically and earnestly dissented. He closes his very ably written opinion, in dissent, with the following recapitulation of the grounds on which he would have awarded the writ.

"1. At common law, and by our statute of 1785, the writ of habeas corpus ad subjiciendum,is a writ of right, demandable whenever a petition in due form asserts what, if true, would entitle the party to relief.

2. That an allegation in a petition that the petitioner is restrained of his liberty by an order of a Judge or Court without jurisdiction, shows such probable cause as to leave it no longer discretionary with the Court or Judge to whom application is made whether the writ shall or shall not issue.

3. That where a person is imprisoned by an order of a Judge of the District Court of the United States for refusing to answer a writ of habeas corpus, he is entitled to be discharged from such imprisonment if the Judge of the District Court had no authority to issue the writ.

4. That the power to issue writs of habeas corpus by the Judges of the Federal Courts is a mere auxiliary power, and that no such writ can be issued by such Judges where the cause of complaint to be remedied by it is beyond their jurisdiction.

5. That the Courts of the Federal Government are Courts of limited jurisdiction, derived from the Constitution of the United States and the acts of Congress under the Constitution, and that when the jurisdiction is not given by the Constitution or by Congress in pursuance of the Constitution, it does not exist.

6. That when it does not appear by the record that the Court had jurisdiction in a proceeding under our habeas corpus act to relieve from an

illegal imprisonment, want of jurisdiction may be shown by proving the facts in the case.

7. That where the inquiry as to the jurisdiction of a Court arises upon a rule for a habeas corpus, all the facts set forth in the petition tending to show want of jurisdiction are to be considered as true, unless they contradict the records.

8. That when the owner of a slave voluntarily brings his slave from a slave to a free State, without any intention of remaining therein, the right of the slave to his freedom depends upon the law of the State into which he is thus brought.

9. That if a slave so brought into a free State escapes from the custody of his master while in said State, the right of the master to reclaim him is not a question arising under the Constitution of the United States or the laws thereof; and therefore a Judge of the United States cannot issue a writ of habeas corpus directed to one who it is alleged withholds the possession of the slave from the master, commanding him to produce the body of the slave before said judge.

10. That the District Court of the United States for the Eastern District of Pennsylvania has no jurisdiction because a controversy is between citizens of different States, and that a proceeding by habeas corpus is in no legal sense a controversy between private parties.

11. That the power of the several Courts of the United States to inflict summary punishment for contempt of Court in disobeying a writ of the Court is expressly confined to cases of disobedience to lawful writs.

12. That where it appears from the record that the conviction was for disobeying a writ of habeas corpus, which writ the Court have no jurisdiction to issue, the conviction is *cordm non judice*, and void.

For these reasons I do most respectfully, but most earnestly, dissent from the judgment of the majority of my brethren refusing the writ applied for."

All honor should be rendered to Judge Knox, for his fidelity to law and the right, in opposition to all his fellow-judges. The people will remember him.

Subsequently to the announcement of the decision of the Court, and the dissenting opinion of Judge Knox, Judge Lowrie published his opinion, wherein he differs, on some points, from the decision. He says:

"I have a very strong impression that no Court is justified in issuing a *habeas corpus* for the purpose of restoring a slave to his master; and that is very plainly the purpose for which the writ was issued out of the District Court. I do not think that our writ has any such purpose, or ever h*d. It was intended to secure the liberty of the subject, and not to try rights of property."

* * * * * * * *

"I have, moreover, a very strong impression that there is no way in which the case before the District Judge can be regarded, that would entitle the Federal Judiciary to take cognizance of it."

He proceeds to say that he had been willing to grant the writ and hear the case ; but after this expression of opinion, he enters upon an argument against the interference of one Court with another, and concludes by concurring in the refusal of the writ. It does not appear what were the reasons and motives which operated in changing his opinion during the interval between the sittings of the Court in Bedford and in Philadelphia, but, more grossly inconsistent than his fellow-judges, in spite of his "very strong impression" that the prisoner is illegally and unjustly imprisoned by a judge who had no jurisdiction in the case, he deliberately refuses to perform his judicial duty in redressing the wrong!

Citizens of Pennsylvania! what shall be the end of these things ? An officer of the Federal Government has usurped authority in a case wholly beyond his jurisdiction, and without law, or the shadow of law, has immured in one of your prisons, a citizen of Pennsylvania. Your own Supreme Bench of Judges fold their hands, and refuse to enforce your laws for his protection. In the person of Passmore Williamson, the rights of every man and woman of this commonwealth have been invaded, and you now hold your possession of personal liberty, and its defense, the *habeas corpus*, in which you have gloried, at the mercy of judicial tyrants who may, at any hour, summon you into their presence, by illegally issued writs of *habeas corpus*, and, on charges of constructive contempt, commit you to prison without bail, and without hope of redress. Will you take warning before it is too late, and arouse yourselves to defend your liberties, and avert the evil which threatens every citizen of this State ? Lord Camden, who has been styled, "one of the purest Judges who ever adorned the English Bench," has said : " *The discretion of a judge is the law of tyrants. It is always unknown. It is different in different men. It is casual, and depends upon constitution, temper, and feeling. In the best, it is oftentimes caprice ; in the worst, it is every vice, folly and passion, to which human nature is liable.*" ,

The Slave power of this nation, which has been long and steadily encroaching upon the rights of the North, emboldened by success, has evidently resolved to re-establish slavery on your soil, by asserting and maintaining, in defiance of your laws, the right to carry and hold their slaves wherever they choose to go, under the Constitution of the United States. In this insolent attempt it seems to have found an assistant in one of your own citizens, who, from his seat in the District Court of the United States, defies and tramples on the laws of Pennsylvania, and perverts " the great remedial process by which *liberty is vindicated and restored,*" to the base purpose of reducing free persons to slavery. John H. Wheeler attempted to carry off, as slaves, from Pennsylvania, persons whom your laws declare to be free, and by so doing rendered himself liable to the legal penalties which you have affixed to the crime of kidnapping. Judge Kane asserts that " he who unites with others to commit a crime, shares with them all the legal liabilities that attend on its commission."— Out of his own mouth and by your laws is he condemned.

If you will tamely submit to these outrages on your laws and on your rights, what can you expect but that the usurped power which has stricken down the habeas corpus, in Pennsylvania, will rob you of the trial by jury, and of the freedom of speech and the press, when it shall serve its purpose so to do. The bold wickedness which dared the one, will be capable of the other. Lay not the flattering unction to your souls that this case concerns the interests of one individual only; it involves the honor and safety of every citizen of the commonwealth. While Passmore Williamson is thus imprisoned, the sovereignty of the State and the true liberty of her citizens lie prostrate in the dust. On you rests the solemn responsibility of choosing whether your dearest rights shall hang upon the caprice of a tyrant, or whether you will assert the sovereignty of the State, and teach these law-defying Judges to tremble before the indignation of a justly incensed people.

_____

Since the foregoing narrative has been prepared for the press, another Decision has been pronounced by Judge Kane, in the District Court of the United States. It was in reply to a petition of Jane Johnson, presented by her counsel, J. B. Townsend and John M. Read, Esqrs., showing that she is one of the three parties named in the writ of Habeas Corpus issued in the case of John H. Wheeler *versus* Passmore Williamson, and stating *First*, that Wheeler had no control over her or her children at the time of issuing the aforesaid writ, they then being free; *Second*, that the writ was issued against her wish; *Third*, that since she left Mr. Wheeler, which, she asserts, she did of her own will and desire, she has not been restrained of her liberty by Mr. Williamson, or any other person; and *Fourth*, that under this writ of habeas corpus, a writ designed to restore freemen to liberty when unduly restrained thereof, John H. Wheeler seeks to recover the petitioner and her children, and reduce them again into slavery. She therefore prays that the writ may be quashed, and that Passmore Williamson may be discharged from his imprisonment.

Judge Kane refused the application to enter this paper among the records of the Court, on the ground that Jane Johnson had no *status* in the Court. A very small part of the decision relates directly to the application before the Judge, the principal portion of it being an elaborate defense of his conduct towards Passmore Williamson. The most important point of his decision is the bold assertion of the right of the slaveholders to pass, *with their slaves*, through Pennsylvania or any other State of the Union. He asserts this on the ground that slaves are *property*, and asks, "How can it be that a State may single out this one kind of property from among all the rest, and deny to it the right of passing over its soil—passing with its owner, parcel of his travelling equipment, as much so as the horse he rides on, his great coat, or his carpet-bag?" The decision is a bold revelation of what a discerning eye could see from the beginning of this case, that the object and determination was and is, to obtain possession of Jane Johnson and her children and re-enslave them, and to this base end he is keeping, and is determined to keep, Passmore Williamson in prison.

Notwithstanding the well-established fact that it is and was utterly beyond the power of Mr. Williamson to bring Jane and her children before the Court; that neither she nor her friends would suffer him to expose her to such peril, even *if he had wished to do so*, Judge Kane says:

"His duty, then as now, was and is, to bring in the bodies, or, if they had passed beyond his control, to declare, under oath or affirmation, so far as he knew, what had become of them." [That is, to give the information which will enable the claimant either to recover his property, or to hold some one else for their value.] "And from this duty, or from the constraint that seeks to enforce it, there can be no escape."

Pennsylvanians are now to decide whether they will submit to the establishment of slavery on their own soil; whether they

will permit slaves to be carried or *driven* across their State sin-
gly or chained in coffles, or whether they will enforce *their
own laws* for the protection of freedom.   If this right of transit bo
granted, who is to decide how long a time slaveholders, or slavedri-
vers with their gangs, may spend in "passing through" a free State,
or what operations peculiar to their trade, though revolting to humanity, they may be permitted to engage in.   Judge Kane's defense
of his persecution of Passmore Williamson, on the ground that Pennsylvania may be made a slaveholding State, whenever a trafficker in
human beings chooses to drive his victims through it, will not
avail for his justification before the tribunal of the PEOPLE.

LETTER FROM PASSMORE WILLIAMSON.

The following letter was written by Passmore Williamson in reply to
one addressed to him by a gentleman of New York city, inquiring respecting further legal means for his relief.   The only just grounds on which he
could obtain redress having been set forth-in his petition to the Supreme
Court of Pennsylvania, and that Court having declined to act in the case,
Mr. Williamson has exhausted the means of legal redress provided by the
State, and he indignantly rejects the other alternative of dishonorable
submission to the tyranny of usurped power.

> "No. 78 PHILADELPHIA COUNTY PRISON,
> Sept. 29, 1855.

DEAR SIR:—Your letter of the 27th inst. is now before me, and in reply
to your inquiry, I may say that I contemplate no further legal proceedings
with reference to my liberation from this jail, in which I am now confined.
I have now been kept here for more than two months, and I can see no
prospect of liberation.   I am a native, and have always been a citizen of
Pennsylvania; and believing myself atrociously wronged, I applied to the
highest tribunal known to our laws, but relief has been withheld.   I can
expect none from the authority that placed me here, without dishonorable
submission.   Having been guilty neither of falsehood, dissimulation, nor
contumacy, I am sure that it is no case for a degrading capitulation.
Such a course would bring with it a diminution of self respect more oppressive than the power now seeking to crush out the highest attribute of
State sovereignty by immuring me within these walls

Accept for yourself, and communicate to others who favor me with
their consideration, my most grateful acknowledgements.

Respectfully yours, &c.,
P. WILLIAMSON."

At the PHILADELPHIA ANTI-SLAVERY OFFICE, No. 31 North Fifth St., Anti-Slavery Books,
Tracts and Newspapers may be always obtained; and a free Reading Room is open to the
public.

PASSMORE WILLIAMSON

vs.

JOHN K. KANE.

ACTION FOR FALSE IMPRISONMENT, BEFORE THE COURT OF COMMON
PLEAS OF DELAWARE COUNTY.

A R G U M E N T O F

JOSEPH J. LEWIS, ESQ.

OF WESTCHESTER,

ON THE PART OF THE PLAINTIFF,

Delivered at Media, December 17th and 18th, 1856.

PHONOGRAPHICALLY REPORTED BY DAVID W. BROWN.

~~~~~~~~~

PHILADELPHIA:
MERRIHEW & THOMPSON, PRINTERS,
Lodge street, north side Pennsylvania Bank.
1857.

451

PASSMORE WILLIAMSON vs. JOHN K. KANE.

This is an action for false imprisonment instituted in the Court of Common Pleas of Delaware County, to recover damages for assaulting the plaintiff and imprisoning him, and detaining him in prison for three months. The complaint is set out in a declaration containing six counts, in some of which the circumstances attending the commission of the offences charged are particularly detailed.

The defendant pleaded five pleas:

1. The first alleges that the defendant was duly commissioned Judge of the District Court of the United States; that being such judge he was privileged from answering in any civil suit for anything done or commanded by him as judge; that, on the 27th of July, 1855, a motion was made in the District Court to commit the plaintiff for contempt, because he had refused to make return to a writ of habeas corpus directed to him by the Court; that the defendant, as judge, had adjudged the plaintiff guilty of the contempt charged; and thereupon a warrant, signed by defendant as judge, issued out of the court to the marshal, by virtue of which the plaintiff was arrested and imprisoned, which were the trespasses complained of in the declaration.

2. The second plea makes substantially the same allegation, with the addition, that by virtue of the warrant issued to the marshal the plaintiff was detained till he purged himself of the contempt; which being done on the 3d day of November, 1855, he was discharged.

3. The third plea embraces all the circumstances alleged in the second, and sets out besides, briefly, the substance of the writ of habeas corpus.

4. The fourth plea only varies from the second in some immaterial particulars.

5. The fifth plea alleges the appointment of the defendant as judge—that on the 18th day of July 1855, John H. Wheeler, a citizen of Virginia, and Minister &c., being temporarily in Pennsylvania, petitioned the District Court for a habeas corpus to be directed to the plaintiff—on the allegation that three persons held to service or labor by the laws of Virginia, and owned by the petitioner, were detained by the plaintiff—that the defendant as judge granted the habeas corpus—that afterwards, to wit, July 19th, 1855, an alias writ issued, directed to the plaintiff, returnable the next day—that the plaintiff appeared at the time appointed, and made his return, stating that the persons named in the writ were not then, nor when the writ was issued, nor at any other time, in the custody or power of the

453

plaintiff—that leave was given to the relator to traverse the return, whereupon the parties were heard by their counsel, and evidence adduced before the defendant as judge—that the defendant as judge, being of the opinion that the return was untrue and illusory, adjudged the plaintiff guilty of contempt, and ordered him to be committed to the custody of the marshal of the district—that neither the plaintiff nor his counsel made any objection to the jurisdiction of the court—that an order of commitment issued, under which the plaintiff was committed to prison, to await the further order of the court—that he remained in prison till he purged himself of the contempt; and that these are the trespasses complained of.

To these pleas the plaintiff replied that the defendant committed the trespass complained of of his own wrong, and without the causes alleged in the pleas.

The defendant thereupon demurred specially, to the replication as applicable to the first, third and fifth pleas, and stated several causes.

1. That by the replication the plaintiff attempts to put in issue mere inference and matter of law.

2. That it attempts to put in issue matter of record.

3. That the replication is double and multifarious.

On the second and fourth pleas he joined issue.

The plaintiff joined in demurrer.

The argument was opened by Mr. Sheppard, one of the defendant's counsel, who addressed the court at an adjourned court in September last.

Mr. Broomall, one of the plaintiff's counsel, who was to have followed Mr. Sheppard, having been obliged to leave the court during Mr. Sheppard's argument, the further hearing of the case was postponed to an adjourned court, to be held on the 17th of December, 1856.

Dec. 17, 1856. On the meeting of the Court, Mr. Broomall rose to address the Court, but being in ill health was able to utter only a few sentences, before he was obliged to withdraw, and Mr. Lewis was called upon, unexpectedly, to proceed.

ARGUMENT.

I am rather disappointed, if the Court please, in the continued indisposition of my colleague, (Mr. Broomall,) inasmuch as it has prevented me, as it did at the last term, from consulting with him as to the course of the argument to be pursued in the present case.

I shall, however, proceed to state the views which present themselves to my mind, following, to a certain extent, the argument which has been exhibited on the other side. I shall not follow it throughout, but merely so far as I think will be sufficient to furnish the answer; for I prefer to reply in a general way to all that has been said, rather than to take up and criticise the various authorities in the order in which they have been presented.

It is objected that the replication is bad in law.

First,—Because it traverses "inference and conclusion of law."

Such is not in effect the traverse.

The issue on the first plea arises thus :—The Plaintiff alleges an assault on his person; the Defendant justifies the trespass on the allegations :

That he was a judge of the District Court;

That, on motion in that Court, that the Plaintiff be committed as for a contempt in refusing to make return to a writ of habeas corpus, the Defendant, *as judge* of the Court, ordered him to be committed.

This is an assertion that the injury was done by the Defendant in his judicial character—as a branch of the government : and if that is true, it is a defence. The important and decisive fact stated is, that the act was done *as judge* of the District Court of the United States.

This fact the Plaintiff controverts, and would place his denial on record. How is that denial to be made? The Defendant says by demurrer. But a demurrer would *admit the fact*. A demurrer, therefore, would not raise the issue desired, and the only issue to be taken on the plea. That can be done only by a denial of the *material fact* alleged. That denial is appropriately made by the replication, which avers that the Defendant committed the trespass in his own wrong, and not for the cause alleged.

Whether the Defendant *acted as judge*, or in his own wrong, does not depend upon any fact stated in the plea, but on facts outside of the plea altogether. The plea sets forth that the Plaintiff was committed for contempt in refusing to make return to a *habeas corpus ad subjiciendum* issued by said Court. Whether this is true or not, depends on the fact as to whether the Court had jurisdiction; for, if the Court had no jurisdiction, the proceedings are *coram non judice.*

In some cases of *habeas corpus ad subjiciendum* the Court has, and in others it has not, jurisdiction. The inquiry then involves the question : for what cause did the writ issue? If for any one of a certain class of cases, the Defendant *acted as judge :* if for any one of another class, he did not act *as judge*—there was in fact, *no writ, no judgment, no order, no court, no judge.* The question is, therefore, a question of fact, depending upon another fact, viz.: the subject of complaint in the *habeas corpus.*

Now it is the Plaintiff's case that the writ issued for a cause of which the District Court and the judge of the District Court had no cognizance, and that, therefore, there was *no writ, no judgment, no order, no court, no judge ;* and that the Defendant's plea in every *material part*—all but the mere matter of inducement—IS UNTRUE.

The denial, therefore, in the replication is not a traverse of "inference or conclusion of law," but of the facts alleged in the plea ; and the issue raised by the replication *de injuria sua propria*, requires an ascertainment of the cause of complaint on which the habeas corpus was founded. Where the matter of right or of law results from facts, it is traversable. Here we have a matter of law resulting from a matter of fact ; and that, in every case, has been held to be traversable. [Commonalty *vs.* Carterbury, 3 Wil. 233–4. Step. on Pl. 216.] In 1 Smith's Leading Cases, 59, we find the same principle laid down in these words :

"If the defendant state in his plea some fact, on the existence or non-existence of which the question whether he be a trespasser *ab initio*, or not, depends, there it will be sufficient to reply *de injuria.*"

As in Kerby *vs.* Denby, trespass for breaking and entering plaintiff's dwelling and imprisoning him, the defendants justified under a ca : sa : "*the outer door being open ;*" it was held that the averment in the plea that the outer door was open was a material averment, for the door being open was a condition precedent to the defendant's right to enter; and therefore the plea was sufficiently traversed by the *general replication, de injuria.* [1 Mees. and Welsb. 336.]

In the case in hand the fact stated in the plea that the defendant *" as judge as aforesaid"* did the act complained of, is one on the existence or non-existence of which the question whether the defendant be a trespasser or not, depends; and that fact is sufficiently traversed by the general replication, *de injuria.*

In Chancey *vs.* Win. [12 Mod. 680] Holt J. says :

" If, in trespass against a constable, he justifies for that he was constable and the plaintiff was breaking the peace, for which he committed him, may not the Plaintiff reply de injuria sua propria absque tali causa ?"

These are the very words, it will be seen, in which the justification is made in this case, and the plea is precisely the same.

In Selby *vs.* Burdons [23 E. C. L. 14] Park J. says :

" As a general proposition, it is untrue that authority of law may not be included in a traverse, it being clear that an arrest by a private individual or peace officer is by an authority of the law ; and yet pleas containing such a justification may be denied by a general traverse."

The modern English courts have departed from the rules adopted in Crogate's case, and admit the replication in many cases in which those rules would not admit it. [See note to Crogate's case, Smith's Leading Cases, 55 : 44 L. L.]

A note to the case of Curry *vs.* Hoffman, [2 Am. L. Reg. p. 252] is as follows :

" The later English cases warrant the use of the replication de injuria, though the plea sets up a justification under an authority given by the law, unless it be at the same time derived mediately or immediately from the plaintiff, or be the process of a court of record. Barden vs. Selby, 9 Bingh. 756. [in error] ; Bowler vs. Nicholson, 12 Ad. & Ellis, 341; Edmunds vs. Penniger, 7 Q. B. 558 ; Price vs. Woodhouse, 16 M. & W. 1 ; See, however, Worsley, vs. The South Devon Rail Road Company, 3 Eng. L. & Eq. 230."

Undoubtedly the plea might have been framed in such a manner as to make the allegation that the defendant acted " as judge as aforesaid" in the matter complained of, a mere inference of law, deduced from the facts previously stated in the plea. In such case it would not have been traversable. Had the plea, after merely setting out that the defendant was judge of the United States District Court, proceeded to state all the proceedings on the *habeas corpus* from Wheeler's petition to the commitment for contempt, and then alleged that the commitment was made *by virtue of his authority as judge*, the *virtute cujus* would have been an inference of law. But the plea does not set out the whole matter: it sets out merely the judgment of contempt. (I am confining my observations now altogether to the first plea, because my remarks in regard to that will apply to the third; the principle raised by the fifth plea is distinct from that which will be involved in the consideration of the others.) The plea does not set out the whole array of facts in justification, but includes in the allegation of the defendant's authority as judge, a matter of law and of fact. Whether the defendant acted as a judge, or not, is not a consequence of facts previously stated. If it were, then the whole matter would be a question of law; but, inasmuch as there is an important fact alleged, (that is, that the defendant acted as judge,) and all the proceedings are not set out, it is competent for us to deny that important fact by the replication *de injuria*. It does not appear by the record whether he acted as judge, or in his own individual character. Such being the fact, they have left that matter at large. The allegation covers all that is not set out in the plea, and therefore it may be denied by a general replication of *de injuria sua propria*. In such case, it is settled beyond controversy, a traverse is proper. [1 Chitty on Pl. 613. Beal *vs.* Simpson, 1 Ld. Ray 410. 1 Wms. Saunders 23, n. 5. Lucas *vs.* Nockells, 4 Bing. 729. 15 E. C. L. 138. Stickle *vs.* Richmond, 1 Hill 81.]

But, secondly, it is alleged that *de injuria*, etc., cannot be replied where plea sets up matter of record by way of justification.

Here it is alleged, on the part of the plaintiff, that *there is no record*. Whether there is, or not, depends upon a fact to be proved: whether, in what he did, the defendant acted, as he has alleged, *as judge*. If he did not act as judge, there was no court and, of course, there was no record. In other words, if the Court had no jurisdiction, there were no such proceedings as those alleged in the plea. *There was no motion, no contempt, no order of commitment.* The *absque tali causa* is a denial that the defendant acted as judge, and of all that is alleged of his proceedings in that character. But, it is said, we cannot deny a matter of record except by a plea of *nul tiel record;* for to do so in this way would be to put a matter of record "in issue to the common people."

This proposition assumes the very fact in issue. It assumes that the defendant did the act as judge, that there is a record, and alleges that we cannot deny the existence of this record because, by the proceedings of a court that had no jurisdiction, it appears that it had jurisdiction. Such is the argument of the other side. The plaintiff denies the jurisdiction of the Court, and to show that all the proceedings set out in the plea are nullities, and the alleged record no record, proposes to prove that the Court had no jurisdiction. Is he to be told that that which is alleged to be a record, is to be judged only by the paper assumed to be a record? That is the sense of the argument (if it has any); and yet the law is undoubted that whether a pretended record is true or false, may be inquired into "by the common people." The Court cannot by recording a falsehood obtain jurisdiction, nor prevent an issue to the country to determine *the fact.*

In Robson *vs.* Eaton [1 T. R. 62], the judgment of the Court of Common Pleas was held a nullity as to a party named in the record, because he had not authorized an appearance for him. In Borden *vs.* Fitch [15 John. 162], it was held that the decree of another Court, duly appearing by the record, was not conclusive, it appearing that the Court had not jurisdiction of the party to be affected by it. The same doctrine is maintained in Andrews *vs.* Montgomery [19 John. 162]. In Shumway *vs.* Stillman [4 Cowen, 294], Justice Sutherland, delivering the opinion of the Court, quotes with approbation from the decision in Borden *vs.* Fitch, that "to give any binding effect to a judgment, it is essential that the Court should have jurisdiction of the person and of the subject matter; and the want of jurisdiction is a matter that may always be set up against a judgment when sought to be enforced, or where any benefit is claimed under it. *The want of jurisdiction makes it utterly void for any purpose.*" The case of Bissell *vs.* Briggs [9 Mass. 467], is to the same point, and also Aldrick vs. Henry [4 Conn. R. 280], where it was decided that if the defendant did not appear, the record was void, though it was averred in it that he did appear. In Starbuck vs. Murray [5 Wend. 148], it was held that in an action on a judgment the defendant may show, under any proper plea, the fact that the Court had not jurisdiction.

The want of jurisdiction need not be pleaded specially : it may be shown under the general issue. On this point I would refer to 1 Kent's Com. 280 (note a), where it is said : "The doctrine in Mills vs. Duryee, is to be taken with the qualification that in all instances the jurisdiction of the Court rendering the judgment may be inquired into, and the plea of *nil debet* will allow the defendant to show that the Court had no jurisdiction over his person."

The most of these cases were suits on judgments recovered in another

State; but the rule is the same whether the judgment was recovered in the same or another State. [Conkling on Jurisdiction, 393.]

It is, therefore, very clear that where a record is set up which is void for want of the jurisdiction of the Court, the trial is not necessarily by the record. There is no such principle as that a void thing shall prove itself.

But here there is no record pleaded. The proceedings in which the defendant claims to have acted as judge, are not pleaded as a record.

In the first plea the defendant has studiously avoided showing the foundation of the proceeding; has omitted the *prout patet per recordum*, essential where a record is pleaded, and has satisfied himself with averring that the defendant *acted as judge* on the motion for judgment, and in ordering the plaintiff to be committed. The replication, therefore, is a denial of the matter of defence as stated in the plea.

Had the plaintiff replied *nul tiel record*, there would have been a departure, and a rejoinder of *tali habetur recordum* would have raised an issue outside of the prior pleading, for the reason that there is no record pleaded. When there is a general allegation in a plea of the facts which, it is said, a record would prove, if given in evidence, without any proffer of the record or any *prout patet per recordum*, do we ever see an answer, by plea, of *nul tiel record?* Such an answer would be insensible—it would have no meaning; for no record being pleaded, you cannot properly reply that there is no such record. The party upon the other side could, without exposing himself to any objection, set out the facts which he expects to prove by record; but, unless he pleads the record in the technical manner in which records only can be pleaded, it is impossible for us to reply *nul tiel record*, and all that we can do is to deny the existence of the facts which he has alleged upon the face of his plea.

In the third instance, it is alleged as a cause of demurrer, that the replication is multifarious and double. Now, no replication has ever been held bad upon that ground, if the several facts put in issue constitute one single ground of defence. [Smith's Leading Cases, note to Crogate's case, p. 57; 44 L. L. 124; Curry *vs.* Hoffman, 2 Am. L. Reg. 251; Stickle *vs.* Richmond, 1 Hill, 77.]

In this case the whole plea is one consistent defence, the point of which is that the trespass complained of was committed by virtue of a warrant issued by the defendant as judge of the District Court of the United States; and in pleading to that effect he necessarily states,

First, That he was judge.

Secondly, That *as judge* he held the plaintiff in contempt.

Thirdly, That, being in contempt, the plaihtiff was, by a regular order, committed to the custody of the marshal.

All these were necessary allegations—not one could be spared ; without any one of them, the plea would have been insensible. They make but one matter of defence ; they tender but one single issue ; and such being the case, it was competent to deny the allegations contained in the plea. In contradicting the whole, we contradict but one single cause or point of defence : the denial raises but the one question : whether or not the matters contained in the plea are true.

In Stickle *vs.* Richmond and Curry *vs.* Hoffman the replication, it is true, protests the authority of the officer, and, by protesting, admits it: then it goes on to deny, under a general allegation for the residue of the cause, the facts stated in the plea. But this protestation of the matter of inducement, in the introduction to the plea, was merely as a measure of precaution, *ex majori cautelâ.* It was not necessary to the singleness of the replication, for without this matter of inducement, which introduced all that followed, the plea would have been imperfect. The replication denies in substance only the facts which are alleged in the body of the plea ; it does not affect to traverse matter that was *mere* inducement, and, therefore, merely necessary to be alleged in order to introduce what followed.

The allegation, in this case, that the defendant was a judge, is certainly as much an integral part of the *unit* which a plea ought to be, and which the plea here is, as any other allegation. Without it the plea would want a member necessary to its legal constitution and completeness.

These observations, made in a general way, dispose of the first three points. The fourth cause of demurrer has been already considered in connection with the first. The third plea is not materially different from the first, as it contains all the facts there set forth, omitting merely the insensible and extraneous matter as to the legal obligation of the defendant.

It may be remarked that these technical questions with regard to the form of the replication are not matters of much interest in pleading at any time. The only effect which can result from raising them is to create delay, for, if your Honor, thinking the replication informal, should be inclined, on that ground, to give judgment in favor of the defendant, the universal practice at present is, not to give judgment, but to allow the party an opportunity to amend ; and even after a case has gone to the Supreme Court, it repeatedly happens that that Court, rather than give judgment upon a special demurrer, will send the case back, in

12

order that the pleadings may be amended and the cause be determined upon its merits.

The raising of these questions of special pleading is, therefore, a mere matter of experiment, and can answer no valuable purpose, unless, indeed, by a special defence some advantage is to be obtained which the party cannot have by submitting all the facts to the jury under the general issue; but, wherever the general issue can be pleaded, and the party can have under it the full benefit of his defence, the courts now will compel him to take his defence in that way, and he will not be allowed to load the record with special pleas that are not necessary to exhibit the merits of the cause. The practice of our courts in this respect is every day becoming more liberal. Avoiding all determinations resting upon mere matters of form, and endeavoring to reach the substance and justice of the case, they make the rules of pleading subservient to that object.

I have looked at this question, therefore, with less interest than I have felt in other and more important points in the case; and those I shall now proceed to discuss somewhat more at length and with a greater degree of attention.

The fifth plea sets out the facts which show, as we think, that the defendant had not jurisdiction, and, therefore, on demurrer, the plaintiff has the same advantage as if he had demurred. This is admitted upon the other side. We are brought, then, to the consideration of the question, whether these pleas are good in law and an answer to the action.

The defendant takes his stand on the principle of judicial inviolability. Called on to answer for an act of official usurpation, by which a peaceable citizen, who had violated no law and infringed upon no right, was treated as a common malefactor, and shut up for three months in prison, he points to his ermine as his protection, and insists on complete immunity from accountability for the outrages, because it was perpetrated in his character as judge. Such an answer is an insult to the law: the plea is a libel on our free institutions. According to every principle of reason and justice, the fact that the injury was inflicted under color of official prerogative but sharpens its sting and gives it ten-fold aggravation.

The proposition that a judge is not responsible to a party injured for anything he may do in abuse of his power and beyond his jurisdiction as judge, is, if not new, at least *startling* to the professional mind of this country, and requires to be sustained by irrefragable argument.

What is the argument? It is this: that the right to issue the writ of habeas corpus and to commit for contempt, is a question under the constitution and laws of the United States; that, the defendant having decided that right, his decision is a judicial determination of the question, and binds all the State courts till that judgment is reversed on appeal. Such is the argument of the other side. It comes from an expected quarter. It was long since said by Jefferson that the most formidable enemy to the liberty of the citizen, under our system, was the usurping tendencies of the Federal Judiciary. Here is a manifestation of the cloven hoof, the sound of whose tread was caught afar off by that sagacious and vigilant friend of constitutional freedom.

But our State courts have not yet bowed the knee so low in servility to the Moloch of Federal power as to sanction this argument. Even Judge Lowrie, (whose opinion has been referred to, and who, in voluntary abnegation of State authority when solicited for the protection of personal liberty against Federal usurpation, has shown most reverence to the highest power,) has excepted as out of the terms of his submission, the case of an action for damages against the wrong-doer. "I speak not here," (says he in his opinion,) "of the action for damages for excess of authority." [P. Williamson's case.]

Now it is an elementary principle that where a court has no jurisdiction, all the proceedings are *coram non judice;* there is no court and consequently no judgment. The proceedings may be inquired into in every other court in which they are brought by a party claiming a benefit under them. An authority in this point is the case of *Ex parte* Randolph, [2 Brockenbrough's Reports, 472.] The words of that decision are as follows:

"It was settled as early as the great Marshalsea case in 10 Coke, 76, and the principle has never been departed from, that where a court has jurisdiction, and proceeds *in verso ordine*, or erroneously, there the proceeding is only voidable; but where the court has not jurisdiction of the case, there the whole proceeding is *coram non judice* and void; and the books, both English and American, abound in cases exemplifying this principle."

In *Ex parte* Watkins [3 Peters 203] the same principle is laid down.

If the District Court then had no jurisdiction in the proceeding against Mr. Williamson, there is no judgment of that court that stands in the way of your adjudging between the parties. Whether that court had jurisdiction is to be decided here, not by the void record of a void judgment, but by an inquiry into the fact as to whether the allegation of jurisdiction is true or false.

A void thing can prove nothing, and whether it be void or valid is to be made out by proof recognized as valid. Whether a court has jurisdiction is usually a mixed question of law and of fact, or rather of law depending on fact. That question is to be determined by our courts, as all other questions of judicial cognizance are determined,—by the evidence laid before them. When such a question is presented to a State court it must be determined by the law of the State, and the court will look to all proper sources for the evidence of what the law is, as well the decisions of the United States courts as of other courts. Whether the defendant was right or wrong in assuming jurisdiction is not to be decided by his own determination to assume jurisdiction, (for that would be to make his will the law,) but by the Constitution and acts of Congress, and by the construction given to them by other and better judges.

As was said in the case of Starbuck vs. Murray [5 Wend. 158 :]

" Unless a court has jurisdiction, it can never make a record which imports an uncontrollable verity to the party over whom it has usurped jurisdiction ; and he ought not, therefore, to be estopped by any allegation in that record, from having any fact which goes to establish the truth of a plea alleging a want of jurisdiction."

To the defendant's proposition Chief Justice Tilghman in the Olmstead case [Brightley's Reports, 9] puts an emphatic negative. " The United States," (he says,) " have no power, legislative or judicial, except what is derived from the Constitution. When these powers are clearly exceeded, the independence of the States and the peace of the Union demand that the State courts should, in cases brought properly before them, give redress."

The servile doctrine of submission to Federal usurpation received at that day no countenance in our courts.

[Here the Court took a recess till 2¼ o'clock P. M. On the re-assembling of the Court, Mr. Lewis, resuming his argument, said :]

In the course of my remarks this morning I referred to decisions of the Supreme courts of certain States, and to the decision of the Circuit Court of the United States, showing that wherever the court had no jurisdiction there its proceedings were *coram non judice* and void. Those cases also show that the question whether a court had jurisdiction was not to be determined by the void record of a void judgment, but by an examination into the fact as to whether the jurisdiction assumed was rightfully exercised. I now proceed to show by other cases of still higher authority, as far as regards the District Court of the Eastern District of Pennsylvania, that that is the law of the courts of the United States.

In the case of Elliott *vs.* Piersol [1 Peters, 328], Judge Trimble, in delivering the opinion of the court, remarks :

"It is argued that the Circuit Court of the United States had no authority to question the jurisdiction of the county court of Woodford county, and that its proceedings were conclusive upon the matter, whether erroneous or not. We agree that, if the county court had jurisdiction, its decision would be conclusive, but we cannot yield an assent to the proposition, that the jurisdiction of the county court could not be questioned, when its proceedings were brought collaterally before the Circuit Court. We know nothing of the organization of the Circuit Courts of the Union which can contradistinguish them from other courts in this respect.

" When a court has jurisdiction, it has a right to decide every question which occurs in the cause, and whether its decision be correct or otherwise, its judgment, until reversed, is regarded as binding in every other court. But, *if it act without authority, its judgments and orders are regarded as nullities.* They are not voidable, but simply void ; and form no bar to a recovery sought, even prior to a reversal, in opposition to them. *They constitute no justification ; and all persons concerned in executing such judgments or sentences, are considered, in law, as trespassers.*

" This distinction runs through all the cases on the subject, and it proves that the jurisdiction of any court exercising authority over a subject, may be inquired into in every other court, when the proceedings of the former are relied on and brought before the latter by the party claiming the benefit of such proceedings."

This doctrine is approved in the Chemung Canal Bank *vs.* Judson [4 Selden, 254,] decided in June, 1853, before the New York Court of Errors, the highest court of record in the State of New York. After citing at length the passage which I have read, Justice Ruggles says :

" The power of this court, therefore, to inquire into the jurisdiction of the District Court of the United States, is undoubted ; and the power of that court to inquire into the jurisdiction of this, is equally clear."

The principle is re-affirmed in Thompson *vs.* Tolmie, [2 Peters, 156.] Justice Thompson in that case observes :

" If there is a total want of jurisdiction, the proceedings are void, and a mere nullity, and confer no right and afford no jurisdiction, and may be rejected when collaterally brought into question."

In the case of Voorhees *vs.* Bank of U S., [10 Peters, 449,] decided as late as January, 1836, Justice Baldwin says :

" The line which separates error in judgment from the usurpation of power, is very definite. In one case it is a record importing absolute verity ; in the other, mere waste paper."

In Wilcox *vs.* Jackson, [23 Peters, 498,] decided in January, 1839,

Justice Barbour, after speaking of the judgments of courts acting within their jurisdiction, remarks :

" But directly the reverse of that is true in relation to the judgment of any court acting beyond the pale of its authority. The principle on this subject is concisely and accurately stated by the court in the case of Elliott *vs.* Piersol [1 Peters, 340] in these words." He then quotes the whole passage already read.

In the case of Grignon *vs.* Astor, [2 Howard, 319,] Justice Baldwin says :

" This is the line which denotes jurisdiction and its exercise in cases *in persona:* where there are adverse parties, the court must have power over the subject matter and the parties."

In the case of Hickey *vs.* Stewart, [3 Howard, 850,] the proceedings of the Court of Chancery of Mississippi were brought in question, and it was decided that they are wholly void, the court having no jurisdiction. Justice McKinley, delivering the opinion in that case, says :

" According to the decision in the case of Henderson *vs.* Poindexter, above referred to, Starke's claim, when submitted by his heirs to the Court of Chancery, was utterly void ; and no power having been conferred by Congress on that court to take or exercise jurisdiction over it for the purpose of imparting to it legality, the exercise of jurisdiction was a mere usurpation of judicial power, and the whole proceeding of the court void.

" In the case of Rose *vs.* Himely, Chief Justice Marshall said : ' A sentence professing on its face to be the sentence of a judicial tribunal, if rendered by a self-constituted body, or by a body not empowered by its government to take cognizance of the subject it has decided, could have no legal effect whatever. The power of the court, then, is of necessity examinable, to a certain extent, by that tribunal which is compelled to decide whether its sentence has changed the right of property. The power under which it acts must be looked into, and its authority to decide the questions which it professes to decide, must be considered.' Upon principle, it would seem that the operation of every judgment must depend on the power of the court to render that judgment ; or, in other words, on its jurisdiction over the subject matter which it has determined."

After quoting the passage from Elliott *vs.* Piersol, which has been already referred to, Justice McKinley continues :

" The same doctrine was maintained by this Court in the case of Wilcox and Jackson, [13 Peters, 511,] and the case of Elliot and others *vs* Piersol and others, referred to, and the decision approved. These cases being decisive of the question of jurisdiction, we deem it unnecessary to refer to any other authority on that point. From the view we have taken of the whole subject, it is our opinion, the decree of the Supreme Court of Mississippi would have been no bar to the action of the plaintiffs in this case, if the subject-matter of the suit had been within its jurisdiction. But we are of the opinion that the court had no jurisdiction of the subject-matter, and that the whole proceeding is a nullity."

A still more recent case is that of Williamson *vs.* Berry, [8 Howard, 495,] which was decided in the year 1850. The court there said :—

" We concur that neither orders nor decrees in chancery can be reviewed as a whole in a collateral way. But it is an equally well-settled rule in jurisprudence, that the jurisdiction of any court exercising authority over a subject, may be enquired into in every other court, when the proceedings in the former are relied upon and brought before the latter by a party claiming the benefit of such proceedings. The rule prevails whether the decree or judgment has been given in a court of admiralty, chancery, ecclesiastical court, or court of common law, or whether the point ruled has arisen under the law of nations, the practice in chancery, or the municipal laws of States.

" This court applied it as early as the year 1794, in the case of Glass et al *vs.* Sloop Betsey, [8 Dall. 7 ;] again, in 1808, in the case of Rose *vs.* Himely,]4 Cranch, 241 ;] afterwards in 1828, in Elliot *vs.* Piersol, a case of ejectment, [1 Peters, 328, 340.] This is the language of the court in that case, not stronger though than it was in the preceding cases."

The passage from Elliot *vs.* Piersol, already referred to, is here quoted at length, and the opinion continues :—

" This distinction runs through all the cases on the subject. This court announced the same principle in Wilcox *vs.* Jackson, [13 Peters, 499] and twice since in the second and third volumes of Howard's Supreme Court Reports. [Shriver's Lessee *vs.* Lynn et al., 2 How., 59 ; Lessee of Hickey *vs.* Stewart et al., 3 How., 750.]"

The court then go on to decide that the Chancellor of the State of New York had improperly assumed jurisdiction of the case that was before him, and that all his proceedings were void.

Thus the authority is ample for the proposition that the proceedings of a court beyond its jurisdiction are nullities, and afford no protection to any officer executing its judgments or decrees. Such an officer is merely a trespasser. If the officer who executes the process is a trespasser, it follows necessarily that the judge who orders it, is at least equally so. Upon no reasonable principle can the ministerial officer be held responsible, and the judicial officer, (whose ignorance or whose error was the cause of the mischief,) be excused. The reason that avoids the judgment and process together, makes all concerned answerable, from t e judge to the marshal or the deputy to whom the last service was confided. It is a well known legal principle, that in trespass all are principals; and it is not easy to perceive how one who has been active in causing a trespass, by his order or decree for its commission, can be less a wrong-doer than the agent, who merely obeys the command of his superior.

Still the question recurs : had the defendant jurisdiction in the proceedings against the plaintiff?

The fifth plea assumes to exhibit the ground on which the writ of *habeas corpus* issued : that Wheeler was the owner of three persons held to service or labor by the laws of Virginia; that they were detained from his possession by the plaintiffs ; and that the *habeas corpus* issued to the plaintiff, commanding him to bring before the defendant the bodies of the persons detained.

Had the defendant jurisdiction, as judge of the District Court of the United States, to issue a writ of *habeas corpus* on such a complaint? Whether he had or not, depends on the question whether the power to issue the writ in such a case is conferred by any act of Congress compatible with the Constitution of the United States.

It was long ago decided that the Supreme Court of the United States, being created by written law, and their jurisdiction being defined by written law, cannot transcend that jurisdiction, and that the power to award the writ of *habeas corpus* by any of the courts of the United States, must be given by written law. [Ex parte Bollman, 4 Cranch, 75.]

The fourteenth section of the Judicial Act, is that to which we are referred as containing a grant of the power. That section provides that :—

" All the before mentioned courts of the United States [the Supreme, Circuit and District courts,] shall have power to issue writs of *scire facias, habeas corpus*, and all other writs not specially provided for by statute, which may be necessary for the exercise of their respective jurisdictions and agreeable to the principles and usages of law. And that either of the justices of the Supreme Court, as well as justices of the District Court, shall have power to grant writs of *habeas corpus* for the purpose of an inquiry into the cause of commitment : provided that writs of *habeas corpus* shall in no case extend to prisoners in gaol, unless where they are in custody under or by color of the authority of the United States, or are committed for trial before some court of the same, or are necessary to be brought into court to testify."

Whatever difficulties may at one time have existed as to the construction of this act, it has been so often considered and construed by the courts, that its meaning may be said to be definitively ascertained. The suggestion of a controversy as to whether the words, " which may be necessary for the exercise of their respective jurisdictions," apply to writs of *scire facias* and *habeas corpus*, or only to the writs "not specially provided for by statute," is too late by nearly half a century. This question was fully considered and decided more than fifty years ago in the case of *Ex parte* Bollman, by Chief Justice Marshall, to whose exposition nothing can be advantageously added, and who put a construction upon this statute which has been acquiesced in ever since. It is a little remarkable that the judges of the Supreme Court of Pennsylvania have overlooked that decision altogether, and have treated this statute as if the words, "which may be necessary for the exercise of of their respective jurisdictions," were to be applied to the writs of *habeas corpus*.

Chief Justice Marshall, in the case I have mentioned, determines the sense, not by verbal criticism nor by grammatical construction, but "by the nature of the provision and by the context;" and he makes it clear that the phrase in question was not intended to limit the power of the courts to issue writs.

But the Chief Justice proceeds in that case to consider other parts of the act of Congress, and finds in them the true limit to the exercise of the power conferred. In the sentence which follows that which authorizes the courts to issue writs of *habeas corpus*, it is said that "either of the judges of the Supreme Court, as well as the judges of the District Courts, shall have power to grant writs of *habeas corpus for the purpose of inquiring into the cause of commitment.*"

By comparing this provision with the previous grant of the power, and considering, in connection with it, the subsequent proviso and the thirty-third section in reference to admitting prisoners to bail, the construction arrived at is that the power to award writs of *habeas corpus* is confined to those cases in which prisoners have been committed under or by color of the authority of the United States, or are to be brought into court to give testimony; that the power of the United States courts to issue writs of *habeas corpus* is restricted wholly to those cases in which the authority of the United States is in some way involved.

[MR. HENRY WHARTON here begged leave to correct Mr. Lewis, who, he conceived had mistaken the language of Chief Justice Marshall. He thought that the interpretation given by the court, was that the words referred to were not restrictive upon the exercise of the power to grant writs of *habeas corpus*. According to his recollection, the Chief Justice in the course of his decision, had said with reference to this argument: "This may be grammatically correct, but we prefer to rest our decision on the general principle that by the terms of the act itself,

2

and by its intention, all the courts of the United States have the right to issue writs of *habeas corpus.*" It had been expressly decided (Mr. Wharton thought) that the Supreme Court have the right to issue writs of *habeas corpus* generally, and the writ which they were empowered to issue was the *habeas corpus ad subjiciendum*—not any writ peculiar to their jurisdiction.]

MR. LEWIS. Undoubtedly Chief Justice Marshall decided that the term "*habeas corpus,*" as contained in the Constitution and in the 14th section of the Judicial Act, referred to the writ of *habeas corpus ad subjiciendum*, and that all the courts of the United States had authority to issue that writ; but Chief Justice Marshall did not decide that they had authority to issue that writ in all cases where the party applying for it was under confinement;—and it is on just this point that the question arises. That the District Court of the United States has authority *in certain cases* to issue the writ there can be no kind of doubt; but that it has no authority to issue the writ in any case except where the prisoner is in confinement " under or by color of the authority of the United States" is just as clear as any principle in the law.

Mr. Rawle, in the second edition of his work on the Constitution, page 118, remarks :

" It is at any rate certain that Congress, which has authorized the courts and judges of the United States to issue writs of *habeas corpus* in cases within their jurisdiction, can alone suspend their power, and that no State can prevent those courts and judges from exercising their regular functions, *which are, however, confined to cases of imprisonment professed to be under the authority of the United States.*" " But the the State courts and judges possess the right of determining of the legality of imprisonment under either authority."

This principle is also laid down in Com. *vs.* Fox, 7 Barr, 336; Com. *vs.* Smith, before Chief Justice Tilghman in 1809 ; and in many other cases.

Judge Story observes in the second chapter of his Commentaries :

" The statute of Charles Second has been in substance incorporated into the jurisprudence of every State in the Union, and the privilege has been secured in most, if not in all, of the State constitutions by a provision similar to that existing in the Constitution of the United States."

" Congress have vested in the courts of the United States full authority to issue this great writ in cases *falling properly within the jurisdiction of the National Government.*"

Curtis, in the first volume of his Commentaries (page 252) observes :

" It was then settled upon great consideration that the first sentence of the statute grants the great writ of habeas corpus to all the courts of the United States when in session; but as they are not always in session, the second sentence vests the power in every judge of those courts also."

After observing that the Supreme Court could issue the writ as a part of its appellate jurisdiction, he says: "This, however, went no farther than to decide that the Supreme Court may always by *habeas corpus inquire into the cause of commitment by any other court of the United States.*"

In the case of *Ex parte* Dorr [3 How. 104], the power conferred by this 14th section of the Judicial Act came again to be considered by the Supreme Court, and Justice McLean, in delivering the opinion of the court, held this language :

" The power given to the courts in this section to issue writs of *scire facias, habeas corpus,* etc., as regards the writ of *habeas corpus* is restricted, by the proviso, to cases where a prisoner is 'in custody under or by color of the authority of the United States, or has been committed for trial before some court of the same, or is necessary to be brought into court to testify.' This is so clear from the language of the section, that any illustration of it would seem to be unnecessary. The words of the proviso are unambiguous; they admit of but one construction, and that they qualify and restrict the preceding provisions of the section is indisputable.

" Neither this, nor any other court of the United States, or judge thereof, can issue a *habeas corpus* to bring up a prisoner who is in custody under a sentence or execution of a State court, for any other purpose than to be used as a witness. And it is immaterial whether the imprisonment be under civil or criminal process. As the law now stands an individual who may be indicted in a Circuit Court for treason against the United States is beyond the power of Federal Courts and judges, if he be in custody under the authority of a State."

In the case of *Ex parte* Barry, before Judge Betts, in the Circuit Court of the United States for the Southern District of New York, he decided that he had no jurisdiction by *habeas corpus* in a controversy as to the custody of a minor. This, if it be law, is decisive of the question which we are now considering. The case appeared subsequently, in a somewhat different shape, before the Supreme Court of the United States, under the name of Barry *vs.* Mercein, and in the report of that case [5 How. 108], I find the opinion of Judge Betts quoted as follows :

" A procedure by *habeas corpus* can in no legal sense be regarded as a suit or controversy between private parties. It is an inquisition by the government, at the suggestion and instance of an individual most probably, but still in the name and capacity of sovereign, to ascertain whether the infant in this case is wrongfully detained and in a way conducing to its prejudice."

" What question can be regarded as, in principle, more local or intro-territorial than those which pertain to the domestic institutions of a State,—the social and domestic relations of its citizens? Or what could probably be less within the meaning of Congress than that, in regard to these interesting matters, the courts of the United States should be empowered to.introduce rules or principles, because found in the ancient common law, which should trample down and abrogate the policy and cherished usages of a State, authenticated and sanctified as a part of her laws by the judgment of her highest tribunals?"

" We must tread the direct and narrow path prescribed for us. As this court has never grasped at ungranted jurisdiction, so it never will, we trust, shrink from that which is conferred upon it."

These quotations go to show distinctly that in a case falling clearly within the cognizance of the municipal law, and not in any way affecting the power of the United States government or coming under its authority, the courts of the State or territory being vested with jurisdiction of the case, the courts of the United States are excluded and have no authority to interfere.

It has been decided that the inquiry into the cause of commitment extends to cases of imprisonment under both civil and criminal process. [*Ex parte* Randolph, 9 Peters, 12; 2 Brock. 447.] This was a case from a circuit court and turned on the want of jurisdiction of auditors. It was decided that the jurisdiction of court and judges was the same, and was controlled by the clause limiting it to inquiry into the cause of commitment.

In referring to the source of jurisdiction (on page 476) the court say : " Now, the act of Congress authorizes us to issue the writ '*for the purpose of inquiring into the cause of commitment;*' " and on page 477 it is observed :

" And, certainly, we are well warranted in making this reference to the common law ; because, although it is admitted by all that it is not a source of jurisdiction, yet it is habitually, rightfully—nay, necessarily —referred to for the definition and application of terms; indeed, there are many terms in the Constitution which could not otherwise be understood."

That is to say, that for the explanation of terms in the constitution and acts of Congress, and for no other purpose in relation to this writ, is the common law referred to.

Conkling in the last edition of his Treatise on the Jurisdiction of the Courts of the United States, referring to the interpretation given to the 14th section of the Judicial Act by Chief Justice Marshall, says :

" It will be seen from this brief review of the judicial decisions relative to the writ of *habeas corpus ad subjiciendum*, that the power conferred upon the courts and judges of the United States to grant it, by the Judicial Act, is strictly limited to the cases therein specified. *It is only in behalf of persons in confinement 'under or by color of the authority of the United States,' or ' committed for trial before some court of the same,' that the power can be exercised.* In all such cases, except after final conviction before a court of competent jurisdiction, the writ may be awarded either by a Circuit or District court, or by a judge of the District court, and, it is presumed, also by a justice of the Supreme Court.' This power was accordingly exercised, as we have seen, by the Circuit Court for the Eastern District of Virginia in the case of Randolph, who was in custody under a warrant of distress issued by the Solicitor of the Treasury; and by the Circuit Court for the Southern District of New York in the case of Kaine, who had been committed by a commissioner. In virtue of the same authority, a person committed on a warrant issued by a commissioner under the act commonly known as the Fugitive Slave Act, was brought up on a writ of habeas corpus awarded by the District Judge of the Northern District of New York.

"In all these cases it was sufficient that applicants were ' in custody under or by color of the authority of the United States.' But, as we have seen, according to the interpretation given to the Constitution in Marbury *vs.* Madison, and in *Ex parte* Bollman and Swartwout, there is a further and very comprehensive limitation to the power of the Supreme Court, although no such distinction is made by the fourteenth section of the Judicial Act. The *original* jurisdiction of that court being specified in the Constitution, Congress, it was held, had no power to enlarge it; and, consequently, the authority of the Supreme Court to grant a writ of *habeas corpus* is restricted to cases falling within the scope of its appellate power, and cases (should any such arise, requiring this form of redress) affecting an ambassador, other public minister or consul, or to which a State is party."

" The highly important powers to be exercised by means of the writ of *habeas corpus* confided to the national judiciary by later acts of Congress for the purpose of preventing undue obstruction of the laws and breaches of the international obligations of the United States, have not happily as yet, so far as I am aware, called for judicial exposition."

" In the first sentence of the fourteenth section of the act of 1789, conferring upon the courts of the United States power to issue writs of habeas corpus, it will be noticed these writs are simply named, without any descriptive words expressive of their nature or uses ; while in the next sentence it is said ' that either of the justices of the Supreme Court, as well as the judges of the District courts, shall have power to grant writs of *habeas corpus for the purpose of. inquiring into the cause of commitment.*'

" The reason of this doubtless is that, there being several species of writs of *habeas corpus,* all of which it was proper to empower the courts to grant, it was necessary in conferring the power on them to use the word in its generic sense ; while, on the other hand, the writ of *habeas corpus ad subjiciendum* being the only species of writ properly issuable by a single judge, it was deemed expedient to describe it. Next and lastly comes the proviso : ' provided, that writs of *habeas corpus* shall in no case extend to prisoners in gaol, unless where they are in custody under or by color of the authority of the United States, or are committed for trial before some court of the same, or are necessary to be brought into court to testify.'

" Speaking of this proviso, the Chief Justice took occasion to observe that ' it extends to the whole section ;' or, in other words, it defines and limits the scope of the power to award writs of *habeas corpus* conferred upon the courts as well as upon the judges. This interpretation, the only one indeed of which the language of the act is susceptible, has ever since been assumed and uniformly acted upon by the Supreme court as unquestionable."

The learned author, whose accuracy and ability are strongly exhibited on every page of his valuable work, adds to the sentence last quoted from the text, the following significant note :

" *It seems, nevertheless, to have been altogether overlooked in a case of recent occurrence in the Eastern District of Pennsylvania*—a case that has elicited no inconsiderable degree of public attention and interest. The proceedings I allude to have been strongly marked throughout by features of a most extraordinary and anomalous character, and seem destined to occupy a conspicuous place in the judicial history of this country."

It may be remarked that Alfred Conkling, the author of the book from which I have just read, was himself for a number of years United States District judge for the Northern District of New York. He had no inconsiderable experience in regard to all these matters, and was thoroughly acquainted with the practice and the decisions of the Supreme Court upon the subject. He sums up the whole matter in the remarks which I have read, and distinctly says that the authority of the judges of the United States courts to issue writs of *habeas corpus* is confined to cases in which the person seeking to be relieved is confined under or by color of the authority of the United States ; and he declares that this distinction, which was first shadowed out in the case of *Ex parte* Bollman and Swartwout, and has since been observed in every case in which the subject has undergone investigation, was in a most remarkable manner overlooked in a late case in the Eastern District of Pennsylvania—alluding to this very case in terms sufficiently intelligible.

An application was made during the year 1830 by a recruiting officer at Albany to Judge Conkling, to bring before him, by *habeas corpus*, for the purpose of discharge, an enlisted private soldier, arrested for a small debt upon process from an inferior court of the State;

but the judge, considering it perfectly clear that he had no authority to issue the writ in virtue of the general power conferred by the Judicial Act, and entertaining doubts as to the act of 1799, advised an application to the Supreme Court of the State. [See note to p. 239 of Conkling's Treatise.]

In the case of United States *vs.* French, [Gallison's Reports, page 1,] decided as long ago as 1812, the same distinction is laid down. The language of the court in that case is :

" We have no authority in this case to issue a *habeas corpus*. The authority given by the Judicial act of 1789, ch. 20, sec. 14, is confined to cases where the party is in custody under color of process under the authority of the United States, or is committed for trial before some court of the United States, or is necessary to be brought into court to testify. It does not extend to cases where the process is from a State court, and the object is to surrender the party in discharge of bail."

In the case of *Ex parte* Smith, [3 McLean, 121,] the jurisdiction of the United States court to issue a *habeas corpus* was sustained expressly on the ground that the petitioner was detained by virtue of authority emanating from the United States.

From the cases to which I have referred, and others which are noted in the work of Judge Conkling, it appears unquestionable that the courts of the United States have power to issue the writ of *habeas corpus* only in certain prescribed cases, of which this is not one. It is unnecessary, therefore to pursue farther this branch of the argument.

It is certain that the act of 1833, called the " Force Act," has no application to this case. That was an act passed by Congress for the purpose of preventing any interference with the authority of the general government, by the State of South Carolina; and there is nothing either in the words or intention of the act, that can be supposed to give jurisdiction to the District court of the United States in such a case as this.

It is unnecessary, in fact, under these decisions to inquire specially into the jurisdiction of the District Court of the United States, which is of a most limited character. That court has not the remotest color of power or authority over such a case as this or the parties to it. The only court that could pretend to such authority is the Circuit Court of the United States ; and that court, as has been shown, has denied that it has it.

If the defendant acted as judge, and not as a court, he clearly had no jurisdiction, because the persons for whose production the writ issued were not alleged to be under commitment of any kind, either under civil or criminal process. If he acted as a District Court, his power was no larger than that which he' possessed as judge of such court, and his action was equally beyond his jurisdiction. Such being the case, the whole proceeding is a nullity, and affords no justification to anybody.

As far as I can understand the language of the act, and the judicial interpretations given to it, the court and the judge have equal power to issue the writ of *habeas corpus* whenever any case calls for the intervention of the authority of the United States—the court, when it is in session; the judge, when the court is not in session; but in both instances the power to issue the writ is confined by the proviso, to those cases in which the persons seeking relief are " in custody under or by color of the authority of the United States, or are committed for trial. before some court of the same, or are necessary to be brought into court to testify."

If this be the correct construction of the Judicial Act—if in all these decisions the United States judges themselves have not erred in determining as to their jurisdiction, then it must be certain that the District Court of the United States had no jurisdiction of the present case. It is shown upon the very face of the fifth plea that no jurisdiction actually existed, for that plea sets forth that the writ of *habeas corpus* issued upon complaint of John H. Wheeler, of Virginia, for the purpose of relieving from custody certain persons whom he claimed as slaves—a case that did not come within the provisions of the act of Congress, and which did not, for any reason that can be imagined, call for the interference of any United States court. It was a case falling clearly within the municipal laws of the State, and in which an appeal might have been made with great propriety to the courts of the State, charged with the protection of her own citizens. The courts of the United States could not interfere in this case for any purpose to which the United States could properly be a party. By the petition itself, it would appear that these persons were not fugitive slaves, and whether they were fugitive slaves or whether they were freemen, does not affect the question. The power of the United States courts in either case is precisely the same ; there is no power given to any court of the United States to interfere upon the subject.

This construction of the Judicial Act is not only reasonable in view of its words, but necessary in reference to its spirit and the objects which it was designed to answer. All questions relating merely to the domestic relations of the citizens of Pennsylvania on our own soil, are properly cognizable by our local tribunals. The government of the United

States has nothing to do with them; its interference in regard to them is wholly uncalled for. Our own courts are competent to afford every remedy, and nothing but a disposition to intermeddle with what does not belong to them, can prompt the action of the Federal courts in such cases. The framers of the Judicial Act never contemplated conferring upon the courts of the United States the right to issue the great writ of *habeas corpus ad subjiciendum* where the authority of the general government was not in some way concerned. The genius of the Constitution gives no sanction to such an idea; the whole theory of our complex system repudiates it. One great object, ever kept in view both in framing the Constitution and in the enactment of laws to carry out its purposes and provisions, was to prevent a conflict of authority. This was regarded as a vital point, involving the stability of the government. But the construction given to the statute, on the part of the defendant, would tend to bring the powers of the Federal and of the State courts into perpetual collision. Under that construction, process would clash with process; sheriff and marshal would be continually crossing each other's path.

It is said that the jurisdiction here assumed has been repeatedly exercised. If such is the fact, it only shows the tendency of Federal power to usurpation and the necessity of giving it a check. There is one reported case, (United States *vs.* Green,) in which Judge Story took cognizance of a question relating to the custody of a minor; but nothing was said on the subject of jurisdiction, and no final order was made. In his Commentaries on the Constitution, that eminent judge has given no countenance to a doctrine that seeks to break down the proper barriers to the ambition of Federal authority, and make the United States courts common arbiters of the rights of citizens under State laws and institutions. Those barriers it is the incumbent duty of the State courts to protect. They have been hitherto observed by all United States judges, (except, as Judge Conkling says, in one case of "a most extraordinary and anomalous character,") wherever the question has been made, but how long such will continue to be the case, if our tribunals are unmindful of an unjustifiable infringement upon their rightful prerogatives, let the history of all past usurpations answer.

It is insisted for the defendant that whether he acted within or without his jurisdiction as judge, he is not answerable civilly in a court of justice to the party injured. This position cannot be maintained upon principle; for, as I have already said in substance, where there is no jurisdiction there is no process, and the ground of justification fails.

He that orders the arrest, and he that executes the order, are equally liable. The extent of the liability is the only question; and that is to be judged by the proper tribunal, after weighing all the facts.

The modern precedents conform to the legal principle. Beaurain vs. Sir William Scott [3 Camp. 388] was decided March 6, 1813. An action was instituted against the defendant, judge of the ecclesiastical court, on the ground that he had made a decree in excess of jurisdiction. The case was tried before Lord Ellenborough, and that the action was maintainable was not denied. [See note to this case.] "Where the judge of any spiritual court excommunicates for a cause of which he has not the legal cognizance, he is also liable to be indicted at the suit of the king. 2 Inst. 623 ; 2 Bl. Com. 101."

In the case of Dicas vs. Ld. Brougham, [25 E. C. L. 418] before Lord Lyndhurst, December 3rd, 1833, it was contended by Campbell, Solicitor General, that no action lay against a judicial officer, and the English authorities cited in the defendant's paper-book were all referred to. Platt, in answer, cited Beaurain vs. Scott :

"Lord Lyndhurst, C. B. There the judge had no jurisdiction. The judge is protected only where he has jurisdiction."

The whole controversy turned on that point—whether the Chancellor, in sending Dicas to prison, acted within his jurisdiction.

In Houlden vs. Smith [68 E. C. L. 382,] decided February 26, 1850, Justice Patterson said : "We have found no authority for saying that he [a judge of a court of record] is not answerable for an act done by his command and authority, where he has no jurisdiction ;"—and the plaintiff had judgment.

If, therefore, the doctrine of judicial inviolability ever obtained (and, whatever may be said in some old cases, I am far from admitting that it did,) it is now thoroughly exploded; and a judge is no further protected from the proper consequences of his acts of trespass than any other person. It would be indeed strange if he should be exempt from liability, while those executing his orders are held liable,—especially as his first duty consists in ascertaining the just boundaries of his powers, while theirs is deemed to be discharged only by the most implicit and unquestioning obedience.

Having referred to the cases which seem to bear directly upon the question of judicial responsibility, it is unnecessary to labor the argument further on that point; and I shall proceed to lay before the court the reasons why, in my apprehension, these pleas ought to be stricken off.

The first case to which I will refer is that of McBride *vs.* Duncan [1 Wharton, 269.] This was an action of trespass brought against the Sheriff of the city and county of Philadelphia for carrying away certain goods and chattels alleged to be the property of the plaintiff. The defendants pleaded "not guilty, with leave to give the special matter in evidence," but afterwards obtained a rule to show cause why the general issue should not be withdrawn and special pleas filed in its stead. This rule was made absolute at the March term, 1835. They then filed six special pleas. To the first four of these pleas the plaintiff put in a replication concluding to the country; to the fifth and sixth, he replied "*nul tiel record.*" To the replication to the first plea the defendants demurred specially; to the replication to the second, third and fourth pleas they rejoined the *similiter.* The case then came up on the issue of *nul tiel record,* and the demurrer to the replication to the first plea, and the questions, were very ably argued by Mr. J. A. Phillips and Mr. W. M. Meredith for the plaintiff, and Mr. F. W. Hubbell for the defendant. In that case, *without any formal motion,* (as appeared from the report, and as I have also learned from one of the eminent gentlemen who were engaged in the argument of the cause,) but on a mere suggestion made in the course of the argument by one of the counsel, the Supreme Court struck off the pleas. Judge Sergeant, delivering the opinion of the court, said: "It has been contended that the matter of these pleas was not admissible under the general issue;" and he then proceeds to show that the whole matter in defence might be given under the general issue. He then observes:

"Still, though the general rule is that a defendant is not permitted to put in special pleas which amount to the general issue, and the court will strike them off, yet there are exceptions; for, in some cases, by the English rules the defendant may take his choice and frame his plea so as to escape being liable to the objection. This is effected by the device of giving color, as in these pleas is done, by alleging that the plaintiff was in possession of the goods by a bailment from Linn for safe-keeping, and by fraudulent conveyances from him. And where such course reserves to the defendant any serious advantage he might otherwise lose, he would, strictly speaking, be entitled to take his choice, and resort to the circuity of special pleading, instead of this plain path of 'not guilty.'

"No important advantage can attend the defendant's special pleading in the case before us, while it leads to delay and burthens the records with volumes which serve little or no purpose but the exercise of ingenuity and learning. It is said [Hob. 127] that it is a good reason for pressing the general issue, instead of special pleading, that 'it makes long records where there is no cause.' In Pennsylvania this remark applies with peculiar force. The genius of our jurisprudence is not favorable to the practice of special pleading, and the cases are rare in which the time and attention of the court have been occupied by disputes upon it. There is no class of the profession employed peculiarly in its study, nor would our trivial attorney's fee compensate for the labor of it. Our system has been to try causes on the general issue with notice of the special matter. To that system our laws and practice conform; and justice, it is believed, is as well administered as where another system prevails. It is remarkable that in some actions which the courts have invented and fostered as best calculated for the trial of right, such as ejectment and trover, there is no special pleading; and in *assumpsit* it is not required.

"It is not meant by these remarks to intimate that there are not cases in which special pleas are necessary and proper, and in which the law of the case cannot be administered without them; or that an intimate knowledge of that branch of the law is not indispensable to the advocate. But where justice may be fully attained without it, where special pleading involves the cause in prolixity and delay without conferring any real benefit on him who resorts to it, the court ought, in the exercise of their legal discretion, and for the prevention of the evils that would result, to enforce the rule that the defendants shall not plead specially what amounts to the general issue."

In Troubat and Haly's Digest this case is referred to as settling the practice of Pennsylvania in this particular.

The question then remains whether the defendant could have the benefit of all his defence under the general issue; and we have only to refer to the English cases in order to be satisfied that that is the fact, for there is no one of those cases where the general issue was pleaded, in which the defendant had not the full benefit of his defence under that plea.

In the case of Houlden vs. Smith, already referred to, the plea was "not guilty," and under that all the defence was given.

In the case of Rosset vs. King [17 E. C. L., 595] the court refused to allow the defendant, in an action of *assumpsit*, to plead the general issue, and also several special pleas that the money mentioned in the declaration was due only for differences arising out of stock-jobbing transactions; as such matter might be given in evidence under the general issue All the pleas, therefore, were stricken off, with the exception of the general issue plea, under which the defence was given.

The case of Coster vs. Wilson, [3 M. & W., 411,] was an action of trespass for assault and false imprisonment, brought against a justice of the peace, who, as it was supposed, had improperly assumed jurisdiction. On an investigation, the opinion of the court was that he had jurisdiction, and his right to issue the writ complained of was therefore sustained. In this case the plea was "not guilty," and under that plea the whole defence was given.

In the case of Hammond *vs.* Teague, [19 E. C. L., 97,] the opinion of the court, as stated in the syllabus, was, "The court will not allow a party to plead, in *assumpsit*, matter which may be given in evidence under the general issue, unless the plea be simple and not likely to perplex the plaintiff."

As far as concerns the merits of the case before us, no party can be deprived of any possible advantage by granting the motion which we make to strike off the pleadings. If the general issue plea had been entered, the case would have been fairly at issue and might have been tried at the last term of the court. The only effect of perplexing the case by these questions of pleading is delay.

Whether or not the general replication *de injuria* is applicable in a case of this kind, is a question of very considerable nicety. In two cases to which I have already referred, the plea of *de injuria* was used and allowed. In another case, the inquiry was made by Lord Holt, why it might not be used. Other cases which have been referred to, have shown that the use of the *de injuria* or general traverse, is not now in the English courts a matter of the same nicety as formerly; and that the plea is now used in many cases where a century ago it was disallowed. Still, if we go to the older cases—if we refer to Crogate's case, and consider the principles there settled as still in force, and applicable to all cases of a similar kind, it requires much accuracy of judgment and a familiar knowledge of the science of special plead. ing, to determine in what cases it is applicable. There are a great number of decisions upon the subject, many of which are conflicting and contradictory. Judge Tyndal has said, in a recent decision in the court of King's Bench, that the cases are not to be reconciled. What is the result? We are involved in a labyrinth of special pleading in relation to a subject which requires no plea but the general issue to afford the defendant every advantage he can desire as to the production of his proof.

But it is argued on the other side, that the rules of pleading require that a single point shall be made in answer to the plea ; that we cannot answer it generally, but must reply some particular fact, and thus raise an issue upon that fact alone. The only object to be accomplished by this is to have the cause decided without reference to all the facts, but only upon that single fact which, according to the argument of the other side, must be presented in answer to the plea. This course will bring up but one single point without eliciting the evidence in relation to the general merits of the case, and will thus prevent the jury from having all the light which a proper investigation of the subject would afford. If such be the object of these pleadings, it cannot find sanction in the spirit of the law or in the sense of justice entertained by the court. On the contrary, inasmuch as our custom has been not to burden our records with elaborate pleadings—inasmuch as the studies of the profession have been of an entirely different nature, and our practice from the earliest period has been in conformity with a more liberal and enlarged system of pleading, there seems to be no propriety in an attempt to revive in a case of this kind (or, in fact, in any case) this recondite and almost extinct science, for the purpose of raising single issues of this character. Under the general issue the defendant can have the benefit of every defence which can be suggested. He can have the opinion of the court upon every question of law as it may arise, and if he be not satisfied with the instructions of the judge he can have them reviewed. The tendency of all recent practice and of all recent legislation, both in this country and in England, is favorable to general issue pleading in preference to special pleading. I have here a book, which is an exposition of the forms of practice in England under the Procedure Acts of 1852—54. The system of pleading is there reduced to the simplest possible elements. A declaration can be written in three lines, and a plea in three words; and in general the business of the courts is conducted upon this system to the entire satisfaction of the profession.

[Mr. Lewis here read specimens of the legal forms, as abridged and simplified under the new system.]

This is the nature of the pleading under the recent Procedure Acts, and it has revolutionized the whole system of English pleading, although that had been already greatly simplified by the rules adopted some years ago. This is another, and a far longer step towards attaining that simplicity which now seems to be the object of the courts. While in England the courts are casting off every shred of the old vesture of the English law, there is no reason why we should clothe ourselves in their discarded garments, instead of following the example which they have set, or, at least, adhering to our own precedents and being governed by our own system which, from the first, has favored simplicity in pleading.

And, as I observed this morning, whatever might be the ultimate decision upon these technical questions, no useful purpose can be subserved by their discussion. A motion to amend the pleadings would at any time obviate all objections. Our courts will not now allow the merits of a cause to be strangled in a mesh of special pleading, by an attempt of either party to show his skill in the practice of this abstruse and now almost obsolete science.

[Mr. Lewis having closed, he was followed on the same afternoon by Mr. G. M. Wharton, and the subsequent morning by Mr. Henry Wharton, both on the part of the defendant. When the latter gentleman had concluded, Mr. Lewis replied as follows:]

If anything could clearly illustrate the propriety of the motion that has been made, it would be the several arguments upon the other side which we have had here three months ago, yesterday and to-day, on the subject of these special pleas.

Such is the state of the law upon the particular matter now before the court, raised by the special demurrer of the opposite side, that it is very difficult for the most experienced man in practice and the most astute legal logician to understand what is to be the result; and if we must necessarily go through with this case as it has been commenced, with the pleadings in their present shape, the final determination of the judges, who have as little experience in these matters as the bar, must be very uncertain. For there is not a judge of any common pleas court of the State of Pennsylvania, nor one sitting upon the bench of the Supreme Court, who is familiar with the law relating to special pleading; and, even though familiar, not one of them could, without considerable difficulty, embarrassment, study and labor, satisfy his mind as to what ought to be the result of an argument upon the pleadings as they now stand. The only way to rid the record of the embarrassment which its present condition produces, is to strike off all the pleas and compel the party to plead the general issue, upon which every question, both of law and of fact, can be judged by the appropriate tribunal. We thus bring the record to such a condition that we all understand our rights; we are all at home, and each party can have the benefit of the facts as he is able to prove them, and of the law as it arises from those facts, by asking the instruction of the court with regard to matters of law and the decision of the jury with regard to matters of fact.

This motion to strike off the pleas is met upon the other side by several objections. One is, that the defendant by his pleas has shown matter of justification in law and is entitled to an issue of law to be determined by the judges. This position is untenable: it is not shown by the record—it is not the fact. The question of jurisdiction is undoubtedly a question of law *where the facts are ascertained*. The gentleman who has just closed his argument upon the other side asserts that the facts are ascertained and truly set down in the plea; but in that respect he is entirely mistaken. The facts are not ascertained in the plea. The plea, it is true, contains a general *allegation* that in this matter the defendant acted as judge; but whether he did act as judge is not a question of law, but is actually a question of fact. Taking the facts as stated in the first and third pleas, without anything more, they would, without doubt, constitute a case in which the defendant would be entitled to judgment. But the facts there stated *are denied.* The all-important fact that the defendant acted as judge in relation to this whole matter is precisely the question upon which we take issue by the general plea. Therefore, the fact is not ascertained; it is not truly represented; we are at issue upon that particular matter by the pleas as they now stand.

That is the issue admitted to be raised by these pleadings—whether or not the defendant did act as judge. If he had joined issue on that plea, then undoubtedly the facts pertaining to the question of jurisdiction, (which we are entitled to give in evidence,) would necessarily come up, and it would be for the court to say whether those facts constituted a defence. The defendant then would have the benefit of the law as applied to such a state of facts, in a charge to the jury that he had or had not jurisdiction.

But he refuses to take issue upon those facts, and insists that we shall offer in reply some single fact, or deny some one of the several allegations which he has made. Were we to do what he thus suggests, we would be bound to take issue either upon the allegation that there is such a record as is there referred to, or upon some other allegation contained in his plea, or allege some fact on which an issue involving the question of jurisdiction might be raised.

But, (as I observed in my argument yesterday,) he has not set out the whole proceedings, but only a part. He does not show how this question came before him. He begins by stating that he is commissioned as judge, and then goes on to say that on a certain motion in the court in a matter of contempt, the judgment of the court was had, and that Mr. Williamson was committed under that judgment. He does not set out any of the intermediate proceedings; and on those intermediate proceedings depends the question whether he had any jurisdiction of the cause. In order, therefore, that your Honor may correctly expound the law in relation to the question of jurisdiction, and in order to enable the jury to decide as to the facts on which that question depends, we must necessarily have those facts before us. How can we have them? We must have them either by a general denial of what is stated upon the record—that he has committed the act complained of as judge—or by stating some particular fact in regard to that matter.

It is contended upon the other side that we must either plead that there is no such record, or must state some particular fact which will show that Judge Kane had no jurisdiction; that we may do either, but cannot do both. The necessary conclusion from this is that we cannot have the benefit of our whole defence, but only of a defence arising upon a single allegation; that we must, at the hazard of losing our cause, select and take issue upon some particular fact, without having the benefit of all the facts which bear upon the case. The object which the defendant proposes to gain in driving us, by this system of special pleading, into a direct replication with regard to his plea is, that we shall tender issue upon some one, single, particular fact. In speaking of this matter yesterday, Mr. G. M. Wharton observed, that such was our only course; and if we are not permitted to put in the replication *de injuria*, his observation is certainly correct : we must then select and take issue upon some one particular fact stated in his plea, or must set up in reply some one particular fact within our own cognizance which he has not there stated, and on that single fact we must stand or fall. This is to narrow down the issue—to prevent the plaintiff from having the benefit of all the facts—to compel us to select and rely upon only a part of our case; thus incurring the hazard of making an erroneous selection by which we may jeopard a judgment in our favor. Now, I submit to your Honor, that a resort to special pleading having such consequences. and, therefore, presumptively for the purpose of attaining them, is not to be favored.

But what is the present state of the record ? Here are five pleas ; they are replied to generally; issue is taken upon two, and a special demurrer put in to the replication as to the others. What arises necessarily from this condition of the record ? We must have a trial before a jury to determine the matters of fact as to the pleas which are at issue; and in addition to that, we have these questions of law which are raised upon the demurrer. When your Honor has given a judgment upon the questions raised on the demurrer, that does not settle the issue raised upon the pleas; that issue must still be tried; and when that trial has been had, what will be the result ? Your Honor must give judgment upon the whole record ; and then the question will arise, what is the effect of these pleas, and this judgment and the verdict of the jury altogether, as far so regards that record ? Thus another embarrassing question must come up, and another argument.

Mr. Henry Wharton, (interrupting:) Certainly, it will be admitted that if judgment be given in our favor on the pleas, that it is an answer to the action.

3

Mr. Lewis. That depends upon what view the court shall take of the law on that subject—it is a question yet to be decided.

I have explained the state of the record. Now, is not that issue to the country upon the matter of fact to be tried?

We had it stated here yesterday, that in the city of Philadelphia it is very usual to try the matters of fact, first and afterwards argue the matters of law arising on the demurrer. In this district we usually determine matters of law first, and afterwards try the issues of fact. But, at all events, when the issues both of law and of fact have been determined, then comes a motion for entering judgment. That motion is for the consideration of the court; and upon the whole record the judgment of the court is to be rendered.

Now, the simplest, easiest, readiest way of determining this whole matter, and avoiding these embarrassing questions with regard to what is to be the effect of the proceeding from beginning to end, is to present a question of this kind in the accustomed way, by a plea under which the defendant can have the full advantage of his defence in the broadest latitude, and under which the plaintiff, unembarrassed in the conduct of his case, can have the full benefit of whatever evidence he may be able to adduce.

In the present state of the pleadings, other difficult points may arise, when we come to the trial of the issues of fact. These relate to the admissibility of evidence. Under the familiar issue of not guilty no embarrassing questions of evidence can arise; but under an issue in which technicality has been accustomed to be regarded more than the merits of the parties or the justice of the cause, the same cannot be said. The artificial logic of special pleading pinches everywhere and has no sympathy for fair play.

It is said by the counsel on the other side that the defendant is entitled to be regarded as having acted honestly, and that he should not be precluded from any possible means of defence. I do not wish to say any thing here in relation to the position which the defendant occupies. Whether he acted honestly in the present case is not a question upon these pleadings. When the subject shall come before the jury, it may be a question how far he can avail himself of the presumption in favor of the honesty of his purposes. Perhaps it may appear that, though no *particular* malice existed, yet a species of malice equally the subject of animadversion and punishment did exist; and if the jury should happen to think so, they, judging from all the circumstances of the case, may render their verdict accordingly. I suppose Lord Chief Justice Jeffreys could be charged with no personal ill feeling against Alice Lee, when she was tried before him; but he had the infamous object of serving those in power; and such an object as that may be in the eye of a modern judge as well as of one that lived two hundred years ago; and wherever that is the case, it is as much malice deserving castigation as if he were actually moved by a feeling of spite against the person who is the victim of his illegal proceeding.

It is said that the defendant here is entitled to the benefit of the judgment of the court upon the matters of law. Undoubtedly he is; but he can more readily and directly have the benefit of those matters of law by instructions upon the subject from the bench, than by pleas, and replications, and demurrers, such as now exist upon this record; because those questions of law will be presented in such a shape that all difficulty as to the true points involved in the case will be relieved.

But if the defendant is entitled to the benefit of the decision of the court on the questions of law, the plaintiff is equally entitled to the benefit of a trial before a jury with regard to the questions of fact; and it is for the purpose of bringing the questions of fact fairly before a jury, the proper tribunal for questions of fact, that we wish these pleas stricken off. We do not desire to deprive the defendant of any reasonable advantage which should be allowed him, but we wish to preserve to ourselves the reasonable advantage to which we are entitled. We want to have the questions of law decided by the court—the questions of fact determined by the jury; and the only way to attain this, is to have the general issue plea entered, by which all the questions will be thus properly presented.

It is reason enough for striking off these pleas, that they render the proceedings embarrassing to both court and counsel. Why, what is the state of the law as regards questions arising upon this very record? The ancient guides are one way, the modern guides directly another. The opinion given by Judge Kent, when on the bench of the Supreme Court of New York, is referred to as showing what he regarded as law. He considered that the record of a court was not to be disregarded, even though it was alleged to be the record of a court not having jurisdiction, and an argument in opposition to this opinion he pronounced "miserable sophistry;" whereas, a subsequent judge of the same court has declared that that very defence is available, and that the record which Judge Kent considered good evidence of all it contained, was in fact no record whatever; and Chief Justice Marshall, in one of his opinions, has said the same thing.

I mention this for the purpose of showing how differently judges have regarded this subject, and how, following one set of guides, you go one way, and following another set of guides you go another. Now, which are we to follow? That is a question, we all know, for the decision of the tribunal to which this case shall ultimately go, if these pleas remain. We do not wish a question of this uncertain character to be presented to any tribunal; and, I submit to your honor, it is fair in us to desire to avoid questions of uncertain solution—questions depending upon the construction which shall be given to the law by the tribunal which is finally to determine it, whose decision must depend altogether upon which set of guides they will follow. Whichever way a judge might incline to give judgment, he could very easily find law enough to support his decision. The judges of the Supreme Court would have no difficulty, as the record now stands, in giving judgment either way, *and well the defendant knows that;* and that may be one of the objects that he has in view in presenting this case in its present shape, for it would be very easy for a court of the last resort to find support in a multitude of authorities (for " their name is legion ") for any judgment which it might be their pleasure to pronounce.

The proper course to be pursued in this case is, I think, settled, if anything can be considered as settled, by the decision of the Supreme Court in the case of McBride vs. Duncan, referred to yesterday. An attempt has been made to criticise that case; but when your Honor shall come to examine it, you will see that it was an action of trespass, as this is an action of trespass; that the pleas there are pleas of justification, as these are pleas of justification.

MR. HENRY WHARTON.—(Interrupting.) They amount directly to a traverse of the plaintiff's allegations.

MR. LEWIS.—They are pleas in which the defendant as sheriff justifies his levying upon the property of the defendant on a *fieri facias.*

MR. WHARTON. They *pretend* to be so; they are not so in fact.

MR. LEWIS. Exactly what *they* are in shape *these* are in shape; these are pretended justifications, just as those are.

What were the replications? To the first four of these pleas the plaintiff put in a replication concluding to the country; to the fifth and sixth he replied, *nul tiel record.* Then there were special demurrers to those pleas. An endeavor was made in that case to raise a question of special pleading; why, I do not know, unless it was to compel the plaintiff to reply to a single fact, so as to have a single issue before the jury, instead of presenting all the facts of the case for their determination. What did the court do? Upon the case coming up before them, after the replication and the special demurrer to the replication and an argument by counsel, they struck off the pleas *of their own motion.*

This case is then a most emphatic reprehension of this form of pleading, by which it is attempted to get up special issues with regard to a case where a party can have the full benefit of his defence under the general issue. This case has no resemblance whatever to the case of Bower *vs.* Roth, [4 Rawle, 83.] In that case it was decided that "it is no cause of demurrer to a special plea that the facts set forth in it may be given in evidence under the general issue;" and certainly it is not, but it is a cause for striking off the pleas, in order that the facts may be given in evidence under the general issue.

I know that in the last edition of Troubat and Haley's Digest, the case of McBride *vs.* Duncan is referred to as over-ruling the decision in Bower *vs.* Roth; but on examining the cases we will find that such is not an accurate statement of the law; for one decides merely that "it is no cause of demurrer to a special plea that the facts set forth in it may be given in evidence under the general issue;" the other decides that it is cause for striking off the pleas. If we had considered it cause of special demurrer, we would have demurred to the pleas; but under the decision in Bower *vs.* Roth, we could not demur on that ground. We can, however, at any time ask to have the pleas stricken off; not because they *amount* to the general issue, (and the whole argument on the other side seems to have been directed against that idea,) but for the reason given in the case of McBride *vs.* Duncan; that everything alleged by the defendant as a matter of defence, can be given in evidence under the general issue; that he can have the same advantages under the general issue as under the pleas which he has offered.

Mr. Henry Wharton.—I find that in the case of Bower *vs.* Roth, the court put their judgment on the general ground, and distinctly affirm the right of the defendant to put on record matters of law.

Mr. Lewis.—He may put them on record; but the question of striking off, when it arises, is a different matter. If a motion had been made in that case to strike off the pleas, according to the principle of the decision in McBride *vs.* Duncan, it would have prevailed; but a special demurrer would not prevail for the same cause.

But it is said that this motion to strike off the pleadings comes too late. That cannot be. The case of McBride *vs.* Duncan settles that. In that case, not only was the general issue plea (which we ask to have pleaded here) waived, but it appears that the general issue was pleaded and afterwards withdrawn, these special pleas being substituted.

Then there was a replication and a special demurrer, and an argument before the court; and after all this the pleas were stricken off.

Undoubtedly, in England, some fifty years ago, it would have been too late after issue had been joined to make a motion to strike off. It is too late there (or *was*, not long since,) to amend your pleas upon special demurrer after you have joined in demurrer. In England you never see leave given to amend after argument on demurrer; the judgment of the court is always rendered upon the pleadings as they stand; but in this country we universally allow an amendment after an argument and judgment in demurrer. The right to amend in Pennsylvania is secured by the act of Assembly, for the reason that, in our State, the science of special pleading is little cultivated or regarded, and it serves the purposes of justice to allow the party to amend his pleading at any time before the verdict is rendered. The idea, therefore, of our motion being too late is an obsolete idea—like the Bank of the United States, it is a thing that does not belong to modern times, and is not to be found in any Pennsylvania book of practice—at all events, in none written within the last twenty-five years.

I hold, therefore, that it is perfectly clear, not only that the motion to strike off in this case comes within time, according to the precedent of McBride *vs.* Duncan, but also that these pleadings are, in their character, such as come within the purview of the judgment in that case, and that to them the reasons there assigned fully apply.

Here there is no necessity even for notice of special matter. The mere entry of the general issue plea of " not guilty" puts every question at issue of which the defendant can avail himself in his defence. This I have shown not only to be the case of McBride *vs.* Duncan, but even by the cases cited in the English books. Thus in the case of Sir William Scott, a judge of the highest court of admiralty in the kingdom—

Mr. Henry Wharton, (interrupting): That case was brought against him not as a judge in admiralty, but as an assistant to one of the ecclesiastical courts—not a court of record.

Mr. Lewis.—That distinction, as far as regards the ecclesiastical and admiralty courts in England, is more nominal than real. Though *technically* not courts of record, they are *actually* so to all intents and purposes.

Mr. Henry Wharton.—Their proceedings are matters for the jury.

Mr. Lewis.—Their proceedings are shown by a certificate instead of a record.

Mr. Henry Wharton.—They are proved as matter of fact.

Mr. Lewis.—Yes, sir; the judge certifies the proceedings, and his certificate is taken as evidence. It is, to be sure, in contemplation of law not taken as importing absolute verity like a record, but in practice it is treated with equal respect, and differs from record evidence only technically.

Mr Henry Wharton.—The regularity of those proceedings is to be determined by the jury, not by the court.

Mr. Lewis.—Technically it is to be determined by the jury, but under the instructions—the *binding* instructions—of the court. Whenever a matter of that kind comes before a jury, the court will instruct them as to the manner in which they must find; and the certificate of a judge of admiralty or a judge of any of the consistorial courts, is considered by the courts as having the essential virtues of record evidence; for it is as much binding upon the court, and they will instruct the jury that it is just as much to be regarded. So that whether the judge is a judge of admiralty or of one of the ecclesiastical courts, and whether his record is to be treated as a matter of fact or a matter of law, is a mere technicality: it has nothing of substance in it.

But it is said in regard to this fifth plea, that in it everything is alleged that constitutes a matter of defence, as well as everything of which the plaintiff can avail himself upon his side. This is not exactly the fact. There are matters outside of this fifth plea; and, although they are referred to, perhaps, in the general allegation, and are therefore to be shown under the general traverse which we have filed; yet, if that traverse is, as they say, irregular, and we are bound to stand upon this fifth plea in its present form, what is the question that then arises? It is this: Do the facts set forth in it constitute a full justification of the defendant? Now, why does the defendant desire that this plea in this particular shape shall constitute the matter to be adjudged, either in this court or the court above. The object is very easily seen—it is perfectly transparent. Judge Black, in his opinion in reference to the present case, has already decided that the presumption arising from this record is that the slaves referred to were fugitive slaves. He uses these words:

" A part of the Jurisdiction of the District Court consists in restoring fugitive slaves; and the habeas corpus may be used in aid of it when necessary. It was awarded here upon the application of a person who complained that his slaves were detained from him. *Unless they were fugitive slaves they could not be slaves at all*, according to the petitioner's own doctrine; and if the Judge took that view of the subject, he was bound to award the writ."

It having thus been decided by Judge Black that the persons named in the application for the habeas corpus are to be presumed, from the state of the record, to have been slaves, it follows, that if the defendant can get us into court upon a demurrer to a plea which sets forth this state of things, he is sure of Judge Black's opinion in his favor when the case shall come before the Supreme Court, for it must be presented there in precisely the shape in which it was when Judge Black delivered his opinion. If on the other hand, we be permitted to show that the persons named in this petition were not fugitive slaves, but were indeed free persons, having been brought into Pennsylvania by the voluntary act of Mr. Wheeler, their former master, then Judge Black's opinion has no bearing whatever upon the case : we then have a new case, not presented by the record before, in which we are to have the opinion of the judge anew upon a state of the law in regard to which he is not committed.

It was therefore very desirable to the defendant that he should compel us to demur to this plea in its present shape, corresponding, as I presume it does, with the proceedings of the defendant's court as now appearing on the face of what is here assumed to be the record. We have several certified copies of that record obtained at different times. They do not happen to agree. This plea, I presume, shows what the alleged record could now show. But we do not consider that this alleged record exhibits the true state of the facts. There are many circumstances outside of it that give a color and character to the proceedings, and to every mind desirous of embracing the whole case and weighing it with a view to an honest judgment, vitally important These can be exhibited on the general issue. Why shall they not ? Does the defendant wish to keep them out of sight? Is he unwilling the country shall have a faithful history of this anomalous and remark-able proceeding from the beginning? We court the exhibition of the truth and the whole truth, and circumstances require of the defendant that he should do no less. The country expects a full and open inquiry. Justice to him and to us can be done in no other way. In order to this end the pleas must be struck off.

[The argument here closed, the Court announcing that the decision would be rendered at its session at Media, on the fourth Monday in February.]